AMERICA⸗
POLITICAL WRITING
DURING THE
FOUNDING ERA

1760–1805

LIBERTY FUND
LIBRARY OF THE AMERICAN REPUBLIC

Works of Fisher Ames
W.B. Allen, ed.

Union and Liberty
John C. Calhoun

In Defense of the Constitution
George W. Carey

American Political Writing During the Founding Era: 1760-1805
Charles S. Hyneman and Donald S. Lutz, eds.

Political Sermons of the American Founding Era: 1730-1805
Ellis Sandoz, ed.

George Washington: A Collection
W.B. Allen, ed.

AMERICAN
Political Writing
during the
Founding Era
1760–1805

Volume II

CHARLES S. HYNEMAN

DONALD S. LUTZ

Liberty Fund

INDIANAPOLIS
1983

This book is published by Liberty Fund, Inc., a foundation established to encourage study of the ideal of a society of free and responsible individuals.

The cuneiform inscription that serves as our logo and as the design motif for our endpapers is the earliest-known written appearance of the word "freedom" (amagi), or "liberty." It is taken from a clay document written about 2300 B.C. in the Sumerian city-state of Lagash.

Library of Congress Cataloging-in-Publication Data
Main entry under title:

American political writing during the founding era,
    1760–1805.

    Includes bibliographies and index.
    1. United States—Politics and government—Colonial
period, ca. 1600–1775—Sources. 2. United States—
Politics and government—Revolution, 1775–1783—Sources.
3. United States—Politics and government—1783–1809—
Sources. I. Hyneman, Charles S., 1900– .
II. Lutz, Donald S., 1943– .
JK113.A716 1983   973.3.   82-24884
ISBN 0-86597-038-6 (set)
ISBN 0-86597-039-4 (v. 1)
ISBN 0-86597-040-8 (v. 2)
ISBN 0-86597-041-6 (pbk. : set)
ISBN 0-86597-042-4 (pbk. : v. 1)
ISBN 0-86597-043-2 (pbk. : v. 2)

94 93 92 91 90 C 6 5 4 3 2
01 00 99 98 97 P 7 6 5 4 3A

TABLE OF CONTENTS

Preface, xi

Acknowledgments, xvii

VOLUME I

[v]

CONTENTS

Contents

CONTENTS

CONTENTS

CONTENTS

VOLUME II

[49]

AN ELECTOR

To the Free Electors of This Town

BOSTON, 1788

The theory of republican government took for granted a number of institutions and practices rarely written about, yet logical and important consequences of that theory. One of these was the view that electioneering was a corrupt practice. The virtuous man was to run for office sitting quietly in his house after offering himself. This brief essay discusses the practice and its rationale. It appeared in the *Boston Gazette* on April 28, 1788. The fact that even James Madison, when he first ran for the Virginia legislature in 1777, refused to campaign or solicit votes shows the strength of the practice. That Madison lost to a tavern keeper also illustrates why the practice was in serious decay by 1788.

───────

It is a criterion of republican principles that they never induce their possessor to seek for an office—and however fashionable it may be, to make professions of gratitude for the suffrages of the people, such professions are alien from true republicanism. The PUBLIC GOOD is, or ought to be, the only object of pursuit to every servant of the public: "Offices should therefore seek for men, not men for offices." The character of a SEEKER should be detestable in the view of every free and independent Elector; such persons constantly exhibit themselves at every return of the present season—and the arts of electioneering are openly and shamelessly practised. Our papers for several years past, have been crouded with essays and declamations, graced with this corrupt borough term, ELECTIONEERING:—Yea, it is supposed that persons, whose characters have been emblazoned as models of political virtue, have modestly employed their own pens to depict themselves, or prevailed on some dependent friend to do this immaculate business for them:—such persons must have a superlative opinion of their own merits, or a very contemptible one of the public discernment. Such, ought never to be the objects of our suffrages. The public good is a secondary consideration with candidates of this sort, and is never attended to as a matter of importance, any further than their own INDIVIDUAL interest can be promoted at the same time.

At the present day, there are many Candidates or Seekers; in bestowing our suffrages, let us not lose sight of real republican principles, and the great interests of the Commonwealth, from too eager a desire to promote a FRIEND, a RELATION, or CONNECTION; who may, perhaps, need a public employment. This principle has a very dangerous tendency, and may, finally introduce an influence fatal to the liberties of the people.

That ARISTOCRACY, of which we have heard so much, may creep upon us through this medium; for in proportion to the DEPENDENT and STRAITENED circumstances of men in public life, in the same proportion (generally speaking) is the probability of their sacrificing their sentiments, to coincide with the view of ambitious men, who have (experience verifies) always established their INFLUENCE and POWER by the assistance of needy expectants.

The important choice of Representatives is now approaching— from that solicitude and concern which the citizens of this metropolis have discovered on this occasion, from year to year, there can be no doubt of their being equally attentive to characters, the ensuing election.

You will doubtless have many exhortations upon the subject, and many excellent qualifications will be treated of, as ESSENTIAL REQUISITES. ALL that I have to say at present is, that so far as any of those persons who were the objects of your choice the last year, have discovered an attachment to the great principles of FEDERALISM—they will doubtless obtain your suffrages the ensuing year.

AN ELECTOR

[50]

BENJAMIN FRANKLIN 1706–1790

An Account of the Supremest Court of
Judicature in Pennsylvania, viz., The Court of
the Press

PHILADELPHIA, 1789

Franklin had multiple careers as printer, sage of wide renown (through *Poor Richard's Almanac*), civic leader, scientist and inventor, superb representative of America in Europe, and towering figure in conventions that produced written constitutions for the state of Pennsylvania and the United States of America. It is his first career that is germane here because, having spent most of his life printing and distributing the works of others as well as writing a great deal on his own for publication, Franklin was very familiar with the strengths and weaknesses of a free press. American pamphleteers loved to imitate the pamphleteers in England, where there was a long tradition of vicious satire, biting irony, parody, and inventive prose forms. While on the whole less sophisticated than their English counterparts, American pamphleteers did display the entire range of formats and literary styles found in England, and the fact that many published under pseudonyms did not always reflect fear of political reprisal so much as fear of a suit for libel. It is not possible to convey the literary richness of the era in a book focusing upon *theoretical* excellence, but this satire by Franklin is good enough to do double duty as a statement by an experienced professional on the limits of a free press and as an example of a more literary style of argument. It was published in the Philadelphia *Federal Gazette* on February 12, 1789, approximately a year before his death. One prominent author has dubbed the piece "On Freedom of the Press and Freedom of the Cudgel."

Power of This Court. It may receive and promulgate accusations of all kinds against all persons and characters among the citizens of the State, and even against all inferior courts; and may judge, sentence, and condemn to infamy, not only private individuals, but public bodies, & c., with or without inquiry or hearing, *at the court's direction.*

In Whose Favor and for Whose Emolument This Court Is Established. In favor of about one citizen in five hundred who, by education or practice in scribbling, has acquired a tolerable style as to grammar and construction, so as to bear printing; or who is possessed by a press and a few types. This five hundredth part of the citizens have the privilege of accusing and abusing the other four hundred and ninety-nine parts at their pleasure; or they may hire out their pens and press to others for that purpose.

Practices of The Court. It is not governed by any of the rules of common courts of law. The accused is allowed no grand jury to judge of the truth of the accusation before it is publicly made, nor is the name of the accuser made known to him, nor has he an opportunity of confronting the witnesses against him, for they are kept in the dark as in the Spanish court of Inquisition. Nor is there any petty jury of his peers, sworn to try the truth of the charges. The proceedings are also sometimes so rapid that an honest, good citizen may find himself suddenly and unexpectedly accused, and in the same morning judged and condemned and sentence pronounced against him, that he is a *rogue* and a *villain.* Yet, if an officer of this court receives the slightest check for misconduct in this his office, he claims immediately the rights of a free citizen by the constitution and demands to know his accuser, to confront the witnesses, and to have a fair trial by a jury of his peers.

The Foundation of Its Authority. It is said to be founded on an article in the State Constitution, which established *the liberty of the press;* a liberty which every Pennsylvanian will fight and die for, though few of us, I believe, have distinct ideas of its nature and extent. It seems indeed somewhat like *the liberty of the press* that felons have by the common law of England before conviction, that is, to be *pressed* to death or hanged. If by *the liberty of the press* were understood merely the liberty of discussing the propriety of public measures and political opinions, let us have as much of it as you please; but if it means the liberty of affronting, calumniating, and defaming one another, I, for my part, own myself willing to part with my share of it whenever our legislators shall please so to alter the law, and shall cheerfully consent to exchange my *liberty* of abusing others for the *privilege* of not being abused myself.

By Whom This Court is Commissioned or Constituted. It is not by any commission from the Supreme Executive Council (who might previously judge of the abilities, integrity, knowledge, & c. of the persons to be appointed to this great trust of deciding upon the characters and good fame of the citizens) for this court is above that Council, and may *accuse, judge, and condemn it,* at pleasure. Nor is it hereditary, as in the court of *dernier resort* in the peerage of England. But any man who can procure pen, ink, and paper, with a press, a few types, and a huge pair of Blacking balls, may commissionate himself, and [thereby] his court is immediately established in the plenary possession and exercise of its rights. For if you make the least complaint of the judge's conduct, he daubs his blacking balls in your face wherever he meets you; and, besides tearing your private character to flitters, marks you out for the odium of the public, as an *enemy to the liberty of the press.*

Of the Natural Support of These Courts. Their support is founded in the depravity of such minds as have not been mended by religion, nor improved by good education:

> "There is a lust in man no charm can tame,
> Of loudly publishing his neighbour's shame."

Hence

> "On eagle's wings immortal scandals fly,
> While virtuous actions are but born and die."
> Dryden.

Whoever feels pain in hearing a good character of his neighbour, will feel a pleasure in the reverse. And of those who, desparing to rise into distinction by their virtues, are happy if others can be depressed to a level with themselves, there are a number sufficient in every great town to maintain one of these courts by their subscriptions. A shrewd observer once said that, in walking the streets in a slippery morning, one might see where the good-natured people lived by the ashes thrown on the ice before their doors; probably he would have formed a different conjecture of the temper of those whom he might find engaged in such a subscription.

PHILADELPHIA, 1789

Of the Checks Proper to be Established Against the Abuse of Power in These Courts. Hitherto there are none. But since so much has been written and published on the federal Constitution, and the necessity of checks in all other parts of good government has been so clearly and learnedly explained, I find myself so far enlightened as to suspect some check may be proper in this part also; but I have been at a loss to imagine any that may not be construed an infringement of the sacred *liberty of the press*. At length, however, I think I have found one that, instead of diminishing general liberty, shall augment it; which is, by restoring to the people a species of liberty of which they have been deprived by our laws, I mean the *liberty of the cudgel*. In the rude state of society prior to the existence of laws, if one man gave another ill language the affronted person would return it by a box on the ear, and, if repeated, by a good drubbing; and this without offending against any law. But now the right of making such returns is denied and they are punished as breaches of the peace, while the right of abusing seems to remain in full force, the laws made against it being rendered ineffectual by the *liberty of the press*.

My proposal then is to leave the liberty of the press untouched, to be exercised in its full extent, force, and vigor; but to permit the *liberty of the cudgel* to go with it *pari passu*. Thus, my fellow-citizens, if an impudent writer attacks your reputation, dearer to you perhaps than your life, and puts his name to the charge, you may go to him as openly and break his head. If he conceals himself behind the printer and you can nevertheless discover who he is, you may in like manner way-lay him in the night, attack him behind, and give him a good drubbing. Thus far goes my project as to *private* resentment and retribution. But if *the public* should ever happen to be affronted, as it ought to be, with the conduct of such writers, I would not advise proceeding immediately to these extremities but that we should in moderation content ourselves with tarring and feathering and tossing them in a blanket.

If, however, it should be thought that this proposal of mine may disturb the public peace, I would then humbly recommend to our legislators to take up the consideration of both liberties, that of the *press* and that of the *cudgel*, and by an explicit law mark their extent and limits; and, at the same time that they secure the person of a citizen from *assaults* they would likewise provide for the security of his *reputation*.

[51]

[ANONYMOUS]

Ambition

CHARLESTON, 1789

Americans during the founding era held many assumptions that greatly affected their political thinking but were rarely discussed in print. This essay on political economy illustrates the point. It appeared in the *City Gazette and Daily Advertiser* of Charleston, South Carolina, on June 6, 1789. Compare this with the article on poverty in the same paper printed on December 8, 1789.

To none, except those who are ignorant of its nature, can it be matter of surprize, that the minds of men are frequently occupied with thoughts on ambition; a passion that vies in [ ] with any that is connected with the human mind; and though so often under discussion, it is still unexhausted; though it has long been chosen for a daring theme, though veterans in knowledge, and in virtue, have been lavish in its praise, it has still material that calls for the exertions and [ ], of our ablest writers.

Ambition, by many writers, has been condemned as a source of evil; nothing that is human is perfect; for this censure therefore they have undoubtedly had some grounds: but might not the heavy charges imputed to her influence, be set with much more justice, to the account of malice and revenge? For who is so despicable, as to feel ambitious of being mean? Who so proud as to wish to be despised? No! The man who runs great lengths in vice, and delights to persecute his fellow creatures, is not only a stranger to every feeling that genuine ambition would inspire, but is actuated by the meaner passions of envy, jealousy or revenge. That we may be able to form a right judgement of this passion, and get the full measure of its merit, let us revert to those ages in which its influence was hardly known; to those times of simplicity, when man for his subsistence depended on the fruits of the chase; whose only discipline, was from the rod of necessity and in that school of adversity, taught to postpone his hunger, until time or chance, shall supply him with food. His only care, like the brutal herd, was to satisfy his present and most pressing wants. Like the beasts did he range the fields for prey; like them did he fly to the woods for shelter; like them did he live; and like them would have remained, had not ambition awakened a sense of the indignity, and taught him, by her secret force that man was made for nobler ends.

Ambition then, "is the wings on which we have soared above the brute creation," by which we have been wafted from a barbarous, to an enlightened age; and without which, we should grovel through life, like the vile insect that crawls upon the ground. The human system is a machine; ambition the spring that puts it in motion. The whole world of mankind, either see and admire its operations; or feel themselves its quickening influence. The venturous horseman meets with proud assurance, the fiercest enemy; he handles the launce with active skill; makes regular, dextrous, and not unfrequently successful attacks; but if defeated, and beaten from the field, "leaves his arrows in the wind to meet his pursuers."

The needy husbandman, from an emulation of the enjoyments and possessions of his neighbors, quits the prospect of present ease, for an industrious and laborious life, instead of submitting to the impulse of passion, which would easily triumph over the unaspiring mind; and instead of submitting to the many invitations to pleasure and the allurements of the world, which would lead him a giddy dance, and expose him alike to poverty and disgrace, he seeks a more rational and profitable exercise; and persuades himself to be constantly and usefully employed for an increase of property and the support of a family. Are there not thousands amongst us, who for a disdain of being dependent on others have denied themselves the pleasures and even the comforts of life; and retired to uncultivated regions, where, shut out from society, and the enjoyments of improved life, they have contented themselves for a while to endure the pains of abstinence, and combat the stubborn globe.

ANONYMOUS

A love of excellence spurs them on to industry, and by increasing their desires and uniting their efforts, leads them to improvement. The grateful earth yields to the hand of culture, and crowns their labor with success. When necessaries are found, convenience and ornament are fought for, until by their continued and united exertion, they make the "wilderness to blossom like a rose." The plains they behold speckled with their flock; their meadows waving with stores for the barn; and their field nodding with treasures of corn. "The hills rejoice, the vallies smile," and every thing looks glad! Thus by their industry, the offspring of ambition, they became the support of their families, and honor to themselves, and a blessing to their country.

What but the love of enterprise, and of applause, would induce the soldier to exchange the peaceful joys of a domestic life for the rougher scenes, the hardships and dangers of a camp? What but the grateful tribute of his country's thanks, could persuade him to leave security, and jeopardy his life in the field of battle? The thought of sharing the honors of the brave, and of rising to glory, gives courage to the hero, and adds strength to the warrior's arm. What is a man without ambition? Let us for a moment admit the painful thought that the men of interest and influence in this country, were lost to ambition! Those whom fortune has favoured and raised to wealth and dignity—Should we see them struggling for the liberty and happiness of the people? Should we find ourselves the happy objects of their care, patronage and protection? Should we not rather behold them regardless of their fellow creatures, carelessly basking in the sunshine of prosperity, and lolling on the bed of affluence? "Ignobly great, and impotently vain," their only excellence would be to be wretched in state; and all they could boast of, supremacy of misery!

After having learned from experience the worth of this virtue, may we encourage its influence, that we may enjoy more extensive and lasting blessings; instead of being contented with these short lived exertions, which are made only upon the spur of occasion, may we be constant in pursuit of those virtues and excellencies to which our ambition prompts us to aspire.

[52]

BENEVOLUS

Poverty

CHARLESTON, 1789

This selection appeared in the *City Gazette and Daily Advertiser* (Charleston, South Carolina) on December 8, 1789. It is couched in a flowery, labored style often used in newspaper pieces, but a careful reading shows that under the quasi-metaphors there is a serious discussion on the effects of poverty. It is easy to imagine a debate between this author and the author of the piece on ambition—from the same paper—set in the 1980's. The style of expression would change, but the liberal and conservative viewpoints of 1789 would be the same today on these issues.

Poverty is so prevalent an evil among the human race, that it may be said, few or none at one period or other of their lives, escape to the grave without (either directly in their own proper persons, or indirectly through the collateral medium of their connexions) being made sensible of its direful effects. Yes, gentlemen, poverty is a never failing source of misery and woe! a perennial spring of sorrow and wretchedness! a prolific mother whose ever-teeming womb is incessantly pregnant with hunger, nakedness, disease, and in a word, with every species of human misery! Woe then to him on whom she siezes with her baleful talons! for poverty is more dreadful in its ravages and effects than Smyrnia plague—since during its influence, the suffering patients may be said to be buried *alive*! I say buried alive; being deserted, abandoned, and forgot of all the world; and thus in a manner, become non entities on earth! Friendship and poverty are incompatible, and therefore poverty has no friend! Pity indeed, sometimes yields a momentary

BENEVOLUS

relief to distress; but this delicate lady, Pity, alas! is of so frail a texture and frame of constitution, that of all beings she is the most short lived and transitory! The good doctor Goldsmith of philanthropic memory, humourously defines pity thus—a species of satire by the bye, extremely apposite to my present purpose. "Pity, says that benevolent character, is at best but a short lived passion, and seldom affords *distress* more than a transitory assistance, with some (and I may add, the greater sum of mankind) it scarce lasts from the first impulse till the hand can be put into the pocket; with others (a very small number) it may continue for twice that space; and on some extraordinary sensibility I have seen it operate for half an hour together. But still, last as it may, it generally produces but beggarly effects; and where, from *this* motive we give *five farthings,* from others we give *five pounds*. Whatever be our first feelings, (continues this ingenious observer of the human passions and propensities) from the *first impulse* of distress, when the same distress solicits a second time, we then feel with diminished sensibility; and like the repetition of an echo, every stroke becomes more and more faint, till at last our sensations lose all mixture of *sorrow,* and degenerate into downright *contempt."* I shall not apologize for the length of this quotation, which I consider thus pertinently interwoven with my coarser stuff, as a precious jewel set in an ordinary collar; and therefore must stamp merit on this my feeble essay to be serviceably to my fellow creature, which, without such an ornament, would have but little value of its own to recommend it to public attention. But to return—*Contempt* did I say? Yes, poverty outdoes even familarity in giving birth to this vile fruit; a bantling that upon all occasions sticks so close to its unhappy parent, that nothing less powerful than the omnipotent influence of gold can ever charm it from her side.

Whatever may have been his birth, his talents, his merits, his accomplishments in life, a man of broken fortune will necessarily find himself indiscriminately involved among the common class of wretch, without any other difference or exception [   ] what must aggravate his case and heighten the pungency of his sufferings, from the uncommon delicacy of his feelings. Poverty (which is an unpardonable kind of crime) strips such a man for ever of every pretence to favor, protection, and esteem, and makes him an object of obloquy and severe animadversion to the uncharitable and conscious part of mankind! Even in *this* region of more than common felicity—in *this* land of freedom and plenty; nay in *this* our rich and populous city may be found at *this* hour, (a circumstance sure, that must deeply affect and interest every feeling bosom of our fellow citizens, and pall the relish and enjoyment of those pleasures which the benignity of our more indulgent stars has put into our possession) numbers of such as I have been describing, (and whose various situations and conditions, though nevertheless uniformly miserable, *all* description) pining in the last stages of human woe! Let us for a moment turn our *minds eye* (it is our duty—it is our interest as men and christians to [do] it) towards the widow and the fatherless—let us take a survey of the state of many a poor, unprovided family, struggling with adversity, and trying to stem the tide of misfortune—let us contemplate (it is an attention worthy of our nature) the undescribably melancholy state of *those*, at this (*to them*) severe and inclement season of the year; among whom are many old, decrepid, and utterly helpless individuals. Let us consider how deplorable a case it is to be in a little cabin or hovel, open to the wind and weather on all sides, without fuel, without food, without raiment, without furniture, and in a word *sans* everything! Aye, without any thing, save their *efforts,* amidst their calamities, to support themselves by resignation and fortitude; and to conceal their *hard* lot from the public eyes! How many such are now, while we are perusing this paper, realizing my assertion, by bravely drying up their involuntary tears, and suppressing their bosum heaving sighs! Methinks I see this moment (alas it is no uncommon sight) methinks I see the obdurate constable, the minion of *justice;* but never the messenger of *mercy,* in the execution of his office; and committing utter ravage and devastation in many parts at once this opulent town—yes, this is no imaginary spectacle, or creature of the fancy, for the thing really and substantially exists! Already lies before my view the *little all,* the last resource of an unfortunate family, (who knew better days, and certainly deserve a better fate) tumbled out of doors upon the pavement, and going to be sold off, probably for a debt of fifty shillings, what cost as many pounds! What, the myrmidons have spared nothing, I see— nothing has been saved from unhallowed fangs! Let me see—two old chairs, a broken pot, an old matress, one door rug, the poor man's mechanic tools, which brought his family a morsel of bread—the poor woman's little holiday thing—all gone! Nothing saved! Now flow ye tears, my eyes open your briny juices, or my distended heart must burst!—Well, this won't do, I'll go and comfort them a little—where

BENEVOLUS

are they? alas! they are gone too! O, what will become of them? I must and I will find them out. I am interested in their welfare; for I too am a man. This day will I abstain from my wonted luxuries and delicacies, that these my fellow creatures, my brethren, may feed upon my self-denial; that they too may eat and bless our common God!

O, would to the almighty, our common benefactor and father, and who is no respector of persons, we were all like dutiful children and loving brethren, more sedulously attentive to the duties and command of charity than we are! However, good christian readers let us one and all, who can, always and at *this* season of the year more especially, step forward to the relief of the poor; a small matter from time to time will do, *much* is not necessary. For this truly pious and good purpose let subscriptions be set on foot, charity sermons preached—societies instituted, and private donations be dispensed, that so a fund may be accumulated; and in order that the proper objects may be known and discovered, the different wards of the city should make true returns of their respective poor; at the same time specifying particulars for the regulation of the Christian Charitable Board. This is undoubtedly the only plan adequate to the occasion and competent to the exigency in question. Partial and precarious eleemosynary donations, amounting to no more than a temporary trivial relief. We may very conveniently relieve the poor without any sensible injury to our own affairs, be our circumstances ever so moderate; for *Charity* does not require that we should go beyond what we can afford; but then she requires and even *commands* what we *can* afford; as being in fact, none of our property; but *bona fide belongs to the poor*. 'Tis therefore our indispensable duty (and for which before the throne of God we are accountable) not to withhold it from them, as in that case, such a derelection would be the most execrable, reprehensible of all frauds; and God forbid, that any who rejoices in being a christian, should be guilty of it! There is no man but may make room (if I may so express myself) for his charity and benevolence to operate, if he will, for that end, curtail his sumptuary expences; and this may be done a thousand different ways—among the most feasible, as well as laudable of these, are retrenching the idle and ostentatious luxury of our pampering tables; we may change our rich and costly wines *sometimes* for cheaper, as well as more wholesome beverage; we may on some *particular days* dine upon plain beef, rather than vension or mutton; and not unfrequently in order to accomplish this heavenly design, we may forbear the company of a *half-friend;* or ask a cruel acquaintance who drops in, to stay for dinner. Tho' much more might have been urged upon this affecting subject, yet, considering the limits of your valuable paper, and the variety of important matters which uniformly crowd in upon the City Gazette, I shall conclude this address, which I think as applicable to every great town throughout the united states, as to our own capitals; and hope and wish accordingly, its influence and effects will pervade the union! For charity should know no bounds, but those of discretion and prudence; and no limits but the ends of the world.

BENEVOLUS

[53]

DAVID RAMSAY 1749–1815

The History of the American Revolution
(Selections)

PHILADELPHIA, 1789

David Ramsay was born in eastern Pennsylvania, was educated at the New Jersey College, which became Princeton University, studied medicine in Philadelphia's newly launched college of medicine, and shortly after took off to Charleston, South Carolina, to win fame and fortune. He enjoyed moderate success in the latter ambition, and his very considerable claims to fame stemmed less from the practice of medicine than from an extended period of service in legislative bodies and an avid interest in compiling histories of his times. Altogether he served nearly twenty years in two houses of the South Carolina legislature and some three years in the Congress organized under the Articles of Confederation and sitting in Philadelphia. Throughout his recording of contemporary history, Ramsay demonstrated a persistent concern to interrelate the aspirations and ideals, the beliefs and commitments, the events and the interplay of events with overriding and enveloping conditions that shaped the mold in which republican government was given its essential character. Americans had long been readers of history as witnessed by constant historical references in their political writings, whether it be the *Federalist Papers* or the writings reproduced in these volumes. It is not surprising, therefore, that they turned at an early date to writing their own history as a people. The best of these early American historians was David Ramsay. The two chapters excerpted here are from a two-volume work which, while efficiently laying out the events leading up to 1787, also proceeds to inject order and meaning into those events. Through the selection of what to include, and frequent explanations and generalizations, Ramsay produces a history of America's founding experience which reinforces and teaches its readers the basics of American political thought as they were generally accepted in 1789.

CHAPTER II

The first emigrants from England for colonising America, left the Mother Country at a time when the dread of arbitrary power was the predominant passion of the nation. Except the very modern charter of Georgia, in the year 1732, all the English Colonies obtained their charters and their greatest number of European settlers, between the years 1603 and 1688. In this period a remarkable struggle between prerogative and privilege commenced, and was carried on till it terminated in a revolution highly favourable to the liberties of the people. In the year 1621, when the English House of Commons claimed freedom of speech, "as their ancient and undoubted right, and an inheritance transmitted to them from their ancestors;" King James the First replied, "that he could not allow of their style, in mentioning their ancient and undoubted rights, but would rather have wished they had said, that their privileges were derived from the grace and permission of their sovereign." This was the opening of a dispute which occupied the tongues, pens and swords, of the most active men in the nation, for a period of seventy years. It is remarkable that the same period is exactly co-incident with the settlement of the English Colonies. James, educated in the arbitrary sentiments of the divine right of Kings, conceived his subjects to be his property, and that their privileges were [27] matters of grace and favour flowing, from his generosity. This high claim of prerogative excited opposition in support of the rights of the people. In the progress of the dispute, Charles the First, son of King James, in attempting to levy ship-money, and other revenues without consent of Parliament, involved himself in a war with his subjects, in which, after various conflicts, he was brought to the block and suffered death as an enemy to the constitution of his country. Though the monarchy was restored under Charles the Second, and transmitted to James the Second, yet the same arbitrary maxims being pursued, the nation, tenacious of its rights, invited the Prince of Orange to the sovereignty of the island, and expelled the reigning family from the throne. While these spirited exertions were made, in support of the liberties of the parent isle, the English Colonies were settled, and chiefly with inhabitants of that class of people, which was most hostile to the claims of prerogative. Every transaction in that period of English history, supported the position that the people have a right to resist their sovereign, when

DAVID RAMSAY 1749–1815

he invades their liberties, and to transfer the crown from one to another, when the good of the community requires it.

The English Colonists were from their first settlement in America, devoted to liberty, on English ideas, and English principles. They not only conceived themselves to inherit the privileges of Englishmen, but though in a colonial situation, actually possessed them.

After a long war between King and Parliament, and a Revolution—these were settled on the following fundamental principles. "That it was the undoubted right of English subjects, being freemen or freeholders, to give their property, only by their own consent. That the House of Commons exercised the sole right of granting the money of the people of England, because that house alone, represented them. That taxes were the free gifts of the people to their rulers. That the authority of sovereigns was to be exercised only for the good of their subjects. That it was the right of the people to meet together, and peaceably to consider of their grievances—[28] to petition for a redress of them, and finally, when intolerable grievances were unredressed, to seek relief, on the failure of petitions and remonstrances, by forcible means."

Opinions of this kind generally prevailing, produced, among the colonists, a more determined spirit of opposition to all encroachments on their rights, than would probably have taken place, had they emigrated from the Mother Country in the preceding century, when the doctrines of passive obedience, non resistance, and the divine right of kings, were generally received.

That attachment to their sovereign, which was diminished in the first emigrants to America, by being removed to a great distance from his influence was still farther diminished, in their descendants. When the American revolution commenced, the inhabitants of the colonies were for the most part, the third and fourth, and sometimes the fifth or sixth generation, from the original emigrants. In the same degree as they were removed from the parent stock, they were weaned from that partial attachment, which bound their forefathers to the place of their nativity. The affection for the Mother Country, as far as it was a natural passion, wore away in successive generations, till at last it had scarcely any existence.

That mercantile intercourse, which connects different countries, was in the early periods of the English Colonies, far short of that degree, which is necessary to perpetuate a friendly union. Had the first great colonial establishments been made in the Southern Provinces, where the suitableness of native commodities would have maintained a brisk and direct trade with England—the constant exchange of good offices between the two countries, would have been more likely to perpetuate their friendship. But as the Eastern Provinces were the first, which were thickly settled, and they did not for a long time cultivate an extensive trade with England, their descendants speedily lost the fond attachment, which their forefathers felt to their Parent State. The bulk of the people in New England knew little of the Mother Country, having only heard of her as a distant kingdom, the rulers [29] of which, had in the preceding century, persecuted and banished their ancestors to the woods of America.

The distance of America from Great Britain generated ideas, in the minds of the colonists, favourable to liberty. Three thousand miles of ocean separated them from the Mother Country. Seas rolled, and months passed, between orders, and their execution. In large governments the circulation of power is enfeebled at the extremities. This results from the nature of things, and is the eternal law of extensive or detached empire. Colonists, growing up to maturity, at such an immense distance from the seat of government, perceived the obligation of dependence much more feebly, than the inhabitants of the parent isle, who not only saw, but daily felt, the fangs of power. The wide extent and nature of the country contributed to the same effect. The natural seat of freedom is among high mountains, and pathless deserts, such as abound in the wilds of America.

The religion of the colonists also nurtured a love for liberty. They were chiefly protestants, and all protestantism is founded on a strong claim to natural liberty, and the right of private judgement. A majority of them were of that class of men, who, in England, are called Dissenters. Their tenets, being the protestantism of the protestant religion, are hostile to all interference of authority, in matters of opinion, and predispose to a jealousy for civil liberty. They who belonged to the Church of England were for the most part independents, as far as church government and hierarchy, were concerned. They used the liturgy of that church, but were without Bishops, and were strangers to those systems, which make religion an engine of state. That policy, which unites the lowest curate with the greatest metropolitan, and connects both with the sovereign, was unknown among the colonists. Their religion was their own, and neither imposed by authority, nor made subservient to political purposes. Though there was a variety of sects, they all agreed in the communion of liberty, and all reprobated the courtly doctrines of passive obedience, and non-resistance. The same dispositions were fostered by the usual [30] modes of education in the colonies. The study of law was common and fashionable. The infinity of disputes, in a new and free country, made it lucrative, and multiplied its followers. No order of men has, in all ages, been more favourable to liberty, than lawyers. Where they are not won over to the service of government, they are formidable adversaries to it. Professionally taught the rights of human nature, they keenly and quickly perceive every attack made on them. While others judge of bad principles by the actual grievances they occasion, lawyers discover them at a distance, and trace future mischiefs from gilded innovations.

The reading of those colonists who were inclined to books, generally favoured the cause of liberty. Large libraries were uncommon in the New World. Disquisitions on abstruse subjects, and curious researches into antiquity, did not accord with the genius of a people, settled in an uncultivated country, where every surrounding object impelled to action, and little leisure was left for speculation. Their books were generally small in size, and few in number: A great part of them consisted of those fashionable authors, who have defended the cause of liberty. Catos' letters, the Independent Whig, and such productions, were common in one extreme of the colonies, while in the other, histories of the Puritans, kept alive the rememberance of the sufferings of their forefathers, and inspired a warm attachment, both to the civil and the religious rights of human nature.

In the Southern Colonies, slavery nurtured a spirit of liberty, among the free inhabitants. All masters of slaves who enjoy personal liberty will be both proud and jealous of their freedom. It is, in their opinion, not only an enjoyment, but a kind of rank and privilege. In them, the haughtiness of domination, combines with the spirit of liberty. Nothing could more effectually animate the opposition of a planter to the claims of Great-Britain, than a conviction that those claims in their extent, degraded him to a degree of dependence on his fellow subjects, equally humiliating with that which existed between his slaves and himself.

[31] The state of society in the Colonies favoured a spirit of liberty and independence. Their inhabitants were all of one rank,

Kings, Nobles and Bishops, were unknown among them. From their first settlement, the English Provinces received impressions favourable to democratic forms of government. Their dependent situation forbad any inordinate ambition among their native sons, and the humility of their society, abstracted as they were from the splendor and amusements of the Old World, held forth few allurements to invite the residence of such from the Mother Country as aspired to hereditary honors. In modern Europe, the remains of the feudal system have occasioned an order of men superior to that of the commonalty, but, as few of that class migrated to the Colonies, they were settled with the yeomanry. Their inhabitants, unaccustomed to that distinction of ranks, which the policy of Europe has established, were strongly impressed with an opinion, that all men are by nature equal. They could not easily be persuaded that their grants of land, or their civil rights, flowed from the munificence of Princes. Many of them had never heard of Magna Charta, and those who knew the circumstances of the remarkable period of English history, when that was obtained, did not rest their claims to liberty and property on the transactions of that important day. They looked up to Heaven as the source of their rights, and claimed, not from the promises of Kings but, from the parent of the universe. The political creed of an American Colonist was short but substantial. He believed that God made all mankind originally equal: That he endowed them with the rights of life, property, and as much liberty as was consistent with the rights of others. That he had bestowed on his vast family of the human race, the earth for their support, and that all government was a political institution between men naturally equal, not for the aggrandizement of one, or a few, but for the general happiness of the whole community. Impressed with sentiments of this kind, they grew up, from their earliest infancy, with that confidence which is well calculated to inspire a love for liberty, and a prepossession in favour of independence.

[32] In consequence of the vast extent of vacant country, every colonist was, or easily might be, a freeholder. Settled on lands of his own, he was both farmer and landlord—producing all the necessaries of life from his own grounds, he felt himself both free and independent. Each individual might hunt, fish, or fowl, without injury to his neighbours. These immunities which, in old countries, are guarded by the sanction of penal laws, and monopolized by a few, are the common privileges of all, in America. Colonists, growing up in the

enjoyment of such rights, felt the restraint of law more feebly than they, who are educated in countries, where long habits have made submission familiar. The mind of man naturally relishes liberty— Where from the extent of a new and unsettled country, some abridgements thereof are useless, and others impracticable, the natural desire of freedom is strengthened, and the independent mind revolts at the idea of subjection.

The Colonists were also preserved from the contagion of ministerial influence by their distance from the metropolis. Remote from the seat of power and corruption, they were not over-awed by the one, nor debauched by the other. Few were the means of detaching individuals from the interest of the public. High offices, were neither sufficiently numerous nor lucrative to purchase many adherents, and the most valuable of these were conferred on natives of Britain. Every man occupied that rank only, which his own industry, or that of his near ancestors, had procured him. Each individual being cut off from all means of rising to importance, but by his personal talents, was encouraged to make the most of those with which he was endowed. Prospects of this kind excited emulation, and produced an enterprising laborious set of men, not easily overcome by difficulties, and full of projects for bettering their condition.

The enervating opulence of Europe had not yet reached the colonists. They were destitute of gold and silver, but abounded in the riches of nature. A sameness of circumstances and occupations created a great sense of equality, and disposed them to union in any common cause, [33] from the success of which, they might expect to partake of equal advantages.

The colonies were communities of separate independent individuals, under no general influence, but that of their personal feelings and opinions. They were not led by powerful families, nor by great officers, in church or state. Residing chiefly on lands of their own, and employed in the wholesome labours of the field, they were in a great measure strangers to luxury. Their wants were few, and among the great bulk of the people, for the most part, supplied from their own grounds. Their enjoyments were neither far-fetched, nor dearly purchased, and were so moderate in their kind, as to leave both mind and body unimpaired. Inured from their early years to the toils of a country life, they dwelled in the midst of rural plenty. Unacquainted with ideal wants, they delighted in personal independence. Removed from the pressures of indigence, and the indulgence of affluence, their bodies were strong, and their minds vigorous.

The great bulk of the British colonists were farmers, or planters, who were also proprietors of the soil. The merchants, mechanics and manufacturers, taken collectively, did not amount to one fifteenth of the whole number of inhabitants. While the cultivators of the soil depend on nothing but heaven and their own industry, other classes of men contract more or less of servility, from depending on the caprice of their customers. The excess of the farmers over the collective numbers of all the other inhabitants, gave a cast of independence to the manners of the people, and diffused the exalting sentiments, which have always predominated among those, who are cultivators of their own grounds. These were farther promoted by their moderate circumstances, which deprived them of all superfluity for idleness, or effeminate indulgence.

The provincial constitutions of the English colonies nurtured a spirit of liberty. The King and government of Great-Britain held no patronage in America, which could create a portion of attachment and influence, sufficient to counteract that spirit in popular assemblies, which, when left to itself, illy brooks any authority, that intereferes with its own.

[34] The inhabitants of the colonies from the beginning, especially in New-England, enjoyed a government, which was but little short of being independent. They had not only the image, but the substance of the English constitution. They chose most of their magistrates, and paid them all. They had in effect the sole direction of their internal government. The chief mark of their subordination consisted in their making no laws repugnant to the laws of their Mother Country.— Their submitting such laws as they made to be repealed by the King, and their obeying such restrictions, as were laid on their trade, by parliament. The latter were often evaded, and with impunity. The other small checks were scarcely felt, and for a long time were in no respects injurious to their interests.

Under these favourable circumstances, colonies in the new world had advanced nearly to the magnitude of a nation, while the greatest part of Europe was almost wholly ignorant of their progress. Some arbitrary proceedings of governors, proprietary partialities, or democratical jealousies, now and then, interrupted the political calm, which generally prevailed among them, but these and other occasional

DAVID RAMSAY 1749–1815

impediments of their prosperity, for the most part, soon subsided. The circumstances of the country afforded but little scope for the intrigues of politicians, or the turbulence of demagogues. The colonists being but remotely affected by the bustlings of the old world, and having but few objects of ambition or contention among themselves, were absorbed in the ordinary cares of domestic life, and for a long time exempted from a great proportion of those evils, which the governed too often experience, from the passions and follies of statesmen. But all this time they were rising higher, and though not sensible of it, growing to a greater degree of political consequence. . . .

[50] Immediately after the peace of Paris, 1763, a new scene was opened. The national debt of Great-Britain, then amounted to 148 millions, for which an interest of nearly 5 millions, was annually paid. While the British minister was digesting plans for diminishing this amazing load of debt, he conceived the idea of raising a substantial revenue in the British colonies, from taxes laid by the parliament of the parent state. On the one hand it was urged that the late war originated on account of the colonies—that it was reasonable, more especially as it had terminated in a manner so favourable to their interest, that they should contribute to the defraying of the expences it had occasioned. Thus far both parties were agreed, but Great-Britain contended, that her parliament as the supreme power, was constitutionally vested with an authority to lay them on every part of the empire. This doctrine, plausible in itself, and conformable to the letter of the British constitution, when the whole dominions were represented in one assembly, was reprobated in the colonies, as contrary to the spirit of the same government, when the empire became so far extended, as to have many distinct representative assemblies. The colonists believed that the chief excellence of the [51] British constitution consisted in the right of the subjects to grant, or withhold taxes, and in their having a share in enacting the laws, by which they were to be bound.

They conceived, that the superiority of the British constitution, to other forms of government was, not because their supreme council was called Parliament, but because, the people had a share in it, by appointing members, who constituted one of its constituent branches, and without whose concurrence, no law, binding on them, could be enacted. In the Mother Country, it was asserted to be essential to the unity of the empire, that the British Parliament should have a right of taxation, over every part of the royal dominions. In the colonies, it was believed, that taxation and representation were inseparable, and that they could neither be free, nor happy, if their property could be taken from them, without their consent. The common people in America reasoned on this subject, in a summary way: "If a British Parliament," said they, "in which we are unrepresented, and over which we have no controul, can take from us any part of our property, by direct taxation, they may take as much as they please, and we have no security for any thing, that remains, but a forbearance on their part, less likely to be exercised in our favour, as they lighten themselves of the burthens of government, in the same proportion, that they impose them on us." They well knew, that communities of mankind, as well as individuals, have a strong propensity to impose on others, when they can do it with impunity, and, especially, when there is a prospect, that the imposition will be attended with advantage to themselves. The Americans, from that jealousy of their liberties, which their local situation nurtured, and which they inherited from their forefathers, viewed the exclusive right of laying taxes on themselves, free from extraneous influence, in the same light, as the British Parliament views its peculiar privilege of raising money, independent of the crown. The parent state appeared to the colonists to stand in the same relation to their local legislatures, as the monarch of Great-Britain, to the British [52] Parliament. His prerogative is limited by that palladium of the people's liberty, the exclusive privilege of granting their own money. While this right rests in the hands of the people, their liberties are secured. In the same manner reasoned the colonists "in order to be stiled freemen, our local assemblies, elected by ourselves, must enjoy the exclusive privilege of imposing taxes upon us." They contended, that men settled in foreign parts to better their condition, and not to submit their liberties—to continue the equals, not to become the slave of their less adventurous fellow-citizens, and that by the novel doctrine of parliamentary power, they were degraded from being the subjects of a King, to the low condition of being subjects of subjects. They argued, that it was essentially involved in the idea of property, that the possessor had such a right therein, that it was a contradiction to suppose any other man, or body of men, possessed a right to take it from him without his consent. Precedents, in the history of England, justified this mode of reasoning. The love of property strengthened it, and it had a peculiar force on

DAVID RAMSAY 1749–1815

the minds of colonists, 3000 miles removed from the seat of government, and growing up to maturity, in a new world, where, from the extent of country, and the state of society, even the necessary restraints of civil government, were impatiently born. On the other hand, the people of Great-Britain revolted against the claims of the colonists. Educated in habits of submission to parliamentary taxation, they conceived it to be the height of contumacy for their colonists to refuse obedience to the power, which they had been taught to revere. Not adverting to the common interest, which existed between the people of Great-Britain, and their representatives, they believed, that the same right existed, although the same community of interests was wanting. The pride of an opulent, conquering nation, aided this mode of reasoning. "What," said they, "shall we, who have so lately humbled France and Spain, be dictated to by our own colonists? Shall our subjects, educated by our care, and defended by our arms, presume to question the rights of Parliament, to which we are obliged to [53] submit." Reflections of this kind, congenial to the natural vanity of the human heart, operated so extensively, that the people of Great-Britain spoke of their colonies and of their colonists, as of a kind of possession, annexed to their persons. The love of power, and of property, on the one side of the Atlantic, were opposed by the same powerful passions on the other.

The disposition to tax the colonies, was also strengthened by exaggerated accounts of their wealth. It was said, "that the American planters lived in affluence, and with inconsiderable taxes, while the inhabitants of Great-Britain were born down, by such oppressive burdens, as to make a bare subsistence, a matter of extreme difficulty." The officers who have served in America, during the late war, contributed to this delusion. Their observations were founded on what they had seen in cities, and at a time, when large sums were spent by government, in support of fleets and armies, and when American commodities were in great demand. To treat with attention those, who came to fight for them and also to gratify their own pride, the colonists had made a parade of their riches, by frequently and sumptuously entertaining the gentlemen of the British army. These, judging from what they saw, without considering the general state of the country, concurred in representing the colonists, as very able to contribute, largely, towards defraying the common expences of the empire.

The charters, which were supposed to contain the principles on which the colonies were founded, became the subject of serious investigation on both sides. One clause was found to run through the whole of them, except that which had been granted to Mr. Penn. This was a declaration, "that the emigrants to America should enjoy the same privileges, as if they had remained, or had been born within the realm;" but such was the subtilty of disputants, that both parties construed this general principle, so as to favour their respective opinions. The American patriots contended, that as English freeholders could not be taxed, but by representatives, in chusing whom they had a vote, neither could the colonists: But [54] it was replied, that if the colonists had remained in England, they must have been bound to pay the taxes, imposed by parliament. It was therefore inferred, that, though taxed by that authority, they lost none of the rights of native Englishmen, residing at home. The partizans of the Mother Country could see nothing in charters, but security against taxes, by royal authority. The Americans, adhering to the spirit more than to the letter, viewed their charters, as a shield, against all taxes, not imposed by representatives of their own choice. This construction they contended to be expressly recognized by the charter of Maryland. In that, King Charles bound, both himself and his successors, not to assent to any bill, subjecting the inhabitants to internal taxation, by external legislation.

The nature and extent of the connection between Great-Britain and America, was a great constitutional question, involving many interests, and the general principles of civil liberty. To decide this, recourse was in vain had to parchment authorities, made at a distant time, when neither the grantor, nor grantees, of American territory, had in contemplation, any thing like the present state of the two countries.

Great and flourishing colonies, daily increasing in numbers, and already grown to the magnitude of a nation, planted at an immense distance, and governed by constitutions, resembling that of the country, from which they sprung, were novelties in the history of the world. To combine colonies, so circumstanced, in one uniform system of government, with the parent state, required a great knowledge of mankind, and an extensive comprehension of things. It was an arduous business, far beyond the grasp of ordinary statesmen, whose minds were narrowed by the formalities of law, or the trammels of office.

DAVID RAMSAY 1749–1815

An original genius, unfettered with precedents, and exalted with just ideas of the rights of human nature, and the obligations of universal benevolence, might have struck out a middle line, which would have secured as much liberty to the colonies, and as great a degree of supremacy to the parent state, as their common good required: But [55] the helm of Great-Britain was not in such hands. The spirit of the British constitution on the one hand, revolted at the idea, that the British parliament should exercise the same unlimited authority over the unrepresented colonies, which it exercised over the inhabitants of Great-Britain. The colonists on the other hand did not claim a total exemption from its authority. They in general allowed the Mother Country a certain undefined prerogative over them, and acquiesced in the right of Parliament, to make many acts, binding them in many subjects of internal policy, and regulating their trade. Where parliamentary supremacy ended, and at what point colonial independency began, was not ascertained. Happy would it have been, had the question never been agitated, but much more so, had it been compromised by an amicable compact, without the horrors of a civil war.

The English colonies were originally established, not for the sake of revenue, but on the principles of a commercial monopoly. While England pursued trade and forgot revenue, her commerce increased at least fourfold. The colonies took off the manufactures of Great-Britain, and paid for them with provisions, or raw materials. They united their arms in war, their commerce and their councils in peace, without nicely investigating the terms on which the connection of the two countries depended.

A perfect calm in the political world is not long to be expected. The reciprocal happiness, both of Great-Britain and of the colonies, was too great to be of long duration. The calamities of the war of 1755, had scarcely ended, when the germ of another war was planted, which soon grew up and produced deadly fruit.

At that time sundry resolutions passed the British parliament, 1764. relative to the imposition of a stamp duty in America, which gave a general alarm. By them the right, the equity, the policy, and even the necessity of taxing the colonies was formally avowed. These resolutions being considered as the preface of a system of American revenue, were deemed an introduction to evils of much greater magnitude. They opened a prospect of oppression, [56] boundless in extent, and endless in duration. They were nevertheless not immediately followed by any legislative act. Time, and an invitation, were given to the Americans, to suggest any other mode of taxation, that might be equivalent in its produce to the stamp act: But they objected, not only to the mode, but the principle, and several of their assemblies, though in vain, petitioned against it. An American revenue was in England, a very popular measure. The cry in favour of it was so strong, as to confound and silence the voice of petitions to the contrary. The equity of compelling the Americans to contribute to the common expences of the empire, satisfied many, who, without enquiring into the policy or justice of taxing their unrepresented fellow subjects, readily assented to the measures adopted by the parliament, for this purpose. The prospect of easing their own burdens, at the expence of the colonists, dazzled the eyes of gentlemen of landed interest, so as to keep out of their view, the probable consequences of the innovation.

The omnipotence of parliament was so familiar a phrase on both sides of the Atlantic, that few in America, and still fewer in Great-Britain, were impressed in the first instance, with any idea of the illegality of taxing the colonists.

The illumination on that subject was gradual. The resolutions in favour of an American stamp act, which passed in March, 1764, met with no opposition. In the course of the year, which intervened between these resolutions, and the passing of a law grounded upon them, the subject was better understood and constitutional objections against the measure, were urged by several, both in Great-Britain and America. This astonished and chagrined the British ministry: But as the principle of taxing America, had been for some time determined upon, they were unwilling to give it up. Impelled by partiality for a long cherished idea, Mr. Grenville brought into the house of commons his long expected bill, for laying a stamp duty in America. By this after passing through the usual forms, it was enacted, that the [57] instruments of writing which are in daily use among a commercial people, should be null and void, unless they were executed on stamped paper or parchment, charged with a duty imposed by the British parliament.

March, 1765.

When the bill was brought in, Mr. Charles Townsend concluded a speech in its favour, with words to the following effect, "And now will these Americans, children planted by our care, nourished up by our indulgence, till they are grown to a degree of strength and opulence, and protected by our arms, will they grudge to contribute their mite to relieve us from the heavy weight of that burden which we lie under." To which Colonel Barré replied, "They planted by your care? No, your oppressions planted them in America. They fled from tyranny to a then uncultivated and unhospitable country, where they exposed themselves to almost all the hardships to which human nature is liable; and among others to the cruelty of a savage foe the most subtle, and I will take upon me to say, the most formidable of any people upon the face of God's earth; and yet, actuated by principles of true English liberty, they met all hardships with pleasure compared with those they suffered in their own country, from the hands of those that should have been their friends. They nourished up by your indulgence? They grew by your neglect of them. As soon as you began to care about them, that care was exercised in sending persons to rule them in one department and another, who were perhaps the deputies of deputies to some members of this house, sent to spy out their liberties, to misrepresent their actions and to prey upon them.—Men, whose behaviour on many occasions, has caused the blood of those sons of liberty to recoil within them.—Men promoted to the highest seats of justice, some who to my knowledge were glad by going to a foreign country, to escape being brought to the bar of a court of justice in their own.—They protected by your arms? They have nobly taken up arms in your defence, have exerted a valour amidst their constant and laborious industry, for the defence of a country whose frontier was drenched in blood, while its interior parts yielded all its little savings to your emolument. And believe [58] me, remember I this day told you so, that same spirit of freedom which actuated that people at first will accompany them still: but prudence forbids me to explain myself farther. God knows, I do not at this time speak from any motives of party heat, what I deliver are the genuine sentiments of my heart. However superior to me in general knowledge and experience, the respectable body of this house may be, yet I claim to know more of America than most of you, having seen and been conversant in that country. The people I believe are as truly loyal as any subjects the King has, but a people jealous of their liberties, and who will vindicate them, if ever they should be violated: but the subject is too delicate—I will say no more."

During the debate on the bill, the supporters of it insisted much on the colonies being virtually represented in the same manner as

Leeds, Halifax, and some other towns were. A recurrence to this plea was a virtual acknowledgment, that there ought not to be taxation without representation. It was replied, that the connexion between the electors and non-electors of parliament in Great-Britain, was so interwoven, from both being equally liable to pay the same common tax, as to give some security of property to the latter: but with respect to taxes laid by the British parliament, and paid by the Americans, the situation of the parties was reversed. Instead of both parties bearing a proportionable share of the same common burden, what was laid on the one, was exactly so much taken off from the other.

The bill met with no opposition in the house of Lords, and on the 22d of March, it received the royal assent. The night after it passed, Dr. Franklin wrote to Mr. Charles Thompson. "The sun of liberty is set, you must light up the candles of industry and oeconomy." Mr. Thompson answered, "he was apprehensive that other lights would be the consequence," and foretold the opposition that shortly took place. On its being suggested from authority, that the stamp officers would not be sent from Great-Britain: but selected from among the Americans, the colony agents were desired to point out proper persons [59] for the purpose. They generally nominated their friends which affords a presumptive proof, that they supposed the act would have gone down. In this opinion they were far from being singular. That the colonists would be ultimately obliged to submit to the stamp act, was at first commonly believed, both in England and America. The framers of it, in particular, flattered themselves that the confusion which would arise upon the disuse of writings, and the insecurity of property, which would result from using any other than that required by law, would compel the colonies, however reluctant, to use the stamp paper, and consequently to pay the taxes imposed thereon. They therefore boasted that it was a law which would execute itself. By the terms of the stamp act, it was not to take effect till the first day of November, a period of more than seven months after its passing. This gave the colonists an opportunity for leisurely canvassing the new subject, and examining it fully on every side. In the first part of this interval, struck with astonishment, they lay in silent consternation, and could not determine what course to pursue. By degrees they recovered their recollection. Virginia led the way in opposition to the stamp act. Mr. Patrick Henry brought into the house of burgesses of that colony, the following resolutions which were substantially adopted.

1765.

1765.

May 28, 1765.

DAVID RAMSAY 1749–1815

Resolved, That the first adventurers, settlers of this his Majesty's colony and dominion of Virginia, brought with them and transmitted to their posterity, and all other, his Majesty's subjects, since inhabiting in this, his Majesty's said colony, all the liberties, privileges and immunities, that have at any time been held, enjoyed and possessed by the people of Great-Britain.

Resolved, That by two royal charters, granted by King James the first, the colonies aforesaid are declared, and entitled to all liberties, privileges, and immunities of denizens, and natural subjects, to all intents and purposes, as if they had been abiding, and born within the realm of England,

Resolved, That his Majesty's liege people, of this, his ancient colony, have enjoyed the rights of being thus governed [60] by their own assembly, in the article of taxes, and internal police, and that the same have never been forfeited, or yielded up, but have been constantly recognized by the King and people of Britain.

Resolved, therefore, That the general assembly of this colony, together with his Majesty, or his substitutes, have, in their representative capacity, the only exclusive right and power, to lay taxes and imposts, upon the inhabitants of this colony, and that every attempt to vest such power in any other person or persons, whatsoever, than the general assembly aforesaid, is illegal, unconstitutional, and unjust, and hath a manifest tendency to destroy British, as well as American Liberty.

Resolved, That his Majesty's liege people, the inhabitants of this colony, are not bound to yield obedience to any law, or ordinance whatever, designed to impose any taxation whatever upon them, other, than the laws or ordinances of the general assembly aforesaid.

Resolved, That any person, who shall, by speaking, or writing, assert, or maintain, that any person, or persons, other than the general assembly of this colony, have any right or power, to impose, or lay any taxation on the people here, shall be deemed an enemy to this, his Majesty's colony.

Upon reading these resolutions, the boldness and novelty of them affected one of the members to such a degree, that he cried out, "Treason! Treason!" They were, nevertheless, well received by the people, and immediately forwarded to the other provinces. They circulated extensively, and gave a spring to all the discontented. Till they appeared, most were of opinion, that the act would be quietly adopted. Murmurs, indeed, were common, but they seemed to be such, as would soon die away. The countenance of so respectable a colony, as Virginia, confirmed the wavering, and emboldened the timid. Opposition to the stamp act, from that period, assumed a bolder face. The fire of liberty blazed forth from the press; some well judged publications set the rights of the colonists, in a plain, but strong point of view. The tongues and the pens of the well informed [61] citizens laboured in kindling the latent sparks of patriotism. The flame spread from breast to breast, till the conflagration, became general. In this business, New-England had a principal share. The inhabitants of that part of America, in particular, considered their obligations to the Mother Country for past favours, to be very inconsiderable. They were fully informed, that their forefathers were driven, by persecution, to the woods of America, and had there, without any expence to the parent state, effected a settlement on bare creation. Their resentment, for the invasion of their accustomed right of taxation, was not so much mitigated, by the recollection of late favours, as it was heightened by the tradition of grievous sufferings, to which their ancestors, by the rulers of England, had been subjected. The descendants of the exiled, persecuted, Puritans, of the last century, opposed the stamp act with the same spirit, with which their forefathers were actuated, when they set themselves against the arbitrary impositions of the House of Stuart.

The heavy burdens, which the operation of the stamp-act would have imposed on the colonists, together with the precedent it would establish of future exactions, furnished the American patriots with arguments, calculated as well to move the passions, as to convince the judgments of their fellow colonists. In great warmth they exclaimed, "If the parliament has a right to levy the stamp duties, they may, by the same authority, lay on us imposts, excises, and other taxes, without end, till their rapacity is satisfied, or our abilities are exhausted. We cannot, at future elections, displace these men, who so lavishly grant away our property. Their seats and their power are independent of us, and it will rest with their generosity, where to stop, in transferring the expences of government, from their own, to our shoulders."

It was fortunate for the liberties of America, that News-papers were the subject of a heavy stamp duty. Printers, when uninfluenced by government, have generally arranged themselves on the side of liberty, nor are they less remarkable for attention to the profits of

DAVID RAMSAY 1749–1815

their profession. A stamp duty, which openly invaded the first, [62] and threatened a great diminution of the last, provoked their united zealous opposition. They daily presented to the public, original dissertations, tending to prove, that if the stamp-act was suffered to operate, the liberties of America, were at end, and their property virtually transferred, to their Trans-Atlantic fellow-subjects. The writers among the Americans, seriously alarmed for the fate of their country, came forward, with essays, to prove, that agreeably to the British constitution, taxation and representation were inseparable, that the only constitutional mode of raising money from the colonists, was by acts of their own legislatures, that the Crown possessed no farther power, than that of requisition, and that the parliamentary right of taxation was confined to the Mother Country, and there originated, from the natural right of man, to do what he pleased with his own, transferred by consent from the electors of Great-Britain, to those whom they chose to represent them in Parliament. They also insisted much on the mis-application of public money by the British ministry. Great pains were taken to inform the colonists, of the large sums, annually bestowed on pensioned favorites, and for the various purposes of bribery. Their passions were inflamed, by high coloured representations of the hardship of being obliged to pay the earnings of their industry, into a British treasury, well known to be a fund for corruption. . . .

[68] The expediency of calling a continental Congress to be composed of deputies from each of the provinces, had early occurred to the people of Massachusetts. The assembly of that province passed a resolution in favour of that measure, and fixed on New-York as the place, and the second Tuesday of October, as the time, for holding the same. Soon after, they sent circular letters to the speakers of the several assemblies, requesting their concurrence. This first advance towards continental union was seconded in South-Carolina, before it had been agreed to by any colony to the southward of New-England. The example of this province had a considerable influence in recommending the measure to others, who were divided in their opinions, on the propriety of it.

1765.
June 6.

The assemblies of Virginia, North-Carolina, and Georgia, were prevented, by their governors, from sending a deputation to this Congress. Twenty eight Deputies from Massachusetts, Rhode-Island, Connecticut, New-York, New-Jersey, Pennsylvania, Delaware, Mary-

land, and South-Carolina met at New-York; and after mature deliberation agreed on a declaration of their rights, and on a statement of
their grievances. They asserted in strong terms, their exemption from
all taxes, not imposed by their own representatives. They also concurred
in a petition to the King, and memorial to the House of Lords, and
a petition to the House of Commons. The colonies that were prevented from sending their representatives to this Congress, forwarded petitions, similar to those which were adopted by the deputies which attended. . . .

[334]   CHAP. XIII.

1777.   In former ages it was common for a part of a community to
migrate, and erect themselves into an independent society. Since the
earth has been more fully peopled, and especially since the principles
of Union have been better understood, a different policy has prevailed.
A fondness for planting colonies has, for three preceding centuries,
given full scope to a disposition for emigration, and at the same time
the emigrants have been retained in a connexion with their Parent
State. By these means Europeans have made the riches both of the
east and west, subservient to their avarice and ambition. Though they
occupy the smallest portion of the four quarters of the globe, they
have contrived to subject the other three to their influence or command.

The circumstances under which New-England was planted, would
a few centuries ago have entitled them from their first settlement, to
the privileges of independence. They were virtually exiled from their
native country, by being denied the rights of men—they set out on
their own expence, and after purchasing the consent of the native
proprietors, improved an uncultivated country, to which, in the eye
of reason and philosophy, the king of England had no title.

If it is lawful for individuals to relinquish their native soil, and
pursue their own happiness in other regions and under other political
associations, the settlers of New-England were always so far independent, as to owe no obedience to their Parent State, but such as
resulted from their voluntary assent. The slavish doctrine of the divine
right of kings, and the corruptions of christianity, by undervaluing
heathen titles, favoured an opposite system. What for several centuries
after the christian era would have been called the institution of a new

DAVID RAMSAY 1749–1815

government, was by modern refinement denominated only an extension of the old, in the form of a dependent colony. Though the prevailing ecclesiastical and political creeds [335] tended to degrade the condition of the settlers in New-England, yet there was always a party there which believed in their natural right to independence. They recurred to first principles, and argued, that as they received from government nothing more than a charter, founded on ideal claims of sovereignty, they owed it no other obedience than what was derived from express, or implied compact. It was not till the present century had more than half elapsed, that it occurred to any number of the colonists, that they had an interest in being detached from Great-Britain. Their attention was first turned to this subject, by the British claim of taxation. This opened a melancholy prospect, boundless in extent, and endless in duration. The Boston port act, and the other acts, passed in 1774 and 1775, which have been already the subject of comment, progressively weakened the attachment of the colonists to the birth place of their forefathers. The commencement of hostilities on the 19th of April, 1775, exhibited the Parent State in an odious point of view, and abated the original dread of separating from it. But nevertheless at that time, and for a twelve month after, a majority of the colonists wished for no more than to be re-established as subjects in their antient rights. Had independence been their object even at the commencement of hostilities, they would have rescinded these associations, which have been already mentioned and imported more largely than ever. Common sense revolts at the idea, that colonists unfurnished with military stores, and wanting manufactures of every kind, should at the time of their intending a serious struggle for independence, by a voluntary agreement, deprive themselves of the obvious means of procuring such foreign supplies as their circumstances might might make necessary. Instead of pursuing a line of conduct, which might have been dictated by a wish for independence, they continued their exports for nearly a year after they ceased to import. This not only lessened the debts they owed to Great-Britain, but furnished additional means for carrying on the war against themselves. To aim at independence, and at the same time to transfer their resources to their enemies, could not have been [336] the policy of an enlightened people. It was not till some time in 1776, that the colonists began to take other ground, and contend that it was for their interest to be forever separated from Great-Britain. In favour of this opinion it was said, that in case of their continuing subjects, the Mother country, though she redressed their present grievances, might at pleasure repeat similar oppressions.—That she ought not to be trusted, having twice resumed the exercise of taxation, after it had been apparently relinquished. The favourers of separation also urged, that Great-Britain was jealous of their increasing numbers, and rising greatness—that she would not exercise government for their benefit, but for her own. That the only permanent security for American happiness, was to deny her the power of interfering with their government or commerce. To effect this purpose they were of opinion, that it was necessary to cut the knot, which connected the two countries, by a public renunciation of all political connections between them.

The Americans about this time began to be influenced by new views.—The military arrangements of the preceding year—their unexpected union, and prevailing enthusiasm, expanded the minds of their leaders, and elevated the sentiments of the great body of their people. Decisive measures which would have been lately reprobated, now met with approbation.

The favourers of subordination under the former constitution urged the advantages of a supreme head, to control the disputes of interfering colonies, and also the benefits which flowed from union. That independence was untried ground, and should not be entered upon, but in the last extremity.

They flattered themselves that Great-Britain was so fully convinced of the determined spirit of America, that if the present controversy was compromised, she would not at any future period, resume an injurious exercise of her supremacy. They were therefore for proceeding no farther than to defend themselves in the character of subjects, trusting that ere long the present hostile measures would be relinquished, and the harmony [337] of the two countries re-established. The favourers of this system were embarrassed, and all their arguments weakened, by the perseverance of Great-Britain in her schemes of coercion. A probable hope of a speedy repeal of a few acts of parliament, would have greatly increased the number of those who were advocates for reconciliation. But the certainty of intelligence to the contrary gave additional force to the arguments of the opposite party. Though new weight was daily thrown into the scale, in which the advantages of independence were weighed, yet it did not preponderate till about that time in 1776, when intelligence reached the colonists of the act of parliament passed in December 1775, for throwing them out of British protection, and of hiring foreign troops to assist in effecting their conquest. Respecting the first it was said, "that protection and allegiance were reciprocal, and that the refusal of the first was a legal ground of justification for withholding the last." They considered themselves to be thereby discharged from their allegiance, and that to declare themselves independent, was no more than to announce to the world the real political state, in which Great-Britain had placed them. This act proved that the colonists might constitutionally declare themselves independent, but the hiring of foreign troops to make war upon them, demonstrated the necessity of their doing it immediately. They reasoned that if Great Britain called in the aid of strangers to crush them, they must seek similar relief for their own preservation. But they well knew this could not be expected, while they were in arms against their acknowledged sovereign. They had therefore only a choice of difficulties, and must either seek foreign aid as independent states, or continue in the aukward and hazardous situation of subjects, carrying on war from their own resources both against their king, and such mercenaries as he chose to employ for their subjugation. Necessity not choice forced them on the decision. Submission without obtaining a redress of their grievances was advocated by none who possessed the public confidence. Some of the popular leaders may have [338] secretly wished for independence from the beginning of the controversy, but their number was small and their sentiments were not generally known.

While the public mind was balancing on this eventful subject, several writers placed the advantages of independence in various points of view. Among these Thomas Paine in a pamphlet, under the signature of Common Sense, held the most distinguished rank. The stile, manner, and language of this performance were calculated to interest the passions, and to rouse all the active powers of human nature. With the view of operating on the sentiments of a religious people, scripture was pressed into his service, and the powers, and even the name of a king was rendered odious in the eyes of the numerous colonists who had read and studied the history of the Jews, as recorded in the Old Testament. The folly of that people in revolting from a government, instituted by Heaven itself, and the oppressions to which they were subjected in consequence of their lusting after kings to rule over them, afforded an excellent handle for prepossessing the colonists in favour of republican institutions, and prejudicing them against kingly government. Hereditary succession was turned into ridicule. The absurdity of subjecting a great continent to a small island on the other side of the globe, was represented in such striking language, as to interest the honor and pride of the colonists in renouncing the government of Great-Britain. The necessity, the advantages, and practicability of independence, were forcibly demonstrated. Nothing could be better timed than this performance. It was addressed to freemen, who had just received convincing proof, that Great-Britain had thrown them out of her protection, had engaged foreign mercenaries to make war upon them, and seriously designed to compel their unconditional submission to her unlimited power. It found the colonists most thoroughly alarmed for their liberties, and disposed to do and suffer any thing that promised their establishment. In union with the feelings and sentiments of the people, it produced surprising effects. Many thousands were convinced, and were led to approve [339] and long for a separation from the Mother Country. Though that measure, a few months before, was not only foreign from their wishes, but the object of their abhorrence, the current suddenly became so strong in its favour, that it bore down all opposition. The multitude was hurried down the stream, but some worthy men could not easily reconcile themselves to the idea of an eternal separation from a country, to which they had been long bound by the most endearing ties. They saw the sword drawn, but could not tell when it would be sheathed. They feared that the dispersed individuals of the several colonies would not be brought to coalesce under an efficient government, and that after much anarchy some future Caesar would grasp their liberties, and confirm himself in a throne of despotism. They doubted the perseverance of their countrymen in effecting their independence, and were also apprehensive that in case of success, their future condition would be less happy than their past. Some respectable individuals whose principles were pure, but whose souls were not of that firm texture which revolutions require, shrunk back from the bold measures proposed by their more adventurous countrymen. To submit without an appeal to Heaven, though secretly wished for by some, was not the avowed sentiment of any. But to persevere in petitioning and resisting was the system of some misguided honest men. The favourers of this opinion were generally wanting in that decision which grasps at great objects, and influenced by that timid policy, which does its work by halves. Most of them dreaded the power of Britain. A few, on the score of interest or an expectancy of favours from royal government, refused to concur with the general voice. Some of the natives of the Parent State who, having lately settled in the colonies, had not yet exchanged European for American ideas, together with a few others, conscientiously opposed the measures of Congress: but the great bulk of the people, and especially of the spirited and independent part of the community, came with surprising unanimity into the project of independence.

[340] The eagerness for independence resulted more from feeling   1776. than reasoning. The advantages of an unfettered trade, the prospect of honours and emoluments in administering a new government, were of themselves insufficient motives for adopting this bold measure. But what was wanting from considerations of this kind, was made up by the perseverance of Great-Britain, in her schemes of coercion and conquest. The determined resolution of the Mother Country to subdue the colonists, together with the plans she adopted for accomplishing that purpose, and their equally determined resolution to appeal to Heaven rather than submit, made a declaration of independence as necessary in 1776, as was the non-importation agreement of 1774, or the assumption of arms in 1775. The last naturally resulted from the first. The revolution was not forced on the people by ambitious leaders grasping at supreme power, but every measure of it was forced on Congress, by the necessity of the case, and the voice of the people. The change of the public mind of America respecting connexion with Great-Britain, is without a parallel. In the short space of two years, nearly three millions of people passed over from the love and duty of loyal subjects, to the hatred and resentment of enemies.

The motion for declaring the colonies free and independent, was   June 7. first made in Congress, by Richard Henry Lee of Virginia. He was warranted in making this motion by the particular instructions of his immediate constituents, and also by the general voice of the people of all the states. When the time for taking the subject under consideration arrived, much knowledge, ingenuity and eloquence were displayed on both sides of the question. The debates were continued for some time, and with great animation. In these John Adams, and John Dickinson, took leading and opposite parts. The former began one of his speeches, by an invocation of the god of eloquence, to assist him in defending the claims, and in enforcing the duty of his countrymen. He strongly urged the immediate dissolution of all political connexion of the colonies with Great-Britain, from the voice of the [341] people, from the necessity of the measure in order to obtain foreign assistance, from a regard to consistency, and from the prospects of glory and happiness, which opened beyond the war, to a free and independent people. Mr. Dickinson replied to this speech. He began by observing that the member from Massachusetts (Mr. Adams) had introduced his defence of the declaration of independence by invoking an heathen god, but that he should begin his objections to it, by solemnly invoking the Governor of the Universe, so to influence the minds of the members of Congress, that if the proposed measure was for the benefit of America, nothing which he should say against it, might make the least impression. He then urged that the present time was improper for the declaration of independence, that the war might be conducted with equal vigor without it, that it would divide the Americans, and unite the people of Great-Britain against them. He then proposed that some assurance should be obtained of assistance from a foreign power, before they renounced their connexion with Great-Britain, and that the declaration of independence should be the condition to be offered for this assistance. He likewise stated the disputes that existed between several of the colonies, and proposed that some measures for the settlement of them should be determined upon, before they lost sight of that tribunal, which had hitherto been the umpire of all their differences.

After a full discussion, the measure of declaring the colonies free and independent was approved, by nearly an unanimous vote. The anniversary of the day on which this great event took place, has ever since been consecrated by the Americans to religious gratitude, and social pleasures. It is considered by them as the birth day of their freedom. . . .

[346] From the promulgation of this declaration, every thing assumed a new form. The Americans no longer appeared in the character of subjects in arms against their sovereign, but as an independent people, repelling the attacks of an invading foe. The propositions and supplications for reconciliation were done away. The dispute was brought to a single point, whether the late British colonies should be conquered provinces, or free and independent states.

The declaration of independence was read publicly in all the states, and was welcomed with many demonstrations of joy. The people were encouraged by it to bear up under the calamities of war, and viewed the evils they suffered, only as the thorn that ever accompanies the rose. The army received it with particular satisfaction. As far as it had validity, so far it secured them from suffering as rebels, and held out to their view an object, the attainment of which would be an adequate recompense for the [347] toils and dangers of war. They were animated by the consideration that they were no longer to risque their lives for the trifling purpose of procuring a repeal of a few oppressive acts of parliament, but for a new organization of government, that would forever put it out of the power of Great-Britain to oppress them. The flattering prospects of an extensive commerce, freed from British restrictions, and the honours and emoluments of office in independent states now began to glitter before the eyes of the colonists, and reconciled them to the difficulties of their situation. What was supposed in Great-Britain to be their primary object, had only a secondary influence. While they were charged with aiming at independence from the impulse of avarice and ambition, they were ardently wishing for a reconciliation. But, after they had been compelled to adopt that measure, these powerful principles of human actions opposed its retraction, and stimulated to its support. That separation which the colonists at first dreaded as an evil, they soon gloried in as a national blessing. While the rulers of Great-Britain urged their people to a vigorous prosecution of the American war, on the idea that the colonists were aiming at independence, they imposed on them a necessity of adopting that very measure, and actually effected its accomplishment. By repeatedly charging the Americans with aiming at the erection of a new government, and by proceeding on that idea to subdue them, predictions which were originally false, eventually became true. When the declaration of independence reached Great-Britain the partisans of ministry triumphed in their sagacity. "The measure, said they, we have long foreseen, is now come to pass." They inverted the natural order of things. Without reflecting that their own policy had forced a revolution contrary to the original design of the colonists, the declaration of independence was held out to the people of Great-Britain as a justification of those previous violences, which were its efficient cause.

The act of Congress for dissevering the colonies from their Parent State, was the subject of many animadversions.

[348] The colonists were said to have been precipitate in adopting a measure, from which there was no honourable ground of retreating.

They replied that for eleven years they had been incessantly petitioning the throne for a redress of their grievances. Since the year 1765, a continental Congress had at three sundry times stated their claims, and prayed for their constitutional rights. That each assembly of the thirteen colonies had also, in its separate capacity, concurred in the same measure.—That from the perseverance of Great-Britain in her schemes for their coercion, they had no alternative, but a mean submission, or a vigorous resistance; and that as she was about to invade their coasts with a large body of mercenaries, they were compelled to declare themselves independent, that they might be put into an immediate capacity for soliciting foreign aid.

The virulence of those who had been in opposition to the claims of the colonists, was increased by their bold act in breaking off all subordination to the Parent State. "Great-Britain, said they, has founded colonies at great expence—has incurred a load of debt by wars on their account—has protected their commerce, and raised them to all the consequence they possess, and now in the insolence of adult years, rather than pay their proportion of the common expences of government, they ungratefully renounce all connexion with the nurse of their youth, and the protectress of their riper years." The Americans acknowledged that much was due to Great-Britain, for the protection which her navy procured to the coasts, and the commerce of the colonies, but contended that much was paid by the latter, in consequence of the restrictions imposed on their commerce by the former. "The charge of ingratitude would have been just," said they, "had allegiance been renounced while protection was given, but when the navy, which formerly secured the commerce and seaport towns of America, began to distress the former, and to burn the latter, the previous obligations to obey or be grateful, were no longer in force."

That the colonists paid nothing, and would not pay to the support of government, was confidently asserted, and [349] no credit was given for the sums indirectly levied upon them, in consequence of their being confined to the consumption of British manufactures. By such illfounded observations were the people of Great-Britain inflamed against their fellow subjects in America. The latter were represented as an ungrateful people, refusing to bear any part of the expences of a protecting government, or to pay their proportion of a heavy debt, said to be incurred on their account. Many of the inhabitants of Great-Britain deceived in matters of fact, considered their American brethren as deserving the severity of military coercion. So strongly were the two countries rivetted together, that if the whole truth had been known to the people of both, their separation would have been scarcely possible. Any feasible plan by which subjection to Great-Britain could have been reconciled with American safety, would at any time, previous to 1776, have met the approbation of the colonists. But while the lust of power and of gain, blinded the rulers of Great-Britain, mistated facts and uncandid representations brought over their people to second the infatuation. A few honest men properly authorized, might have devised measures of compromise, which under the influence of truth, humility and moderation, would have prevented a dismemberment of the empire; but these virtues ceased to influence, and falsehood, haughtiness and blind zeal usurped their places. Had Great-Britain, even after the declaration of independence, adopted the magnanimous resolution of declaring her colonies free and independent states, interest would have prompted them to form such a connexion as would have secured to the Mother Country the advantages of their commerce, without the expence or trouble of their governments. But misguided politics continued the fatal system of coercion and conquest. Several on both sides of the Atlantic, have called the declaration of independence, "a Bold, and accidentally, a lucky speculation," but subsequent events proved, that it was a wise measure. It is acknowledged, that it detached some timid friends from supporting the Americans in their opposition to Great-Britain, but it increased the [350] vigour and union of those, who possessed more fortitude and perseverance. Without it, the colonists would have had no object adequate to the dangers to which they exposed themselves, in continuing to contend with Great-Britain. If the interference of France was necessary to give success to the resistance of the Americans, the declaration of independence was also necessary, for the French expressly founded the propriety of their treaty with Congress on the circumstance, "that they found the United States in possession of independence."

All political connexion between Great-Britain and her colonies being dissolved, the institution of new forms of government became unavoidable. The necessity of this was so urgent that Congress, before *May 15.* the declaration of independence, had recommended to the respective assemblies and conventions of the United States, to adopt such governments as should, in their opinion, best conduce to the happiness and safety of their constituents. During more than twelve months the colonists had been held together by the force of antient habits, and by laws under the simple stile of recommendations. The impropriety of proceeding in courts of justice by the authority of a sovereign, against whom the colonies were in arms, was self-evident. The impossibility of governing, for any length of time, three millions of people, by the ties of honour, without the authority of law, was equally apparent. The rejection of British sovereignty therefore drew after it the necessity of fixing on some other principle of government. The genius of the Americans, their republican habits and sentiments, naturally led them to substitute the majesty of the people, in lieu of discarded royalty. The kingly office was dropped, but in most of the subordinate departments of government, antient forms and names were retained. Such a portion of power had at all times been exercised by the people and their representatives, that the change of sovereignty was hardly perceptible, and the revolution took place without violence or convulsion. Popular elections elevated private citizens to the same offices, which formerly had been conferred by royal appointment. The people felt an uninterrupted continuation of the blessings [351] of law and government under old names, though derived from a new sovereignty, and were scarcely sensible of any change in their political constitution. The checks and balances which restrained the popular assemblies under the royal government, were partly dropped, and partly retained, by substituting something of the same kind. The temper of the people would not permit that any one man, however exalted by office, or distinguished by abilities, should have a negative on the declared sense of a majority of their representatives, but the experience of all ages had taught them the danger of lodging all power in one body of men. A second branch of legislature, consisting of a few select persons, under the name of senate, or council, was therefore constituted in eleven of the thirteen states, and their concurrence made necessary to give the validity of law to the acts of a more numerous branch of popular representatives. New-York and Massachusettes went one step farther. The former constituted a council of revision, consisting of the governor and the heads of judicial departments, on whose objecting to any proposed law, a reconsideration became necessary, and unless it was confirmed by two thirds of both houses, it could have no operation. A similar power was given to the governor of Massachusetts. Georgia and Pennsylvania were the only states whose legislature consisted of only one branch. Though many in these states, and a majority in all the others, saw and acknowledged the propriety of a compounded legislature, yet the mode of creating two branches out of a homogeneous mass of people, was a matter of difficulty. No distinction of ranks existed in the colonies, and none were entitled to any rights, but such as were common to all. Some possessed more wealth than others, but riches and ability were not always associated. Ten of the eleven states, whose legislatures consisted of two branches, ordained that the members of both should be elected by the people. This rather made two co-ordinate houses of representatives than a check on a single one, by the moderation of a select few. Maryland adopted a singular plan for constituting an independent senate. By her constitution the members of that body [352] were elected for five years, while the members of the house of delegates held their seats only for one. The number of senators was only fifteen, and they were all elected indiscriminately from the inhabitants of any part of the state, excepting that nine of them were to be residents on the west, and six on the east side of the Chesapeak Bay. They were elected not immediately by the people, but by electors, two from each county, appointed by the inhabitants for that sole purpose. By these regulations the senate of Maryland consisted of men of influence, integrity and abilities, and such as were a real and beneficial check on the hasty proceedings of a more numerous branch of popular representatives. The laws of that state were well digested, and its interest steadily pursued with a peculiar unity of system; while elsewhere it too often happened in the fluctuation of public assemblies; and where the legislative department was not sufficiently checked, that passion and party predominated over principle and public good.

Pennsylvania instead of a legislative council or senate, adopted the expedient of publishing bills after the second reading, for the information of the inhabitants. This had its advantages and disadvantages. It prevented the precipitate adoption of new regulations, and gave an opportunity of ascertaining the sense of the people on those laws by which they were to be bound; but it carried the spirit of discussion into every corner, and disturbed the peace and harmony of neighbourhoods. By making the business of government the duty of every man, it drew off the attention of many from the steady pursuit of their respective businesses.

The state of Pennsylvania also adopted another institution peculiar to itself, under the denomination of a council of censors. These were to be chosen once every seven years, and were authorised to enquire whether the constitution had been preserved—whether the legislative and executive branch of government, had performed their duty, or assumed to themselves, or exercised other or greater powers, than those to which they were constitutionally entitled. To enquire whether the public taxes had [353] been justly laid and collected, and in what manner the public monies had been disposed of, and whether the laws had been duly executed. However excellent this institution may appear in theory, it is doubtful whether in practice it will answer any valuable end. It most certainly opens a door for discord, and furnishes abundant matter for periodical altercation. Either from the disposition of its inhabitants, its form of government, or some other cause, the people of Pennsylvania have constantly been in a state of fermentation. The end of one public controversy, has been the beginning of another. From the collision of parties, the minds of the citizens were sharpened, and their active powers improved, but internal harmony has been unknown. They who were out of place, so narrowly watched those who were in, that nothing injurious to the public could be easily effected, but from the fluctuation of power, and the total want of permanent system, nothing great or lasting could with safety be undertaken, or prosecuted to effect. Under all these disadvantages, the state flourished, and from the industry and ingenuity of its inhabitants acquired an unrivalled ascendency in arts and manufactures. This must in a great measure be ascribed to the influence of habits, of order and industry, that had long prevailed.

The Americans agreed in appointing a supreme executive head to each state, with the title either of governor or president. They also agreed in deriving the whole powers of government, either mediately or immediately from the people. In the eastern states, and in New-York, their governors were elected by the inhabitants, in their respective towns or counties, and in the other states by the legislatures: but in no case was the smallest tittle of power exercised from hereditary right. New-York was the only state which invested its governor with executive authority without a council. Such was the extreme jealousy of power which pervaded the American states, that they did not think proper to trust the man of their choice with the power of executing their own determinations, without obliging him in many cases to take the advice of such counsellors as they thought proper to nominate. [354] The disadvantages of this institution far outweighed its advantages. Had the governors succeeded by hereditary right, a council would have been often necessary to supply the real want of abilities, but when an individual had been selected by the people as the fittest person for discharging the duties of this high department, to fetter him with a council was either to lessen his capacity of doing good, or to furnish him with a skreen for doing evil. It destroyed the secrecy, vigor and dispatch, which the executive power ought to possess, and by making governmental acts the acts of a body, diminished individual responsibility. In some states it greatly enhanced the expences of government, and in all retarded its operations, without any equivalent advantages.

New-York in another particular, displayed political sagacity superior to her neighbours. This was in her council of appointment, consisting of one senator from each of her four great election districts, authorised to designate proper persons for filling vacancies in the executive departments of government. Large bodies are far from being the most proper depositaries of the power of appointing to offices. The assiduous attention of candidates is too apt to biass the voice of individuals in popular assemblies. Besides in such appointments, the responsibility for the conduct of the officer, is in a great measure annihilated. The concurrence of a select few on the nomination of one, seems a more eligible mode for securing a proper choice, than appointments made either by one, or by a numerous body. In the former case there would be danger of favoritism, in the latter that modest unassuming merit would be overlooked, in favour of the forward and obsequious.

A rotation of public officers made a part of most of the American constitutions. Frequent elections were required by all, but several still farther, and deprived the electors of the power of continuing the same office in the same hands, after a specified length of time. Young politicians suddenly called from the ordinary walks of life, to make laws and institute forms of government, turned their attention to the histories of ancient republics [355] and the writings of speculative men on the subject of government. This led them into many errors and occasioned them to adopt sundry opinions, unsuitable to the state of society in America, and contrary to the genius of real republicanism.

The principle of rotation was carried so far, that in some of the states, public offices in several departments scarcely knew their official duty, till they were obliged to retire and give place to others, as ignorant as they had been on their first appointment. If offices had been instituted for the benefit of the holders, the policy of diffusing these benefits would have been proper, but instituted as they were for the convenience of the public, the end was marred by such frequent changes. By confining the objects of choice, it diminished the privileges of electors, and frequently deprived them of the liberty of choosing the man who, from previous experience, was of all men the most suitable. The favourers of this system of rotation contended for it, as likely to prevent a perpetuity of office and power in the same individual or family, and as a security against hereditary honours. To this it was replied, that free, fair and frequent elections were the most natural and proper securities, for the liberties of the people. It produced a more general diffusion of political knowledge, but made more smatterers than adepts in the science of government.

As a farther security for the continuance of republican principles in the American constitutions, they agreed in prohibiting all hereditary honours and distinction of ranks.

It was one of the peculiarities of these new forms of government, that all religious establishments were abolished. Some retained a constitutional distinction between Christians and others, with respect to eligibility to office, but the idea of supporting one denomination at the expence of others, or of raising any one sect of protestants to a legal pre-eminence, was universally reprobated. The alliance between church and state was completely broken, and each was left to support itself, independent of the other.

The far famed social compact between the people and their rulers, did not apply to the United States. The [356] sovereignty was in the people. In their sovereign capacity by their representatives, they agreed on forms of government for their own security, and deputed certain individuals as their agents to serve them in public stations agreeably to constitutions, which they prescribed for their conduct.

The world has not hitherto exhibited so fair an opportunity for promoting social happiness. It is hoped for the honor of human nature, that the result will prove the fallacy of those theories, which suppose that mankind are incapable of self government. The ancients, not knowing the doctrine of representation, were apt in their public meetings to run into confusion, but in America this mode of taking the sense of the people, is so well understood, and so completely reduced to system, that its most populous states are often peaceably convened in an assembly of deputies, not too large for orderly deliberation, and yet representing the whole in equal proportions. These popular branches of legislature are miniature pictures of the community, and from the mode of their election are likely to be influenced by the same interests and feelings with the people whom they represent. As a farther security for their fidelity, they are bound by every law they make for their constituents. The assemblage of these circumstances gives as great a security that laws will be made, and government administered for the good of the people, as can be expected from the imperfection of human institutions.

In this short view of the formation and establishment of the American constitutions, we behold our species in a new situation. In no age before, and in no other country, did man ever possess an election of the kind of government, under which he would choose to live. The constituent parts of the antient free governments were thrown together by accident. The freedom of modern European governments was, for the most part, obtained by the concessions, or liberality of monarchs, or military leaders. In America alone, reason and liberty concurred in the formation of constitutions. It is true, from the infancy of political knowledge in the United States, there were [357] many defects in their forms of government. But in one thing they were all perfect. They left the people in the power of altering and amending them, whenever they pleased. In this happy peculiarity they placed the science of politics on a footing with the other sciences, by opening it to improvements from experience, and the discoveries of future ages. By means of this power of amending American constitutions, the friends of mankind have fondly hoped that oppression will one day be no more, and that political evil will at least be prevented or restrained with as much certainty, by a proper combination or separation of power, as natural evil is lessened or prevented by the application of the knowledge or ingenuity of man to domestic purposes. No part of the history of antient or modern Europe, can furnish a single fact that militates against this opinion, since in none of its governments have the principles of equal representation and checks been applied, for the preservation of freedom. On these two pivots are suspended the liberties of most of the states. Where they are wanting, there can be no security for liberty, where they exist they render any farther security unnecessary.

The rejection of British sovereignty not only involved a necessity of erecting independent constitutions, but of cementing the whole United States by some common bond of union. The act of independence did not hold out to the world thirteen sovereign states, but a common sovereignty of the whole in their united capacity. It therefore became necessary to run the line of distinction, between the local legislatures, and the assembly of the states in Congress. A committee was appointed for digesting articles of confederation between the states or united colonies, as they were then called, at the time the propriety of declaring independence was under debate, and some weeks previously to the adoption of that measure, but the plan was not for sixteen months after so far digested, as to be ready for communication to the states. Nor was it finally ratified by the accession of all the states, till nearly three years more had elapsed. In discussing its articles, many difficult questions occurred. One was to ascertain the ratio of [358] contributions from each state. Two principles presented themselves, numbers of people, and the value of lands. The last was preferred as being the truest barometer of the wealth of nations, but from an apprehended impracticability of carrying it into effect, it was soon relinquished, and recurrence had to the former. That the states should be represented in proportion to their importance, was contended for by those who had extensive territory, but they who were confined to small dimensions, replied, that the states confederated as individuals, in a state of nature, and should therefore have equal votes. From fear of weakening their exertions against the common enemy, the large states for the present yielded the point, and consented that each state should have an equal suffrage.

It was not easy to define the power of the state legislatures, so as to prevent a clashing between their jurisdiction, and that of the general government. On mature deliberation it was thought proper, that the former should be abridged of the power of forming any other confederation or alliance—of laying on any imposts or duties that might interfere with treaties made by Congress—or keeping up any vessels of war, or granting letters of marque or reprisal. The powers of Congress were also defined. Of these the principle were as follows: To have the sole and exclusive right of determining on peace and war—of sending and receiving ambassadors—of entering into treaties and alliances,—of granting letters of marque and reprisal in terms of peace.—To be the last resort on appeal, in all disputes between two or more states—to have the sole and exclusive right of regulating the

DAVID RAMSAY 1749–1815

alloy and value of coin, of fixing the standard weights and measures—regulating the trade and managing all affairs with the Indians—establishing and regulating post offices—to borrow money or emit bills on the credit of the United States—to build and equip a navy—to agree upon the number of land forces, and to make requisitions from each state for its quota of men, in proportion to the number of its white inhabitants.

No coercive power was given to the general government, nor was it invested with any legislative power over [359] individuals, but only over states in their corporate capacity. As at the time the articles of confederation were proposed for ratification, the Americans had little or no regular commercial intercourse with foreign nations, a power to regulate trade or to raise a revenue from it, though both were essential to the welfare of the union, made no part of the federal system. To remedy this and all other defects, a door was left open for introducing farther provisions, suited to future circumstances.

The articles of confederation were proposed at a time when the citizens of America were young in the science of politics, and when a commanding sense of duty, enforced by the pressure of a common danger, precluded the necessity of a power of compulsion. The enthusiasm of the day gave such credit and currency to paper emissions, as made the raising of supplies an easy matter. The system of federal government was therefore more calculated for what men then were, under these circumstances, than for the languid years of peace, when selfishness usurped the place of public spirit, and when credit no longer assisted, in providing for the exigencies of government.

The experience of a few years after the termination of the war, proved, as will appear in its proper place, that a radical change of the whole system was necessary, to the good government of the United States.

[54]

ROBERT CORAM 1761–1796

Political Inquiries, to which is Added A Plan for the Establishment of Schools Throughout the United States

WILMINGTON, 1791

A great deal was written about education for youth in the founding era. Making education available to a broad public was seen as critical to preparation for citizenship and the development of virtues necessary for continued support of republican government. There was no shortage of plans for national or statewide systems, some coming very close to what we have in fact developed. Robert Coram was born in England but migrated with his family to South Carolina while a boy. He fought in the revolutionary war, serving for a time under John Paul Jones aboard the *Bonhomme Richard*. After the war he moved to Wilmington, Delaware, where, among other things, he was the editor of the *Delaware Gazette*. Coram was a strong Anti-Federalist during the ratification period. Ironically, Robert Coram did not himself receive a formal education, but was self-taught in the political and literary classics well enough to run a night school in Wilmington providing instruction in Latin and French. His essay reproduced here is considered by many to be the most advanced and thoughtful piece on education written during the era. It is notable for carrying the discussion far beyond mere formal education to consider it in the context of what we would today recognize as socialization broadly conceived.

ROBERT CORAM 1761–1796

Above all, watch carefully over the education of your children. It is from public schools, be assured, that come the wise magistrates—the well trained and courageous soldiers—the good fathers—the good husbands—the good brothers—the good friends—the good man.— RAYNAL.

This work is intended merely to introduce a better mode of education than that generally adopted in the country schools throughout the United States.

INTRODUCTION

It is serious truth, whatever may have been advanced by European writers to the contrary, that the aborigines of the American continent have fewer vices, are less subject to diseases, and are a happier people than the subjects of any government in the Eastern world.

From the first of these facts may be drawn two important consequences—first, that the proneness to vice, with which mankind have always been charged and to check which is the ostensible purpose of government, is entirely chimerical; secondly, that vice in civilized nations is the effect of bad government. It is plain, if men are virtuous without laws, they may be virtuous with good [iv] laws, for no reason can be given why good laws should make men vicious. Government is, no doubt, a very complicated machine; but vice in the subject cannot be the mere consequence of complexity in the form of government: for if one good law would not necessarily produce vice, neither would one hundred. These truths are simple, but they are not the less useful.

Europeans have been taught to believe that mankind have something of the Devil ingrafted in their nature, that they are naturally ferocious, vicious, revengeful, and as void of reason as brutes, etc., etc. Hence their sanguinary laws, which string a man to a gibbet for the value of twenty pence. They first frame an hypothesis, by which they prove men to be wolves, and then treat them as if they really were such.

But notwithstanding the Europeans have proved men to be naturally wolves, yet they [v] will assert that "men owe everything to education. The minds of children are like blank paper, upon which you may write any characters you please." Thus will they every day refute the fundamental principles upon which their laws are built, and yet not grow a jot the wiser.

Whoever surveys the history of nations with a philosophic eye will find that the civilized man in every stage of his civilization and under almost every form of government has always been a very miserable being. When we consider the very splendid advantages which the citizen seems to possess, the grand scheme of Christianity, the knowledge of sciences and of arts, the experience of all ages and nations recorded in his libraries for a guide, how mortifying must it be to him to reflect that with all his boasted science and philosophy he had made but a retrograde advance to happiness and that the savage, by superior instinct or natural reason, has attained what [vi] he, the citizen, by all his powers of refined and artificial intellect could never reach.

There must be some fundamental error, therefore, common to all civilized nations, and this error appears to me to be in education. In savage state education is perfect. In the civilized state education is the most imperfect part of the whole scheme of government or civilization; or, rather, it is not immediately connected with either, for I know of no modern governments, except perhaps the New England states, in which education is incorporated with the government or regulated by it.

In the savage state, as I said before, the system of education is perfect. To explain this, it will be necessary to define the word *education,* or at least what I mean by it. Education, then, means the instruction of youth in certain rules of conduct by which they will be enabled to support themselves when they come to age and to know [vii] the obligations they are under to that society of which they constitute a part. Nature, then, in the savage state is the unerring instructor of their youth in the first or principal part of education, for, when their bodily powers are complete, that part of education which relates to their support is complete also. When they can subdue the wild animals, they can procure subsistence. The second, or less essential part, is taught by their parents: their laws, or rather *customs,* being few and simple, are easily remembered and understood.

But the unfortunate civilized man, to obtain a livelihood, must be acquainted with some art or science, in which he is neither instructed by nature, by government, by his parents, or oftentimes by any means at all. He is then absolutely unable to procure himself subsistence without violating some law, and as to the obligations he is under to society, he knows indeed but very little if anything about them. In this state of the case, the situation of the civilized man is infinitely worse than that of the savage, nay, [viii] worse than that of the brute creation, for the birds have nests, the foxes have holes, and all animals in their wild state have permanent means of subsistence, but the civilized man has nowhere to lay his head: he has neither habitation nor food, but forlorn and outcast, he perishes for want and starves in the midst of universal plenty.

To alleviate, therefore, in some measure the miseries of this unhappy being is the intent of the following sheets. And in pursuit of an object of such importance the author shall not be afraid to follow truth wherever it may lead him. As an American, he asserts his claim to this privilege, and he hopes it may be allowed him, upon the double score of his birthright and the task he has undertaken, to plead the cause of humanity.

CHAP. I

Inquiry into the Origin of Government; and a Comparative View of the Subjects of European Governments with the Aborigines of America.

No question has puzzled philosophers of all ages more than the origin of government. The wants and vices of mankind have been generally held out to be the causes of all the good and bad governments with which mankind have alternately been blessed or cursed from the earliest ages to the present day. But there is no satisfactory reason to believe that government originated from either of those causes. We can never believe it originated from his wants, considering the very small proportion of [10] cultivated land in proportion to the uncultivated at this day in every part of the globe, some small islands excepted; nor will his vices afford a better solution of the question, since the savages of North America are infinitely more virtuous than the inhabitants of the most polished nations of Europe.

How the first government originated we are entirely in the dark. Scripture is silent on this head, and all that we know is that Cain founded a city and called it after the name of his son Enoch. As to the origin of modern governments, they seem chiefly to have been founded by conquest: their origin is, however, involved in much obscurity.

Since, then, we are unable to discover the origin of government from the impenetrable obscurity in which it is involved, let us consider its end as equally applicable to our purpose. The end of government, we are told, is public good, by which is to be understood the happiness of the community. The great body of the people in Europe are unhappy, not to say miserable: there needs no other argument to prove that all the European governments have been founded upon wrong principles, since the means used have not produced the end intended.

[11] The following description from the Abbé Raynal may perhaps be with truth applied to the body of the people throughout Europe: "In our provinces the vassal or free mercenary digs and ploughs the whole year round lands that are not his own and whose produce does not belong to him, and he is even happy, if his labor procures him a share of the crops he has sown and reaped. Observed and harassed by a hard and restless landlord who grudges him the very straw on which he rests his weary limbs, the wretch is daily exposed to diseases which, joined to his poverty, make him wish for death rather than for an expensive cure followed by infirmities and toil. Whether tenant or subject, he is doubly a slave; if he has a few acres, his lord comes and gathers them where he has not sown; if he has but a yoke of oxen or a pair of horses, he must employ them in the public service; if he has nothing but his person, the prince takes him for a soldier. Everywhere he meets with masters and always with oppression." Let us now consider the state of the American Indians.

This inquiry is attended with more difficulty than at first sight would appear. Indeed, if the present race of American Indians should shortly [12] become extinct, it would be impossible for posterity to form any judgment of them, whether they were a species of orangutan or rational beings. The European libraries have been stuffed with such monstrous caricatures of the American that they have influenced their ablest philosophers, and Raynal and Buffon have both endeavored to account for the supposed defects in the man of the Western world. Excepting Clavijero's *History of Mexico*, the short account given by Mr. Jefferson, Carver's *Travels*, *The History of the Five Nations*, and Bancroft's *History of Guiana*, I do not recollect an account of the American which deserves the name of history. The translations from French and Spanish writers are generally full of the most glaring prejudice and absurdity.

I once saw a history of Louisiana, translated from the French, in which some curious person had, in a fine hand in the margin, refuted almost the whole of the text.

And for a specimen of Spanish history, take the following from the *History of California* by Miguel Venegas: "The characteristics of the Californians as well as of all the other Indians are stupidity, an insensibility, want of knowledge and reflection, inconstancy, impetuosity, and blindness of appetite; an excessive sloth and abhorrence of all labor and fatigue, an incessant love of pleasure and amusement of every kind, however [13] trifling or brutal; pusilanimity and relaxity; and, in fine, a most wretched want of everything which constitutes the real man and renders him rational, inventive, tractable, and useful to himself and society. It is not easy for Europeans who never were out of their own country to conceive an adequate idea of those people. For even in the least frequent corners of the globe there is not a nation so stupid, of such contracted ideas, and so wretched both in body and mind as the unhappy Californians."

Some of the features of this miserable picture are of so heterogeneous a cast that one can hardly be induced to believe them copied from the same original. Stupidity, excessive sloth, and abhorrence of all labor and fatigue but ill agrees with impetuosity and incessant love of pleasure. I shall not be at the trouble of refuting this banter upon history, only to be equaled in absurdity by the philosophical researches of Mr. De Pauw, but will content myself with quoting a little more from Mr. Miguel Venegas and leave the reader to judge for himself:

"However, in the Californians are seen few of those bad dispositions for which the other Americans are infamous; no inebriating liquors [14] are used among them, and the several members of a rancheria live in great harmony among themselves and peaceably with others. What little everyone has is safe from theft. Quarrels are rarely known among them. All their malice and rage they reserve for their enemies, and so far are they from obstinacy, harshness, and cruelty that nothing could exceed their docility and gentleness; consequently they are easily persuaded to good or evil . . . They make their boats of the bark of trees, and every part of the workmanship, the shaping, joining, and covering them, is admired even by Europeans. The men likewise make nets for fishing, for gathering fruits, and for carrying the children, and even those worn by the women. But in this particular they show such exquisite skill, making them of so many different colors, sizes, and variety of workmanship, that it is not easy to describe them."

Father Taraval says, "I can affirm that of all the nets I ever saw in Europe and New Spain none are comparable to these, either in whiteness, the mixture of the other colors, or the strength and workmanship in which they represent a vast variety of figures." I hope the contradiction and absurdity are manifest.

The citizens of the United States differ as widely in their opinions and in many instances seem [15] as much prejudiced against the Indians as the Europeans. Mutual jealousies among those who reside near the frontier, the ferocity with which the Indians conduct their wars, but principally the numerous forged accounts published in our newspapers of horrid murders perpetrated by them have given the citizens of these states such an antipathy against the Indians as will not easily be removed. I traveled with one of Mr. McGillivray's men from Philadelphia to New York last summer and had the mortification to see him insulted in almost every public house at which we stopped on our route. One of the landlords did not scruple to tell him that he, the landlord, would as leave shoot an Indian as a rattlesnake. And take the following account from the *Delaware Gazette:*

"Extract of a letter from Sunbury, Northumberland County, Pennsylvania, dated November 13, 1790.—

"One of the men who murdered the Indians at Pine Creek was tried on Saturday evening; and though a number of witnesses clearly proved the hand he had in perpetrating the horrible deed, and the confession of his counsel at the bar, which confirmed it; yet, notwithstanding [16] an express charge from the judges to bring him in guilty, the jury, in a few minutes, returned with a verdict in his favor and a subscription to pay the costs of suit, that he might be set at liberty. And all this from a most absurd idea, which the Attorney General could not, with all his endeavors, beat out of them, that the crime was not the same to kill an Indian as a white man. For some minutes the Chief Justice was struck with astonishment. How the state can pacify the Indians now, Heaven knows; while at this moment the other murderers are at large in this country, and none will arrest them."

It is said that the inhabitants of Canada and the other French settlements are very seldom troubled by the Indians. The French government has kept a watchful eye over the conduct of its subjects and never suffered any injury done to the Indians to pass unpunished. It is indeed in vain to expect peace with those people while the present rancor, too visible in the conduct of the citizens of those states, continues. But as this is rather foreign to my present purpose, I shall proceed with what I have to offer on the subject of the aborigines of America, from Carver's *Travels* and Bancroft's *History of Guiana,* as the least prejudiced testimony applicable to the present purpose which has fell under my observation.

[17] "The Indians," says Mr. Carver, "in their common state are strangers to all distinction of property, except in the articles of domestic use, which everyone considers as his own and increases as circumstances may admit. They are extremely liberal to each other and supply the deficiency of their friends with any superfluity of their own. In dangers they readily give assistance to those of their band who stand in need of it, without any expectation of return, except of those just rewards which are always conferred by the Indians on merit. Governed by the plain and equitable laws of nature, everyone is rewarded solely according to his deserts, and their equality of condition, manners, and privileges, with that constant and sociable familiarity which prevails throughout every Indian nation, animates them with a pure and truly patriotic spirit which tends to the general good of the society to whom they belong.

"If any of their neighbors are bereaved by death or by an enemy of their children, those who are possessed of the greatest number of slaves supply the deficiency; and those are adopted by them and treated in every respect as if they really were the children of the person to whom they are presented.

"The Indians, except those who live adjoining to the European colonies, can form to themselves no idea of the [18] value of money; they consider it, when they are made acquainted with the uses to which it is applied by other nations, as the source of innumerable evils. To it they attribute all the mischiefs which are prevalent among Europeans, such as treachery, plunderings, devastation, and murder. They esteem it irrational that one man should be possessed of a greater quantity than another and are amazed that any honor should be annexed to the possession of it. But that the want of this useless metal should be the cause of depriving persons of their liberty and that on account of this partial distribution of it great numbers should be immured within the dreary walls of a prison, cut off from the society of which they constitute a part, exceeds their belief. Nor do they fail, on hearing this part of the European system of government related, to charge the institutors of it with a total want of humanity and to brand them with the names of savages and brutes."

The following character of the Caribbee Indians is taken from Bancroft's *Guiana:* "In reviewing the manners of these Indians, some few particulars excepted, I survey an amiable picture of primeval innocence and happiness, which arises chiefly, from the fewness of their wants, and [19] their universal equality. The latter destroys all distinctions among them, except those of age and personal merit, and promotes the ease, harmony and freedom of their mutual conversation and intercourse [   ] The fewness and simplicity of their wants, with the abundance of means for their supply, and the ease with which they are acquired, renders all division of property useless. Each amicably participates [in] the ample blessings of an extensive country without rivaling his neighbor or interrupting his happiness. This renders all governments and all laws unnecessary, as in such a state there can be no temptations to dishonesty, fraud, injustice, or violence, or indeed any desires which may not be gratified with innocence; and that chimerical proneness to vice, which among civilized nations is thought to be a natural propensity, has no existence in a state of nature like this, where everyone perfectly enjoys the blessings of his native freedom and independence without any restraints or fears.

"To acquire the art of dispensing with all imaginary wants and contenting ourselves with the real conveniences of life is the noblest exertion of reason and a most useful acquisition, as it elevates the mind above the vicissitudes of fortune. Socrates justly observes 'that those who want least approach nearest to the gods, who want nothing.' The simplicity, however, which is [20] so apparent in the manners of those Indians is not the effect of a philosophical self-denial but of their ignorance of more refined enjoyments, which, however, produces effects equally happy with those which result from the most austere philosophy; and their manners present an emblem of the fabled Elysian fields where individuals need not the assistance of each other but yet preserve a constant intercourse of love and friendship.

" 'O FORTUNATOS NIMIUM, SUA SI BONA NORINT. VIRO.' "

"It is doubtless," says the immortal Raynal, "of great importance to posterity to record the manners of savages. From this source, perhaps, we have derived all our improvements in moral philosophy. Former metaphysicians sought for the origin of society in those very societies which had been long established. Supposing men guilty of crimes, in order that they may have the merit of giving them saviours; blinding their eyes, in order that they may become their guides and masters, they call *mysterious, supernatural,* and *divine* what is only the operation of time, ignorance, weakness, and chicane. But after perceiving that social institutions neither originated from natural wants nor from religious opinions—since many nations live independent without any [21] worship—they discovered that all corruptions, both in morals and legislation, arose from society itself and that vice originally proceeded from legislators, who generally instituted laws more for their own emolument than public good, or whose views towards equity and right were perverted by the ambition of their successors or by the alteration of times and manners.

"This discovery has already thrown great light upon the subject, though it is still to mankind but as the dawn of a fine day. Its opposition to established opinions prevents it from suddenly producing those immense benefits which it will confer on posterity, and this latter circumstance ought to give consolation to the present generation. But however this may be we may assert with confidence that the ignorance of savages has contributed greatly to enlighten polished nations."

In the comparative view of the civilized man and the savage, the most striking contrast is the division of property. To the one, it is the source of all his happiness: to the other, the fountain of all his misery. By holy writ we are informed that God gave to man dominion over the earth, the living creatures, and the herbs; human laws have, however, limited this jurisdiction to certain orders or classes of men; the rest are to feed upon air if they can or fly to another world [22] for subsistence. This parceling out to individuals what was intended for the general stock of society leads me to inquire farther into the nature and origin of property. I am not quite so visionary as to expect that the members of any civilized community will listen to an equal division of lands: had that been the object of this work, the author had infallibly lost his labor. But a substitute, and perhaps the only one, is highly practicable, as will hereafter appear.

CHAP. II

Inquiry into the Origin of Property; and a Refutation of Blackstone's Doctrine on That Subject.

"There is nothing which so generally strikes the imagination," says Dr. Blackstone, "and engages the affections of mankind as the right of property or that sole and despotic dominion which one man claims and exercises over the external things of this world, in total exclusion of the right of any other individual in the universe. And yet there are very few that will give themselves the trouble to consider the origin and foundation of this right. Pleased [23] as we are with the possession, we seem afraid to look back to the means by which it was acquired, as if fearful of some defect in our title; or at best we rest satisfied with the decisions of the laws in our favor, without examining the reason or authority upon which those laws have been built.

"We think it enough that our title is derived by the grant of the former proprietor, by descent from our ancestors, or by the last will and testament of the dying owner not caring to reflect that (accurately and strictly speaking) there is no foundation in nature, or in natural law, why a set of words upon parchment should convey the dominion of land, why the son should have a right to exclude his fellow creatures from a determinate spot of ground because his father had done so before him, or why the occupier of a particular field or of a jewel, when lying on his death bed and no longer able to maintain possession, should be entitled to tell the rest of the world which of them should enjoy it after him.

"These inquiries, it must be confessed, would be useless, and even troublesome, in common life. It is well, if the mass of mankind will obey the laws, when made, without scrutinizing too nicely into the reasons of making them. But when law is to be considered, not only as matter of practice but also as a rational science, it cannot be improper or useless to examine [24] more deeply the rudiments and grounds of those positive constitutions of society."

Doctor Blackstone seems to have been extremely cautious how he ventured upon his inquiry into the origin of property, as if fearful of some defect in his title; and his caution has, notwithstanding his profound sagacity, evidently run him into contradiction and absurdity. He tells us, in his chapter on the study of the law, that "every subject is interested in the preservation of the laws; it is therefore," says he, "incumbent upon every man to be acquainted with those at least with which he is immediately concerned, lest he incur the censure of living in society without knowing the obligations which it lays him under."

And in the part we have just now quoted he obliquely censures the conduct of the generality of mankind, who, he says, will not give themselves the trouble to consider the origin and foundation of the right of property. But when he reflects upon the probable consequences of a rational investigation of this subject, he flies his ground. "These inquiries," says he, "it must be owned would be useless, and even troublesome, in common life. It is well, if the mass of mankind will obey the laws, when made, without scrutinizing too nicely into the reasons of making them."

But though the mass [25] of mankind are prohibited to scrutinize too nicely into the reasons of making laws, it seems that it is not improper for those who consider law as a matter of practice, and a rational science, to examine more deeply into their rudiments and grounds. That is, in plain English, lawyers may know the obligations of society, but the people not. Thus it was when corrupt priests despised the ordinances of a just God, defiled his altars with unhallowed sacrifices, and stained them with innocent blood, they hid their creed beneath the impenetrable veil of a dead language, that their iniquity might not be detected.

Thus it is, that those who should direct the opinions of mankind descend to contemptible sophistry and contradiction, turn traitors to their own principles, apostates to the sacred cause of truth, and while they pretend that their system of law is founded upon principles of equity tell us in plain terms that it will not bear investigation. The right to exclusive property is a question of great importance, and, of all others, perhaps, deserves the most candid and equitable solution. Such a solution will afford a foundation for laws which will totally eradicate from the civilized man a very large portion of those vices which such legislators as Dr. Blackstone pretend to be natural to the human race. One deplorable [26] iniquity, at least, which has filled the earth with tears and the hearts of all good men with deep regret— I mean the slave trade—could never have existed among any people who had distinct ideas of property, but this subject has been treated of in such an obscure, vague, and contradictory manner by the European lawyers that it is impossible to determine by them what is property and what is not.

"In the beginning of the world," says Dr. Blackstone, "we are informed by holy writ the all bountiful Creator gave to man 'dominion over all the earth, and over the fish of the sea, and over the fowl of the air, and over every living thing that moveth upon the earth.' This is the only true and solid foundation of man's dominion over external things, whatever airy metaphysical notions may have been started by fanciful writers upon that subject."

The Doctor, not the least fanciful of metaphysical writers, quotes the text in Genesis as a demonstration of his creed, to tell us that he believes in the Bible, which is in some measure necessary, as many of his arguments militate against such belief. If then the text in Genesis is the only true and solid foundation of man's dominion over external things, every son and daughter of Adam is co-heir to this paternal inheritance, for the gift [27] was made in common to the whole race of Adam. How then have part of mankind forfeited their right to the bounties of Providence? Or from what source does the monopoly of lands originate, since it is plain it cannot be derived from the text in Genesis? The Doctor, indeed, tells us that "the earth, and all things thereon, are the general property of all mankind, exclusive of other beings from the immediate gift of the Creator. And while the earth continued bare of inhabitants, it is reasonable to suppose that all was in common among them and that everyone took from the public stock to his own use such things as his immediate necessities required."

And why not take from the public stock, when men multiplied? The command from the Creator was, increase and multiply. And must men then forfeit their right to the bounties of Providence, by acting in obedience to this precept? Or does Dr. Blackstone suppose that the earth can support only a part of mankind, and that the rest live upon air, light, fire, or water, the only inheritance he has left them? It is plain, if the earth supports its inhabitants in the present unequal division of property, it will support them under an equal division. "These general notions of property," continues the Doctor, "were then sufficient to answer all the purposes of human life." That is, the solid foundation of man's dominion over external [28] things, is a notion: this notion was, however, sufficient to answer all the purposes of human life; "and might still have answered them," continues the Doctor, "had it been possible for mankind to have remained in a state of primeval simplicity, as may be collected from the manners of many American nations when first discovered by the Europeans."

It is upwards of 5,000 years since the creation of the world. At the creation men were in a state of primeval simplicity; the American Indians are at this day in a state of primeval simplicity; ergo, it is not possible for men to remain in a state of primeval simplicity. Here is logic elegantly displayed! Thus it is that the sophistry of this English doctor flies before the test of investigation. It is therefore possible for men to remain in a state of primeval simplicity, since some of them are so at this day; unless indeed the Doctor supposes the Indians to be the offspring of a creation subsequent to Adam. This primeval simplicity, the Doctor supposes, was the case with the ancient Europeans, according to the memorials of the golden age.

"*Sed omnia communia et indivisa omnibus fuerint, veluti unum cunctis patrimonium esset.* Not," says the Doctor, "that this communion of goods seems ever to have been applicable, even in the earliest ages, to aught but the substance of the thing; nor could it be extended to the use of it." Why not? Let us [29] translate the passage. All things were common and undivided to all, even as one inheritance might be to all. The sense of this passage is so obvious and plain that a person could hardly think it possible to be misunderstood, but Dr. Blackstone is determined to understand it not as common sense but as unintelligible jargon. By a peculiar application of the participle *indivisa,* the Doctor infers that the community of goods could not be extended to the use of such goods, which is making downright nonsense of the sentence: it is making the patrimony left in such manner that not a single heir can enjoy the least use or benefit of it at all. Why should so much stress be laid on the participle *indivisa,* in the first part of the sentence, when the second part of the sentence is explanatory of the first? The goods were left *communia & indivisa;* but in what manner? *Veluti unum cunctis patrimonium esset:* even as one inheritance might be to all. The Doctor appears designedly obscure in this very paragraph and seems rather desirous to perplex his reader than to throw any light upon the subject.

"For by the law of nature and reason," continues the Doctor, "he who first began to use a thing acquired therein a kind of transient property that lasted so long as he was using it, and no longer: or to speak with greater precision, the right of possession continued for the same time only that [30] the act of possession lasted. Thus the ground was in common, and no part of it was the permanent property of any man in particular; yet, whoever was in the occupation of any determinate spot of it for rest, for shade, or the like, acquired, for the time, a sort of ownership, from which it would have been unjust and contrary to the law of nature to have driven him by force, but the instant that he quitted the use or occupation of it another might seize it without injustice."

According to this vague account of natural law, it appears that men had a right to that quantity of ground which happened to be in immediate contact with their feet, when standing up; with their backsides, when sitting; and with their body, when lying down; and no more. No provision is made for agriculture; indeed it would not have suited the Doctor to have allowed the existence of agriculture at that period of the world for reasons which will hereafter appear.

Any person possessed of common sense and some erudition who was not previously bent upon establishing a favorite system at the expense of truth might give us a rational account in what manner property should be regulated under the law of nature. Such a person would probably say all things subject to the dominion of man may be included in two classes, land and movables; [31] the rational foundation of the tenure of each is labor. Thus fruit growing on a tree was common, but when collected it became the exclusive property of the collector; land uncultivated was common but when cultivated, it became the exclusive possession of the cultivator. Men, then, according to the laws of nature, had an exclusive property in movables and an exclusive possession in lands, both which were founded on labor and bounded by it. For as labor employed in the collection of fruit could give an exclusive right only to the fruit so collected, so labor in the soil could give exclusive possession only to the spot so labored. But this kind of reasoning would by no means suit Dr. Blackstone.

"But," continues the Doctor, "when mankind increased in number, craft, and ambition, it became necessary to entertain conceptions of more permanent dominion and to appropriate to individuals, not the immediate use only, but the very substance of the thing to be used." Query: could a man eat an apple without entertaining conceptions of permanent dominion over the substance? Those conceptions existed then anterior to the increase of men in number, craft, and ambition, and were not the consequence of it.

"Otherwise," continues the Doctor, "innumerable tumults must have arisen, and the good order of the world been continually broken and disturbed, while a variety of persons [32] were striving who should get the first occupation of the same thing or disputing which of them had actually gained it." From a system so vague as the Doctor's, and which he would pawn upon us for natural law, nothing but disputes could be expected, for nothing is determinate. His futile distinctions between the use of a thing and the substance of a thing and his notions of possession are truly ridiculous. But those contests for occupancy, this mighty bugbear so fatal to the good order of the world, we can easily prove to be a mere phantom of the Doctor's brain; like the raw head and bloody bones with which ignorant nurses scare their children, it has no existence in nature.

As labor constitutes the right of property in movables and the right of possession in lands, it is evident no disputes could arise merely from the nature of the right, for before labor was employed there could be no right to squabble about, and after labor was employed the right was completely vested. In fact, the whole of Blackstone's chapter on property was artfully contrived to countenance the monopoly of lands as held in Europe. "When men increased in number, craft, and ambition, it became necessary to entertain conceptions of more permanent dominion." If the Doctor means anything he means that [33] more permanent dominion was established as a check to craft and ambition; or, in other words, that the laws vested a permanent property in lands in some persons, to prevent their being dispossessed by unruly individuals. But this clearly demonstrates the Doctor to be as ignorant of the affections of the human heart as he is of natural law. For a community of lands is the most effectual check which human wisdom could devise against the ambition of individuals. What is the civilized man's ambition? To procure a property in the soil. But there is no such ambition among savages, for no man, civilized or savage, is ambitious of what is common to every man: land is common among savages; therefore they set no value upon it. In most civilized nations land is held only by a few and also made essential to the qualification of candidates for public offices: hence, to possess property in lands is the ambition of civilized nations.

But, continues the Doctor, "As human life also grew more and more refined, abundance of conveniences were contrived to render it more easy and agreeable, as habitations for shelter and safety and raiment for warmth and decency. But no man would be at the trouble to provide either, so long as he had only a *usufructuary* property in them, which was to cease the instant that he [34] quitted possession, if, as soon as he walked out of his tent or pulled off his garment, the next stranger who came by would have a right to inhabit the one and wear the other."

If his wise head would have suffered him to reason and not sophisticate, Dr. Blackstone would have found that there never was nor could be a *usufructuary* property in a garment or a house; the property in this case was from its nature always absolute. For a house or a garment in *statu quo* is no production of the earth and was certainly never considered as a part of the general stock of society. The materials of which the house or the garment was formed might have been common stock, but when by manual labor or dexterity the materials became converted into a house or a garment, it became the exclusive property of the maker. And this is not merely a scholastic or speculative distinction, but a distinction founded in nature and well known to the American Indians.

"The Indians," says Carver, "are strangers to all distinction of property, except in the articles of domestic use, which everyone considers as his own." And this miserable sophist, Dr. Blackstone, knew better: he knew that a house or a garment could not be usufructuary property, for he establishes the position, which will hereafter appear, that "bodily labor bestowed upon any subject which before lay in [35] common to all men gives the fairest and most reasonable title to exclusive property therein."

It is a little surprising, if anything from Dr. Blackstone can surprise us, that he will not suffer men to have been so well provided for, under the law of nature, as the brute creation. "For," says he, "the brute creation, to whom everything else was in common, maintained a kind of permanent property in their dwellings, especially for the protection of their young; the birds of the air had nests and the beasts of the fields had caverns, the invasion of which they esteemed a very flagrant injustice and would sacrifice their lives to preserve." The argument, therefore, of the necessity of more permanent dominion than was exercised under the law of nature, to secure a man's right to his house or garment, is totally false, seeing that not a usufructuary but an absolute and exclusive property was vested in him by the laws of nature.

"And there can be no doubt," continues the Doctor, "that movables of every kind became sooner appropriated than the permanent substantial soil, partly because they were susceptible of a long occupancy, which might be continued for months together, without any sensible interruption, and at length by usage ripen into an established right, but principally because few of them [36] could be fit for use till improved and meliorated by the bodily labor of the occupant, which bodily labor bestowed upon any subject, which before lay in common to all men, is universally allowed to give the fairest and most reasonable title to an exclusive property therein." But movables never were common stock, for by the very act by which they become movables, they become absolute and exclusive property. Thus fruit growing on a tree was not movable until collected, but when collected it became absolute and exclusive property. A tree standing was not movable, but when cut down it became exclusive property. Again, the animal creation could not be esteemed movables until they were caught; but when caught they became exclusive property.

"As the world by degrees grew more populous, it daily became more difficult to find out new spots to inhabit without encroaching upon former occupations; and by constantly occupying the same individual spot, the fruits of the earth were consumed and its spontaneous produce destroyed, without any provision for a future supply or succession. It therefore became necessary to pursue some regular method of providing a constant subsistence and this necessity produced, or at least promoted and encouraged, the art of agriculture."

The Doctor had well nigh forgot his [37] Bible. He should have recollected that the first man born was a tiller of the ground, and agriculture therefore nearly coeval with the creation. And although it may be objected that the art was lost in the deluge, yet we are certain that it was revived in the person of Noah, who, we are informed in the 9th Genesis, "began to be an husbandman, and he planted a vineyard."

The President Goguet, in his *Origin of Laws, Arts, and Sciences,* teaches much the same doctrine with Dr. Blackstone; it may therefore be necessary to attend to him also. "There was a time," says M. Goguet, "when mankind derived their whole subsistence from the fruits which the earth produced spontaneously, from their hunting, fishing, and their flocks. Such was the ancient manner of living till agriculture was introduced; in this manner several nations still live, as the Scythians, Tartars, Arabians, savages, etc."

By savages, M. Goguet means the aborigines of America, and here he is clearly mistaken, for agriculture is known and practiced by every Indian tribe throughout the continent of America. Maize or Indian corn is a grain peculiar to this continent, and we have never heard of its growing wild; it must therefore have been cultivated by the aborigines of the continent. From the multitude of authorities which M. Goguet cites, when he treats of the saveages, one would [38] conclude that he had better information concerning them than of the Tartars, Arabians, and Scythians, and that if he is mistaken in regard to the savages, he may also be mistaken concerning the others.

But as the authors of false theories generally contradict themselves, so M. Goguet tells us that "Homer, in *Odyss.* L. vi. 10, says that in those remote ages it was one of the first cares of those who formed new establishments to divide the lands among the members of the colony . . . And the Chinese say that Gin Hoand, one of their first kings, who reigned 2,000 years before the vulgar era, divided the whole of his lands into nine parts, one of which was destined for dwelling, and the other eight for agriculture—" *Martini hist. de la Chine.* "And by the history of Peru, we find that their first Incas took great pains in distributing their lands among their subjects—" *Accost hist. des Ind.*

But further, M. Goguet tells us that agriculture introduced *landmarks,* the practice of which, he says, is very ancient: "We find it very plainly alluded to in Gen. xlix. 14."*[39] Now if landmarks be the consequence of agriculture (and landmarks existed in the days of the patriarch Jacob), it follows that agriculture existed then also. But M. Goguet, had he believed or read his Bible, might have found texts enough to convince him that agriculture was known and practiced in the earliest ages. The example of Cain was surely pretty early, and although, as has before been observed, it might be said the art was lost in the deluge, yet we find frequent mention of it shortly after: Genesis xxx, 14—"And Reuben went in the days of wheat harvest and found mandrakes in the field," etc.

It seems difficult to account for the opinions of European authors, in denying agriculture to the first race of men, especially when the

---

* In turning to the text which M. Goguet says alludes to landmarks, in the edition of the Bible dedicated to King James, I find the text, "Issachar is a strong ass, crouching down between two burdens." As I could perceive nothing here alluding to landmarks, I at first suspected the chapter or verse wrong quoted, but having recourse to the Vulgate edition, I found the text, "Issachar shall be a strong ass lying down between two borders," which borders, I presume, M. Goguet thought alluded to landmarks.

Bible which they all pretend to believe is so directly opposed to them. But as the Americans are always quoted to support this doctrine, it would seem that this opinion was founded upon the stupid productions, entitled Histories of America: inferences drawn from those relations, which bear every mark of prejudice and absurdity, are to be believed in preference to holy writ. Some of the Americans, say those authors, live on acorns: hence [40] acorns were the original diet of mankind, for [that] men in early ages knew nothing of agriculture is plain from the practice of those savages. Here is first a false statement of fact and then a conclusion in opposition to holy writ.

M. Goguet, it is very plain, has fell into this error, for he says, "Travelers inform us that even at this day in some parts of the world they meet with men who are strangers to all social intercourse, of a character so cruel and ferocious that they live in perpetual war, destroying and devouring each other. Those wretched people, void of all the principles of humanity, without laws, polity, or government, live in dens and caverns, and differ but very little from the brute creation; their food consists of some roots and fruits, with which the woods supply them; for want of skill and industry, they can seldom procure more solid nourishment. In a word, not having the most common and obvious notions, they have nothing of humanity but the external figure."

Here he quotes his authorities: *Voyage 5 le Blanc. Hist. nat. de Island. Hist. des Isles Marianes. Lettres edifiantes. N. Relat. de la France equinox. Hist. gen. des Voyages. Voyages de Frezier. Rec. des Voyages au Nordt.* Many of them, no doubt, of equal authority with Robinson Crusoe. But, M. Goguet says, those savage people exactly answer the description given us by historians of the ancient state of mankind. [41] Does M. Goguet believe that we are in possession of any history of the ancient primitive state of mankind except the Bible? But M. Goguet has established his opinion and will not flinch from it. He says, "But all the rest of mankind, except a few families of Noah's descendants who settled in Persia, Syria, and Egypt, I repeat it again, led the life of savages and barbarians."

We will give up to M. Goguet's repetitions and his obstinacy, but we will think as we please; we know of no such orangutan as he has just described from ignorant voyages. So much for M. Goguet; let us hear what is said on the other side of the question: The editors of the *Encyclopedia* say, "Nor is there any solid reason for concluding that all nations were originally unskilled in agriculture." See article

WILMINGTON, 1791

[on] "Agriculture," *Encyclopedia.* Modern discoveries also prove that agriculture is everywhere known. For of all the rude and uncivilized inhabitants of our vast continent, of all the numerous islands in the Pacific Ocean,† of those under the equator, [42] where reigns an

---

†   CAROLINE ISLES.

Father Cantova, speaking of the Caroline Islands, says, "The principal occupation of the men is to make boats for fishing and to cultivate the earth." *Lettres edifiantes & curieuses. Tom. 15, p. 313.*

FRIENDLY ISLES.

"The province alloted to the men is as might be expected far more laborious and extensive than that of the women: agriculture, architecture, boat building, fishing, and other things that relate to navigation are the objects of their care; cultivated roots and fruits being their principal support, this requires their constant attention to agriculture, which they pursue very diligently and seem to have brought to almost as great perfection as circumstances will permit."

OTAHEITE.

In the account of the agriculture of Otaheite, Captain Cook seems in some measure to contradict himself. He says, "It is doubtless the natural fertility of the country, combined with the mildness and serenity of the climate, that renders the natives so careless in their cultivation that in many places, though overflowing with the richest productions, the smallest traces cannot be observed. The cloth plant, which is raised by seeds brought from the mountains, and the ava or intoxicating pepper are almost the only things to which they pay any attention." Capt. Cook afterwards tells us that he supposes the inhabitant of Otaheite prevents the progress of the bread plant to make room for others, to afford him some variety in his food, the chief of which are the cocoanut and plantain, the first of which he says can give "no trouble after it has raised itself a foot or two above the ground; but the plantain requires more care." Hence we may enumerate four species of vegetables cultivated at Otaheite, viz. the cloth plant, the ava, the cocoanut, and the plantain. But as the cocoanut and the plantain were the chief among other substitutes to the bread plant, here is a fair inference that some other species of vegetables were cultivated.

SANDWICH ISLES.

"What we saw of their agriculture furnished sufficient proofs that they were not novices in that art. The vale ground is one continued plantation of taro and a few other things which have all the appearance of being well attended to. The potato fields and spots of sugar cane or plantains on the higher grounds are planted with the same regularity and always in the same determinate figure, generally as a square or oblong, but neither those nor the others are enclosed with any kind of fence, unless we reckon the ditches in the low grounds such, which, it is more probable, are intended to convey water to the taro. The great quantity and goodness of those articles may also perhaps be as much attributed to skillful culture as to natural fertility of soil." *Cook's last Voyage.*

eternal spring—where a luxuriant soil and a vertical sun produce fruits in abundance and seem most to preclude the necessity of agriculture— it is notwithstanding universally known and practiced.

Dr. Blackstone's remarks on the origin of property are in many instances so similar to those of President Goguet [43] that one would be apt to think that the Doctor did not come honestly by them but that he pilfered them from the *Origin of Laws, Arts, and Sciences.* "When husbandry was unknown," says the President, "all lands were common. There were no boundaries nor landmarks, everyone sought his subsistence where he thought fit. By turns they abandoned and repossessed the same districts, as they were more or less exhausted. [44] But after agriculture, this was not practicable. It was necessary then to distinguish possessions and to take necessary measures that every member of society might enjoy the fruits of his labors."

The President here supposes that vices which receive their existence with bad government are natural to the heart of man. The Indians pursue agriculture, but their land is in common; and they enjoy the fruits of their labor, without any boundaries, enclosures, or divisions of land. Theft is unknown among them; this is an incontrovertible fact, which totally overturns and demolishes the crazy theories of President Goguet and Doctor Blackstone.

"The art of agriculture," says the Doctor, "by regular connection and consequence, introduced the idea of more permanent property in the soil than had been hitherto received and adopted. It was clear that the earth could not produce her fruits in sufficient quantities without the assistance of tillage. But who would be at the pains of tilling it, if another might watch an opportunity to seize upon and enjoy the product of his industry, art, and labor. Had not, therefore, a separate property in lands, as well as movables, been vested in some individual, the world must have continued a forest and men have been mere [45] animals of prey, which according to some philosophers is the genuine state of nature." But we deny that by any connection or consequence the art of agriculture necessarily introduced more permanent property in the soil than was known in the days of Cain or than is now known by the American Indians. We deny that by the laws of nature any man could seize upon the product of the art, industry, or labor of another, and surely the Doctor forgets not only the Bible but his own words, for he has already established the position that bodily labor bestowed upon any subject which before lay in common gives the fairest and most reasonable title to exclusive property therein.

We deny that by any necessary consequence a community of lands would have detained the world a forest. A right to exclusive possession in lands, founded on the equitable and rational principle of labor, would at all times have been sufficient for all the purposes of men. What does the Doctor mean by *mere animals of prey?* The savage, as we are pleased to call him, takes his bow and repairs to some forest, to obtain subsistence by the death of some animal: the polished citizen takes his pence and repairs to some butcher; the brute creation are equally victims, and men equally animals of prey.

Civilized or savage, bowels entombed in bowels is still his delight; but the savage slays to satisfy his natural [46] wants, the citizen often murders for purposes of riot and ostentation; and before he should upbraid the savage on this score, he should have profited by the precepts which the poet puts into the mouth of Pythagoras: *"Parcite mortales, dapibus temerare nefandis corpora! sunt fruges, sunt deducentia ramos pondere poma suo tumidæque in vitibus uvæ, sunt herbæ dulces sunt quæ mitescere flamma mollirique queant,"*‡ etc. Precepts which were never conveyed to the savage, but which the citizen has been in possession of for ages past.

The doctor's premises being therefore false, his conclusions of the necessity of a separate property [47] in lands being vested in some individuals falls to the ground of course. But, continues the Doctor, "Whereas now (so graciously has Providence interwoven our duty and our happiness together) the result of this very necessity has been the ennobling of the human species, by giving it opportunity of improving its rational faculties, as well as of exerting its natural [faculties], necessity begat property and order to insure that property, recourse

---

‡ Spare, O mortals! to pollute your bodies with horrid feasts. There are fruits, there are apples, which bend the branches by their weight, and juicy grapes on the vine. There are sweet herbs, and herbs which may be made sweeter and softer by fire, etc. *Ov. Met. lib. 15.*

It may be indeed doubted whether butcher's meat is anywhere a necessary of life. Grain and other vegetables, with the help of milk, cheese, and butter, or oil where butter is not to be had, it is known from experience, can without any butcher's meat afford the most plentiful, the most wholesome, the most nourishing, and the most invigorating diet. Decency nowhere requires that any man should eat butcher's meat, as it in most places requires that he should wear a linen shirt or a pair of leather shoes. *Smith's Wealth of Nations.*

was had to civil society, which brought with it a train of inseparable concomitants, states, governments, laws, punishments, and the public exercise of religious duties."

That is to say, God created man imperfect and ignoble, a mere animal of prey, but when, with the sword of violence and the pen of sophistry, a few had plundered or cheated the bulk of their rights, the few became ennobled and the many were reduced from mere animals of prey to beasts of burden. But why not mention a few more concomitants of civil society, such as poverty, vices innumerable, and diseases unknown in the state of nature. Look around your cities, ye who boast of having established the civilization and happiness of man, see at every corner of your streets some wretched object with tattered garments, squalid look, and hopeless eye, publishing your lies, in folio to the world. Hedged in the narrow strait, between your sanguinary laws and [48] the pressing calls of hunger, he has no retreat, but like an abortive being, created to no manner of purpose, his only wish is death. For of what use can life be but to augment his sufferings by a comparison of his desperate lot with yours?

But to continue, "The only question remaining," says the Doctor, "is how this property became actually vested, or what is it that gave a man an exclusive right to retain in a permanent manner that specific land which before belonged generally to everybody but particularly to nobody. And as we before observed that occupancy gave a right to the temporary use of the soil, so it is agreed upon all hands that occupancy gave also the original right to the permanent property in the substance of the earth itself, which excludes everyone else but the owner from the use of it.

"There is indeed some difference among the writers of natural law concerning the reason why occupancy should convey this right and invest one with this absolute property, Grotius and Pufendorf insisting that this right of occupancy is founded upon a tacit and implied assent of all mankind, that the first occupant should become the owner; and Barbeyrac, Titius, Mr. Locke, and others holding that there is no such implied assent, neither is it necessary that there should be, for that the [49] very act of occupancy alone being a degree of bodily labor is from a principle of natural justice without any consent or compact sufficient of itself to gain a title . . . A dispute that favors too much of nice and scholastic refinement! However, both sides agree in this, that occupancy is the thing by which the title was in fact originally gained, every man seizing to his own continued use such spots of ground as he found most agreeable to his own convenience, provided he found them unoccupied by any man."

But why this snarl at Barbeyrac, Titius, Mr. Locke, and others? It is plain that Dr. Blackstone had predetermined when he wrote his *Commentaries* to exclude the great body of mankind from any right to the boundaries of Providence—light, air, and water excepted—or else why would he turn up his nose at a distinction absolutely necessary to set bounds to the quantum and prevent a monopoly of all the lands among a few? The position has been before established "that bodily labor bestowed on any subject before common gives the best title to exclusive property."

But the act of occupancy is a degree of bodily labor; that is, the occupancy extends as far as the labor, or, in other words, a man has a right to as much land as he cultivates and no more, which is Mr. Locke's doctrine. This distinction is therefore absolutely necessary to determine the quantum [50] of lands any individual could possess under the laws of nature. For shall we say a man can possess only the ground in immediate contact with his feet, or if he climbs to the top of a mountain, and exclaims, "Behold, I possess as far as I can see!," shall there be any magic in the words or the expression which shall convey the right of all that land, in fee simple, to him and his heirs forever? No: as labor constitutes the right, so it sensibly defines the boundaries of possession.§

How then shall we detect the empty sophist who in order to establish his system of monopoly would fain persuade us that the Almighty did not know what he was about when he made man. That he made him an animal of prey and intended him for a polished citizen; that he gave his bounties in common to all and yet suffered a necessity to exist by which they could be enjoyed only by a few. Had Dr. Blackstone been disposed to give his readers a true account of the origin of landed property in Europe he might have said exclusive property in lands originated with government; but most of the governments that we have any knowledge of were founded by conquest: property therefore in its origin seems to have been [51] arbitrary. He might then have expiated upon the difficulty and inconvenience of

§ The Europeans have long supposed that the mere walking upon a piece of vacant ground gave them a right to it. Hence the Spaniards upon their first landing on this continent, set up a post, by which they claimed a right to it.

attempting any innovations upon the established rules of property. This would have sufficiently answered his purpose and saved him much sophistry and absurdity and not a little impiety: for it is surely blasphemy to say that there is a necessity of abrogating the divine law contained in the text of Genesis to make room for human laws which starve and degrade one half of mankind to pamper and intoxicate the rest.

"But after all," continues the Doctor, "there are some few things which must still unavoidably remain in common: such (among others) are the elements of light, air, and water." Thank you for nothing, Doctor. It is very generous, indeed, to allow us the common right to the elements of light, air, and water, or even the blood which flows in our veins. Blackstone's *Commentaries* have been much celebrated, and this very chapter, so replete with malignant sophistry and absurdity, has been inserted in all the magazines, museums, registers, and other periodical publications in England and cried up as the most ingenious performance ever published. Dr. Priestley and Mr. Furneaux both attacked Mr. Blackstone on the subject of some invectives against the dissenters and a mal-exposition of the [52] toleration act, but no champion was to be found to take the part of poor forlorn Human Nature, and the Doctor was suffered, unmolested, to quibble away all the rights of the great brotherhood of mankind.

Reduced to light, air, and water for an inheritance, one would have thought their situation could not be easily made worse, but it is not difficult to be mistaken. The bulk of mankind were not only cheated out of their right to the soil but were held ineligible to offices in the government because they were not freeholders. First cruelly to wrest from them the paternal inheritance of their universal Father, and then to make this outrageous act an excuse for denying them the rights of citizenship. This is the history of civil society in which our duty and happiness are so admirably interwoven together. We will, however, never believe that men originally entered into a compact by which they excluded themselves from all right to the bounties of Providence; and if they did, the contract could not be binding on their posterity, for although a man may give away his own right, he cannot give away the right of another.

"The only true and natural foundations of society," says Dr. Blackstone, "are the wants and fears of individuals." The word *society* here is a vague term, by which we are at liberty to understand any government which has existed from the creation of the world [53] to the present day. But if the European governments were erected to supply the wants and lessen the fears of individuals, we may venture to assert that the first projectors of them were errant blockheads. The wants of man, instead of having been lessened, have been multiplied, and that in proportion to his boasted civilization; and the fear of poverty alone is more than sufficient to counterbalance all the fears to which he was subject in the rudest stage of natural liberty.

From this source arise almost all the disorders in the body politic. The fear of poverty has given a double spring to avarice, the deadliest passion in the human breast; it has erected a golden image to which all mankind, with reverence, bend the knee regardless of their idolatry. Merit is but an abortive useless gift to the possessor, unless accompanied with wealth; he might choose which tree whereon to hang himself, did not his virtuous mind tell him to "dig, beg, rot, and perish well content, so he but wrap himself in honest rags at his last gasp and die in peace."

It is a melancholy reflection that in almost all ages and countries men have been cruelly butchered for crimes occasioned by the laws and which they never would have committed, had they not been deprived of their natural means of subsistence. But the governors of mankind seem [54] never to have made any allowance for poverty, but like the stupid physician who prescribed bleeding for every disorder, they seem ever to have been distinguished by an insatiable thirst for human blood. The altars of a merciful God have been washed to their foundation from the veins of miserable men; and the double-edged sword of Justice, with all its formality and parade, seems calculated to cut off equally the innocent and guilty. Between religion and law, man has had literally no rest for the sole of his foot.

In the dark ages of Gothic barbarity ignorance was some excuse for the framing of absurd systems, but in the age in which Dr. Blackstone lived, he should have known better, he should have known that the unequal distribution of property was the parent of almost all the disorders of government; nay, he did know it, for he had read Beccaria, who treating upon the crime of robbery, says, "But this crime, alas!, is commonly the effect of misery and despair, the crime of that unhappy part of mankind to whom the right of exclusive property (a terrible and perhaps unnecessary right) has left but a bare subsistence." There is no necessity for concealing this important truth, but much benefit may be expected from its promulgation—It offers a foundation whereon to erect a system, which like the sun in the universe, will transmit light, life, and harmony to all under its influence—I mean—A SYSTEM OF EQUAL EDUCATION.

[55]   CHAP. III

Consequences Drawn from the Preceding Chapters by Which It Is Proved that All Governments Are Bound To Secure to Their Subjects the Means of Acquiring Knowledge in Sciences and in Arts.

In the first part of this work, we have shown that the most obvious difference between the situation of the savage and the civilized man is the division of property. We have shown also that this difference is the origin of all the miseries and vices of the one and of all the innocence and happiness of the other. We have also demonstrated that the civilized man has been unjustly deprived of his right to the bounties of Providence and that he has been rendered, as much as human laws could do it, an abortive creation.

We will now inquire the best mode of alleviating his miseries, without disturbing the established rules of property. In the savage state, as there is no learning, so there is no need of it. Meum & tuum, which principally receives existence with civil society, is but little known in the rude stages of natural liberty; and where [56] all property is unknown, or rather, where all property is in common, there is no necessity of learning to acquire or defend it. If in adverting from a state of nature to a state of civil society, men gave up their natural liberty and their common right to property, it is but just that they should be protected in their civil liberty and furnished with means of gaining exclusive property, in lieu of that natural liberty and common right of property which they had given up in exchange for the supposed advantages of civil society; otherwise the change is for the worse, and the general happiness is sacrificed for the benefit of a few.

In all contracts, say civilians, there should be a *quid pro quo*. If civil society therefore deprives a man of his natural means of subsistence, it should find him other means; otherwise civil society is not a contract, but a self-robbery, a robbery of the basest kind: "It represents a madman, who tears his body with his arms, and Saturn, who cruelly devours his own children." Society should then furnish the people with means of subsistence, and those means should be an inherent quality in the nature of the government, universal, permanent, and uniform, because their natural means were so. The means I allude to are the means of acquiring knowledge, as it is by the knowledge of some art or science that man is to provide for subsistence in civil society. These [57] means of acquiring knowledge, as I said before, should be an inherent quality in the nature of the government: that is, the education of children should be provided for in the constitution of every state.

By education I mean instruction in arts as well as sciences. Education, then, ought to be secured by government to every class of citizens, to every child in the state. The citizens should be instructed in sciences by public schools, and in arts by laws enacted for that purpose, by which parents and others, having authority over children, should be compelled to bind them out to certain trades or professions, that they may be enabled to support themselves with becoming independency when they shall arrive to years of maturity.

Education should not be left to the caprice or negligence of parents, to chance, or confined to the children of wealthy citizens; it is a shame, a scandal to civilized society, that part only of the citizens should be sent to colleges and universities to learn to cheat the rest of their liberties. Are ye aware, legislators, that in making knowledge necessary to the subsistence of your subjects, ye are in duty bound to secure to them the means of acquiring it? Else what is the bond of society but a rope of sand, incapable of supporting its own weight? A heterogenous jumble of contradiction and absurdity, from which the subject knows not how to extricate himself, [58] but often falls a victim to his natural wants or to cruel and inexorable laws—starves or is hanged.

In the single reign of Henry VIII, we are informed by Harrison that seventy-two thousand thieves and rogues were hanged in England. How shall we account for this number of executions? Shall we suppose that the English nation at this period were a pack of thieves and that everyone of this number richly deserved his fate? Or shall we say that the lives of so many citizens were sacrificed to a wretched and barbarous policy? The latter seems to be the fact.

The lands in England, at this time, were held under the feudal system, in large tracts, by lords; the people were called vassals; but the conditions of their servitude were so hard, their yoke so grievous to be borne, that numbers left the service of their lords. But where could they fly or how were they to provide for subsistence? The cultivation of the soil was denied them, except upon terms too vile and degrading to be accepted, and arts and commerce, which at this day maintain the bulk of the people, were then in their infancy and probably employed but a small proportion of the people.

We despise thieves, not caring to reflect that human nature is always the same: that when it is a man's interest to be a thief he becomes one, but when it is his interest to support a good character he becomes an honest man; [59] that even thieves are honest among each other, because it is their interest to be so. We seldom hear of a man in independent circumstances being indicted for petit felony: the man would be an idiot indeed who would stake a fair character for a few shillings which he did not need, but the greatest part of those indicted for petit felonies are men who have no characters to lose, that is—no substance, which the world always takes for good character.

If a man has no fortune and through poverty or neglect of his parents he has had no education and learned no trade, in such a forlorn situation, which demands our charity and our tears, the equitable and humane laws of England spurn him from their protection, under the harsh term of a vagrant or a vagabond, and he is cruelly ordered to be whipped out of the county.

From newspapers we often gather important and curious information. In the *Baltimore Advertiser* of the 16 Nov. 1790 is the following extract from an English newspaper: "The French exult in having been the first nation who made their King confess himself a citizen. With all due deference to the French, we manage those things as well in England. In the last reign there was a good deal of dispute between the parish of [60] St. Martin and the Board of Green Cloth about the payment of poor rates for the houses in Scotland Yard. The Board would not pay, because they belonged to the King! 'And if they do belong to the King, is not the King a parishioner?,' was the reply; *'but if the thing is at all doubtful, we will put it beyond dispute;'* and they accordingly elected his majesty to the office of church warden. The King served the office by deputy and was thankful they had not made him a constable. They might have made him an overseer of the poor, which every King is, or ought to be, in right of his office, but in that case, by the old constitution of St. Martin, he might have had the flogging of vagrants to perform with his own hands, for there is in the books of the parish a curious item of expense: *'To furnishing the Overseer of the poore with one cloke, maske and cappe; to whippe the beggars out of the parish.' "*

So much for English parish law, a remnant of which, says a writer in the *Delaware Gazette,* has more than once been put in execution in this state. Strangers suspected of being poor have been imprisoned because they could produce no pass from the place they last left. Unfortunate civilized man! Too much reason had Raynal to say, "Everywhere you meet with masters and always with oppression." How often, says this venerable philosopher, have we heard the poor man expostulating [61] with heaven and asking what he had done, that he should deserve to be born in an indigent and dependent station.

How can those English vagrant acts be reconciled to that law which pretends to protect every man in his just rights? Or have poor men no rights? How will they square with the doctrines of the Christian religion which preach poverty, charity, meekness, and disinterestedness, after the example of their humble founder. "Let us dwell no longer," says a French writer, "upon those miseries, the detail of which will only grieve and tire you; believe that the ornaments of your churches would better cover the nakedness of Jesus Christ in the sacred and miserable persons of your poor: yes, you would have more merit to cover his terrestrial members than to entertain a pomp foreign to his laws and the charity of his heart. The Church, the spouse of a God, poor and humble, hath always had a terrible fear of poverty: she has preserved wisely, and in good time, resources against this terrifying sin. The immense wealth she has amassed by preaching poverty hath put her at her ease, until the consummation of ages."

Is it any wonder that poverty should be such a formidable terror to civilized nations, when it never meets with quarter, [62] but always with persecution, when both religion and law declare it to be the object of their most implacable hatred and disgust. English vagrant acts, although they are a manifest abuse of civilization, have been hitherto impregnable to the attacks of sound reason and elegant satire. Many English authors have honestly reprobated them; Mr. Fielding in several of his novels has highly ridiculed them; and Doctor Goldsmith has exposed them in a vein of inimitable satire, in his history of a poor soldier. Pity such philosophers were not magistrates!

"In vain," says Raynal, "does custom, prejudice, ignorance, and hard labor stupify the lower class of mankind, so as to render them insensible of their degradation; neither religion nor morality can hinder them from seeing, and feeling, the injustice of the arrangements of policy in the distribution of good and evil."

But how comes this injustice in the arrangements of policy? Is it not evident that it is all the work of men's hands? Thus it is that the sins of the fathers are visited upon the children unto the third and fourth generation. A tyrant, a madman, or a fool forms a society; to aggrandize his own family and his dependants, he creates absurd and unnatural distinctions; to make one part of the people fools, he makes the other part slaves. His posterity [63] in a few generations mix with the mass of the people, and they then suffer for the despotism, the folly, or the ignorance of their ancestor. The distinctions, however, which are the root of their misery, still exist, although their author is extinct; thus it is that the folly of man outlives himself and persecutes his posterity.

"To live and to propagate," says the before-mentioned author, "being the destination of every living species, it should seem that society, if it be one of the first principles of man, should concur in assisting this double end of nature." We should be cautious how we unite the words *society* and *government,* they being essentially different. Society promotes but bad governments check population. In bad governments, only, is celibacy known, and it is of little consequence what class of subjects practice it, whether the clergy, as in France, or the servants, as in England—it is always baneful. It estranges the affections of the human heart from its proper object and gives the passions an unnatural direction. Poverty, the great scourge of civilized nations, is the immediate cause of celibacy in the lower class of people.

Celibacy in the higher ranks proceed from the same cause, though not so immediately. The [64] fear of poverty has made the love of gain the ruling passion: hence parents to secure an estate to their children marry them in their infancy: hence money is always title good enough to procure a husband or wife: hence those preposterous matches which unite beauty and deformity, youth and old age, mildness and ferocity, virtue and vice. In Europe the inclination of a girl is seldom consulted in regard to a husband: hence the infidelity to the marriage bed so common in those countries and the matrimonial strife so frequent, which deter many from entering into that state who have both ability and inclination.

It has been observed that the attraction of the sexes is in many circumstances similar to gravity, the spring of motion in the universe, that it always acts in the same degree in the same climate. If the design of Providence in the creation of man was that he should multiply and replenish the earth, why endeavour to destroy this natural propensity? Why encourage celibacy repugnant to nature and death to society? Men do not, in fact, practice celibacy through inclination but necessity: in short, nothing is wanting to induce men to marry, but [what is wanting is what is required] to enable every man to maintain a wife, and should the care of government extend to the proper education of the subject, every man would be enabled to do it.

[65] We have already demonstrated that government should furnish the subject with some substitute in lieu of his natural means of subsistence, which he gave up to government when he submitted to exclusive property in lands. An education is also necessary in order that the subject may know the obligations he is under to government.

The following observations of a celebrated English historian are very applicable: "Every law," says Mrs. Macaulay in her *History of England,* "relating to public or private property and in particular penal statutes ought to be rendered so clear and plain and promulgated in such a manner to the public as to give a full information of its nature and extent to every citizen. Ignorance of laws, if not wilful, is a just excuse for their transgression, and if the care of government does not extend to the proper education of the subject and to their proper information on the nature of moral turpitude and legal crimes and to the encouragement of virtue, with what face of justice can they punish delinquency? But if, on the contrary, the citizens, by the oppression of heavy taxes, are rendered incapable, by the utmost exertion of honest industry, of bringing up or providing for a numerous family, if every encouragement is given to licentiousness for [66] the purpose of amusing and debasing the minds of the people or for raising a revenue on the vices of the subject, is punishment in this case better than legal murder? Or, to use a strong yet adequate expression, is it better than infernal tyranny?"

Time was when the laws were written in a language which the

people did not understand, and it seemed the policy of government that the people should not understand them, contrary to every principle of sound policy in legislation. If the system of English law was simplified and reduced to the standard of the common sense of the people, or were the understanding of the people cultivated so as to comprehend the system, many absurdities which exist at this day would have been rejected.

We are told by Sir William Blackstone that it is a settled rule at common law that no counsel shall be allowed a prisoner upon his trial upon the general issue in any capital crime unless some point of law shall arise proper to be debated. This is without doubt a barbarous law, and it is a little surprising that while every other art and science is daily improving, such inconsistencies should have been suffered to continue to this time of day in a science on which our lives depend. Men are every day liable to suffer in their property by their ignorance [67] of the forms of legal writings adopted by lawyers. But although a man should be under the necessity of suffering in his property by not knowing which form of writing would best secure his debts or preserve his estate, yet certainly he might be allowed to know some little of the statute law in which his life is concerned. Those governments, therefore, which think the instruction of youth worthy [of] their attention, would do well to cause an abridgement of their statute law to be read in their schools at stated times, as often as convenient.

Mankind, ever inclined to the marvelous, run astray in search of a phantom, an *ignis fatuus,* while they neglect those simple and palpable truths which could only conduct them to that happiness they are so eagerly in search of. How many volumes have been wrote upon predestination, free will, liberty, and necessity, topics which are not properly the objects of the human understanding and of which after we have wrote a thousand volumes we are not a whit wiser than when we began, while the economy of society is but little understood and the first and simplest principles of legislation entirely neglected.

Nothing is more obvious than that every person in a civilized society should contribute towards the support of government. How stupid, then, is the [68] economy of that society conducted, which keeps one half of the citizens in a state of abject poverty, saddling the other half with the whole weight of government and the maintenance of all the poor beside? Every citizen ought to contribute to the support of government, but all obligations should bind within the limits of possibility; a man, at least, should be able to pay a tax before he is compelled to do it as a duty. But the pauper who cannot procure even the vilest food to spin out a miserable existence may indeed burden but can never support the government.

The English, whose absurdities we are at all times proud to imitate, in this respect seem justly to have deserved the keen satire of Dr. Swift, who says the sage professors of Laputa were employed in extracting sunbeams out of cucumbers, calcining ice into gunpowder, and making fire malleable. The policy of the English government appears to have been to make the mass of people poor and then to persecute them for their poverty, as their vagrant acts abundantly testify; those acts, as has been said before, are a manifest abuse of civilization—they are impolitic, barbarous, inhuman, and unjust, and would disgrace even a society of satyrs.

In an essay on trade, written in the reign of George II, are the following paragraphs:

[69] "The *Spectator* calculates 7 parts in 8 of the people to be without property and get their bread by daily labor. If so, will trade pretend to employ all hands equally and constantly? If not, it will be worth considering how they live in the present situation of things. Mr. Gee, a very intelligent author, computes three millions unemployed in the three kingdoms: the truth of which appears by divers particulars. Prisons, workhouses, transports, and beggars are so many instances to confirm the truth of this observation. Some preposterously complain that in any labor or business that requires expedition a sufficiency of hands is wanting.

"But what numbers are there continually traveling from one country to another, from nation to nation, who would work day and night for a little more pay—which argues that the choice is to live by honest means, and if they are hurried into others less justifiable, it is for want of employment. And as such men must eat and drink whether they work or no, they are put to many shifts for a subsistence; no wonder, then, if the empty stomach fills the head with dangerous projects. It is unnatural to think that many of those poor wretches who are doomed to death or exile would have run the hazard of their lives, or liberty, in such trifles as it is frequently forfeited for (the 10d. or 12d. convicts) were they not compelled to it by griping necessity; [70] for it is well known that many of those who are sent abroad alter their sentiments with their circumstances, and this is a principle argument to recommend the christianity of transportation.

"Rapin, in his history of Edward VI, thus speaks of the people's complaints—for they were so early that they were not able to gain their livelihoods—1st, because business was fallen into more hands, meaning the vagabond monks; 2d., by inclosures; 3d., by breeding sheep, which took fewer hands and lessened the wages. Dean Swift gives much the same reasons for the miserable poverty of Ireland.

"Philips, Esq., argues thus—If, says he, there were full employment, labor would rise to its just value, as everything else does when the demand is equal to the quantity; and therefore [he] denies that there is work enough, or that property is reasonably and sufficiently diffused, till necessaries are rendered so plentiful and thereby so cheap that the wages of the laboring man will purchase a comfortable support.

"Vanderlint's late pamphlet adjusts every article of expense and at the lowest computation supposes a laborer cannot support himself, a wife, and four children at less than £.50 a year. Now if he works daily as a laborer, the top wages he can get exceeds not 18d. a day. Masons, carpenters, etc. have half a crown, but both fall [71] short of the sum, though in full employ, so that beggary and thievery from this account seem their inevitable destiny; and while one part of the world condemns and punishes the delinquents, the other ought to rejoice, for the greater the numbers that go into idle and unwarrantable ways of living, the better and securer state it makes for those behind.

"Dr. Garth has ingeniously described the use of such contingencies in higher life:

> For sickly seasons the physicians wait,
> And politicians thrive in broils of state;
> In sessions the poor lay all their stress,
> And hope each month their crowds will be the less.

"Poverty makes mankind unnatural in their affections and behavior. The child secretly wishes the death of the parent, and the parent thinks his children an incumbrance and has sometimes robbed their bellies to fill his own. Many yield themselves up to the unnatural lusts of others for a trifling gratuity, and the most scandalous practices are often the effects of necessitous poverty. Is it not therefore of consequence to provide for the growing evil, and worthy a legislative inquiry how the poor people are brought up? Men also come to renounce their generative faculty or destroy that fruit whose misery they cannot [72] prevent.

"The difficulty of getting money to purchase food is the same thing now which dearths were formerly, with this little difference, that as famine might vex them once in an age or two, this sticks close every year for the lifetime of laborers who are at low wages and at an uncertainty even in that, numbers of them being driven to great straits, sitting in the market place till the eleventh hour, and then called perhaps a servant to the plantations; some through a meekness of disposition starve quietly and in private; others associate in crimes and are hanged or in fear of that, hang themselves. It is in vain to argue against fact, no nation on earth, nor perhaps all the absolute kingdoms together, affording so many instances of suicides and executions as England, and plainly for a care in most of them about this mortal body how it shall subsist."

But if such has been the situation of the poor, in the nation whose government has been so much boasted of, how have they fared in the rest of Europe? Take the following description of the galley slaves of Italy, from the Sieur Dupaty. "All sorts of wretches are fastened indiscriminately to the same chain; malefactors, smugglers, dealers, Turks taken by the corsairs, and volunteers, galley slaves. Voluntary galley slaves! Yes—These are poor men, whom government get [73] hold of between hunger and death. It is in this narrow passage they wait and watch for them. Those wretched beings, dazzled with a little money, do not perceive the galleys and are enlisted. Poverty and guilt are bound in the same chain! The citizen who serves the republic suffers the same punishment with him who betrays it!

"The Genoese carry their barbarity still further; when the term of their enlisting is near expiring, they propose to lend a little money to those miserable creatures. Unhappy men are eager for enjoyment; the present moment alone exists for them; they accept—but at a week's end nothing remains to them but slavery and regret, insomuch that at the expiration of that time they are compelled to enlist again, to discharge their debt, and sell eight years' more of their existence. Thus do the greatest part of them consume, from enlistments to loans, and from loans to enlistments, their whole lives at the galleys in the last degree of wretchedness and infamy: there they expire . . . Let us add one more trait to this picture of the galleys. I saw the wretches selling from bench to bench, coveting, disputing, stealing even the fragments of aliment which the dogs of the street had refused—Genoa! thy palaces are not sufficiently lofty, spacious, numerous, nor brilliant, we still perceive thy galleys!"

[74] We may apostrophize more generally. Civilization, thy benefits are not sufficiently solid, numerous, nor splendid; we everywhere perceive that degradation and distress which thy daughter poverty has entailed upon our race.

Finally, the security of all governments must in a great measure depend upon the people. Should a savage be introduced into a civilized society and denied all means of improving himself, could it be expected that he could form any accurate notions of the policy, economy, or obligations of that society? And yet among the great body of the people in polished Europe, among the laboring poor, how rare is it to find a man possessed of anything equal to the general knowledge of an ingenious savage?

The European artist is expert in the particular article of his trade or art. Thus a pin maker is dexterous at making pins, but in everything else he is as grossly stupid, his understanding is as benumbed and torpid, as it is possible for any intellectual faculty to be. The number of executions in England has been already observed to be occasioned more by the wretched policy of the government than by any innate depravity of the people, who, generally speaking, are ignorant to a proverb. They have, it is true, universities and [75] colleges, with a few charity schools, but the former receive none but the sons of wealthy subjects and the latter are very circumscribed; few poor children have even the chance of balloting for admittance. Hence the body of the people are ignorant.

And in France, if one hundredth part of the money expended in the maintenance of legions [of] fat, lazy, lubberly ecclesiastics had been employed in instructing the people in public schools, the nation would be a nation of men instead of a rude and ignorant rabble, utterly incapable of profiting by the golden opportunity which now offers and which, were it not for the exertions of their leaders, would, instead of emancipating them, only serve more strongly to rivet their fetters. Humanity is wounded by the outrages of the mob in France, but what better can be expected from *ignorance,* the natural parent of all enormity?

The actions of mobs are always characteristic of the people who compose them, and we will find the most ignorant always guilty of the greatest outrages: hence the striking difference between American and European mobs. The mob that burnt the tea at Boston, and even that under Shays, was a regular and orderly body, when compared with that of Lord George Gordon or any of the late mobs in France. We know of [76] no such outrages committed in America.

But as there will be sometimes disorders in the very best of governments, such as keep the mass of people in profound ignorance must abide by the consequences when the body politic is convulsed. Mr. Noah Webster is the only American author, indeed the only author of any nation, if we except perhaps Montesquieu, who has taken up the subject of education upon that liberal and equitable scale which it justly deserves. I had the present work in idea some time before Mr. Webster's essays made their appearance and was not a little pleased to think he had anticipated my idea.

Although I am sensible that I have dealt pretty freely with quotations in this work already, yet I think it a debt due to Mr. Webster to introduce part of his sentiments on this subject—"A good system of education," says this author, "should be the first article in the code of political regulations, for it is much easier to introduce and establish an effectual system for preserving morals than to correct by penal statutes the ill effects of a bad system. I am so fully persuaded of this that I shall almost adore that great man who shall change our practice and opinions and make it respectable for the first and best men to superintend the education of youth.

[77] "It is observed by the great Montesquieu that 'the laws of education ought to be relative to the principles of the government.' In despotic governments the people should have little or no education, except what tends to inspire them with a servile fear. Information is fatal to despotism. In monarchies education should be partial and adapted to each class of citizens. But 'in a republican government,' says the same writer, 'the whole power of education is required.' Here every class of people should *know* and *love* the laws. This knowledge should be diffused by means of schools and newspapers, and an attachment to the laws may be formed by early impressions upon the mind.

"Two regulations are essential to the continuance of republican governments: 1. Such a distribution of lands and such principles of descent and alienation as shall give every citizen a power of acquiring what his industry merits. 2. Such a system of education as gives every citizen an opportunity of acquiring knowledge and fitting himself for places of trust. These are fundamental articles, the *sine qua non* of the existence of the American republics."

"Hence the absurdity of our copying the manners and adopting the institutions of monarchies. In several states we find laws passed [78] establishing provisions for colleges and academies where people of property may educate their sons, but no provision is made for instructing the poorer rank of people even in reading and writing. Yet in these same states every citizen who is worth a few shillings annually is entitled to vote for legislators. This appears to me a most glaring solecism in government. The constitutions are *republican* and the laws of education are *monarchical.* The *former* extend civil rights to every honest industrious man, the *latter* deprive a large proportion of the citizens of a most valuable privilege.

"In our American republics, where government is in the hands of the people, knowledge should be universally diffused by means of public schools. Of such consequence is it to society that the people who make laws should be well informed that I conceive no legislature can be justified in neglecting proper establishments for this purpose.

"Such a general system of education is neither impracticable nor difficult, and excepting the formation of a federal government that shall be efficient and permanent, it demands the first attention of American patriots. Until such a system shall be adopted and pursued, until the statesman and divine shall unite their efforts in *forming* the human mind, rather than in lopping its excrescences after it has been neglected, until legislators discover that the only [79] way to make good citizens and subjects is to nourish them from infancy, and until parents shall be convinced that the *worst* of men are not the proper teachers to make the *best,* mankind cannot know to what degree of perfection society and government may be carried. America affords the fairest opportunities for making the experiment and opens the most encouraging prospect of success."

Suffer me then, Americans, to arrest, to command your attention to this important subject. To make mankind better is a duty which every man owes to his posterity, to his country, and to his God; and remember, my friends, there is but one way to effect this important purpose—which is—by incorporating education with government.— *This is the rock on which you must build your political salvation!*

[80]   CHAP. IV

The System of Education Should Be Equal. Equality of Men Considered. Raynal Mistaken in His Notions of Equality.

THAT the system of education should be equal is evident, since the rights given up in the state of nature and for which education is the substitute were equal. But as I know it will be objected by some that the natural inequality of the human intellect will obviate any attempt to diffuse knowledge equally, it seems necessary to make some inquiry concerning the natural equality of men.

That all men are by nature equal was once the fashionable phrase of the times, and men gloried in this equality and really believed it, or else they acted their parts to the life! Latterly, however, this notion is laughed out of countenance, and some very grave personages have not scrupled to assert that as we have copied the English in our form of federal government, we ought to imitate them in the establishment [81] of a nobility also.

For my part, I do believe that if there was any necessity for two distinct hereditary orders of men in a society that men would have been created subordinate to such necessity and would at their birth be possessed of certain characteristic marks by which each class would be distinguished. However, as much has been said of late upon grades and gradations in the human species, I will endeavor to add my mite to the public stock.

In the dark ages of the world it was necessary that the people should believe their rulers to be a superior race of beings to themselves, in order that they should obey the absurd laws of their tryants without "scrutinizing too nicely into the reasons of making them." As neither the governors nor governed understood any other principle of legislation than that of fear, it was necessary in order that the people should fear their rulers to believe them of a superior race to themselves.

Hence in the Jewish theocracy their rulers came in under a *jure divino* title, consecrated and anointed by the Deity himself. Hence the Mexican emperors were descended in a direct line from the sun, and in order to conduct the farce completely the descendants of the female line only inherited, in order that the blood line of the sun might never be lost. This was a master stroke of policy, perhaps never equalled in the eastern [82] world, but it sufficiently shows that the emperors were apprehensive that if the people suspected an extinction of the blood line that they would conclude they were governed by men like themselves, which would be subversive of the principle of fear on which their government was erected.

But until the light of letters be again extinct, vain will be the attempt to erect a government on the single principle of fear or to introduce a nobility in America. If the Americans could be brought seriously to believe that by giving a few hereditary titles to some of their people, such people would immediately upon their being invested with such titles become metamorphosed into a superior race of beings, an attempt for a nobility might succeed.

But to return to our inquiry—If an elegant silver vase and some ore of the same metal were shown to a person ignorant of metals, it would not require much argument to convince him that the vase could never be produced from the ore. Such is the mode of reasoning upon the inequality of the human species. Effects purely artificial have been ascribed to nature, and the man of letters who from his cradle to his grave has trod the paths of art is compared with the untutored Indian and the wretched African in whom slavery has deadened all the springs of the soul.

[83] And the result of this impartial and charitable investigation is that there is an evident gradation in the intellectual faculties of the human species. There are various grades in the human mind [—this] is the fashionable phrase of the times. Scarce a superficial blockhead is to be met with but stuns you with a string of trite commonplace observations upon gradation, and no doubt thinks himself *in primo gradu* or at the top of the ladder.

Nature is always various in different species, and except in cases of *lusus naturæ,* always uniform in the same species. In all animals, from the most trifling insect to the whale and elephant, there is an evident uniformity and equality through every species. Where this equality is not to be found in the human species it is to be attributed either to climate, habit, or education, or perhaps to all. It must be obvious to every intelligent person the effect which habit alone has upon men. Awkward boobies have been taken from the ploughtail into the Continental army in the late war and after a few campaigns have returned home, to the surprise and admiration of their acquaintances, elegant, ornamental, and dignified characters. Such astonishing metamorphoses have been produced by the army that to habit alone may be ascribed all the inequality to be found in the human species.

[84] If then education alone (for in this sense, the army may be properly called a school) is capable of producing such astonishing effects, what may not be ascribed to it when united with climate? Indeed we have numberless commonplace observations which have been always read as true and which are entirely founded upon this idea of equality in the intellectual faculties of the human race. Take the following—The minds of children are like blank paper, upon which you may write any characters you please. But what tends most to establish this idea of natural equality [is that] we find it always uniform in the savage state.

Now if there was a natural inequality in the human mind, would it not be as conspicuous in the savage as in the civilized state? The contrary of which is evident to every observer acquainted with the American Indians. Among those people all the gifts of Providence are in common. We do not see, as in civilized nations, part of the citizens sent to colleges to learn to cheat the rest of their liberties who are condemned to be hewers of wood and drawers of water. The mode of acquiring information, which is common to one, is common to all; hence we find a striking equality in form, size, and intellectual faculties nowhere to be found in civilized nations.

It is only in civilized nations where extremes are to be found in the human species—it is here where wealthy and dignified mortals [85] roll along the streets in all the parade and trappings of royalty, while the lower class are not half so well fed as the horses of the former. It is this cruel inequality which has given rise to the epithets of nobility, vulgar, mob, canaille, etc. and the degrading, but common observation—Man differs more from man, than man from beast—The difference is purely artificial. Thus do men create an artificial inequality among themselves and then cry out it is all natural.

If we would give ourselves time to consider, we would find an idea of natural intellectual equality everywhere predominant but more particularly in free countries. The trial by jury is a strong proof of this idea in that nation; otherwise would they have suffered the unlettered peasant to decide against lawyers and judges? Is it not here taken for granted that the generality of men, although they are ignorant of the phrases and technical terms of the law, have notwithstanding sufficient mother wit to distinguish between right and wrong, which is all the lawyer with his long string of cases and reports is able to do? From whence also arises our notion of common sense? Is it not from an idea that the bulk of mankind possess what is called common understanding?

This common understanding must be supposed equal, or why should we apply the term common which implies equality? But it will perhaps be [86] objected that the minds of some men are capable of greater improvement than others, which daily experience testifies: to which I answer that there is perhaps as great a variety in the texture of the human mind as in the countenances of men. If this be admitted, the absurdity of judging of the genius of boys by the advances they make in any particular science will be evident. But a variety is by no means inconsistent with an equality in the human intellect. And although there are instances of men who by mere dint of unassisted genius have arose to excellence, while others have been so deficient in mental powers as not to be capable of improvement from the combined efforts of art, yet when we enumerate all the idiots and sublime geniuses in the world, they will be found too few in number when compared with the rest of mankind to invalidate the general rule that all men are by nature equal.

But why should a strict mathematical equality be thought necessary among men, when no such thing is to be found in nature? In the vegetable creation, the generality of plants arrive to perfection, some reach only half way, and some are blights, yet the vegetable creation is perfect. The soil is to plants what government is to man. Different soils will produce the same species of vegetables in different degrees of perfection, [87] but there will be an equality in the perfection of vegetables produced by the same soil in the same degree of cultivation. Thus governments which afford equal rights to the subjects will produce men naturally equal; that is, there will be the same equality in such men as is to be found in all the productions of nature. As one soil, by manuring it in patches, will produce vegetables in different degrees of perfection, so governments, which afford different privileges to different classes of people will produce men as effectually unequal as if the original germ of stamina of production was essentially different.

The notion of a natural inequality among men has been so generally adopted that it has created numerous obstacles to the investigation of their rights and biased the most discerning of modern writers. The Abbé Raynal, whose philanthropy I revere and of whose works I am far from being a willing critic, seems to have adopted this erroneous opinion.

"It has been said," says the Abbé, in his *Revolution of America,* "that we are all born equal; that is not so—that we had all the same rights; I am ignorant of what are rights, where there is an inequality of talents, of strength, and no security or sanction—that nature offered to us all the same dwelling, and the same resources; that is not so— that we were all endowed indiscriminately with the same means of defense; [88] that is not so; and I know not in what sense it can be true that we all enjoy the same qualities of mind and body. There is amongst men an original inequality for which there is no remedy. It must last forever, and all that can be obtained by the best legislation is not to destroy it but to prevent the abuse of it.

"But in making distinctions among her children like a stepmother, in creating some children strong and others weak, has not nature herself formed the germ or principal of tyranny? I do not think it can be denied, especially if we look back to a time anterior to all legislation, a time in which man will be seen as passionate and as void of reason as a brute."

But how is it that we are not all born equal? There may be a difference between the child of a nobleman and that of a peasant, but will there not also be an inequality between the produce of seeds collected from the same plant and sown in different soils? Yes, but the inequality is artificial, not natural. It has been already observed that there is a striking equality in form, size, and intellectual faculties among the American Indians nowhere to be found in what we call civilized nations. Men are equal where they enjoy equal rights. Even a mathematical equality in powers among men would not necessarily secure their [89] rights.

It had escaped the Abbé's reflection that nature, when she formed more men than two, formed the germ or principle of tyranny as effectually as when she created one man of double powers to another, for among three men of equal powers two could as effectually overpower the third as one man of six feet could overcome one of three. But although a mathematical equality among men neither exists nor is necessary, yet the generality of men educated under equal circumstances possess equal powers. This is the equality to be found in all the productions of nature, the equality and the only equality necessary to the happiness of man.

The inhabitants of the United States are more upon an equality in stature and powers of body and mind than the subjects of any government in Europe. And of the United States, the states of New England, whose governments by charter verged nearest to democracies, enjoy the most perfect equality. Those who live ashore are all legislators and politicians;|| and those who follow the sea are all captains and owners; yet their governments are orderly and their ships navigated with as much success as if they were commanded with all the etiquette and subordination of royal navies. But though the constitution of the New England states were democratical, yet their laws [90] were chiefly borrowed from the British code, many of which were unequal, such as vagrant acts, acts which confer rights of residence and citizenship, and the like—hence the equality of the citizens of New England, though striking when compared with any of the European governments, is not strictly natural. But among the American Indians, where no vestige of European absurdity is found interwoven in their laws, where they are governed by the plain and equitable code of nature, here is perfect natural equality.

The Abbé Raynal seems to be mistaken in his opinion concerning the origin of government. Speaking of the miseries to which man is subject in his civilized state, he says, "In this point of view, man appears more miserable and more wicked than a beast. Different species of beasts subsist on different species, but societies of men have never ceased to attack each other. Even in the same society, there is no condition but devours and is devoured, whatever may have been or are the forms of government or artificial equality which have been opposed to the primitive and natural inequality."

Men educated under bad governments, who see nothing but vice and infamy around them, who behold hardened wretches falling victims to the laws daily, are apt to conclude that man is naturally wicked— that in a state of [91] nature, he is a stranger to morality, he is barbarous and savage, the weak always falling a prey to the strong— that government was instituted to protect the weak and to restrain the bold and to bring them more upon an equality.

But this is all a mistake—the man of America is a living proof

|| See Morse's Geography.

to the contrary. He is innocent and spotless when compared with the inhabitants of civilized nations. He has not yet learned the art to cheat, although the traders have imposed upon him by every base and dirty fraud which civilized ingenuity could invent, selling him guns which are more likely to kill the person who fires them than the object at which they are presented; and hatchets without a particle of steel—incapable of bearing an edge or answering any use. I have seen whole invoices of goods, to a very considerable amount imported for the Indian trade, in which there was not an article which was not a palpable cheat.

Some excuse indeed seems necessaary to those who have brought men under the yoke of cruel and arbitrary governments, and nothing is more easy than to say, it is all their own faults; that is, the faults of the people. They had given themselves up to the full possession of their unruly passions, appetites, and desires, every man tyrannizing over his neighbor. Government, therefore, [92] arose out of necessity. This they will assert with as much confidence and maintain with as much obstinacy as if, forsooth, they had been personally present at the first conventions of men in a state of nature—and although no vestige is to be found of the foundation of any of the governments now existing being laid in any such convention, and although the conduct of individuals in those societies which approach nearest to the state of nature are so very far from supporting this opinion that they rather teach us to believe that men excel in wickedness in proportion to their civilization.

Therefore, instead of supposing with Abbé Raynal a primitive inequality which was found necessary to be lessened by the artificial equality opposed to it in different forms of government, we will suppose a primitive equality, and this equality to be disturbed and broken by an external force, not by members of the same society opposed to each other, but the conquest of one society by another, when the conquering society became the governors and the conquered society the governed.

This is clearly the case in regard to the English government, which we know was founded by conquest, and which Mr. Blackstone, with much eloquence but more sophistry, would fain persuade us had a much more equitable origin. The English, indeed, seem in their theory of [93] the gradation of the human species to have forgotten the state of their ancestors when conquered by the Romans—a rude and barbarous people, dwelling in caverns, feeding on roots, their only clothing the uncouth representation of the sun, moon, and stars, daubed in barbarous characters on their skins; yet the descendants of these wretched savages pretend that there is an evident gradation in the intellectual faculties of the human species. Since, therefore, men are naturally equal, it follows that the mode of education should be equal also.

It is generally observed that most of the American legislatures are composed of lawyers and merchants. What is the reason? Because the farmer has no opportunity of getting his son instructed without sending him to a college, the expense of which is more than the profits of his farm. An equal representation is absolutely necessary to the preservation of liberty. But there can never be an equal representation until there is an equal mode of education for all citizens. For although a rich farmer may, by the credit of his possessions, help himself into the legislature, yet if through a deficiency in his education he is unable to speak with propriety, he may see the dearest interest of his country basely bartered away and be unable to make any effort except his single vote against it. Education, therefore, to be generally useful should be brought home to every man's door.

[94]   CHAP. V

Wretched State of the Country Schools throughout the United States, and the Absolute Necessity of a Reformation.

The country schools through most of the United States, whether we consider the buildings, the teachers, or the regulations, are in every respect completely despicable, wretched, and contemptible. The buildings are in general sorry hovels, neither windtight nor watertight, a few stools serving in the double capacity of bench and desk and the old leaves of copy books making a miserable substitute for glass windows.

The teachers are generally foreigners, shamefully deficient in every qualification necessary to convey instruction to youth and not seldom addicted to gross vices. Absolute in his own opinion and proud of introducing what he calls his European method, one calls the first letter of the alphabet *aw*. The school is modified upon this plan, and the children who are advanced are beat and cuffed to forget the former mode they have been taught, which irritates their minds and retards their progress. The quarter being finished, the children lie idle until another master offers, few remaining in one place more than a quarter. [95] When the next schoolmaster is introduced, he calls the first letter *a,* as in *mat*—the school undergoes another reform and is equally vexed and retarded. At his removal, a third is introduced, who calls the first letter *hay.* All these blockheads are equally absolute in their own notions and will by no means suffer the children to pronounce the letter as they were first taught, but every three months the school goes through a reform—error succeeds error—and dunce the second reigns like dunce the first.

The general ignorance of schoolmasters has long been the subject of complaint in England as well as America. Dr. Goldsmith says, "It is hardly possible to conceive the ignorance of many of those who take upon them the important trust of education. Is a man unfit for any profession, he finds his last resource in commencing schoolmaster— Do any become bankrupts, they set up a boarding school and drive a trade this way when all others fail—nay, I have been told of butchers and barbers who have turned schoolmasters, and more surprising still, made fortunes in their new profession." And I will venture to pronounce that however seaport towns, from local circumstances, may have good schools, the country schools will remain in their present state of despicable wretchedness unless incorporated with government.

[96]   *Now, blame we most the nurslings or the nurse?*
          The children crook'd, and twisted, and deform'd
          Through want of care, or her whose winking eye
          And slumb'ring oscitancy mars the brood?
          The nurse, no doubt. Regardless of her charge,
          She needs herself correction. Needs to learn
          That it is dang'rous sporting with the world,
          With things so sacred as a nation's trust,
          The nurture of her youth, her dearest pledge.

If education is necessary for one man, my religion tells me it is equally necessary for another, and I know no reason why the country should not have as good schools as the seaport towns, unless indeed the policy of this country is always to be directed, as it has been, by merchants. I am no enemy to any class of men, but he that runs may read.

A blind adherence to British policy seems to have pervaded both the general and state governments, notwithstanding there is no analogy between the two countries; and this will be the case until we can raise men in the country who will think for themselves and be able to arrange and communicate their ideas. Towns have the advantages of libraries, the country of retirement—the youth of the former may become elegant imitators; those of the latter, bold originals; being out of the sphere of vice so attractive in cities, their productions will bear the stamp of virtuous energy.

[97] When I say that the policy of this country, has been hitherto directed by merchants, etc., I mean that the inhabitants of seaport towns have a very considerable influence in all our public proceedings and that from education and local circumstances such inhabitants appear to me to have an improper bias in favor of commercial and mercantile habits and interests, habits and interests which do not appear to me to be congenial with the true interest of the United States.

The necessity of a reformation in the country schools is too obvious to be insisted on, and the first step to such reformation will be by turning private schools into public ones. The schools should be public, for several reasons—1st. Because, as has been before said, every citizen has an equal right to subsistence and ought to have an equal opportunity of acquiring knowledge. 2d. Because public schools are easiest maintained, as the burden falls upon all the citizens.

The man who is too squeamish or lazy to get married contributes to the support of public schools as well as the man who is burdened with a large family. But private schools are supported only by heads of families, and by those only while they are interested, for as soon as the children are grown up their support is withdrawn, which makes the employment so precarious that men of ability and merit will [98] not submit to the trifling salaries allowed in most country schools and which, by their partial support, cannot afford a better.

Let public schools then be established in every county of the United States, at least as many as are necessary for the present population; and let those schools be supported by a general tax. Let the objects of those schools be to teach the rudiments of the English language, writing, bookkeeping, mathematics, natural history, mechanics, and husbandry—and let every scholar be admitted gratis and kept in a state of subordination without respect to persons.

The other branch of education, I mean, instruction in arts, ought also to be secured to every individual by laws enacted for that purpose, by which parents and others having authority over youth should be compelled to bind them out at certain ages and for a limited time to persons professing mechanical or other branches, and the treatment of apprentices during their apprenticeship should be regulated by laws expressly provided, without having recourse to the common or statute law of England. I mention this because, independent of the difference of circumstances between these United States and England, I think a more humane and liberal policy might be established than that now [99] in usage in England and better adapted to the present circumstances of America; and indeed it is high time to check that blind adherence to transatlantic policy which has so generally prevailed.

It would be superfluous to insist on the necessity of trades—their use is obvious. I shall only remark that, considering the transitory nature of all human advantages, how soon a man may be dispossessed of a very considerable property—how many avenues there are to misfortunes; a good trade seems to be the only sheet anchor on which we may firmly rely for safety in the general storms of human adversity. How much then is it to be lamented that ever the tyranny of fashion or pride of birth gave an idea of disgrace to those virtuous and useful occupations.

To demonstrate the practicability of establishing public schools throughout the United States, let us suppose the states to be divided into districts according to the population, and let every district support one school by a tax on the acre on all lands within the district. Let us suppose for argument's sake, six miles square, which will be 36 square miles—sufficient for a district for the mean population of the United States. The schoolhouse should be built of brick and in the center of the district; it would be then three miles from the schoolhouse door to the boundary [100] of the district. The building might be two stories, with a large hall on the lower floor for the schoolroom; the rest of the house should be for the master's family and might consist of two rooms on the lower floor and three or four in the second story, with perhaps an acre of ground adjoining.

We will suppose the ground to cost £10, the building £800, the master's salary £150 per annum, and £50 for an assistant, with £50 for mathematical instruments; in all £1060, of which £800 is for building the schoolhouse; and as people enough will be willing to contract for building the house, to wait a year for half the money, we will suppose £400 to be paid the first year. Now in 36 square miles are 23,040 acres, which is little better than 4d. per acre; the next year's payment will be £660, which will be about 7d.; then the succeeding years there will be the teacher's salary, £150, the assistant £50, and £50 for contingent expenses, books, etc. will be £250. per annum, which will not amount to 3d. per acre.

Now when we consider that such a trifling tax, by being applied to this best of purposes, may be productive of consequences amazingly glorious, can any man make a serious objection against public schools? "It is unjust," says one, "that I should pay for the schooling of other people's children." But, my good sir, it is more unjust that your posterity should go [101] without any education at all. And public schools is the only method I know of to secure an education to your posterity forever. Besides, I will suppose you to be the father of four children—Now, sir, how can you educate these four children so cheap, even in your present paltry method? The common rate at present is 8s. 4d. per quarter, which is 33s. 4d. per year, which for 4 children is £6 13 4. Now if you hold 300 acres of land, you will pay towards the support of decent public schools, at 3d. per acre, 900d. or £3 15 per annum.

Perhaps no plan of private education can ever be so cheap as public. In the instances of public schools a considerable part of the master's salary would be spent in the district. The farmer might supply him with provisions, and the receipts might be tendered as a part of his tax to the collector. Thus the farmer would scarcely feel the tax.

No modes of faith, systems of manners, or foreign or dead languages should be taught in those schools. As none of them are necessary to obtain a knowledge of the obligations of society, the government is not bound to instruct the citizens in any thing of the kind—No medals or premiums of any kind should be given under the [102] mistaken notion of exciting emulation. Like titles of nobility, they are not productive of a single good effect but of many very bad ones: my objections are founded on reason and experience. In republican governments the praises of good men, and not medals, should be esteemed the proper reward of merit, but by substituting a bauble instead of such rational applause, do we not teach youth to make a false estimate of things and to value them for their glitter, parade, and finery? This single objection ought to banish medals from schools forever.

I once knew a schoolmaster who besides being an arithmetician was a man of observation: this person had a school of upwards of 90 scholars and at every quarterly examination a gold medal was given to the best writer and a silver one to the best cipherer. I requested him one day candidly to inform me of the effects produced by those medals; he ingenuously told me that they had produced but one good effect, which was [that] they had drawn a few more scholars to his school than he otherwise would have had, but that they had produced many bad effects.

When the first medal was offered, it produced rather a general contention than an emulation and diffused a spirit of envy, jealousy, and discord through the whole school; boys who were bosom friends before became fierce contentious rivals, and when the prize was [103] adjudged became implacable enemies. Those who were advanced decried the weaker performances; each wished his opponent's abilities less than his own, and they used all their little arts to misrepresent and abuse each other's performances. And of the girls' side, where perhaps a more modest and more amiable train never graced a school, harmony and love, which hitherto presided, were banished, and discord reigned triumphant—jealousy and envy, under the specious semblance of emulation, put to flight all the tender, modest, amiable virtues, and left none but malignant passions in their stead. But the second quarter, things changed their faces.

There must indeed be almost a mathematical equality in the human intellect, if in a school of nearly 100 scholars, one or two do not, by superior genius, take the lead of the rest. The children soon found that all of them could not obtain the medal, and the contention continued sometimes among three, but seldom with more than two. But although the contention was generally confined to two, yet the ill effects produced by the general contention of the first quarter still remained and discord as generally prevailed. But more, the medal never failed to ruin the one who gained it and who was never worth a farthing afterwards; having gained the object of his ambition, he conceived there [104] was no need of further exertion or even of showing a decent respect either to his tutor or his schoolmates; and if the losing competitor happened to be a girl, she sometimes left the school in tears and could never be prevailed upon to enter it afterwards.

Those are the effects of medals as they operated on the school, but they extended their mischief still further. The flame of jealousy was kindled in the breasts of the mothers, who charged the master with partiality in the distribution of the medals, although they were adjudged by four of five indifferent persons of merit in the town, and although the tutor uniformly refused to give his opinion on the merit of any performance, and care was taken that the authors of none of the performances were known by the persons who adjudged the prize.

To conclude, to make men happy, the first step is to make them independent. For if they are dependent, they can neither manage their private concerns properly, retain their own dignity, or vote impartially for their country: they can be but tools at best. And to make them independent, to repeat Mr. Webster's words, two regulations are essentially necessary. First, such a distribution of lands and principles of descent and [105] alienation as shall give every citizen a power of acquiring what his industry merits. Secondly, such a system of education as gives every citizen an opportunity of acquiring knowledge and fitting himself for places of trust. It is said that men of property are the fittest persons to represent their country because they have least reason to betray it. If the observation is just, every man should have property, that none be left to betray their country.

"It has been observed that the inhabitants in mountains are strongly attached to their country, which probably arises from the division of lands, in which, generally speaking, all have an interest. In this, the Biscayners exceed all other states, looking with fondness on their hills as the most delightful scenes in the world and their people as the most respectable, descended from the aborigines of Spain. This prepossession excites them to the most extraordinary labor, and to execute things far beyond what could be expected in so small and rugged a country, where they have few branches of commerce. I cannot give a greater proof of their industry than those fine roads they have now made from Bilboa to Castile, as well as in Guypuscoa and Alaba. When one sees the passage over the tremendous mountains of Orduna, one cannot behold it without the utmost surprise and admirations."¶

It is with infinite satisfaction that I have seen a similar sentiment

---

¶ Dillon's Travels in Spain.

adopted by the Court of Errors and [106] Appeals, in the Delaware state, in the case of Benjamin Robinson and William Robinson appellants, against the lessee of John Adams, respondent. "Estates in fee tail," say the court, "are not liable to division by will, or upon intestacy, as estates in fee simple are; & those distributions are very beneficial.* It is much to be wished that *every citizen could possess a freehold,* though some of them might happen to be small. Such a disposition of property cherishes domestic happiness, endears a country to its inhabitants, and promotes the general welfare. But what ever influence such reflections might have upon us, on other occasions they can have but little if any on the present for reasons that will hereafter appear."

From the last sentence in the foregoing paragraph, and the note beneath, it would appear that this republican sentiment was introduced by the court, not from any immediate relation, reference, [107] or application, which it had to the cause under consideration, but merely that it might be generally diffused.

And now, my fellow citizens, having thus, though in an indigested manner, shown you the great cause of all the evils attendant on an abuse of civilization, it remains with you to apply the remedy. Let it not be said, when we shall be no more, that the descendants of an Eastern nation, landed in this Western world, attacked the defenseless natives and "divorced them in anguish, from the bosom of their country," only to establish narrow and unequitable policies, such as the governments of our forefathers were.

But let us, since so much evil has been done, endeavor that some good many come of it. Let us keep nature in view and form our policy rather by the fitness of things than by a blind adherence to contemptible precedents from arbitrary and corrupt governments. Let us begin by

---

* "It is greatly to be desired that the persons appointed by our courts, for viewing and dividing lands among the children of intestates, would not suffer themselves so easily to be prevailed upon to report that the lands will not bear a division. Thus, very often an estate is adjudged as incapable of division, to one of the children that might well be divided into five or six, if not more farms, as large as many in the Eastern states; upon which the industrious and prudent owners live happily. By the usual way of proceeding among us, one of the children is involved in a heavy debt that frequently proves ruinous to him; or if the debt of valuation is paid to the other children, it is in a number of such trifling sums and at such distances of time, one from another, that they are of very little use to those who receive them. This matter deserves very serious consideration."

perfecting the system of education as the proper foundation whereon to erect a temple to liberty and to establish a wise, equitable, and durable policy, that our country may become *indeed* an asylum to the distressed of every clime—the abode of liberty, peace, virtue, and happiness—a land on which the Deity may deign to look down with approbation—and whose government may last till time shall be no more!

FINIS.

[55]

JOEL BARLOW 1754–1812

---

*A Letter to the National Convention of France
on the Defects in the Constitution of 1791*

NEW YORK, 1792

Born in Redding, Connecticut, and educated at Yale, Barlow went on to a successful double career in letters and diplomacy. His literary efforts include one epic, *The Columbiad,* and a number of famous lighter pieces such as *The Hasty Pudding.* Barlow was also a perceptive theoretical analyst of politics. This piece, an analysis of the French Constitution from the view of American principles, won him an honorary citizenship awarded by the French General Assembly. He later served as United States consul to Algiers, where he negotiated the release of American prisoners, and negotiated treaties with Algiers, Tunis, and Tripoli. Sent to France to negotiate a commercial treaty with Napoleon, Barlow was caught in the confused retreat by French forces from Moscow and died of exposure. The present piece reflects the confidence the Americans had developed in their own institutions and the reasoning underlying them.

A LETTER, &c.

GENTLEMEN,

The time is at last arrived, when the people of France, by resorting to their own proper dignity, feel themselves at liberty to exercise their unembarrassed reason, in establishing an equal government. The present crisis in your affairs, marked by the assembling of a National Convention, bears nearly the same relation to the last four years of your history, as your whole revolution bears to the great accumulated mass of modern improvement. Compared therefore with all that is past, it is perhaps [4] the most interesting portion of the most important period that Europe has hitherto seen.

Under this impression, and with the deepest sense of the magnitude of the subject which engages your attention, I take a liberty which no slight motives could warrant in a stranger, the liberty of offering a few observations on the business that lies before you. Could I suppose however that any apology were necessary for this intrusion, I should not rely upon the one here mentioned. But my intentions require no apology; I demand to be heard, as a right. Your cause is that of human nature at large; you are the representatives of mankind; and though I am not literally one of your constituents, yet I must be bound by your decrees. My happiness will be seriously affected by your deliberations; and in them I have an interest, which nothing can destroy. I not only consider all mankind as forming but one great family, and therefore bound by a natural sympathy to regard each other's [5] happiness as making part of their own; but I contemplate the French nation at this moment as standing on the place of the whole. You have stepped forward with a gigantic stride to an enterprize which involves the interests of every surrounding nation; and what you began as justice to yourselves, you are called upon to finish as a duty to the human race.

I believe no man cherishes a greater veneration, then I have uniformly done, for the National Assembly who framed that Constitution, which I now presume your constituents expect you to revise. Perhaps the merits of that body of men will never be properly appreciated. The greatest part of their exertions were necessarily spent on objects which cannot be described; and which from their nature can make no figure in history. The enormous weight of abuses they had to overturn, the quantity of prejudice with which their functions called them to contend, as well in their own minds as in those of all the European world, the open [6] opposition of interests, the secret weapons of corruption, and the unbridled fury of despairing faction,— these are subjects which escape our common observation, when we contemplate the labours of that Assembly. But the legacy they have left to their country in their deliberative capacity will remain a lasting monument to their praise; and though while searching out the defective parts of their work, without losing sight of the difficulties under which it was formed, we may find more occasion to admire its wisdom, than to murmur at its faults; yet this consideration ought not to deter us from the attempt.

The great leading principle, on which their constitution was meant to be founded, is *the equality of rights*. This principle being laid down with such clearness, and asserted with so much dignity in the beginning of the code, it is strange that men of clear understandings should fail to be charmed with the beauty of the system which nature must have taught them to build [7] on that foundation. It shows a disposition to counteract the analogy of nature, to see them at one moment, impressing this indelible principle on our minds, and with the next breath declaring, That France shall remain a monarchy,— that it shall have a king, hereditary, inviolable, clothed with all the executive, and much of the legislative power, commander in chief of all the national force by land and sea, having the initiative of war, and the power of concluding peace;—and above all, to hear them declare, that "The nation will provide for the splendour of the throne," granting in their legislative capacity to that throne more than a million sterling a year, from the national purse, besides the rents of estates which are said to amount to half as much more.

We must be astonished at the paradoxical organization of the minds of men who could see no discordance in these ideas. They begin with the open simplicity of a rational republic, and immediately plunge into all the labyrinths of royalty; and a [8] great part of the constitutional code is a practical attempt to reconcile these two discordant theories. It is a perpetual conflict between principle and precedent,—between the manly truths of nature, which we all must feel, and the learned subtilties of statesmen, about which we have been taught to reason.

In reviewing the history of human opinions, it is an unpleasant consideration to remark how slow the mind has always been in seizing the most interesting truths; although, when discovered, they appear to have been the most obvious. This remark is no where verified with more circumstances of regret, than in the progress of your ideas in France relative to the inutility of the kingly office. It was not enough that you took your first stand upon the high ground of natural right; where, enlightened by the sun of reason, you might have seen the

clouds of prejudice roll far beneath your feet—it was not enough that
you began by considering royalty, with its well-known scourges, as
being the cause of [9] all your evils,—that the kings of modern Europe
are the authors of war and misery, that their mutual intercourse is a
commerce of human slaughter,—that public debts and private oppressions, with all the degrading vices that tarnish the face of nature, had
their origin in that species of government which offers a premium for
wickedness, and teaches the few to trample on the many;—it was not
enough that you saw the means of a regeneration of mankind in the
system of equal rights, and that in a wealthy and powerful nation you
possessed the advantage of reducing that system to immediate practice,
as an example to the world and a consolation to human nature. All
these arguments, with a variety of others which your republican orators
placed in the strongest point of light, were insufficient to raise the
public mind to a proper view of the subject.

It seems that some of your own philosophers had previously
taught, that royalty was necessary to a great nation. Montesquieu,
among his whimsical maxims about [10] laws and government, had
informed the world, that a limited monarchy was the best possible
system, and that a democracy could never flourish, but in a small
tract of country. How many of your legislators believed in this doctrine,
how many acted from temporising motives, wishing to banish royalty
by slow degrees, and how many were led, by principles less pardonable
than either, it is impossible to determine. Certain it is, that republican
ideas gained no ground upon the monarchical in your constituting
assembly, during the last six months of their deliberations. It is
likewise certain, that the majority of that assembly took much pains
to prevent the people from discovering the cheat of royalty, and to
continue their ancient veneration, at least for a while, in favour of
certain principles in government which reason could not approve.

It is remarkable that all the perfidy of your king, at the time of
his flight, should have had so little effect in opening the eyes of so
enlightened a people as the French. [11] His flight, and the insulting
declaration which he left behind him, were sufficient not only to give
the lie to the fiction, with which common sense has always been put
to the blush, and to which your assembly had attempted to give a
sanction, *that kings can do no wrong,* but they were sufficient to show,
at least to all who would open their eyes, that the business of
government required no such officer. There is no period during your

revolution, if there is any to be found in the history of France, when business went on with more alacrity and good order, than during the suspension of the royal functions in the interval from the time that the king was brought back to the capital in June, until the completion of the constitution in September. Every thing went right in the kingdom, except within the walls of the assembly. A majority of that body was determined to make an experiment of a limited monarchy. The experiment has been made. Its duration has indeed been short, being less than eleven months; but, although in [12] some respects it has been almost as fatal to the cause of liberty as any system could have been within the time, yet in other respects it has done more good than all the reasonings of all the philosophers of the age could have done in a much longer time: it has taught them a new doctrine, which no experience can shake, and which reason must confirm, *that kings can do no good.* So that, if the question were now to be agitated by the people of France, as it may be by you in their behalf, whether they will have a king or not, I should suppose the following would be the state of the calculation: A certain quantity of evils are to be expected from the regal office; and these evils are of two classes, *certain* and *probable.* The *certain* evils are, 1. The million and a half sterling a year drawn from the people to "support the splendour of the throne;" 2. A great variety of enormous salaries paid to ministers at home, to ambassadors abroad, and to bishops in the church; while the only business of these men and their salaries [13] is, to support the fiction, that kings can do no wrong. It will always cost more to support this fiction, than it would to support the whole national government without it. 3. The worst of all the certain evils is, that the million and a half will be nearly all spent in bribery and corruption among the members of the legislature, to increase the power of the throne, and the means of oppression. If the money, after it is extorted from the people, could be thrown into the sea, instead of being paid to the king and his satellites, the evil would be trifling; in that case the wickedness would cease with the first act of injustice; while in this it multiplies the weapons of destruction against themselves. It creates a perpetual scrambling for power, rewards knavery in the higher ranks, encourages falsehood in others, and corrupts the morals of the whole. This it is that debases and vilifies the general mass of mankind, and brings upon them the insulting remarks of many men, who even wish them well, *that the people are unfit for liberty.*

JOEL BARLOW 1754–1812

[14] Among the *probable* evils resulting from the kingly office, the principal one, and indeed the only one that needs to be mentioned, is the chance of its being held by a *weak or a wicked man.* When the office is hereditary, it is scarcely to be expected but that this should always be the case. Considering the birth and education of princes, the chance of finding one with practical common sense is hardly to be reckoned among possible events; nor is the probability less strong against their having virtue. The temptations to wickedness arising from their situation are too powerful to be resisted. The persuasive art of all their flatterers, the companions of their youth, the ministers of their pleasures, and every person with whom they ever converse, are necessarily employed to induce them to increase their revenue, by oppressing the people, whom they are taught from their cradle to consider as beasts of burthen. And what must almost insure the triumph of wickedness in their tempers, is the idea that they act totally and for ever without restraint. This is an allurement [15] to vice that even men of sense could scarcely resist. Impress it on the mind of any man that he *can do no wrong,* and he will soon convince you of your mistake.

Take this general summary of the evils arising from hereditary monarchy, under any restriction that can be proposed, and place it on one side of the account,—and state, on the other side, the truth which I believe no man of reflection will hereafter call in question, *that kings can do no good,* and the friends of liberty will no longer be in doubt which way you will decide the question relative to that part of your constitution.

I cannot feel easy in dismissing this part of my subject, without offering some remarks on that general vague idea which has long been floating about in the world, that a people under certain circumstances are unfit for liberty. You know in what insulting language this observation has been perpetually applied to the French during the course of the [16] revolution. Some have said that, they were too *ignorant* to form a government of their own, others, that they were too *poor,* others that they were too *numerous,* and others, that they were too *vitious.* I will not descend to the examination of the particular parts of this charge, nor of the whole as applied to the French, or to any other particular people; I will only remark on the general observation, as aplicable to any possible nation existing in a state of nature. By a state of nature I mean a state of peace; where the intention is, as a nation, to live by industry at home, not by plunder from abroad.

I think Montesquieu has said, that virtue must be the foundation of a republican government. His book is not now by me, or I would try to discover what he means by virtue. If he means those moral habits by which men are disposed to mutual justice and benevolence, which is the common idea of virtue, it cannot be the foundation of a republican government, or of any government. These qualities require [17] no restraints: the more general their influence should be among any people, the less force would be necessary in their government; and could we suppose a nation in which they should exist in a perfect degree, that nation would require no government at all. It is the vices, not the virtues of men which are the objects of restraint, and the foundation of government. The expression of the general will, operating on the mind of an individual, serves with him as a substitute for virtue. This general will may always be expressed by a nation in any possible circumstances; and, if the nation be in a state of nature, this expression will always be *moral virtue,* according to their ideas of the word; and it will always *tend* to moral virtue, in the most extensive sense in which we have yet been able to define it.

It has been said, that man differs from man, as much as man from beast; it is said also to be fit, that the wise and virtuous should make laws for the ignorant and vitious. It is not to my purpose: to call in [18] question the first of these assertions: but the second, plausible as it is, I must totally deny; at least in the sense in which it is generally understood. That some men in the same society should be wiser and better than others, is very natural; and it is as natural, that the people should choose such to represent them in the formation of laws. But in this case the laws originate from the people at large, ignorant and vitious as they are; and the representatives are only the organs by which their will is declared. This is not the sense in which the assertion is intended. It is meant, that if kings were always wise and good, or if a band of nobles were always wise and good, it would be best that they should de [*sic*] the hereditary legislators. This is the sense in which I deny the assertion, because it is contrary to the analogy of nature. It being a subject on which we cannot look for experience, we must reason only from analogy; and it appears extremely evident to me, that, were a succession of the wisest and best men that ever have, or ever will be known, to be perpetuated in any country

[19] as independent legislators for the people, the happiness and good government of the nation would be greatly injured by it. I am confident that any people, whether virtuous or vitious, wise or ignorant, numerous or few, rich or poor, are the best judges of their own wants relative to the restraint of laws, and would always supply those wants better than they could be supplied by others.

In expressing these ideas on the peace and happiness to be expected from a free republic, I have been often accused of holding too favourable an opinion of human nature. But it appears to me, that the question, whether men, on any given portion of the earth, are able to make their own laws, does not depend in the least on their moral character. It has no relation to their state of improvement, or their state of morals. The only previous enquiry is, What is the object to be aimed at in the government? If it be the good of the whole community, the whole can best know the means of pursuing it; If it be to exalt a [20] few men at the expense of all the rest, the decision, perhaps, may take a different turn.

A republic of beavers or of monkies, I believe, could not be benefited by receiving their laws from men, any more than men could be in being governed by them. If the Algerines or the Hindoos were to shake off the yoke of despotism, and adopt ideas of equal liberty, they would that moment be in a condition to frame a better government for themselves, than could be framed for them by the most learned statesman in the world. If the great Mr. Locke, with all his wisdom and goodness, were to attempt the task, he would probably succeed as ill as he did in his constitution for the colony of South Carolina.

Colonies have always been teazed and tormented more or less (and probably always will be as long as colonies shall exist) by the overweening wisdom of the mother-country, in making their laws and constitutions. This is often done without [21] any wish to tyrannize, and sometimes with the best intentions to promote the good of the people. The misfortune more frequently lies in the legislator's not knowing the wants and wishes of the people, than in any wanton desire to counteract them. The sure and only characteristic of a good law is, *that it be the perfect expression of the will of the nation;* its excellence is precisely in proportion to the universality and freedom of consent. And this definition remains the same, whatever be the character of the nation, or the object of the law. Every man, as an individual, has a will of his own, and a manner of expressing it. In forming these individuals into society, it is necessary to form their wills into a government; and in doing this, we have only to find the easiest and clearest mode of expressing their wills in a national manner. And no possible disadvantages relative to their state of morals or civilization can render this a difficult task.

I have gone into these arguments, not merely to prove that the *French* are fit for [22] liberty, who are certainly at this moment the most enlightened nation in Europe; but to show that the calumny contained in the contrary assertion need not be repeated against any other nation, who should make the like exertions, and whose pretensions, in this respect, might appear more questionable in the eye of fashionable remark.

But it will be said, I am too late with all these observations on the necessity of proscribing royalty from your constitution. The cause is already judged in the minds of the whole people of France; and their wishes will surely be the rule of your conduct. I suppose that, without being reminded of your duty by a stranger, one of your first resolutions would be, to fix a national anathema on every vestige of regal power, and endeavour to wipe out from the human character the stain which it received, with its veneration for kings and hereditary claims. But it requires much reflection to be well aware to what extent this duty should carry you. There are many vices in your constitution, which, [23] though not apparently connected with the king, had their origin in regal ideas. To purify the whole code from these vices, and to purge human nature from their effects, it will be necessary to resort to many principles which appear not to have struck the minds of the first assembly.

You will permit me to hint at some of the great outlines of what may be expected from you, under the peculiar advantages with which you meet to form a glorious republic. Although many of my ideas may be perfectly superfluous, being the same as will occur to every member of your body, yet it is possible that some of them may strike the mind in a new point of light, and lead to reflections which would not rise from any other quarter. Should this be the case in the smallest degree, it ought to be considered, both by you and me, as an ample reward for our pains, in writing and in reading this letter.

On considering the subject of government, when the mind is once set loose from [24] the shackles of royalty, it finds itself in a new world. It rises to a more extensive view of every circumstance of

JOEL BARLOW 1754–1812

the social state. Human nature assumes a new and more elevated shape, and displays many moral features, which, from having been always disguised, were not known to exist. In this case, it is a long time before we acquire a habit of tracing effects to their proper causes, and of applying the easy and simple remedy to those vices of our nature which society requires us to restrain. This, I apprehend, is the source of by far the greatest difficulties with which you have to contend. We are so much used, in government, to the most complicated systems, as being necessary to support those impositions, without which it has been supposed impossible for men to be governed, that it is an unusual task to conceive of the simplicity to which the business of government may be reduced, and to which it must be reduced, if we would have it answer the purpose of promoting happiness.

[25] After proscribing royalty, with all its appendages, I suppose it will not be thought necessary in France to support any other errors and superstitions of a similar complexion; but that undisguised reason in all things will be preferred to the cloak of imposition. Should this be the case, you will conceive it no longer necessary to maintain a *national church*. This establishment is so manifestly an imposition upon the judgment of mankind, that the constituting assembly must have considered it in that light. It is one of those monarchical ideas, which pay us the wretched compliment of supposing that we are not capable of being governed by our own reason. To suppose that the people of France are to learn the mode of worshipping God from the decrees of the Council of Trent, is certainly as absurd as it would be to appeal to such a Council to learn how to breathe, or to open their eyes. Neither is it true, as is argued by the advocates of this part of your constitution, that the preference there given to one mode of worship [26] by the payment of the Catholic priests, from the national purse, to the exclusion of others, was founded on the idea of the property supposed to have been possessed by that church, and which by the assembly was declared to be thenceforward the property of the nation.

The church, in this sense of the word, signifies nothing but a *mode of worship;* and to prove that a mode can be a proprietor of lands, requires a subtilty of logic that I shall not attempt to refute. The fact is, the church considered as an *hierarchy,* was always necessary to the support of royalty; and your assembly, with great consistency of design, wishing to preserve something of the old fabric, preserved something of this necessary prop, but as the fabric is now overturned, the prop may be safely taken away. I am confident that monarchy and hierarchy will be buried in the same grave; and that in France they will not survive the present year.

[27] I know it is asserted and believed by some well-wishers to society, that religion would be lost among men, if they were to banish all legal establishments with regard to the manner of exercising it. I should not be so perfectly convinced as I am of the absurdity of this opinion, were it not easy to discover how it came to be introduced. It is an idea, as I believe, purely political; and it had its origin in the supposed necessity of governing men by fraud,—of erecting their credulity into an hierarchy, in order to sustain the despotism of the state. I hold religion to be a natural propensity of the mind, as respiration is of the lungs. If this be true, there can be no danger of its being lost: and I can see no more reason for making laws to regulate the impression of Deity upon the soul, than there would be, to regulate the action of light upon the eye, or of air upon the lungs. I should presume therefore, that, on stripping this subject of all the false covering which unequal governments have thrown upon it, you will make no national provision for the support of any class of men, [28] under the mock pretence of maintaining the worship of God. But you will leave every part of the community to nominate and pay their own ministers in their own way. The mode of worship which they will thus maintain, will be the most conducive to good order, because it will be that in which the people will believe.

Much has been said, since the beginning of your revolution, on the difference between the business of framing constitutions, and that of ordinary legislation. Indeed I am afraid that either too much or too little has been inculcated on this subject; because it appears to me, that the doctrine now received is not that which the subject would naturally suggest. It teaches us to consider those laws that are called *Constitutions,* in a light so sacred, as to favour too much of the old leaven of veneration for precedent; and every degree of such veneration is so much taken from the chance of improvement. To suppose that our predecessors were wiser than ourselves is not an extraordinary thing, though [29] the opinion may be ill-founded; but to suppose that they can have left us a better system of political regulations than we can make for ourselves, is to ascribe to them a degree of discernment to which our own bears no comparison; it supposes them to have known our condition by prophecy better than we can know it by experience.

There was not only a degree of arrogance in your first assembly, in supposing that they had framed a constitution, which for a number of years would require no amendment; but they betrayed a great degree of weakness in imagining that the ridiculous barriers with which they fenced it round would be sufficient to restrain the powerful weight of opinion, and prevent the people from exercising the irresistible right of innovation, whenever experience should discover the defects of the system. It is partly to these barriers, as well as to the inherent vices of the constitution, that we are to attribute the late insurrections in Paris. If we would trace the causes of [30] popular commotions, we should always find them to have originated in a previous unjust restraint.

I would not however be understood to mean, that there should be no distinction between the constitutional code, and other occasional laws. There is room for a considerable difference, both as to the mode of expressing them, and as to the formalities proper to be observed in repealing or amending them. I will offer some remarks on a plan for amendments toward the close of my letter. With regard to the general complexion of the code, it ought to be as simply expressed and easy to be understood as possible; for it ought to serve not only as a guide to the legislative body, but as a political grammar to all the citizens. The greatest service to be expected from it is, that it should concentrate the maxims, and form the habits of thinking, for the whole community. For this purpose, it is not sufficient that it be purified from every vestige of monarchy, and hierarchy, with all the impositions and [31] inequalities which have sprung insensibly from these ideas; but it should contemplate the whole circle of human propensities, and cut off the temptations and opportunities for degenerating into those evils which have so long afflicted mankind, and from which we are now but beginning to arise.

After laying down the great fundamental principle *that all men are equal in their rights,* it ought to be the invariable object of the social compact to insure the exercise of that equality, by rendering them as equal in all sorts of enjoyments, as can possibly be consistent with good order, industry, and the reward of merit. Every individual ought to be rendered as *independent* of every other individual as possible; and at the same time as *dependent* as possible on the whole community.

On this undeniable maxim, I think the following positions ought to be founded and guaranteed in the constitutional code:

[32] *First,* The only basis of representation in the government should be *population;* territory and property, though absurdly stated by your first assembly as making part of the basis of representation, have no interest in it. Property, in itself, conveys no right to the possessor, but the right of enjoying it. To say that it has the right of claiming for itself the protection of society, is absurd; because it is already protected, or it would not be property. It is the *person,* not the property, that exercises the will, and is capable of enjoying happiness; it is therefore the person, for whom government is instituted, and by whom its functions are performed. The reason why property has been considered as conveying additional rights to the possessor in matters of government, is the same as has blinded the understandings of men relative to the whole order of nature in society. It is one of those appendages of monarchy and oligarchy, which teaches that the object of government is to increase the splendour of the few, and the misfortunes of the [33] many. And every step that such governments take has a tendency to counteract the equality of rights, by destroying the equality of enjoyments.

Second, If you take the population as the only basis of representation in the departments, the next step will be, to declare every independent man to be an active citizen. By an independent man, I mean every man whom the laws do not place under the control of another, by reason of nonage or domesticity. The laws of France, in my opinion, have always placed the period of majority by several years too late; that is, later than nature has placed it. This however, was of little consequence in a political view, as long as the government remained despotic; but now, when the rights of man are restored, and government is built on that foundation, it is of consequence to increase as far as possible the number of active citizens. And for this purpose I should suppose the period of majority ought to be placed at least as early as the age of twenty years. [34] To make this change in France would be attended with many advantages. I[t] would increase the stock of knowledge, and of industry, by inspiring young men with early ideas of independence, and the necessity of providing for themselves by some useful employment: it would be a great inducement to early marriages; and, by that means, increase population, and encourage purity of morals.

JOEL BARLOW 1754–1812

I am likewise fully convinced, that the assembly was wrong in supposing that a state of domesticity ought to deprive a man of the rights of a freeman. This is a relick of those ideas which the ancient government has inspired. Where a servant is absolutely dependent on the caprice of a master for his place, and consequently for his bread, there is indeed much force in the argument, that he can have no political will of his own; and will give his suffrage as directed by the master. But when every man shall be absolutely free to follow any profession, every kind of useful industry being equally encouraged and rewarded; [35] and especially when every man shall be well instructed in his duties and his rights, which will certainly be the consequence of the system you have now begun,—such arguments will fall to the ground with the system which they support. The servant and his master, though not equal in property or in talents, may be perfectly so in freedom and in virtue. Wherever the servant is more dependent on the master, than the master on the servant, there is something wrong in the government. The same remarks I believe may be repeated, with little variation, in the case of insolvent debtors, another class of men disfranchised by the first assembly.

Third, The manner in which citizenship may be acquired or lost, is a subject which ought to be reconsidered by you; as your predecessors have left in it some room for improvement. Their regulation was indeed a liberal one, compared with what other governments have done; but not so, when compared with what the subject required. I am confident that when society [36] shall be placed on the right footing, the citizens of any one state will consider those of any other state as their brothers and fellow citizens of the world; and in this case, when those who are called foreigners come to settle among them, a mere declaration of their intention of residence will be sufficient to entitle them to all the rights which the natives possess. I was anxious that the French should set the example in this species of liberality, as they have done in so many other good things, and I still believe, that on reviewing the subject, you will do it.

But according to your constitution there are many ways in which the rights of citizens may be lost, for one of which I can see no reason; it is naturalization in a foreign country. This is so manifestly illiberal and unjust, that I am almost sure it will be altered. It is an old feudal idea of allegiance; and goes upon the supposition that fidelity to one country is incompatible with our duty to another. When a citizen of one state is complimented with the [37] freedom of another, it is generally an acknowledgment of his merit; but your constituting assembly considered it as an object of punishment. Many of your citizens have been naturalized in America; but the American governments certainly did not foresee that this act of theirs would disfranchise those gentlemen at home. You have lately conferred the rights of a French citizen on George Washington. If he should accept the honour you have thus done him, and the American constitution were in this respect the same as your own, he must immediately be turned out of office, and for ever disfranchised at home.

Fourth, You will doubtless consider the important subject of the *frequency of popular elections,* as claiming a farther deliberation. It is an article on which too much reflection cannot be bestowed. It influences the habits of the people and the spirit of the government in a variety of ways, that escape our common observation. I mentioned before, that one of the first objects of society is to render every [38] individual perfectly dependent on the whole community. The more completely this object is attained, the more perfect will be the equality of enjoyments and the happiness of the state. But of all individuals, those who are selected to be the organs of the people, in making and in executing the laws, should feel this dependence in the strongest degree. The easiest and most natural method of effecting this purpose is, to oblige them to recur frequently to the authors of their official existence, to deposit their powers, mingle with their fellows, and wait the decision of the same sovereign will which created them at first, to know whether they are again to be trusted.

There are doubtless some limits to this frequency of election, beyond which it would be hurtful to pass; as every subject has a medium between two vitious extremes. But I know of no office, in any department of state, that need to be held for more than one year, without a new election. Most men, who give in to this [39] idea with respect to the legislative, are accustomed to make an exception with regard to the executive, and particularly with regard to that part which is called the judiciary. I am aware of all the arguments that are usually brought in support of these exceptions; but they appear to me of little weight, in comparison to those in favour of universal annual elections. Power always was, and always must be, a dangerous thing. I mean, power collected from the great mass of society, and delegated to a few hands; for it is only in this sense that it can properly be called power. The physical forces of all the individuals of a great nation cannot be brought to act at once upon a single object; and the same may be said of their moral forces. It is necessary therefore that the exercise of these should always be performed by delegation; the moral in legislation, the physical in execution. This is the proper definition of national power; and in this sense it is necessarily dangerous; because, strictly speaking, it is not exercised by those whose property it is, and for whose [40] good it is intended to operate. It is in the nature of this kind of trust to invert in some measure the order of things; it apparently sets the servant above the master, and disposes him to feel a kind of independence which ought never to be felt by any citizen, particularly one who is charged with a public function.

It has ever been the tendency of government to divide the society into two parties,—the governors and the governed. The mischiefs arising from this are almost infinite. It not only disposes each party to view the other with an eye of jealousy and distrust, which soon rise to acts of secret or open enmity, but it effectually corrupts the morals of both parties, and destroys the vital principles of society; it makes government the trade of the few, submission the drudgery of the many, and falsehood the common artifice of the whole. To prevent this, I would have no man placed in a position in which he can call himself governor, for a moment longer than while he performs the duties of his trust [41] to the satisfaction of his fellow citizens, nor even then, but for a short period. He should feel at all times as though he were soon to change places with any one of his neighbours, whom he now sees submissive to his authority.

But to answer this purpose, the frequent return of elections is not of itself sufficient. I am fully of the opinion, that with regard to all discretionary officers, there ought to be an exclusion by rotation. Those functions that are purely ministerial, such as those of sheriffs, constables, clerks of courts, registers, &c. perhaps may form exceptions; but legislators, executive counsellors, judges and magistrates of every description, should not only feel their dependence on the people by an annual election, but should frequently mingle with them by an exclusion from office. The effect of this would be, not what is often asserted, that no one would understand government but the contrary, that every one would understand it. This would form a prodigious stimulus to the [42] acquisition of knowledge among all descriptions of men, in all parts of the country. Every man of ordinary ability would be not only capable of watching over his own rights, but of exercising any of the functions by which the public safety is secured. For whatever there is in the art of government, whether legislative or executive, above the capacity of the ordinary class of what are called well informed men, is superfluous and destructive, and ought to be laid aside. The man who is called a *politician,* according to the practical sense of the word in modern Europe, exercises an office infinitely more destructive to society than that of a highwayman. The same may be said, in general, of the *financier;* whose art and mystery, on the funding system of the present century, consist in making calculations to enable governments to hire mankind to butcher each other, by drawing bills on posterity for the payment.

I would therefore suggest the propriety of your reviewing the article of biennial [43] elections, as instituted by your first assembly, and of your making them annual; the same term, if not the same manner of election, ought to extend to all executive officers, whose functions are in any manner discretionary. I think it would likewise be essential, that no office of this description should be held by one man, more than two years in any term of four years. This would send into the departments, and into every part of the empire, at frequent periods, some thousands of men with practical knowledge of public business; it would at least be the means of doubling the number of such well-instructed men; and, by holding out the inducement to others, to qualify themselves to merit the confidence of their fellow citizens, it would multiply the number of men of theoretical knowledge, at least ten fold. All these men will be watchful guardians of the public safety. But these are not all the advantages of frequent elections. They habituate the people to the *business* of election, and enable them to carry it on with order and regularity, like their daily [44] labour; they habituate the candidates to be gratified with the public confidence, or to be disappointed in the expectation of obtaining it; so that their success or disappointment ceases to make that deep impression on their minds, which it otherwise would do. It is thus that you would cut off an infinite source of that intrigue and corruption, which are foretold with so much horror by those who have not well-studied the effects of a well organized popular government. But another method, not less effectual, to prevent the arts of scrambling for power and places, will be hinted at in the following article.

Fifth, Among the fatal misconceptions of things which monarchy has entailed upon us, and which are extremely difficult to eradicate from the mind, must be reckoned that prevalent opinion, that all governments should gratify their agents with *enormous salaries.* This idea has usually been more particularly applied in favour of the executive officers of government and their dependants; and it had its origin in [45] the antecedent principle, that government divides the people into two distinct classes, and that the same quantity of business, coming within the verge of one of these classes, must be paid for at a higher price than it would be, within that of the other; though it should be performed by the same man, and required the same exertion of talents. Your constitution is silent as to the quantity of salary that shall be paid to any particular officer; it only says, that "the nation will provide for the splendour of the throne" (which indeed is a declaration of war against the liberties of the people) but the authors of that constitution, in their legislative capacity, after providing for that splendour with a sum sufficient to purchase the majority of almost any corps of seven hundred legislators, went on to provide for the splendour of the ministers. They gave to one, if my memory does not deceive me, one hundred and fifty thousand livres, and one hundred thousand to each of the rest. This on an average is about three times more than ought to have been [46] given, unless the object were to carry on the government by intriguing for places.

I mention this article, not on the score of œconomy. That consideration, however weighty it may appear, is one of the least that can strike the mind on the subject of public salaries. The evil of paying too much is pregnant with a thousand mischiefs. It is almost sufficient of itself to defeat all the advantages to be expected from the institution of an equal government. The general rule to be adopted in this case (which perhaps is all that can be said of it in the constitution) appears to me to be this, *That so much, and no more, shall be given for the performance of any public function, as shall be sufficient to induce such men to undertake it whose abilities are equal to the task.* If this rule were strictly observed, it is rational to conclude, that there would be no more contention or intrigue among candidates to obtain places in the government, than there is among manufacturers, to find a market [47] for their goods. This conclusion becomes more probably just, when we consider that your intention is to cut off from the servants of the public all hopes of obtaining the public money by any indirect and fraudulent measures. When there shall be no more civil list, or livre

rouge, no more ministerial patronage in church or state, no more sale
of justice or purchase of oppression, or any kind of perquisite of office,
but the candidate shall be assured, that all the money he shall receive,
will be the simple sum promised by the legislature, that sum being
no more than the work is honestly worth, he will accept or relinquish
the most important trust, as he would an ordinary occupation.

This single circumstance of salaries, being wisely guarded on
every side, would, in the course of its operation, almost change the
moral face of government. It would silence all the clamours against
the republican principle, and answer many of the fashionable calumnies
against the character of the human heart.

[48] There is another questionable opinion now extant, even in
republican countries; which, as it has made some figure in France,
and is connected with the subject of salaries, I will mention in this
place. It is supposed to be necessary, for the energy of government,
that its officers should assume a kind of external pomp and splendour,
in order to dazzle the eye, and inspire the public mind with a veneration
for their authority. As this pomp cannot be supported without some
expence, the supposed necessity for assuming it is always offered as a
reason for high salaries; and, allowing the first position to be true,
the consequence is certainly reasonable and just. If we are to be
governed only by deception, it is right that we should pay for this
deception. But the whole argument is wrong; that is, if we allow
monarchy and hierarchy to be wrong; it is a badge of that kind of
government which is directly the reverse of republican principles, or
the government of reason. I do not deny, that this official pomp has
in a great measure the effect which is intended from [49] it; it imposes
on the unthinking part of mankind, and has a tendency to secure their
obedience. This effect, however, is not so great as that of simplicity,
and the native dignity of reason would be; but on the moral habits of
society, its operation is more pernicious than at first view we are ready
to imagine. So far as the people are caught by the imposition, it leads
them to wrong ideas of themselves, of their officers, and of the real
authority of laws. This is a fatal deviation from the true design of
government; for its principal object certainly ought to be, to rectify
our opinions, and improve our morals.

For my own part, when I see a man in private life assuming an
external splendour, for the sake of gaining attention, I cannot but feel
it an insult offered to my understanding; because it is saying to me,

that I have not discernment enough to distinguish his merit, without this kind of *ecce fignum*. And when an officer of government exhibits himself in the foppery of a puppet, and is drawn by six or eight [50] horses, where two would be really more convenient to himself, I am grieved at the insult offered to the nation, and at their stupidity in not perceiving it. For the language of the mummery is simply this, That the officer cannot rely upon his own personal dignity as a title to respect, nor the laws be trusted to their own justice, to insure their execution. It is a full acknowledgment on his part, that the government is bad, and that he is obliged to dazzle the eyes of the people, to prevent their discovering the cheat. When a set of judges on the bench take the pains to shroud their head and shoulders in a fleece of horse-hair, in order to resemble the bird of wisdom, it raises a strong suspicion, that they mean to palm upon us the emblem for the reality.

It is essential to the character of a free republic, that every thing should be reduced to the standard of reason; that men and laws should depend on their own intrinsic merit, and that no shadow of deception should ever be offered to the people; [51] as it cannot fail to corrupt them; and pave the way to oppression. I make these remarks, not that they will form an article proper to enter into your constitution, but to remove every appearance of argument in favour of high salaries. And I think the constitution ought to contain a general declaration, *that every public salary should be restricted to a sum not more than sufficient to reward the officer for his labour;* which sum must, of course, be left to be fixed by the legislature.

Seventh, There appears to me to be an error of doctrine in France, with respect to the relation which ought to subsist between the representative, and his immediate constituents. It is said, that when a representative is once chosen, and sent to the Assembly, he is no longer to be considered as representing the people of the particular department which sent him, but of the nation at large; and therefore, during the term for which he is chosen, he is not accountable to the people who chose him, but is to be controuled, removed or [52] suspended, only by the National Assembly. This appears to have been established, in order to get rid of a contrary doctrine, which was found to be inconvenient; which was, that a delegate should be bound at all times to follow the *instructions* of his constituents; as thereby all the advantages to be expected from discussion and deliberation would be lost. If the first of these be an error, as I believe it is, it may easily be avoided, without running into the last. When the delegate receives instructions, which prove to be contrary to the opinion which he afterwards forms, he ought to presume that his constituents, not having had the advantage of hearing the national discussion, are not well informed on the subject, and his duty is to vote according to his conscience. It is to be supposed that, for his own sake, he will explain to them his motives; but if for this, or any other circumstance, they should be dissatisfied with his conduct, they have an undoubted right at any time to recall him, and nominate another in his place. This will tend to maintain a proper relation between [53] the representative and the people, and a due dependence of the former upon the latter. Besides, when a man has lost the confidence of his fellow-citizens of the department, he is no longer their representative; and when he ceases to be theirs, he cannot in any sense be the representative of the nation; since it is not pretended that he can derive any authority, but through his own constituents. This, however, cannot deprive the assembly of its right to expel or suspend a member for any refractory conduct, which may be deemed an offence against the state,

Eighth, The article of *inviolability,* as applied to the members of the assembly, or to any other officers of the state, is worthy of re-consideration. But before it be again decided in the affirmative, you ought to take a general view of that interesting subject of *imprisonment for debt.* It is a species of civil cruelty which all modern governments have borrowed from the Roman law, which considered a debtor as a criminal, and committed the care of his punishment [54] into the hands of the creditor, lending the public prison as an instrument of private vengeance. It is a disgrace to the wisdom of a nation, and can never be allowed in a well regulated state. If no citizen could be arrested or deprived of his liberty, for debt, there would be no need of making an exception in favour of the officers of government; and thus you would remove a distinction which must always appear unjust.

Ninth, You will scarcely think that your duty is discharged, so as to satisfy your own minds on the establishment of a constitution, from which the friends of humanity will anticipate a total regeneration of society, until you shall have given a farther declaration on the subject of criminal law. All men of reflection are agreed, that punishments in modern times have lost all proportion to the crimes to which they are annexed, even on that scale of barbarous justice by which they were introduced. Few, however, have had the wisdom to discover, or the boldness to declare [55] the true cause of the evil; and while we remain ignorant of the cause, it is no wonder that we fail in finding the remedy. In the glooms of meditation on the miseries of civilized life, I have been almost led to adopt this conclusion, That society itself is the cause of all crimes; and, as such, it has no right to punish them at all. But, without indulging the severity of this unqualified assertion, we may venture to say, that every punishment is a new crime; though it may not in all cases be so great as would follow from omitting to punish.

There is a manifest difference between *punishment* and *correction;* the latter, among rational beings, may always be performed by instruction; or at most by some gentle species of restraint. But punishment, on the part of the public, arises from no other source but a jealousy of power. It is a confession of the inability of society, to protect itself against an ignorant or refractory member. When there are factions in a state, contending for the supreme command, the pains inflicted by each party [56] are summary; they often precede the crime; and the factions wreak their vengeance on each other, as a prevention of expected injuries. Something very similar to this is what perpetually takes place in every nation, in what is called a state of tranquillity and order. For government has usually been nothing more than a regulated faction. The party which governs, and the party which reluctantly submits to be governed, maintain a continual conflict; and out of that conflict proceed the crimes and the punishments, or, more properly speaking, the punishments and the crimes. When we see the power of the nation seizing an individual, dragging him to a tribunal, pronouncing him worthy of death, and then going through the solemn formalities of execution, it is natural to ask, what is the meaning of all this? It certainly means, that the nation is in a state of civil war; and even in that barbarous stage of war, when it is thought necessary to put all prisoners to death. In deciding the question, whether a particular criminal should be put to death, I never would ask what is the [57] nature of his offence; it has nothing to do with the question; I would simply enquire, what is the condition of the society. If it be in a state of internal peace, I would say it was wicked and absurd to think of inflicting such punishment. To plead that there is a necessity for that desperate remedy, proves a want of energy on the government, or of wisdom in the nation.

When men are in a state of war, with the enemy's bayonets

pointed at their breasts, or when they are in the heat of a revolution, encompassed by treason, and tormented by corruption, there is an apology for human slaughter; but when you have established a wise and manly government, founded on the moral sense, and invigorated by the enlightened reason of the people, let it not be sullied by that timid vengeance, which belongs only to tyrants and usurpers. I could wish that your constitution might declare, not merely what it has already declared, that the penal code shall be reformed, but, that within a certain period after the return of peace, [58] *the punishment of death shall be abolished*. It ought likewise to enjoin it on the legislative body to soften the rigour of punishments in general, until they shall amount to little more than a tender paternal correction. Whoever will look into the human heart, and examine the order of nature in society, must be convinced, that this is the most likely method of preventing the commission of crimes. But

Tenth, In order to be consistent with yourselves in removing those abuses which have laid the foundation of all offences against society, both in crimes and punishments, you ought to pay a farther attention to the necessity of *public instruction*. It is your duty, as a constituting assembly, to establish a system of government that shall improve the morals of mankind. In raising a people from slavery to freedom, you have called them to act on a new theatre; and it is a necessary part of your business, to teach them how to perform their parts. By discovering to a man his rights, you impose upon him a new [59] system of duties. Every Frenchman, born to liberty, must now claim, among the first of his rights, the right of being instructed in the manner of preserving them. This the society has no authority to refuse; and to fail of enjoining it on the legislative body, as a part of its constant care, would be to counteract the principles of the revolution, and expose the whole system to be overturned.

From what the constitution has already declared on this head, and from the disposition of the two last assemblies, I have no doubt but considerable attention will be paid to it; but I wish in this place to recommend it to a more particular consideration, as a subject connected with criminal law. It is certain that no obedience can be rationally expected from any man to a law which he does not know. It is not only unjust, but absurd and even impossible, to enforce his obedience. It is therefore but half the business of legislators to make good laws; an indispensable part of their duty is to see that every person in [60] the state shall perfectly understand them. The barbarous maxim of jurisprudence, *That ignorance of the law is no excuse to the offender,* is an insolent apology for tyranny, and ought never to disgrace the policy of a rational government. I think therefore it would do honor to your constitution, and serve as a stimulus to your legislature and to your magistrates, in the great duty of instruction, to declare, *That knowledge is the foundation of obedience, and that laws shall have no authority but where they are understood.*

Eleventh, Since I am treating of morals, the great object of all political institutions, I cannot avoid bestowing some remarks on the subject of *public lotteries.* It is a shocking disgrace to modern governments, that they are driven to this pitiful piece of knavery, to draw money from the people. But no circumstance of this kind is so extraordinary, as that this policy should be continued in France, since the revolution; and that a state lottery should still be reckoned among the permanent [61] sources of revenue. It has its origin in deception; and depends for its support, on raising and disappointing the hopes of individuals, on perpetually agitating the mind with unreasonable desires of gain, on clouding the understanding with superstitious ideas of chance, destiny, and fate, on diverting the attention from regular industry, and promoting a universal spirit of gambling, which carries all sorts of vices into all classes of people. Whatever way we look into human affairs, we shall ever find, that the bad organization of society is the cause of more disorders than could possibly arise from the natural temper of the heart. And what shall we say of a government, that avowedly steps forward with the insolence of an open enemy, and creates a new vice, for the sake of loading it with a tax? What right has such a government to punish our follies? And who can look without disgust on the impious figure it makes, in holding the scourge in one hand, and the temptation in the other? You cannot hesitate to declare in your constitution, that all state lotteries shall be for ever abolished.

[62] *Twelfth,* As yours is the first nation in the world, that has solemnly renounced the horrid business of conquest, you ought to proceed one step farther, and declare, that you will have no more to do with *colonies.* This is but a necessary consequence of your former renunciation. For colonies are an appendage of conquest; and to claim a right to the one would be claiming a perpetual, or reiterated right to the other. Supposing your colonies were to declare independence, and set up a government of their own (which your own principles and

the first laws of nature declare they have a right to do) in that case, the same pretences which you now have to hold them under your controul, would certainly justify you in reconquering and subjecting them. But it would be a mere waste of argument, to prove that you have no *right* to retain a sovereignty over them; and if I could bring myself to pay so ill a compliment to your justice, as to suppose that you could wish to violate a right, for the sake of what is called *policy,* it would be easy to show, that to maintain foreign [63] possessions, is in all cases as impolitic, as it is unjust and oppressive. Policy, in this respect, can have no other object, but the advantages of trade; and it may be laid down as a universal position, that whatever solid advantages can flow to the mother country from the trade of her colonies, would necessarily flow to her, if they were independent states. The experience of mankind has not yet enabled us even to suppose a case, in which it would be otherwise. Whatever is free and mutually advantageous in trade, would be natural, and would be carried on by each party for its own interest: whatever is unnatural and forced must be secured by means that will probably lessen the quantity of the whole; but at all events, the cost of maintaining it will for ever exceed the profits. This is not only found to be true, from the experience of every nation which has maintained colonies abroad; but the nature of the subject requires, that it should always be the case. It is a theory, for the proof of which no experience could have been [64] necessary; and it is to the pride of kings, and the mistaken rapacity of governments, to the false glare of extended sovereignty, and the desire of providing predatory places for the sycophants of courts, that we are to attribute the train of calamities which has tormented the maritime nations of Europe, in maintaining colonies for the monopoly of trade. And where are we to look for reason and reformation, but to France? The English and other governments, to support a consistency of character, and fill up the measure of their sins, are faithful only to this one point, that the more they are convinced of the truth, the more obstinate is their perseverance in error.

I cannot but think it unnecessary, if not impertinent, to enter into farther arguments to prove, that justice, policy, and the true principles of commerce, require you to set the example of the world, of declaring your colonies absolutely free and independent states, and of inviting [65] them to form a government of their own. The example would soon be followed by other nations; if not from reason and from choice, at least from the more imperious argument of necessity.

Thirteenth, I cannot close my letter, without some reflections on the policy of maintaining any thing like what is called *a standing army in time of peace,* which seems to have been the intention of your first Assembly. Such a force would have many fatal effects on the spirit of a republican government, without answering any good purpose that can be expected from it. According to your own principles, you will have no more to do with foreign wars, unless you are invaded; and it is probable, that the present is the last invasion that will ever be formed against France. But, be that as it may, a standing military force is the worst resource that can be found for the defense of a free republic. In this case, the strength of the army is the weakness of the nation. If [66] the army be really strong enough to be relied on for defence, it not only imposes on the people a vast unnecessary expence, but it must be a dangerous instrument, in the hands of dangerous men; it may furnish the means of civil wars, and of the destruction of liberty. If, on the contrary, it be not sufficient for external defence, it will only serve to disappoint the people. Being taught to believe that they have an army, they will cease to trust in their own strength, and be deceived in their expectations of safety.

But the greatest objection against a standing army is, the effect it would have on the political sentiments of the people. Every citizen ought to feel himself to be a necessary part of the great community, for every purpose to which the public interest can call him to act; he should feel the habits of a citizen and the energies of a soldier, without being exclusively destined to the functions of either. His physical and moral powers should be kept in equal [67] vigour; as the disuse of the former would be very soon followed by the decay of the latter. If it be wrong to trust the legislative power of the state for a number of years, or for life, to a small number of men; it is certainly more preposterous to do the same thing with regard to military power. Where the wisdom resides, there ought the strength to reside, in the great body of the people; and neither the one nor the other ought ever to be delegated, but for short periods of time, and under severe restrictions. This is the way to preserve a temperate and manly use of both; and thus, by trusting only to themselves, the people will be sure of a perpetual defence against the open force, and the secret intrigues of all possible enemies at home and abroad.

Fourteenth, After tracing the outlines of your constitution, according to your present ideas, and proclaiming it in the most solemn manner, as the foundation of law and right, it will still be vain to think of restraining the people from making [68] alterations and amendments, as often as experience shall induce them to change their opinions. The point you have to aim at in this, is to agree upon a method in which amendments can be made, without any of those extraordinary exertions, which would occasion unnecessary insurrections. The more easy and expeditious this method shall appear, the less likely it will be to provoke disorders, and the better it will answer the purpose, provided it always refers the subject to the real wishes of the people. I would propose, therefore (on the presumption that your legislative body shall be chosen only for one year at a time) that every annual National Assembly shall have power to propose, and the next succeeding one to adopt and ratify, any amendments that they shall think proper in the constitutional code. But it should always be done under this restriction, that the articles to be proposed by any one Assembly, should be agreed to, and published to the people in every department, within the first six months of the sessions of that [69] Assembly. This would give time to the people to discuss the subject fully, and to form their opinions, previous to the time of electing their members to the next Assembly. The members of the new Assembly, when they should come together, would thus be competent to declare the wishes of the people on the amendments proposed, and would act upon them as they should think proper. The same power of proposing and adopting would be continued from year to year with perfect safety to the constitution, and with the probability of improvement.

Thus, gentlemen, I have given a hasty sketch of some leading ideas, that lay with weight upon my mind, on a subject of much importance to the interests of a considerable portion of the human race. If they should be thought of no value, they will of course occupy but little of your attention, and therefore can do no injury. If I have said any thing from which a useful reflection shall be drawn, I shall feel [70] myself happy in having rendered some service to the most glorious cause that ever engaged the attention of mankind.

JOEL BARLOW.

[56]

TIMOTHY STONE 1742–1797

Election Sermon

HARTFORD, 1792

I n this sermon before the Connecticut governor and legislature,
Timothy Stone, Congregationalist minister from Lebanon, Connecticut, appeals to the need for true community if liberty is to
survive. The result is a good summary of what Americans during the
founding era felt important for the continued success of their experiment in self-government, leadership and unity being prominent in the list.

ELECTION SERMON.

DEUTERONOMY IV. 5, 6.

> *Behold, I have taught you statutes and judgments, even as the Lord
> my God commanded me, that ye should do so in the land whither ye
> go to possess it.*
> *Keep therefore, and do them; for this is your wisdom and your
> understanding in the sight of the nations, which shall hear all these
> statutes, and say, Surely this great nation is a wise and understanding
> people.*

We are not left in doubt, concerning the wisdom and salutary
nature of that constitution under which the Hebrews were placed, as
it proceeded immediately from GOD; and, in reference to the particular
circumstances of that people, was the result of unerring perfection. It

was a free constitution, in which, [6] all the valuable rights of the community were most happily secured. The public good, was the great object in view, and, the most effectual care was taken to preserve the rights of individuals. Proper rewards were promised to the obedient, and righteous punishments allotted for the disobedient. GOD designed, for special reasons, that the seed of Abraham, should be distinguished in a peculiar manner from all other nations; he therefore undertook the government of them himself, in all matters respecting religion, civil policy, and that military establishment, which he saw to be necessary for their happiness and defence. We find Moses, who received this constitution from GOD, and delivered it to his people, frequently exhorting them, to maintain a sacred regard for this divine institution, and to pay a conscientious obedience to all its laws: in doing of which, they might secure to themselves national prosperity, and enjoy, the unfailing protection of Almighty GOD.

To deter them from disobedience, he called up their attention to that solemn scene which opened to their view, when they stood before the LORD their GOD in Horeb: when there were thunders, and lightnings, and a thick cloud upon the mount, and the voice of the trumpet exceeding loud; so that all the people that was in the camp trembled. And the LORD commanded, saying, *gather me the people together, and I will make them hear my words, that they may learn to fear me all the days that they shall live upon the earth, and that they may teach their children.* [7] *For the* LORD *thy* GOD, *is a consuming fire, even a jealous* GOD.

The argument made use of in the text, to excite in that people, a spirit of obedience to their constitution and laws, was this, that it would raise their character in the sight of the nations: who from thence would be led, to entertain a veneration for them, as a great nation, a wise and understanding people. This sacred passage, in connection with the important occasion, which hath called us to the house of GOD, this morning, may direct our attention to the following enquiry.

In what, doth the true wisdom of a people, a civil community, consist?

The general answer to this question, may not be difficult; it will no doubt, be readily admitted, that the highest wisdom of a community of intelligent beings, must consist, in pursuing that line of conduct, which shall have the most direct and sure tendency to promote the best good of the whole, both in time, and eternity. What ever creatures, may conceive to be a good, either, through imperfection of understanding, or degeneracy of heart; yet, if that which they call good, is inseparably connected with more pain than pleasure, taking in the whole of their existence; then it cannot with propriety be styled good, certainly not the best good, consequently wisdom will not choose it. The province of wisdom, is, to discover and elect the most valuable objects; and, to adopt the best means to obtain them. These [8] observations, apply with equal force, to individuals, and communities; to all classes of men, whether in the higher, or, lower walks of life. Communities, most certainly, as well as individuals, under the guidance of wisdom, will pursue that conduct which shall be productive of their highest happiness, in every period of their existence. But the question returns, what is that conduct, which shall have the desired tendency, and will effect the highest good? This question, as it respects mankind at large in their present state, might admit, a great variety of answers: some of which, may demand particular notice on the present occasion. As,

I. Wisdom will direct a community to establish a good system of government. It may be a question whether the allwise GOD ever designed, that any of his intelligent creatures, even in a state of perfection, should exist without some kind of government, and subordination amongst themselves. All creatures, have not the same capacities; neither are they placed under equal advantages; and, if those may be found, whose capacities are equally extensive, still they are different; and seem to be designed for different purposes, and stations, in the great system. We read, of thrones, dominions, principalities, and powers amongst the angelic hosts: Which titles, denote various stations among those sinless beings, that they are differently employed, in degrees of subordination to each other, in the government of that holy family of which, GOD, is the father. But, however this may be, as our acquaintance with that world of glory, is very imperfect—[9] yet it is beyond a doubt, that government was designed, and is absolutely necessary for men on earth, in their present state of degeneracy.

Creatures, who have risen in rebellion, against the holy and perfect government of JEHOVAH; have partial connections, selfish interests, passions and lusts, which often interfere with each other, and which, will not always be controlled by reason, and the mild influence of moral motives, however great: but these in their external expressions, must be under the restraint of law, or there can be no peace, no safety among men. Some kind of government, is therefore indispensibly necessary for the happiness of mankind, that they may partake of the security, and other important blessings resulting from society; which cannot be enjoyed in a state of nature. Without any consideration, of the various forms of government which have been adopted, in different ages and countries; that, may be the best for a particular people, which in the view of all their circumstances, affords the fairest prospect of promoting righteousness, and of securing the most valuable privileges of the community, in its administration.

Civil liberty is one of the most important blessings which men possess of a temporal nature, the most valuable inheritance on this side heaven. That constitution may therefore be esteemed the best, which doth most effectually secure this treasure to a community. That liberty consists in freedom from restraint, [10] leaving each one to act as seemeth right to himself, is a most unwise mistaken apprehension. Civil liberty, consists in the being and administration of such a system of laws, as doth bind all classes of men, rulers and subjects, to unite their exertions for the promotion of virtue and public happiness. That happy constitution enjoyed by the Hebrews, of which, the Supreme Lawgiver was the immediate author, was no other, than a system of good laws, and righteous statutes: which limited the powers and prerogatives of magistrates, designated the duties of subjects, and obliged each to that obedience to law, and exchange of services, which tended to mutual benefit.† "And what nation is there so great, that hath statutes and judgments so righteous, as all this law which I set before you this day." A state of society necessarily implies reciprocal dependence in all its members; and rational government, is designed to realize and strengthen this dependance, and to render it, in such sense equal in all ranks, from the supreme magistrate, to the meanest peasant, that each one may feel himself bound to seek the good of the whole: when individuals do this, whether rulers or subjects, they have a just right to expect the favor and protection of the whole body. The laws of a state, should equally bind every member, whether his station be the most conspicuous, or, the most obscure. Rulers in a righteous government, are as really under the control of laws, as the meanest

† Deut. iv. 8.

TIMOTHY STONE 1742–1797

subject: and the one equally with the other, should be subjected to punishment, when ever he becomes criminal, by a violation of the law. [11] Rewards and punishments, should be equally distributed to all, agreeably to real merit or demerit, without respect of persons. A constitution, founded upon the general and immutable laws of righteousness and benevolence, and corresponding to their particular circumstances, will therefore become a primary object with a wise and understanding people.

2. The wisdom of a people will appear, in their united exertions to support such a system of government, in its regular administration.

Enacting salutary laws, discovers the wisdom and good design of legislators: but the liberty and happiness of the community, essentially depend upon their regular execution. The best code of laws can answer no good purposes, any further than it is executed. Every member in society is bound, in duty to the community, himself, and posterity, to use his endeavours that the laws of the state be carried into execution.

Laws, point out the existing offices, relations and dependancies of the community: they serve for the direction, support and defence of all characters; but considered as restraints, they more especially respect the unruly members.† "Knowing this, that the law is not made for a righteous man, but for the lawless and disobedient, for the ungodly and for sinners, for unholy and profane, for murderers of fathers, and murderers of mothers, for manslayers, for whoremongers, for them that defile themselves with mankind, for liars, for perjured persons, [12] and if there be any other thing that is contrary to sound doctrine." It is unreasonable to expect, that the vices of man which are inimical to society, will be restrained by silent laws existing upon paper: they must be carried into execution, and be known to have an active existence, that such as contemn the law, may not only read, but feel the resentment of the community.

It is not within the reach of human understanding, to look with precision into futurity, to discover all the circumstances and contingencies which may take place among a people: neither is it certain, that every person who may possess a fair character for ability and integrity, and who may be called into public life, will be governed in all his actions, by public and disinterested motives. Through necessary imperfection, or corrupt design, statutes may be enacted, which may

---

† 1. Tim. i. 9, 10.

not prove salutary in their execution; but greatly prejudicial to the common good: Hence ariseth the necessity of alterations and amendments, in all human systems.

Changes however, should be few as possible; for the strength and reputation of government, doth not a little depend upon the uniformity and stability observed in its administration. Laws while they remain such, ought to be executed, when found to be useless or hurtful, they may be repealed: to have laws in force and not executed, or to obstruct the natural course of law in a free state, must be dangerous; will have many hurtful tendencies, will greatly weaken government, and render all the interests of the community insecure. Liberty, property and [13] life, are all precarious, in a state where laws cease in their execution. When known breaches of law pass with impunity, and open transgressors go unpunished; when executive officers grow remiss in their duty, especially, when they connive at disobedience: all distinctions betwixt virtue and vice will vanish, authority will sink into disrepute, and government will be trampled in the dust—for which reasons, with others that might be named, it must be the wisdom, the indispensible duty of all characters in society, to unite their exertions, for the support of righteous laws, in their regular administration. As it would be exceedingly unreasonable to expect, that any people, can ever realize the benefits of good government, under a weak, or a wicked administration—in which, persons destitute of abilities, or, of stable principles of righteousness and goodness, fill the various departments of the state. Hence,

3. The wisdom of a people will appear in the election of good rulers.

The peace and happiness of communities, have a necessary dependence, under GOD, upon the character and conduct of those who are called to the administration of government. A bad constitution, under the direction of wise and pious rulers, who have capacity to discern, disposition and resolution to pursue the public good, may become a blessing; being made to subserve many valuable purposes. But the best constitution, committed to rulers of a contrary description, may be subverted; or so abused, as to become a curse; and be rendered [14] productive of the most mischievous consequences. The understanding, or folly, of a people in reference to their temporal interests, is in nothing more conspicuous, than in the choice of civil rulers. In free states the body of electors have it in their power to be governed well; if faithful to themselves and the public, in raising those to offices of trust and importance, who are possessed of abilities and have merited their confidence by former good services.

Knowledge and fidelity, are qualifications indispensibly necessary to form the character of good magistrates. No man, ever possessed natural or acquired abilities, too great for the discharge of the duties constantly incumbent upon those, who act as the representatives of the Most High GOD, in the government of their fellow creatures: multitudes however well disposed, are totally incapable of such trust. The interests of society are always important, they are many times involved in extreme difficulty, through the weakness of some, and the wickedness of others; and there is need of the most extensive knowledge, wisdom and prudence, to direct the various opposing interests of individuals into one channel, and guide them all to a single object, the public good. Woe to that people, to whom GOD by his providence in judgment shall say; "I will give children to be their princes, and babes shall rule over them. And the people shall be oppressed, every one by another, and every one by his neighbour: the child shall behave himself proudly against the antient, and the base against the honourable. And judgment is turned away backward, and justice standeth afar off: for truth is fallen in [15] the street and equity cannot enter; and he that departeth from evil maketh himself a prey."†

But knowledge alone, will qualify no person to fill a public station with honor to himself, or advantage to others. The greatest abilities the most extensive knowledge are capable of abuse; and when misapplied to selfish ambitious purposes, may be improved to the destruction of every thing valuable in society.

Fidelity therefore, is another essential characteristic in a good ruler. This is a qualification so absolutely essential, that *when known to be wanting,* no conceivable abilities can atone for its absence. Fidelity hath no sure unshaken foundation, but in the love and fear of the one true GOD: that love, which extends its benign influence to all the creatures of GOD. This is a branch of that benevolent religion, which the Son of GOD came down from Heaven to establish, in the hearts of men on earth: this when seated on the soul of man, becomes a stable principle of action, and will have an habitual influence in all his conduct, whether in public or private life—this will enable rulers

† Isa. iii, 4, 5, and lix: 14, 15.

to maintain the dignity of their elevated stations, amidst the strong temptations with which they may be assaulted—feeling their just accountableness to those of their fellow men, who have placed such confidence in them, as to entrust them with all their valuable temporal interests: and what is infinitely more, feeling their accountableness to GOD; they will labor to discharge the important duties of their office; remembering that the day is fast approaching, [16] when, notwithstanding, "they are gods, and children of the Most High, yet they shall die like men, an[d] fall like one of the princes." Able pious magistrates, who wish to answer the end of their appointment, will not wish to hide their real characters from the public eye—they will come to the light that their deeds may be manifest.

It is the interest and privilege of an enlightened free people, to be acquainted with the characters of their most worthy citizens, who are candidates for public offices in the community; and, it is equally their interest and privilege, to make choice of those only to be rulers, who are known among their tribes, for wisdom and piety. Following the salutary counsel of the prince of Midian, they will provide out of all the people, able men, such as fear GOD, men of truth, hating covetousness.

Free republicans, as observed above, have it in their power to be governed well: but they are in the utmost danger through a wanton abuse of this power. Actuated, by noble public spirited motives, and a primary regard to real merit in their elections; they will have the heads of their tribes, as fathers to lead them in paths of safety and peace: under the guidance of such rulers, who consider their subjects as brethren, and children, and all the interests of the community as their own; a people can hardly fail of all that happiness of which societies are capable in this degenerate state.

But when party spirit, local views, and interested motives, direct their suffrages, when [17] they loose sight of the great end of government the public good, and give themselves up, to the baneful influence of parasitical demagogues, they may well expect to reap the bitter fruits of their own folly, in a partial wavering administration. Through the neglect, or abuse of their privileges, most states have lost their liberties; and have fallen a prey to the avarice and ambition of designing and wicked men. "When the righteous are in authority, the people rejoice: but when the wicked beareth rule, the people mourn." This joy, or mourning, among a people, greatly depends on

their own conduct in elections—bribery here, is the bane of society—
the man who will give or receive a reward in this case, must be
extremely ignorant, not to deserve the stigma of an enemy to the
state—and should he have address to avoid discovery, he must be
destitute of sensibility, not to feel himself to be despicable. All private
dishonorable methods to raise persons to office, convey a strong
suspicion to the discerning mind, that merit is wanting: real merit
may dwell in obscurity, but it needeth not, neither will it ever solicit,
the aids of corruption to bring itself into view. When streams are
polluted in their fountain they will not fail to run impure—offices in
government obtained by purchase, will always be improved to regain
the purchase money with large increase: and a venal administration
will possess neither disposition nor strength to correct the vices of
others, but will lose sight of the public happiness, in the eager pursuit
of personal emolument.

[18] 4. Wisdom will lead a people to maintain a sacred regard
to righteousness, in reference to the public, and individuals.

Moral righteousness is one of those strong bonds by which all
public societies are supported. Heathen nations ignorant of divine
revelation, and the particular duties and obligations which are enlightened and inforced by the word and authority of GOD have nevertheless
been sensible, of the great importance of moral righteousness. Greece
and Rome, in the beginning of their greatness, before they sunk into
effeminacy and corruption, were careful to encourage and maintain
public and private justice: they laboured to diffuse principles of
righteousness among all ranks of their citizens. Many of their writings
on this subject, deserve attention so far as the observance of moral
duties respect civil communities, and the well-being of mankind in
the present world. As all civil communities have their foundation in
compacts, by which individuals immerge out of a state of nature, and
become one great whole, cemented together by voluntary engagements;
covenanting with each other, to observe such regulations, and perform
such duties as may tend to mutual advantage: hence ariseth the
necessity of righteousness, this being the basis on which all must
depend. When this fails, compacts will be disregarded, men will loose
a sense of their obligations to each other, instead of confidence and
harmony, will be a spirit of distrust and fear, every man will be afraid
of his neighbour; jealousies will subsist betwixt rulers and subjects,
the strength of [19] the community will be lost in animosity and

division, all ability for united exertion will be destroyed, and, the bonds of society being broken it must be dissolved. It was long since observed, by one of the greatest and wisest of kings, and will for ever remain true; "That righteousness exalteth a nation: but sin is a reproach to any people." The truth of this divine maxim doth not depend upon any arbitrary constitution, or, positive system of government: but flows from the reason and nature of things.

There is in the constitution of heaven, an established connection, between the practice of righteousness and the happiness of moral beings united in society. Public faith, and private justice, lay a foundation, for public spirit and vigorous exertion to rest upon; in such a state, every one will receive a proper reward for his service, let his station be what it may: and every delinquent, will realize such punishment, as his offence, or neglect of duty may deserve. In a fixed regular course of communicative and distributive justice, all may know before hand, what the reward of their conduct will be. What the apostle hath said concerning the natural body, and applied to the church of CHRIST: may with equal propriety and little variation, be applied to political societies. These bodies are composed of various members, the members have various offices, but all of them are necessary, for the well being of the whole; there is something due from the body to every member, and from every member to the body: every part is to be regarded, [20] and righteousness maintained throughout the whole.

The members of a well organized civil community, under an equal and just administration, have no more reason to complain of the station alloted to them in providence; than the members of the natural body, have of the place, by GOD assigned them in that. "The eye cannot say unto the head, I have no need of thee; nor again the head to the feet, I have no need of you. But that the members should have the same care one for another. And whether one member suffer, all the members suffer with it: or one member be honoured, all the members rejoice with it." No member of the natural body, of a civil community, or of GOD's moral kingdom, can be required to do more, than observe the proper duty of its own station: when this is performed, all is done which can reasonably be demanded, it hath done well, and may expect the approbation and protection of the whole body.

Men may indeed complain, because they are not angels; and do it with as much propriety, as to feel discontented, because they are not all placed at the head of civil communities. The allwise GOD, hath given us our capacities, and fixed our stations, and when righteousness is observed by us, and the community of which we are members, we shall then do, and receive, what belongs to us, and this is all we can reasonably desire.

5. The wisdom of a people essentially consists, in paying an unfeigned obedience to the [21] institutions of that religion, which the Supreme Lawgiver hath established in his church on earth.

That religion, which GOD hath enjoined upon rational beings, is not only necessary for his glory, but essential to their happiness. To establish a character as being truly religious, under the light of divine revelation, it is by no means sufficient, that men should barely acknowledge the existence, and general providence of one supreme DIETY. From this heavenly light, we obtain decided evidence, that the Almighty Father, hath set his well beloved Son the blessed IMMANUEL, as King upon his holy hill of Zion. This DIVINE person, in his mediatorial character, "is exalted, far above all principality, and power, and might, and dominion, and every name that is named, not only in this world, but also, in that which is to come. And all things are put under his feet. That at the name of JESUS, every knee should bow, of things in heaven, and things in earth, and things under the earth; and that every tongue should confess, that JESUS CHRIST is LORD, to the glory of GOD the Father."

In vain, do guilty mortals worship the great Jehovah, and present their services before him, but, in the name, and for the sake of this glorious Mediator. For it is his will "that all men should honor the Son, even as they honor the Father."

Communities, have their existence in, and from, this glorious personage. The kingdom is his, and he ruleth among the nations. [22] Through his bounty, and special providence, it is, that a people enjoy the inestimable liberties and numerous advantages of a well regulated civil society: through his influence, they are inspired with understanding to adopt, with strength and public spirit to maintain, a righteous constitution: He gives able impartial rulers, to guide in paths of virtue and peace; or gets up over them the basest of men. By his invisible hand, states are preserved from internal convulsions, and shielded by his Almighty arm from external violence: or, through his providential displeasure, they are given as a prey to their own vices; or to the lusts and passions of other states, to be destroyed.

Thus absolutely dependent, are temporal communities, and all human things, upon HIM who reigneth King in Zion. "Be wise now therefore, O ye kings; be instructed, ye judges of the earth. Kiss the Son lest he be angry, and ye perish from the way, when his wrath is kindled but a little: blessed are all they that put their trust in him."

The holy religion of the Son of GOD, hath a most powerful and benign influence upon moral beings in society. It not only restrains malicious revengeful passions, and curbs unruly lusts; but will in event, eradicate them all from the human breast—it implants all the divine graces and social virtues in the heart—it sweetens the dispositions of men, and fits them for all the pleasing satisfactions, of rational friendship—teaches them self denial—inspires them with a generous public spirit—fills them [23] with love to others, to righteousness and mercy—makes them careful to discharge the duties of their stations—diligent and contented in their callings—this, beyond any other consideration, will increase the real dignity of rulers—will give quiet and submission to subjects—this is the only true and genuine spirit of liberty, which can give abiding union and energy to states— and will enable them to bear prosperity without pride—and support them in adversity without dejection—this will afford all classes of men consolation in death, and render them happy in GOD, their full eternal portion, in the coming world.

Religion, therefore is the glory of all intelligent beings, from the highest angel, to the meanest of the human race: and will for ever happify its possessors, considered, either individually, or, as connected in society: for this assimilates the hearts of creatures, to the great fountain of being in the exercise of general and disinterested affection; and is, the consumation of wisdom.

If the preceding observations, have their foundation in reason, and the word of GOD: we see the happy connection between religion and good government. The idea that there is, and ought to be, no connection between religion and civil policy, appears to rest upon this absurd supposition; that men by entering into society for mutual advantage, become quite a different class of beings from what they were before, that they cease to be moral beings; and consequently, loose their relation and obligations [24] to GOD, as his creatures and subjects: and also their relations to each other as rational social creatures. If these are the real consequences of civil connections, they are unhappy indeed, as they must exceedingly debase and degrade

TIMOTHY STONE 1742–1797

human nature: and it is readily acknowledged, these things being true, that religion can have no further demands upon them. But, if none of the relations or obligations of men to their Creator, and each other are lost by entering into society; if they still remain moral and accountable beings, and, if religion is the glory and perfection of moral beings, then the connection, between religion and good government is evident—and all attempts to separate them are unfriendly to society, and inimical to good government, and must originate in ignorance or bad design.

Religion essentially consists in friendly affection to GOD, and his rational offspring; and such affection, can never injure that government which hath public happiness for its object.

Attempts have been made to distinguish between moral and political wisdom—moral and political righteousness—as tho there were two kinds of wisdom and righteousness, distinct in their nature, and applicable only to different subjects: that which is moral, belonging to the government of men as subjects of GOD's dominion; and that which is political, to men as subjects of civil rule—But, if wisdom and righteousness, are the same in the fountain, as in the streams, in GOD, as in his creatures; differing [25] not in nature and kind, but only in degree, then all such distinctions are manifestly without foundation. We read it is true, of a particular kind of wisdom, the fruit of which is "bitter envying and strife and every evil work: and that this wisdom, is earthly, sensual and devilish." But, until it is made to appear, that this is more friendly to civil government, than the wisdom "from above, which is pure and peaceable, full of mercy and good fruits, without partiality, and without hypocrisy:"* the supposed distinction, will not apply to human governments with advantage—nor, destroy the connection between religion and good government.

Religion and civil government, are not one and the same thing: tho' both may, and are designed to embrace some of the same objects, yet the former, extends its obligations and designs immensely beyond what the latter can pretend to: and it hath rights and prerogatives, with which the latter may not intermeddle. Still, there are many ways, in which civil government may give countenance, encouragement, and even support to religion, without invading the prerogatives

---

* Lam. xiv.—18.

of the Most High; or, touching the inferior, tho sacred rights of conscience: and in doing of which, it may not only shew its friendly regard to christianity, but derive important advantages to itself.

The friends of true happiness, whether ministers of state, or ministers of religion, or, in whatever character they may act, will therefore [26] exert themselves to promote that cause, which aims at no less an object, than the glory of JEHOVAH, and the highest felicity of his unlimited and eternal kingdom.

A civil community, formed, organized, and administered, agreeably to the principles which have been suggested, will possess internal peace and energy; its strength and wealth may easily be collected for necessary defence, consequently will ever be prepared to repel foreign injuries: it will enjoy prosperity within itself, and become respectable amongst the nations of the earth.

Could this, and the other states in the American Republic in their separate and united capacities, be established upon the principles of true wisdom, that righteousness and goodness, which have their foundation in the nature of things, and are essential parts, of the christian system—could we build upon this foundation, we might set forth a good example, and become a blessing to mankind—in this way we might establish our character as a wise and understanding people—become* "beautiful as Tirzah, comely as Jerusalem"—we should "look forth as the morning, fair as the moon, clear as the sun, and terrible as an army with banners."

Those deserve well of their brethren, who have devoted their time and superior abilities to the public, in the establishment and administration of civil constitutions, which are calculated to answer purposes, importantly beneficial to mankind.

[27] These thoughts, may call our grateful attention, to the honourable and venerable characters, collected this morning in the house of GOD. Some respectful, serious addresses, to the different characters here present may conclude this discourse.

MAY IT PLEASE YOUR EXCELLENCY,

Seats of dignity in free republics are truly honorable, where merit, and the voice of uncorrupted citizens are the only causes of elevation. The first Magistrate in such a state, is more respectable than the most

---

* Solomons Song vi. 4, and 10.

powerful Monarch, who obtains his throne, either by arbitrary usurpation, the arts of venality, or even the fortunate circumstance of hereditary succession. In either of the instances supposed, the throne may be filled without personal worth, may be supported by the same means by which it was at first obtained, and may be improved for the purposes of idleness and dissipation: or what is worse, to consume the wealth, destroy the liberties, and even sport with the lives of subjects. By means of such abuse of power, a people will be rendered vastly more wretched, than they would have been in a state of nature; and yet find it extremely difficult, to extricate themselves from these complicated evils. But such abuse of power cannot so easily take place, or be continued, in free republican governments; where places of honor are inseparably connected with important duties; duties which must be performed, otherwise such places will not long be supported, under the jealous inspection of a people, possessed of the knowledge, [28] and love of liberty, together with the means of its preservation.

These considerations, add to the merit, and increase the lustre of those worthy characters, which have been repeatedly called by the united voice of their brethren to preside in this State. The understanding of this people and their knowledge of worth, have been conspicuous, in the attention generally paid, to deserving personages in the election of their rulers: especially in the long succession of wise religious governors, whose eminent talents, and pious examples, have been so extensively beneficial to this community. May your Excellency's name, in this honourable catalogue, remain a lasting memorial, of the many services which you have rendered to this people, as a public testimony of the respect of your enlightened fellow citizens: and may your unremitted exertions for their prosperity be continued, and all your benevolent endeavours to promote their temporal and eternal interests, meet the divine blessing—may you never bear that sword in vain, which the exalted MEDIATOR, through the instrumentality of men, hath put into your hand; let this be a shield to the innocent, the widow, and the orphan, in their oppressions; while it remains a terror, to all such as do evil: you will if possible, scatter the wicked with your eyes, but when coercion becomes necessary, you will bring the wheel over them. Sensible of the weighty cares, and strong temptations of your exalted station, may your dependance, be increasingly fixed on that glorious and gracious Being, who hath called you to office; esteeming [29] his approbation infinitely superior to the applause of mortals. By the weight of your example, and the influence of that authority with which you are clothed, may you, sir, do much for the honor of GOD the Redeemer, for the advancement of his holy religion among men—for the promotion of righteousness and peace, in this, and the United States of America—for the abolition of slavery and every species of oppression—for the increase of civil and religious liberty, in the earth—And when, by the Supreme Disposer of all events, you may be called, to relinquish the honors, and cares of this mortal life, our prayer to Almighty GOD; is, that in that solemn hour, you may enjoy the supports of conscious integrity, meet with the approbation of your Judge, and be graciously received to the society of the blessed.

The public address, may now, be respectfully presented, to his Honor the Lieutenant-Governor, the Council, and House of Representatives.

HONORED GENTLEMEN,

The trust, which GOD, and this respectable commonwealth, have reposed in you is truly important. All the temporal interests of this people, in a sense, are put into your hands and committed to your management, for the general good. Children place strong confidence, in the wisdom and tender care of their natural parents; so, do this people in you, gentlemen, as their civil fathers: this confidence is not only implied, but expressed, in the designation [30] of your persons to those offices which you hold, in the government of your fellow citizens. Civil liberty, is an inheritance descending from the Father of Lights, a talent which, individuals may not despise, or misimprove without guilt: how vastly important then, must this, with its connected blessings in society, be, to a large community? The extensive views, and patriotic feelings, of wise and virtuous magistrates, cannot fail, deeply to impress their minds with the weight and solemnity of the trust reposed in them. Great anxiety for preferment, betrays a weak mind, or a vicious heart. Those only, deserve the honors of an elevated station, who are willing to bear the burdens, and perform the duties which belong to it: and to reap the rewards which righteousness and benevolence will bestow: and who, in the ways of well doing, can meet with calmness, the temporary ingratitude, of a misguided misjudging people. Not that the preacher would be understood to mean, that great esteem, with an ample pecuniary recompense, are

TIMOTHY STONE 1742–1797

not due, to those, whose time, and superior talents are employed, in promoting the happiness of their fellow men.

You, gentlemen, are vested with an authority which men of wisdom and virtue will ever revere; which properly exercised, none can resist, without resisting the ordinance of GOD: and persevering in their resistance "must receive to themselves damnation." May you ever exercise such authority, in the meekness of wisdom, for the best good of your brethren: agreeably to those unchangeable laws of righteousness [31] and goodness, which the Supreme Lawgiver hath established in his moral kingdom.* "That no iniquity, be found in the place of righteousness, or, wickedness, in the place of judgment; your eyes will be upon the faithful of the land, that they may dwell with you: those who walk in a perfect way," will be designated by you for all important executive trusts. Viewing yourselves, in the light of truth, as the ministers of GOD, to this people for good, you will realize the important connection between the moral government of JEHOVAH, and those inferior governments which he hath ordained to exist among men. In this light, you will esteem it your highest glory, to manifest a personal, supreme regard, to the benevolent institutions of the Son of GOD: by the weight of your example, and the force of all that influence you possess, you will study to commend his holy religion to all men; that you may be instrumental, in promoting the temporal peace and eternal happiness of this people. Public sentiments have a vast influence upon the conduct of mankind; public sentiments receive their complexion from public men; the rulers of a people can do more than some may imagine, to promote real godliness: if this, is recommended in their conversation, and exemplified in their lives, it will attract the attention of multitudes; it may lead some to a happy imitation, and will not fail, to give strong support, to all the friends of GOD. But men, sufficiently disposed at all times to cast off the fear of GOD, need slender aid, from public influential characters, to become professed [32] advocates, for infidelity and licentiousness. How exceedingly interesting, gentlemen, to yourselves and the community, is the station assigned to you in providence? May unerring wisdom guide all your steps, and the God of Abraham be your shield, and exceeding great reward.

The Ministers of GOD's sanctuary, will accept some thoughts

---

* Eccl. iii. 16—Ps. ci. 6.

addressed to them, not indeed for their instruction, but, to "stir up their pure minds by way of remembrance."

REVEREND FATHERS AND BRETHREN,

Our character as christians, obligeth us to be righteous before GOD, walking in all the commandments and ordinances of the Lord blameless: not forgetting that, of civil magistracy, as one of the wise and gracious appointments of heaven, which, rightly improved, will extend its happy influence beyond the present life. And, our office as ministers, calleth us to exhort all the disciples of Jesus, that they "submit themselves to every ordinance of man for the Lord's sake: unto kings and governors as unto them that are sent by him for the punishment of evil doers, and for the praise of them that do well. For so is the will of GOD, that with well doing ye may put to silence the ignorance of foolish men." The ignorance and folly of that principle, that there is no connection between religion and civil policy, is most happily refuted, when the followers of JESUS act in character, and demonstrate to the world, that real christians are the best members of society in every station. We are not then acting out [33] of character, when pointing out the advantages of a righteous government, and the necessity of subjection to magistrates. This however, is not the principal object of our ministry: our wisdom and understanding will eminently appear, in converting sinners from the error of their ways—in winning souls to CHRIST. To effect which our speech and our preaching must not be with enticing words of man's wisdom, but in demonstration of the spirit and of power.

Confiding, in the unerring wisdom, and boundless goodness, of GOD, we need not be ashamed, nor afraid, to declare all his counsel—being well assured, that no doctrine, or duty, can be found in his revealed will, but such as are profitable for men to believe and practice. The great comprehensive design of the christian ministry, is the glory of GOD, in the salvation of sinners, through JESUS CHRIST. In pursuing this noble all important design, we shall labor to exhibit, the divine excellency of the christian religion, in the holiness of our lives and conversation, as well, as in the simplicity, and uncorruptness of our doctrines: that our example and our preaching, may unite in their tendency, to persuade sinners, to become reconciled to GOD. "How beautiful upon the mountains are the feet of him that bringeth good tidings; that publisheth peace, that saith unto Zion, thy GOD reigneth!"

and how is this beauty increased? when the spiritual watchmen upon the walls of Zion, "sing together with the voice, and see eye to eye."*

[34] That this beauty may appear and shine, in all the ministers and churches of CHRIST; let us become more fervent, and united, in supplications, to our Father in Heaven, that he may shed forth plentiful effusions of that spirit of love, and of a sound mind, which is the only abiding principle of union, between moral beings. Under the influence of this holy spirit, awakened to activity and diligence, by the repeated instances of mortality, among the ministering servants of GOD, in the past year; may we all pursue the sacred work assigned to us, with increasing joy, and success, until called from our labors, to receive the free rewards of faithful servants, in the kingdom of our Lord and Saviour JESUS CHRIST.

A brief address, to the numerous audience present on this joyful anniversary, will close this discourse.—

BRETHREN AND FELLOW CITIZENS,

Let us not vainly boast, in our truly happy constitution—nor in the number of wise, and pious personages, whom GOD hath called to preside in its administration. We have abundant occasion indeed, to bless, and praise, the GOD of Heaven; for all our distinguishing privileges, both civil and religious—few of our lapsed race, enjoy immunities, equal to those which we possess: but we do well to remember, that profaneness and irreligion, infidelity and ungodliness, when connected with such advantages, will exceedingly enhance the guilt of men, and without repentance will awfully increase the [35] pains of damnation. Would we become a wise understanding people, we must learn the statutes, and judgments, which the LORD our GOD, hath commanded, and obey them—we must be a religious, holy people, "for without holiness, no man shall see the LORD." Let all be exhorted, to become wise to salvation, through faith, which is in CHRIST JESUS.—AMEN.

* Isa. lii. 7, 8.

[57]

DAVID RICE 1733–1816

*Slavery Inconsistent With Justice and
Good Policy*

AUGUSTA, KENTUCKY, 1792

Born and reared in rural Virginia, David Rice was attracted to the
Presbyterian Church while a youth, studied theology, and took
up a career of evangelical preaching and organization for the Presbyterian
Church, first in Virginia and North Carolina and later in Kentucky.
He made the provision of low-cost or free education an important
aspect of his mission and was instrumental in founding Hampden-
Sydney College, in Virginia, and Transylvania University, in Kentucky.
His travels and stands for preaching in the back country acquainted
him thoroughly with the conditions and consequences of slavery and
brought him early to a stubborn opposition to human bondage. In this
speech Rice is, as an elected member, addressing the constitutional
convention that drew up the first Kentucky Constitution. His objective
is a provision in the fundamental document that will make slavery
unlawful in Kentucky. Both in terms of rhetorical force and theoretical
sophistication, this is as thoughtful and effective a statement
on the subject as one can find during the founding era.

Mr. Chairman,
I rise Sir, in support of the motion now before you. But my reverence
for this body, the novelty of my present situation, the great importance
and difficulty of the subject, and the thought of being opposed by
gentlemen of the greatest abilities, has too sensible an impression on
my mind. But, Sir, I know so much of my natural timidity, which

DAVID RICE 1733–1816

increases with my years, that I foresaw this would be the case: I therefore prepared a speech for the occasion.

Sir, I have lived free, and in many respects happy for near sixty years; but my happiness has been greatly diminished, for much of the time, by hearing a great part of the human species groaning under the galling yoke of bondage. In this time I lost a venerable father, a tender mother, two affectionate sisters, and a beloved first born son; but all these together have not cost me half the anxiety as has been occasioned by this wretched situation of my fellow-men, whom without a blush I call my brethren. When I consider their deplorable state, and who are the cause of their misery, the load of misery that lies on them, and the load of guilt on us for imposing it on them; it fills my soul with anguish. I view their distresses, I read the anger of Heaven, I believe that if I should not exert myself, when, and as far, as in my power, in order to relieve them, I should be partaker of the guilt.

Sir, the question is, Whether slavery is consistent with justice and good policy? But before this is answered, it may be necessary to enquire, what a slave is.

A slave is a human creature made by law the property of another human creature, and reduced by mere power to an absolute unconditional subjection to his will.

This definition will be allowed to be just, with only this one exception, that the law does not leave the life and the limbs of the slave entirely in the master's power: and from it may be inferred several melancholy truths, which will include a sufficient answer to the main question.

In order to a right view of this subject, I would observe, that there are some cases, where a man may justly be made a slave by law. By vicious conduct he may forfeit his freedom; he may forfeit his life. Where this is the case, and the safety of the public [4] may be secured by reducing the offender to a state of slavery, it will be right; it may be an act of kindness. In no other case, if my conceptions are just, can it be vindicated on principles of justice or humanity.

As creatures of God we are, with respect to liberty, all equal. If one has a right to live among his fellow creatures, and enjoy his freedom, so has another; if one has a right to enjoy that property he acquires by an honest industry, so has another. If I by force take that from another, which he has a just right to according to the law of nature, (which is a divine law) which he has never forfeited, and to which he has never relinquished his claim, I am certainly guilty of injustice and robbery; and when the thing taken is the man's liberty, when it is himself, it is the greatest injustice. I injure him much more, than if I robbed him of his property on the high-way. In this case, it does not belong to him to prove a negative, but to me to prove that such forfeiture has been made, because, if it has not, he is certainly still the proprietor. All he has to do is to shew the insufficiency of my proofs.

A slave claims his freedom, he pleads that he is a man, that he was by nature free, that he had not forfeited his freedom, nor relinquished it. Now unless his master can prove that he is not a man, that he was not born free, or that he has forfeited or relinquished his freedom, he must be judged free; the justice of his claim must be acknowledged. His being long deprived of this right, by force or fraud, does not annihilate it, it remains; it is still his right. When I rob a man of his property, I leave him his liberty, and a capacity of acquiring and possessing more property; but when I deprive him of his liberty, I also deprive him of this capacity; therefore I do him greater injury, when I deprive him of his liberty, than when I rob him of his property. It is in vain for me to plead that I have the sanction of law; for this makes the injury the greater, it arms the community against him, and makes his case desperate.

If my definition of a slave is true, he is a rational creature reduced by the power of legislation to the state of a brute, and thereby deprived of every privilege of humanity, except as above, that he may minister to the ease, luxury, lust, pride, or avarice of another, no better than himself.

We only want a law enacted that no owner of a brute, nor other person, should kill or dismember it, and then in law the case of a slave and a brute is in most respects parallel; and where they differ, the state of the brute is to be preferred. The brute may steal or rob, to supply his hunger; the law does not condemn him to die for his offence, it only permits his death; but the slave, though in the most starving condition, dare not do either, on penalty of death or some severe punishment.

Is there any need of arguments to prove, that it is in a high degree unjust and cruel, to reduce one human creature to such an [5] abject wretched state as this, that he may minister to the ease, luxury, or avarice of another? Has not that other the same right to have him

DAVID RICE 1733–1816

reduced to this state, that he may minister to his interest or pleasure? On what is this right founded? Whence was it derived? Did it come from heaven, from earth, or from hell? Has the great King of heaven, the absolute sovereign disposer of all men, given this extraordinary right to white men over black men? Where is the charter? In whose hands is it lodged? Let it be produced and read, that we may know our privilege.

Thus reducing men is an indignity, a degradation to our own nature. Had we not lost a true sense of its worth and dignity, we should blush to see it converted into brutes. We should blush to see our houses filled, or surrounded with cattle in our own shapes. We should look upon it to be a fouler, a blacker stain, than that with which the vertical suns have tinged the blood of Africa. When we plead for slavery, we plead for the disgrace and ruin of our own nature. If we are capable of it we may ever after claim kindred with the brutes, and renounce our own superior dignity.

From our definition it will appear, that a slave is a creature made after the image of God, and accountable to him for the maintenance of innocence and purity; but by law reduced to a liableness to be debauched by men, without any prospect or hope of redress.

That a slave is made after the image of God no Christian will deny; that a slave is absolutely subjected to be debauched by men, is so apparent from the nature of slavery, that it needs no proof. This is evidently the unhappy case of female slaves; a number of whom have been remarkable for their chastity and modesty. If their master attempts their chastity, they dare neither resist or complain. If another man should make the attempt, though resistance may not be so dangerous, complaints are equally vain. They cannot be heard in their own defence, their testimony cannot be admitted. The injurious person has a right to be heard, may accuse the innocent sufferer of malicious slander, and have her severely chastised.

A virtuous woman, and virtuous Africans no doubt there are, esteems her chastity above every other thing; some have preferred it even to their lives: then forcibly to deprive her of this, is treating her with the greatest injustice. Therefore since law leaves the chastity of a female slave entirely in the power of her master; and greatly in the power of others, it permits this injustice; it provides no remedy, it refuses to redress this insufferable grievance; it denies even the small privilege of complaining.

AUGUSTA, KENTUCKY, 1792

From our definition it will follow, that a slave is a free moral agent legally deprived of free agency, and obliged to act according to the will of another free agent of the same species; and yet he is accountable to his Creator for the use he makes of his own free agency.

[6] When a man, though he can exist independent of another, cannot act independent of him, his agency must depend upon the will of that other; and therefore he is deprived of his own free agency; and yet, as a free agent, he is accountable to his Maker for all the deeds done in the body. This comes to pass through a great omission and inconsistency in the legislature. They ought farther to have enacted, in order to have been consistent, that the slave should not have been accountable for any of his actions; but that his master should have answered for him in all things, here and hereafter.

That a slave has the capacities of a free moral agent will be allowed at all. That he is, in many instances, deprived by law of the exercise of these powers, evidently appears from his situation. That he is accountable to his Maker for his conduct, will be allowed by those, who do not believe that human legislatures are omnipotent and can free men from this allegiance and subjection to the King of heaven.

The principles of conjugal love and fidelity in the breast of a virtuous pair, of natural affection in parents, and a sense of duty in children, are inscribed there by the finger of God; they are the laws of heaven; but an inslaving law directly opposes them, and virtually forbids obedience. The relation of husband and wife, or parent and child, are formed by divine authority, and founded on the laws of nature. But it is in the power of a cruel master, and often of a needy creditor, to break these tender connections, and forever to separate these dearest relatives. This is ever done, in fact, at the call of interest or humour. The poor sufferers may expostulate; they may plead; may plead with tears; their hearts may break; but all in vain. The laws of nature are violated, the tender ties are dissolved, a final separation takes place, and the duties of these relations can no longer be performed, nor their comforts enjoyed. Would these slaves perform the duties of husbands and wives, parents and children; the law disables them, it puts it altogether out of their power.

In these cases, it is evident that the laws of nature, or the laws of man, are wrong; and which, none will be at a loss to judge. The divine law says, Whom God hath joined together, let no man put asunder; the law of man says, to the master of the slave, Though the

DAVID RICE 1733–1816

divine law has joined them together, you may put them asunder when you please. The divine law says, Train up your child in the way he should go; the law of man says, You shall not train up your child, but as your master thinks proper. The divine law says, Honor your father and mother, and obey them in all things; but the law of man says, Honor and obey your master in all things, and your parents just as far as he shall direct you.

Should a master command his slave to steal or rob, and he should presume to disobey, he is liable to suffer every extremity of punishment short of death or amputation, from the hand of his [7] master; at the same time he is liable to a punishment equally severe, if not death itself, should he obey.

He is bound by law, if his master pleases, to do that, for which the law condemns him to death.

Another consequence of our definition is, That a slave, being a free moral agent, and an accountable creature, is a capable subject of religion and morality; but deprived by law of the means of instruction in the doctrines and duties of morality, any further than his master pleases.

It is in the power of the master to deprive him of all the means of religious and moral instruction, either in private or in public. Some masters have actually exercised this power, and restrained their slaves from the means of instruction, by the terror of the lash. Slaves have not opportunity, at their own disposal, for instructing conversation; it is put out of their power to learn to read; and their masters may restrain them from other means of information. Masters designedly keep their slaves in ignorance lest they should become too knowing to answer their selfish purposes; and too wise to rest easy in their degraded situation. In this case the law operates so as to answer an end directly opposed to the proper end of all law. It is pointed against every thing dear to them; against the principal end of their existence. It supports in a land of religious liberty, the severest persecutions and may operate so as totally to rob multitudes of their religious privileges, and the rights of conscience.

If my definition is just, a slave is one who is bound to spend his life in the service of another, to whom he owes nothing, is under no obligation; who is not legally bound to find him victuals, clothes, medicine, or any other means of preservation, support or comfort.

That a slave is bound to spend his life in the service of his master, no one will dispute; and that he is not indebted to his master, is under no obligations to him, is also evident. How can he possibly be indebted to him, who deprives him of liberty, property, and almost every thing dear to a human creature. And all he receives is the bare means of subsistence; and this not bestowed until he has earned it; and then not in proportion to his labor; nor out of regard to him, but for selfish purposes. This bare support the master is not bound by law to give; but is left to be guided by his own interest or humour; and hence the poor slave often falls short of what is necessary for the comfortable support of the body.

The master is the enemy of the slave; he has made open war against him, and is daily carrying it on in unremitted efforts. Can any one then imagine, that the slave is indebted to his master, and bound to serve him? Whence can the obligation arise? What is it founded upon? What is my duty to an enemy that is carrying on war against me? I do not deny, but, in some circumstances, it is the duty of the slave to serve; but it is a duty he owes himself, [8] and not his master. The master may, and often does, inflict upon him all the severity of punishment the human body is capable of bearing; and the law supports him in it: if he does but spare his life and his limbs, he dare not complain; none can hear and relieve him; he has no redress under heaven.

When we duly consider all these things, it must appear unjust to the last degree, to force a fellow creature, who has never forfeited his freedom, into this wretched situation; and confine him and his posterity in this bottomless gulph of wretchedness for ever. Where is the sympathy, the tender feelings of humanity? Where is the heart that does not melt at this scene of woe? Or that is not fired with indignation to see such injustice and cruelty countenanced by civilized nations, and supported by the sanction of the law?

If slavery is not consistent with justice, it must be inconsistent with good policy. For who would venture to assert, that it would be good policy for us to erect a public monument of our injustice, and that injustice is necessary for our prosperity, and happiness? That old proverb, that honesty is the best policy, ought not to be despised for its age.

But the inconsistency of slavery with good policy will fully appear, if we consider another consequence of our definition, viz.

A slave is a member of civil society bound to obey the law of

DAVID RICE 1733–1816

the land; to which laws he never consented; which partially and feebly protect his person; which allow him no property; from which he can receive no advantage; and which chiefly, as they relate to him, were made to punish him. He is therefore bound to submit to a government, to which he owes no allegiance; from which he receives great injury; and to which he is under no obligations; and to perform services to a society, to which he owes nothing and in whose prosperity he has no interest. That he is under this government, and forced to submit to it, appears from his suffering the penalties of its laws. That he receives no benefit by the laws and government he is under, is evident, from their depriving him of his liberty, and the means of happiness. Though they protect his life and his limbs, they confine him in misery, they will not suffer him to fly from it; the greatest favours they afford him chiefly serve to perpetuate his wretchedness.

He is then a member of society, who is, properly speaking, in a state of war with his master, his civil rulers, and every member of that society. They are all his declared enemies, having, in him, made war upon almost every thing dear to a human creature. It is a perpetual war, with an avowed purpose of never making peace. This war, as it is unprovoked, is, on the part of the slave, properly defensive. The injury done him is much greater than what is generally esteemed a just ground of war between different nations; it is much greater than was the cause of war between us and Britain.

It cannot be consistent with the principles of good policy to keep a numerous, a growing body of people among us, who add no [9] strength to us in time of war; who are under the strongest temptations to join an enemy, as it is scarce possible they can lose, and may be great gainers, by the event; who will count so many against us in an hour of danger and distress. A people whose interest it will be whenever in their power, to subvert the government, and throw all into confusion. Can it be safe? Can it be good policy? Can it be our interest or the interest of posterity, to nourish within our own bowels such an injured, inveterate foe, a foe, with whom we must be in a state of eternal war? What havock would a handful of savages, in conjunction with this domestic enemy, make in our country! Especially at a period when the main body of the inhabitants were softened by luxury and ease, and quite unfitted for the hardships and dangers of war. Let us turn our eyes to the West-Indies; and there learn the melancholy effects of this wretched policy. We may there read them written with the blood of thousands. There you may see the fable, let me say, the brave sons of Africa engaged in a noble conflict with their inveterate foes. There you may see thousands fired with a generous resentment of the greatest injuries, and bravely sacrificing their lives on the altar of liberty.

In America, a slave is a standing monument of the tyranny and inconsistency of human governments.

He is declared by the united voice of America, to be by nature free, and entitled to the privilege of acquiring and enjoying property; and yet by laws past and enforced in these states, retained in slavery, and dispossessed of all property and capacity of acquiring any. They have furnished a striking instance of a people carrrying on a war in defence of principles, which they are actually and avowedly destroying by legal force; using one measure for themselves and another for their neighbours.

Every state, in order to gain credit abroad, and confidence at home, and to give proper energy to government, should study to be consistent; their conduct should not disagree with their avowed principles, nor be inconsistent in its several parts. Consistent justice is the solid basis on which the fabric of government will rest securely; take this away, and the building totters, and is liable to fall before every blast. It is, I presume, the avowed principles of each of us, that all men are by nature free, and are still entitled to freedom, unless they have forfeited it. Now, after this is seen and acknowledged, to enact that men should be slaves, against whom we have no evidence that they have forfeited their right; what would it be but evidently to fly in our own face; to contradict ourselves; to proclaim before the world our own inconsistency; and warn all men to repose no confidence in us? After this, what credit can we ever expect? What confidence can we repose in each other? If we generally concur in this nefarious deed, we destroy mutual confidence, and break every link of the chain that should bind us together.

[10] Are we rulers? How can the people confide in us, after we have thus openly declared that we are void of truth and sincerity; and that we are capable of enslaving mankind in direct contradiction to our own principles? What confidence in legislators, who are capable of declaring their constituents all free men in one breath; and, in the next, enacting them all slaves? In one breath, declaring that they have a right to acquire and possess property; and, in the next, that they shall neither acquire nor possess it during their existence here? Can I

DAVID RICE 1733–1816

trust my life, my liberty, my property in such hands as these? Will the colour of my skin prove a sufficient defence against their injustice and cruelty? Will the particular circumstance of my ancestors being born in Europe, and not in Africa, defend me? Will straight hair defend me from the blow that falls so heavy on the wooly head?

If I am a dishonest man, if gain is my God, and this may be acquired by such an unrighteous law, I may rejoice to find it enacted; but I never can believe that the legislature were honest men; or repose the least confidence in them, when their own interest would lead them to betray it. I never can trust the integrity of the judge who can sit upon the seat of justice, and pass an unrighteous judgment, because it is agreeable to law; when that law itself is contrary to the light and law of nature.

Where no confidence can be put in men of public trust, the exercise of government must be very uneasy, and the condition of the people extremely wretched. We may conclude, with the utmost certainty, that it would be bad policy to reduce matters to this unhappy situation.

Slavery naturally tends to sap the foundations of moral, and consequently of political virtue; and virtue is absolutely necessary for the happiness and prosperity of a free people. Slavery produces idleness; and idleness is the nurse of vice. A vicious commonwealth is a building erected on quicksand, the inhabitants of which can never abide in safety.

Young gentlemen, who ought to be the honour and support of the state, when they have in prospect an independent fortune consisting in land and slaves, which they can easily devolve on a faithful overseer or steward, become the most useless and insignificant members of society. There is no confining them to useful studies, or any business that will fit them for serving the public. They are employed in scenes of pleasure and dissipation. They corrupt each other, they corrupt the morals of all around them; while their slaves, even in time of peace, are far from being equally useful to society with the same number of freemen; and, in time of war, are to be considered as an enemy within our walls. I said they were useless, insignificant members of society. I should have said more; I should have said, they are intolerable nuisances, pernicious pests of society. I mean not to reproach men of fortune; I mean only to point out the natural tendency of slavery, in order to shew, how inconsistent it is with good policy.

AUGUSTA, KENTUCKY, 1792

[11] The prosperity of a country depends upon the industry of its inhabitants; idleness will produce poverty: and when slavery becomes common, industry sinks into disgrace. To labour, is *to slave,* to work, is *to work like a Negro:* and this is disgraceful; it levels us with the meanest of the species; it sits hard upon the mind; it cannot be patiently borne. Youth are hereby tempted to idleness, and drawn into other vices; they see no other way to keep their credit, and acquire some little importance. This renders them like those they ape, nuisances of society. It frequently tempts them to gaming, theft, robbery, or forgery; for which they often end their days in disgrace on the gallows. Since every state must be supported by industry, it is exceedingly unwise to admit what will inevitably sink it into disgrace; and that this is the tendency of slavery is known for matter of fact.

Slavery naturally tends to destroy all sense of justice and equity. It puffs up the mind with pride: teaches youth a habit of looking down upon their fellow creatures with contempt, esteeming them as dogs or devils, and imagining themselves beings of superior dignity and importance, to whom all are indebted. This banishes the idea, and unqualifies the mind for the practice of common justice. If I have, all my days, been accustomed to live at the expence of a black man, without making him any compensation, or considering myself at all in his debt, I cannot think it any great crime to live at the expence of a white man. If I rob a black man without guilt, I shall contract no great guilt by robbing a white man. If I have been long accustomed to think a black was made for me, I may easily take it into my head to think so of a white man. If I have no sense of obligation to do justice to a black man, I can have little to do justice to a white man. In this case, the tinge of our skins, or the place of our nativity, can make but little difference. If I am in principle a friend to slavery, I cannot, to be consistent, think it any crime to rob my country of its property and freedom, whenever my interest calls, and I find it in my power. If I make any difference here, it must be owing to a vicious education, the force of prejudice, or pride of heart. If in principle a friend to slavery, I cannot feel myself obliged to pay the debt due to my neighbor. If I can wrong him of all his possessions, and avoid the law, all is well.

The destruction of chastity has a natural tendency to introduce a number of vices, that are very pernicious to the interest of a commonwealth; and slavery much conduces to destroy chastity, as it puts so great a number of females entirely in the power of the other sex; against whom they dare not complain, on peril of the lash; and many of whom they dare not resist. This vice, this bane of society, has already become so common, that it is scarcely esteemed a disgrace, in the one sex, and that the one that is generally the most criminal. Let it become as little disgraceful in the other, and there is an end to domestic tranquility, an end to the public prosperity.

[12] It is necessary to our national prosperity, that the estates of the inhabitants of the country be greatly productive. But perhaps no estates, possessed in any part of the world, are less productive than those which consist in great numbers of slaves. In such estates there will be old and decrepid men and women, breeding women, and little children; all must be maintained. They labour only from servile principles, and therefore not to equal advantage with free men. They will labour as little, they will take as little care, as they possibly can. When their maintenance is deducted from the fruit of their labour, only a small pittance remains for the owner. Hence many, who are proud of their estates, and envied for their wealth, are living in poverty, and immersed in debt. Here are large estates to be taxed; but small incomes to pay the taxes. This, while it gives us weight in the scale of the Union, will make us groan under the burden of our own importance.

Put all the above considerations together, and it evidently appears, that slavery is neither consistent with justice nor good policy. These are considerations, one would think, sufficient to silence every objection; but I foresee, notwithstanding, that a number will be made, some of which have a formidable appearance.

It will be said, Negroes were made slaves by law, they were converted into property by an act of the legislature; and under the sanction of that law I purchased them; they therefore became my property, I have a legal claim to them. To repeal this law, to annihilate slavery, would be violently to destroy what I legally purchased with my money, or inherit from my father. It would be equally unjust with dispossessing me of my horses, cattle, or any other species of property. To dispossess me of their offspring would be injustice equal to dispossessing me of my annual profits of my estate. This is an important objection, and it calls for a serious answer.

The matter seems to stand thus: many years ago, men, being deprived of their natural right to freedom, and made slaves, were by law converted into property. This law, it is true, was wrong, it established iniquity; it was against the law of humanity, common sense, reason, and conscience. It was, however, a law; and under the sanction of it, a number of men, regardless of its iniquity, purchased these slaves, and made their fellow men their property.

The question is concerning the liberty of a man. The man himself claims it as his own property. He pleads, that it was originally his own; that he has never forfeited, nor alienated it; and therefore, by the common laws of justice and humanity, it is still his own. The purchaser of the slave claims the same property. He pleads, that he purchased it under the sanction of a law, enacted by the legislature; and therefore it became his. Now, the question is, who has the best claim? Did the property in question belong to the legislature? Was it vested in them? If legislatures are possessed of such property as this, may another never exist! [13] No individual of their constituents could claim it as his own inherent right; it was not in them collectively; and therefore they could not convey it to their representatives. Was it ever known, that a people chose representatives to create and transfer this kind of property? The legislatures were not, they could not be possessed of it; and therefore could not transfer it to another; they could not give what they themselves had not. Now does the property belong to him, who received it from a legislature that had it not to give, and by a law they had no right to enact; or to the original owner, who has never forfeited, nor alienated his right? If a law should pass for selling an innocent man's head, and I should purchase it; have I in consequence of this law and this purchase, a better claim to this man's head than he has himself?

To call our fellow-men, who have not forfeited, nor voluntarily resigned their liberty, our property, is a gross absurdity, a contradiction to common sense, and an indignity to human nature. The owners of such slaves then are the licenced robbers, and not the just proprietors, of what they claim; freeing them is not depriving them of property, but restoring it to the right owner; it is suffering the unlawful captive to escape. It is not wronging the master, but doing justice to the slave, restoring him to himself. The master, it is true, is wronged, he may suffer and that greatly; but this is his own fault, and the fault of the enslaving law; and not of the law that does justice to the oppressed.

You say, a law of emancipation would be unjust, because it

would deprive men of their property; but is there no injustice on the other side? Is nobody intitled to justice, but slave-holders? Let us consider the injustice on both sides; and weigh them in an even balance. On the one hand, we see a man deprived of all property, and all capacity to possess property, of his own free agency, of the means of instruction, of his wife, of his children, of almost every thing dear to him: on the other, a man deprived of eighty or an hundred pounds. Shall we hesitate a moment to determine, who is the greatest sufferer, and who is treated with the greatest injustice? The matter appears quite glaring, when we consider, that neither this man, nor his parents had sinned, that he was born to these sufferings; but the other suffers altogether for his own sin, and that of his predecessors.—Such a law would only take away property, that is its own property, and not ours: property that has the same right to possess us, as its property, as we have to possess it: property that has the same right to convert our children into dogs, and calves, and colts, as we have to convert theirs into these beasts: property that may transfer our children to strangers, by the same right that we transfer theirs.

Human legislatures should remember, that they act in subordination to the great Ruler of the universe, have no right to take the government out of his hand nor to enact laws contrary to his; that if they should presume to attempt it, they cannot make that right, [14] which he has made wrong; they cannot dissolve the allegiance of his subjects, and transfer it to themselves, and thereby free the people from their obligations to obey the laws of nature. The people should know, that legislatures have not this power; and that a thousand laws can never make that innocent, which the divine law has made criminal; or give them a right to that, which the divine law forbids them to claim. But to the above reply it may be farther objected, that neither we nor the legislature, enslaved the Africans: but they enslaved one another, and we only purchased those, whom they had made prisoners of war, and reduced to slavery.

Making prisoners of war slaves, though practised by the Romans and other ancient nations, and though still practised by some barbarous tribes, can by no means be justified; it is unreasonable and cruel. Whatever may be said of the chief authors and promoters of an unjust war, the common soldier who is under command and obliged to obey, and as is often the case, deprived of the means of information as to the grounds of the war, certainly cannot be thought guilty of a crime so heinous, that for it himself, and posterity deserve the dreadful punishment of perpetual servitude. It is a cruelty that the present practice of all civilized nations bears testimony against. Allow then the matter objected to be true, and it will not justify our practice of enslaving the Africans. But the matter contained in the objection is only true in part. The history of the slave trade is too tragical to be read without a bleeding heart and weeping eyes.

A few of these unhappy Africans, and comparatively very few, are criminals, whose servitude is inflicted as a punishment for their crimes. The main body are innocent, unsuspecting creatures, free, living in peace, doing nothing to forfeit the common privileges of men. They are stolen, or violently borne away by armed force, from their country, their parents, and all their tender connections; treated with an indignity and indecency shameful to mention, and a cruelty shocking to all the tender feelings of humanity; and they and their posterity forced into a state of servitude and wretchedness for ever. It is true they are commonly taken prisoners by Africans; but it is the encouragement given by Europeans that tempts the Africans to carry on these unprovoked wars. They furnish them with the means, and hold out to them a reward for their plunder. If the Africans are thieves, the Europeans stand ready to receive the stolen goods: if the former are robbers, the latter furnish them with arms, and purchase the spoil. In this case who is the most criminal, the civilized European, or the untutored African? The European merchants know, that they themselves are the great encouragers of these wars, as they are the principal gainers by the event. They furnish the sinews, add the strength, and receive the gain. They know, that they purchase these slaves of those, who have no just pretence to claim them as theirs. The African can give the European no better claim than [15] he himself has; the European merchant can give us no better claim than is vested in him; and that is one founded only in violence or fraud.

In confirmation of this account might be produced many substantial vouchers, and some who had spent much time in this nefarious traffic. But such as are accustomed to listen to the melancholy tales of these unfortunate Africans cannot want sufficient evidence. Those who have seen multitudes of poor innocent children driven to market, and sold like beasts, have it demonstrated before their eyes.

It will be farther objected, that in our situations, the abolition of slavery would be bad policy; because it would discourage emigrants

DAVID RICE 1733–1816

from the Eastward, prevent the population of this country, and consequently its opulence and strength.

I doubt not but it would prevent a number of slave-holders from coming into this country, with their slaves. But this would be far, very far from being an evil. It would be a most desirable event; it would be keeping out a great and intolerable nuisance, the bane of every country where it is admitted, the cause of ignorance and vice, and of national poverty and weakness. On the other hand, if I mistake not, it would invite five useful citizens into our state, where it would keep out one slave-holder; and who would not rejoice in the happy exchange? Turn your eyes to the Eastward; behold numerous shoals of slaves, moving toward us, in thick succession. Look to the Westward; see a large, vacant, fertile country, lying near, easy to access, an asylum for the miserable, a land of liberty. A man, who has no slaves, cannot live easy and contented in the midst of those, who possess them in numbers. He is treated with neglect, and often with contempt: he is not a companion for his free neighbours, but only for their more reputable slaves: his children are looked upon and treated by theirs as underlings. These things are not easy to bear; they render his mind uneasy, and his situation unpleasant. When he sees an open way to remove from this situation, and finds it may be done consistent with his interest, he will not long abide in it. When he removes, his place is filled up with slaves. Thus, this country will spew out its white inhabitants; and be peopled with slave-holders, their slaves, and a few, in the highest posts of a poor free man, I mean that of an overseer. When we attentively view and consider our situation, with relation to the East and the West, we may be assured that this event will take place, that the progress towards it will be exceedingly rapid, and greatly accelerated by the fertility of our soil.

That this, on supposition that slavery should continue, would soon be the state of population in this country, is not only possible, but very probable; not only probable but morally certain. But is this a desirable situation? Would it be safe, and comfortable? Would it be so, even to masters themselves? I presume not: especially when I consider, that their near neighbors, beyond the [16] Ohio, could not, consistent with their principles, assist them, in case of a domestic insurrection. Suppose our inhabitants should be fewer; they would be useful citizens, who could repose a mutual confidence in each other. To increase the inhabitants of this state by multiplying an enemy within our own bowels; an enemy, with whom we are in a state of perpetual war, and can never make peace, is very far from being an object of desire: especially if we consider, that a belief of the iniquity of this servitude is fast gaining ground. Should this sentiment obtain the general belief, what might be the event? What the condition of this country?

Another frightful objection to my doctrine is, That should we set our slaves free, it would lay a foundation for intermarriages and an unnatural mixture of blood, and our posterity at length would all be Mulattoes.

This effect, I grant, it would produce. I also grant, that this appears very unnatural to persons labouring under our prejudices of education. I acknowledge my own pride remonstrates against it; but it does not influence my judgment, nor affect my conscience.

To plead this as a reason for the continuation of slavery, is to plead the fear that we should disgrace ourselves, as a reason why we should do injustice to others: to plead that we may continue in guilt, for fear the features and complexion of our posterity should be spoiled. We should recollect, that it is too late to prevent this great imaginary evil; the matter is already gone beyond recovery; for it may by proved, with mathematical certainty, that, if things go on in the present channel, the future inhabitants of America will inevitably be Mulattoes.

How often have men children by their own slaves, by their fathers' slaves, or the slaves of their neighbours? How fast is the number of Mulattoes increasing in every part of the land? Visit the towns and villages in the Eastward, visit the seats of gentlemen, who abound in slaves; and see how they swarm on every hand. All the children of Mulattoes will be Mulattoes, and the whites are daily adding to the number; which will continually encrease the proportion of Mulattoes. Thus this evil is coming upon us in a way much more disgraceful, and unnatural, than intermarriages. Fathers will have their own children for slaves, and leave them as an inheritance to their children. Men will possess their brothers and sisters as their property, leave them to their heirs, or sell them to strangers. Youth will have their grey-headed uncles and aunts for slaves, call them their property, and transfer them to others. Men will humble their own sisters, or even their aunts, to gratify their lust. An hard-hearted master will not know whether he has a blood relation, a brother or a sister, an uncle or an aunt, or a stranger of Africa, under his scourging hand. This is not the work of imagination; it has been frequently realized.

[17] The worst that can be made of this objection, ugly as it is, that it would be hastening an evil in an honest way which we are already bringing on ourselves in a way that is absolutely dishonest, perfectly shameful, and extremely criminal. This objection then can have no weight with a reasonable man, who can divest himself of his prejudices and his pride, and view the matter as really circumstanced. The evil is inevitable; but as it is a prejudice of education, it would be an evil only in its approach; as it drew near, it would decrease; when fully come, it would cease to exist.

Another objection to my doctrine, and that esteemed by some the most formidable, still lies before me: an objection taken from the sacred scriptures. There will be produced on the occasion, the example of faithful Abraham, recorded Gen. xvii and the law of Moses, recorded in Lev. xxv. The injunctions laid upon servants in the gospel, particularly by the Apostle Paul, will also be introduced here. These will all be directed, as formidable artillery, against me, and in defence of absolute slavery.

From the passage of Genesis, it is argued, by the advocates for perpetual slavery, that since Abraham had servants born in his house and bought with money, they must have servants for life, like our negroes: and hence they conclude, that it is lawful for us to purchase heathen servants also. From the law of Moses it is argued, that the Israelites were authorised to leave the children of their servants, as an inheritance to their own children for ever: and hence it is inferred that we may leave the children of our slaves as an inheritance to our children forever. If this was immoral in itself, a just God would never have given it the sanction of his authority; and, if lawful in itself, we may safely follow the example of Abraham, or act according to the law of Moses.

None, I hope, will make this objection, but those who believe these writings to be of divine authority; for if they are not so, it is little to the purpose to introduce them here. If you grant them to be of divine authority, you will also grant, that they are consistent with themselves, and that one passage may help to explain another. Grant me this; and then I reply to the objection.

In the 12th verse of the 17th of Genesis, we find that Abraham was commanded to circumcise all that were born in this house, or bought with money. We find in the sequel of the chapter, that he obeyed the command without delay; and actually circumcised every male in his family, who came under this description. This law of circumcision continued in force; it was not repealed, but confirmed by the law of Moses.

Now, to the circumcised were committed the oracles of God; and circumcision was a token of that covenant by which, among other things, the land of Canaan, and their various privileges in it, were promised to Abraham and his seed; to all that were included in that convenant. All were included, to whom circumcision, [18] which was the token of the covenant, was administered, agreeably to God's command. By divine appointment, not only Abraham and his natural seed, but he that was bought with money of any stranger that was not of his seed, was circumcised. Since the seed of the stranger received the token of this covenant, we must believe, that he was included, and interested in it; that the benefits promised were to be conferred on him. These persons bought with money were no longer looked upon as uncircumcised and unclean, as aliens and strangers; but were incorporated with the church and nation of the Israelites; and became one people with them; became God's covenant people. Whence it appears, that suitable provision was made by the divine law that they should be properly educated, made free, and enjoy all the common privileges of citizens. It was the divine law enjoined upon the Israelites; thus to circumcise all the males born in their houses; then if the purchased servants in question had any children, their masters were bound by law to incorporate them into the church and nation. These children then were the servants of the Lord, in the same sense as the natural descendants of Abraham were; and therefore, according to the law, Lev. xxv. 42, 55. they could not be made slaves. The passages of scripture under consideration were so far from authorising the Israelites to make slaves of their servants' children, that they evidently forbid it; and therefore are so far from proving the lawfulness of our enslaving the children of the Africans, that they clearly condemn the practice as criminal.

These passages of sacred writ have been wickedly pressed into the service of Mammon, perhaps more frequently than any others: but does it not now appear, that these weighty pieces of artillery may be fairly wrested from the enemy, and turned upon the hosts of the Mammonites, with very good effect?

DAVID RICE 1733–1816

The advocates for slavery should have observed, that in the law of Moses referred to, there is not the least mention made of the children of these servants, it is not said that they should be servants or any thing about them. No doubt some of them had children, but it was unnecessary to mention them; because they were already provided for by the law of circumcision.

To extend the law of Moses to the children of these servants, is arbitrary and presumptuous; it is making them include much more than is expressed or necessarily implied in the expression, *They shall be your bond men forever*; because the word *forever* is evidently limited by the nature of the subject; and nothing appears, by which it can be more properly limited, than the life of the servants purchased. The sense then is simply this, they shall serve you and your children as long as they live.

We cannot certainly determine how these persons were made servants at first; nor is it necessary we should. Whether they were persons who had forfeited their liberty by capital crimes; [19] or whether they had involved themselves in debt by folly or extravagance, and submitted to serve during their lives, in order to avoid a greater calamity; or whether they were driven to that necessity in their younger days, for want of friends to take care of them, we cannot tell. This however we may be sure of, that the Israelites were not sent by a divine law to nations three thousand miles distant, who were neither doing, nor mediating any thing against them, and with whom they had nothing to do; in order to captivate them by fraud or force, tear them away from their country and all their tender connections, bind them in chains, crowd them into ships, and there murder them by thousands, with the want of air and exercise; and then condemn the survivors and their posterity to slavery for ever.

But it is further objected, that the Apostle advises servants to be contented with their state of servitude, and obedient to their masters; and though he charges their masters to use them well, he no where commands them to set them free.

In order rightly to understand the matter, we should recollect the situation of Christians at this time. They were under the Roman yoke, the government of the heathen; who were watching every opportunity of charging them with designs against their government, in order to justify their bloody persecutions. In such circumstances, for the Apostle to have proclaimed liberty to the slaves, would probably have exposed many of them to certain destruction, brought ruin on the Christian cause, and that without the prospect of freeing one single man; which would have been the height of madness and cruelty. It was wise, it was humane in him not to drop a single hint on this subject, farther than saying, *If thou mayest be made free, use it rather.*

Though the Apostle acted with this prudent reserve, the unreasonableness of perpetual unconditional slavery, may easily be inferred from the righteous and benevolent doctrines and duties taught in the New Testament. It is quite evident, that slavery is contrary to the spirit and genius of the Christian religion. It is contrary to that excellent precept laid down by the divine author of the Christian institution, viz. *Whatsoever ye would that men should do to you do ye even so to them.* A precept so finely calculated to teach the duties of justice, to inforce their obligation, and induce the mind to obedience, that nothing can excel it. No man, when he views the hardships, the sufferings, the excessive labours, the unreasonable chastisements, the reparations between loving husbands and wives, between affectionate parents, and children, can say, were I in their place, I should be contented; I so far approve this usage, as to believe the law that subjects me to it, to be perfectly right: that I and my posterity should be denied the protection of law, and by it be exposed to suffer all these calamities; though I never forfeited my freedom, nor merited such treatment, more than others. No; there is an honest SOMETHING in our breasts, that hears testimony against this, as unreasonable and wicked. I found it in my own breast near forty years ago, and [20] through all the changes of time, the influence of custom, the arts of sophistry, and the facinations of interest, remains here still. I believe, it is a law of my nature; a law of more ancient date than any act of parliament; and which no human legislature can ever repeal. It is a law inscribed on every human heart; and may there be seen in legible characters, unless it is blotted by vice, or the eye of the mind blinded by interest. Should I do any thing to countenance this evil, I should fight against my own heart; should I not use my influence to annihilate it, my own conscience would condemn me.

It may be farther objected, this slavery, it is true, is a great evil; but still greater evils would follow their emanciption. Men who have laid out their money in purchase of slaves, and now have little other property, would certainly be great sufferers; the slaves themselves are unacquainted with the arts of life, being used to act only under the direction of others; they have never acquired the habits of industry; have not that sense of propriety and spirit of emulation necessary to make them useful citizens. Many have been so long accustomed to the meaner vices, habituated to lying, pilfering and stealing, that when pinched with want, they would commit these crimes, become pests to society, or end their days on the gallows. Here are evils on both hands, and of two evils, we should take the least.

This is a good rule, when applied to natural evils; but with moral evils it has nothing to do; for of these we must chuse neither. Of two evils, the one natural, the other moral, we must always chuse the natural evil; for moral evil, which is the same thing as sin, can never be a proper object of choice. Enslaving our fellow creatures is a moral evil; some of its effects are moral, and some natural. There is no way so proper to avoid the moral effects as by avoiding the cause. The natural evil effects of emancipation can never be a balance for the moral evils of slavery, or a reason why we should prefer the latter to the former.

Here we should consider, on whom these evils are to be charged; and we shall find they lie at our own doors, they are chargeable on us. We have brought one generation into this wretched state; and shall we therefore doom all the generations of their posterity by it? Do we find by experience, that this state of slavery corrupts and ruins human nature? And shall we persist in corrupting and ruining it in order to avoid the natural evils we have already produced? Do we find, as the ancient Poet said, that the day we deprive a man of freedom, we take away half his soul? and shall we continue to maim souls, because a maimed soul is unfit for society! Strange reasoning indeed! An astonishing consequence! I should have looked for a conclusion quite opposite to this, viz. that we should be sensible of the evil of our conduct, and persist in it no longer. To me this appears a very powerful argument against slavery, and a convincing proof of its iniquity. It is ruining God's creatures whom he has made free moral agents and accountable [21] beings; creatures who still belong to him; and are not left to us to ruin at our pleasure.

However, the objection is weighty, and the difficulty suggested great. But I do not think, that it is such as ought to deter us from our duty, or tempt us to continue a practice so inconsistent with justice and sound policy: therefore I give it as my opinion, that the first thing to be done is TO RESOLVE, UNCONDITIONALLY, TO PUT

AUGUSTA, KENTUCKY, 1792

AN END TO SLAVERY IN THIS STATE. This, I conceive, properly belongs to the convention; which they can easily effect, by working the principle into the constitution they are to frame.

If there is not in government some fixed principle superior to all law, and above the power of legislators, there can be no stability, or consistency in it; it will be continually fluctuating with the opinions, humours, passions, prejudices, or interests, of different legislative bodies. Liberty is an inherent right of man, of every man; the existence of which ought not to depend upon the mutability of legislation; but should be wrought into the very constitution of our government, and be made essential to it.

The divising ways and means to accomplish this end, so as shall best consist with the public interest, will be the duty of our future legislature. This evil is a tree that has been long planted, it has been growing many years, it has taken deep root, its trunk is large, and its branches extended wide; should it be cut down suddenly, it might crush all that grew near it; should it be violently eradicated, it might tear up the ground in which it grows, and produce fatal effects. It is true, the slaves have a just claim to be freed instantly: but by our bad conduct, we have rendered them incapable of enjoying, and properly using this their birth-right; and therefore a gradual emancipation only can be adviseable. The limbs of this tree must be lopped off by little and little, the trunk gradually hewn down, and the stump and roots left to rot in the ground.

The legislature, if they judged it expedient, would prevent the importation of any more slaves: they would enact that all born after such a date should be born free: be qualified by proper education to make useful citizens, and be actually freed at the proper age.

It is no small recommendation of this plan, that it so nearly coincides with the Mosaic law, in this case provided; to which even suppose it a human institution, great respect is due to its antiquity, its justice and humanity.

It would, I think, avoid in a great measure, all the evils mentioned in the objection. All that was the master's own, at the time fixed upon in the act, would still be his own: All that should descend from them would be his own until he was paid for their education. All he would lose would be the prospect of his children's being enriched at the expence of those who are unborn. Would any man murmur at

DAVID RICE 1733–1816

having this prospect, which was given him by a righteous law, that frees from oppression future generations?

[22] Is there any such man to be found? Let us stop a moment to hear his complaint. "I have long lived happy by oppression. I wanted to leave this privilege as an inheritance to my children. I had a delightsome prospect of their living also in ease and splendor at the expence of others; this iniquity was once sanctified by a law, of which I hope my children's children would have enjoyed the sweets; but now this hard-hearted, this cruel convention has cut off this pleasing prospect.

"They will not suffer my children to live in ease and luxury, at the expence of poor Africans. They have resolved, and alas! the resolution must stand forever, that black men in the next generation shall enjoy a fruit of their own labour, as well as white men; and be happy according to the merit of their own conduct. If justice is done to the offspring of negroes, mine are eternally ruined. If my children cannot, as I have done, live in injustice and cruelty, they are injured, they are robbed, they are undone. What—must young master saddle his own horse?—Must pretty little miss sweep the house and wash the dishes? and these black devils be free!—No heart can bear it!— Such is the difference between us and them, that it is a greater injury to us to be deprived of their labour, then it is to them to be deprived of their liberty and every thing else. This wicked convention will have to answer another day for the great injury they have done us, in doing justice to them."

Emancipation on some such plan as above hinted, would probably in many instances, be a real advantage to children in point of wealth. Parents would educate them in such a manner, and place them in such circumstances, as would be more to their interest, than possessing such unproductive estates as slaves are found to be.

The children would imbibe a noble independent spirit, learn a habit of managing business, and helping themselves. They would learn to scorn the mean and beggarly way of living, at the expence of others, living in splendour on plunder of the innocent. Where estates were wisely managed, children would not find their fortunes diminished. They would not be mocked with nominal, but possess real wealth; wealth that would not merely feed their vanity, but fill their coffers.

The children of the slaves, instead of being ruined for want of education, would be so brought up as to become useful citizens. The country would improve by their industry; manufacturers would flourish; and, in time of war, they would not be the terror, but the strength and defence of the state.

It may be farther objected, that to attempt, even in this gradual way, the annihilation of slavery in this country, where so many are deeply interested, might so sensibly touch the interest of some unreasonable men, as probably to stir up great confusion, and endanger the tranquility of our infant state.

Though I doubt not but some men of narrow minds, under the influence of prejudice or covetousness, might be made uneasy and [23] disposed to clamour; yet I apprehend but little danger of any ill effects. The measure would be so agreeable to the honest dictates of conscience, the growing sentiments of the country, and of many even of the slave-holders themselves, that any opposition they might make would not be supported; and they would be too wise to hazard the hastening an event they so much dread.

If the growing opinion of the unlawfulness of slavery should continue to grow, holding men in that state will soon be impracticable; there will be no cause existing sufficient to produce the effect, when this shall happen a certain event may suddenly take place, the consequences of which may be very disagreeable. This I take to be the proper time to prevent this evil. We may now do it in a peaceable manner, without going a step out of the way of our duty, and without hazarding what might be attended with tenfold more confusion and danger.

The slavery of the negroes began in iniquity; a curse has attended it, and a curse will follow it. National vices will be punished with national calamities. Let us avoid these vices, that we may avoid the punishment which they deserve; and endeavour so to act, as to secure the approbation and smiles of Heaven.

Holding men in slavery is the national vice of Virginia; and while a part of that state, we were partakers of the guilt. As a separate state, we are just now come to the birth; and it depends upon our free choice whether we shall be born in this sin, or innocent of it. We now have it in our power to adopt it as our national crime; or to bear a national testimony against it. I hope the latter will be our choice; that we shall wash our hands of this guilt; and not leave it in the power of a future legislature, ever more to stain our reputation or our conscience with it.

THE END

This work is re-printed at the request of many persons, some of whom belong to the SOCIETY OF FRIENDS, to whom it is now dedicated. It may, with their assistance, tend to aid the views of our Legislature in abolishing the representation of slaves, and eventually of the existence of slavery in this country.

[58]

THEODORE DWIGHT 1764–1846

*An Oration, Spoken Before the Connecticut
Society, for the Promotion of Freedom and the
Relief of Persons Unlawfully
Holden in Bondage*

HARTFORD, 1794

Dwight was educated at Yale University and later studied law. He earned his living mainly in the practice of law in Hartford, Connecticut, where he was a frequent contributor to newspapers and other journals, writing principally on political subjects. Public discussion of the conditions and consequences of slavery had become a common occurrence in New England and the Middle Atlantic States by the time Dwight entered the controversy. His effort is distinguished by his dealing with the issue in more than the abstract terms of rights. The effects of slavery on the slaves, their masters, and government and society in general are discussed in a rather comprehensive fashion.

If this assembly were convened, for the purpose of listening to a dissertation on the general subjects of freedom and slavery, the fact would appear singular, in the view of a stranger. For certainly, a nation, which has led the rest of the world to the consideration of these most interesting topics, and fully disclosed the nature of the latter, ought to furnish no employment for the advocate of the former. And if any thing can sound like a solecism in the ears of mankind, it will be this story—That in the United States of America, societies are formed for the promotion of freedom. Will not the enquiry instantly

THEODORE DWIGHT 1764–1846

be made—"Are the United States of America not free? Possessed of the best country, the wisest government, and the most virtuous inhabitants, on the face of the earth; are they still enslaved?" No— America is not enslaved; she is free. Her country is still excellent, her government wise, and her inhabitants virtuous. But this reply must be mixed with one base ingredient. The slavery of negroes is still suffered to exist. The answer being given, the astonishment will immediately [4] cease, and the enquiry become cool and spiritless. Whether negroes are enslaved, or free; miserable, or happy; are questions not interesting to their whiter masters. Placed by Providence in a more fortunate situation, and impelled by that love of domination, which is inherent in man, they become much more active in securing the subjects of their tyranny, than in the extension of human happiness. Nor is this all. Such is the depravity of our nature and the force of habit, that Reason is too often called in to aid the dictates of Passion, and sanction the cruelties of Tyranny.

The existence of African slavery then even in the State of Connecticut, being a fact which admits not of contradiction, the propriety of institutions like that, which has brought this audience together, will sufficiently appear. Nor will the frequent recurrence of this meeting, in the smallest degree lessen the importance of its duty. For tho' to the ear of cold and nerveless Apathy, the frequent detail of iniquities steadily committed, and of duties too often neglected, may be a tedious and painful talk; yet the benevolent heart can never be uninterested, when contemplating the prospect of his encreasing felicity.

There is not a point of view, in which African slavery has not been considered by men of the first talents for research, for detail, and for description. The labours of the poet, the historian, the legislator, and the divine, have often presented the subject in the strongest, and most odious colours. Still the evil exists; and Interest [5] alone has been able to withstand the united force of imagination, of eloquence, of truth, and of religion. I say interest alone; for I will venture to assert, that when it shall cease to be for the interest if mankind, to torture their fellow creatures in this wicked commerce, not one solitary individual will be found trafficking in human flesh. Those commands of the Deity, which are now impiously appealed to, as a sanction for barbarity and murder, will then be passed by unregarded; and these defenceless objects of cruelty, will be left in the quiet enjoyment of their native simplicity, innocence, and happiness. Where is the zealous apostle of truth, who, believing it to be the will of the compassionate God, that every being, among his creatures, who wears a sable complexion, should be reduced to the most abject servitude, would risque his property, his health, and his life, on a tedious and dangerous voyage, merely to fulfil the decrees of Heaven. It is presumed, that such an instance cannot be found, among the sons of men. And those persons who justify slavery by the permission, or command of God, must believe that the omniscient Jehovah paid but a slender regard to a part of his will, which is opposed by every emotion of generosity, compassion and sensibility, when he submitted the chance of its propagation, to the uncertain management of human interest.

Persuaded that Interest then is the only support of a practice so wicked, so detestable, and so destructive in its effects on the human mind, I shall be pardoned for the manifestation, at least of earnestness, in the following desultory remarks, on some of the reasons, urged against [6] that total abolition of slavery, in the State of Connecticut. These remarks may perhaps be interspersed, or succeeded by others, in some measure descriptive of its nature, and of its effects on the human mind.

Within a few years past, the subject of slavery has been repeatedly discussed, in the legislature of this state, with great force of reasoning, and eloquence. The injustice of it has been generally, if not uniformly acknowledged; and the practice of it severely reprobated. But, when the question of total abolition has been seriously put, it has met with steady opposition, and has hitherto miscarried, on the ground of political expediency—That is, it is confessed to be *morally wrong,* to subject any class of our fellow-creatures to the evils of slavery; but asserted to be *politically right, to keep them in* such subjection. Without attending to this strange, and unfounded doctrine, in itself, I will consider some of the arguments, used in support of that political rectitude.

It is said, that the slavery of negroes was introduced *by our ancestors*—who, are acknowledged to have been generally humane and pious, and yet never questioned its rectitude; from them it *descended to us;* therefore, as *we inherit* the evil, we are at liberty to extricate ourselves from it *by degrees;* and are not bound to do it *immediately.* In support of this doctrine, we are told—that, tho' *the blacks* have a claim to justice, *the whites* have also a claim; that by doing *strict justice* to them, we shall do *injustice* to ourselves; and that we ought not to consult the interests of *one part of the community, at the expense of another.*

[7] It being then acknowledged that the enslaving of Africans was wrong in the first instance, it must necessarily follow, that the continuance of it is wrong: for a continued succession of unjust actions, can never gain the pure character of justice. If it was originally wrong, it has never ceased to be wrong for a moment since; and length of time, instead of factioning, aggravates the transgression. This mode of reasoning is uniformly adopted by courts of justice, when deciding on questions of property, by the rules of municipal law. No tribunal ever admitted a plea of injustice on the part of a father in vindication of his son, to whom the fruits of his illegal, or wicked conduct had descended. So far is this from the fact, that every person, found guilty of withholding strict justice from his neighbour, on such a frivolous pretence, is forced by the laws of his country to compensate the person injured, for every moment, during which the claim remains unanswered. And certainly, the moral law enjoins a very different doctrine from that, against which I am contending. "I the Lord, am a jealous God, visiting the iniquities of the fathers, upon the children"—is a strong, and unequivocal language of the decalogue. And if any man should deny substantial right to another, for the reasons which I have mentioned, the voice of common sense, as well as of law, would justify his creditor in casting him into prison, until he should pay the uttermost farthing. And what is the real ground of this difference, in the administration of justice, between white men, and negroes? Simply this—the white men can appeal to the laws of their country, and enforce their rights. The negroes whom our fathers, and ourselves have enslaved, [8] have no tribunal to listen to their complaints, or to redress their injuries. Forced from their country, their friends, and their families, they are dragged to the sufferance of slavery, of torture, and of death, with no eye, and no arm, but the eye and arm of God, to pity, and to punish their wrongs. Society recognizes their existence, only for the purposes of injustice, oppression, and punishment.

By doing strict justice to the negroes, I presume is meant, totally to abolish slavery, and place them on the same ground, with free white men. The injustice, which, it is contended, will proceed from the immediate accomplishment of this end, in the first place respects the property of the persons who hold slaves. It is said that they were purchased under the sanction of the laws of the country; and therefore, arbitrarily to deprive the owners of such property without any retribution would be injustice. This is combining two questions which have no relation to each other. The right of the slave to liberty, in a distinct consideration, from the right of the master to a compensation for the loss of his slave. Nor will the act of government, in granting freedom to the slave, weaken the master's claim for that compensation; but if it is just, at the time when the slave is set at liberty, it will forever remain just until it is satisfied. Emancipating the slave then, subjects the master to no disadvantage in claiming from government the value of the slave; and therefore holding the slave in bondage, until compensation is made to the master, is clearly unjust.

[9] But this question must be considered on very different grounds. "The rights of persons," says a sensible writer on the laws of England, "considered in their natural capacities, are of two sorts, absolute and relative. By the absolute rights of mankind, we mean those, which are from their primary, and strictest sense; such as would belong to their persons merely in a state of nature, and which every man is entitled to enjoy, whether out of society, or in it. And these may be reduced to three principal, or primary articles, the right of personal security, the right of personal liberty, and the right of private property."* No person, who hears me, will deny the justice or reasonableness of this doctrine. Concerning it, then, as acknowledged, it is evident that the right of private property, standing in a station, subordinate to the right of personal security, and the right of personal liberty, means an inferiour consideration. Therefore, previously in discussing, and establishing the right of private property, the rights of personal security, and personal liberty, must be discussed, and established. If this reasoning be just, it is impossible, in any situation, or under the authority of any laws to acquire a property in a human being. For it cannot be acquired without violation of rights, to which he has a prior, and absolute claim; and which are of inconceivably greater importance. The result, then, must necessarily be, that, in abolishing African slavery, no injury is done to private property.

But granting, for the moment, that property [10] can be gained in the body and mind of man; a concession which can scarcely be made, for the sake of argument, without horror; I deny, that any such property ever was gained, in this state, under the sanction of law.

* Blackstone's Commentary.

THEODORE DWIGHT 1764–1846

Search the statute books of Connecticut, from the date of its Charter to the present moment, and tell me where is the law which establishes such an inhuman privilege? Happily for the honour of the state, those books were never stained with so black a statute. But it will be replied, that slavery is sanctioned by Prescription, and implicitly allowed by laws of the land. "To make a particular Custom good," says the accomplished jurisprudent, from whom I have already quoted, "the following are necessary requisites—That it have been used so long, that the memory of man runneth not to the contrary. So that if any one can shew the beginning of it, it is no good custom." It would not be a difficult task, to discover the beginning of the Custom under consideration. "It must have been continued. Which must be understood of the right; for if the right be any how discontinued for a day, the Custom is quite at an end."—The right of the Custom of slavery, is given up by much the greater part of the community. "It must have been peaceable—It must be reasonable." Surely no man will contend that this Custom is either peaceable, or reasonable. The reason of man rises in uniform opposition to it; and it is marked in every stage with war, barbarity, and murder.

But if this Prescription, or Custom, when tried by the rules of the English common law, would stand the test, still I contend, that no prescriptive right, can infringe the absolute rights of [11] mankind. These, especially personal security, and personal liberty, cannot be violated but by the positive laws of society. Such laws, I have already remarked, do not exist, in the code of Connecticut. But in that code there does exist a law, which speaks emphatically the opposite language. "No man's person shall be arrested, restrained, or any ways punished— No man shall be deprived of his wife, or children—No man's goods or estate shall be taken away from him, nor any ways indamaged, under colour of the law, or countenance of authority, unless clearly warranted by the laws of this state." Are not negroes men? Are they not arrested, restrained, and punished? Are they not deprived of their wives, and children? Are not their goods and estate taken from them, and endamaged, under colour of law, and countenance of authority alone? For the Custom, so often mentioned, can have no force, if there is a positive statute authorizing African slavery; and if there is no such statute, African slavery must owe its existence, solely to the countenance of authority.

But to make a still stronger concession, in favour of the friends

of slavery than those already made, viz. That the absolute rights of
individuals *are* subject to violation, under the authority of custom,
and that such custom, having obtained, *is* clearly warranted by the
laws of this state, yet I venture to assert, that no Custom and no Law,
which a state where slavery is practised, either has made, or can make,
ought to affect the enslaved negroes at all, unless designed as a partial
compensation for the injuries which they have suffered—injuries, for
which all the wealth of man can never atone. The right of society to
make [12] laws of any description, depends entirely on the original
compact, which formed the society. This compact, must have the real,
or implied assent of every person, who is to be bound by the regulations
of the society. Every person, then, who is forced to submit to the
laws, and institutions of society, has a right to be heard, either in
person, or by his representative, when those laws, and institutions are
framed; and every person, who is forced to submit to such laws and
institutions, without the opportunity of being thus heard, is forced
to submit to the hard, and oppressive hand of Tyranny. Slaves then,
having never really, nor impliedly agreed to any social compact, and
never being heard, either personally, or representatively in the
legislature, form no part of the social body; and therefore cannot justly
be the object of laws, except in the case I have already instanced. On
the contrary, so far from uniting voluntarily with societies, in this
country, they are bro't into them by force, and by force subjected to
the laws, and regulations of powers, which they never acknowledged,
and to which they owe neither obedience, nor gratitude. Being thus
forced into a state of hostility, if defensive war is susceptible of
justification, in any possible instance, this is that instance. Their lives,
their property, their liberty, their happiness, are perpetually exposed
to the inroads of every merciless invader. And tho', as the finishing
stroke to their systems of guilt, societies think fit to punish those acts
in slaves, which indeed in their own members, would be both civil
and moral evils; yet, probably on the strength of reasoning similar to
that which I have adopted, an elegant English writer, pronounces it
"impossible for a slave, to be guilty of a civil crime." The same law,
[13] which justifies the enormities, committed by civilized nations,
when engaged in war, will justify slaves for every necessary act of
defence, against the wicked, and unprovoked outrages, committed
against their peace, freedom, and existence.

But this question of expediency, is entitled to a still further

consideration. It is said by the opposers of abolition, that the slaves
are happier with their masters, than they could be, if possessed of
freedom. Who is it that decides for them? Have the slaves been asked
the question? Shall the man, whose heart rejoices in the opportunity
of tyrannizing over the happiness of an abject wretch, whom force has
subjected to his domination, prescribe enjoyments for that wretch?
Let the inestimable jewel of freedom, be held out to their acceptance
by the hand of legislation, and with it some shadow of compensation
for their indescribable sufferings, and then, if they refuse it, let them
serve their masters forever. But, until that has been done, let decency
forbid the mouth of the savage, to utter the shameful falsehood.

Perhaps the strain, in which I have spoken, may be censured, as
dangerous to the peace of society. But if I have spoken the words of
truth and soberness, I will risque the charge. Few men love their
country with a more sincere, and ardent affection, than myself. Dear
as it is to me, I am more solicitous for its justice, than for its peace.
But when justice can be rendered, without disturbing the public
tranquillity, it becomes a duty of the most peremptory and indispensible
nature.

[14] In surveying the history of those countries, where domestic
slavery has been carried to its greatest length, the mind is forcibly
impressed with its detestable consequences on the human character.
One of the most obvious, is a disposition to cruelty and injustice.
Children are trained up from the cradle, in habits of punishment and
revenge. Unrestrained, by their parents, from an implicit obedience
to the dictates of passion, they regard slaves only as objects of
convenience, oppression, and torture; and often embrue their infant
hands in the blood of Innocence. Under the influence of such an
education, they advance in life, improving in the most inhuman, and
destructive qualities. For the most trifling offence, and frequently for
the sake of amusement, the slave is doomed to the sufferance of the
most ingenious barbarity. And when grown to adult years, with a
mind as debased as cruel, the imperious, and unprincipled master,
satiates his brutal passion on violated chastity. And when the offspring
of his guilty embraces, opens its eyes on the light of the sun, instead
of the protection, the support, and the affection of a father, it
experiences the injustice, the barbarity, and the vengeance of a tyrant.
Nay, masters procreate the slaves, which not only perform every
menial, and degrading office for them, but often are sold by them in

market, like the beasts of the field. And however shocking it may
sound to our ears, the instances are doubtless too frequent, in which
the innocent offspring of the master and servant, not only becomes
the slave of her unnatural brother, but is also forced to submit to his
horrid and incestuous passion.

[15] Another consequence of slavery, is a spirit of denomination.
For proof of this, we may apply to those parts of the United States,
where slavery is most extensively practiced. In the four southern states,
there exists the strongest spirit of aristocracy to be found in the union.
This assertion I dare to make, in defiance of all the clamour, which
can be raised to contradict it. Where is that spirit of republicanism,
equality, freedom, and emnity to tyranny, of which they so arrogantly
boast? Believe me, they exist but in sound. Domestic despotism rides
triumphantly over the liberties, and happiness of thousands of our
fellow-creatures, in each of those pretended republics. In no other
country on earth, is slavery carried to such a length of oppression.
Not contented with the common round of cruelty and wickedness,
the masters there mock their slaves with the name of privileges, which
they never enjoy; and thus force them to contribute to the strengthening
of the powers, which hold them in bondage. Enjoying no rank in the
community, and possessing no voice, either in elections, or legislation,
the slaves are bro't into existence, in the Constitution of the United
States, merely to afford opportunity for a few more of their masters,
to tyrannize over their liberties. And no event could fill these states
with such alarming apprehensions, as the erection of the standard of
Freedom among their enslaved subjects. Therefore, before they upbraid
the citizens of the northern states, with an attachment to the principles
of aristocracy, or monarchy, let them begin the equal communication
of those privileges, which *in theory,* they confess to be the birth right
of man. Let them visit New-England, and learn the rudiments [16]
of freedom. Here they will find, at least in some places, and God
grant I may speedily say in all, that instead of the lawful distance
between the master and the slave, each inhabitant is as independent
as the insolent planter. That here,

> "Tho' poor the peasant's hut, his feast tho' small,
> He sees his little lot the lot of all;
> Sees no contiguous palace rear its head
> To shame the meanness of his humble shed;
> No costly lord the sumptuous banquet dear,

To make him loath his healthful, homely meal;
But calm, and bred in innocence and toil,
Each wish contracting fits him to the soil.
Cheerful at morn he wakes from short repose,
Breathes the keen air, and carols as he goes.
At night returning, every labour sped,
He sits him down the monarch of a shed,
Smiles by his cheerful fire, and round surveys
His children's looks, which brighten at the blaze."*

On the whole, every species of wickedness results from slavery, wherever it exists. The inhabitants, in the common course of events, become licentious in the commission of every immorality. All the honest, and virtuous employments of life, falling to the share of the slaves, the master naturally avoids them as unworthy of his dignity, and plunges into habits of indolence, and vice, equally destructive, and disgraceful to society. Even the females, forgetting those amiable, and endearing qualities, which bend the fiercer nature of man to gentleness and love, indulge themselves in paroxisms of rage; and under the influence of the most ferocious passions, seize the engines of torture, [17] and with their feeble force, inflict on their unhappy servants the keenest misery. See a picture, drawn by one of the most humane and ingenious of her sex.

"Lo! where reclin'd, pale Beauty courts the breeze,
Diffused on sofas of voluptuous ease,
With anxious awe, her menial train around,
Catch her faint whispers of unutter'd sound.
See her in monstrous fellowship unite
At once the Scythian, and the Sybarite;
Blending repugnant vices, misallied,
Which frugal nature purpos'd to divide.
See her with indolence, to fierceness join'd,
Of body delicate, infirm of mind,
With languid tones imperious mandates urge,
With arm recumbent wield the household scourge,
And with unruffled mien, and placid sounds,
Contriving torture, and inflicting wounds."†

* Goldsmith.
† Mrs. Barbauld

HARTFORD, 1794

At the present period, when the principles of liberty are so highly revered, and the practice of them so justly admired, every question, in which they are involved, ought to be discussed by the soundest reason, and established on the most substantial justice. For when the persons interested in the event of such discussion, are of sufficient force to be formidable, those who are hardy enough to withhold their unalienable rights, will find themselves plunged in a deluge of calamity. Every instance on historical record, and every example before our eyes, abundantly teaches this solemn truth. Without wasting time in multiplying cases, I will only resort to one of the latter description. The situation of France, and some of her most important [18] colonies, affords a melancholy proof, that a deviation from the path of reason and justice, in the pursuit of freedom, is necessarily attended, with the most distressing evils. When the councils of the nation were guided by discretion and integrity, the surrounding world beheld with admiration and applause, a stupendous object in the great system of Providence—one of the most numerous and mighty nations, on the earth, led by the hand of Reason alone to the acquisition of freedom and happiness. But when the government was siezed by a profligate, and blood-thirsty junto, which, for a period, forced the infatuated republic to assassination and ruin.

> "Then fell the flower of Gallia, mighty names,
> Her scary senators, and gasping patriots.
> The Mountain spake, and their licentious band
> Of blood-train'd ministry were loos'd to ruin,
> Invention wanton'd in the toil of servants
> Stabb'd on the breast, or reeking on the points
> Of sportive javelins. Husbands, sons and sires,
> With dying ears drank in the loud despair
> Of shrieking Chastity. The waste of war
> Was peace and friendship to their civil massacres."*

From France, turn your attention to the island of St. Domingo. A succession of unjust, and contradictory measures, in both the national and colonial governments, at length highly exasperated the negroes, and roused their spirits to unanimity and fanaticism. Seized by the phrenzy of oppressed human nature, they suddenly awoke from the lethargy of slavery, attacked their tyrannical masters, spread desolation

* Brooke.

THEODORE DWIGHT 1764–1846

and blood over the face of the colony, and by a series of vigorous efforts, established themselves on [19] the firm pillars of freedom and independence. Driven from their houses and possessions, by new and exulting masters, the domestic tyrants of that island wander over the face of the earth, dependent on the uncertain hand of Charity for shelter, and for bread. To the honour of Americans, it is true, that in this country, they have realized the most liberal humanity. But by a dispensation of Providence which Humanity must applaud, they are forced to exhibit, in the most convincing manner, this important truth—that despotism and cruelty, whether in the family, or the nation, can never resist one angry, or enraged and oppressed man, struggling for freedom.

These evils may perhaps appear distant from us; yet to some of our sister states they are probably nigh, even at the doors. Ideas of liberty and slavery, have taken such stronghold of the negroes, that unless their situation is suddenly ameliorated, the inhabitants of the southern states, will have the utmost reason to dread the effects of insurrection. And with the example of the West-Indies before their eyes, they will be worse than mad, if they do not adopt effectual measures to escape their danger. To oppose the slaves by force when in a state of rebellion, or to hold them in their present condition, for any considerable length of time in future, will be beyond their strength. Courage and discipline, form but a feeble front to check the onset of freedom.

> "For what are fifty, what a thousand slaves,
> Match'd to the sinew of a single arm
> That strikes for liberty?"*

And when hostilities are commenced, where shall they look for auxiliaries in such an iniquitous [20] warfare? Surely, no friend to freedom and justice will dare to lend them his aid. In the case, not essentially different in principle from the one under consideration, except its being less aggravated, the God of Heaven has uttered the following denunciation. "Therefore thus saith the Lord, ye have not harkened unto me, in proclaiming liberty every one to his neighbour, and every man to his brother: Behold I proclaim a liberty for you, saith the Lord, to the sword, to the pestilence, and to the famine.

* Brooke.

And I will make you to be removed into all the face of the earth. And I will give the men that have transgressed my covenant, into the hand of their enemies, and into the hand of them, which seek their life. And their dead bodies shall be for meat unto the fowls of heaven, and to the beasts of the earth."* Nor can the threatenings in this passage be avoided, under the idea, that it is a prophecy, remote, and uninteresting to us. It contains nothing more than the natural and necessary consequences of slavery, in every country, where the slaves are more numerous than their masters. Indeed the prophecy has been most minutely fulfilled in the island already mentioned.

In this state indeed, and with the sincerest pleasure I make the remark, in consequence of the small number of slaves, the advancement of civilization, and the diffusion of a liberal policy, the situation of the negroes is essentially different. Exposed to few severe punishments, and indulged in many amusements, compared with what is found in most other countries, they are here flourishing, and happy. But even here they are slaves. The very idea embitters every enjoyment. [21] So necessary is freedom to happiness, that the mind, well informed of its nature, and acquainted with its blessings, if subjected to the will of an arbitrary and cruel master, would be wretched and solitary, altho' surrounded by all the pleasures of the garden of God. But as slaves do in fact exist in Connecticut, the inhabitants of the state, as it respects this great subject, must be divided into two classes—those, who justify slavery in the abstract—and those, who condemn it. And this general division will be found to comprehend every intermediate stage of character. For tho' the number of persons is small, who will avowedly advocate the principles of slavery; yet such persons do not only exist, but have the hardihood to appeal for arguments to support their barbarous sentiments, to the fountain of our holy religion, which breathes nought but peace and good will to man. But there is another more specious description of persons, which I class among the enemies of the freedom and happiness of mankind. These persons professedly acknowledge the wickedness of slavery, and still, on the pretence of political expedience, use every artifice of ingenuity and fraud, to rivet the fetters, which bind their fellow creatures in bondage. Such persons, deaf to the voice of Reason, and the supplications of Humanity, bend every object to the advancement of their wealth, and the gratification

---

* Jeremiah, Chap. xxxiv, 17, 20.

of their ambition; while the groans of dying Innocence, the screams of violated Chastity, and the ravings of tortured Maniacks, would sleep on their ears like the gentle musick of the passing gale. To such persons, as well as to those of the second class, which I have mentioned, a few enslaved, wretched beings, appeal for the blessings of freedom. [22] On the part of the slaves, it is a question of right; and on that of the state, a question of justice—a question, which cannot be suppressed by the strong pleadings of Avarice, nor hidden in the subterfuges of Sophistry. The first of these spirits is not more opposed to humanity, than the latter is to integrity. Sophistry may at times assist the advocate at the bar, when espousing the cause of iniquity; but in a legislator it must ever be infamous, and the conscience of an honest man will never submit to its imposition. Nor should motives of ambition be suffered to operate, to the destruction of human happiness. It is a possession of too much value, to be held by so frail a tenure. Depraved indeed must be the heart of that man, who will swerve from the rigid rules of justice and duty, to aid his ambitious projects. Equally depraved, and if possible more execrable is the unfeeling savage, who will lengthen out the misery of a fellow being with a smile of sarcastic pleasure on his fraudful countenance. In the hour of distress and apprehension, gloomy and bitter must be the reflections of such a mind. But to the mind animated with a love of justice, and glowing with the purest benevolence, the valley of the shadow of death, will open a peaceful passage to the preference of his God.

If the arguments which I have used, as well as innumerable others which are constantly urged in opposition to slavery, cannot be fully answered and refuted, may it not be hoped, that this relique of oppression, so odious and so wicked, will be speedily extirpated in the state of Connecticut. Why should a countenance in this happy land, be saddened with the melancholy evil! [23] Can it be urged as a reason for its continuance, that the slaves, not being numerous enough to become troublesome, are unworthy of the public attention? A regard to the happiness of beings, occupying but a point in his dominions, destitute even of the claim of justice, and dependent on his will for existence, induced the Son of the living God to exchange the bosom of his Father, for a cruel, and ignominious death. And shall we refuse so slightly to imitate this illustrious example? The slaves are sufficiently numerous, and sufficiently important, to be highly injured, by being stripped of the only blessing, which can render life worth enjoying. For where is the being, who would not rather yield up his life a sacrifice, than part with his freedom? The wretch, if such an one can be found, is unworthy of the name of man.

Who then can charge the negroes with injustice, or cruelty, when "they rise in all the vigour of insulted nature," and avenge their wrongs? What American will not admire their exertions, to accomplish their own deliverance? Every friend to justice and freedom, while his heart bleeds at the recital of the devastation and slaughter, which necessarily attend such convulsions of liberty, must thank his God for the emancipation of every individual from the miseries of slavery. This is the language of freedom; but it is also the language of truth—a language which ever grates on the ears of tyrants, whether placed at the head of a plantation, or the head of an empire. Every description of them, sooner than be deprived of domination—

> Would rather see
> This earth a desart, desolate, and wild,
> And like a lion stalk his lonely round,
> Famish'd, and roaring for his prey."*

[24] But this spirit, has neither charms to allure, nor terrors to awe the inhabitants of America. Having resisted it in the full vigour of manhood, they will disdain to yield to it in the imbecility of infancy. And indeed, submission would not only be deeply degrading, but extremely dangerous—dangerous, not to liberty alone, but to security and peace. Those tender plants can never flourish, on the bleak and barren soil of Slavery. For the same principles, which lead nations to the attainment of freedom, urge individuals to pursue the same important object; and the struggles of the latter, are as often marked with desperation as the efforts of the former. Indeed, from individuals, the spirit is generally communicated to states, and from states to nations. And since the mighty, and majestic course of Freedom has begun, nothing but the arm of Omnipotence can prevent it from reaching to the miserable Africans. But let the domestic tyrants of the earth, tremble at the approaches of such a destructive enemy. For should they even attempt to oppose it, either by strategem or force—

"Devouring War, shall wake his bloody band

---

* Brooke

THEODORE DWIGHT 1764–1846

At Freedom's call, and scourge their guilty land.
And while this thundering chariot rolls along,
And scatters discord o'er the fated throng,
Death in the man, with Anger, Hate, and Fear,
And Desolation stalking in the rear,
Revenge, by Justice guided, with his train,
Shall drive impetuous o'er the trembling plain."**

** Altered from Churchill

[59]

AMERICANUS

[TIMOTHY FORD 1762–1830]

The Constitutionalist: Or, An Inquiry How
Far It Is Expedient and Proper to Alter the
Constitution of South Carolina

CHARLESTON, 1794

Born and raised in New Jersey, Ford graduated from Princeton and studied law in New York. Thereafter he practiced law in Charleston, South Carolina, where he was prominent in public life and civic affairs. Between September 29 and November 10, 1794, Ford published ten essays in Charleston's *City Gazette and Daily Advertiser* under the name Americanus. At issue was the demand by those in the uplands of South Carolina, the Piedmont area west of the first set of falls, for a redistricting of the legislature to take into account population shifts during the previous two decades. Those in the eastern tidewater region, now in a minority among the voting population, naturally opposed such reapportionment, as well as any attempt to reapportion the upper house on the basis of anything but wealth. Ford, speaking for the tidewater interests, outlines a theory of representation drawn from a conservative Whig perspective that looks back to the pre-Revolution era for its roots, and foreshadows the Southern view until the Civil War. Only the first seven essays are reproduced here because the last three are taken up with specific and technical details of proposed districts.

No. I.

It has been customary amongst theoretical writers on government, to deduce the rights of man from an ideal state, called a state of nature.

AMERICANUS

This is a state in which the human race is supposed to have been placed by their Maker, the world being a great common, and man the incumbent; a state in which each one had a right to take what he wanted from the objects that surrounded him but acquired no property in what he did take, except while using or consuming it; that the moment he laid it out of his hand, it reverted to the general mass, and became the equal property of all, by ceasing to be the peculiar property of any. Possession was the only legitimate mode of acquiring right, and that right could be secured only by consuming the subject. The part that remained unconsumed, though only laid down upon the turf while the possessor could go to the spring and drink, immediately belonged to the byestander, who, in his absence might incline to take it up. To make the hypothesis better answer the ends of its creation, it goes on to say, that in this state *might* and *right* were synonimous terms; and he who wrested from the hands of his weaker neighbour the root which he had dug out of the ground, or the prey which he had hunted in the forest, acquired the privilege of calling it his own. That the state of nature was by this means a scene of constant strife, and man the most barbarous savage of the wilderness; that victory and defeat were the only events that could be recorded, and alternate plunder the only intercourse amongst God's creation; that the moral principle had no place amongst men, mere inclination being the only incentive to action, and their will the only law they knew. The hypothesis then supposes, that men, grown weary of a state so barbarous and bloody, at length took up the idea of associating together in a compact, in order that they might, by the united strength, curb the outrageous, and protect the weak and pusilanimous; that by this means the world was transformed [4] from a state of nature to a state of society, from a state of war to a state of peace.

There is a rule in arithmetic called the *rule of false,* which teaches us by assuming some numbers known not to be true, but working with them as though they were true, to find out that which is really so. Fortunately, arithmetic furnishes other methods of arriving at the truth, and I should be sorry if it were the only science that could boast of that prerogative. Indeed, the very rule itself requires, that as there should be some other rule by which it can be tested; no man could ever know that the conclusions to which he might be conducted by the *rule of false* were just, unless he had the result of a true rule to compare them with. The only advantage derivable from the fact is, that we are thereby taught that falsehood may be so disguised under the garb of truth, as to confound all distinction between them, unless the mind be guarded by caution.

Now, it is manifest, that such a state as is called a state of nature never in fact existed since the creation of Adam and Eve. Man was no sooner born, than he was associated under some common tie, which bound the human race together. The first knowledge he had of himself was this. Nature implanted the ties, habit confirmed them, and experience approved them. Man knew his powers and his rights, before the fancy of philosophers ever engendered this ideal state; and felt the relation in which he stood to his fellowmen, by rules superior to those which were metaphysically deduced from it. The laws of nature he knew from his own experience; but a state of nature was neither intelligible nor credible. When he was told, that what he acquired by his own industry was *his own,* he understood it; but when he was talked to of a state of nature, in which nothing was his own, but that he had felt the inconveniencies of his weak and destitute situation, and had transferred himself into a state of society in order to acquire property, he recollected nothing of it. He attended to the narrative concerning it, as to a fairy tale which amused his curiosity; but when he sat down soberly to reflect upon his rights and his duties, he placed himself under the direction of his senses, and deduced his rule of conduct from the real situation which he found he occupied in the world, and which he understood to be much the same as [5] the generations of men who had gone before. It appeared safer to reason upon things *as they are,* than *as they might have been;* rather upon that which was real, than upon that which feigned. Nor was he destitute of sufficient lights to guide his reason. Observing that every man came into the world equally naked and helpless, and all returned to a state of perfect equality in the grave, he easily inferred that each was by nature as good as his neighbour. When he experienced hunger and thirst, cold and nakedness, he learnt the necessity and the means of remedying them at the same time. Feeling that the benevolencies and affections of the heart rewarded their possessor with peculiar gratification, and made all around him contented and happy; and perceiving that the angry passions harrowed up his own repose, and threw all around him into a state of ferment and confusion; he at once learnt the value of the social duties and kindred virtues. When he trangressed the rules which these virtues invariably suggested, he felt a degree of self reproach; and when he performed them, of self-approbation; which taught him to mark the difference between good and evil, virtue and vice. The principles of honor and shame sprung spontaneously from the evolutions of the moral sense; and man was at once referred to a monitor within, to which he entrusted the government of his actions. When he surveyed his strength and his faculties, and found that they were subjected by nature to his own volition only, and that each was endowed with his portion thereof, he easily learnt that the portion allotted to each individual belonged exclusively to himself. When he perceived that in the exercise of them he could procure what nature prompted him to desire he learnt that the things procured belonged to himself in the same manner. The rules of justice resulted from every thing he saw and felt. It was easy to conclude, that no one could take from another the fruits of his faculties, since he could not command the faculties themselves. Each one was of course entitled to his acquisitions in proportion to his own exertions, or to the degree of ability which nature had conferred; for it was soon evinced that she had her favorites. In a word, the moral principle aided by experience, and unfolding itself at every turn, became the able instructor and the unerring guide of man; his rights, his interests, his duties and his obligations naturally [6] sprung from this source; he felt it in every emotion, and saw it exemplified in all the works of nature. But, as the first station he found himself in was the social, so his first and all his subsequent reflections arose in it; its benefits and conveniencies, which every day's experience demonstrated, were not considered as the moving cause with man to form that state, but as the substantial reason why he was placed in it. Unbiassed nature could never believe that the Maker of man placed him in a state excessively bad, and that he altered it for the better by a contrivance of his own. The inference which man naturally drew from every thing he saw, knew and felt, was, that God placed him in a social state, but left the regulation of the terms of association to himself. To be associated, therefore, was the law of his nature; but the modification of the social compact was to be governed by those various circumstances in which each society might find themselves; each was at liberty to form their own contract, and fix their own principles.

The Scythians might choose one mode, the companions of Cecrops another, and the followers of Romulus, a third; each might bind themselves by their own institutes, but could not be bound by those of one another. Men did not, therefore, learn their rights from the form of the compact they made, but made the compact the means of protecting the rights which they had previously ascertained to belong to them as associating beings. To say then, that this or that particular right is the offspring of a social compact, if true at all, is not the whole truth, and therefore misleads. Every substantial right depends as much upon society as every other. The right of property is generally adduced as an instance of what is derived merely from the social compact. To prove this, it is said, that the strong rob the weak of their acquisitions in a state of nature, and therefore that the institution of society is necessary to guarantee the possession and enjoyment of them. Yielding for a moment to the supposition of such a state as is called a state of nature, I will prove that the right to life depends on the same principle: for, let me ask, if the same superiority of strength in that state, is not equally sufficient to take the life? and not the combined force of society equally necessary to protect it? It follows then, that life, and every other right, are as much the gift [7] or emanation of society, as the right of property; because, it must be confessed, that in a state of nature they are equally subject to the invasion of the strong. Will it be answered, that life being the gift of nature, and necessarily existent under her laws, is to be distinguished from property, which being a subsequent acquisition made by man, has no dependence on the laws of nature? It will not avail; for the preservation of life is nature's first law, and she herself points out the means. These consist in the fruits of the earth, or the prey of the forest, acquired by him whose existence is to be preserved thereby; to take these away, is to take life itself. If, therefore, the right to the property thus acquired be not a natural right, neither is the right to life such: for, I can see no substantial difference between taking away the life of a man by intercepting his food, or by strangling. Nor is this right of property confined to mere present subsistence, as it is very easy to evince. Nature has ordained a period to the bodily powers, short of that she has assigned for life. She has implanted in man as strong an attachment to his existence when those powers have sunk under the elapse of years, as when the vigor of youth enabled him to provide the requisites of life. She has bestowed upon him in youth more strength and activity than the current exigencies of life require, with an evident reference to the wants and imbecility of his declining years. She has, therefore, announced to him, that the time will come when he will wish to live, and shall not be able, unless he devotes the surplus of his youthful strength to provide for his helpless condition when age shall have dissolved his nerves. Thus having implanted in every man the right to future as well as present existence, and appointed the same means for both, the right and the means are as clear and inviolable in the one case as the other. To this we may add, that she has laid her strongest injunctions on man to provide for the infant years of his offspring; the right to that provision, when made, is therefore as strong as is the right of his offspring to life.

The conclusion then is, that the right of property, as well as those of life and liberty, are the gifts of nature. The end of civil society is to guard them by stronger sanctions, the moral sense being too weak and too unequal amongst men for that purpose. The two last are common to all men in [8] equal degrees; the first is common to all, but the degree depends upon the endowments of nature, and industry and success in the pursuit. The idle and the indigent acquire no title, under the social compact to supply their own remissness out of the acquisitions of the industrious; yet this is ever the tendency of human nature: against this the social institutions ought chiefly to be directed. If an individual attempt it, he is instantly punished by the sentence of the laws, as an invader both of natural and social right. No aggregation of numbers can sanction the act; and that social compact or constitution must be exceedingly imperfect, which does not protect the industrious as well against public rapacity as against private robbery. The latter we know can be at all times suppressed; it is from the former that most is to be apprehended, and against it therefore the civil institutions ought chiefly to be directed. When men confederate for wicked purposes, their numbers keep them in coun-tenance; and under the plausible pretence of being a majority, they may be led to attempt that which, as individuals, they would blush to avow. And when by deceitful casuistry, they are reconciled to the attempt of preying upon the possessions of the wealthy, the point of satiety is the only one at which they will be likely to stop. Where this point is, would be hard to know. The merely malevolent passions expire of their own violence, or subside with the blood; perfidy and fraud may out-run their means, or grow tired: but rapacity, when once put into motion, knows no bounds short of exhausting the objects. Small successes are the parents of greater desires; the sweets of enjoyment tempt on the pursuit, and that which began in vice becomes sanctioned by precedent.

No. II.

[9] The natural rights of men undoubtedly form the rational foundation of the social compact. I say the *rational* foundation; for, it cannot be doubted, that if man be a free agent, endowed by nature with the power of disposing of his own situation in the world, he may in this and every other instance make a compact or agreement irrational and foolish. I have shewn, in a former number, that these natural rights are derived from the laws of necessities of nature; that is, what is common and necessary to all men, as such, must spring from nature. It is not requisite to frame the fanciful system of a *state of nature,* in order to learn what these are; for, as the laws of nature cannot be changed, so neither can they be beholden to any contrivances of man. They illustrate and prove themselves. *Life, liberty* and *property,* have been adduced as the chief among the natural rights of men. The two former are common to all men, and in equal degree; the latter is indeed common to all, but the degree depends upon industry and success. That very industry, while it produces the personal benefit of each individual, constitutes the prosperity, strength and comfort of the whole. It is as necessary to the *existence* of the body-politic, under its best organization, as to the *existence* of the individual in the supposed natural state. A variety of writers have attempted to shew what a people ought to do when they form a social compact for the purpose of perpetuating or securing their rights. If the *natural rights* were the only matters to be regarded, perpetuated or secured by the institution of society, the rules which they commonly frame would be liable to fewer exceptions. It is here that their fancied state of nature misleads them; they first of all place man naked and destitute amongst the roving animals of the forest, where they run for some time without connection, and almost without knowledge of one another; then they collect their rude materials into a plain and form a horde, and out of this horde springs a social compact. Here, as every man comes out of the same rude situation of nakedness and savage barbarity, all are to start even and equal in the career of society, no interest being acquired by any, with nothing in possession, but every thing in pursuit, the

object of the association may be summed up in a short sentence—
"Life, liberty and property shall be secured [10] to all;" and all that
would be required of a constitution would be to provide the means of
accomplishing that end. But as such a previous state never existed but
in the dreams of theorists, so the rules that are formed upon it must
be imperfect for a practical system. If men, at the formation of a
compact or constitution, are in fact possessed of acquired rights, and
vested interests, these must be regarded, or the compact will embrace
but one half of its object. Instead of being founded upon the principles
of reason and justice, it would be evidently partial; and the descriptions
of people, whose peculiar rights and interests were thus discarded from
the compact, in subscribing to it, would authenticate the evidence of
their own folly.

A late ingenious author* seems to have had a view to this
distinction, when he says, "Besides the general maxims of legislation
which apply to all, there are particular circumstances confined to each
people, which must influence their establishment, and render their
regulations proper only for themselves. Thus we see that the Hebrews
formerly, and the Arabs in later times, have had religion for their
principal object; the Athenians, literature; Tyre and Carthage, commerce; Rhodes, her marine; Sparta, war; and Rome, virtue." If the
accidental state into which society may be thrown after the formation
of a constitution, ought to influence the laws and regulations, by
parity of reason ought the pre-existent state of the people themselves
to influence the consitution. For what purpose is it made, if not to
suit the state and condition of men? The natural rights of man ought
indeed to be common to all constitutions; but the real situation of
each people ought to govern their own institutes, and make them
peculiar to themselves. The natural rights of man can never vary in
any society, because they are built upon the eternal principles of
nature; but the interests of man are subject to all those vicissitudes to
which the state of society is itself liable. Where there is but one specie
of interest among the people who are about to adjust their association
it will be as easy to adopt their constitution to their acquired interests
as to their natural rights. If they were all shepherds, whatever
guaranteed the interests of one, would serve for all.[11] If they were
all huntsmen or husbandmen, the rules would still be simple and

* Rousseau

plain. But if the husbandmen should come to associate with the shepherds, the latter would necessarily stipulate, that the pastures should not all be turned up by the plow; and if the huntsmen should join both, the one would stipulate that they should not frighten away or scatter the flocks; the other that they should not trample the fields of grain. And here it is proper to distinguish the rights of prior occupants from those of subsequent emigrants. It can never be contended under any laws, human or divine, that a body of husbandmen have a right to enter upon the peaceful society of shepherds, and prescribe their own terms of association.

This would be neither a social nor a *civil* compact; it would be a forcible invasion of right, which is the very thing the social compact is intended to avoid. If the prior occupants were free, they would surely have a right to prescribe to the new comers such stipulations as would effectually guard their acquired interests; and all that the latter could in decency ask, would be such stipulations as would secure to them the enjoyment of all the natural rights, and the benefit of all their acquired interests. If the interests of the two were of such a nature as to be utterly inconsistent and incapable of union, the emigrants ought to seek some other place, or some other people, and leave the prior occupants to themselves, none the worse for their visit. But if a union should be still insisted upon by the visitants, they ought to take the benefit, willing to yield their interests or their claims in those points where they could not be made consistent with the condition of the other party. Natural reason and unbiassed justice would dictate such a concession.

The superior right was on the side of the occupants, and no people can have a right to set down amongst them upon terms subversive of the rights they antecedently possessed; at least such a pretence can spring from nothing better than mere conquest which at this time of day no person will, I believe, contend to be a legitimate source of right. The occupants may indeed concede some of their rights, in order to facilitate the union, but the very idea of concession supposes a liberty of refusal. It at once involves the idea of a mere contract, in which each party may propose their terms [12] of union, but neither can be compelled to accept; but, when they do accept, the compact then takes its rise, and is equally obligatory upon all, and is to be the touchstone of all future claims. The very essence of the compact, when made, is *mutual obligation*, which is obviously inconsistent with a power reserved in either party to rescind or remodel the stipulations so as to suit only themselves.

Force or conquest can be the only source of such a claim, and its advocates must equally contend for a right in the hunters of setting down, under terms prescribed by *themselves*, upon the prior occupancy of the peaceful shepherds. The party who would attempt either, place themselves at once in a state of war, and depend on force, and not on reason, for the accomplishment of their ends.

An intrusion like this into the domains of a settled people can claim no more pretence of right than Alexander, when he passed the Granicus, or Caesar when he passed the Rubicon. A wandering horde has just as good a right to set down amongst a people, *and be their law givers*, as they have, after having formed an association upon mutual principles, to change them at pleasure, as their varying interests, their passions, or their caprice may dictate. Power is in each case the only source of right, and arbitrary will the measure of its exercise. The common notions of a contract utterly exclude the idea of a right residing in one party to alter or rescind it—*mutual obligation* forms its very essence. To bind one party, and leave the other at large, is to impose a law upon a conquered people, instead of forming a contract between free and equal parties.

Mere power can never constitute a legitimate right, and yet by what other claim can one party presume, of their own accord, to change the compact? It is said indeed, that the majority ought to govern. This principle is true under modifications, but it is not indefinitely so. It is a principle very capable of being perverted, and likely always to be enlisted on the side of those who have or hope to have a majority, let their views or principles be what they may.

But I contend, 1st. That the majority of an associated people have no right to infringe the social compact. If they have, then it follows that the compact has no existence longer than while the contracting interests are equal in point of number or power. It would derive its sanctions not from [13] mutual assent, nor from moral obligation, but from physical force. It would be no breach of civil duty to attempt a subversion of the government at any time, provided the enterprizing leader had a tolerable prospect of gaining a successful majority; for it never can be unlawful to attempt that which would be lawful if attended with success; and on this principle Cataline's name ought to be erased from the records of infamy, and inscribed in the brightest page of Roman virtue. The weaker party in society would literally have *no right whatever*: neither life, liberty or property would be guaranteed to *them* by the social compact, seeing the majority are not bound by it, but might destroy the whole, and by the same rule any part of it at pleasure. In the case which we have supposed above of the husbandmen associating with the shepherds, the farmers, if a majority, would be justifiable in commiting rapine upon the flocks of their associates. Virtue and vice would lose their distinction; the most vicious views would be sanctified, if pursued by the greater number, and the most virtuous resistance punishable in the less. 2d. If the principles of justice are derived from a higher source than human institutions, (and who will deny it?) I contend that the majority have no right to infringe them. Society is made up of different descriptions of men; between each description a common interest creates a common sympathy. The merchants, the farmers, the planters and the manufacturers, each have their common interests; each of these interests have their respective rights annexed to them, independently of the great natural rights which are common to all.

Suppose one of these communities of interest (as the mercantile) to include a majority of the whole society—May they infringe the rights of any or of all of the others? May they do to the others as in return they would be unwilling should be done to themselves? (This I take as the best criterion of justice or injustice.) If they may, then a majority have a right to infringe the laws of nature, and every other law which dictates the rules of justice. These cease to be obligatory of course when three men chuse to abolish them, and but two men vote to observe them. In fine, justice would import no obligation *per se*, and must always count the number of her votaries against that of her opponents, to *know* whether she had any existence at all. The truth is, that the [14] term majority is a *relative term*, and supposes a compact already made; by which compact it is stipulated or implied, that the general will *in the functions of government* shall be taken to be that which a majority declares. But take away the idea of a compact or association, and to what does this term then relate? It relates to nothing; or, which is the same thing, to an indefinite number of unassociated men, none of whom have any power or controul over the others. If then the rights of the majority (be they what they may) derive themselves from a previous compact, the compact is the *principal*, and those rights the *accessory* dependant upon it; and whenever the latter attempt to destroy the former, it in the same instant destroys itself. And what sort of right must that be, the exercise of which necessarily works its own destruction? A phantom raised up in the dark recesses of brooding theory, where "airy nothing often gains a local habitation and a name," but which the light of practical reason dissolves away "like the baseless fabric of a vision."

No. III.

In my first number I took the liberty of refusing my assent to the doctrine of a state of nature as being precedent to a state of society; because it is a mere creature of theory, and as such capable of being so managed and moulded as to mislead the candid enquirer. If any person will, however, point out to me the time and place, when and where it had existence, I will still acknowledge myself a convert to the doctrine. It would be sufficient for all my present purposes to deny, (which I believe I may safely do) that it ever existed in Carolina. I contended also, that a state of society is the natural state; that nature placed man in it the moment she produced him, but left the regulation of the terms of association to himself, as she did every thing else which respected his transactions and circumstances in this world. That without resorting to a state of nature, the natural rights of men may be easily known and understood, being in fact nothing more than what nature has obviously conferred or made necessary to [15] every man. Of these were enumerated *life, liberty* and *property*. The first is conferred, the second and third made necessary by the decrees of nature. We might have included the intellectual right: but it might have led to a prolixity of metaphysical discussion unnecessary for the present purpose. These rights being common to all men, necessarily formed the foundation of the social compact. In the second number, however, it has been shewn, that they do not form the only foundation of it. The acquired interests of the different parties in society necessarily enter into the constitution of it. If this were not the case a party of merchants could never voluntarily associate with a party of planters, or a party of manufacturers with either. If their several interests be precious to each, neither can ever be supposed to assent to a compact, in which those interests are disregarded. What temptation could they have to associate? The rights about which they would be most solicitous (being most liable to invasion) would be those which the social compact would not provide for. This compact then, rationally understood, supposes the contracting parties to be of two descriptions. When it immediately regards the natural rights of man, each individual is a party *per se*, because each individual, *as such*, possesses those rights. When the rights of certain descriptions are to be provided for, each description, composed of many individuals, forms a contracting party. In no country under heaven is the latter better exemplified than in Carolina, being composed of the mercantile, the planting, the farming and the manufacturing interests. Each of these is as much entitled to consideration, in forming a compact, as any of the others; and neither submitted to it upon the principle of holding their peculiar rights and interests at the courtesy of any of the others. Such a submission, as I have before shewn, would import an act of necessity, and not of free agency and assent. There is a more general division, into which the society we live in may be viewed; I mean, the holders of slaves, and those who have none; or, more properly, those who pursue and must pursue their occupations by *slaves*, and those who pursue, or may pursue, their occupations of themselves. This latter division is, perhaps, the most comprehensive of any that can be made, and forms two interests very distinguishable from each other. This distinction [16] must be qualified by a very important consideration. Not every one who holds slaves merely, is to be considered as forming a branch of the former description; but those whose cultivation is of such a nature, as that the very existence of it depends on that property. Nature has decreed, that the race of white people shall not labour in the fertile swamps of this climate; but she has not interdicted their labouring in the up lands, particularly above the falls of the rivers. These truths none will, I presume, undertake to controvert in the face of every day's experience. It follows necessarily that, on the one hand, an upland farmer may part with all his slaves and be a farmer still; while, on the other, a swamp planter parting with them is broken up entirely, and is a planter no more. Let not, therefore, these distinct circumstances be confounded; for in confounding them we confound the rights of different parties, and open the door for erroneous reasoning. The slave is *essential* to the one; he is but *convenient* to the other. In the second number I have stated what I conceive to be rights of *prior occupants*, of those who have first discovered and settled a country, compared with the rights of those who afterwards emigrate and join them. A union between two such people can arise from but two sources, conquest or compact. As the former claims every thing, the occupants can have nothing but what is derived from courtesy. It is vain to attempt to reason upon rights unreasonably acquired. Instead of rights, reason declares them to be *wrongs* ab initio; and disclaims the having of any connexion with them.

There is, as yet, no *avowed* pretence in Carolina, of any rights being derived from this source. It is to be passed over as unworthy of discussion in a free country.

Compact then is the foundation on which we stand, subsisting as I have already shewn, between each individual of the one part, and the *whole mass* on the other, so far as respects life, liberty and property, and the other natural rights of men; and between each description of interest, and the residue collectively, so far as regards the common interests of each description. Thus the common mercantile interest contracts that the planting, farming and manufacturing interests shall be sacredly regarded, while they, on the other hand, guarantee the mercantile. Each of these interests alternately contract [17] with all the others; and this branch of the social compact is as necessary, as obvious, and as indispensible as the former: as *necessary*, because the danger of invasion is as great; as *obvious*, because the title of each party is as clear; and as *indispensible*, because the inducements are as cogent as any right to which the social compact can have relation. Nay, *the danger of invasion is greater than in the case of the natural rights*, as I have hinted in a former number; for although these interests are the emanation of one of the natural rights, vis. *property*, yet there are a thousand ways in which arbitrary restrictions, preferences, monopolies, or unequal taxation may be brought to bear upon some one or more of them, without a direct invasion of the natural right of property. The sacredness of the natural rights forms in a great degree their protection, and throws a sudden and forcible check upon the effects of power.

But when interest has seduced the heart, insidious glosses dazzled the understanding, and consciousness of power tempted the act, the subverted interests of particular classes have been made to bear reluctant testimony to the truth of the assertion. Every citizen then in society, who was of a particular description of interest, may be said to have contracted in a double capacity. If a planter, he stipulated as a man, that his natural rights should be preserved, and as a planter, that the planting interest should not be swallowed up by the other interests in the state. It would be a piece of mockery, if the former only were provided, and the latter left unsecured. The same may be said of all the other descriptions. In this view of the compact, there is no mystery, no far fetched theory; it is what every man feels when he refers to himself, and all must approve when applied to others. It takes man as it finds him, with all his real rights, interests and circumstances attending him. The social compact appears what it ought to be; a bargain, in which a variety of interests are concerned, adopted by common consent for the safety of all. In adjusting such a compact, amongst a people extensive in numbers and territory, unequal in population and riches, diverse in habits and manners, many difficulties must be expected to occur. Some will be natural, some fictitious. That effort which self-interest always makes to gain the advantage of a contract, will be no less employed on an occasion like this. Each party will set off their respective interests, and state [18] their demands with peculiar ferver. It is here that the different interests which I have been contending for, but which the common theory takes no notice of, make their appearance. Each interest unites in distinct views, and makes an integral party in the discussion. The natural rights, as all men agree in them, are found easy to adjust; the difficulty made no account of in theory, turns out in practice to be the subject most agitated in arranging the social compact. It is morally impossible that the several interests should be composed of equal numbers. Nor is it necessary they should, in order that they may be entitled to weight as an interest in the adjustment of the social compact, because it would at once be estimating the rights and interests of man by the number of votes, and not by principle; a position which I trust has been refuted in a former number. As in a free constitution, no man is so poor or contemptible, but his natural rights are to be sacredly regarded, so no existing interest is to be set at nought or sacrificed, because of its comparative smallness in point of number. If it forms in reality a *contracting party*, that is sufficient to entitle it to every claim it could have, were the numbers never so much augmented. If this were not so, the master interest, like Aaron's serpent, might constitutionally swallow up all the rest; and an Agrarian law be engrafted upon legitimate right, under a system which professes to secure to every man his possessions. When by a compact, a people have determined that the society shall be governed by laws made for the common good (so they do not oppugn the compact) it is natural indeed, that they should agree to take the sense of the majority of the constituted bodies as the touch stone of such laws; because there is no other method for them to fix upon. But they could never make a compact, and then submit to the majority of the people, who contract, whether it is a compact or not, or whether it should continue as they made it. Three men might as well sign and seal a mutual obligation, and after they had done, leave it to the determination of any two of them, whether it is obligatory or not; any two might in that *case* collude together for the purpose of defrauding the third.

It follows from this, that, as to all *legislative acts*, the majority of the constituted body has a right to determine; but [19] that the right is derived from the very compact itself, and not from any pre-existent quality supposed to reside in the people during the time they were in an unconnected state, or were passing from that to another state. It has been shewn before, that any attempt to exercise such a right upon a contract itself, would be the same thing as an attempt to rescind and destroy it. Thus, then, the minority are bound to the majority in the making of *laws*; but in the making of *constitutions* the obligation is reciprocal, and therefore equal upon both. This is a distinction of the utmost consequence to a free government. Laws spring from constantly varying circumstances of the society: their objects, and of course, their duration, are often temporary; they are sometimes founded in mistake, sometimes made for experiment, and are therefore in all cases subject to be varied or abrogated.

The good of society requires that the laws should change with its exigencies; and the power of deciding when these exigencies occur, must be referred to the majority of the constituted bodies. This majority may speak the sense of a majority of the people, or it may not; but I know of no constitution which prescribes a mode of ascertaining the fact, or that requires the ascertainment of the fact as a prerequisite to give force and validity to the law. The people having, in their charter of association, drawn certain rules for the government of the bodies they constitute, surrender to those bodies the right of judging upon matters of public expediency; reposing their safety and tranquility in this, that let them institute what they may, there are certain rights and interests which they cannot invade, certain prescribed boundaries which they cannot pass. Their constitution is a strong citadel which commands every part that is without, and, having been built by the aid of all, nothing less than the strength of all can demolish it. But when a part of the association, perhaps a bare majority *by one*, assumes the privilege of destroying this goodly fabrick of pleasure, it then becomes rather a place of annoyance than of defence. Nothing is, from that moment, safe in society. A majority—it is an appellation easy to assume, a thing which every man in society (no matter by what means) will assume the right to form if he can. The vilest of factions may sometimes acquire it in the moments of popular delusion, and invoke its sanction in [20] the worst of causes. A compact which cannot secure society against such efforts or pretensions, is unworthy of a free people. It ensures no tranquility to the peaceable, no success to the industrious, and no prospect of reward to any, but those who would break all the bands of society and commence a general plunder.

No. IV.

In the three former numbers I have stated certain principles which influence men upon entering into society, as well as in adjusting the association; or, in other words, in framing a constitution. These have been deduced from practice and experience, from acknowledged rights and interests, and not from any particular theory. They have been illustrated and proved in a manner at least satisfactory to myself. They are before the public, who will form their own judgment concerning them. Persuaded as I am myself, of their solidity, it will not be inconsistent in me to build upon them as upon a solid foundation. It has probably struck the reader already, that these papers have a reference to a subject which has lately been made public, and which is likely to become highly interesting to the people of this country. It has been announced that a number of gentlemen in the upper country, have associated together as reformers; have organized themselves into a systematic body, and have dispersed their subordinate bodies through-out the country, under prescribed principles and special instructions. They have addressed themselves to the people at large, telling them that they had made a new discovery which had astonished them; though they had indeed suspected before, from some facts within their knowledge, that matters were as they turned out to be upon their

AMERICANUS

"careful and attentive examination."* This new discovery, it seems, [21] was of an inequality in the representation of this country: from whence it was inferred, that our government possesses the form of freedom without the substance; and the constitution being radically defective or oppressive, the people are called upon to join the reformers in setting it right. The latter have promised to draw petitions for the people to sign, and to support them before the legislature in such a manner as will not be unworthy of the cause. They tell the people, that attempts had before been made to obtain a partial redress, but the legislature was of opinion that the people did not wish it. They are therefore exhorted to refute this opinion by the unanimity of their measures; although the evil itself was announced by the association as a recent discovery, which they were then giving the first notice of to the people. These communications have been followed by a series of letters, signed *Appius*, addressed in a familiar style to the people of South-Carolina; but upon a perusal of them, we find, that they are particularly addressed to that part of the state commonly called the upper or back country. The object seems to be to convince the inhabitants that they are exceedingly oppressed under the existing form of government in this state, and to reinforce the address from the reform association. To remodel the constitution, in point of representation, so as to place the wealth of the low country, and all its interests and concerns, under the immediate administration of the back country, seems to be the direct view both of the association and of the address. It is declared, that *wealth ought not be represented; that a rich citizen ought to have fewer votes than his poor neighbour; that wealth should be stripped of as many advantages as possible, and it will then have more than enough; and finally, that in giving property the power of protecting itself, government becomes an aristocracy.* The advocates for such a system, have, in my view, but one step further to go. These principles are well pointed, and their aim pretty well disclosed, in the 31st page of the pamphlet, where it is said, "The upper and lower countries have opposite habits and views in almost every particular. One is accustomed to expence, the other to frugality. One will be inclined to numerous offices, large salaries, and an expensive government; the other, from

---

* It is wonderful that the fact should be announced with the pompous affectation of a *new discovery*, seeing that a very large number, if not a majority of the association, were members of that convention which instituted the very inequality they complain of.

the moderate fortunes of the inhabitants, and their simple way of life, will prefer low [22] taxes, small salaries, and a very frugal civil establishment. One imports almost every article of consumption, and pays for it in produce; the other is far removed from navigation, has very little to export, and must therefore supply its own wants. Consequently one will favor commerce, the other manufactures; *one wishes slaves, the other will be better without them.* Where two classes of people in the same community have such opposite inclinations and customs, it is fit that the most numerous should govern."

I cannot think that the people of this country, and particularly of the lower country, have been tranquil readers of these doctrines. To them it involves a question no less than "to be or not to be." I profess myself to be one who considers it of the utmost magnitude, who views the attempt now making, as of the most dangerous and alarming kind, and one which ought to arouse our most steady and determined opposition. Under this impression, I shall proceed, in the course of a few remaining numbers, to discuss these claims under the principles which I have already laid down with that freedom which becomes a citizen, and I trust with that respectful deference which is due to the public. It is observable, that not only the *right to govern*, but the manner in which the government is to be exerted, are plainly disclosed in this pamphlet; *commerce and slaves,* and the other points which constitute "the opposite views and interests," are to be governed (perhaps abolished) by the "most numerous," whose manufacturing interests are repugnant to the first, and who would "be better without the second." One unavoidable inference results from the whole, which is, that the upper and lower country, as they are at present situated, never can be connected under any form which does not explicitly lay all the *peculiar rights* of the latter at the feet of the former. I shall, however, refer observations of this kind to a future paper, and at present resume my plan. I trust I have demonstrated already, that certain rights attach to the prior occupants of a country, which subsequent emigrants can claim no right to divest, unless it is the right of conquest.

I have also hinted, and in some measure exemplified what these rights are; and now lay it down as a principle, that *the right of prior occupancy comprehends all those advantages and immunities which are essential to the nature of the industry and* [23] *pursuits which led the prior occupants to settle and attach themselves to the country in which the emigrants found them*. If the latter cannot associate with the former under any other terms than compelling them to abandon their original occupations, the latter have no right to associate at all; because their union becomes inconsistent with the very existence of one of the parties; and if so, who ought to give way? Appius tells us the prior occupants: then Appius must contend for the *right of conquest*. Let the republicans of Carolina weigh well the principles of such a pretence, before they decide upon it.

Here then we come to the question, in whom doth the rights of prior occupancy reside? A short survey of the history of Carolina will answer the question. Indeed Appius himself tells us who are not the prior occupants, by setting forth the great rapidity with which the *upper country* has become peopled within the few last years. He tells us that "all that is now called the back country, *and even the middle districts,* were for a long time held by the savages; that population and wealth were confined to a few leagues along the sea coast; and that the lower country was flourishing and wealthy, while the middle was either wholly unsettled, or contained only a few indigent and scattering inhabitants, and the more remote, interior parts now called the back country, entirely unknown or occupied by savages." Those Carolinians who have formed any acquaintance with the history of their own country, know, that some where about the year 1670, a number of adventurers, under the auspices of the first proprietors, fled from want and religious persecution at home, and took refuge amongst the forests of this country. The first settlement was made under governor Sayle, upon the spot where Charleston now stands. Those poor occupants, and such as joined them from year to year, encountered every possible hardship incident to their situation, and braved the hostile tribes of barbarians that surrounded them; fondly imagining that they would enjoy themselves and transmit to their children all the rights, civil and religious, which they sacrificed so much to obtain. After twenty years labour, expended with little reward, in clearing and cultivating the sandy uplands near the coast, accident discovered that the riches of the country lay in the swamps; and the rice was the grain congenial both to the soil and the climate. It was soon found, [24] however, that the race of white people could not labour there, and that he who attempted it, seldom cleared more ground than sufficed for his own grave, in which he was very shortly deposited. Captive Indians were soon substituted, and in process of time, labourers were drawn from

Africa. The cultivation of the swamps, by their agency, became a system which made the low country flourishing and wealthy; while the upper country was the habitation of savages, and the place from whence the settlers were constantly invaded. Inconsiderable in numbers as they were, their blood and treasure were often drawn upon to purchase that peaceable territory now enjoyed by their brethren of the upper country. Children are now alive, who have wept a father slain by the hands of the savages; nay, there are now many citizens whose feet have trodden the wilderness of that country, and who, at the risk of their lives, have derived to the present inhabitants the privilege of setting down upon lands uninfested by the barbarous tribes. Not more than twenty-one years before the late war, the territory which now claims to govern the low country, was acquired from the Indians, and forts were built for the defence of it. And who are the present occupants? Those who have gathered from all quarters of late years, and associated themselves with the people of the low country; the first occupants of the one place, and for the most part the first proprietors of the other. The latter were in possession of their country, their slaves, their rights, and their properties, as they now stand; while the former were in other countries and associated with other people. Hither they came, acquiescing in the country as they found it; they found it a country abounding in wealth, but weak in numbers; they held out their numbers as the guarantee, and not as the destroyer of its wealth; and in return acquired the equal right of pursuing their fortunes and partaking of its privileges.

The population of the low country was nearly as great as it is at the present time, when that of the middle country was but inconsiderable, and when the trees of the back forest had never felt the axe. In the low country it spread from the sea coast; in the back country it arose from a current of migrations setting down the continent on each side of the mountains. The settlers of the low country, for the most [25] part, brought with them a stock of wealth which they threw into the common fund. In the back country the settlers brought little else but their persons. I mean no offence by this distinction; but the fact is not controvertible. All the emigrants who joined the low country, found it peculiarly situated both with regard to its government and its slaves; they acquiesced in a system which they saw so necessary and proper for a people so peculiarly situated.

They felt many advantages in their indigent situation, of sitting down amongst a people whose resources of wealth were abundantly competent for all the exigencies both of government and defence. The people with whom they associated, cheerfully recognized their title to all the privileges of freemen, and all the rights of protection; they were even content to see the fruits of their labour enure to themselves with little or no exactions to government; but they uniformly said, "that our very existence as a people, depends upon the perpetual observance of certain fundamental institutions, and we cannot submit to any people on earth the power of abrogating or altering them." We have embarked all that is dear to us in this system, which our forefathers planted and transmitted to us; and we must cease *to be* altogether, the instant we cease to be *just what we are*. To you who are settling a different country, we chearfully guarantee every benefit and immunity you can possibly derive from it; our ancient system possesses nothing that opposes any obstacle to you; but on the contrary, our wealth purchases the means of your protection, and our commerce affords reward to your industry. We are willing to share with you every interest and every right which we possess; but we cannot surrender the power of regulating our great and peculiar concerns. Though we take you into our association, content that you should share the government, yet we can never surrender ourselves into your hands with power to dispose of us as you please; being bound by no natural or moral obligation to do so, and feeling that it would be reposing too much in the hands of a people, strangers to our interests, our customs and our concerns. The nature of the country you are about to settle, and of the pursuits of the settlers, point out that its numbers will soon transcend those of the low country; and we must at this moment stipulate [26] for our ultimate safety, or by admitting you into our body, we surrender ourselves to your disposal. As an alliance upon such terms would probably be fatal unto us at some time or another, we would rather decline its present advantages; but if your object be, as you profess, to embark with us, content that wealth should form the ballast, as it does in fact the sinews of the state, we welcome you as fellow citizens, and embrace you as brethren. The language was natural, the compact reasonable, and therefore acquiesced in. The emigrants in the back country felt an honest disposition to subscribe to the superior rights of the prior occupants; they pretended no claim of setting down amongst the latter, and being their law-givers; they did that from principle which they clearly felt they should themselves have required under like circumstances. They stipulated that man should be free, and all his natural rights sacredly regarded; and under these stipulations they were content to associate and pursue their industry. They saw that the occupants of the low country could never, with safety, blend themselves with a people who were likely to be superior in numbers, and in every respect so differently circumstanced, upon any other terms; they were conscious of no right themselves to negative the terms, being free to accept them, or seek some other people, whose interests, habits and views were more congenial with their own. They found them advantageous and accepted them. Under the union thus formed, they have lived happy and free; their numbers have increased almost beyond example, and the later emigrants have discovered nothing in the state of the connexion to prevent their placing themselves, their interests, and their families under it. Bad as it is, in the opinion of the reformers, thousands have thought it more eligible than any thing offered by the neighboring states, and, without any view of altering the system, have planted their vines and fig trees in confidence of peace and happiness.

No. V.

[27] I hope that it has been evinced in the last number, to every candid and unprejudiced mind, that the inequality of representation between the low and the back country, so much exclaimed against by Appius hath sprung from no *usurpation*, nor from any novel principles incorporated into the government of this country. Instead, therefore, of announcing it as a discovery just made, as a horrible thing just burst upon them, the association might have read it in every period of the Carolina history, and traced it through every vestige of its government. They might have seen it not only at the original settlement of the upper and back country, but found it running through the progress of the connexion to the present day; and some of them might perhaps have recognized it as the system under which they were born. Had they been willing, they might also have surveyed the *causes* that produced it. They would have noticed it as the production of assent, always implicitly and often expressly given. As relating to the people of the low country, they would have recognized in it nothing but

what common prudence and self preservation would dictate; as relating to the back country, nothing but reasonable and just acquiescence. Placing *themselves* amongst the former, they would have felt at once that they would themselves have stipulated for it, placing themselves *candidly* amongst the latter, that they could not with reason refuse it. They must in the one case feel all the solicitude of prior occupants, who had grown old and wealthy under a system, the violation of which would be their ruin; as emigrants on the other hand, who had acquired every thing but the mere balance of the government, or a power to violate the established system, they must feel every reason to be satisfied. The emigrants having acquired every thing necessary to the success of their own views in joining a settled people, and all that was consistent with the safety of that people could claim no more under professions of a peaceable connexion. To have *then* demanded more, would have betrayed an overweening ambition; and would have suggested to the occupants well founded apprehensions that the demand was prompted by other views than those of sitting down peaceably and pursuing their fortunes under equal laws. They might have [28] began to dread, that in fostering these emigrations, they would plant in their own bosoms the seeds of their ruin. Under such an impression, instead of draining their treasury, and even mortgaging their future industry, as they often did, to drive from the back country those who were constantly opposing the progress of that settlement; they would rather have entered into an everlasting treaty with *Moytoy* and *Skijogustah*, and the nations they represented, to stand a barrier to foreign migrations. Better might they conceive it, to resort occasionally to arms to repel savage invasions, than to surrender themselves by compact to the unqualified disposal of people from all countries, little better acquainted with the pre-existent institutions and peculiar circumstances of the country than the *aborigines*, and restrained by no constitutional check from the violation of them. Had the settlers, in fact, announced or avowed one half of what Appius has done, instead of being welcomed as associates by the occupants, under the persuasion that by such accessions, strength and prosperity would be derived to the state, the latter would have been shocked at every emigration, viewing as a reinforcement to an internal enemy. The usual means of public safety would have become the harbingers of real danger; and the low country must have considered themselves as *a crop* ripening for the sickle, to be cut down and divided when the upper country should have increased in labourers sufficient to begin the harvest. For to what principle of probable safety could they have entrusted themselves and their posterity, after putting into the possession of indefinite numbers of needy settlers, in the back country, all the power that could be requisite for invading and subverting their essential interests? Human nature, it is well known, is too frail to be always true to the principles of virtue and justice; too often tempted, too seldom rectified to be safely relied on. Could then its mere clemency and moderation form a safe depository of all that was precious, to a people in all respects so differently circumstanced as Appius has described them? Though virtue and justice sometimes bind men to the right, yet their efficacy is not uniform; if it were there would be no need of laws or constitutions. Interest, the most powerful impulse of the human breast, often overlooks or out runs the dictates of the regular virtues. In the mad career of [29] its pursuits, when thoroughly excited, laws themselves form feeble obstacles; and what could be expected from those rights or possessions of other people, which were the objects of the excitement? It was obvious to the slightest observation, that the emigrants to the back country, for some time, at least, must be poor and necessitous, they therefore could not want *temptation*; that they must soon become very numerous, and therefore could not want *the power*. In the same part of society then must soon unite the two requisites which seldom fail to set mankind in motion, vis. *temptation*, or an ardent desire to obtain an object; and *power* to accomplish what they wish. The *power* and *temptation* to do wrong have seldom found any successful restraint or opposition. To unite these two in any one party, or in any one person, is always dangerous in the extreme. If he must necessarily be cloathed with the *power*, prudence required that every thing be thrown in which can mitigate or destroy the temptation; if he must be placed in a way of *temptation*, all proper checks ought to be directed against the power.

From hence it is plain, that the low country occupants preserved to themselves no more than the principle of mere self preservation dictated, and that the emigrants as reasonable beings, were content to acquiesce in an arrangement which left them every thing, but the mere power of oppressing by numbers, the few, but wealthy people with whom they associated. Increasing as they were every day, by accessions of people from all quarters, with whom they had no prior acquaintance, however honest their own intentions might have been,

AMERICANUS

it was strictly impossible for them to ensure the low country against abuses, otherwise than by leaving in their hands those checks which they found them in possession of. If then, there ever subsisted between the back and the low country anything of that *original compact* upon which, the association tells us, all lawful governments rests, it is to be found here; and its leading feature is that very inequality of representation which they have so recently discovered. Hence the people of the low country, so far from being chargeable with usurpation, or with wresting the government from its original institution, have adhered to original terms and stipulations; while the association, guided by some new lights or smitten by some new impulse, are attempting the destruction [30] of the fundamental system, to make way for a government all their own. They have claimed the right *to govern* in explicit terms, and yet talk about "the origin of the society when the mutual contract was formed." At the *origin* of society in Carolina, I have shewn that the people they address were no parties to the compact. And if ever any compact was made, which conferred upon them the right they now contend for, let them shew it. Perhaps I shall yet produce them a compact to the contrary. The association further alledges, that "all the contracting parties, that is all the people, were equal and stipulated to continue so." Reserving for another occasion, the particular consideration of the perverted term *equality,* I will here examine a little this general and unqualified position, as relating to this country. 1st. All the people were not equal in *rights.* In *natural rights* I admit they were. But the rights of *prior occupancy* have been, in my view, clearly defined and brought home to the people of the low country. In this respect, therefore, the emigrants to the back country, have at no time been upon terms of equality. 2nd. I believe it will hardly be affirmed, that the people between whom the question is at issue, were equal in their *circumstances.* 3rd. The efficient motives which induced the association were not equal. One party had everything to gain from it; the other could gain nothing but the additional benefits that might be derived from an augmentation of the settlement. All that the one could want was the peaceable enjoyment of what they already possessed; the other sat down to gain that which was unpossessed. The one was happy before the union; the other fought the union as the means of happiness.

Thus then, though the association may have read of people who were in all respects equal at the time they formed an association it is manifest that it is improperly affirmed of the people of Carolina.

It is as far from being true that any stipulation was ever made, that all the people should in all respects continue equal. If the rights of prior occupancy, if the rights of extensive wealth did in fact exist, it remains for the association to shew us when the stipulation was made to give them up and equalize them. I have shewn, from the history of this country, that the reverse was the fact. There can be but two modes of [31] parting with a right of any kind: voluntarily surrender, or forcible divestment. The latter has never taken place, as yet, in Carolina, whatever may happen under the auspices of the association. They indeed, seem to have taken liberty, *one* of the natural rights of man, and erected it into a deity mighty to destroy: cloathed it with omnipotence and fallen down to invoke it's aid, in bringing to the dust every other right, natural and acquired. In the blaze of glory with which they have incircled the god, all the rights of property are lost. One would almost imagine that, in their views, a free government is to consist of nothing but mere freedom; that *liberty* and *property* have no affinity to each other. But on the contrary, that true liberty confers the divine right of "stripping property of all its advantages," and of presenting the proprietors, like Charon's passengers, in the form of naked skeletons. But let them beware, lest in arraying liberty with the omnipotence of a deity, or the captiousness of an arbitrary monarch, they convert her into a tyrant; and on the placid brow which naturally beams peace and all the charming virtues, they stamp the scowl of malevolence and the terrific bodings of civil discord.

No. VI.

When a favorite principle has gone forth in society, and every person smitten with its captivating qualities, has given it a cordial admission, any attempt to lop off its excrescences, or to bound its extent is apt to meet with a cold reception. The fancy wrought up by degrees to the highest pitch, and indulging an enthusiastic rapture, is disturbed by the smallest break or diminution; like the ear of the amateur, when the full chorus is invaded by the grating discords of an untuned instrument. The term *equality* has of late been chaunted with so much delight, and echoed from all quarters with so much fervor, that it has become almost the only *carmen necessarium;* the centre and substance of all that is precious. It has been said, with truth, "that best things spoiled, corrupt to worst." Liberty abused to licentiousness has become [32] a curse; religion pushed to enthusiasm has drenched the earth in blood. From hence the enemies of both have taken occasion to infer that there is no reality in either; or that they are inconsistent with human happiness. Their advocates, on the other hand, have always exerted themselves to restrain the one within the bounds of temperate enjoyment, and the other within those of rational exercise; and in effecting these they have always had the sublime satisfaction of evincing the reality and the blessings of both. *Equality,* like liberty, its sister, and religion, its supporter, when the notions concerning it are confined to the boundaries nature has prescribed, displays at once the reality of its existence, the divinity of its origin, and the substantial blessings of its institution. But when carried to an excess which nature never intended; when employed to support a set of illusions which experience must sooner or later explode, (as cool deliberating reason always disclaims) it is in danger of expiring with its own unnatural works; and its real utility of being at length questioned or denied. If we wish to ensure its permanency, and transmit it as a blessing to posterity, we ought to avoid connecting it with any thing that is impure or unnatural; assured that nothing of that kind can last longer than the fleeting passion of the times in which they subsist; and that posterity judging coolly, will be urged in vain to accept the legacy. To form extravagant or erroneous notions upon almost any subject whatever, is not a difficult matter. We need only let the mind or the fancy run without the curb of reason, and their own vagaries will soon effect it. But to rectify and reform them, is always a work arduous in the attempt, slow and doubtful in the progress and effect. There is a reluctance in human nature to confess its error and to tread back its mazes, which is always forward. These considerations point out the propriety of our guarding against erroneous notions respecting so valuable a principle as that of equality. So much has it been the theme of popular eulogy, so animated and extravagant the praises lavished upon it, and so copiously have its qualities been described, that it is no wonder if men should begin to call for a general plan of equalization. A few degrees more of the calorific principle would probably produce ebullition or inflammation, beyond the power of the body politic to endure. Already has it been carried so far as to intimate that [33] it would not be improper to strip wealth of its advantages; and to assert roundly that it ought to have no representation or influence in civil society. It is but one gradation to say it ought to have no specific protection. Thus the term *equality* has been made to signify the *state and condition* of men, though the abusers of the principle have not avowed it. We observe inequality of condition so constantly set in contrast with civil liberty, that the implication cannot be disguised. Yet, however, the most extravagant advocates of these notions, profess to draw their principles from nature—from a state of nature. I will then discuss this point upon their own grounds, and the institutes of nature shall decide. That she created all men free and equal *in their rights;* and that in this respect she has not one favorite in all her progeny, I most religiously believe. But in the endowment of natural gifts and faculties, nature has instituted almost every gradation, from the confines of inferior animals to the state of superior creation. Her views in the *human condition* are evidently to inequality. Why hath she made one man strong and another weak; one nimble and alert, another heavy and inactive; one industrious and another slothful? Why hath she dropped scarcely a solitary spark of her celestial fire into one mind, and beamed into another the richest and most copious effulgence? Why are some men bold and others timid; some sagacious and others dull; some successful and others unfortunate?

Delivering mankind out of her hands so differently and unequally endowed in these respects, can it for a moment be imagined that nature ever intended they should be equal in their circumstances? If she did she stands fairly convicted of instituting means which must of necessity frustrate her own ends; of making war upon her own purposes. If nature then has not only made men unequal at first, but has put them into a situation in which the fruits of that inequality must be constantly accumulating; if in all the combinations into which men have been thrown in the world, it has ever been preserved, the unavoidable conclusion is, that inequality of condition is one of nature's laws. If we consider this matter in a civil view, the result will be the same. If inequality of condition be in fact the institution of nature herself, it would be rather presumptuous to attempt to establish civil society upon principles repugnant to her laws. Indeed those civil [34] institutions have seldom lasted long which have counteracted them. All seem to agree however, that the fundamental rights of men in

AMERICANUS

civil society are to be inferred from the laws of nature. It will appear then that *equality of rights* and *equality of conditions* are matters entirely distinct; and that the former is so far from implying the latter, that it is the true parent of the very reverse. For instance the equal rights of men require that each individual should be the exclusive proprietor of the fruits of his own industry.

Take then a strong man and a weak one, or one who is industrious, and another who is indolent, and let them start even in a course of labor. At the expiration of any given period, how will matters stand amongst them? Obviously, the former must have acquired abundantly more than the latter. Now society, by the very principles of the social compact, guarantees to each what each acquires; and in so doing must necessarily guarantee *inequality of condition.*

Let us, for the sake of argument, take this matter upon a larger scale. Suppose 100 men, with a bow and a hatchet each should set down together in a wilderness; these men, it is obvious, would be all equal *in condition* as well as in *rights;* all at full liberty to pursue the plan they like best: in the course of the first year, 20 of these clear ten acres of land each, build a house and set down to agriculture: twenty more catch and tame ten head of cattle each, and subsist upon the milk and the young of their flocks. The remaining sixty wander about the settlement, and depend upon the precarious chance of their bow, perhaps upon pilfering, for daily subsistence; will it be said at the end of the first year, that their circumstances or their rights, are equal; obviously not the first, nor also the second; because the industrious forty have acquired rights in *property,* which the idle sixty have not. Yet Appius will tell us, that because the latter are most numerous, and possess the natural right of *liberty* (in common with the others) they are unquestionably entitled to govern the whole; to dispose of the hard earned property of the industrious forty, at pleasure. Strange state indeed, must that be, where the rights of the citizen diminish in proportion as his industry and acquisitions increase, and where he who contributes nothing, has a right to dispose of all! It might afford a subject of curious speculation, to enquire [35] what sort of laws they would be likely to make *for the good government and police of the settlers?* They would pass no criminal laws against pilfering and plundering, robbery or rapacity; no laws to check idleness and vagrancy; no laws to protect property, and no other laws in short, but such as would authorize the lounging crew to prey upon the industrious.

If some public exigency should require the raising of a common fund, the other party would, of course, be called upon to raise it. If personal services should be requisite, the government party, too idle to afford them, would call as readily upon the *habits of industry* of the others, as they had usually done upon the *fruits* of their industry on other occasions. The honest minority would probably be obliged first to labour in building fortifications, and then to pay themselves for it. These proceedings of the majority would naturally arise from the strong principle of self love, moving in concert with absolute authority; or rather, as I have stated in my last number, from the dangerous and destructive union of *power* with *temptation*. If such a government as I have been describing is not perfectly consistent with the political dogmas avowed by the association and supported by Appius, I shall be glad they will point out the difference. But to return to the question of equality. I think it must be manifest that men cannot be considered equal in their natural endowments, nor in their personal acquisitions; nor in their civil rights, so far as regards such acquisitions: that is to say, that though the man worth but 10£ has as clear a right to what he holds, as the one worth 10,000£ yet the latter surely has more extensive civil rights guaranteed by society, than the former. In a word, equality of *condition* is inconsistent with the laws of nature, not derivable from the rights of man, and not to be found in any of the institutions of civil society. It is as absurd to look for it, or to attempt to force the human condition to it, as *equality of happiness*.

To what then does this term equality relate? I will answer in the words of the French constitution; "men are born and always continue free, and equal in respect of *their rights*." Thus, my personal liberty is equal to that of any other man; my life is *equally* sacred and inviolable, my bodily powers are *equally* my own; my power over my own actions is *equally* great and *equally* secured from external restraint; [36] my will is *equally* free; what I acquire, be it greater or less, I have an *equal* right to possess, to use and to enjoy. I have an equal claim upon the protection of the laws; an *equal* right to serve my country, and an *equal* claim to be exempted from service. If I am the most weak, the most indigent man in society, the laws of the land, no person, no description of persons can do to me what might not *equally* be done to the most powerful and the most wealthy. And finally, when I dislike the government under which I live, I have an equal right to transport myself into another country, and associate with another people. Here is matter sufficient for the republican to prize; sufficient to constitute honest contentment with his lot in other respects. He may be happy even in indigent circumstances and placid, though unfortunate.

In the possession of rational liberty, he may pursue his industry under the most flattering omens; and enjoy the fruits of it, with the highest relish. But when his mind is poisoned with notions of equality *of condition* (which the incautious and undiscriminating use of the term is apt to effect) he is at once soured with discontentment with his own lot; and with envy at the lot of others. Private repose and public tranquility are alike sacrificed; and one of the best principles of reformed government becomes the bane of society. And so it must ever be when men refine on theory, and endeavor forcibly to warp every thing into a mathematical agreement. When in spite of nature's decrees, her inequalities are to be broken down for the purpose of making equal fractions; when an artificial frame is made, like Dionysius's bedstead, and every thing is to be cut and spliced to suit it; no wonder if society should be found in tatters and fragments. Short, however, must be the reign of such politics; nature will speak out; a little experience must soon condemn, and sober reason explode the delusion. If the effects would instantly expire with the cause, good men might always wait the event with patience. But in such cases the sentiment of the poet is too often verified.

> "One moment gives occasion to destroy
> What to re-build, would a whole age employ."

No. VII.

[37] We are told by Appius, "that wealth will always acquire influence enough in every government to protect itself. That the influence it does acquire, is a dangerous disease, which ought to be checked." Let us enquire a little how these observations apply, as between the lower and the back country; for it is to be remembered that the present controversy is between them. And here we shall find that Carolina, so distinguishable in many other respects from all other countries, has also her peculiarities in this respect. Appius himself, has drawn the picture of the two. He has pointed all his arguments

respecting the *influence of wealth* against the *low country;* and has also said, that *in the upper country, a great equality of property prevails, and that the fortunes of the inhabitants are moderate.* The lower country then is generally wealthy, or in easy circumstances; the upper or back country generally possessed of but moderate acquisitions. Now I can easily conceive that a very rich man, if he be also a good man, seated in the midst of a circle of poor people, will acquire amongst *those people,* a considerable degree of influence. He has it in his power to employ their industry, to relieve their necessities, and to bestow many comforts upon them. In this respect, a rich man on the bank of the Keowee, and another on the Santee, would be similarly situated. But the question is, how the man at Keowee is to acquire his influence upon the Santee, and *vice versa.* I believe Appius would not very readily solve it. Here it is, as in many other parts, that the mind would be misled by a general principle, unqualified by circumstances. It is generally true, that great riches are apt to acquire influence; but it is as true, that the influence is acquired only in and about the place where the riches are seated. The association have given pretty good proofs of late, that the "protecting *influence,*" of low country riches, acts rather feebly beyond the falls of the rivers. Nor do present omens leave it much to confide in, when divested of all other means of protection. It is not probable that a poor man at Enoree or Tyger, being told that the low country was very rich, would feel himself much influenced to *protect* those riches; it would be well if he did not feel a persuasion that they were "a dangerous disease," which required a remedy. The truth is, [38] that in countries where wealthy men are dispersed, pretty equally throughout, some influence may attach to their situation, and that influence will act in every part of society; but in countries like Carolina, where a geographical line may be drawn, so as to divide the rich from those of moderate property; the influence of riches, however it may act within the tract to which it is confined, can take no effect beyond it. Low country wealth therefore, will have as little influence in Pinckny and Washington, as beyond the Atlantic. Instead of acquiring influence enough to protect itself, as Appius tells us, it is manifest, that by placing the government of Carolina in the hands of the back country, the wealth of the low country will be divested of every means of protection; even that silent influence which it possesses in almost every other country, by being dispersed equally throughout. It may not be amiss to enquire a little into the effect of the government as it now stands, with a view to the safety and protection of all parties. The controversy resolves itself indeed into a question of *right,* and a question of *expediency.* The right to govern has been already variously considered with relation to prior occupancy, to the claims of majority, and those other claims deducible from the natural rights of man. I shall add here, that the low country possesses in common with the upper country, every thing that comes under the denomination of personal right; over and above these, the rights of superior property, clearly appertain to the low country. If the latter does not include the balance (and in the opinion of Appius, it seems it does not) it must be for this only reason, *that property is entitled to no consideration in a free government.* Let the maintainers of this doctrine tell us for what purpose, in reality, men enter into and support society? If it be not to strengthen the right of property, and to make each one the sovereign master and sole possessor of his goods and chattels, houses and land. I confess I see no temptation to adopt or support it. Assuming the affirmative however, as a principle, I must believe *that he* will be most attached to the government, who has most at stake in it. So universal is this opinion amongst men that I belive there are but few constitutions in the United States, which do not like our own, make the possession of property to a certain extent, [39] most commonly a freehold, an essential qualification for a seat in the legislature.

Appius might upon his principles as well complain, that the citizen who owns nothing but his cloaths and his gun is excluded from the legislature, as that the superiority of more numbers does not govern. The principle to be complained against is precisely the same in both cases, only differing in degree. But take it upon the point [of] expediency. That mode of government is surely the most proper and expedient *which gives the most reasonable prospect of protecting the rights of all parties;* because this is the end of government. The question then is whether it is most likely that the low country, possessing the balance of the government, will invade the personal rights of the back country (which the low country hold in common with them) or that the back country would be more likely to invade the rights of wealth, which they do not hold in common with the low country; that is to say in extent. In the one case the personal right could not be subverted by the low country, without injuring themselves; in the other, the possessions of the wealthy may be infringed not only without injury to the back country, but perhaps in pursuance of their own interests. Here then is a distinguishing mark of probability in favor of the present system, and against the reform.

While the spirit of liberty prevails in the low country, they must regard as sacredly as their own, the personal rights of their back country brethren. That this spirit does now exist in equal degree, I presume will not be questioned; that it will continue as long, if not longer, I will endeavor to prove. Liberty is a principle which naturally and spontaneously contrasts itself with slavery. In no country on earth can the line of distinction ever be marked so boldly as in the low country. Here there is a standing subject of comparison, which must be ever present and ever obvious. The instant a citizen is oppressed *below par* (if I may so express myself) in point of freedom, he approaches to the condition of his own slave, his spirit is at once aroused, and he necessarily recoils into his former standing. The constant example of slavery stimulates a free man to avoid being confounded with the blacks; and seeing that in every instance of depression he is brought nearer to a par with them, his efforts must invariably force him towards an opposite point. In the country [40] where personal freedom, and the principles of equality, were carried to the greatest extent ever known, domestic slavery was the most common, and under the least restraint. I shall at once be understood as speaking of the Spartans. They threw all property into common stock, abolished gold and silver circulation, and no man could call any one thing his own. The Helots, like our negroes, were slaves. The citizens exercised the most savage authority over them. Children might hunt them and kill them, provided they did it skillfully, in order to exercise themselves in the art of insidious warfare. Yet the Spartans possessed freedom in the greatest extent, and were abundantly jealous of it.

If then domestic slavery, so far from being inconsistent, has in fact, a tendency to stimulate and perpetuate the spirit of liberty in the low country, it is to be fairly inferred, that under their management, the personal rights would receive as effectual and as permanent protection, as under any other people. Consistently with the constitution we live under, all laws must be general; of course any act calculated to invade personal rights, must operate every where, and by necessity, upon the low country people themselves. The question of expediency then is, whether the low country, are as likely to subvert the personal rights of the back country as the latter would be to invade the property of the former? If the same tie does not secure the latter, which (as I have shewn) secures the former, the answer must be in the negative. And it follows of course, that the back country are much safer under the present system, then the low country would be under the change proposed by the association. Upon the whole, then, the superior right to govern, as claimed by the back country, has been discussed under a variety of views, independently of the constitution, and proved to be without foundation. The question of expediency, situated as Carolina is, has also been considered, and results in favor of the government as it now stands for the safety, as well of the personal rights, as of the rights of property. That both parties are safe as matters now stand, one might be unsafe after the proposed alteration. It is a thing therefore not demandable of right, and not adviseable in point of expediency.

AMERICANUS

[60]

JAMES KENT 1763–1847

An Introductory Lecture to a Course of
Law Lectures

NEW YORK, 1794

Son of a successful lawyer on the Connecticut–New York border, James was from an early age coached for entry to Yale University. The careful selection of preparatory schools and special tutors paid off. Interrupted by military maneuvers in his freshman year at Yale, he fell upon the four volumes of Blackstone's *Commentaries* and read them from end to end. They "inspired me, at the age of fifteen, with awe," and that stroke of luck also incited great rewards. The mature James Kent may be said to have pursued three careers. As professor of law at Columbia he did not attract students, but he wrote a series of lectures that, after revision several years later, marked him as one of the country's foremost students of American law and the English common law in which it is rooted. Simultaneous with his study, teaching, and practice of law, Kent was for some thirty years active in politics as a Federalist in pronounced opposition to Jeffersonian Republicans. This phase of his career saw him for three terms a member of the New York legislature and an influential member of the New York Constitutional Convention of 1820–21. Finally, he established his greatest claim to renown in a quarter-century of service as chief judge of two of New York's highest courts. By common accord, persons who study the development of American law seriously count Kent one of the half-dozen jurists who have put the deepest imprint on American jurisprudence. The *Introductory Lecture,* which appears here, was written in his first year as a teacher of law and does not stand intact in the *Commentaries* published over thirty years later. It fits into this collection of writings vital to the establishment of republican government because it clearly enunciates the doctrine of judicial review in somewhat different terms than Hamilton did in *The Federalist.* Stressing the American basis of the doctrine, Kent makes it sound more like an established, traditional part of American law.

JAMES KENT 1763–1847

INTRODUCTORY LECTURE.

Mr. President, and Gentlemen,

In entering upon a COURSE of LECTURES on the Government and Laws of our Country, I cannot refrain from expressing what I have long felt, a deep sense of the greatness of the undertaking, and a just diffidence of my own qualifications to execute it with success. This is the first instance in the annals of this Seat of Learning, that the Science of our Municipal Laws has thus been admitted into friendship with her Sister Arts, and been invited to lend her aid to complete a course of public Education. The experiment is however well deserving of a favorable reception; and none I am persuaded will be more ready to bestow it, than those Gentlemen who are the most truly sensible of the importance and difficulty of the inquiries which this experiment involves. No persons will more cheerfully regard this attempt with the indulgence it will greatly need, than those who have been accustomed to liberal pursuits, and have taken a comprehensive survey of the natural foundation of Laws, and the complicated System of our National Jurisprudence.

Institutions of the present kind seem to be peculiarly proper at this day, when the general attention of mankind is strongly engaged in [4] speculations on the Principles of Public Policy. The Human Mind, which had been so long degraded by the fetters of Feudal and Papal Tyranny, has begun to free herself from bondage, and has roused into uncommon energy and boldness. The Theory of Government, and the Elements of Law, have been examined with a liberal spirit, and the profoundest discernment. Nor have our American Constitutions been neglected abroad; they have excited scrutiny, and merited and received applause. A learned French Professor* has incorporated them, although in a very imperfect manner, into his plan of Juridical Lectures; and he even expressed a concern, lest the picture he drew of the purity of our Legislation should promote Emigrations from Europe. How inexcusable should WE probably be deemed by mankind, if we neglected to make our own Laws and Constitutions an interesting object of Public Instruction?

But the People of this Country are under singular obligations, from the nature of their Government, to place the Study of the Law

---

* De la Croix's Review of Constitutions, vol. 2, 419.

at least on a level with the pursuits of Classical Learning. The Art of maintaining Social Order, and promoting Social Prosperity, is not with us a mystery fit only for those who may be distinguished by the adventitious advantages of birth or fortune. The Science of Civil Government has been here stripped of its delusive refinements, and restored to the plain Principles of Reason. Every office in the vast chain of political subordination, [5] is rendered accessible to every man who has talents and Virtue to recommend him to the notice of his Country. There is no individual in any station, art, or occupation, who may not entertain a reasonable expectation in some period of his life, and in some capacity, to be summoned into public employment. If it be his lot however to be confined to private life, he still retains the equal and unalienable Rights of a Citizen, and is deeply interested in the knowledge of his social duties; and especially in the great duty of wisely selecting, and attentively observing those who may be entrusted with the guardianship of his Rights; and the business of the Nation. But those who are favoured with nobler and superior parts, with a brighter portion of moral and intellectual accomplishments, (and such I hope will from time to time be the ornaments and pride of this Seat of Learning) have a still louder invitation to a knowledge of the Law, and stronger obligations to obtain it. Such persons are reared up by Providence, not to slumber away their lives in the obscurity of retreat, but to be useful, eminent, and illustrious in public stations. Their usefulness will not be confined merely to the exercise of the inferior offices of the local districts in which they may live, although in such offices a competent share of legal information is required. A wider field is opened for the virtuous and generous Youth of our Universities. The free Commonwealth of the United States, which in all its ties, relations and dependencies, is animated with the pure spirit of popular representation, offers the highest rewards to a successful cultivation of the Law, and the utmost encouragement to genius. The numerous seats in our State Legislatures, in Congress, in the [6] higher Judicial and Executive Departments, ought in general to be filled with a succession of men, who to the indispensable virtues of probity and patriotism, unite a masterly acquaintance with the leading principles of our Constitutional Polity, and the maxims and general detail of our Municipal Institutions. A moment's reflection must surely convince every one what an amazing trust is confided to those who are placed in the administration of our

Government, and what extensive legal and political knowledge is requisite to render them competent to discharge it. Our political Fabrics and Systems of Jurisprudence, which have been reared with great pains, and perfected with much wisdom, are to be guarded and preserved not only from the open assaults of violence, but the insidious operations of Faction, which are more hostile and dangerous to the Principles of Liberty.

A general initiation into the elementary learning of our Law, has a happy tendency to guard against mischief, and at the same time to promote a keen sense of Right, and a warm love of Freedom. This is strikingly illustrated in the historical progress of our Colony Governments, and manners. It is well known that the influence of the Common Law was strongly felt and widely diffused by our American Ancestors, from the time of their emigration from Europe, and settlement on this side of the Atlantic. The History of their Colonial Proceedings, (an inquiry too much neglected at the present day) discovers clearly the marks of a wise and resolute People, who understood the best securities of political happiness, and the true foundation of the social ties. [7] The earliest inhabitants of the present State of Massachusetts declared by law that the free enjoyment of the Liberties of Humanity was due to every Man in his place and proportion, and ever had been, and ever would be, the tranquility and stability of the Commonwealth. They also avowed that they came over with the Privileges of Freemen, and they ascertained and defined those Privileges, and established a Charter of Rights, with a caution, sagacity, and precision, rarely, if at all, surpassed by their descendants.* In the distant History of this State, we meet with traces of the same enlightened sense of civil security. Early in the present century, our Colonial Assembly declared, that it was, and always had been, the unquestionable Right of every Freeman to have a perfect and entire property in his goods and estate; and that no money could be imposed or levied upon him without the consent of his Representatives.† Testimonies of the same flattering nature are probably to be found in the Records of all our Colony Legislatures. But no higher evidence need or can be produced of the prevailing knowledge of our Rights, and the energy of the freedom of the Common Law, than the spirit

---

* Hazard's State Papers, 408, 487.
† Colony Journals, vol. 1, 224.

which pervaded and roused every part of this Continent on the eve of the late Revolution; when the same power which had once nourished us, jealous of our rising greatness, attempted to abridge our immunities, and check our prosperity. The first Congress, which assembled in the year 1774, discovered a familiar acquaintance with the sound [8] principles of Government, and just notions of the social Rights of Mankind. They declared and asserted these Rights with a perspicuity, force, manliness and firmness, which threw much lustre on the American Character. The late Earl of Chatham said he could discover no Nation or Council that surpassed them, notwithstanding he had read Thucydides, and had studied and admired the master-states of antiquity.

By thus comparing the excellent Principles of our Civil Policy, with their effects upon the progress of our Government, and the spirit of our People, we are insensibly and properly led to feel for them an uncommon share of reverence and attachment. I cannot but be of opinion, that the Rudiments of a Law, and Senatorial Education in this Country, ought accordingly to be drawn from our own History and Constitutions. We shall by this means imbibe the principles of Republican Government from pure fountains; and prevent any improper impressions being received from the artificial distinctions, the oppressive establishments, or the wild innovations which at present distinguish the Trans-Atlantic World.

The British Constitution and Code of Laws, to the knowledge of which our Lawyers are so early and deeply introduced by the prevailing course of their professional inquiries, abounds, it is true, with invaluable Principles of Equity, of Policy, and of Social Order; Principles which cannot be too generally known, studied and received. It must however be observed at the same time, that many of the fundamental doctrines of their Government, and Axioms of their Jurisprudence, are [9] utterly subversive of an Equality of Rights, and totally incompatible with the liberal spirit of our American Establishments. The Student of our Laws should be carefully taught to distinguish between the Principles of the one Government, and the Genius which presides in the other. He ought to have a correct acquaintance with genuine Republican Maxims, and be thereby induced to cultivate a superior regard for our own, and I trust more perfect systems of Liberty and Justice. In the words of a discerning writer in this country, who has very ably unfolded the doctrine of Representative Republics, "the

JAMES KENT 1763–1847

Student should be led thro' a System of Laws applicable to our Governments, and a train of reasoning congenial to their Principles."*

But there is one consideration, which places in a strong point of view, the importance of a knowledge of our constitutional principles, as a part of the education of an American Lawyer; and this arises from the uncommon efficacy of our Courts of Justice, in being authorised to bring the validity of a law to the test of the Constitution. As this is however a subject of a very interesting tendency, and has in many cases inspired doubts and difficulties,† I will take the liberty of devoting a few reflections to it, even in this Introductory Discourse.

The doctrine I have suggested, is peculiar to the United States. In the European World, no [10] idea has ever been entertained (or at least until lately) of placing constitutional limits to the exercise of the Legislative Power. In England, where the Constitution has separated and designated the Departments of Government with precision and notoriety, the Parliament is still considered as transcendently absolute; and altho some Judges have had the freedom to observe, that a Statute made against natural equity was void,** yet it is generally laid down as a necessary principle in their Law, that no Act of Parliament can be questioned or disputed.†† But in this country we have found it expedient to establish certain rights, to be deemed paramount to the power of the ordinary Legislature, and this precaution is considered in general as essential to perfect security, and to guard against the occasional violence and momentary triumphs of party. Without some express provisions of this kind clearly settled in the original compact, and constantly protected by the firmness and moderation of the Judicial department, the equal rights of a minor faction, would perhaps very often be disregarded in the animated competitions for power, and fall a sacrifice to the passions of a fierce and vindictive majority.

No question can be made with us, but that the Acts of the Legislative body, contrary to the true intent and meaning of the Constitution, ought to be absolutely null and void. The only inquiry which can arise on the subject is, whether the Legislature [11] is not of itself the competent Judge of its own constitutional limits, and its

---

* Chipman's Sketches, 238.

† See the case, Trevett and Weeden, in Rhode-Island, 1786.

** Hob. 87.—12. Mod. 687.

†† Wooddeson's Elm. 81.4 Inst. 36. Mr. Paley in his principles of moral and political philosophy says, the Legislature must of necessity be absolute.

acts of course to be presumed always conformable to the commission under which it proceeds; or whether the business of determining in this instance, is not rather the fit and exclusive province of the Courts of Justice. It is easy to see, that if the Legislature was left the ultimate Judge of the nature and extent of the barriers which have been placed against the abuses of its discretion, the efficacy of the check would be totally lost. The Legislature would be inclined to narrow or explain away the Constitution, from the force of the same propensities or considerations of temporary expediency, which would lead it to overturn private rights. Its will would be the supreme law, as much with, as without these constitutional safeguards. Nor is it probable, that the force of public opinion, the only restraint that could in that case exist, would be felt, or if felt, would be greatly regarded. If public opinion was in every case to be presumed correct and competent to be trusted, it is evident, there would have been no need of original and fundamental limitations. But sad experience has sufficiently taught mankind, that opinion is not an infallible standard of safety. When powerful rivalries prevail in the Community, and Parties become highly disciplined and hostile, every measure of the major part of the Legislature is sure to receive the sanction of that Party among their Constituents to which they belong. Every Step of the minor Party, it is equally certain will be approved by their immediate adherents, as well as indiscriminately misrepresented or condemned by the prevailing voice. The Courts of Justice which are organized with peculiar advantages to exempt them from the [12] baneful influence of Faction, and to secure at the same time, a steady, firm and impartial interpretation of the Law, are therefore the most proper power in the Government to keep the Legislature within the limits of its duty, and to maintain the Authority of the Constitution.

It is regarded also as an undisputed principle in American Politics, that the different departments of Government should be kept as far as possible separate and distinct. The Legislative body ought not to exercise the Powers of the Executive and Judicial, or either of them, except in certain precise and clearly specified cases. An innovation upon this natural distribution of power, has a tendency to overturn the balance of the Government, and to introduce Tyranny into the Administration. But the interpretation or construction of the Constitution is as much a JUDICIAL act, and requires the exercise of the same LEGAL DISCRETION, as the interpretation or construction of a Law.

JAMES KENT 1763-1847

The Courts are indeed bound to regard the Constitution what it truly is, a Law of the highest nature, to which every inferior or derivative regulation must conform. It comes from the People themselves in their original character, when defining the permanent conditions of the social alliance. And to contend that the Courts must adhere implicitly to the Acts of the Legislature, without regarding the Constitution, and even when those Acts are in opposition to it, is to contend that the power of the Agent is greater than that of his Principal, and that the will of only one concurrent and co-ordinate department of the subordinate authority, ought to controul the fundamental Laws of the People.

[13] This power in the Judicial, of determining the constitutionality of Laws, is necessary to preserve the equilibrium of the government, and prevent usurpations of one part upon another; and of all the parts of government, the Legislative body is by far the most impetuous and powerful. A mere designation on paper, of the limits of the several departments, is altogether insufficient, and for this reason in limited Constitutions, the executive is armed with a negative, either qualified or complete upon the making of Laws. But the Judicial Power is the weakest of all, and as it is equally necessary to be preserved entire,* it ought not in sound theory to be left naked without any constitutional means of defence. This is one reason why the Judges in this State are associated with the Governor, to form the Council of Revision, and this association renders some of these observations less applicable to our own particular Constitution, than to any other. The right of expounding the Constitution as well as Laws, will however be found in general to be the most fit, if not only effectual weapon, by which the Courts of Justice are enabled to repel assaults, and to guard against encroachments on their Chartered Authorities.†

Nor can any danger be apprehended, lest this principle should exalt the Judicial above the Legislature. They are co-ordinate powers, and equally bound by the instrument under which they [14] act, and if the former should at any time be prevailed upon to substitute arbitrary will, to the exercise of a rational Judgment, as it is possible it may do even in the ordinary course of judicial proceeding, it is not

---

* Montesq, Spirit of Laws, Book xi, Chap. 6.
† See the decision of the Circuit Court of the United States, for the District of New York, April 5, 1972.

left like the latter, to the mere controul of public opinion. The Judges may be brought before the tribunal of the Legislature, and tried, condemned, and removed from office.

I consider then the Courts of Justice, as the proper and intended Guardians of our limited Constitutions, against the factions and encroachments of the Legislative Body. This affords an additional and weighty reason, for making a complete knowledge of those Constitutions to form the Rudiments of a public, and especially of a law Education. Nor are the accomplishments of Academical learning any ways repugnant to a rapid improvement in the Law. On the contrary, the course of instruction which is taught within these walls, will greatly assist the researches of the Student into the nature and history of all Governments,—will give him a just sense of the force of moral and political obligation, and will especially crown the career of his active life, with increasing honour and success. A Lawyer in a free country, should have all the requisites of Quinctilian's orator. He should be a person of irreproachable virtue and goodness. He should be well read in the whole circle of the Arts and Sciences. He should be fit for the administration of public affairs, and to govern the commonwealth by his councils, establish it by his Laws, and correct it by his Example. In short, he should resemble Tully, whose fruitful mind, as this [15] distinguished Teacher of oratory* observes, was not bounded by the walls of the Forum, but by those of nature. Nor do I recollect any material part of the attractive chain of classical studies, but which may be useful as well as ornamental in our legal pursuits.

The perusal of the best Greek and Roman Authors, the purest models of composition and correctness, is highly important to those who wish to form their taste and animate their genius. The ancient Classic Writers, are in general so distinguished for their good sense and manly graces, and have formed their Works on such sure principles of nature, that they have always been diligently studied in countries, and by scholars, the most celebrated for learning and accomplishments, and no doubt they will receive the admiration of the most distant ages. But it is not only with a general view to taste and elegance, or even for the glowing exhibition of public examples, that I would thus warmly recommend the original compositions of the ancients. The

* De Institutione oratoria, Lib. XII.

knowledge of the civil law, the most durable monument of the wisdom of the Romans, is extremely interesting, whether we consider the intrinsic merit of the system, or its influence upon the Municipal Laws of the land. That venerable body of Law, which was compiled under the auspices of the Emperor Justinian, and which has fortunately come down for the delight and improvement of modern times, discovers almost every where, the traces of an enlightened age of the Roman Jurisprudence. And it is a well known [16] fact, that altho the Taste and Philosophy of the Romans declined with their freedom, a succession of eminent Civilians continued to shine with equal lustre far under the Emperors, and Papinian, Paul, and Ulpian still preserved the sound sense and classic purity of the civil law.

The art of close reasoning, which is greatly helped by the Sciences of Logic and Mathematics, is of indispensable importance to those who wish to possess weight and reputation at the Bar. A distinguishing mind is to be sure not an ordinary gift. An accurate acquaintance with the general Principles of Universal Law, and an acute discernment of the minute and often latent circumstances which discriminate the operation of causes, and enable the means to be justly applied to the end, are the fruits only of great capacity and consummate application. Such fortunate geniuses are destined like Hardwicke or Mansfield, to enlighten and meliorate the Jurisprudence of their own times, and to render their names familiar with future generations. But as an eminent Author has observed,* legal studies require only a state of peace and refinement, and may even be pursued with a common share of judgment, experience and industry: and it will be found in almost every degree of natural talents, that mathematical and logical exercises, contribute to collect and strengthen the powers of the human mind.

The doctrines of Moral Philosophy form the foundation of Human Laws and must be deemed [17] an essential part of Juridical Education. It is the business of this Science to examine the nature and moral character of Man, the relations he stands in to the Great Author of his being, and to his Fellow-Men; the duties, the rights and happiness resulting from those relations. We are led by these inquiries to a knowledge of the nature, extent, and fitness of moral obligation, the object and efficacy of punishment, the necessity and final end of government, the justness and harmony of obedience.

* Gibbon's Hist. Vol. 8, 26.

But the Art of Public Speaking is singularly applicable to the Profession of the Law, which by its Bar and Senatorial Employments, possesses a field, which next to that of the Pulpit, is eminently within the region and under the influence of Eloquence. The object of public speaking is to illustrate and enforce the truth. To this end, it is necessary to remove prejudices, engage the attention, state the cause with clearness, arrange the arguments with skill, and deliver them with justness of expression and the force of sincerity. "Perhaps there is no scene of public speaking, says an elegant Teacher of the Science of Rhetoric,* where eloquence is more necessary than at the Bar. The dryness and subtilty of the subjects, generally agitated in such places, require more than any other a certain kind of eloquence in order to command attention; in order to give proper weight to the arguments that are employed, and to [18] prevent any thing which the pleader advances from passing unregarded." And when we recollect the intimate connection that subsists between the pursuits of Law and General Policy, and the path which is opened in this and in all free countries, from the laborious duties of the Bar into the deliberate Assemblies of the Nation, the Student is strongly invited to aim at something higher than the calm and temperate eloquence which is proper in his profession. He should strive to make himself a Master of the great variety of Public Interests, and the Springs of Public Action. He should cultivate a glowing Attachment to his Country and the best good of Mankind, and awaken in his breast those lively Passions which give the highest energy to the understanding, and the boldest efforts to eloquence. It was by virtues like these, added to the force of universal Education, that the ancient orators, most of whom were Lawyers, attained to such distinguished Pre-eminence in their age and country. And in like manner the principal ornaments of the English Bench and Bar, within the period of the present times, have been not more remarkable for their consummate knowledge of the Law, than for their Talents, Oratory and acquisitions as Scholars.

But I have ventured perhaps sufficiently far, in endeavouring to point out for the benefit of the Student, the principal advantages of a knowledge of our Government and Laws, and the utility of Academical Learning in aiding his pursuits. It remains only, that I designate the

* Blair's Lec. Vol. 2, 272.

[19] general path I intend to pursue in the course of the following LECTURES.

This is not the proper place to prescribe a System of Rules for the mere Mechanical Professor of our Laws. The design of this Institution, is undoubtedly of a more liberal kind. It is intended to explain the Principles of our Constitutions, the reason and History of our Laws, to illustrate them by a comparison with those of other Nations, and to point out the relation they bear to the spirit of Representative Republics. Nothing I apprehend is to be taught here, but what may be usefully known by every Gentleman of Polite Education, but is essential to be known by those whose intentions are to pursue the science of the Law as a practical Profession.

I propose to begin with an Examination of the nature and duties of Government in general, and a brief Historical Review of the several Forms of Government which have hitherto appeared in the World. The Political History of the United States, will then be considered from the earliest dawn to Union to the settlement of the present Constitution. The final establishment of our Independence, will naturally lead us to examine the consequence of our separate situation, by a summary review of the Law of Nations, as applicable to the several Conditions of Peace, of War and of Neutrality. With these preliminary dissertations, we shall be prepared to enter into a systematic View of the Constitution and Laws of the National Government.

[20] I shall consider the structure, rights, and Powers of Congress, the Constitution and Powers of the President, and of the subordinate Executive Departments, with a survey of the several subjects of a fiscal and military nature, which are incident to those departments. The Judicial System will next occupy our attention. This will involve a consideration of the organization, powers and jurisdiction of the Federal Courts, with an historical and critical examination of the elementary parts of a Suit at Law. The powers and objects of the Admiralty, and Equity side of those Courts will also be the subject of a distinct inquiry. I shall then conclude the Subject of the Federal Government and its Jurisprudence, with a detail of the Criminal Law, and the various proceedings in public prosecutions.

The constitutions of the several States, their structure and residuary portion of power, and particularly the Constitution of this State, in all its Branches, Legislative, Executive, and Judicial, will be the next and extensive subject of our inquiries. The remainder of this Course, will be principally if not entirely confined to the Municipal Laws of this State. This will lead me to examine the Rights of Property, both real and personal, in all their several gradations and modifications, and the several ways in which property is acquired and transferred. The interesting subject of Personal Contracts, will naturally involve itself in this examination. Our attention will probably be finally directed to the diffusive subject of Private Actions, and of Crimes [21] and Punishments, but with respect to some of these latter subjects I have not as yet been able to make the ultimate arrangements.

This is a SKETCH of the outlines of the Course of Lectures which are before me. The anxieties which are felt for the execution, are in some measure proportioned to the impressions which result from the dignity of the subject, and the interesting nature of this Institution. The Science of Law, has expressly for its object the advancement of social happiness and security. It reaches to every tie which is endearing to the affections, and has a concern in every action which takes place in the extensive circles of public and private life. According to the lively expression of Lord Bacon, it may justly be said to *come home to every man's business and bosom.* But there are other considerations which naturally arise in connection with our Reflections on the happy System of our Constitutions and Laws.

The events which are rapidly crowding the present æra, are to be deemed among the most solemn, and the most important in their consequences, of any which have hitherto been displayed in the History of Mankind. Great Revolutions are taking place in the European World, in Government, in Policy and in morals, and a new turn will be given to the habits of thinking, and probably to the destination of human society. A total demolition of the ancient fabrics, and the most daring hand of innovation, may possibly be expedient in the eastern continent, to recall [22] Society to its original Principles of simplicity and freedom; and to dissolve the long, intricate and oppressive chain of subordination, which has degraded the principal Nations of Europe, and who have been doomed so severely to suffer in the first instance by the violence of the Roman Power, and afterwards by the Genius of the Feudal System. But amidst the universal passion for novelty, which threatens to overturn every thing which bears the stamp of time and experience, we in this country ought to be extremely careful, not to pass along unconscious of the labours of the Patriots who effected our Revolution; nor let the admirable Fabrics of our Constitutions, and the all pervading Freedom of our Common Law, be left unheeded or despised. I am most thoroughly, most deeply persuaded, that we are favoured with the best Political Institutions, *take them for all in all,* of any People that ever were united in the Bonds of Civil Society. The goodness of these Institutions will brighten on free investigation, and faithful experiment, and be respected according as they are understood.

To preserve these best Fruits of our Independence, is a trust to be confided to the rising hopes of the day, to such of our Young Gentlemen as are animated with the generous passion of becoming hereafter distinguished as Lawyers, Magistrates and Statesmen; and permit me to add, it is a trust which they ought not to contemplate, but with a reverence due to its importance, and with a manly determination to deserve it. If he to whom is entrusted in this seat of Learning the cultivation of our Laws, can have any effect in elevating [23] the attention of some of our Youth from the narrow and selfish objects of the Profession, to the nobler study of the General Principles of our Governments, and the Policy of our Laws:—If he can in any degree illustrate their Reason, their Wisdom, and their propitious Influence on the freedom, order, and happiness of Society, and thereby produce a more general Interest in their support, he will deem it a happy consolation for his labors.

FINIS.

[61]

SAMUEL WILLIAMS 1743–1817

The Natural and Civil History of Vermont
(Chapters XIII, XIV, and XV)

WALPOLE, NEW HAMPSHIRE, 1794

In addition to sermons, pamphlets, and newspaper essays, a surprising number of books on politics, some of them multi-volume treatises, were published during the founding era. The present selection is an example. Since it is impossible to print here the four hundred pages and more that Williams wrote, three successive chapters in which political matters are most directly treated are reproduced—pages 324–351 of the original edition. The book enjoyed a long life as a textbook in the schools of Vermont and was reprinted as late as 1944. The author, son of a Massachusetts Congregationalist minister, was blessed with fine mental equipment, betrayed by excessive vanity, and enticed into moral lapses that led to his forced resignation from the Harvard College faculty at the age of forty-five. He instituted his career as a Congregational minister but from the day of his ordination found time for serious study of astronomy and mathematics, published occasional papers, and claimed to possess "the best astronomical apparatus in America" when he accepted a chair in Natural and Experimental Philosophy at Harvard. Forced out of this position ten years later, he made his way in disgrace to Rutland, Vermont, where he mustered a miserable income by publishing a newspaper and a magazine and doing odd jobs for the state government. Apparently not embittered by his previous defeats and current disfavor with fortune, Williams and his family were kindly received in the frontier capital. He responded by writing an analysis and critique of the state and its problems that is worth careful reading two hundred years later. A man with Samuel Williams' diverse interests and profound learning could not be satisfied writing a simple history, and in the sections reproduced here, the eye of an anthropologist is turned upon the American experience. The result is an analysis of American politics combining traditional, theoretical discourse with early social, scientific analysis.

CHAP. XIII.

STATE OF SOCIETY.—*Customs and Manners: Education, early Marriages, Activity, Equality, Economy, and Hospitality of the People.*

The customs and manners of nations are derived from descent, situation, employment, and all those regulations which have an influence upon the state of the people; and they serve better than other circumstances to ascertain the character of nations, and to denote the state of society at any given period in their history.—The customs and manners of the people of Vermont, are principally derived from the people of Newengland, from whom they are descended: But in a few particulars they have received a direction, from the state of society which takes place among the settlers in a new country.

EDUCATION.—Among the customs which are universal among the people, in all parts of the state, one that seems worthy of remark, is, the attention that is paid to the education of children. The aim of the parent, is not so much to have his children acquainted with the liberal arts and sciences; but to have them all taught to read with ease and propriety; to write a plain and legible hand; and to have them acquainted with the rules of arithmetic, so far as shall be necessary to carry on any of the most common and necessary occupations of life. All the children are trained up to this kind of knowledge: They [325] are accustomed from their earliest years to read the Holy Scriptures, the periodical publications, newspapers, and political pamphlets; to form some general acquaintance with the laws of their country, the proceedings of the courts of justice, of the general assembly of the state, and of the Congress, &c. Such a kind of education is common and universal in every part of the state: And nothing would be more dishonourable to the parents, or to the children, than to be without it. One of the first things the new settlers attend to, is to procure a schoolmaster to instruct their children in the arts of reading, writing, and arithmetic: And where they are not able to procure or to hire an instructor, the parents attend to it themselves. No greater misfortune could attend a child, than to arrive at manhood unable to read, write, and keep small accounts: He is viewed as unfit for the common business of the towns and plantations, and in a state greatly inferiour to his neighbours. Every consideration joins to prevent so degraded and mortifying a state, by giving to every one the customary education, and advantages.—This custom was derived from the people of New-england; and has acquired greater force in the new settlements, where the people are apprehensive their children will have less advantages, and of consequence, not appear equal to the children in the older towns.—No custom was ever better adapted to private, or public good. Such kind of education and knowledge, is of more advantage to mankind, than all the speculations, disputes, and distinctions, that metaphysics, logic, and scholastic theology, have ever produced. In the plain common good sense, promoted by the one, virtue, utility, freedom, and public happiness, have their foundations. In the useless speculations produced by the other, common sense is lost, folly becomes refined, and the useful branches of knowledge are darkened, and forgot.

[326] EARLY MARRIAGES.—Another custom, which every thing tends to introduce in a new country, is early marriage. Trained up to a regular industry and economy the young people grow up to maturity, in all the vigour of health, and bloom of natural beauty. Not enervated by idleness, weakened by luxury, or corrupted by debauchery, the inclinations of nature are directed towards their proper objects, at an early period; and assume the direction, which nature and society designed they should have. The ease with which a family may be maintained, and the wishes of parents to see their children settled in the way of virtue, reputation, and felicity, are circumstances, which also strongly invite to an early settlement in life. The virtuous affections are not corrupted nor retarded by the pride of families, the ambition of ostentation, or the idle notions of useless and dangerous distinctions, under the name of honour and titles. Neither parents nor children have any other prospects, than what are founded upon industry, economy, and virtue.—Where every circumstance thus concurs to promote early marriages, the practice becomes universal, and it generally takes place, as soon as the laws of society suppose the young people of sufficient age and discretion to transact the business of life.—It is not necessary to enumerate the many advantages, that arise from this custom of early marriages. They comprehend all the society can receive from this source; from the preservation, and increase of the human race. Every thing useful and beneficial to man, seems to be connected with obedience to the laws of his nature: And where the state of society coincides with the laws of nature, the inclinations, the duties, and the happiness of individuals, resolve themselves into

customs and habits, favourable, in the highest degree, to society. In no case is this more apparent, than in the customs of nations respecting marriage. When [327] wealth, or the imaginary honour of families, is the great object, marriage becomes a matter of trade, pride, and form; in which affection, virtue, and happiness, are not consulted; from which the parties derive no felicity, and society receives no advantage. But where nature leads the way, all the lovely train of virtues, domestic happiness, and the greatest of all public benefits, a rapid population, are found to be the fruit.

ACTIVITY AND ENTERPRIZE.—A spirit of activity and enterprize is every where found in a new state. Depending upon their own industry, and having nothing to expect from speculation and gaming in public funds, or from the errors or vices of government, the views of the people are directed to their own employments and business, as the only probable method of acquiring subsistence, and estate. Hence arises a spirit of universal activity, and enterprize in business. No other pursuits or prospects are suffered to divert their attention; for there is nothing to be acquired in any other way. Neither begging, or gaming, or trading upon public funds, measures, and management, can be profitable employments to the people who live at a distance from wealthy cities, and the seat of government. The only profitable business, is to pursue their own profession and calling.—To this pursuit their views become directed; and here, their activity and enterprize become remarkable. No difficulty or hardship seem to discourage them: And the perseverance of a few years generally serves to overcome the obstacles, that lay in their way at first. It is only those who are of this enterprising spirit, who venture to try their fortunes in the woods; and in a few years, it generally raises them into easy and comfortable circumstances.—To the most essential and necessary duties of man, heaven has annexed immediate and important blessings. The people thus active, laborious, [328] and perpetually in hard exertions, are destitute of many of the conveniences of life; and of what, in every populous city, would be esteemed its necessaries. Can their health and spirits remain unimpaired, amidst this scene of hard living, and hard labour? Will they not waste away thus labouring in the woods, without good living, able physicians, and the advantages of medicine? So far from it, that no people have so few diseases, multiply so fast, or suffer so little from sickness. Temperance and labour do more for them, than art and medicine can do for others.

The disorders which wear away the inhabitants of wealthy cities, are almost unknown in the woods. Very few die, but under the unavoidable decays of nature; and the deaths are to the births, in no higher a proportion than 1 to 4,8. Unacquainted with the improvements which are made in the medical art in Europe, the people of the new settlements neither know the names of the diseases, or their remedies; nor stand in any need of their discoveries, or prescriptions. The benevolent Author of Nature has annexed that health to their temperance, industry, and activity, which is never found in drugs, medicines, or any attainments of art. And while the people are thus active and industrious in performing their duty, the property and health of individuals, and the prosperity of the state, are all found to flourish together.

EQUALITY.—The nearest equality that ever can take place among men, will also be found among the inhabitants of a new country. When a number of men are engaged in the same employments and pursuits, and have all of them to depend upon their own labour and industry for their support, their situation, views, and manners, will be nearly the same; the way to subsistence, to ease, and independence, being the same to all. In this stage of society the nearest equality will take place, that ever can subsist among [329] men. But this equality will be nothing more than an equality of rights; and a similarity of employment, situation, pursuit, and interest. In a new country this similarity will be so great, as to form a near resemblance of manners and character; and to prevent any very great inequalities of privilege from taking place in society, either from rank, offices of government, or any other cause.—But nothing ever did, or ever can produce an equality of power, capacity, and advantages, in the social, or in any other state of man. By making men very unequal in their powers and capacities, nature has effectually prevented this. The whole race resemble one another in the make and form of their bodies; in their original appetites, passions, and inclinations; in reason, understanding, and the moral sense, &c. But in these respects it is similitude, not equality, which nature has produced. To some, the Author of Nature has assigned superiour powers of the mind, a strength of reason and discernment, a capacity of judging, and a genius for invention, which are not given to others. To others, the Deity has assigned a strength, vigour, and firmness of constitution, by which the bodily powers are more favoured in one, than in another. Causes thus natural and original, will be followed with their natural and proper effects.

Superiour wisdom and abilities, will have superiour influence and effect in society. Superiour strength and activity of body, will also have advantages peculiar to themselves. In making these natural distinctions, nature evidently designed to qualify men for different attainments, and employments. And while she gave to all the nature and the rights of man, she assigned to some a capacity and a power, to make a much more useful improvement and exercise of that nature, and of those rights, than she has given to others.—Thus a state of nature is itself a state of society, or at least naturally tends to produce [330] it. And in the earliest stages of society, all that equality will take place among mankind, which is consistent with it. Placed in a situation nearly similar, the employments, views, and pursuits of the people, become nearly the same. The distinctions derived from birth, blood, hereditary titles and honours, and a difference of rights and privileges, are either unknown or resolve themselves into nothing, among a people in such a situation; in every view, they cease to be of any use or importance to them. Their situation naturally leads them to discern the tendencies, and designs of nature. They all feel that nature has made them equal in respect to their rights; or rather that nature has given to them a common and an equal right to liberty, to property, and to safety; to justice, government, laws, religion, and freedom. They all see that nature has made them very unequal in respect to their original powers, capacities, and talents. They become united in claiming and in preserving the equality, which nature has assigned to them; and in availing themselves of the benefits, which are designed, and may be derived from the inequality, which nature has also established. Wherever a number of people are engaged in a common, economical, laborious pursuit of subsistence, property, and security; such views of their equality, and rights, immediately occur to their minds; they are easily discerned, and they are perfectly well understood.

ECONOMY.—Every thing in the situation and employments of the people, in a new country, will naturally tend to produce economy. There are no large estates, or cultivated farms, prepared beforehand for the heir. Every thing for food, raiment, and convenience, must be procured by the labour and industry of the planter; and it is not without much difficulty and hardship, that the people can procure the necessaries of life at first, or the conveniences [331] of it afterwards. What is thus procured with labour and difficulty, will be used with prudence and economy. The custom will not be to fall into scenes of expensive entertainments, amusement, and dissipation: But to provide for the calls and demands of nature, to preserve the health and vigour of the body, and to be able to raise up and support a family. And this will of course, introduce a steady regard to economy, in all their expenses, habits, and customs.—The influence that this has on the affairs of individuals, and on the state of society, is every where apparent. No such degrees of wealth can ever exist in any place, as shall be equal to the demands of luxury. And where custom has introduced a habit of living and expense, above the annual income, dependence, venality, and corruption, with constant want and distress, is the never failing consequence. But the most pernicious of all the effects of luxury, is the degradation it brings on the nature of man. It destroys the vigour and powers of men, and by constantly enfeebling the body and mind, seems to reduce them to a lower order of beings. The body, weakened by excessive indolence and indulgence, loses health, vigour, and beauty, and becomes subject to a thousand emaciating pains and maladies. The mind, subdued by indolence and inactivity, scarcely retains its rational powers; and becomes weak, languid, and incapable of manly exertions, or attainments. To a state thus degraded, effeminate, and unmanly, luxury frequently reduces those, who bear the remains of the human form. Political writers have frequently argued that luxury was of real service to the nations of Europe; that it tended to find employments for the poor, and was necessary to keep the money in circulation. This reasoning cannot be contradicted: But it supposes the state of society to be essentially bad; and that it cannot be supported but [332] by the management, operations, and balance of vices. In such a state of society, luxury is certainly a benefit: And the highest degree of it, would be the greatest benefit of all. It would be the best thing that could happen in such a society, for the corrupted venal part to spend their estates, by luxury and dissipation, and to have them pass into other hands. This would be far better for mankind than to have them live useless, be constantly corrupting others, or train up an emaciated feeble race, degraded by effeminacy and weakness, below the rest of the human race. Whatever might be done to load such with honours, titles, and distinctions, it will be impossible ever to make them men; or at least such kind of men, as shall be upon terms of equality with the rest of the human race.—Activity, industry, and economy, will prevent such a race from appearing, or such effects from taking place, in any of the new states of America.

HOSPITALITY.—That benevolent friendly disposition, which man should bear to man, will appear under different forms, in different stages of society. In the first combinations of mankind, when all are exposed to danger, sufferings, and want, it appears in one of its most amiable forms, and has been called hospitality. In this form it exists among the people who are subjected to the common danger, fatigue, and sufferings, which attend the forming of new settlements. Feeling every moment their own wants and dangers, they are led by their situation, to assist each other in their difficulties and danger. The traveller finds among them, all the relief their circumstances will enable them to afford him: And before they are able to erect houses for public entertainment, the stranger is sure to find the best accommodations, the situation of private families will admit.—This hospitable disposition seems to be universal, in all the new settlements: And the [333] unfortunate and poor man finds a relief from it, which he never expects to find among a more wealthy people. No custom was ever better adapted to afford relief to an individual, or to promote the advantage of the state. A beggar or robber is scarcely ever to be seen in a country, where there is nothing to be obtained by the business. The poor find their relief in labour, and not from a multiplicity of laws, which extract large sums from others, but afford little relief to them: And from the profits of their labour, they will soon cease to be in distress. Those that appear to be objects of distress, are generally such in reality: And where the public has not been abused by such pretences, few will be exposed to suffer on such accounts. In such a state of society, hospitality naturally performs what it ought to perform: It encourages none in idleness and dissipation, but relieves those whose circumstances require relief. It provides only for those, who cannot find other resources; and aims only to put such into a situation, in which they may support themselves, and be of use to the public.

[334]   CHAP. XIV.

STATE OF SOCIETY.—*Religion: Importance of this Principle, Danger of any Controul in it, Equality of all Denominations, Effect of this Equality,*

*Grants and Laws for the Support of Religion, Extent of Religious Liberty,
Connexion of Religion with Science and Education.*

Religion is one of those concerns, which will always have great influence
upon the state of society. In our original frame and constitution, the
Benevolent Author of our Natures, has made us rational and accountable
creatures: Accountable to ourselves, to our fellow men, and to our
God. These foundations of religion, are so strong, and universal, that
they will not fail to have an effect upon the conduct of every one:
And while they thus enter into the feelings and conduct of all the
members, they will unavoidably have a great influence upon the state
and conduct of society. Nor can society either set them aside, or carry
on the public business without them. Instead of this, in one form or
another, society will be perpetually calling in the aids of religion.
When human declarations and evidence are to receive their highest
force, and most solemn form, or when the most important transactions
are to be performed, and offices of the highest trust and consequence
are committed [335] to men, the last appeal will be to religion, in
the form of solemn affirmation or oath.

The most pure and benevolent system of religion, which has ever
prevailed among men, is that of Christianity. This religion founded
in truth, and adapted to the nature and state of man, has proposed
for its end and aim, that which is of the highest importance to men
and to society, universal benevolence, the love of God and man, or
universal virtue. But neither this, nor any other system of moral truth,
can impart infallibility to men. Whatever infallibility there may be
in moral, in mathematical, or in revealed truths, men may greatly
mistake when they come to explain, and apply them: And instead of
being above all possibility of error, they will find that infallibility
belongs only to the government of God; and that it certainly is not
entailed upon any parties, or denominations of men.—Nothing
therefore could be more dangerous, than to allow to any of these
denominations the power to make laws to bind the rest, in matters of
religion. The ruling party would vote themselves to be the only pure
denomination, they would make the rest contribute to their support,
and establish their own sentiments and practice, as the perfection of
knowledge, wisdom, and religion; and in this way adopt measures,
which tend to entail all their imperfections and errors, upon future
ages. The dominion of one party over another in matters of religion,

has always had this effect: It has operated to confirm error, oppress the minority, prevent the spirit of free inquiry and investigation; and subjected men to the most unrelenting of all persecutions, the persecution of priests and zealots, pleading principle to justify their vilest actions.—At the same time, every good man feels himself bound not to renew or admit any such authority in matters of religion. The obligations of religion are antecedent to, and more [336] strong than any obligations derived from the laws of society. The first and the most important obligation any man can feel, is to obey his Maker, and the dictates of his own heart. The peace of our minds depends more essentially upon this, than any other circumstance in the course of human life.—What then has society to do in matters of religion, but simply to follow the laws of nature: To adopt these, and no other; and to leave to every man a full and perfect liberty, to follow the dictates of his own conscience, in all his transactions with his Maker?

The people of Vermont have adopted this principle, in its fullest extent. Some of them are episcopalians, others are congregationalists, others are of the presbyterian, and others are of the baptist persuasion; and some are quakers. All of them find their need of the assistance of each other, in the common concerns and business of life; and all of them are persuaded, that the government has nothing to do with their particular and distinguishing tenets.—It is not barely *toleration,* but *equality,* which the people aim at. Toleration implies either a power or a right in one party, to bear with the other; and seems to suppose, that the governing party are in possession of the truth, and that all the others are full of errors. Such a toleration is the most that can be obtained by the minority, in any nation, where the majority assume the right and the power, to bind society, by established laws and forms in religion. The body of the people in this commonwealth, carry their ideas of religious liberty much further than this: That no party shall have any power to make laws or forms to oblige another; that each denomination may lay themselves under what civil contracts and obligations they please; but that government shall not make any distinctions between them; that all denominations shall enjoy [337] equal liberty, without any legal distinction or preeminence whatever.

The effect of this religious freedom, is peace, quietness, and prosperity to the state. No man is chosen to, or excluded from civil offices, on account of his particular religious sentiments. The clergy of the several denominations, have no chance to assume any powers,

but among their own party. The people are under no obligation to
support any teachers, but what they choose to lay themselves under.
And no civil advantages are to be gained, or lost, by belonging to
one denomination, rather than to another. The causes and the motives
to contention, being thus taken away, there is scarcely any thing left
to influence men to join one denomination rather than another, but
belief, sentiment, and conscience. In this equality of all parties,
religious professions become what they always ought to be; not matters
of gain, profit, or civil distinctions; but matters of opinion, persuasion,
and conscience: Sentiments and faith respecting the Deity, in which
none expect to find the power of oppressing or ruling over others; but
the same protection and benefit from the government, which they are
at equal expense in supporting.

The settlement and support of the ministers of religion, has been
encouraged and assisted by the government. The earliest grants of
land in this state, were made by Benning Wentworth, governor of
Newhampshire. This gentleman was of the communion of the church
of England. In the grants of land that were made by him, there were
three rights in each township reserved for religious purposes: One to
the society for propagating the gospel in foreign parts; one for a glebe,
designed for the use of an episcopal clergy; a third for the first settled
minister, intended for his private property, to [338] encourage the
settlement of a minister in the new plantations. In the grants of
townships, which have been made by the government of Vermont,
two rights have been reserved for the support of a clergy: One for a
parsonage, designed for the support of a minister, and unalienable
from that purpose; another to become the property, and designed to
encourage the settlement of the first minister. This right accrues to
the first clergyman who is settled in the town, of whatever denomination
he may be.—The salary of the minister ariseth wholly from the
contract which the people may make with him. These contracts are
altogether voluntary: But when made, by a law passed October 18,
1787, are considered as being of equal force and obligation as any
other contracts; but no persons of a different denomination are obliged
by them. The law has no reference to any particular denomination,
but considers them all as having a right to make what contracts they
please, with the minister they choose; and being of course bound by
their own act, to fulfil their contract. A law designed to confirm the

equal rights of all, is not subject to the exceptions or complaints of any party.

No embarrassments have attended any of the grants of land, which have been made for religious purposes, but those designed for a glebe, and those made to the society for propagating the gospel in foreign parts. In most of the towns there are not any persons of the episcopal persuasion, nor any incumbent to have the care of the glebe lots. The society for propagating the gospel in foreign parts, have not concerned themselves about the lands, which were granted to them. Both these rights have remained unimproved and uncultivated, except where individuals have gained possession of them; and it has been a disadvantage to the state, to have such tracts of land lying waste. It has been repeatedly a [339] matter of consideration in the general assembly, what ought to be done with these lands.—Instead of coming to any decision upon the matter, in October, 1787, the general assembly passed an act, authorising the selectmen of the several towns, to take care of and improve the glebe and society lands, for the space of seven years; and to apply the incomes to the improvements of the lands, those excepted, which were in the possession of an episcopal minister. This law has been but little attended to, and is not at all competent to the improvement of the lands, or to render them beneficial to the state, or to any valuable purpose.—In any view of the matter, these lands ought not to be suffered to remain useless, and detrimental to the state. If the society for propagating the gospel in foreign parts, had made such as assignation of them, as would have served to promote religious instruction and knowledge, the people would have had the benefit that was intended by the grantor. If this be neglected an unreasonable time, it becomes the duty of the legislature, to prevent their remaining a public disadvantage to the state, by continuing uncultivated and useless.

The principles of religious liberty, are asserted in their fullest extent, in the constitution of Vermont. In the declaration of rights, there is a clause which seems to be adequate to the subject, and clearly expresses the religious rights of the people.—"Nor can any man be justly deprived or abridged of any civil right as a citizen, on account of his religious sentiments, or peculiar mode of religious worship; and no authority can, or ought to be vested in, or assumed by any power whatever, that shall in any case interfere with, or in any manner controul the rights of conscience, in the free exercise of religious worship."* In the plan of government formed in [340] 1778, and revised in 1786, a religious test was imposed upon the members of the assembly, inconsistent with the above declaration: In the late revisal of the constitution (1792) this imperfection has been done away; and religious liberty has acquired a complete establishment, by a declaration that "no religious test shall be required of any member of the legislature."†

A greater attention to the liberal arts and science, would be of great advantage to the religious and civil interests of the state. The people of Vermont have not the advantages for the education of their youth, or the improvement of knowledge, which the people in the other states have. The disadvantages and dangers, which arise for want of literary institutions, are greater than they are aware of. The religion of ignorance, will either be, infidelity, or superstition; and it often produces an unnatural mixture of both, greatly unfavourable to the moral, and civil interests of men. When folly, in its own view, is become infallible and sacred, it opposes with obstinacy, all improvements in society; and requires, with a peculiar insolence, the submission of all other men, to its own weakness and bigotry. The only remedy for the difficulties which arise in society, from this cause, is the increase of knowledge and education. And where society is destitute of the means and institutions, which are requisite to promote knowledge, it is without one of its most essential advantages; the means of her own cultivation, and improvement.

The education of children for the common business of life, is well attended to. But the customary methods of education for the professions of divinity, law, or physic, are extremely deficient; and do not promise either eminence, or improvement. The [341] body of the people appear to be more sensible of this defect, than professional men themselves. From the first assumption of all of the powers of government, the assembly had in contemplation, the establishment of an university in the state; and with this view, reserved one right of land in all the townships which they granted, for the use of such a seminary. In November, 1791, the legislature passed an act establishing the university at Burlington, upon a liberal, catholic, and judicious foundation. It has not as yet, entered upon the business of instruction.

---

* Declaration of rights, Article III.
† Plan or frame of government, Section V.

If it should be furnished with able and judicious instructors, by extending the benefits of education, and promoting an attention to the arts and sciences, it would greatly assist the intellectual and moral improvement of the people: These improvements are of essential importance to men, in every stage of society; but most of all necessary, when they are forming a new state.

[342]   CHAP. XV.

STATE OF SOCIETY—*Nature of the American Government. Constitution of Vermont, Laws.*

NATURE OF THE AMERICAN GOVERNMENT. The object and the principle of government is the same, in every part of the United States of America. The end or the design of it, is the public business; not the power, the emolument, or the dignity, of the persons employed, but only that public business which concerns either the whole federal territory, or some particular state.—The *principle* on which all the American governments are founded, is *representation.* They do not admit of sovereignty, nobility, or any kind of hereditary powers; but only of powers granted by the people, ascertained by written constitutions, and exercised by representation for a given time.

Governments founded on this principle, do not necessarily imply the same form. They do not admit of monarchy, or aristocracy; nor do they admit of what was called democracy by the ancients. In the ancient democracies the public business was transacted in the assemblies of the people: The whole body assembled to judge and decide, upon public affairs. Upon this account, the ancient democracies were found to be unfit, and inadequate to the government of a large nation. In America this [343] difficulty never occurs: All is transacted by representation. Whatever may be the number of the people, or the extent of the territory, representation is proportioned to it; and thus becomes expressive of the public sentiment, in every part of the union. Hence the government in different states, though chiefly republican, varies in its form; committing more or less power to a governor, senate, or house of representatives, as the circumstances of any particular state may require. As each of these branches derive their whole power from the people, are accountable to them for the use and exercise they make of it, and may be displaced by the election of others; the security of the people is derived not from the nice ideal application of checks, ballances, and mechanical powers, among the different parts of the government; but from the responsibility, and dependence of each part of the government, upon the people.

This kind of government seems to have had its form and *origin*, from nature. It is not derived from any of the histories of the ancient republics. It is not borrowed from Greece, Rome, or Carthage. Nor does it appear that a government founded in representation ever was adopted among the ancients, under any form whatever.—Representation thus unknown to the ancients, was gradually introduced into Europe by her monarchs; not with any design to favour the rights of the people, but as the best means that they could devise to raise money. The monarchs who thus introduced it, with a view to collect money from the people, always took care to check it when it ventured to examine the origin and extent of the privileges of the sovereign, or of the rights of the people.—In America every thing tended to introduce, and to complete the system of representation. Made equal in their rights by nature, the body of the people were in a situation nearly [344] similar with regard to their employments, pursuits, and views. Without the distinctions of titles, families, or nobility, they acknowledged and reverenced only those distinctions which nature had made, in a diversity of talents, abilities, and virtues. There were no family interests, connexions, or estates, large enough to oppress them. There was no excessive wealth in the hands of a few, sufficient to corrupt them. Britain tried in vain to force upon them a government, at first, derived from the decrees of her parliament; afterwards, from conquest. Nothing remained for such a people, but to follow what nature taught; and as they were too numerous to attempt to carry on their governments in the form of the ancient democracies, they naturally adopted the system of representation: Every where choosing representatives, and assigning to them such powers as their circumstances required. This was evidently the system of government, that nature pointed out: And it is a system that has no where been suffered to prevail but in America, and what the people were naturally lead to by the situation, in which Providence had placed them. The system of government then in America, is not derived from superstition, conquest, military power, or a pretended compact between the rulers and the people; but it was derived from nature, and reason; and is

SAMUEL WILLIAMS 1743–1817

founded in the nature, capacities, and powers, which God hath assigned to the race of men.

All the *Power* that such governments can have, is derived from the public opinion. The body of the people while they remain industrious and economical, will be steadily attached to the public interest, which will entirely coincide with their own. They will more readily discern what their interest is, and be more steadily attached to it, than is to be expected from men who are placed in offices of honour and profit. The public opinion will be much [345] nearer the truth, than the reasonings and refinements of speculative or interested men: The former will be founded wholly in a desire, and aim, to promote the public safety; the latter will be unavoidably more or less governed, by private views, interests, and aims: And when the government has the general opinion of the people to support it, it can act with the greatest force and power; that is, with the collected force and power of the whole nation: And this is the greatest force that ever can be exerted by any government, in any situation whatever.— Despotism never acquires a force equal to this. When a whole nation unite, and the public spirit moves and operates in the same direction, nothing can withstand its force, and the powers of despotism, with all their standing troops and regular armies, fall before it. It is only when the public sentiment and spirit is thus united, and brought into action, that government has acquired, or is able to exert the whole force of the national power.—With this strength, the governments of America amidst every kind of difficulty, rose superiour to all opposition; firmly established themselves, in fifteen different states; and gave uncommon vigour and efficacy to a federal establishment, which was designed and adapted to manage the public business of the whole system.

But whatever be the form or the power of government, it cannot attain its greatest perfection, unless it contains within itself, the means of its own *improvement*. The men of civilized countries, are making gradual and constant improvements in knowledge, in the sciences, and in all the arts by which life is made more secure and happy. Hence, that form of government which was best suited to their state in one stage of society, ceases to be so, in another: And unless the government itself improves, with the gradual improvement of society, it will lose much of its respectability, and power; become unsuited to [346] the state, and injurious to the people. Despotism has always contemplated the body of the people, as mere mob; and has aimed and operated to keep them in that situation. To governments founded in this principle, the improvement of mankind proves fatal and destructive: And there is nothing, such governments are more anxious to prevent, than knowledge, property, and improvement, in the body of the people.—Built upon the rational and social nature of man, the American government expects to find its surest support, and greatest duration, in the gradual improvement, in the encreasing knowledge, virtue, and freedom, of the human race. The present government of America, is therefore proposed to her citizens, not as the most perfect standard of what man can ever attain to, but only as the best form, which we have as yet been able to discover: Not as a form, which is to bind our heirs and posterity forever, but as a form which is referred to them, to alter and improve, as they shall find best. Upon this idea, it is one of the constituent and essential parts of American government, that conventions shall be called at certain periods of time, to alter, amend, and improve the present form and constitution of government; as the state, circumstances, and improvements of society, shall then require. Thus provision is made, that the improvement of government, shall keep pace with the improvement of society in America. And no policy would appear more puerile or contemptible to the people of America, than an attempt to bind posterity to our forms, or to confine them to our degrees of knowledge, and improvement: The aim is altogether the reverse, to make provision for the perpetual improvement and progression of the government itself.

As this kind of government is not the same as that, which has been called monarchy, aristocracy, or democracy; as it had a conspicuous origin in America, [347] and has not been suffered to prevail in any other part of the globe, it would be no more than just and proper, to distinguish it by its proper name, and call it, *The American System of Government*.

CONSTITUTION OF VERMONT.—The government of Vermont is of the same nature, and founded upon the same principles, as the other governments in the United States. By their constitution, formed in 1778, and revised in 1786, and 1792, the supreme legislative power is vested in a house of representatives of the freemen. Every town has a right to choose a representative, on the first Tuesday of September annually. The representatives so chosen, are to meet on the second Thursday of the succeeding October, and are styled *The General*

SAMUEL WILLIAMS 1743–1817

Assembly of the state of Vermont. They have power to choose their own officers; to sit on their own adjournments; prepare bills, and enact them into laws; they may expel members, but not for causes known to their constituents antecedent to their election; impeach state criminals; grant charters of incorporation, constitute towns, boroughs, cities, and counties; in conjunction with the council they are annually to elect judges of the supreme, county, and probate courts, sheriffs and justices of the peace; and also with the council, may elect majorgenerals, and brigadiergenerals, as often as there shall be occasion: They have all other powers necessary for the legislature of a free and sovereign state: But have no power to add to, alter, abolish, or infringe any part of the constitution.

The supreme executive power is vested in a governor, or lieutenantgovernor, and a council of twelve persons, chosen by the freemen, at the same time they choose their representative. The governor, or the lieutenantgovernor and council, are to commission all officers; prepare such business as may appear to them necessary to lay before the general [348] assembly: They are to sit as judges to hear and determine on impeachments, taking to their assistance, for advice only, the judges of the supreme court. They have power to grant pardons, and remit fines, in all cases whatsoever, except in treason and murder, in which they have power to grant reprieves, but not to pardon until after the end of the next session of assembly, and in cases of impeachment, in which there is no remission or mitigation of punishment, but by act of legislation. They may also lay embargoes, or prohibit the exportation of any commodity, for any time not exceeding thirty days, in the recess of the house only.—The governor is captaingeneral and commander in chief of the forces of the state, but shall not command in person, except advised thereto by the council, and then only so long as they shall approve: And the lieutenantgovernor by virtue of his office, is lieutenantgeneral of all the forces of the state.

That the laws before they are enacted may be more maturely considered, and the inconvenience of hasty determinations as much as possible prevented, all bills which originate in the assembly are laid before the governor and council for their revision and concurrence, or proposals of amendment; who return the same to the assembly with their proposals of amendment (if any) in writing; and if the same are not agreed to by the assembly, it is in the power of the governor and

council, to suspend the passing of such bills, until the next session of
the legislature. But no negative is allowed to the governor and council.

The formers of the constitution were aware that the plan of
government, which they had drawn up, would not be adequate to the
affairs of government, when the state of the people should become
different, but must necessarily vary with it: And they wisely made
provision to have the whole examined [349] and revised, at the end
of every seven years. The provision they made for this purpose was a
council of censors, to consist of thirteen persons, to be elected by the
people every seventh year, on the last Wednesday in March; and to
assemble on the first Wednesday in June. The duty assigned to them,
is to inquire whether the constitution has been preserved inviolate in
every part; whether the legislative and executive branches of government
have performed their duty, as guardians of the people; or assumed to
themselves, or exercised other or greater powers, than they are entitled
to by the constitution; whether the public taxes have been justly laid,
and collected; in what manner the public monies have been disposed
of; and whether the laws have been duly executed. Powers fully
competent to these purposes, are committed to them. They may send
for persons, papers, and records: They have authority to pass public
censures, to order impeachments, and to recommend to the legislature
the repealing such laws, as shall appear to them to have been enacted
contrary to the principles of the constitution. These powers they may
exercise during the space of one year, from the time of their election;
and they may call a convention to meet within two years after their
sitting, if they judge it necessary.

In examining a constitution of government, the most capital
circumstance to be taken into consideration, is, the condition and
circumstances of the people, or the state of society among them. At
the first assumption of government in Vermont, the form of it differed
but little from the democracy of the ancients. From that period, it
has been constantly tending to give more power to the house of
representatives,—But it is found by experience, that in so popular a
government, nothing is more necessary than some provision, like that
of the council of censors, to have all the public proceedings revised at
[350] certain periods of time; and such alterations made in the
constitution, as time, events, or the circumstances of the people, may
require. As the state of society is progressive, there is no way to have

the government adapted to the state of society, but to have the government also progressive; that both may admit of the improvements, that are gradually made in human affairs. With this provision, a constitution of government which contains many faults, will gradually mend and improve itself, without being forced to the dangers and convulsions of a revolution: And it seems to be the only provision which human wisdom has yet found to prevent the interposition of such calamities.

LAWS.—So much of the common law of England as is not repugnant to the constitution, or to any act of the legislature, is adopted as law within this state: And such statute laws, and parts of laws of the kingdom of England and Greatbritain, as were passed before the first day of October, 1760, for the explanation of the common law, and are not repugnant to the constitution, or some act of the legislature, and are applicable to the circumstances of the state, are also adopted and made law in Vermont.—The criminal law of Greatbritain seems to be adapted only to a very degraded, vicious, and barbarous state of society. No less than one hundred and sixty crimes are punishable by death. Sanguinary laws and executions have there made death so common and familiar, that it seems to have become one of those common occurrences, which is constantly to be expected, and is very little regarded. Several of the punishments, in the contrivances of their cruelty, are fully equal to any thing that has ever been perpetrated by the Indians of America: In brutal rage and inhuman torture, the punishment assigned to high treason, fairly exceeds any thing the Indian genius could ever conceive.—Such a code of [351] criminal law is wholly unfitted to the uncorrupted state of the people in America; nor would they in any part of the continent, be persuaded to admit it. Instead of one hundred and sixty, there are only nine crimes, to which the laws of Vermont have assigned the punishment of death: And since the first assumption of government in 1777, there has not been any person convicted of any of these crimes.—What relates to the internal affairs of government, the regulations necessary for a new country, or such as are suited to our particular state of society, are provided for by statutes made for such particular cases and purposes.—To form a code of laws suited to the state of a large nation, has been justly esteemed the most difficult part of government. It does not appear that human wisdom has ever been able to effect this without great errors, in any part of the earth. If it is to be obtained, the particular states of America have now a fair opportunity to make the experiment, how far human wisdom can proceed at present, in effecting this arduous but most important attainment.

[62]

JACK NIPS

[JOHN LELAND 1754–1841]

The Yankee Spy

BOSTON, 1794

John Leland could point to ancestors who had been in North America a full century before his birth. At the age of eighteen, having only the education provided in elementary schools, he was licensed as a Baptist preacher. His first pastorates were in Virginia where he was deeply moved by his observations of slavery. At age 37 he returned to the Bay State to complete a career that won him repute as a worthy successor of Isaac Backus, great founder and leader of the church in New England. As a Baptist clergyman, John Leland had a vested interest in the doctrine of separation of Church and State, since any connection between the two would invariably work to the detriment of the Baptists, who were in a distinct minority everywhere. It is not surprising, then, that Leland was influential in the passage of the Virginia Statute of Religious Freedom, in 1786. He supported the United States Constitution only after James Madison assured him that a bill of rights guaranteeing freedom of religion would be added. The essay reproduced here, which begins in catechism form, is surprisingly modern, and relevant to issues that still exercise American politics in the late twentieth century.

———

THE YANKEE SPY.

Question. Why are men obliged, every year, to pay their taxes?
Answer. To support government.
Q. What is government?
A. The government here intended, is the mutual compact of a

certain body of people, for the general safety of their lives, liberty, and property.

Q. Are all systems of civil government founded in compact?

A. No: successful robbers and tyrants have founded their systems in *conquest*—enthusiasts and priest-ridden people have founded theirs in *grace*—while men without merit have founded their system in *birth;* but the true principle, that all Gentile nations should found their government upon, is, *compact.*

Q. Was civil government appointed by the Almighty from the beginning?

A. It was not; nor was it necessary until sin had intoxicated man with the principle of self-love. The law was not made for a righteous man, but for the disobedient.

Q. What form of government prevailed first among mankind?

A. Patriarchal. The father of a family used to exercise some sovereignty over his successors, until they moved from the city of their father, and became patriarchs themselves.

Q. How long did the world stand without any government in it but patriarchal?

[4] A. There was no other kind before the flood, (which was more than one thousand six hundred and forty-five years,) nor afterwards till Nimrod, two generations after the flood.

Q. What was Nimrod?

A. He was the first that began to be a *mighty one* in the earth. He was a mighty hunter before the Lord, who hunted beasts to support his army with, and hunted men to reduce them to his will.

Q. What form of government did he adopt?

A. A kingly form; for the beginning of his kingdom was Babel, Erech, Accad, and Calneh. He was the first of those pretty creatures called kings, who reduced others to subjection by hunting them like beasts.

Q. Did the Almighty ever give a code of political laws to any nation? or, are nations left to act at discretion in establishing forms of government and codes of laws?

A. The Almighty did certainly give the nation of Israel a complete code of laws on Sinai, and in the wilderness, for their rule of conduct in religious, civil and military life.

Q. Were those laws obligatory on other nations?

A. Laws, that are in themselves just, are binding on all men,

JACK NIPS

but the particular form of many of those laws was peculiar to that nation. The transgression of many of those precepts was criminal in that nation, which the Gentiles were never accused of by their great apostle, Paul.

Q. What did other nations do, in point of government, while Israel was in the wilderness and under the regulation of judges?

A. When Nimrod usurped the monarch's crown, the spirit of domination ran through the world like a raging plague. Ashur went out to the land of Shinar, where Nimrod's seat was, and built Nineveh, and founded the Assyrian monarchy, and the contagion of having kings, and being kings, prevailed so greatly, that every little village had a king. Abraham, with three hundred and eighteen servants, conquered four of them and their hosts—Joshua destroyed thirty-one—and Adonibezek cut off the thumbs and great toes of seventy; also eight kings and eleven dukes reigned over Edom, before any in Israel.

Q. In what condition was the nation of Israel, after they left Egypt, before Saul reigned over them, in regard to their police?

A. They were in a state of theocracy, the best of all states when people have virtue enough to bear it.

Q. Were there no men among them who exercised dominion over the rest?

[5] A. Moses and Aaron exercised divine orders among them; the princes of the tribes and the officers bore authority, and the judges, of whom there were thirteen, had some pre-eminence, but neither of them had the power of making laws; when God appointed them, they were to execute his laws, and no other.

Q. Was the code of laws, ordained for the government of Israel, sufficient to govern other nations by, in their very different circumstances?

A. It was not. Canaan was an inland country—the people were forbidden to trade with other nations, so that no laws were made for navigation, commerce, or union; all of which are necessary in Gentile nations. And, beside, their civil and religious laws were all blended together. The sabbath of the seventh day—seventh year, and fiftieth year—the three grand feasts, and a multitude of sacrifices, ceremonies, and oblations were enjoined on that people, which things Gentile nations have nothing to do with.

Q. Has the *political* part of that constitution ever been abused by Gentile legislatures?

A. Abundantly so, among Gentile nations that have become Christian; for by bringing Christian states upon the same footing with the commonwealth of Israel, they have supposed that Christian nations have a just right to dispossess the heathen of their lands and make slaves of their persons, as Israel served the Canaanites and Jebusites: for no better claim than this had the European nation to make a seizure of America. Nor is this all: civil rulers, in Christian countries, have taken the liberty of adopting such precepts of the Mosaic constitution as suited them, and punished those who would not submit, when, at the same time, they have left unnoticed a great number of the precepts of Moses which were equally obligatory.

Q. Has the *ecclesiastical* part of the Mosaic constitution ever been abused as well as the political part?

A. Yes, and that to a great degree. The church of Israel took in the whole nation, and none but that nation: whereas, Christ's church takes no whole nation, but those who fear God and work righteousness in every nation. But almost all Christian nations and states, since the reign of Constantine, have sought to establish national churches: in order to effect which, they have brought in all the *natural seed* of the professors into the pales of the church, making no difference between the precious and the vile; and from this foundation they have appealed to the laws of state, instead of the laws of Christ, to direct their mode of discipline. What a [6] scandal it is to the Christian name to see church discipline executed in a court-house, before the judges of the police—to see censures given at the whipping-post, and excommunications at the gallows;* and for smaller breaches, to be admonished by a sheriff's seizing and selling cows, etc., or wiping off the admonition by a pecuniary mulet! Yet such has been, and still is the case, even in New England, that has made her boast of religion and liberty.† Circumcision, as to its first institution, was not of Moses, but of the fathers that lived before Moses, yet it was enjoined by Moses to be performed on all the males of Israel. From this a great number of ecclesiastics have changed blood for water, and sprinkle their children

* The Baptists and Newlights have been imprisoned, fined, and whipped, and witches and Quakers have been hung in Massachusetts.
† Seizing and selling, for ministerial tax, is still practised in many towns to this day.

instead of bleeding them, in order to make the gospel church as extensive as the church of Israel was. Yet many of them will not admit a person to go back as far as John for the origin of baptism, because, say they, John's administration was under the law; yet they will run back two thousand four hundred years before John for a precedent of baptism.‡

Q. Was not circumcision, to the church of Israel, the same that water-baptism is to the church of Christ?

A. If so, the following absurdities arise.

First. None but the males were circumcised: whereas, both males and females are sprinkled with water. To say that the females were *virtually* circumcised in the males, is just as good sense as to say the females are *virtually sprinkled* in the males.

Second. None were ever circumcised under eight days old, which was the general time appointed; but children are sprinkled sometimes [7] before they are eight hours old. Midwives have been empowered to do it, in case death was nearer than a priest.

Third. Circumcision was never a priestly rite: fathers, masters, mothers, and friends did the work; but sprinkling is supposed to be a ministerial rite.

Fourth. Whatever circumcision figured out, it was something that was wrought in the *spirit* and done *without hands;* and as there is nothing done by men, that is called *baptism by water,* either sprinkling, pouring, or dipping, that can possibly change the spirit, so neither of them are effected without the hands of men. The conclusion, therefore, is, that the first did not figure out the last.

Fifth. None but those who were circumcised were to inherit Canaan; of course, then, none but those who are baptized with water can inherit heaven, which is a consequence inadmissible.

Q. What do you think of the British constitution of government?

A. There is no constitution in Britain. It is said, in England, that there are three things unknown, viz. the prerogatives of the

---

‡ A Reverend Gentleman in the county of Worcester, who, like many of his brethren, views John's baptism under the law, contends for infant baptism from Genesis, ix., 27. That the laws of Moses was in force while John lived, and even to the death of Jesus, I do not deny; but that John baptized in Jordan and Enon, such, and such only, as brought forth fruits of repentance, by an order of the law, will be denied until it can be proved. If no institution, appointed before the death of Christ, is imitable for Christians, the holy supper should be neglected.

crown—the privileges of parliament—and the liberty of the people. These things are facts, for although they consider the seventy-two articles of the Magna Charta as the basis of their government, yet from that basis they have never formed a constitution to describe the limits of each department of government. So that precedents and parliamentary acts are all the constitution they have.

Q. How does government operate in England?

A. A hereditary king of the Protestant faith, must always fill the throne, whether he be a wise man or a dunce. A house of lords, of the hereditary mould, must always check the house of commons.

Q. What is the house of commons?

A. It is a representative body of a small part of the nation, chosen once in seven years. It is called the house of *commons,* because the house of lords is a house of *uncommons,* supposed to be a species of beings like the *Genii* of the Mahometans, between angels and men, born only to rule, without having a fellow-feeling with those whom they rule over.

Q. What condition has that form of government reduced the people to?

A. It has sunk them in a debt of more than two hundred and eighty millions, so that the interest of their debt, together with the support of the civil and military lists, imposes an annual tax [8] on the people equal to thirty shillings sterling per soul, and at the expiration of the year the nation is a million of pounds more in debt than at the beginning.

Q. How stand religious concerns in England?

A. The thirty-nine articles and book of common prayer are established by law. No man can fill any office in the civil or military departments without taking an oath to support them, and upon receiving a commission he must seal his oath with the eucharist: this is true of all, saving the members of parliament, who are obliged only to take the oath of abjuration, *Curse the Pope and Papistry.*

Q. But are there none in England that dissent from the established religion?

A. Many of them, of various denominations.

Q. How do they fare?

A. They are deprived of such advantages as the conformists enjoy. In addition to all their proscriptions, the tenth part of all their income is taken from them to support priests that they never hear, and in whom they place no confidence.

Q. Is it supposed that the articles and forms of the church of England are so perfect that they cannot be mended?

A. They are always perfect when dissenters are handled. Edward Wrightman was burnt to death at Litchfield, by a warrant from prince James, for saying that the worship of God was not fully described in the thirty-nine articles and book of common prayers, and nearly eight thousand lost their property, liberties, and lives in the reign of the merciful king Charles, because they could not, would not say, that they believed what they could not believe, and so conform to the established worship.

They are also always perfect when a candidate enters into holy orders, for all of them do solemnly declare that they give their unfeigned assent and consent to all and every thing contained in that book, and yet, from the first formation of that book, it has passed above six hundred alterations, and to this day, many parts of it are complained of by many of the Episcopal clergymen.

Q. What have you to say about the Federal Constitution of America?

A. It is a novelty in the world: partly confederate, and partly consolidate—partly directly elective, and partly elective one or two removes from the people; but one of the great excellencies of the Constitution is, that no religious test is ever to be required to qualify any officer in any part of the government. To say that the Constitution is perfect, would be too high an encomium upon [9] the fallibility of the framers of it; yet this may be said, that it is the best national machine that is now in existence.

Q. What think you of the Constitution of Massachusetts?

A. It is as good a performance as could be expected in a state where religious bigotry and enthusiasm have been so predominant.

Q. What is your opinion of having a *bill of rights* to a constitution of government?

A. Whenever it is understood that all power is in the monarch—that subjects possess nothing of their own, but receive all from the potentate, then the liberty of the people is commensurate with the bill of rights that is squeezed out of the monarch.

After the conquest of William, the government of England was completely monarchical, until the reign of king John, when the Magna

Charta was given to the people: this has often been mentioned in America as a sufficient reason for a *bill of rights,* to preface each constitution: but in republican, representative governments, like those of America, where it is understood that all power is originally in the *people,* and that all is still retained in their hands, except so much as for a limited time is given to the rulers, where is the propriety of having a bill of rights? In this view, no such bill is found in the Federal Constitution.

But it is not my intention, at this time, to dispute the point of propriety or impropriety of a bill of rights, but shall only add that the liberty of the people depends more upon the organization of government, the responsibility of rulers, and the faithful discharge of the officers, than it does upon any bill of rights that can be named.

The illustrious patriots of Massachusetts, in framing their Constitution of government, in 1780, prepared a bill of rights, which is adopted in the state, on which I shall make some remarks. The bill contains thirty articles, upon a few of which I shall animadvert.

In the second article it is said, "it is the right and duty of all men publicly, and at stated seasons, to worship the Supreme Being." This article would read much better in a catechism than in a state constitution, and sound more concordant in a pulpit than in a statehouse.

Suppose there are, in Massachusetts, a number of Pagans and Deists: the Pagans, upon hearing that it is their *duty* to worship *one* Supreme Being only, must consequently renounce all other deities whom they have been taught to adore; here their consciences must be dispensed with, or the constitution broken. The Deist, who believes all religion to be a cheat, must either act the [10] hypocrite, or disregard the supreme law of the State. This duty is called a *right:* if every man has this *right,* then he has a *right* to judge for himself, and will hardly thank any body for turning his right into what they may call a duty. That it is the duty of men, and women too, to worship God publicly, I heartily believe, but that it is the duty or wisdom of a convention or legislature to enjoin it on others, is called in question, and will be, until an instance can be given in the New Testament, that Jesus, or his apostles, gave orders therefor to the rulers of this world.

It is the duty of men to repent and believe—to worship God in their closets and families as well as in public—and the reason why

JACK NIPS

public worship is enjoined by authority, and private worship is omitted, is only to pave the way for some religious establishment by human law, and force taxes from the people to support avaricious priests.

What leads legislators into this error, is confounding *sins* and *crimes* together—making no difference between *moral evil* and *state rebellion:* not considering that a man may be infected with moral evil, and yet be guilty of no crime, punishable by law. If a man worships one God, three Gods, twenty Gods, or no God—if he pays adoration one day in a week, seven days, or no day—wherein does he injure the life, liberty or property of another? Let any or all these actions be supposed to be religious evils of an enormous size, yet they are not crimes to be punished by the laws of state, which extend no further, in justice, than to punish the man who works ill to his neighbor.

When civil rulers undertake to make laws against moral evil, and punish men for heterodoxy in religion, they often run to grand extremes. The eating of a potatoe for food, and using emetics for physic, were once considered in France as religious evils. Galileo was once excommunicated and banished by the Pope's bull, as a man of dangerous heresy, because he believed in the Copernican system. The ancients were treated as heretics, who believed they had antipodes. The court of Zurich made a law to drown Felix Mentz with water, because he was baptized in water. In short, volumes might be written, and have been written, o show what havoc among men the principle of mixing *sins* and *crimes* together has effected, while men in power have taken their own opinions as infallible tests of right and wrong.

The third article of the bill of rights is similar to the second in its structure. It is said, "The people of this commonwealth have a right to invest their legislature with power to authorise and [11] require, and the legislature shall from time to time authorise and require the several towns, parishes, etc., to make suitable provision, at their own expense, for the institution of the public worship of God, and for the support and maintenance of public Protestant teachers, in all cases where such provision shall not be made voluntarily."

If the legislature of this commonwealth have that power to institute and establish that religion, which they believe is the best in the world, by the same rule, all the legislatures of all the commonwealths, states, kingdoms and empires that are in the world, and that have been in the world, may claim the same.

If dumb idols are called devils, and idolatry is the religion of the devil, this claim of power brings all the Gentile nations under the government of the devil. Idolatry was established by this pretended power in the Gentile nations, when the Christian religion was first sent among them; now if that establishment was right, then the apostles were wrong in separating so many thousands from the established religion. They were guilty of effecting a schism, and government was innocent in inflicting such punishment upon them and their adherents. In process of time, the religion of Christ prevailed so far that it was established in the empire of Rome; at which epoch it received a deadly wound, which gradually reduced it to superstition, fraud and ignorance; so that, in the sixteenth century, a number of kingdoms and principalities protested against the church of Rome; but this was a grand piece of obstinacy, if rulers have the power that the article under consideration says belongs to the legislature of Massachusetts. These Protestants, especially in England, retained so many of the Papal relics, that great numbers became nonconformists; here they repeated their crime, rejecting the English establishment, as well as that of Rome. Some of those nonconformists came into New-England, and soon began to exercise that power which the bill of rights says they have a right to.

Now, how shall all these evils be remedied? answer—all who have dissented from the established religion of New-England must return to that fold, and confess their errors; then all must return to the church of England, and submit to that establishment; then, joining with the Episcopalians, all must apply to the Pope for pardon, and submit to his uncontrolable authority; then, with the Papists, all must return to the Pagans, and submit to the Polytheism. If the power spoken of is right, then this mode of procedure is right; and, therefore, it is not the natural consequence of religious [12] establishments by human law, to bring all men under the government and religion of the devil, it is because there is neither devil nor devilish religion in the world.

It is observed, that "the people of this commonwealth have a right to invest their legislature with this power." But where do they get this right? The universe is composed of a multitude of units; so this commonwealth is formed by a number of individuals. The confederacy is the sovereign, and rulers are agents; and how can the creature have more power than the Creator? *Propter quod unum quodque*

JACK NIPS

est tale, illud ibsum est magis tale. Whatever is found in the common-wealth, in aggregate, is found in small, essential particles among all the individuals; if, therefore, this power is in the commonwealth, each individual has a little of it in his own breast; and has a right to exercise it towards his neighbor, and force him to worship God, when, where, and in such a manner as he himself shall choose; and if this be the case, what means the first article in the bill of rights; where it is said, "all men are born free and equal." To be consistent, either that clause should be erased, or the power contended for given up.

This power is to be used to oblige the people "to make suitable provision at their own expense, for the institution of the public worship of God." I have long been of the belief that Jesus Christ instituted his worship; and if my faith is well founded, then it is not left for rulers to do in these days; but, surely nothing more can be meant by it, than that the legislature shall incorporate religious societies, and oblige them to build houses for public worship. Parishes, precincts, and religious societies politically embodied, are phrases not known in the New Testament; convey ideas contrary to the spirit of the gospel, and pave the way for force and cruelty, inadmissible in Christ's kingdom, which is not of this world. If any number of real saints are incorporated by human law, they cannot be a church of Christ, by virtue of that formation, but a creature of state.

This power is further to be exercised, to require the people to be at expense "for the support and maintenance of public Protestant preachers."

Preaching by the day, by the month, by the year, annual taxes for preaching; what strange sounds these are! not strange in these days; but such strangers in the New Testament, that they are not to be found there. How insignificant would the federal government be, if it was dependant on the laws of the states to support its officers! That government that has not force enough [13] in it to support its officers, will soon fall; just so with the government of Jesus. The author of our religion has appointed a maintenance for his teachers; but has never told the rulers of this world to interfere in the matter.

How much did John the Baptist, Jesus, Peter, James or John, ask per year? Answer: I know not. If a man preaches Jesus, he cannot talk enough for it; the gold of Ophir cannot equal it; if he preaches himself, it is good for nothing.

Strange it is, that men should pretend to be sent by God to

preach to sinners, and yet will not do the work of the Lord, unless they can get men to be legal bondsmen for Jehovah.

To read in the New Testament, that the Lord has ordained that those that preach the gospel shall live by its institutions and precepts, sounds very harmonical; but to read in a state constitution, that the legislature shall require men to maintain teachers of piety, religion and morality, sounds very discordant.

We may next observe, that the legislature of Massachusetts have not power to provide for any public teachers, except they are Protestant. Pagans, Turks and Jews, must not only preach for nothing; but Papists, those marvellous Christians, cannot obtain a maintenance for their preachers by the laws of their commonwealth. Such preachers must either be supported voluntarily, support themselves, or starve. Is this good policy? Should one sect be pampered above others? Should not government protect all kinds of people, of every species of religion, without showing the least partiality? Has not the world had enough proofs of the impolicy and cruelty of favoring a Jew more than a Pagan, Turk, or Christian; or a Christian more than either of them? Why should a man be proscribed, or any wife disgraced, for being a Jew, a Turk, a Pagan, or a Christian of any denomination, when his talents and veracity as a civilian, entitles him to the confidence of the public.

The next thing to be noticed is, that the legislature of Massachusetts is invested with power and "authority to enjoin upon all the subjects an attendance upon the instructions of the public teachers, at stated times and seasons." By which stated times, no doubt, is meant the days called Sabbaths, Sundays (Sondays,) First-days or Lord's-days. I shall not dispute the point about the holy-day, whether it was enjoined on men from the beginning, or never before the manna was given in the wilderness; whether the fourth commandment in the decalogue, was of a moral or ceremonial nature; whether it was binding on all nations, or only on Israel; [14] whether the same day of the week is to be kept to the end of the world; whether the seventh part of time answers the end of the law, or whether the seventh day is changed for the first; but shall use the liberty of saying, that the appointment of such stated holy-days, is no part of human legislation. I cannot see upon what principle of national right, the people of Massachusetts could invest their legislature with that power; and as I cannot deduce it from the source of natural right, so neither can I

JACK NIPS

find a hint in the New Testament, that Jesus or his apostles, ever reproved any for the neglect of that day; or that they ever called upon civil rulers to make any penal laws about it. And it is curious to see what havoc rulers make of good sense, whenever they undertake to legalize said day. No longer ago than 1791, the legislature of this commonwealth made a sabbatical law; wherein, for the groundwork, they say, that the seventh part of time is to be kept holy; but how do they calculate time? A man on a journey may travel until Saturday night, midnight, and begin again on Sunday at sundown; if eighteen hours is the seventh part of a week, then their calculation is good; but being conscious that it is not, they make it up (i. e. pay what they have borrowed) out of recreation; for such exercise must cease on Saturday at the going down of the sun, and continue to cease till Sunday midnight. It may further be observed, that the law of God, and the laws of men, differ widely in phrase; the law that enjoined the observance of the seventh day on the nation of Israel, which came from Jehovah, did not except the works of necessity and mercy; neither man, maid, nor beast were to work—but a little way were they to travel—a bundle of sticks was not to be gathered and laid on the fire—nor had they any orders to assemble on that day, in a stated manner, to read the laws of Moses. It was to be a day of rest, which gave it the name Sabbath; but the laws of men have so many exceptions, that nothing, and anything, are done on said day.

But however these things are, the legislature of this state is to oblige the people to assemble on these stated times, to hear the instructions of these teachers of piety, religion and morality, if there be any on whose instructions they can conscientiously and conveniently attend. Here is a gap wide enough for any man to creep out. If neglecting to go to meeting is not justified by pleading inconveniency, his conscience will soon do it; but whether he goes to church or not, his pennies must go to the treasurer's purse.

It is true that one sect of Protestant Christians has as fair an opportunity to be incorporated as another, but there are many who [15] justly despise the idea of religious incorporation by human law, and therefore those who do not, have an undue advantage over others. Supposing, in France, the National Convention should decree that all sects of Christians, that believed that kings, in certain cases, might wear their heads and crowns upon them, should have equal privileges in France, I ask, whether the Jacobin party should share equal favors with the royalists? So, in this case, all sects of Protestant Christians that choose to be incorporated, may elect their own teachers and contract with them for their maintenance, and assess it upon all within their respective precincts; but those who cannot, in conscience, accord with this legal religion, must pay their tax with the rest, and be at the trouble of drawing it out of the treasury again, which sometimes occasions vexatious lawsuits.

Now, if it should be argued that a great many in this commonwealth believe, in their consciences, that it is the best way to serve God, to have societies incorporated by law, and levy a tax upon all to support their worship and maintain their teachers, how easily the above evils might be prevented, and all enjoy liberty of conscience. If those only, who are conscientious in legal religion, are incorporated, and tax none but themselves, there will be no cruel distraining from those whose consciences dictate another mode of worship. A man can cheerfully work when he verily believes he is doing God service; a man, therefore, who believes in religious incorporation, can joyfully give in his name to be taxed; and he who believes that the law has nothing to do about religious worship, can as joyfully stay at home. The last of these have as good grounds to judge that the first plead conscience for cruelty, as the first have to judge that the last plead conscience for covetousness.

But there is no need for a constitutional clause about things of this nature; for if a number of men contract with a preacher, for a year, or for life, the bond which they give him, is as recoverable by law as any bond whatever; but the poison of such contracts is, including those who do not act voluntarily, and perpetuating them upon their successors or natural offspring.

The last clause of the third article reads thus:

"And every denomination of Christians, demeaning themselves peaceably, and as good subjects of the commonwealth, shall be equally under the protection of the law; and no subordination of any one sect or denomination to another, shall ever be established by law."

[16] On this section I have several remarks to make:

First. The first part of it is very liberal, to a certain degree; but if it read *all men* instead of *every denomination of Christians,* it would be unexceptionable.

When the Pagans were favored by law, more than Christians, what devastation it made in the empire of Rome, in the first introduction

of the Christian religion, until the reign of Constantine. In the first
three centuries, almost two millions of lives were lost for conscience
sake. These were men, women and children, who were as good subjects
of state as any in the empire. After the change in the empire, when
the Christian religion became established by law, the Pagans suffered
in the same manner that the Christians had done in the ten preceding
persecutions. Who can read the history of these sufferings without
seeing the bad policy of establishing either of the religions in the
empire?

Second. Although the clause now under consideration is some
what liberal, indeed entirely so among Christians, yet it nowise accords
with a former clause in the same article, where the legislature is
forbidden to incorporate any Christians but *Protestants,* at least, are
not vested with power to do it. *Protestants* only can be formed into
religious societies and distrain for a maintenance for their teachers.

One of two things must be granted; either that Papists are no
Christians, or that there is a partiality established. Among little souled
bigots, who believe nobody right but themselves, who confine the
Christian religion to their own sect, and conclude that they have the
exclusive right to monopolize salvation, it would not be strange to
hear that Papists, and all others who differed with them in sentiment,
were no Christians; but this cannot be the case here. The framers of
the constitution were men of information and acquaintance with the
world; the result is, then, that there is a contradiction in the two
clauses of the same article.

Such is the state of things in Massachusetts, that the legislature,
according to the power vested in them by the first part of the third
article, have made such laws as have effected a subordination of one
sect to another, contrary to the last clause in the same article.

On March 23, and June 28, 1786, two acts passed; the first
respecting towns, the other precincts, which effect the subordination
just mentioned. These two laws were somewhat uniform in structure,
and therefore a quotation from one of them may [17] suffice in this
place. Each inhabitant has the power of voting in town or precinct
affairs, who pays two-thirds more in one tax than a poll tax; and then
follows, "That the freeholders and other inhabitants, in each respective
town, qualified as aforesaid, at the annual meeting for the choice of
town officers, or at any other town-meeting regularly warned, may
grant and vote such sums of money as they shall judge necessary for

the settlement, maintenance and support of the ministry, to be assessed upon the polls and property *within the same,* as by law provided."

Now if any Christians but Protestants are thus incorporated, the constitution is violated; and if none but Protestants, what may the Catholics say? But this is not all; by this act, property entitles a man to church privileges. A degree of simony is contained in the act. The wisest man that was ever born of a woman could not estimate *wisdom,* by all the gold and pearls on earth; but here a little property procures it; at least, an annual tax entitles a man to the rights of it. Whether these voters are spiritual, moral, or profane, they have an equal suffrage in the choice of spiritual teachers, who have, or should have, the cure of souls at heart.

It is well known, that there are a number of Baptists in this state; in some towns they and their adherents form a majority; but in the greatest part of the towns, those called the *standing order* are superior to all the rest. As the Baptists are Protestants, where they form a majority, they might be incorporated as well as others, and tax all in the town or precinct to part with their money for religious uses. But it is well known that they are principled against it. They do not believe that the legislature have any proper authority, upon the scale of good policy, to make any laws to incorporate religious societies and require a maintenance for the ministry. Now the question is, Do their sentiments prevent their demeaning themselves as peaceable subjects of state? Let those who differ with them in judgment answer. Yet from their known and conscientious principles, how are they reduced to subordination in various places?

In a town or precinct where the Baptists are a minority, the major part choose and settle a minister; the expense is levied upon all according to poll and property; the Baptists, in this case, must either part with their money to support a religion that they do not fully believe in, or be subordinate enough to get a certificate to draw it out of the treasurer's hands. Some have condescended to the last mode, as being the best alternative they had; while others have had such a disgust to submit to a power, belonging [18] neither to the kingdom of the Messiah, nor the civil government on earth, that they would not bow let the consequences be what they would. The distraining law-suits and oppressions that have risen from this source, even since the ratification of the present constitution, need not be mentioned at this time.

JACK NIPS

One observation more shall close my strictures on this article. It is well noticed that none shall be protected by law, but those who properly demean themselves as peaceable subjects of the commonwealth. This, however should be extended to all men, as well as to Christian denominations.

For any man, or set of men, to expect protection from the law, when they do not subject themselves to government, is a vain expectation. Let a man's motive be what it may, let him have what object soever in view; if his practice is opposed to good law, he is to be punished. Magistrates are not to consult his motive or object, but his actions.

Without adverting to Bohemia, Munster, or any part of Europe or Asia for instances, we shall pay attention to a few recent transactions of our own. A Shaking-Quaker, in a violent manner, cast his wife into a mill-pond in cold weather; his plea was, that God ordered him so to do. Now the question is, Ought he not to be punished as much as if he had done the deed in anger? Was not the abuse to the woman as great? Could the magistrate perfectly know whether it was God Satan, or ill-will, that prompted him to do the deed? The answers to these questions are easy.

In the year of 1784, Matthew Womble, of Virginia, killed his wife and four sons, in obedience to a Shining One, who, he said, was the Son of God, to merit heaven by the action; but if the court had been fearful of offending that Shining One, and pitied Womble's soul, they would never have inflicted that punishment upon him which they did the October following. Neither his motive, which was obedience, nor his object, which was the salvation of his soul had any weight on the jury.

Should magistrates or jurors be biased by such protestations, the most atrocious villains would always pass with impunity.

I shall here add, that in Scotland, two women were brought before the sessions for fornication; one of them was a church member and the other was not. She who was a daughter of Zion was pitied, and the man who had defiled her was judged a vile seducer, and severely fined; but she who was not a member of the church, was judged a lewd slattern, and was driven out of the parish, that she might not deceive honest men any more.

[19] Should a man refuse to pay his tribute for the support of government, or any wise disturb the peace and good order of the civil

police, he should be punished according to his crime, let his religion be what it will; but when a man is a peaceable subject of state, he should be protected in worshipping the Deity according to the dictates of his own conscience.

It is often the case, that laws are made which prevent the liberty of conscience; and because men cannot stretch their consciences like a nose of wax, these non-conformists are punished as vagrants that disturb the peace. The complaint is: "These men, being Jews, do exceedingly trouble the city." Let any man read the laws that were made about Daniel and the three children, and see who were the aggressors, the law makers or the law breakers. The rights of conscience should always be considered inalienable—religious opinions as not the objects of civil government, nor any way under its jurisdiction. Laws should only respect civil society; then if men are disturbers they ought to be punished.

Among the many beautiful traits of the constitution of Massachusetts, the provision made for its revision shines with great effulgence.

Permanency and improvement should be mixed together in government. But few nations have ever had patriotism sufficient to remove the radical deficiencies of government, without falling into convulsion and anarchy. There are certain ebbs and tides in men, and bodies of men, which often break over all proper bounds, without a proper check. To leave government, therefore, so mutable that a bare majority can alter it, when under some prevailing passion, exposes that permanency that the good of the whole, and the confidence of allies, call for. In this last view of things, some real, confessed evils had better be borne with, than to make government too fluctuating. In the federal government, it requires two-thirds of the states, or two-thirds of the members of Congress, to change the constitution. In Massachusetts the same; but not till after the experiment of fifteen years. However this may appear to others, to me it appears one of the fairest lines in the constitution; a signal of a patriotic people, conscious of their liability of mistake, wishing to improve in policy, attached to energy and freedom. And there is no doubt but, in the year 1795, the citizens of this state may meet by their delegates, and coolly improve upon the constitution, and remove its defects, that time and experience have discovered, without the least danger of [20] tumult or noise. Should that be the case, it is hoped that some things respecting religion will be altered, which is the chief end of the publishing of this small tract.

If the constitution should be revised, and anything about religion should be said in it, the following paragraph is proposed:—

"To prevent the evils that have heretofore been occasioned in the world by religious establishments, and to keep up the proper distinction between religion and politics, no religious test shall ever be requested as a qualification of any officer, in any department of this government; neither shall the legislature, under this constitution, ever establish any religion by law, give any one sect a preference to another, or force any man in the commonwealth to part with his property for the support of religious worship, or the maintenance of ministers of the gospel."

[63]

PERES [PEREZ] FOBES
1742–1812

An Election Sermon

BOSTON, 1795

In a day when Harvard listed its students according to their social rank, as perceived by the Harvard faculty, Perez Fobes was fifth from the bottom in a graduating class of forty-seven. He was born in Massachusetts, served as a chaplain in the Revolutionary Army, and held pastorates in the Congregational Church for some twenty years. At the age of forty-four he took up a professorship in Natural Philosophy at Rhode Island College (later called Brown University) and thereafter pursued a mixed career of preaching, teaching, and administration at preparatory school and college levels. In this sermon before the governor and General Court of Massachusetts, Fobes makes evident the problems and pitfalls encountered in extending a liberal theory of politics, developed to justify a revolution, to the practicalities of establishing republican government on a continental scale. What are the characteristics of a good public official? What is acceptable behavior toward such an official by citizens with freedom of speech and press and a habit of criticizing government? At what point does behavior that was once considered purely patriotic cease being patriotic and become subversive? Fobes here previews the problems surrounding the passage of the Alien and Sedition Acts of 1798.

PERES [PEREZ] FOBES 1742–1812

[AN ELECTION SERMON]

II. PETER, II. *Chap. part of the* 10*th and* 12*th Verses.*

> They despise government—are not afraid to speak evil of
> dignities—and things they understand not.

An honest man is a character more frequently claimed than deserved.
But of all claims, that of a calumniator is one of the most unfounded.
The pen of inspiration has left a stigma in the evil of detraction. It is
condemned by the voice of nature, and the verdict of reason. Whether
it is vented by the tongue, the pen, or the press; whether it is conveyed
under the disguise of dark insinuation, affected silence, or the
contumelious brow; whether it arises from competitions of honour, or
the jealousies of interest from prejudice, or rancorous passion; or is
retailed only for amusement, to supply the vacancy of reason, or the
barrenness of conversation; from whatever source it springs, whatever
form it assumes, [16] or however confined in its walks, slander is a
crime of the deepest dye, base in itself, and baneful to society. But if
such is the criminality of "speaking evil one of another" in the circle
of private life, what is their crime *"who dare to speak evil of dignities?"*
Presumptuous and self willed are they called, and in company joined with
characters of such infamy, that the most copious language on earth,
under the control of genius and inspiration, was found too barren to
describe them, without the aid of metaphors, the most degrading that
could be borrowed from Heaven, Earth, and Sea.

"*Fallen angels, wandering stars, raging waves of the sea, foaming out
their own shame, filthy dreamers, spots and blemishes in society, trees twice
dead, cursed children, brute beasts made to be taken and destroyed,"* with
such company are *they* ranked *who despise government.* And is there not
a cause amply sufficient to justify this marked distinction between evil
speaking in common, and *speaking evil of dignities?* An attempt to
investigate this distinction, while it diversifies a common topic, will
perhaps suggest some useful observations on civil government. I feel
on this occasion, the want of more than all the apologies that have
ever been made in this place: but to ask the candour and patience of
such an audience as this, might be "to speak evil of dignities;" and
to speak evil, is in the original Greek, to *blaspheme:* to open the mouth
against the civil magistrate, the vicegerent of God on earth, is *"to set
the mouth against heaven."* [7] The word, *dignities,* is here taken in the

abstract, and signifies political authority; in the concrete it is put for persons exercising power and jurisdiction. While it extends to all the grades and departments of public office, it strongly implies, that all men in public office *ought* to be men of dignity. But who are these dignities? What is that government which cannot be spoken against, without incurring the guilt of blasphemy, and the penalty of damnation? The answer is plain: That government, which the Apostle calls *an ordinance of God,* is a government chosen by the people; for he as expressly calls it *the ordinance of man.* Rulers are *ministers ordained of God,* only when they are the *ministers of good to the people.* Obedience therefore, to civil rulers imposed on the people, or to any *form* or *administration* of government contrary to the will of the people, was never inculcated by the inspired Apostle on pain of damnation: for the same authority which in this instance condemns, in others justifies open resistance and opposition to government. The unreasonable humour of Ahab King of Israel, the menacing edicts of Nebuchadnezzar, and the peremptory mandate of the Egyptian Monarch were disregarded with impunity, and even without blame. Was it a crime in Hushai to develop the machinations of Ahitophel? or did Mordecai speak evil of dignities when he exposed the plot of Haman against the whole nation of the Jews? If Sir Edmund Andross is a tyrant, if Arnold is a traitor, or even Lord Bacon is the bribed Judge, let their villany be unmasked, let their guilt be [8] unkennelled. To do this every citizen is bound by prior and superior claims of society. Should the highest officer of any government on earth, flagrantly abuse the authority of his station, even by prosecuting private designs, or by adopting public measures hostile to the public good, it is not a crime, but the duty of a free people to be free enough to speak evil of him. The tongue in this case is the proper weapon to chastise and refrain, where the laws of men cannot reach. This will keep the public mind awake, by adding stimulus to ardour and information.

Hence we conclude, that speaking evil of dignities is a crime on the supposition only, that rulers are both the choice and ministers of good to the people. When this is a fact, those words of the Apostle which seem to carry horror in their sound, do not exaggerate its criminality. This will appear both from the nature and design of government, and from the duties and character of its officers.

In man, the noblest work of God on earth, three worlds co-exist: The material, animal and angelic; or *spirit, soul and body.* These are all governed by Deity, in a manner wisely adapted to their different natures and capacities. The material world is governed by irresistible force, the brute creation by instinct, man by law, he alone is endued with moral life, united with the animal and intellectual. This triple life, which combines all the known powers of nature, renders man a moral agent; amenable to God [9] the moral governor of the world. With the angel and the brute in his composition, he possesses power and propensity to do wrong as well as right. This renders him a fit subject of civil government. The impulses of animal nature render it necessary, and the social principle makes it agreeable, as the author of these powers, God himself is the author of government.

To that astonishing variety in his composition, which renders man a proper subject, we may add, the still greater variety, visible in the human genius and disposition, which demonstrates the necessity of subordination. Different stations in life require different talents and qualifications. If every man had the same degree of taste, of reason, or education, which are the portion of a few individuals, how wretched would be the lot of those who occupy the lowest offices, and perform the drudgeries of life. A sublime genius, a refined imagination, without an object, or the possibility of gratification, would serve only to tantalize and torment the possessor. Such is the difference of intellectual abilities among men, that the condition of an ox or an ass, endued with some human intellect, would not be more wretched, perhaps, than that of some philosophic genius destined only to drive them. This diversity of genius, which is independently the gift of providence, plainly indicates the necessity of those distinctions in life, which are implied in government; it shews moreover, the wisdom and benevolence of the deity, in providing for all, in such manner, as proves at once [10] the indispensability of every man in society; and that the poorest in his humble condition may be as useful, contented and happy as the richest and most elevated officer of government.

Again—The signatures of subordination are legible in the human form. We behold in the countenance of some persons a kind of dignity, which at once beams reverence, and designates for dominion: in others, we observe such vacancy and prostration of dignity, as equally marks them for subjection. This diversity, altho it may arise in part from the original constitution of the mind, or from moral culture and improvement, is so conspicuous and captivating, as none will affirm, that the elevated stature of King Saul, the beauty of Absalom's person, the ruddy complexion of David, and the ennobling form of Washington, had no share in raising them up to the highest stations in life.

There is yet another proof of the divine authority of government, and that is the manner in which we come into existence. Had this been, like the original pair of our race, in a state of adult maturity and independence, it would have been, perhaps, more difficult to reduce fallen men to a state of government than the most savage beast, *"which are tamed, and have been tamed of mankind."* But, happy for us, a different plan has been adopted. By a law of nature we all begin to exist in a state of helpless infancy, under the entire control and direction of parents. By [11] this means children early become members of a family, which is itself an empire in miniature. Having formed in the moulding age of life, proper ideas and habits of government, they become at length prepared for civil society, in larger communities. While this benevolent law of nature announces government coeval with our existence, it speaks louder than the tongue of men or angels, the necessity of early education. Her voice to legislators is, "depend not on the number of your laws, or the severity of fines and punishments; but *lay the axe at the root* of vice, take possession of the heart, and charm, if possible, the young stranger to the love of virtue and country, in the tenderest period of life. Do this, by giving birth and energy to every possible institution for the education of youth." *It teaches* parents also, the ministers of religion and others, that while employed in the humble office of instructing youth, their services may be as patriotic, and perhaps more useful to their country, than the wisdom of their counsels in the senate, or the valour of their arms in the field. In fine, while *it teaches* all this, it *shews,* that to despise government is to violate a law of nature.

But in still blacker colours does this crime appear, if we consider the design of government, and the manner in which it is supported. Its benevolent design embraces the greatest good of the whole community. But this can be effected in that way only which GOD himself has taken, both to instruct mankind, and to govern the world. His will is taught us [12] in the sacred scriptures, not in detail, but by general rules. In like manner GOD governs the world by the laws of a general providence. These laws are calculated to secure the good of the whole. They must therefore, equally affect each individual comprehended under them, without any distinction of personal circumstance or character. Should the thunderbolt be diverted in its course, or stopped in its career, contrary to the fixed laws of electricity, to save one useful citizen, why not to save another? *"But shall the earth be forsaken, or the rock moved out of its place for thee?"* This would introduce such a train of miraculous events, as would subvert the whole constitution of nature, and destroy that established connexion between cause and effect, which is now the principal source of human knowledge and foresight.

Analogous to this divine model, all human governments must be constructed and maintained; i. e. by general laws; laws adapted to the state and happiness of men collectively. That endless variety in the condition and circumstances of individuals who compose by a community, renders it impossible to secure by general laws, the good of the whole, without injury or inconvenience to some individuals. An attempt to avoid by particular laws, the jarring claims, and infinite collisions of interest, which happen in society, would be perfectly nugatory. GOD himself has not done it. Inattention to this subject had been the unhappy cause, not only of strong prejudices against the book [13] of GOD, but of bold censures against GOD and man. Under a mistake of this kind, the friends of Job censured an innocent man. Is it not owing to this, more than to any other cause, that men so often *speak evil of dignities?* Observing that some existing law is less favorable to their own private interest, than to that of some others, or than different regulations might be, they at once let loose the tongue of censure against them; not considering perhaps, not knowing, that the very law which would please them might injure, if not ruin thousands. Let us further observe, that the same object in view, when the legislator frames a law, ought to be in his eye, when the penalty is affixed; that is, the general good: In order to which, he will consider that moral evil is estimated by the intention of the agent; political evil by its consequences in society. Human laws cannot reach the heart; the cognizable actions therefore, of men in society, must be estimated in the abstract only; as such they are denominated political crimes, varying in magnitude, according to their tendency or general consequences to the community; that is, in proportion to the intensity and extent of misery that would follow, if all actions of that description were to be generally tolerated, or become common.

By this standard the penalty of every law should be adjusted; and not by the supposed moral evil of the action, which cannot be known, nor by its particular consequences to a few individuals, which cannot be regarded, but by its general effects on society. This [14] is the pole star of every statesman; by the light of which only it is that we can account for the capital punishment of Uzzah for touching the ark, the zeal of Saint Paul in abstaining from meat, and the necessity of severe punishments for burglary, counterfeiting money, running contraband goods, exercitual desertion for cowardice, and many other actions, which in themselves appear small offences, if not innocent or indifferent.—Inattention to this principle, it is presumed, has been the fruitful source of great misdemeanors and public disturbance. Can it be supposed, that the late insurgents in a sourthern state would have refused the payment of a small excise, had they considered, that the general consequence of that refusal was the certain loss of all public revenue, and the final subversion of all government?—From the same cause, have we not seen, what humanity ever blushes to relate, a reputed honest man, in open town-meeting, hold up his hand to defraud the public, or a public creditor, who would not, scarcely for his right hand, have been seen to injure one of his neighbours?

Inattention, permit me to say, is the best apology I can make for numbers of my fellow-citizens who neglect public worship, perform journeys, and unnecessary business on the LORD's Day. They do not consider, that if every other person, who had an equal right and the same excuse, should follow the example, public worship, that great pillar of civil government, would be entirely overthrown. But [15] more than all, this principle now unfolds its chief design, and shews, as with a sun beam, the enormity of reviling dignities. A ruler is the father of his country; he stands at the head of government, at the helm of the ship, in which our lives and fortunes are all embarked. An attack upon him may sink the whole. Slander in this instance, is more then death; it is parricide, more fatal than all the malignant influences once ascribed to baleful comets, which spread plagues and desolations through a whole country.

But if we consider civil rulers in character of real dignities, it will strike a deeper stain of guilt and baseness into the crime.

If it could be said of *David,* on account of the dignity and importance of his public character, that *he was with* 10,000 *of the people;* was it not a greater crime *to speak evil of such a "dignity,"* than of another man? Dignity is opposed to meanness. It can be applied to no action but what is virtuous, and therefore to no being on earth but man. To him it is applied in point of character, sentiment and behaviour, all which in some degree, must unite in a man of dignity. But to form a ruler of that description, he ought to be—1st. a man of a good discernment and information. Great talents, and erudition may be indispensable in the learned professions, and in the pretorean department of a government, in which the people are governed by laws and not men. The police of some nations may indeed, be a science of operose attainment; but the administration [16] of a government, simple in its structure and formed as our own is, by the common sense of a free, virtuous people, cannot be a subject of vast depth or difficulty. Where men have honesty enough, they rarely will want skill enough, to guide well the affairs of state. The human body is subsisted chiefly by common food. This is the most easily obtained and the most wholesome, otherwise it would not have been *common.* The grand object, let us remember, as well as name of our government, is the *"Common-wealth."* It must however, be granted, that the smallest accession of knowledge adds to every character a dignity which is felt; and were it not for envy, would be acknowledged by all. Children soon feel the superiour authority, it gives a parent even in the government of a family. Rulers may not all be men of science, but if they are not men *"who have understanding in the times, and know what Isreal ought to do,"* it is at the risque of both of their country, and their own reputation, as dignities. 2d. *meekness of wisdom,* a cool dispassionate temper, is a distinguished trait in the character of official dignity. The greatest legislator was the meekest man on earth. It was an excess of diffidence in Moses, to decline, for want of abilities, the office of an embassador to a royal court. But it raises in the mind an idea of greater dignity, than the conduct of that aspiring young man, who spoke the real sentiments of others, besides his own, when he said, *"O that I were made ruler in the land, that every man who hath any suit or cause, might come to me and I* [17] *would do him justice!"* Hypocrites may be found in politics, as well as in divinity. With patriotism on the tongue, there may be faction or tyranny in the heart. High pretensions of friendship to the rights of man, attended with bitter criminations of men in public office, ought never to be admitted as a test of sincerity, or of real qualifications for office; because great zeal and ostentation are seldom united with that cool dispassionate temper which is always necessary to form a just opinion upon any subject. In our coolest moments, *"we see through a glass darkly."* But when we see through a ferment of passion, we see and judge falsely. The medium has a property strange and unknown in optics. It distorts and discolours, magnifies and diminishes every object at the same time. The rash policy of boisterous men at the helm of Government has been compared to a whirlwind at sea. When it happens to blow the right way, it may drive the ship from rocks or shoals, and save the cargo. But tornadoes are always dangerous to navigation.

To this cool dispassionate temper we must unite, 3d. resolution and intrepidity of mind; for this gives great dignity and elevation to a ruler. Unmoved by the fawnings of flattery or the four scowls of ambition, deaf to the croaking of anarchy and blind to the splendid baits of monarchy, he will nobly dare to speak his opinion, and act with firmness and decision. Like a rock in the midst of the ocean, he stands unshaken. The waves of violence, of [18] intrigue and faction may rise, foam and roar against him, but dash and die at his feet. This firmness of mind is directly opposed to that indecisive temper, by which some are perpetually *halting between two opinions,* without forming any at all. It stands opposed also to another temper, which may be called decision in excess, a rapid rotation of opinion.—Men of this cast decide in such haste, and with so little discretion, that *they are given to change;* vibrating from one side to the other, that we know not where to find them. *"A double minded man is unstable in all his ways, unstable as water he shall not excel."* There is another contrast of this mental fortitude, and that is ductility of mind; this renders the possessor too obsequious to flattery, to the lure of interest and popularity; too prone to be duped by the intrigues of disaffected aspiring men. Whatever may be the real cause or composition of these different tempers, certain it is, that the indecisive character, a bivious mind, and the ductile temper, all diminish dignity, and disqualify men for public office.

Firmness of mind must be accompanied with, 4th. consideration; for this, when united as commonly it is with industry and a public spirit, is one of the most prominent and pleasing features in the whole character of dignity. With what mild and gentle rays it shines through the characters of David, Solomon and a Washington, and gives them more real dignity, than all the dazzling splendours of a throne? This will soften the splendors of their stations, and give them an affable deportment, a complacency [19] of behaviour, and such conciliating manners, as cannot fail to secure the most commanding influence over the people.—In this way the greatest monarch of the earth governed *men, who were in debt, in distress, and discontented.* There our exasperated spirits, bankrupts, and broken fortunes, who had no interest in the welfare of the country, he influenced into one common concern for its property.—Such a motley mass of discordant materials he kneaded up, into one useful harmonious compound! It is a unanimous vote in our world, never to respect, but always to despise a haughty disposition. This disposition once degraded from his throne, the royal brute of Babylon, and turned him out a grazing with the beasts of the field! it sunk another as low in the eyes of millions, when in the haughtiness of his spirit, he said "I will bring all America to my feet." *Pride goeth before destruction, and a haughty spirit* is the fall of dignity. How unreasonable in a ruler as well as degrading is such a temper? What has he that he did not receive? Is he superior to others in the dignity of his person? GOD is the author of his frame. Has he more official dignity? It is derived from the sovereignty of the people. Does he shine in the most elevated stations? Like the moon he shines only in borrowed light. We do not particularly mention justice, humanity and patriotism, because they are all included in 5th. "Religion" which above all, gives to a ruler the highest dignity of character. The patriarchal benediction truly applies to religion alone: *"thou art the excellency of dignity and the excellency of power."* [20] This refines, enables and animates all the features that compose dignity, both of character and office.—Emancipated from inglorious passions and pursuits, which rob me of all true honour, religion plants in the heart such undissembled virtue and piety, as will ensure respect and reverence, even to men of the lowest rank, but in men appointed to move in the higher spheres of life, religion casts a lustre on their elevated seats, and "by a strong reflection doubles the beams of dignity." How amiable, how sublime in such a character! Every feature, every action in it, creates esteem, and commands reverence. How sordid then is the wretch who dares *to speak evil of such dignities!* Is it now possible to sully this crime with an additional stain of infamy? Yes, it is done only by considering that the character of a ruler deprives him of the power of retaliation in his own defence. *"When Michael the arch-angel contended with the Devil about the body of Moses, he durst not bring against him a railing accusation;"* the dignity of Michael's character, rendered him an unequal match for Satan, at *railing;* therefore he said, *the Lord rebuke thee, and not I.* From the subject naturally arise the following

BOSTON, 1795

OBSERVATIONS

1. Rulers are involved in the guilt of slander, when their conduct affords a just occasion for the people to speak evil of them. Can it be possible, that a legislator should enter the walls of the Senate, and under the solemnities of an oath, there give his voice and sanction to a law which he sacredly commits to the [21] magistrate for execution; and then both of them be seen to violate *that law*, which the one has made, and the other is sworn to execute? Is it a crime to speak evil of such dignities? there is no dignity in such men. Vice is eternally mean. 2d. The character given of a ruler, leads us to decide a long controverted question, respecting the best form of civil policy, in favor of a free republic. I mean "a democratical aristocracy, resting on the free election of the people, and revocable at pleasure."—The strength and glory of such a republic depend on the virtue of the people, which is real dignity. That of monarchy is supported by the glare of earthly grandeur, by the pageantry of heroism, and the weapons of death, which is royal dignity. This intoxicates the senses, but the other touches the heart. Hence a republican form was the choice and fabric of God himself for his own people. Moses with a senate of seventy, shared the government of Israel. The nature of man, the character of christian rulers, above all the benevolent principles of liberty and equality, embosomed in the religion of JESUS, are congenial to no other form; at least they appear incompatible with monarchical principles and the dynasty of kings. 3d—The advocated principle of calculating laws to embrace the aggregate sum of happiness in a community shews the absurdity of that doctrine, which maintains that moral evil is political good; or that private vice is public virtue. Were this a fact, it would be the duty of legislators to *establish iniquity by law*, i.e. they ought to enact laws to encourage [22] the practice of fraud, rapine, falsehood, robbery, assassination &c. than which nothing can be more absurd, or abhorrent to the principles of reason and common sense. 4th. Since it is a crime of such malignity to *despise government*, it highly concerns every citizen, particularly to know in what manner this may be done. *Government*, I would observe, *may be despised* by fallacious comparisons—by inequality of elections—licentiousness of the press—neglect to diffuse virtue and knowledge—disunion of the magistracy and christian priesthood—exorbitant wealth in the hands of individuals—improper connexions with despotic

PERES [PEREZ] FOBES 1742–1812

governments—neglect to watch and provide for our own government, the means of military defence—in such ways as well as by *speaking evil of dignities,* we may *despise* and even *destroy* a free government. On some of these articles, I would subjoin a few observations.

1st. *The palladium of Liberty may pull down the pillars of freedom.* A licentious press, like the unruly tongue, is full of deadly poison. It sows the seeds of discord, and saps the foundation of all government. By corrupting the source of public information, it becomes the bane both of private and social felicity. When political poison is vomited from the press, few will escape the contagion. When partiality in a printer loses its infamy, or the most uncorrupted integrity ceases to be the summit of his ambition—when he and his readers are not struck with the horror of an earthquake, at the idea of venality and misrepresentation [23] —when they print falsehood *for hire,* publish scandal *for money,* sell the liberties of their country for a *reward, and the wicked bare rule by their means, and the peeple love to have it so—what shall we do in the end thereof?*

2d. Whatever tends to destroy or diminish an equal voice in elections, will endanger the immunities of a people. Associations of every description, whether civil or ecclesiastical, whether self-created or sanctioned by government or by the god of nature, all tend to create in the mind certain byasses and attachments which produce an accretion of power and influence in future elections; nor can this be avoided without eradicating the principles of human nature. The existence of society depends on this principle; similar effects will arise from a natural superiority of genius, from greater acquisitions in knowledge, in wealth and in the arts of address. The Deity never intended a perfect equality among men, not even in their elective power. This would have been a scar, if not a solecism in the analogy of nature. This however, bears no proportion to that inequality which prevails among despotic nations, and which ought to be considered as the horror of all free governments. In nature we always observe variety, but we seldom find extremes. The beauty and utility of the human hand, that badge of human authority, would suffer great diminution, if its fingers were equal, but much more if they were enormous, either in length or size. It is only from an extreme or abuse [24] of this inequality, that danger is apprehended; and over which we ought ever to watch with a jealous eye.

3d. *National wealth, especially when carefully accumulated in the*

hands of a few individuals, is dangerous in the extreme to human liberty.
The experience of ages, the repeated admonitions of our Saviour and
his apostles prove beyond a doubt, *the power of riches corrupt the human
heart.* Hardly can we find one period of prosperity, in the whole history
of the Israelites, or of any other nation on the earth, which has not
been followed with a decay of piety, and a corruption of morals. Shall
we then rejoice and not tremble, when we see a profusion of earthly
good; flowing streams of prosperity, in which multitudes are bathing
themselves at ease, while the rapid current is carrying away the
liberties of mankind? Opulence is the common parent of idleness,
luxury and dissipation &c. The reflection of a moment will convince
us, that wealth is both the object and principal cause of *avarice* and
ambition. These are the common sources of anarchy and despotism,
and these again, are the charybdis and scylla of our country—most of
the disputes and quarrels that happen in the world, originate from
the idea of property. Savages live in tolerable peace almost without
government, because they feel not, as we do, the power of wealth.
While this attracts the gaze of vulgar admiration, it is apt to swell
the heart with pride, "that unsocial and unfriendly passion," *only by
pride cometh contention.* Its influence [25] on civil elections is still more
pernicious. Money is frequently the most forcible logic, and he that
carries the longest purse, will often carry the most votes. In this view
of wealth, we see and admire the policy as well as justice of a late act
of our legislature, which rescinded an old fragment of monarchy too
long worn as the right of primogeniture. We feel also, and revere the
wisdom of GOD in the appointment of a jubilee, as an essential article
in the Jewish policy. This, it is probable, was the great palladium of
liberty to that people. A similar institution perhaps may be the only
method in which liberty can be perpetuated among selfish, degenerate
beings in any government under heaven. But aside from this, and in
full view of the dangers of exorbitant wealth, permit me to say that
the prayer of one good man ever ought to be the united prayer of all
America, *"give us not riches—nor poverty."*

4th. The baneful effects of ignorance among the subjects of a
free government, I need not describe. Inspiration has done it for me
in one of her horrid descriptions of wild beasts and birds of prey,
prowling under the dreary darkness of night, *"Wherein all the beasts of
the forest do creep forth, their houses shall be full of doleful creatures, owls
shall dwell there, and satyrs, not fabulous, shall dance there."* Happy for

us, such darkness is past, and the present is a period of unusual ardour; for inquiry and diffusion of knowledge. Yea, the present is a most luminous period in that regular gradation of human knowledge, [26] which from the beginning of creation down to the present time, has been constantly advancing. By a train of surprising events in providence, calculated to throw light upon each other, the public mind in every age, and among all nations, has been gradually opening, *from the father of lights;* as much light and knowledge have been sent down to earth, as the circumstances of its inhabitants would bear. At certain periods however, knowledge on earth, like the heavenly bodies, has proceeded with unequal velocity; and like them, it has sometimes appeared stationary and even retrograde; but this was in appearance only. Upon the whole it has been progressive, and will probably continue its progress, until its final completion in the full effulgence of millennial glory, when *"the earth shall be full of the knowledge of* GOD." Partial interruptions have only paved the way for accelerating its progress. Great conquests and revolutions in the world, have given the people an opportunity for reforming their systems of government, and for great improvements, in useful arts and knowledge.—The American revolution is an instance of this kind, beyond a parallel. A large portion of the globe inhabited by millions of people, rapid in population, had long been held in subjection to one distant island. But the vision which *the young Hebrew* saw in his dream, *was but for an appointed time.* No longer could *the sun, the moon and stars,* be made to gravitate round a pebble: no longer could they *make obeisance* to Briton's king.—Nature itself revolted. They arose to independence, ascended their native [27] sphere, and formed a new solar system; a system compleat of *federal democracy;* in which equal power, emanating from each individual, uniting, formed one central luminary. This is retained in its station by a balance of gravitating power, accumulated in separate branches of the same body, as well as in a number of separate bodies or states. These are each independent in jurisdiction, different in structure, magnitude and distance from the centre; around them a number of secondaries perform their judicial circuits in periodical times; these are attended with satellites of executive power. A large judiciary body, created and impelled by solar influence, ranges like a comet through the whole system; spreads terror among evil doers; and gives lustre and stability to the whole frame. In a word, the influence of the solar orb pervades every other body, retains each in its own orbit, and gives to all energy and motion, by confederating all into one fast harmonious system. No sooner was this luminary kindled up in America, than it darted its beams of science and liberty across the Atlantic. It dawned in Europe—it glows in France. New discoveries and vast accessions of knowledge, and the arts of life astonished the world. We lived an age in a few years; we saw a *nation born in a day*. Having felt the pangs and pleasures of the parturition of a new empire, we now behold the aurora of science fast rising to meridian lustre. Hardly can we contemplate the present, and anticipate the future state of our country, without moments of triumph. When we reflect on the present improved state of commerce, agriculture and of tactics, the mechanical and fine [28] arts, geography and natural history, surgery and the medical art, chymistry, electricity, areology with the infant, but real science of physiognomy &c. all in progression; then lift up our eyes and behold a new galaxy of American geniuses, lately risen and still rising in our hemisphere, what in the name of science, what may we not expect? At least, we may hope, that modern polish of literature will not, *like Pharoh's lean kine*, eat up the more substantial parts; and that the time will soon arrive, when four years at a college will not roll away, without consecrating a portion of it, to the classical, scientific study of natural history, and those practical principles of chymistry, on which the rationale and improvements of agriculture and the mechanical arts, so much depend; and which at the present day are so highly necessary to the growth and prosperity of this young American empire. May we not also indulge the pleasing hope, that the orthography of our own language, that vehicle and repository of arts and sciences, will soon be purged of its barbaric dross, and become as pure simple, and systematic as our politics. May the genius, the unconquerable spirit of Americans, forbid that a language formed by accident in days of Gothic ignorance, and refined and enriched with so many infusions of elegance and learning, that a language which probably will become the vernacular tongue of more millions than ever spoke one language on earth, should long remain perplexed and incumbered with so many literal defects and redundancies easily corrected. On this account I beg leave to [29] say that the orthography of the English language, in its present state, is a tax on life, the opprobrium of science, a load of expensive lumber on the tender minds of millions of our race. In such a nation as this, it is intolerable. I will not think of it, but proceed to a thought more pleasing, 5th.

virtue and religion above all are the strongest pillars of government. The mask of hypocrisy is a public acknowledgment of the worth of religion. The suggestion even of Atheists, when they dub religion a state engine to awe men into obedience, is a tacit confession of its utility in government. A safe engine it is, and of such force too, that the want, or weakness of but a single spring in it, I mean the belief of a future state, has always proved fatal to the establishment of government over any one whole nation on earth. Inspectors of the public manners, appointed by the law-givers of antiquity, prove that virtue was esteemed essential to the prosperity & even existence of government. Should we appeal to the records of history—to that of the Jewish nation—to the Egyptians, Persians, Grecians, Romans, and to most of the flourishing states in the world, her verdict would be in favor of virtue. The interchange of virtue and vice, graduated the scale, by which the wealth, power and respectability of all nations may be accurately measured. Polybius, who ascribes to irreligion the ruin of his own country, which preceded that of Rome, observes that a tenfold security given by a Grecian trustee for a small sum of public money, was sure to be violated, while the religion [30] of an oath among the Romans was ample security for every engagement. While virtue prevailed in the Roman Empire, her feet in the language of Daniel, were *iron*. But when the people began to degenerate, the iron began to be mixed with clay. Her feet were broken, and the empire fell.—In a word, it can no more be doubted that happiness and misery of public communities, as well as individuals, are connected with virtue and vice, than that gravitation is a property of matter. But if ethical virtue was the existence and prosperity of ancient governments, what may not be expected from the purest system of moral virtue ever taught on earth? Compared with this, the finest morals of Socrates or Confucius, or Plato, or Epictetus, are no more than the light or heat of a glow worm, to that of the meridian sun. The religion of nature teaches men to be just and righteous; but a righteous man is not the character which christianity calls a good man. A good man will do *more* than strict justice can demand of him; *he will do more than others.* His services done for the public are performed not with servility, but affection.—Not merely to escape censure, or for the sake of reward, *"but as a servant of Christ with good will"* to mankind, *"doing service as unto the Lord, and not to men."* Religion requires those *who rule over men to be more than just;* they must *rule in the fear of* GOD: Because gods on earth are the subjects of Heaven, and must give an account of their stewardship to GOD, as well as to men. It was from this principle only, that the vice-roy of Egypt could assure [31] his brethren, that he would be just to them; that he was a man that could be trusted; for says he, *I fear* GOD. This will operate with peculiar force on the people as well as on rulers. This will seize the hearts. And the subject yields to the magistrate, *not for wrath, but for conscience sake.* He will not *despise government;* he is *afraid to speak evil of dignities,* because he believes that one is *the ordinance,* and the other, the *minister of* GOD. And those who resist, however they may escape punishment from men, *will* yet *receive to themselves damnation.* To him *the word of* GOD is *sharper than* the magistrate's *sword;* a guard stronger to human laws, than all their penal sanctions.

A judgment to come awes him more than all the terrors of an earthly tribunal. By those sublime and interesting discoveries which revelation unfolds, a new tribunal of justice is erected in the human breast; where conscience sits as judge, a judge that will be heard, when all others are silent. Such is the energy of religion! O religion the scorn of infidels, "a pitiful and paltry thing," but the everlasting pillar of government; for the sake of which, may heaven save us from the vortex of deism—that old harlot, lately re-baptized by the name of reason—*the age of reason.* Immortalized indeed, for the discovery of a new proof, *that infidelity is only another name for ignorance;* and that a great politician in Europe as well as insurgents in America, may be guilty of speaking evil of "DIGNITIES," *and things they "understand not"*—with proper deference to lord Bolingbrooke, [32] Bill Beadle,* and Tom Paine. I will close this article with an aphorism of the wisest and one of the greatest politicians that ever lived, and presume to recommend it, as *more* than equal to the Spanish proverbs, or even those of the American Franklin—it is this—"RIGHTEOUSNESS EXAL-TETH A NATION, BUT SIN IS A REPROACH TO ANY PEOPLE."

In the presence of an assembly, that contains so many living characters of *dignity;* His *Excellency* claims our first attention. Two annual suns have not yet revolved over the silent corpse of the patriotic, the generous, the amiable *Hancock,* since we saw him here. The man

---

* He pistoled himself at Weathersfield in Connecticut, December 11, 1782, after he had murdered an amiable wife and four children. This appears to have been done in cool blood, and from the genuine principles of his boasted, benevolent deism.

of dignity, the patron of Liberty, the friend of religion, of its ministers, and institutions, must die! But happy for us, his co-patriot lives, and this day fills his vacant seat. Venerable with age, more venerable for his piety and unconquerable love of liberty, we behold him again placed in the first seat of Government, by the United voice of his grateful country. She loved *his brother* in proscription, and still remembers the name of *Adams* enrolled with him, on the immortal list of exemptions from pardon, for no other crime but that of being a friend to his country. If his inflexible attachment to the same principles has since procured him the wounds of censure, *are they not wounds without a cause?* and [33] will he not with his dying breath, forgive his enemies, and pray for the liberties of mankind. His eminent services in the cause of freedom are too deeply engraved on the hearts of all true republicans ever to be forgotten. May the fostering hand of heaven guard him, at this critical period of life, from every adverse event which might shake the few remaining sands, that now measure his important life. With all the sensibilities of an imperfect offending mortal, united with the honest intrepidity of virtue, may he not appeal to heaven and earth, in the language of an inspired patriot of his own name, and say—"I am old and grey headed, I have walked before you from my childhood to this day; behold here I am, witness against me, before the LORD, and before his people, whom have I defrauded? Whom have I oppressed? Or of whose hand have I taken a bribe. And the people will say—thou hast not defrauded, thou hast not oppressed us, the LORD is witness, the LORD think upon you for good according to all that you have done for this people."

The re-election of a distinguished character to the second office in this Commonwealth bears an honorable attestation to his abilities and public virtue.—His early attachment to the principles of republicanism, his patriotic exertions in the accomplishment of our happy revolution, with later services, in promoting the true interests of his country, have fully justified the wisdom, the gratitude and patriotism of his electors. May heaven reward his faithful services with honours unfading and eternal.

[34] With grateful hearts we hail the return of an anniversary, which has once more convened those honored gentlemen who compose the two branches of our happy Legislature. From their known abilities, and the characters of their electors, we presume they have brought with them, to this consecrated spot, real dignity of character.

BOSTON, 1795

We rejoice in the senatorial *branch* of our government—chosen by the people at large. Their influence will operate as a useful check on the more local interest of the other *branch,* which otherwise might interfere and diminish the sum of public happiness.—This influence of the patrician order may indeed operate as a check on the dispatch of business, but repeated discussions of the same subject, in a different branch of the same body, will be more than a compensation for delay. As the object is ever the same, both branches will harmoniously co-operate for the general good. Every member holds an office, that is rendered highly momentous, both by the magnitude of its object, and the solemnity of an oath by which their fidelity is pledged. Guardians of the public rights, great confidence is reposed in them.—The eyes of the people, yea, the eyes of GOD himself are upon them. Unto Heaven may they look for assistance, and to the most perfect models on earth, for imitation.

JESUS was "the prince of the kings of the earth;" but he washed his disciples feet. *He went about doing* [35] *good.* Learn of him, learn industry, condescension, philanthrophy: *"whosoever would be greatest among you, let him be the servant of all."* Moses, when he stood on the mount with the laws of the Hebrew nation in his hand, with what astonishing dignity and splendour did this great magistrate appear in the eyes of the people? But *Moses wist not that his face shone:* "Be instructed ye rulers of the earth." This man had been with his GOD in the mount; *and Judah ruleth with* GOD, *and* therefore *is faithful.*— "The power of godliness" is the supreme dignity of all rulers in Heaven or earth. Acquainted with human nature, our civil fathers will not be disappointed to find honest men, who from ignorance of the duties, the expenditures and responsibility of public office, *will* be apt to consider rulers in a state like drones in the hive, which live on the honey of the poor labouring bees.—Others will mutter against government, and clamour for different measures, when they neither know nor can tell what they want. While they condemn rulers for oppressing the people, they are themselves acting the very part of that tyrant, who having once had a dream, threatened to kill his officers, if they did not interpret it, when he himself could not tell his own dream. When evils or inconveniences are felt in society, too many are apt to imagine the fault is in rulers, when it is in the people: hence they will seek a remedy in a change of the former; not considering, that an army infected with the plague, or composed of cowards, cannot be cured by a new choice of officers. Others will be found turbulent and disappointed—men of desperate [36] minds and fortunes, who constantly carry about them the tinder of faction, waiting only for a spark to produce an explosion. They wish for convulsions in the state, that *they* may rise into view, "ride in the tempest, and direct the storm." From such men, no honest ruler can escape the calumny of the tongue. Envy is the tax of eminence, and must be paid by every man in public office. While the Son of GOD remained in private life, *he increased in favour both with* GOD *and* "*Men.*" But when he assumed his public office he suffered more than the scourge of tongues. If our amiable *President* has made his escape, beyond any human character, it must be remembered, that he, like the amiable and intrepid Daniel, said to the people "*Let thy gifts be to thyself and thy reward to another;*" otherwise HE might have heard the growls of avarice and the curses of clowns.—In proportion to the degree in which a public spirit, or the social principle, prevails over the selfish, rulers will feel their own dignity, and make others feel it too. Conscious integrity will raise them far above the petulance of the tongue, or the virulence of party rage; "none of these things move them." Nothing will abate the ardor of their exertions for the public good. They know that silence is the school of wisdom, and *"with well doing they will put to "silence" the ignorance of foolish men."* We shall see them moving on, in silent majesty, like the full-orbed moon, above the reach of the arrows of slander, and beyond all danger of an eclipse or even a spot, from the little shadows of ten thousand beagles barking at them.—Example unblemished in public life will forever be [37] held sacred: they know that man is an imitative being; that between mind and body there exists such a reciprocity of influence, that even imitating the gestures and manners of others tends to produce a similarity of disposition. The passions of the people are moulded by the inclinations of the great. The actions of rulers, like the rods of Jacob, which he peeled and set before the flocks, will give colour and complexion to all that behold them; yea, more than this, the influence of public example will operate on the people, like the magnetic influence upon iron, which not only attracts or repels, but even communicates its own nature. This theory is authenticated by the most striking facts of inspiration. "As in water face answereth to face," so did the character of GOD's ancient people, both of Israel and Judah, correspond to that of her rulers. Whether they neglected or attended to religion and the worship of GOD, the people generally followed their example. What a lesson is before us! a volume of the most serious instruction in a single fact. May *"the honourable of the earth"* never forget, that character gives currency as well as dignity to their laws and public administrations; and while enforced by example, their own exertions to promote piety and morality, industry and temperance, with all the useful arts of life, will be productive of the most salutary effects.

Among numerous objects that may claim the attention of our honored rulers, and to which their own wisdom is fully competent, I would only suggest [38] that the property of numbers among us while they and their families are attending public worship on the Lord's Day, is liable to invasion, from licentious neighbours who attend no worship at all.—When the people of Israel left their own habitations and went up to Jerusalem to worship, GOD himself interposed; and by a miracle guarded in their absence, the property of his own people against the rapacity of their enemies. But without a miracle, or the least invasion of the rights of conscience, may not our legislators in this instance, place the property of every citizen upon the same ground of security. This would be done, if those who do not, should be obliged either to attend public worship themselves, or to furnish at their own expense a guard to the property of others, *while* they do attend.—*"With that confidence wherewith I am bold* to say, that our civil rulers will not forget their own names as *"dignities,"* it may be presumed, they will not forget that public institution of learning, to which they are so much indebted both for their literary and official dignity. May *"stand as a seal upon their arm, and a signet on their right hand."*—Above all, our venerable fathers will bear it in mind, that while employed in the service of their country, they are all acting a part for eternity. Fired with a noble emulation of transmitting their names to posterity in laurels of honour, they will be infinitely more concerned, to secure an enrolment of their names *on the Lamb's book of life;* where "the righteous shall be had in everlasting remembrance."

[39] *My fellow citizens of this numerous and respectable assembly,*

We know the value of freedom. We can truly appreciate the blessings of a free and happy constitution. When our birth-right was sold, *with a great sum* the purchase was made. Most ardently we wish they may never be abused, despised or lost. May Heaven, auspicious, forever guard them:—but this cannot be done unless men will guard their own tongues. A savage undisciplined tongue is more to be dreaded than undisciplined troops, or the most inhuman savage. Sharper than a two edged sword, it cuts the bands of love which unite man to man, and thrusts its deadly stab into the bosom of society; it is a *pestilence that walks in darkness and wasteth at noon day*. When the cause of liberty bleeds, let the patriotic tongue blow the trumpet, and plead its injured rights. Freedom of speech and of the press, in such a cause, is the terror of tyrants and the scourge of anarchy. But when licentious and ungoverned, they create jealousies, infuse suspicions, weaken public confidence, kindle, and augment the flames of such contention, as may desolate a country, and crimson it with blood! While every man claims, as he justly may, a right to watch his own government, let him watch his own tongue. In this way the poorest man may plant one of the strongest guards around the liberties of his country, by that which will cost him nothing, but silence. If he cannot keep his heart from deceit, he may keep his lips from speaking evil of dignities. Should we ever [40] behold what Solomon saw and lamented in his day, viz. *"Folly set in great dignity;"* the fault must be chiefly in the people who set them up. While therefore, we censure our rulers, we condemn ourselves. Never let us dare to sport with the character of a ruler. Public character especially ought to be treated as one of the most dear and delicate of all possessions. How easily is it tarnished? and how often is it done in ways unknown and unsuspected? Is there a man on earth willing, that his faults should be enumerated without naming his virtues? Partiality in this case is a species of the blackest slander.—Names and epithets of the most honourable import are, from the poverty of language, always liable to this kind of partiality; and when perverted, they become vehicles of the most abusive scandal: Just as the rankest poison may be conveyed in the richest perfumes. The names appropriated to express power, as it resides in the two branches of our own legislature, have not escaped this kind of perversion. Monarchy is exploded; but the idea still remains. Should an appropriate name to express that idea be wanted, etymology will present us with the word, *"Autocratical,"* i.e. the power of self, or self-important. This, it is presumed, truly expresses the feelings of the heart, and is perhaps the best definition of both the others, when they are bandied on the tongues of zealous partizans by way of reproach.

Where encomiums on the one side—ridicule and obloquy on the

other, are both extravagant, it becomes difficult if not impossible to find the truth.

[41] Among a free people there will be a variety of opinions, from whence different plans and systems of civil policy will be adopted, even where the object is the same. In this case, if different paths should not lead us with equal safety to the desired object, candour and moderation are the best remedies.

When political heresy creeps in, the standard must be lifted up against it. "To the law and to the testimony"—to the constitution and to the sovereign people we must appeal—the majority must decide, and all the people shall say Amen. While we are watching our own, and speak with freedom on the great republic of France, let us be *afraid to speak evil of "dignities" and things we understand not.* Let no envenomed tongue or sacrilegious hand dare touch the *ark* of liberty, or presume to make one link in that infernal chain of confederation against human happiness! May heaven secure us from systems of monarchical policy, and the devouring gulph of European politics! In fine, may all the friends of peace and harmony in our own and in the federal government, that admired fabric of human policy; may the friends of union without division, and of union without consolidation, yea, let every individual among us, unite and display his friendship by a strict government over the tongue, that *"unruly, member" of society;* the greatest tyrant, the vilest insurgent on earth! *"fight neither with small nor great, but with the King" of tyrants,* this demagogue of faction. To do this we are bound, both [42] by the highest claims of society and the more sacred ties of christianity. For, "if any man speak with the tongues of men and angels, and bridleth not his own tongue," *this man's religion is vain.* Convinced of this, and knowing that the heart is the guilty source from whence proceed evil thoughts, and speaking *evil of dignities,* let us look up to him, under whose dominion is the heart of man, and pray him to *create within us a pure heart,* and form us anew in CHRIST JESUS, that we may govern our passions, and bridle our tongues. May the most ardent gratitude from every heart, and every tongue arise to the eternal throne of the Supreme Ruler of nations, for the present peace and prosperity of our nation. Luminated with the hope of its continuance, let every one follow the unerring path of national and individual happiness, delineated by the dictates of infinite wisdom in such language as this— *"He that will love life, and see good days, let him refrain his tongue from evil and his lips that they speak no guile, let him depart from evil and do good."* Travelling in this peaceful path of wisdom and rectitude. A few days more the journey of life will be ended, the strife of tongues will cease, all our connexions with civil society be dissolved; while the *renovated* soul, washed in the Redeemer's blood, panting for liberty, will burst the chains of its prison, and bound over the long range of eternity, exploring and triumphing in all the "LIBERTIES OF THE SONS OF GOD."

AMEN.

[64]

JUSTICE [JACOB] RUSH
1746–1820

---

*The Nature and Importance of an Oath—the
Charge to a Jury*

RUTLAND, VERMONT, 1796

Jacob Rush chose to make law his profession rather than to follow in the steps of his elder brother Benjamin, who was destined to become America's first physician to command eminence in the great hospitals of Europe. He also differed from his brother in displaying little disposition to figure in the great debate over grievances with England and the rules to be followed in constructing a republican form of government. His charge to a jury in Philadelphia that is printed here excited enough interest in other places to be printed in a magazine in Vermont, the *Rural Magazine or Vermont Repository,* in 1796. A careful reading of the text will show that Judge Rush took the opportunity to outline a little-understood aspect of American political theory. Many Americans believed that political obligation rested not on any signed contract but rather on the taking of an oath. Many colonies had required oaths before one could vote or become a citizen, and state constitutions often required oaths of a wide range of officials. We still require oaths of jurors, witnesses in court, military personnel, and naturalized citizens, not to mention the president of the United States, and this essay is a reminder that to a completely Christian people the problem of political obligation has a simple, theoretical solution. The text here is taken from the October issue of the Vermont magazine.

JUSTICE [JACOB] RUSH 1746–1820

A Charge, delivered by Judge Rush, at Easton Court, on the 8th Sept. 1796, to the Grand Jury of the County of Northampton, in Pennsylvania.

Gentlemen of the Grand Jury.

As we are constantly employed in the administration of oaths, and every person is liable to be called upon to swear before some competent authority, it cannot be deemed improper, in this place, to address a few observations to you on the importance of an oath. This is the more requisite, from the danger that every idea, with respect to the solemnity of an oath, is likely to be obliterated from the mind, by the indecent manner in which they are daily uttered in familiar conversation, and the almost equally indecent manner in which they are frequently administered in the ordinary course of justice.

An oath, gentlemen, is a very serious transaction, and may be defined, a solemn appeal to God for the truth of the facts asserted by the witness, with an imprecation of the divine justice upon him, if the facts which he relates are false; or in the case of a promissory oath, if the party doth not fulfil his engagement.

We perceive from this definition, that oaths are of two kinds, assertory and promissory. The former included the testimony given by witnesses, and in general all matters of fact that are asserted or related upon oath. Promissory oaths are those taken by officers of government—all oaths of allegiance and protection, and likewise the oaths you have severally taken as grand jurymen.

The use of oaths, as a means of ascertaining the truth, it is impossible to trace to its origin. They have prevailed in different ages and countries, as far back as historical information can carry us, and are in fact as old as the creation. Abraham and Abimeleck ratified their covenant by the solemnity of mutual oaths, as did also Jacob and Laban—in which cases we observe, that Abraham and Jacob received the oaths of Abimeleck and Laban, though they swore by false gods, which are acknowledged by modern writers to be binding, provided the party believes in the existence of one God, the creator of all things. Swearing by inferior deities in such cases is considered as a mode of appealing through them to the Supreme Being; agreeably [470] to the declaration of our Saviour, "He that sweareth by the throne of God, sweareth by him who sitteth thereon, and he that sweareth by the temple, sweareth by him who inhabits the same."

Through these inferior objects the appeal is made, and terminated in a solemn invocation of the God of all Gods.

If we suppose the institution of an oath to be of divine origin, yet there is no doubt, that human authority is competent to establish those forms of swearing that are most calculated to strike with religious awe and veneration. Accordingly the forms of swearing vary in different countries. But in one point all ages and countries have uniformly concurred—namely, that oaths are to be administered to all persons according to their opinion, and in such form as most affects their consciences.

In the Old Testament we find Abraham called upon his servant to swear, and requiring him to place his right hand under Abraham's thigh, while he repeated the words of the oath to him; and Jacob used the same ceremony when he made his son Joseph swear he would not bury him in Egypt.

The persons of the Gentoo religion in India, when they take an oath, fall prostrate before the bramin or priest, and lay the right hand upon the bramin's foot; an oath of this kind has been admitted to be legal evidence in England, because the Gentoos profess a belief in one God, the creator and governor of all things.

A Mahometon swears upon the Alcoran, and places his right hand flat upon it, and his left hand upon his forehead. In this posture he looks steadily a few minutes at the Alcoran, and by this ceremony he conceives himself bound to speak the truth.

A Jew is sworn upon the five books of Moses, upon which he lays his right hand.

The general form in use among Christians, is to lay the right hand upon the Bible, or the New Testament only, and to kiss it. The ceremony of laying the hand upon the book, is undoubtedly of Pagan origin, and was introduced among the primitive Christians from the example of the heathens, who were accustomed to swear in the presence of their false gods—and sometimes by actually touching or laying the hand upon the sacred utensils of their superstition. The mode appeared solemn and affecting to the Christians; and therefore the presence of the Bible when they swore, was substituted in the place of the false gods of the Pagans, and was produced as a sacred memento of the religious obligations they were under to speak the truth. Hence we find some of them swore with the hand laid upon the Bible—some with the Bible spread open before them—some by laying their hand upon the breast, others with the hand stretched out, or lifted up towards heaven, but always with the sacred book in their immediate presence and sight. The insatiable spirit of superstition, which finally terminated in the establishment of popery, had at that time made considerable progress in the christian church; and to this spirit we must ascribe the circumstance of kissing the book and the expressions we sometimes meet with in ancient writers—so help me God and his saints, which last words, viz. and his saints, have been omitted by the protestants: Though they [471] still retain the former, and the ceremony of kissing the book.

Thus we see the mode of swearing amongst us, is partly of pagan, and partly of popish extraction. Among the early Christians, great latitude was admitted with respect to the form of swearing; nor does it appear that any mode whatever was prescribed, but that every person made use of the form most agreeable to his conscience. Even in the reign of Charles the second in England, we meet with an instance of a Doctor Owen, Vice Chancellor of Oxford, who being summoned as a witness, refused to be sworn by laying his hand upon the Bible, and kissing it; but he caused the book to be held open before him, with his right hand lifted up towards heaven, and was sworn in that form. The jury conceiving some doubts, whether he deserved as much credit as a witness sworn in the common form, put the question to the court. The chief justice with the utmost liberality told them that the doctor had taken as strong an oath, as any other witness, and was as much entitled to belief—but added he, if he himself was to be sworn, he would lay his right hand upon the book.

These and many other forms of swearing have been made use of in the world—but an oath does not consist merely in form. It consists in something more than laying the hand upon the Bible—kissing it—looking at it—or having placed it in our sight with the hand held up or stretched out. These are so many shadows, and alter not the nature of the transaction. It is the solemn appeal to God—it is engaging to speak the truth, and calling upon him to witness our sincerity, that constitute the oath and obligation. If this be done, it is immaterial whether any or what form be used. Whether the witness kiss the book, or lay his hand upon it, or whether he does neither, he is equally bound to speak the truth; and if he does not, he is guilty of perjury. But though oaths are obligatory in all religions, however indistinct the views they exhibit of God and his attributes, yet is their force peculiarly binding in Christian countries; because the sanction of rewards and punishments is more fully revealed by the Christian religion, and consequently the degree of guilt in transgressing the rules of moral duty, must be greater.

But can this appeal be made by every body? Can this security for speaking the truth be given by every one? Most certainly, gentlemen, it cannot.

It is impossible this appeal should be made or this security given, by those who do not believe in one God as creator and governor of the world. A Turk, or Indian, believing this, may be a witness, and a Christian renouncing the belief of it, or through ignorance unacquainted with it, is utterly incapable of being sworn in our courts of justice. The ties of religion can have no effect upon a mind, in which no idea of religion can be found, and there can be no religion if you take away a belief in the existence of a God, because it is the foundation of all religion. Upon this ground, Lord Kenyon, the present chief justice of England, rejected a person as incompetent to give evidence, who knew nothing of the obligations of an oath, of a future state of rewards and punishment, had never learned his catechism, and had only heard there was a God, and that [472] those who told lies would go to the gallows. A person discovering a disbelief of these principles, stands in the same predicament with one who is entirely ignorant of them, and consequently cannot be a witness.

If the obligation of an oath depend wholly upon the sense and belief of a deity; that he abhors falsehood, and will punish perjury; and if oaths are necessary for the maintenance of peace and justice among men; it clearly follows that a belief in the existence of God is necessary for the support of civil society. Every thing therefore that tends to unhinge our belief in this important principle, must be reprobated by all good men; because it tends to weaken the security of an oath. Lord Mansfield has asserted, what no person will venture to deny, "that no country can subsist a twelve-month in which an oath is not thought binding: for the want of it, he adds, must necessarily dissolve society." Whatever therefore relaxes the religious sentiment upon which an oath is founded, is injurious to society; because it lessens the restraint which the belief of that salutary principle imposes upon the human mind.

It is with perjury as with other crimes, there are certain paths that lead to it; and though there are some persons who may never arrive at the commission of this horrid crime, yet there is reason to fear, by their practices and example, they may be the means of others falling into it. One deviation from moral rectitude necessarily leads to another. He who has robbed his neighbour, will not hesitate to deny it with a lie or an oath, if such denial may be the means of his acquital. Drunkenness is often the foundation of quarrels, which not unfrequently end in murder or manslaughger.

The two vices that more immediately lead to perjury, are the infamous habits of lying, and swearing in common conversation. With respect to the person who has been accustomed to disregard truth in the ordinary occurrences of life, besides the pernicious example he sets to others, it is much more likely he should fall into the crime of perjury, than the man who is distinguished for strict veracity in his conversation. As to the impious vice of common swearing: to say that least of it—it is so absurd in itself, that nothing can possibly exceed the guilt, unless it be the folly of it. And were it not that it becomes criminal when viewed in its consequences upon civil society, would deserve it be mentioned only to be despised. It is indeed to be lamented that so many persons of rank, and good sense, among us, are addicted to it. They little think while they are invoking the vengeance of heaven upon themselves and others, and confirming the most trivial assertions with the awful name of the diety, that they are scattering firebrands, arrows and death around them. Man is an imitative animal; and the lower rank are eternally copying the manners, and even the expressions of those they have been taught to look upon as their superiors in education and stile of living. Though we are ready to admit, that persons of rank and sense who are guilty of this vice, if called upon to swear in a court, would scrupulously adhere to the truth, yet are they by the force of their example doing infinite mischief by inducing others to treat with contempt the [473] name of the deity, who perhaps may not be restrained from perjury by the advantages of a good education, and better reflection, which their superiors may have enjoyed. It is indeed a self-evident proposition, that an habitual profanation of the name of God by the familiar use of oaths and curses in common conversation, must very much tend to lessen that awe and reverence of the Supreme Being, which is one of the strongest guards against perjury; and consequently be in a high degree injurious to society. It is for this reason our laws have endeavoured to restrain common swearing, and have made it an offence punishable by a magistrate. Such, however, is the unfortunate predominance of custom, that the law is seldom put in execution: And this in fact will be always the case, while men of influence in elevated stations, lead the way in the violation of the laws. Their example like a torrent, sweeps away all before it, and the law seems to be silently repealed, by the rank, the character, and the number of the offenders.

Let the pretensions of a person to virtue be what they may, if he conducts himself in any manner injurious to his country, and forbidden by the laws, he is at best but a pretender to the character of a good citizen. His actions speak louder than his words, and mark him the decided enemy of social order and public happiness. "By their fruit you shall know them"—is not less true when applied to detect the pretender in patriotism, than the hypocrite in religion. The man who by his immoral practices is constantly infringing the laws of order, and spreading confusion through the moral world, contributes his utmost efforts to involve every thing in anarchy and ruin; and whatever may be the language of his lips with his vices, he is stabbing his country to the heart.

I observed, gentlemen, that some oaths are called promissory oaths; such are all oaths of office, and some others. This mode of exacting the performance of a trust, by the additional security of an oath, is universally practised by civilized nations; and though by our law the punishment of perjury cannot be inflicted for the violation of such engagement, yet may it be prosecuted as a misdemeanor; and in the sight of God, the guilt is equal to the case of perjury, where facts are misrepresented or concealed. In the eye of reason there can be no difference, between a person's swearing to a fact that never existed, and swearing that he will perform a particular act, and wilfully omitting it; or swearing that he will not perform a particular act, and afterwards deliberately doing it. There are doubtless different degrees of malignity attending the crime of perjury, as well as all other crimes. Yet I cannot avoid remarking that perjury in the case of violated promises may be, and frequently is, a more aggravated and detestable crime than even swearing to a direct falsehood, because it is accompanied with a perfidious breach of trust. In the case of marriage, for example, which is generally understood to be a contract, fortified with the solemnities of an oath, scarcely any guilt can exceed the violation of it. It is a cruel breach of trust, coupled with perjury; and tends directly to destroy the peace of families, and to tear up the very foundation of society. Contracts [474] and oaths must have some meaning. But if the inconvenience of executing them, or mere whim and pleasure, be admitted as an excuse for the breach of them; then farewell, gentlemen, to all honour and honesty. If one of the parties be discharged, the other cannot remain bound. The consequence of both parties being released from obligations, whenever either party shall feel, or fancy he feels, an inconvenience from adhering to his contract, must be this—that every person will be at liberty to rescind his solemn compact whenever he pleases. A doctrine pregnant with the most horrid confusion, and the entire subversion of society.

The true criterion or standard of any action whatever is this— what would be the result to society, if every other person did the same thing. In this scale man may weigh his actions, with the utmost nicety—by this rule he may measure the innocence or criminality of every step he takes in life. Suppose, for example, all persons to abandon themselves to adulterous courses—or suppose an universal and unre-strained intercourse to take place between the sexes; in either of these cases, such an universal depravity of morals would ensue, as must utterly destroy society.

Every single act therefore, comprized in either of these supposed cases, must be unlawful. If one man has a right to be his own avenger, every other person must have the same right. But if all men were to execute their own revenge, desolation, rapine and murder would quickly overspread the land. Every single act of revenge therefore, is utterly repugnant to social obligation.

From the consequences of any action being injurious to the public welfare, if universally practised, we infer, that every single action of the same kind of description, is criminal. The rule will hold good when applied to lying, stealing, drunkenness, and every other vice. For if one man has a right to steal, to tell a lie, to get drunk, or to violate his solemn promises as often as he pleases, so has every other man. But if all men were to give into these practices, society must be annihilated; for it could not possibly exist, if it were entirely composed of such infamous wretches. In the one case there would be no such thing as property—in the other no truth, or dependence of one man upon the words of another; and in the third, viz. a society consisting of drunkards, universal wretchedness must be the inevitable consequence.

From these observations, gentlemen, we cannot but perceive the destructive tendency of vice, in its very nature; and how utterly incompatible it is, with the interests of society. It is at the same time agreeable to remark, the coincidence, the perfect harmony, between the precepts of heaven, and the necessary consequences of human actions.

The laws of God forbid the indulgence of our passions only in such cases, where their gratification would be injurious to ourselves, or our neighbours, and enjoin the performance of all those duties, that are calculated to improve the heart, or promote the welfare of others. The Christian religion is in fact the surest basis of morality, and consequently of order and good government.

Of this heaven born religion it [475] is the peculiar characteristic, that while obedience to its commands constitutes the highest felicity of the individual, the practice of its benevolent precepts, is at the same time, the firmest foundation of social happiness and public prosperity. In the elegant language of holy writ, "her ways are ways of pleasantness, and all her paths are peace." even in this world. "Righteousness exalts a nation; (that is, makes it flourish) but sin is a reproach to any people; and by slow, but sure steps, under any form of government, inevitably leads to national misery and destruction."

[65]

NATHANAEL EMMONS 1745–1840

A Discourse Delivered on the National Fast

WRENTHAM, MASSACHUSETTS, 1799

Born and raised in Connecticut, Emmons studied at Yale, and spent fifty of his years as a Congregational minister in the Massachusetts village of Franklin, near Rhode Island. Widely sought after for instruction in theology and the art of preaching, he had a favorite dictum: "Have something to say; say it." For a full half-century Americans had been listening to sermons dealing with the nature of civil authority and the right of citizens to resist wrongful acts of rulers. Emmons here looks upon civil disobedience from the other side—the duty to obey constituted authorities in a new nation. Revolutionary principles are not abandoned but discussed in a balanced fashion as Americans struggle to preserve political stability during the 1790s without abandoning their heritage.

A DISCOURSE

TITUS iii. 1.

Put them in mind to be subject to principalities and powers, to obey magistrates, to be ready to every good work.

Heathens and infidels have always been disposed to represent the friends of revealed religion, as enemies to the peace and order of civil society. The nations bordering upon Jerusalem basely insinuated, that "it was a rebellious city, hurtful to kings and provinces." The unbelieving Jews accused our Savior of being opposed to Caesar and to the laws of his country. And it was a very common practice among the Pagans, to cast the odium of their own seditions and insurrections upon the peaceable and harmless Christians. To wipe off this aspersion from the followers of Christ, the Apostle Paul, who was a Roman citizen, and well understood the nature and importance of civil government, abundantly inculcated the duty of submission to those in authority. Nor did he stop here, but exhorted other preachers [6] of the gospel, to inculcate the same duty upon all the professors of religion. Knowing the general reluctance of mankind to legal restraint, and the peculiar prejudice of the Jewish converts against Pagan princes, he expressly enjoined it upon Titus, "to put his hearers in mind to be subject to principalities and powers, and to obey magistrates." By these appellations, he meant to denote all orders and ranks of civil officers, under all forms of civil government. This therefore, is the plain and practical truth, which falls under our present consideration:

That ministers ought to inculcate upon subjects the duty of obedience to civil rulers.

Here it may be proper to show,

I. Who are to be understood by civil rulers.
II. That it is the duty of subjects to obey them: and,
III. That ministers ought to inculcate this duty.

I. Let us consider who are to be understood by civil rulers.

Though God has not seen fit, under the gospel dispensation, to institute any particular form of civil government; yet he has prescribed the qualifications and duties of civil rulers. And we can hardly suppose, that he would delineate the duties and qualifications of a certain order of men, which he neither approved, nor intended should exist. It is, therefore, evidently the will of God, that there should be civil government, and that there should be a certain order of men to administer it. In this sense, we may consider civil government, as the ordinance of God, and civil rulers, as the ministers of God; though they derive all their authority from their fellow citizens. But the question before us is, who are to be [7] understood by civil rulers, to whom submission is due. This seems to be a plain question, though it has been much agitated by the greatest statesmen and divines. Reason and scripture concur to teach us, that the powers that be, or those who are in peaceable possession of civil authority, are the magistrates whom we ought to obey.

There are three ways of men's coming into possession of civil power. One way, and indeed the best way, is by the free and fair election of the people, who, in every republican government, enjoy the right of choosing their own rulers. This right generally is, and always ought to be, restricted to persons of a certain character and interest. Those, who are so dependent, as to have no will of their own, are totally disqualified to give their suffrages for civil magistrates. Such men, however, as are fairly chosen into office by the people, are properly civil rulers, and to be acknowledged and treated accordingly.

Another way in which men may become clothed with civil authority, is by hereditary right. Any people may make their government hereditary, if they please. And after they have adopted such a form of government, men may come into power by succession, without any formal election. The eldest son of a king, for instance, may be the rightful heir to the throne; and, upon his father's decease, abdication, or removal, may take possession of it, without the voice of the people.

The last and worst way of men's coming into the seat of government, is by usurpation. This method of obtaining power has been much practised in all ages of the world. A son has often usurped the throne of his father. A prime minister, or a peculiar favorite, has often usurped the throne of his master. An [8] enterprising and successful general has often turned his arms against his sovereign, and placed himself in his room. Though the conduct of usurpers is to be condemned and detested, yet after the people have, through fear or feebleness, acknowledged their supremacy, they are to all intents and purposes civil rulers, to whom obedience and subjection belong. It must be supposed, that the Apostle meant to include sovereigns of this description, among "principalities and powers" in the text. For it is well known, that many of the primitive Christians lived under the government of usurpers. Most of the sovereigns, in the first ages of Christianity, had unrighteously seized the thrones which they filled. And if Christians were to obey the principalities and powers then in being, they were to obey those who came into power, by unjust and unlawful means. Indeed, there seems to be an obvious reason why such men should be obeyed. After usurpers are peaceably established in their dominions, the people explicitly or implicitly engage to submit to their authority. Though they promised submission with reluctance; yet having promised, their promise is morally binding. Besides, those, who have violently seized the reins of government, may afterwards be very good rulers. And it matters not, whether they rule by written or verbal laws, provided they rule in wisdom and equity. So long as they employ their power to promote the public good, the people have reason to lead peaceable and quiet lives in all godliness and honesty. As Augustus Caesar used his usurped power with great moderation, during his long and gentle reign; so the Romans were so much obliged to obey his authority, as if he had come to the throne, by the free and general voice of the empire. But not to enlarge upon this [9] topic at present, I would say in a word, that by civil rulers in the text and in this discourse, are to be understood all those, who are in the peaceable possession of civil power. I proceed to show,

II. That it is the duty of subjects to obey their civil rulers. And this will appear, if we consider,

1. That the Scripture expressly enjoins this duty upon subjects. The Apostle Paul requires them to "be subject to principalities and powers, and to obey magistrates." The Apostle Peter, in his first Epistle, exhorts believers to be good subjects of civil government, in order to adorn their Christian profession, and recommend their religion to those, who were strongly prejudiced against it. "Dearly beloved," says he, "I beseech you to have your conversation honest among the Gentiles: That whereas they speak against you as evil doers, they may by your good works which they shall behold, glorify God in the day of visitation. Submit yourselves to every ordinance of man, for the Lord's sake: whether it be to the king, as supreme; Or unto governors, as unto them that are sent by him for the punishment of evil doers, or for the praise of them that do well. For so is the will of God, that with well-doing ye may put to silence the ignorance of foolish men." There is another passage in the thirteenth of Romans, which more fully and forcibly inculcates, upon all, the great duty of submission to civil magistrates. "Let every soul be subject unto the higher powers. For there is no power but of God: the powers that be are ordained of God. Whosoever therefore resisteth the power resisteth the ordinance of God: and they that resist shall receive to themselves damnation. For rulers are not a terror to good works, but to the evil. Wilt thou then not be afraid of the power? do that which [10] is good, and thou

NATHANAEL EMMONS 1745–1840

shalt have praise of the same. For he is the minister of God to thee for good. But if thou do that which is evil, be afraid; for he beareth not the sword in vain; for he is the minister of God, a revenger to execute wrath upon him that doeth evil. Wherefore ye must needs be subject, not only for wrath, but also for conscience sake. For, for this cause pay ye tribute also: for they are God's ministers attending upon this very thing." Here submission to those in authority, is most expressly enjoined upon all, as a moral and Christian duty. Many passages of a similar import might be adduced from the Old Testament: but I choose to draw the proof of this duty, from the precepts of Christianity, which are unquestionably binding upon subjects at this day, under whatever form of government they live.

2. The duty of submission naturally results from the relations, which subjects bear to their rulers. There would be no propriety in calling the body of the people subjects, unless they were under obligation to obey those in the administration of government. Every people either directly or indirectly promise submission to their rulers. Those, who choose their civil magistrates, do voluntarily pledge their obedience, whether they take the oath of allegiance or not. By putting power into the hands of their rulers, they put it out of their own; by choosing and authorizing them to govern, they practically declare, that they are willing to be governed; and by declaring their willingness to be governed, they equally declare their intention and readiness to obey. In every free government, the rulers and the ruled lay themselves under mutual obligations to each other. For a free government is founded in compact; and every compact, whether private or public, invariably binds all the parties concerned. [11] The subjects of every elective government, therefore, voluntarily and expressly engage to obey those, whom they raise to places of power and trust. And as to such as live under different forms of government, they also indirectly and implicitly promise submission to the powers that be. Hence all subjects owe obedience to the civil magistrates, by virtue of their own actual engagements. There is not a single exception in this case. The man, who is born after a government is established, is as much obliged to submit to it, as if he had lived while it was framing, and had actually assisted in framing it. The man, who is born after an usurper has taken the supreme power, is as much obliged to submit to him, as if he had lived in the time of the revolution, and had personally consented to his sovereignty. Every person is born the subject of some

government, and has no right, when he comes upon the stage of action, to refuse obedience to those, who are in the peaceable possession of civil power. There are no detached individuals in any civil community; but all are members of the body politic, and universally bound, by their own explicit or implicit consent to pay obedience and subjection to those, whom they have either chosen or allowed to sit in the seats of government.

I may add,

3. All subjects ought to obey their rulers, for the sake of the public good. It is the duty of civil magistrates to seek the general welfare of the people, and so long as they diligently and faithfully attend upon this very thing, they justly merit the obedience and concurrence of every one of their subjects. For every person ought to desire, and as far as he can, contribute to the peace and prosperity of that community to which he belongs. Let a civil constitution [12] be ever so good, it can answer no valuable purpose, unless the people will submit to those in administration. Rulers are mere cyphers, without the aid and concurrence of their subjects. What can a general do to defend his country, if his soldiers refuse to fight? And what can the supreme magistrate do to maintain the peace and order of society, if his subjects refuse to obey? All the benefit to be derived from civil government ultimately depends upon the people's obedience to civil rulers. The subject, therefore, is under moral obligation, resulting from the general good, to submit to the civil magistrate. And agreeably to this, the Apostle says, "He is the minister of God to thee for good. Wherefore ye must needs be subject not only for wrath, but also for conscience sake." As the conscience of every man tells him, he ought to seek the general good; so it equally tells him he ought to obey the higher powers, who are seeking the same desirable and important end.

Thus the people, in every civil society, are universally bound by the general good, as well as by their own engagements and the authority of God, to pay a cordial and conscientious obedience to all the officers of government. I now proceed to show,

III. That ministers ought to inculcate such submission to civil magistrates.

Here permit me to observe,

1. That preachers are expressly required to press this plain and important duty upon the people of their charge. "Put them in mind to be subject to principalities and powers, and to obey magistrates."

NATHANAEL EMMONS 1745–1840

The Apostle wrote this Epistle on purpose to direct a minister of the gospel how to conduct in his sacred office. And instead of warning against him being too officious, in treating upon the delicate subject of [13] submission to government, he commands him, without fear or favor, to admonish his hearers of their indispensable obligation to obey every order of civil magistrates. There appears no circumstance of time or place to restrict this injunction to Titus in particular; and, therefore, we must suppose, that it equally applies to all the preachers of the gospel, in every age of Christianity. It is beyond doubt, that the Apostle intended, by the precept in the text, to teach not only Titus, but all succeeding ministers, the great importance of inculcating upon subjects that obedience and submission, which they owe to all in authority, from the highest to the lowest.

2. It becomes the preachers of the gospel, in this case, to follow the example of the inspired Teachers. John the Baptist repeatedly inculcated submission to civil authority. When some of the Publicans were about to be baptized, they seriously asked him, "Master, what shall *we* do?" Shall we relinquish our civil employment, and no longer gather the public taxes? "And he said unto them, Exact no more than that which is appointed you." Defraud not the public to promote your own private interest; nor disobey the lawful authority under which you act. At the same time, "the soldiers likewise demanded of him, saying, And what shall *we* do?" Shall we cease to be soldiers, and refuse to obey our officers? "And he said unto them, Do violence to no man, neither accuse any falsely; and be content with your wages." Slay only your public enemies; abuse none of your fellow soldiers; and cheerfully take the lot and perform the duties assigned you. Our Saviour taught the same doctrine. On a certain occasion, the Pharisees sent unto him their disciples, with the Herodians, saying, "Master, we know that thou art [14] true, and teachest the way of God in truth, tell us, therefore, what thinkest thou? Is it lawful to give tribute unto Caesar or not? Then said he unto them, Render unto Caesar the things which are Caesar's; and unto God the things that are God's." This was a plain and explicit command to be subject to principalities and powers, and to obey magistrates. The Apostles strictly followed the example of their divine Master, and forcibly inculcated upon subjects the duty of submission to all in authority, whether kings, or governors, or more subordinate rulers. These examples are worthy of the attention and imitation of all the ministers

of the gospel. Though in some cases they have no right to imitate Christ and the Apostles; yet no reason can be assigned, why they should not follow their example in ordinary preaching, and inculcate upon subjects the same submission to government, which those infallible preachers inculcated.

3. It no less belongs to the office of gospel ministers, to teach men their duty towards civil rulers, than to teach them any other moral or religious duty. This appears from the manner, in which the Apostle commands Titus to address the various characters among his people. He first directs him to instruct the aged, the young, and those in a state of servitude; and then immediately exhorts him to "put all persons in mind to be subject to principalities and powers, to obey magistrates, to be ready to every good work, to speak evil of no man, to be no brawlers, but gentle, shewing meekness to all men." In this connection, the Apostle plainly teaches ministers, that they are under the same obligation to inculcate upon their hearers the duty of submitting to civil rulers, as to exhort them to be peaceable, and gentle, and ready to every good work. It is an essential branch of the ministerial [15] office, to explain and inculcate all the duties, which God has enjoined upon all persons of every age, relation, and connection of life. Those in the gospel ministry, therefore, as truly act in character and agreeably to their sacred office, while they teach and exhort subjects to obey magistrates, as while they teach and exhort them to love God with all the heart, or to love their neighbours as themselves. And I may still further observe,

4. That there are some peculiar reasons, why the duty of submission to civil authority should be more especially inculcated upon the minds of subjects. Men are extremely apt to forget that, they are under any moral obligation to obey the rulers of the land. This the Apostle plainly suggests, by his mode of expression in the text. *"Put them in mind* to be subject to principalities and powers." The people are very ready to imagine, that there is no moral evil in violating the laws of their country. They are much more disposed to regard the *power,* than the *authority,* of civil magistrates. If they obey, it is for wrath, and not for conscience sake. If they disobey, they feel no remorse nor regret, unless they receive the due reward of their deeds. How frequently are the good and wholesome laws against gaming, tavern haunting, sabbath breaking, and such like evils, trampled upon by multitudes, without once reflecting, that they have

poured contempt upon the ordinance of God? The general respect paid to civil authority seems to be much more owing to a principle of prudence, than to a sense of duty. Hence there appears to be a peculiar necessity of inculcating the duty of obedience and submission to all orders of civil rulers. As no duty is more generally forgotten or neglected than this; so no duty needs to be more frequently and powerfully inculcated.

[16] Besides, there is scarcely any duty more disagreeable to the human heart, than submission to civil government. Men are naturally unwilling to be controlled, and especially by human laws, the reasons of which they seldom understand. Some have no capacity, some have no inclination, and some have no opportunity, to examine the wisdom and rectitude of public measures. But even supposing, that those in administration could demonstrate to the apprehension of every individual, that all the laws and measures of government were calculated to promote the general good; yet there is no reason to think, that this would satisfy the minds of people in general. For the public good is a light object, when thrown into the scale against private interest. Just so long, therefore, as men are disposed to prefer private good to public, they will feel a strong reluctance to the obedience and submission which they owe to civil rulers. And since it is well known, that this is the prevailing disposition of mankind, it must be granted, that subjects need to be often and solemnly admonished, to sacrifice their private interest to the public good, and submit to every ordinance of man, for the Lord's sake.

There is still another plain and important reason, why submission to government should be strongly inculcated. The safety and happiness of the whole body politic more essentially depend upon each member's performing this, than any other duty. A subject may neglect any other duty, and injure only himself, or a few individuals, with whom he is intimately connected. But if he rise against government, or disobey the laws of the land, his disobedience is like the disobedience of a centinel who exposes both himself and the whole army to destruction. A seditious and disorganizing spirit is extremely contagious. It will [17] suddenly and almost imperceptibly enflame the minds of the largest people. And when this spirit once seizes the majority, neither their numbers, nor their riches, nor their arms can afford them the least protection. The most excellent and patriotic rulers, and the most peaceable and virtuous citizens are liable to fall victims to the fury and revenge of lawless and ungovernable rebels. Where there is no subordination, there can be no government; and where there is no government, there can be no public peace nor safety. Such an absolute necessity of submission to civil authority, in every civil community, renders this duty of the highest political importance. And this importance loudly calls upon the ministers of the gospel of peace, to inculcate upon subjects, in the most plain and pungent manner, their indispensable obligation to be subject to principalities and powers, and to obey magistrates, and every order and distinction.

This subject now suggests some seasonable and useful reflections.

1. There is no ground to complain of the ministers of the gospel, for inculcating political duties. Those who dislike public men and public measures are very apt to complain of preachers, if they undertake to adapt their discourses to the present state of public affairs, and press obedience and subjection to the powers that be. In the beginning of this century, there was a party in Britain friendly to the Pretender, who bitterly complained of Bishop Hoadly and other clergymen, for supporting the house of Hanover, and inculcating loyalty and subjection to those in the peaceable possession of the reins of government. And there are many now in America, who are friendly to France, and who publicly reproach those preachers of the gospel, who presume, at this interesting crisis of public [18] affairs, to step forth in the cause of their country, and inculcate the duty of submission to those patriotic rulers, who are seeking the safety and interest of the nation. But, if what has been said in this discourse be true, their complaint of the clergy is altogether unscriptural, unreasonable, and inconsistent. It is unscriptural, because ministers are required by the precepts of the gospel and the practice of Christ and the Apostles, to inculcate submission to government. It is unreasonable, because ministers have the common right of citizens, to form their own opinions, and to speak their own sentiments, upon such public measures, as relate not merely to the local politics of a town or parish, but to the great body of the nation. And it is inconsistent; because those who complain, are highly pleased to hear ministers preach in favor of the government they like, and in support of the measures they approve. They now condemn the same kind of preaching, which, less than twenty years ago, they highly applauded. They have no real objection against *political* preaching, but against *what* is preached upon *political* subjects. It is readily admitted, if ministers recommend tyranny to rulers, or

sedition to subjects, they deserve to be censured; but on the other hand, if they preach sound doctrine in politics and morals, their preaching ought to be candidly heard, and religiously followed. And for my own part, I verily believe, there is now a special call in providence to all the ministers of the gospel, to put men in mind of the duty and importance of supporting the constitution, and submitting to the administration, of our present free and excellent government.

2. There appears to be no more difficulty in determining the measure of submission to civil government, than the measure of submission to any other human [19] authority. Volumes have been written in favor of passive obedience and non-resistance to the higher powers. And volumes have been written in opposition to this absurd and detestable doctrine. But notwithstanding all the learning and ingenuity which have been displayed on both sides of this question, and the remaining diversity of opinion upon it, it seems to be attended with no peculiar difficulty but what arises from the selfish views and feelings of mankind. Many cannot endure the idea of submission to civil authority, unless it be so qualified, softened, and limited, as to allow them to disobey and resist their rulers, whenever their private opinion, or personal interest requires it. But God enjoins submission to all human authority, in the same general, and unlimited terms. The Scripture requires subjects "to submit themselves to *every ordinance of man,* for the Lord's sake." The Scripture requires children "to obey their parents *in all things,*" and the Scripture requires servants, "to obey, *in all things,* them that are their masters according to the flesh." Who can discover, upon reading these precepts given to subjects, servants, and children, the least difference in the measure of submission? But though the Scripture no where prescribes the measure of submission to government, yet it is the plain dictate of reason, that all submission to human authority is absolutely limited. Servants, and even slaves, have the right of private judgment, and may, in certain cases, justly refuse obedience to their masters, and oppose their authority. Children have the right of private judgment, and may, in certain cases, refuse obedience to their parents, and resist unto blood. So subjects have the right of private judgment, and may, in certain cases, refuse submission to those in authority, and even destroy them. But all moral agents, [20] who have the right of private judgment, are accountable for their exercise of it. If servants resist their masters, without reason, they deserve to be punished. If children resist their parents, without reason,

they deserve to be punished. And if subjects rise in opposition to government, without reason, they deserve to suffer as criminals. In short, every subject, who resists the powers that be, is either a patriot or a rebel, and ought to be considered and treated as such. The reason why no divine nor human law fixes the measure of submission to human authority, is because the cases in which it may be right to resist, cannot be ascertained until they actually occur. Though we know before hand, that there are measures of submission to all human authority; yet no man can determine what they are, until cases actually take place, which will justify resistance. Who can tell when a servant may justly rise against his master, and destroy his life? None will pretend, that every time he feels provoked, or thinks himself injured, he may rise and redress his supposed grievances. Children often imagine they are abused, when their parents reprove, restrain, or correct them; but will any say, that, in all such cases, they have a right to resist parental authority? It also appears from observation and experience, that subjects are apt to think themselves injured and oppressed, when they are heavily taxed, or called upon to support and defend their government; but who will maintain, that every supposed or real grievance will justify resistance to legal authority? Though rulers ought not to injure any of their subjects; yet individuals cannot be justified in disturbing the public peace, for the sake of redressing their own private wrongs. Hence it is easy to see, that there is no more nor less difficulty in ascertaining the proper measure of submission to civil [21] government, than the proper measure of submission to any other human authority. There is nothing but *absolute necessity* can justify a people in breaking the bands of society. It is theirs to judge when such necessity exists, and to judge according to truth. For, if they either ignorantly or wilfully rise against their rulers, without just cause, they act the part of rebels; and if there be power and virtue enough in government, they must be restrained and punished.

3. It is extremely criminal to disobey civil rulers, and oppose the regular administration of government. There is a strong propensity in mankind to trample upon human authority, and obstruct the execution of the most wise and salutary laws. And this unruly spirit infatuates their minds, and leads them to imagine, that there is little or no criminality, in striking at the foundation of public peace and safety. Indeed, many consider a restless, discontented, seditious spirit as virtuous, rather than sinful; and would be thought to be acting a

noble, manly, patriotic part, while they are weakening the hands of rulers, and destroying the energy of government. But such persons ought seriously to consider, that they are violating their own voluntary engagements, opposing the public good, and disobeying the express commands of the Supreme Ruler of the universe. These sacred and solemn obligations bind their consciences to obedience and submission; and their guilt in disobeying and opposing the laws of the land, is in proportion to the obligations they violate. The Scripture calls those, who are enemies and opposers of government, *heady, high minded, truce-breakers,* and *traitors;* and represents them as deserving to be punished not only in this life, but in that which is to come. It is true, indeed, all transgressions of human as well as divine laws are not [22] equally heinous. The violation of some civil laws is so common, and so generally winked at, that it may be supposed to be owing to ignorance, or inattention, rather than to a deliberate and wicked design. But when subjects knowingly and violently oppose the laws of the land, and aim to overturn the pillars of government, they contract a heavy load of guilt, and expose themselves to the heavy hand of human and divine justice.

4. It is criminal not only to disobey and resist civil authority, but also to countenance, cherish, and enflame a spirit of disobedience and rebellion. This is often done by some great and influential men, who are either afraid or ashamed to appear in open opposition to government. Those who wish to weaken the hands of rulers, and to pave the way to anarchy and confusion, very often conceal their views, while they use every mean in their power, to diffuse a spirit of discord and sedition in the minds of the people. They speak evil of dignities. They represent the most wise and upright rulers, as acting from mean, mercenary, and arbitrary motives, and aiming to enrich and aggrandize themselves. They complain of their public measures, and insinuate, that they are systematically calculated to enslave and destroy the people. They represent wise laws to be unwise; just laws to be unjust; necessary laws to be unnecessary; and constitutional laws to be unconstitutional. And if these methods of enflaming the passions of the populace against their rulers be not sufficient to answer their purpose, they have recourse to another, which is next to irresistable, I mean bribery. This engine both antient and modern nations have employed to promote conspiracies, insurrections, and rebellions, against government. The French have of late carried [23] the art of bribery

to the highest degree of perfection. According to the best accounts, they have corrupted every people whom they have subjugated, by this diabolical method. These are the means, which artful and designing men employ to diffuse a disobedient and rebellious spirit into the minds of those, who are unacquainted with public affairs. And we have great reason to believe, that not a few are now secretly exerting all their influence, to propagate such a dangerous spirit. We clearly discover such a strong and zealous opposition to government, as cannot be accounted for, by any visible cause. There must be, therefore, some men behind the curtain, who are pushing on the populace to open sedition and rebellion. It is highly probable, that the late insurgents in Pennsylvania were corrupted and deluded, by some artful and influential characters, who have chosen to lie concealed from the public eye. And it is no less probable, that those unhappy creatures still really believe, many of the populace, and some of the principal men, in all the United States, secretly approve and applaud their insurrection, as a bold and noble act of patriotism. But those, who thus secretly cherish and enflame a seditious and rebellious spirit, are of all subjects the meanest and vilest. They do more mischief, and contract more guilt, than the poor, deluded, infatuated mortals, who actually rise in rebellion, and attempt the subversion of government.

5. Those in executive authority are under indispensable obligation, to give rebels and traitors a just recompense of reward. They are God's ministers to execute wrath upon them that do evil; and they ought not to hold the sword of justice in vain. They are not only to countenance and encourage obedience, but to discountenance and discourage disobedience. [24] They are not only to reward them that do well, but to punish the lawless and disobedient, as a terror to all their subjects. It is true indeed, they ought to make distinctions among the guilty, and proportion their punishments according to the nature and aggravations of their crimes. Though they may with propriety appear lenient towards ignorant and deluded transgressors; yet the general good of society requires them to make examples of some, at least, of the more bold and malignant enemies of government. The best laws will soon lose their force, if they be not duly executed, and the transgressors of them generally entertain a hope of impunity. Though the penalties of the laws should be lenient, yet the execution of them should be speedy and rigid. For it is not the penalty of the law, but the execution of it, that strikes terror into the minds of

rebels. Rebellion is an heinous crime and deserves a severe punishment; and yet there is scarcely any crime, which the great body of the people more ardently desire should be treated with lenity. They can coolly, if not cheerfully, see the murderer, money-maker, or the thief, receive the due reward of his deeds; but they are extremely apt to pity, and endeavor to screen the insurgent, or rebel, from condign punishment. This compassion towards the disturbers of the public peace, has been carried far enough, if not too far, in both the Northern and Southern States. It seriously concerns those who are entrusted with the execution of the laws to reflect, that "the judgment is God's," and that he allows them not to fear the face of man, nor to indulge that tender mercy towards the enemies of government, which would prove cruelty to their most virtuous and peaceable subjects.

[25] 6. The present appearance of a seditious and rebellious spirit in this happy country is extremely alarming. This spirit has often appeared in the world; and produced the most fatal effects. When the spies returned from searching the land of promise, a spirit of rebellion broke out in the camp of Israel. And though Moses and Aaron, on the occasion, fell on their faces before all the assembly of the congregation of the children of Israel; and Joshua the son of Nun, and Caleb the son of Jephunneh, employed the whole force of their eloquence, to persuade the deluded and infatuated rebels, to go forward and take possession of the land of Canaan, yet they absolutely refused to obey the authority of their wise and faithful rulers. This was highly displeasing to God, who doomed them to wander and perish in the wilderness; while he safely conducted the dutiful and obedient to a land flowing with milk and honey. The last time Jerusalem was besieged, a spirit of sedition proved fatal to the city, and to millions of its deluded inhabitants. The French were happy in their new modelled government, until a spirit of rebellion broke out, and destroyed their monarch, their nobility, their clergy, and their wisest and best citizens. Switzerland, which lately contained a number of rich, flourishing, united States, is now groaning under the fatal effects of a seditious and rebellious spirit. The same spirit has once and again disturbed the peace of America. At the close of the last war, a spirit of opposition to the Commutation act appeared in Connecticut; but was easily and happily nipped in the bud. Some time after, a levelling spirit prevailed in this Commonwealth, and produced a formidable insurrection against the courts of justice, which it required a military

[26] force to suppress. Since the establishment of our present general government, some of its enemies, at the Southward, took up arms and violently opposed the collection of duties on distilled liquors. To reduce those sons of sedition to reason and to order, was extremely troublesome and expensive to the public. And this year, the same turbulent and rebellious spirit has appeared again, and rendered it necessary to call forth an armed force against the opposers of government. The present appearance, therefore, is truly alarming. Though but small numbers have yet openly and violently opposed the laws of the land, yet the leaven of rebellion has evidently poisoned the minds of many, in various parts of the Union. It is yet unknown, what will be the effect of either lenient or severe measures towards those, who are now in the hands of public justice. The people feel deeply interested in the fate of disorganizers and insurgents. This, however, is certain, that unless a spirit of sedition can be effectually suppressed, and a spirit of subordination effectually established, there can be no peace nor safety to these United States. A very wise and experienced ruler has said, "Rebellion is as the sin of witchcraft." It is not only very contagious, but extremely infatuating. It deprives men of all sober reasoning and reflection. This is demonstrated by the effects, which it has already produced amongst us. Some very honest, and, in other respects, very judicious people have already become deaf and blind. They cannot *see* the increasing light thrown upon the dark designs of France; nor *hear* the voice of the most wise and enlightened statesmen. This presages a rapid progress of the present spirit of infatuation. And should this continue and increase, it will naturally produce one [27] or the other of these deplorable effects. It will either bring on a general civil war, and reduce us to the dreadful system of liberty and equality; or it will render it absolutely necessary to tighten the reins of government, and lay stronger restraints upon the tongues, the pens, the hands, and the liberties of those, who are now complaining of our free government, and its wise and gentle administration. We may all be satisfied, that our general government will never be altered for the worse, so long as we remain heartily attached to it, and will faithfully exercise our right of choosing upright and able rulers, who understand the nature and estimate the worth of our excellent Constitution. But though the present prospect is, that the prevailing spirit of sedition and rebellion will be eventually suppressed; yet there is ground to fear, that if much time, great exertions, and large sums of money be

employed to suppress it, the body of the people will be so irritated, that they will choose to have government strengthened and their liberties abridged, rather than be perpetually exposed to the dire effects of sedition, insurrection, and rebellion. Nothing, therefore, can prevent the horrors of civil war, or the loss of our civil liberties, but the effectual suppression of that seditious spirit, which refuses to be subject to principalities and powers, and to obey magistrates.

7. It is just ground of humiliation before God, this day, that our free, flourishing, and highly favored nation, have become so averse from submission to civil government. There is no nation in the world, who have better laws, than the people of America; and yet there is no nation, perhaps, who pay so little regard to their own laws, as the enlightened citizens of the United States. How are the laws against gaming, [28] profane swearing, sabbath-breaking, and the use of unjust weights and measures, trampled upon by all classes of people? And what a daring spirit of sedition and rebellion is making its dreadful appearance through every corner of our land? These are national sins; and these national sins are extremely aggravated. No nation on earth know their obligations to obey magistrates, and submit to every ordinance of man for the Lord's sake, better than we do. From the first settlement of our country to nearly the present period, we have been habituated to pay submission to every species of human authority. And we still enjoy the sacred Oracles, and religious instruction from sabbath to sabbath. These circumstances greatly enhance the guilt of our national disobedience and licentiousness. Let us lament the prevalence of these land-defiling iniquities. It is the proper duty and business of the day. And unless we sincerely perform this duty, this day will increase our national guilt, and ripen us for national ruin.

8. It is extremely impolitic, as well as criminal, in civil rulers, to reject Christianity themselves, and to endeavor to make their subjects reject it. It is well known, that some of our civil magistrates, who fill high seats in government, are become apostles of infidelity, and represent it as conducive to liberty and equality, and the most perfect state of civil society. But what evidence can they find in Scripture, in reason, or in experience, to establish their bold and novel opinion. It appears from what has been said in this discourse, that Christianity is calculated to strengthen the sinews of government. It commands rulers to be faithful to their trusts, and subjects to be

obedient to all in authority. And it enforces these commands, [29] by the weighty motives of eternity. It is also the dictate of reason, that the spirit of Christianity, which is the spirit of pure disinterested benevolence, forms the best rulers, and the best subjects, and eminently qualifies both for the different stations they hold in society. And when or where was it ever found, by experience, that atheism, deism, or infidelity had a favorable influence upon the peace and happiness of a civilized people? But one nation in the world have made the experiment, and they have nothing to boast of their new discovery. What tremendous havoc has infidelity made among all orders and classes of men in the French nation, and in all the nations, whom they have sacrilegiously *regenerated?* It is astonishing, that learned statesmen should not only embrace the principles of infidelity, but even propagate such loose and immoral sentiments. If they would consult only their personal power and influence, and the present good of society, they would certainly recommend revealed religion, and sincerely desire that the great body of the people might imbibe its spirit, and act under its powerful and benign influence.

9. It now only remains, my hearers, to put you in mind of your duty, at the present critical and alarming crisis. You see a spirit of disaffection and opposition to government prevailing among your countrymen. You have heretofore felt, and begin to feel again, the bitter effects of such a disorganizing spirit. You know the reasons, or rather pretences, which the uneasy and discontented allege for their opposition to public men and public measures. You have heard the duty and necessity of submitting to government briefly described and inculcated. It now seriously [30] concerns you, as you regard your consciences and your country, to appear openly and decidedly in favor of your laws and of your rulers. Speak well of their characters and duly appreciate their late noble and spirited measures. Reflect upon the plain and obvious reasons, upon which the Sedition and Alien Laws are founded, and upon the urgent necessity of heavy taxes for the public defence. Can you hesitate a moment, whether it be possible to maintain your national independence, without being armed, both by land and sea, against both foreign and domestic enemies? Where can be our safety, if the navies of Europe are suffered to sail into our ports and harbors, without the least obstruction? What can hinder a sudden and awful revolution of government, if the counsels of those be followed, who are insidiously aiming to bring about such a dreadful

catastrophe? Open your eyes upon the fate of other nations, and attend more to the *conduct,* than to the *language,* of the French Republic, who have long fixt their ardent wishes upon the fertile fields of America, and left no measure untried, to deceive us, to our own destruction. Think not, that you shall cease to be subject to principalities and powers, if the great nation take you under their wing. Though they have given different appellations to magistrates, yet they have not weakened their hands, nor shortened their swords. The powers that be in that tyrannical nation, are more to be dreaded than a Nero or Caligula. There appears to be but one way to escape the dangers to which you are exposed, and that is, to obey your present wise, firm, faithful magistrates, and cheerfully concur in their wise and prudent measures, to guard [31] you against French infidelity and French tyranny. Submit yourselves, therefore, to every ordinance of man for the Lord's sake; and lead a quiet and peaceable life in all godliness and honesty. For this is good and acceptable in the sight of God our Saviour.—Amen.

[66]

JONATHAN MAXCY 1768–1820

An Oration

PROVIDENCE, 1799

Born in Massachusetts a few miles west of the Rhode Island border, Maxcy was educated at nearby Rhode Island College, later called Brown University. Shortly after completing his course of study, he was ordained a Baptist preacher but occupied his pastorate for scarcely a year when, at the age of twenty-four, he was made president of the college from which he had graduated five years before. His repute for excellence in administrative skills and his fame as a preacher and orator led to a later appointment as president of Union College in New York, and then a call from South Carolina to organize and become the first president of a college that was to become the University of South Carolina. After his entry into manhood Maxcy took an active interest in the development of the new republic and the welding of the American people into a nation. In this address he injects himself into the debate over the Alien and Sedition Acts, launching into a review of basic political principles supporting rights and equality from a conservative point of view.

Called by your suffrages, Fellow-Citizens, I once more address you on the Anniversary of our National Independence. This event, though glorious in itself, and wonderful in its effects, is, by the peculiar situation of our public affairs, exalted to a point of unprecedented importance. Never has our country been exposed to greater danger; never has our government been assaulted with greater violence, by foreign foes and domestic traitors; never have [there] been more insidious, persevering and malevolent attempts to corrupt public

JONATHAN MAXCY 1768–1820

opinion; to undermine the foundations of religion, to cut asunder the sinews of moral obligation, and to cover this happy land with carnage, desolation and ruin. Let us then with enthusiasm hail the Birth-Day of our Sovereignty. Let us summon all our energies against the artifices of secret intrigue, and the aggressions of open hostility. To animate your patriotism, and inspire you with all the ardour of violated liberty; to render you feelingly alive to the necessity of united vigorous measures of defence, to rouze up your generous indignation at the unprovoked abuses practised by a foreign nation of gigantic power, permit me to call back your attention to that period, not far past, when all that was dear to you as members of society and subjects of government, was suspended over the gulf of ruin; when you rose up with an invincible courage, and, in the voice of united thunders, announced to the world that you were FREE, SOVEREIGN and INDEPENDENT. On that great and trying occasion, what were your feelings? Did you tamely submit [4] to the usurping arm of foreign domination? Did you surrender your liberties, without a struggle or a sigh? No, Americans, you did not; you acted the part of men worthy of liberty; you displayed the standard of freedom; you drew the sword of vengeance; you discharged the thunderbolt of destruction, and, under the protection of heaven, obtained a triumph, which glitters in capitals on the pillars of eternity. Succeeding years crowned the efforts of our wisdom, and the labours of our industry, with a success and prosperity which have astonished the world. The establishment of an energetic government, the culti-vation of the soil, the rapid increase of population, the great extension of commerce, the improvement of arts and sciences—all combined to perpetuate our freedom, to augment our power, and to render us a respectable and invincible nation. Guarded by the immense ocean, we hoped to escape that whirlwind which has long been spending its rage on the devoted nations of Europe. We assumed a neutral station: our right hand held out the branch of peace, while our left welcomed the persecuted stranger. Britain first smote us with her gigantic arm; she listened to our remonstrances, and redressed our wrongs. France, irritated at our success in preserving peace, determined on revenge. She renewed with additional vigour those secret, insidious acts, which she had long practised to controul our public councils, and to destroy the confidence of the people in the government of their choice. Detected and disappointed by the vigilance of our rulers, she threw aside the mask, and disclosed her vengeful countenance on the Atlantic. Our commerce fell a prey to her all-devouring jaws. The overtures made by our government have been neglected with the most haughty disdain, and our messengers of peace treated like the representatives of a nation destitute of wisdom and power. We have now no resource left to vindicate our honour and our rights, but our courage and our force. These we trust are sufficient to defend us against all enemies, whether foreign or domestic.

We must rank among our disgraces as well as among our misfortunes, the existence of a set of men in our country, who have derived their political principles from foreign influence and foreign intrigue who exert their utmost efforts to ruin our government, and to prostrate [5] all permanent establishments. These men discard, as the effects of superstition, all ancient institutions; and, instead of adhering to an uniform order of things, delight in perpetual revolutions. Their systems of rights, like their systems of government, is metaphysic and fantastical. They do not consider that government is a science derived from the experience of ages, and that it ought to embrace the rights and welfare, not of the present age only, but of all posterity. They consider the chief magistrate in no other view than a private citizen; government in no other view than an affair of temporary expediency or advantage. Thus they level that distinction which is the foundation of submission to laws; and reduce a contract the most solemn and important to an equality with a partnership in commerce, which at any hour may be broken off and dissolved. Let their ideas of government be realized in actual operation, and there is an end of all order, peace and prosperity. For how can agriculture and commerce, arts and sciences, be carried on to perfection under an administration perpetually changing? What security has property? What excitement can there be to industry, where it is liable to lose, in one moment, the acquisition of years? A good government will derive assistance from the experience of past ages. It will embrace and perpetuate the complicated mass of individual and public rights and interests. It ought to be considered as an inheritance to be transmitted from one generation to another; and not as the capricious offspring of a moment, perpetually exposed to destruction, from the varying whim of popular phrenzy, or the daring strides of licentious ambition. The great objects of national importance cannot be obtained, except under a political system, rendered permanent by a well regulated balance of power; guarding on the one hand against tyrannical usurpation, and on the

other against democratic violence. Such we conceive is the government
of these United States. Nevertheless, there are many who view it in a
far different light; or, because they are conscious of its energy, are
continually advancing opinions and doctrines which tend to its subversion. They well know that the people of this country are very averse
to a government like that of England. They take advantage from this
circumstance, and are continually ringing it in our ears, that our
government apes the manners of the British, and [6] is rapidly changing
into that complicated system of monarchy, aristocracy and democracy.
This representation is given, either from ignorance of the British
constitution, or from a desire to annihilate our confidence in our own.
Compare for a moment the principal branches of the English government with the principal branches of the American. How great the
contrast! How wide the difference! The king of Great-Britain is
independent; the President of the United States is not. The former
holds his throne by hereditary right; a right not derived from the
consent of the people, nor at the disposal of the people: the latter
holds his office by election, and with the consent of the people. The
President of the United States, after a short space of time, descends
and assumes his place as a private citizen; the king of Great-Britain
holds his crown and his throne through life. The former is accountable
for his conduct, and liable to impeachment whenever he violates the
laws; the latter is accountable to no human power, nor can he be
impeached at any human tribunal. In the king we behold an enormous
power, independent and unimpeachable; in the President we behold
a power limited by the constitution, and incapable of committing
abuses with impunity. Can we descry any resemblance between these
two important branches of the American and British governments?
Why then all this outcry against the enormous power of our supreme
magistrate? Why so many industrious attempts to persuade the people
that he is an aspiring monarch? I will tell you: It is because we are
blessed with a group of government levellers, who cultivate those all-
preserving, democratic virtues, jealousy and ingratitude.

In the government of Great-Britain is an inheritable peerage.
The lords temporal and spiritual are independent: they hold their seats
without the consent of the people, and can hold them against their
consent. How different the American Senators! Chosen by the people
in a constitutional mode, they are wholly dependent for their power
on the people; and must, after a prescribed term, revert to their places

as private citizens. Great-Britain has an house of commons. In this branch lies the only share which the people have in the government, and here their influence is very small. For the commons consist of all such men of property in the kingdom as have [7] not a seat in the house of lords. The knights which represent the counties are chosen by the proprietors of lands; and the citizens and burgesses, who represent the cities and boroughs, are chosen by the mercantile part of the nation. Hence the inequality of representation is so great in the house of commons, that the people rank this among their greatest grievances. We can discover no resemblance between the British house of commons and our house of representatives. In short, the most important branches of the British government are independent and hereditary: all branches of the American government are dependent and elected. Who but a madman, or an enemy to our country, could have had the effrontery to assert, that our government is formed after the British model? Our government is our own, and so long as we adhere to it, we shall be a people free, independent, and invincible.

Another sentiment strenuously maintained by the enemies of our government, is, that the union of the States is an affair of occasional convenience or advantage; and that any State, whenever she sees fit, has a right to denounce the proceedings of Congress, and to secede from the great political body. These positions are advanced with a view to impede the energy of the Federal Government, and even to undermine its foundation. If admitted and reduced to practice, they will render the execution of laws utterly uncertain; and, in case of foreign invasion, will expose the government to destruction and the country to devastation. The advocates of these strange political opinions seem not disposed to profit by past examples. They are like those fanatics who look for all wisdom in themselves: "and such never fail to find it." I would cite them to the states of ancient Greece, at the time of the Persian invasion, under Xerxes. Had these states been united under a common government; had they been responsible to some supreme controlling power; they would not through fear and jealousy, have deserted the public cause, and have left the Athenians and Spartans to oppose the immense army of Asia. One would suppose, that in a time of such pressing danger, a sense of the necessity of indissoluble union, would have had the force of a law, to compel all the states to engage in the common cause. But the reverse took place. The haughty monarch of Persia, taking advantage [8] of the disunion of his enemies, pressed forward, marked his steps with *fire* and *blood*, took the city of Athens, which his general Mardonius soon after entirely destroyed. This example is a loud warning to us, that a country divided into a number of independent states, can have no safety but in union, and no union but in responsibility to a supreme controlling power. I will hazard the assertion, that the states of Greece suffered more from their internal dissentions and divisions, which arose from the want of a Federal Government, possessed of a power over them all, than they did from all their foreign wars. Is it not the part of prudence, to profit by the errors, as well as by the wisdom of past ages? Is it not the part of folly, in the present advanced state of the science of government, to admit an idea which the example of all the ancient independent republics reprobates, as the fruitful source of division, violence and destruction?

Those metaphysic knights in the science of civil policy, who have attempted the subversion of our government, have done no small mischief by the perpetual use of certain words and phrases, which, though they conveyed no definite meaning, yet were calculated like the incantations of magic, to blind, seduce and mislead the unwary. "LIBERTY, EQUALITY, RIGHTS OF MAN;" these are the ensigns armorial of the whole tribe of political speculatists; these they hold up to the people, with a view to change real liberty into licentiousness; real equality into murderous violence; and the real rights of man into indiscriminate plunder. The indefinite phrase, *"Rights of Man,"* seems to imply, that man is born into the world with certain connatural political rights. This cannot be true, for government is a creature of man's invention and wisdom, and is founded on the compact of men in society. If man has any political rights which he can claim, it is because he is a member of the political system, or a partner in the great community of rights attached to the government under which he lives, whether this government is formed by his contemporaries, or inherited from his ancestors. But man, considered as such, has but one right, that of self-preservation. The phrase *"Rights of Man,"* has been lavishly thrown out in this as well as in other countries, with a view to persuade the people that their government was an arbitrary engrossment of power; that it was an unreasonable restraint on their [9] passions and energies; that as it denied them certain rights which they might claim because they were men, it ought to be demolished and buried in ruin. The direct tendency of the doctrine styled *"Rights of Man"* is to disquiet the people, to set them at variance with their rulers, to fill all the grades of society with an unreasonable jealousy of each other, and to change the order of civil institutions into the anarchy of barbarous association.

Let us for a moment contemplate the magical, wonder-working word, "EQUALITY." This, in the French cavalcade of death, is harnessed up behind Liberty. That fair goddess is with reluctance dragged into the train, and thrust forward, that her charms may introduce the infernal procession which troops behind her. The revolutionary demagogues of our country talk much of equality. They assure us, in their indefinite, unqualified language, that all men are equal. To ascertain whether this assertion is true, we must recur to fact and experience. Nature, so far from having made all men equal, has made them very unequal. All men have not the same strength and activity of body— all have not the same endowments and energies of mind. These are facts which speak in a language too plain not to be understood. Nature no where yokes up a dwarf with a giant, or a Newton with an ape. Amidst her mighty profusions of endowments, we discover an instinctive wisdom, fitting the numerous parts of this stupendous whole to their several places; arranging them by orders, differences and contrasts, so as to constitute one perfect system, whose parts are never all young, nor old, nor equal, but supported in a beautiful diversity through a perpetually dying and reviving universe.

Society no less than nature makes great differences and inequalities among men. When the road to acquisition is equally open to all— when the laws equally protect every man's person and property—all men will not make exertions equally great—all will not possess the same spirit of enterprize—all will not obtain accessions of wealth, of learning, virtue and honour, equally extensive and important. The industrious, prudent citizen, will gain vast quantities of property, while the negligent and idle will remain in the depths of poverty. To the last, the doctrine of equality is like the music of angels. Energized by the sound, he rouzes from his lethargy, and revels [10] on the divided spoils of his wealthy neighbour. That men in the social state are equal as to certain rights—that they ought to be protected in their persons and property, while they conduct as good citizens, will undoubtedly be admitted. This, however, is a very different kind of equality from that which the promulgers of this pernicious doctrine intended to introduce. Their schemes of wicked ambition were, to overturn all the established governments in the world, and to obtain an unlimited control over the minds and bodies of men. Nothing could be more immediately conducive to this purpose, than to render all the subordinate ranks of society dissatisfied with their condition. This was to be accomplished by persuading them, that the governments under which they lived were unjust and oppressive; that all religion was a vain and idle superstition; that there was no difference in men, except what arose from arbitrary violence; that the few who had acquired great wealth had no better right to it than the many who had acquired none; and that nothing could restore genuine liberty but the prostration of every dignity and of every advantage, whether derived from the industry of man, or the bounty of God. The advocates of this pernicious system of equality, in the career of their opposition to the laws of nature and society, have expressed their fervent displeasure at that respect which long has been, and I trust long will be, attached to eminent and dignified men, exalted to the higher stations in government. This is an important part in the system of universal disorganization. For if you destroy all respect for magistrates, you destroy all confidence in them; and leave no security for the existence of liberty or laws. The cry of our levelling democrats is, "respect the majesty of the people."—Where are we to look for the majesty of the people, except in the persons exalted to office by the suffrages of the people? These are the characters whose public administrations are to shew whether the people have any majesty. The phrase, "majesty of the people," in its modern acceptation, brings into view such an indefinite object, made of every gradation of character, from wisdom to folly, from virtue to vice, from aspiring ambition to brutal stupidity; that it serves only to perplex the mind, by rendering its views vast and irregular. We hope the American angle of vision is not sufficiently large, to [11] take in that indescribable farrago of majesty, with which our modern levellers are so much enamoured. We hope we have still judgment enough to distinguish merit, and gratitude enough to reward it. We are willing that the laws of nature, and the principles of civil association, should still be followed. We have not yet lost all regard for ancient institutions and ancient wisdom. We respect our magistrates; we esteem and protect the ministers of our holy religion; we embrace as our brethren all our worthy fellow-citizens; we form our political system after the great primeval model which descends from the source of infinite wisdom; which combines into one harmonious whole, principalities and powers, and exhibits in one vast and brilliant assemblage, millions of different dignities, without envy and without revolution. Peace, and order, and rational liberty; these are the objects to which we are invincibly attached. If once illumined by the transforming doctrine of equality, we shall see the whole establishment of nature reversed. Walking on enchanted ground, we shall see vales usurping the place of mountains; rivers whirling back to their sources, and skies falling to embrace the earth. We shall see huge whales sporting on the Andes, and clumsy bears flouncing in the Pacific. The planets in their courses will utter censure at their Maker, and the moon will repine at the splendour of the sun. When we are transformed into complete levellers, we can overleap, at one bound, all the mighty differences established by infinite wisdom; and, without a seeming disgust at the junction of eternally jarring principles, shall congratulate ourselves that we have escaped the drudgery of human prudence, and emerged into a region of perfect day.

Another cause which has had an extensive influence in producing and propagating erroneous notions respecting the nature of civil government, and which has rendered great numbers of people jealous and unhappy, is either an ignorant or designed misrepresentation of liberty. All restraints on the feelings, passions and actions of men, have been considered as the arbitrary mandates of a tyrant. It has generally been asserted, that when man quits the savage for the social state, he resigns a part of liberty to secure the rest. From this erroneous sentiment have orginated the most violent invectives against those measures of government, which limit at a certain boundary the [12] exercise of civil rights, and render men responsible for the abuse of those rights. What liberty has man in the unsocial, uncivilized state? I conceive he has none, which properly comes under the idea of liberty. True, he is exempt from the restraints of law: he is also destitute of the protection of law. He consults no will, and no power but his own. Every man, therefore, in an uncivilized state, is either a tyrant or a slave. No one can be sure of the produce of his labour, or of the safety of his person. Visionary theorists may amuse themselves with their pompous descriptions of the liberty of uncovenanted man; but fact and experience will tell us, that he has no liberty but in a society governed by laws which controul every man's will, and protect the weak against the strong. What is called liberty in any other state, is properly the liberty of doing mischief. It is licentiousness or despotism.

JONATHAN MAXCY 1768–1820

Government is by no means founded on what are called natural rights, but on conventional agreement. Every man in the uncivil state claims a right to every thing. Of consequence, every man sets himself up for a tyrant. War and bloodshed ensue, till the strongest arm determines whose right is best founded. Every man in the uncivil state claims a right to be the judge of his own cause, and the avenger of his own wrongs. He relinquishes both these rights when he enters into society. He now has a claim to assistance and protection from the aggregate wisdom and force of the community. Every right which he now possesses, rests on the social compact. He cannot now conduct himself in any way that is repugnant to established laws and constitutions. These prescribe the rights of every individual, and these alone secure genuine civil liberty. In the social state, every man is at liberty without any responsibility to extend and to use his rights, so far as they do not interfere with the rights of others, or with the general good of the community. The moment a man abuses his rights, with respect to the character, persons or property of others, he becomes responsible, and deserves punishment. For if no man is responsible for the abuse of his rights, society and liberty, with all their advantages, are destroyed.

A good government is a system of restraints on the actions and passions of its subjects. All good citizens will rank these restraints [13] among their rights, and not among their grievances. A spirit of national liberty exults in submission to the controul of just and salutary laws. It considers these as its only asylum against violence and outrage. A spirit of licentiousness is impatient of all restraint, delights in perpetual revolutions, and always measures its right by its power. Some of the citizens of these States consider our government as too complex in its structure, and too expensive in its operations. They confidently assure us, that a simple house of representatives, with a speaker, would fully answer every object of national importance. The simplest forms of government will generally secure some individual object better than the more complex, but they commonly leave the most important concerns unguarded. Every one who is versed in the political history of nations, knows that the ends to be obtained by government are numerous, often difficult of access, and, when obtained, difficult to be secured. No simple direction of power can possibly be accommodated to the complexity of human affairs. Hence it is that the due distribution of powers, so as to secure the greatest number of advantages, with the fewest inconveniences, has been considered, by the most profound politicians, as the most difficult part in the mechanism of civil institutions. In governments where there is but one branch of power, there is no security of liberty. Simple democracies, whether managed by the whole people assembled, or by their representatives, have always proved as tyrannical as the most despotic monarchies, and vastly more mischievous. It is in vain to substitute theoretical speculations in the place of facts. The modern zealots of revolutionary reform may tell us that the science of government is of all others the most simple; that a nation, in order to be free, needs only an exertion of will; but the experience of ancient and modern times will tell us that the science of government is of all others the most intricate: because it is to be deduced from principles which nothing but experiment can develop: and that a nation, in order to be free, needs some wisdom as well as will. But our reeking demagogues, in order to accomplish their designs of demolishing all permanent establishments, address themselves to the stubborn principle of will, and guide it, not by convincing the understanding [14]—not by presenting a certain prospect of improved liberty and happiness—but by irritating the feelings, rouzing up the passions, and loading the soul with a sense of unreal grievances.

The enemies of our own and of all other established governments, in order to give complete success to their schemes of destruction, have attempted to exterminate all religious and moral principles. They well knew, that if men would not fear and obey the Supreme Being, they would not any subordinate being. Hence it is, that such efforts have been made to discredit the doctrines of natural and revealed religion. Hence it is, that cargoes of infidelity have been imported into our country, and industriously circulated to corrupt the minds and morals of the rising generation. Efface the idea of a supreme controlling power from the minds of men, and you leave none of those exalted motives, none of those ennobling virtues, none of those aspiring principles of perfection, which have excited, adorned and animated the greatest geniuses of ancient and modern times. No government, except absolute despotism, can support itself over a people destitute of religion; because such a people possesses no principles on which governmental motives can operate to secure obedience. The most salutary laws can have no effect against general corruption of sentiments and morals. The American people, therefore, have no way to secure their liberty, but by securing their religion; for there is no medium between an entire destitution of religion and the most deplorable servitude. No nation, however ignorant and barbarous, except one, has ever attempted to support a government without some respect to a Supreme Being. Let us then guard with the utmost vigilance against those domineering, abandoned and arrogant philosophists, who consider themselves as the asylums of wisdom, and the oracles of truth; who assert that there is no standard of moral rectitude; and are striving to persuade man, that to be perfect, he needs only forget every thing exterior to himself, and suffer all his actions to be guided by the impulses of his own nature. These sentiments, if reduced to practice, will undoubtedly destroy all moral, civil and social obligations. For how can men form societies, institute governments, and cultivate arts and sciences, who will be guided by no laws, and controlled by no power out of themselves? Each one considers himself a deity, [15] and yet conducts like a brute! Each is an instinctive Animal, and yet a perfect intelligence! Such are the effects of renouncing religion—of substituting speculation in the room of experience!

We are called upon as citizens and as men, by the highest motives of duty, interest and happiness, to resist the innovations attempted on our government; to cultivate in ourselves and others the genuine sentiments of liberty, patriotism and virtue. After a long series of peace, prosperity and happiness, you are threatened with all the horrors and cruelties of war. The tempest thickens around you, and the thunder already begins to roar. A Nation hardened in the science of human butchery; accustomed to victory and plunder; exonerated from all those restraints by which civilized nations are governed, lifts over your heads the iron sceptre of despotic power. To terrify you into an unmanly submission, she holds up to your view Venice, shorn of her glory; Holland, robbed, degraded and debased; Switzerland, with her desolated fields, smoking villages and lofty cliffs, reeking in blood amidst the clouds. In the full prospect of this mighty group, this thickening battalion of horrors, call up all your courage; fly back to the consecrated altar of your liberty, and while your souls kindle at the hallowed fire, invigorate your attachment to the birth-day of your independence; to the government of your choice; feel with additional weight the necessity of united wisdom, councils and exertions, and vow to the God of your fathers, that your lives and fortunes; that every thing you esteem sacred and dear; that all your energies and resources, both of body and mind, are indissolubly bound to your sovereignty and freedom. On all sides you now behold the most energetic measures of defence. All is full of life, and ardour, and zeal. The brave youth, the flower and strength of our country, rush into the field, and the eye of immortal WASHINGTON lightens along their embattled ranks. Approach these hallowed shores, ye butchers, who have slaughtered half Europe—you will find every defile a THERMO-PYLE, and every plain a MARATHON!—We already behold our fleet whitening the clouds with its canvass, and sweeping the ocean with its thunder. The Gallic flag drops to American valour, and our intrepid sailors sing victory in the midst of the tempest.—Brave men! you will fight [16] for your country while an inch of sinew stretches on your bones, or a drop of blood throbs in your veins!—Fellow-Citizens, it is not by tribute, it is not by submission—it is by resolution, it is by courage, that we are to save our country. Let our efforts and our wisdom concentrate in the common cause, and shew to the world, that we are worthy that freedom which was won by the valour and blood of our fathers. Let our government, our religion and our liberty, fostered by our care, and protected by our exertions, descend through the long range of succeeding ages, till all the pride and presumption of human arrangements shall bow to the empire of universal love, and the glory of all sublunary grandeur be forever extinguished.

FINIS.

[67]

ALEXANDER ADDISON 1759–1807

Analysis of the Report of the Committee of the Virginia Assembly

PHILADELPHIA, 1800

Addison, a judge in the Pennsylvania courts for more than a decade, is best remembered today for his compilations of judicial decisions and opinions issued from the Pennsylvania courts over a considerable period of years. As a judge he spoke out vigorously for enforcement of the federal sedition act of 1798. His charges to the grand juries sitting in his circuit are remarkable for their clarity of exposition of the law as it prevailed in America prior to the new act, and for explaining how the act of 1798 affected earlier law. The comprehensive list of writings recommended for further reading at the close of this collection contains one of these jury charges as well as another jury charge on the same topic made eight years before the sedition act was passed. In the essay now to be read, Addison responds to a state legislative attack on the alien and sedition laws, cited as 508 in Selected List of Writings. A report by a majority of the Virginia legislature exalted freedom of speech and press and justified the right of state interposition to protect speech and press from action by the national government that would inhibit it. Taking on this Virginia document almost line by line, Addison defends Congress, tries to define limits to freedom of the press, and attacks the compact theory underlying the doctrine of interposition. Structurally, these theoretical arguments are similar to those to take place in the 1850s on other issues.

ANALYSIS OF THE REPORT OF THE COMMITTEE OF THE VIRGINIA ASSEMBLY

The Legislature of Virginia, having, on the 21st. December 1798, ordered certain resolutions, censuring the administration of the Federal

Government, to be transmitted for the concurrence of the Legislatures of the several states, and receiving in its last session, proceedings of some of the states on those resolutions unfavourable to their views, referred those proceedings to a committee, and received a report, revising, examining, and justifying the resolutions, and solemnly adhering to them, as true, constitutional, and salutary.

The resolutions, embracing a variety of topics, if not intended, were well calculated, as a declaration of war by the state of Virginia against the government of the United States; and the transmission of them to the several states was well calculated to combine every state, under the plausible pretext of preserving the constitution, in a system of hostility against the Union. They [4] have no doubt answered part of the purpose they were intended to effect, in the elections of the several states; and the report now brings them forward, in their best shape, to influence the Union in the election of a President. The report, evidently the work of one man, is drawn up with great art and ingenuity. With some it may be doubtful whether it be the work of a candid mind ingenuously endeavouring to impress on others its own convictions; or the work of an ingenious mind uncandidly endeavouring to persuade others to believe what it believes not itself. Of the end which it prosecutes such is my opinion, that it cannot be prosecuted without a great sacrifice either of principle or of understanding. In this opinion I may perhaps have to claim, and ought therefore to give, much charitable allowance for the steps by which an upright mind may be led to its own deception: but the report will hardly claim apology from defect of understanding. In answers or refutations, a greater diffusion of style is often requisite, than in the propositions which give rise to them. Much of the original subject must be repeated, to make the remarks on it intelligible. And some things, which yet may be doubted, cannot be more shortly expressed. If in the analysis which I am about to undertake of the reasoning in the principal points in this report, I can attain to any considerable degree of its classical brevity of expression, it is more than I expect, and all that I desire.

The 1st. and 2d. resolutions vindicated by the report profess a maintenance of the Constitution, and an attachment to the Union of the United States. This is well if it be sincere: but professions of this kind, put in, by way of protestation; that things in themselves evil, may be construed as favourable as possible, are frequently a preface to matter of very different tendency, and may perhaps be more justly considered as ground of suspicion, than means of justification, of the principal matter.

The 3d. resolution declares *"the powers of the Federal Government as resulting from the compact to which the states are parties, no farther valid, than they are authorized by* [5] *the grants enumerated in that compact; and that, in case of a deliberate, palpable, and dangerous exercise of other powers, the states, who are parties thereto, are bound to interpose, for maintaining within their respective limits, the authorities, rights, and liberties, appertaining to them."*

Without controverting the ground on which this resolution is supported, or remarking on the vague terms in which it is couched, I shall discuss its main purport, *that the states are bound to restrain within their limits the authority of the Federal Government.*

Among a variety of senses, of which the word *states* is susceptible, the report adopts the following, as the sense in which it is to be understood in this resolution; viz. *the people in their highest sovereign capacity.* This sense of the word *states,* the report justly maintains, "because, in this sense the constitution was submitted to the states; in this sense the states ratified it; and in this sense the states are parties to the compact from which the powers of the Federal Government result." In this sense, therefore, the word *states* is equivalent to *the people of each state,* who are parties to the compact of the Union expressed in the constitution of the United States.

This sense of the word states may be farther illustrated and supported by comparing the constitution with the confederation of the United States. The confederation was an act, not of the *people* of each state, but of the *legislature* of each state. The delegates who framed it were chosen not by the people, but by the Legislature of each state; it was ratified not by the people, but by the Legislature of each state; and the members of Congress who acted under it were chosen not by the people, but by the Legislature of each state: it was an Union of the *Governments,* rather than of the *people,* of the several states; and the governments, not the people of the several states, were the parties to this compact. The delegates who framed the constitution were, indeed, also chosen by the Legislatures of the several states, because they were chosen under the confederation; but they framed the constitution, not in the name of the Legislatures, [6] but of the *people* of the several states; and they submitted it to the ratification, not of the Legislatures, but of the people of the several states. The people, not the Legislatures, of the several states did ratify it, and made it their act. And the people, not the Legislatures, of the several states, thus became parties to this compact, and choose members of Congress to act under it.

It appearing then, that the people of the several states are the parties to the compact in the constitution, it will not follow that, because the *parties* to a compact must be the judges whether it has been violated, the *Legislatures* of each state are the judges whether the constitution has been violated. Yet this is the position maintained by the resolution; and, unless this position be maintained, the resolution fails. It seems clear, that the reasoning in the resolution does not support it: and I know no reasoning that can support it. To give the reasoning in the report its full force, it amounts to this, and to this only. The people of the several states in their sovereign capacity are parties to the compact in the constitution; every party to a compact may judge of its violation: the people of Virginia, in their sovereign capacity, are a party to this compact; therefore the people of Virginia, in their sovereign capacity, may judge of its violation. It is manifest that this reasoning will not support the resolution; for it claims a right of the Legislature of Virginia to judge of the violation of the compact. To support the resolution, the reasoning ought to be thus. The Legislature of Virginia is a party to the compact; every party to a compact has a right to judge of its violation; therefore the Legislature of Virginia has a right to judge of its violation. The premises are false, the conclusion is not true, and the resolution fails.

The people never act, in their sovereign capacity, but either in framing or dissolving a constitution. While the constitution is in force, the people are either subjects or agents of the constitution. The powers of sovereignty are divided by the constitution among several agents; the legislative, the judicial, the executive, and the elective agents. One or more of these powers [7] may be exercised by the people; but not as sovereigns, but as agents of the constitution. Each of these powers may be considered as a part of the sovereignty, and the agents may be called the sovereign for that part, and for that part only. For whenever they act on subjects not commited to them, they are usurpers, not sovereigns. And the Legislature, acting on a judicial subject, is no more sovereign, than the Judiciary acting on a legislative subject. It is usurpation in either. The people of the United States have, for general purposes, united all the states into one state, territory, or empire; and have given general legislative, judicial, executive, and elective power to agents for this empire. The people of each state have given legislative, judicial, executive, and elective powers, within their several limits, to agents for those limits. By authority derived from the people of each state, subordinate powers are given to agents for inferior districts of each state. Within their powers, those subordinate agents are as much sovereigns as the Legislature of the state. And the Legislature of Virginia has no more right to arraign the exercise of the powers of the Legislature of the United States, than county Commissioners of Pennsylvania, to arraign the exercise of the powers of the Legislature of Pennsylvania. The right of judging of the exercise of the powers of the Legislature of the United States is vested in the Judiciary, or (to use the words of the report) in "the people in their highest sovereign capacity." The members of the Virginia Assembly were chosen by the people of that state to make laws for Virginia, not to judge of the laws of the United States. When they undertake to judge of the laws of the United States, they act not in a corporate or sovereign capacity, but give their opinion as individuals, and without any public authority.

The exercise of this judicial power, over the acts of the Federal Government, by the state Legislatures, is as dangerous as it is illegal; and, with such exercise of power, it may be averred, that the Union cannot subsist. The Legislature of Virginia consists of more members [8] than the Congress of the United States; and the Legislatures of the other states are numerous. I shall not make any invidious distinction between the capacity and information of the members of the several state Legislatures, and of the Federal Legislature; but I may fairly state that influence is not in proportion to capacity and information, nor these in proportion to number; and I may fairly presume, from the importance of the subject, and the opportunity of discussion, that the capacity and information of the Federal Legislature is superior. Their integrity may be presumed equal: for all are equally bound by the laws; and equally influenced by a contest for power. And the chance, that the Federal Legislature is in the right, may be better, from the habit, under the confederation, of exercise by the state Legislatures of powers vested by the constitution in the Federal Legislature. Extinguished claims do not readily yield to new rights. Supposing therefore the authority of the Federal Legislature to be legal and proper, what chance would there be for its preservation (with a people not always possessing the best means of information, and not seldom corrupted by false information) in a contest between it and the Legislatures of all the states, each claiming to act by authority? In such a contest, the preservation of the Federal Government would seem to be a matter rather of miraculous, than of just, calculation; no reasonable man would calculate upon it; and the dissolution of the Union would be a consequence almost necessary.

If each of the state Legislatures has authority to judge of the acts of the General Legislature, what chance would there be for uniformity of decision? Endless diversities of opinion would exist; the passions of the people would be embarked and distracted; and the Union would be dissolved.

The people of each state, the parties to the compact, have not vested their several Legislatures with this judicial power. They have given it to other agents, the Judiciary departments, rising in various grades, from a Justice of the peace to the Supreme Court of the United [9] States, and all being the agents of the people. By suffering this power to remain where the people have placed it, uniformity of construction can be regularly and happily attained. If corruption is to be presumed, will the Legislature, a numerous body, with little profit or duration attached to their authority, have greater respect for their character, than the Judiciary will have? If there be a paramount judicial authority, its exercise results not to the Legislature, which is but another agent of the people, for another purpose, but to the people of each state, the parties to the compact, who can correct the evil in their elective or sovereign capacity.

The 4th. resolution *"expresses deep regret, that a spirit has been manifested by the Federal Government, to enlarge its powers by forced construction of the Constitution, and a design to expound certain general phrases so as to destroy the effect of the particular enumeration, which necessarily limits them, and so as to consolidate the states into one sovereignty, the tendency and results of which would be to transform the republican system of the United States into an absolute or mixed monarchy."*

As instances of *"a spirit in the Federal Government, to enlarge its powers by forced construction,"* the report enumerates *"The Alien and Sedition acts, the Bank-law, and the Carriage-tax."* The two first are the subjects of very severe censure in a subsequent resolution. I shall on this point only observe, that the judiciary of the United States, the agents of the people for this purpose, have determined, that the

ALEXANDER ADDISON 1759–1807

Sedition act and the Carriage-tax are within the constitutional power of Congress, by a just and not forced construction; and it lies not in the mouth of the Virginia legislature, to controvert this. And, with respect to the Bank law, it will be recollected, that the Congress under the confederation did deliberately, solemnly, and almost unanimously, incorporate and establish the Bank of North America,* which remained in existence at the formation and adoption of the constitution of the United States. So notorious an exercise of [10] this power, by a Congress of far less authority than that which established the Bank of the United States, unrestrained and unnoticed by the constitution, seems a strong argument, that the power to establish Banks existed in Congress under the confederation, and exists under the Constitution. This argument is strengthened by this circumstance, that Mr. Madison, one of the four members of Congress who voted against the establishment of the Bank of North America, and a member of the committee who made the report to the Virginia Legislature, was a member of the general convention, which framed, and of the Virginia convention which adopted, the constitution. Strength is also given to this argument by the general acquiescence in the establishment of the Bank of the United States. So that the censure of the report looks rather like a pettish adherence to an obstinate prejudice than a sound opinion of a constitutional point.

"*The design to expound certain general phrases in the Constitution, so as to destroy the effect of the particular enumeration which necessarily limits them,*" has, it seems never manifested itself in any act of the Federal government; and the report justifies the resolution, from a vague reference to "*debates in the Federal Legislature,*" from "*a report of the late Secretary of the Treasury on manufactures,*" and from "*a report of a committee of Congress on the promotion of agriculture.*" Admitting the censorial power exercised by the Virginia Assembly, their vigilant exercise of it is highly meritorious, since it is not merely corrective but preventive, and, like the laws of Heaven, extends not merely to the conduct but to the heart, not merely to acts but to designs, not merely to any branch of the administration, but to every member and agent of any branch.

The resolution mentions no general phrase, which a design appears so to expound, as to destroy the effect of the particular enumeration

---

* Journals 26th, May and 29th, December 1781.

necessarily limiting them. This defect is supplied by the report, which states, that "the general phrases here meant must be those of *providing for the common defence and general welfare."*

The proofs of a design to pervert the construction of these phrases are debates in Congress, a report of the late [11] Secretary of the Treasury, and a report of a committee of Congress. No debate in Congress is specified as a proof of this. If any were, it would be proof only of a design or mistake of the individual member. It is stated "that in the Secretary's report, it is expressly contended to belong to the discretion of the National Legislature, to pronounce upon the objects which concern the *general welfare,* and for which, under that description, an appropriation of money is requisite and proper. And there seems to be no room for a doubt, that whatever concerns the general interests of LEARNING, of AGRICULTURE, of MANUFACTURES, and of COMMERCE, are within the sphere of the National Councils *as far as regards an application of money."* "The reports of the committee on agriculture" (it is stated) "assumes the same latitude of power in the National Councils, and applies it to the encouragement of agriculture." It was not thought prudent to mention, that these principles had been sanctioned by the judgment of the late President of the United States. The venerable name of WASHINGTON, whom even envy and malice, the constant attendants of living virtue, now cease to disturb in his grave, might have covered these principles with such a shield of integrity and wisdom, that the assaults of the Virginia Assembly would have been harmless. But, without sheltering them in the shade of an ILLUSTRIOUS name, let us examine the reasoning with which they are opposed.

The report of the Virginia committee states, *that the power given to Congress by the constitution, "to provide for the common defence and general welfare of the United States," is limited by the subsequent enumeration of particular cases, and extends not beyond them.* This position it supports, *by the similarity of expression in the 8th. article of the confederation, and in the 8th. section of the 1st. article of the constitution of the United States;* and by a conclusion, *that if the general phrases were so limited in the confederation, they must be so limited in the constitution.* The conclusion might have appeared just, if the constitution had manifested no design to enlarge the powers of Congress; if our union under the constitution had been, as under the confederation, an [12] union of governments, and not, as to general purposes, an union of people; and if Congress were not

ALEXANDER ADDISON 1759–1807

now, what it was not formerly, a representation of the people in each state, as the Assembly of each state is a representation of each county of that state. In such a great change of circumstances, the conclusion, that the powers remain the same, is hardly logical, and surely not necessary.

The Virginia report contends, that, though Congress has power to raise money and apply it to provide for the general welfare of the United States, *it has no power to apply money to any case not specially enumerated in the constitution. Whenever money is to be applied to a particular measure, a question arises whether the particular measure be within the enumerated authorities vested in Congress. If it be, money may be applied, if it be not, no such application can be made. This interpretation is enforced by the clause in the constitution, which declares that no money shall be drawn from the Treasury, but in consequence of appropriations made by law. An appropriation of money to the general welfare, would be deemed rather a mockery, than an observance, of this constitutional injunction.*

The GREAT FATHER of his country, the committee of Congress, and the late Secretary of the Treasury, may be fairly believed as competent to give a just interpretation of the constitution as the Virginia committee, and their interpretation will not be weakened by the interpretation of the Virginia committee, but so far as this is supported by reasoning. The late Secretary of the Treasury says, and he is supported by the late President, and by the committee of Congress, that it belongs "to the discretion of the National Legislature, to pronounce upon the objects which concern the general welfare, and for which, under the description, and appropriation of money is requisite." The necessity of an appropriation before money can be drawn, and the *mockery,* if there were any, of an appropriation to the general welfare, will not operate against this interpretation. Congress will first pronounce, that a certain measure is necessary or conducive to the general welfare of the United States, and direct the manner of its establishment, and then appropriate money to that particular measure.

[13] There is nothing therefore in the Virginia reasoning to invalidate the interpretation of the late President, the committee of Congress, and the late Secretary; and it will not be pretended, that, on mere authority, the interpretation of the Virginia committee or Assembly deserves a preference.

The Virginia report argues not fairly. On the presumption that

Congress has no powers but those specified in the constitution, it concludes, that the power by the first clause of the 8th. section of the 1st. article of the constitution granted to Congress "to raise money to provide for the general welfare," is explained and limited by the subsequent clauses, which specify the instances, and the only instances, in which Congress has power to provide for the general welfare of the United States. On this ground, all the other clauses of this section, are but an explanation of the first clause, and Congress has no power but one, to raise money, or, in the words of the constitution, "to lay and collect taxes, duties, imposts and excises;" and all that follows of this section is only descriptive of the objects, to which this money is to be applied; the first clause describing the object in *general phrases,* and the other clauses detailing the *particular measures* comprehended within those general phrases. This section will then amount to this: Congress shall have power to raise money, *in order to borrow money, in order to regulate commerce, in order to establish an uniform rule of naturalization and uniform laws of bankruptcy, in order to regulate the value of money and fix the standard of weights and measures, in order to provide for the punishment of counterfeiting, in order to secure to authors and inventors the exclusive right to their writings and discoveries, in order to constitute tribunals, in order to define piracies, in order, &c. &c. and for no other purpose whatever.* This interpretation of the constitution will seem absurd, but it is clearly supported by the reasoning of the Virginia committee. If their interpretation can be supported, mine may be also, and if mine fails, so must theirs. For if the phrase "general welfare," do not imply a distinct power, (or duty which involves a power) but be limited by the subsequent phrases, all the subsequent phrases taken together can mean no more than it.

[14] Admitting that Congress has no powers but those specified in the constitution, and that the 8th. section of the 1st. article is a specification of their powers, it seems clear, that (instead of the first clause being general phrases explained and limited by the subsequent clauses) every clause gives a distinct power, and every power is coupled with a duty, the discharge of which is submitted to the discretion of Congress. Thus the first clause imposes on Congress a *duty* "to provide for the common defence and general welfare" of the United States; and submitting to the discretion of Congress what objects or measures are necessary or conducive to these ends, for their accomplishment gives to Congress a *power* "to lay and collect taxes, duties, imposts,

and excises." The second clause gives another power to the exercise of which a duty is necessarily imposed, whenever Congress, in its discretion, shall think its exercise necessary. And so of every other clause of this section.

It seems strange indeed, that expressions in the confederation, which gave no internal legislative powers to Congress, should, by the Virginia committee, be aplied to limit expressions in the constitution avowedly made to give to Congress internal legislative powers. Under the Confederation, it was the *duty* of Congress "to manage the general interests,"* to provide for the common defence and general welfare of the United States; but for this purpose, they had no *power* to raise money. The constitution has, to this duty, united this power; and Congress has, under the constitution all the superintending and provident duty which Congress had under the confederation, together with all the legislative power, for the discharge of this duty, which the confederation had left with the several states. The 8th. article of the confederation was not a limitation of the powers of Congress, but a direction how the money, for the exercise of those powers, should be raised by the states. The necessity of an auxiliary state power, to enable the Federal Government to discharge its duties, and the impossibility of efficaciously obtaining this aid, was the great defect of the confederation. [15] This is supplied by the constitution, which gives to Congress all legislative power, for the execution of their duties; and makes the government of the United States a compleat government with all powers within itself for general purposes. In judging of the power of Congress under the constitution, we must not limit it by the power of Congress under the confederation: for it has now all the power which the former Congress had to prescribe and require, and the power which the state legislatures had to execute or provide means for executing the prescriptions and requisitions of Congress. The proper comparison between the powers would therefore be, that in cases where the former Congress could officially, and for the general welfare, require the state legislatures to pass laws; the present Congress can pass those laws itself. Thus if the former Congress had declared to the several state legislatures, that the United States were in danger from the residence of aliens, and the prevalence of Seditious Libels; and that the general welfare required that each state

* Confederation, Article 5.

should pass Alien and Sedition laws; would any one doubt that it was the duty of each state to obey this requisition? And if it was the duty of each state legislature to do so then; is it not the duty of Congress to do so now when legislative powers have been given to enable Congress itself to discharge all its duties?

As the Constitution thus enlarged the powers of Congress, it enlarged also the control of the people over the exercise of those powers, by giving to the people of the United States the immediate election of Representatives in Congress, without whose consent no act of Congress can be made. So that now the General Legislature having power over all general concerns and care of the general welfare, ought to be deemed as immediately the representatives, and as justly intitled to the confidence of the people of the United States, as the state legislatures are the representatives, and intitled to the confidence of the people of their respective states. The welfare of the several states is intrusted to the care of their several legislatures; and the general welfare to the General Legislature, with competent powers to each for the discharge of the duties imposed.

[16] As the Constitution plainly gives to Congress power over the means to provide for the general welfare, the propriety of exercising this power by the Representatives of the people of the United States can hardly be questioned. The regulations of no state can extend beyond its own limits; and the concurrence of all the states, in every measure necessary for the general welfare, is not to be expected, or must be tardy and incumbered. If Congress, therefore, do not apply their power over the means to every case of general welfare, some cases will be unprovided for; and Congress by neglecting to apply its power, will neglect its duty, and betray the interests of its constituents, the people of the United States.

The condition in which the Virginia report would place the nation of the United States is singularly absurd; a nation without authority to provide for its own welfare. the individual states cannot provide for it: for their authority is limited within their several boundaries. Congress, as the report says, cannot provide for it: for its authority extends only to *some* cases of the general welfare. The constitution is not so absurd. It gives to Congress power over the means, and imposes the duty of providing for the general welfare in all cases whatever, to which in its discretion the means ought to be applied. And this power and discretion is to be controlled, like the power and discretion of the state legislatures, by the judiciary, or by the people in their elective or their sovereign capacity.

If such then be the just construction of the constitution, the objection stated in the report, that it tends to consolidate the states into one sovereignty, has no force; for the constitution is the work of the people of the United States; and an objection to a just construction of the constitution is an objection to the constitution itself, which is an objection to the act of the people of the United States, and will not lie in the mouth of the Legislature of Virginia, who are but agents, for a particular purpose, of a part of the people of the United States.

[17] Ever since the "United States assumed a separate and equal station among the powers of the earth," they have been, as every nation must be, consolidated, as to general purposes into one sovereignty. The confederation vested the powers of this sovereignty in Congress; and the constitution enlarged the powers of this sovereignty, enlarging also the control of the people over the exercise of those powers. The enlargement of the general authority of the United States, become indispensable, was effected by a diminution of the individual authority of the several states. What was taken from one set of agents of the people, was given to another set of agents of the people; and the control of the people over their agents was still preserved. The authority of the people was not diminished, the power only of their agents was altered. That there should be a sovereignty, or power co-extensive with the territory, and adequate to the general wants and welfare, is not an objection, but a praise, to the system of government adopted by the people. If it can be urged as an objection, it will lie only against the extent of territory, not the extent of power, and will conclude, not to a diminution of power, but to a diminution of territory—to a dissolution of the Union—a separation of the states. Is it to this conclusion that the report would lead?

That a power to raise money in order to provide for the general welfare, or a power to provide for the general welfare, should, by any possible construction be so extended as to amount to a power to *legislate in all cases whatever*, and so to consolidate the states into one sovereignty, seems a supposition so extravagant, that I cannot persuade myself, it will ever be honestly and seriously urged. But admitting it possible (probable it is not) is it a greater evil, that the general welfare of the United States should be provided for by one body of representatives of the people, instead of several; or should be left altogether unprovided for?

This dreaded *consolidation of the states,* and its portended result, the *transformation of our republican system into a monarchy,* I cannot consider as the work of honest rational [18] conviction, but as either the fiction of fancy, or the delusion of party on the passions, prejudices, or inexperience of the people. If it have a rational foundation, it must be this, that a general authority of a republican form cannot be exercised over so extensive a territory as that of the United States. From this position the conclusion will be, either that there must be a diminution of territory, in other words, a separation of the Union; or our republican government must be changed to a monarchy; or the welfare of the United States must be unprovided for, which, in other words, is, that the powers shall be incompetent to the purposes of government. Can any fears of a change of government justify the withholding from government the means of providing for the welfare of the people?

The report contends, that the result of consolidation will be monarchy, *"because the legislature will increase the prerogative of the executive, by delegating to it legislative powers; because the consolidation will increase the patronage of the executive; and because this increase of prerogative and patronage will either enable the Chief Magistrate, quietly and repeatedly, to secure his election, and finally to regulate the succession; or will render the elections of Chief Magistrate so violent and corrupt, that the public voice itself might call for an hereditary in place of an elective succession."*

I shall not spend time in discussing conjectures like these; but will just observe that any prerogative, given by the legislature to the executive, may be restrained, or reclaimed by the power which gave it, and the legislature will always be under the control of the people; that the people will always control the election of President in spite of all patronage, while they remain uncorrupted, and fit for the exercise of their rights; that if corruption in the people admit hopes of monarchy, such hopes, with the present or without any patronage, will excite violence sufficient to produce the effect dreaded from it; and that, if the public voice ever call for an hereditary succession, no constitutional provisions can prevent it.

But I am not convinced that a republican form, with a proper distribution of authority and power, is incompetent [19] for the government of an extensive territory. If there be a well organized general and subordinate government; if there be, in the general government, a power to provide for the general welfare; and, in the subordinate governments, a power to provide for the particular welfare; and if there be, in each of these authorities, a force to secure the execution of them, and make the power and benefit of government be every where felt; a republican government may promote and serve the happiness of the people of an extensive territory.

The 5th. resolution *"protests against the palpable and alarming infractions of the constitution in the cases of the Alien and Sedition acts; the first of which exercises a power not delegated to the Federal Government, and by uniting legislative and judicial powers to executive, subverts the principles of free government, and the provisions of the Federal Constitution; and the other of which also exercises a power not delegated, but expressly forbidden by the constitution, a power which, more than any other, ought to produce universal alarm, because leveled against that right of freely examining public characters and measures, and of free communication among the people, which has ever been justly deemed the only effectual guardian of every other right."*

The report, viewing this as the great leading resolution, enters into an ample investigation of it. As the Alien and Sedition acts have been elsewhere so clearly justified, I shall endeavour to confine my observations on this part of the report (interesting as it professes to be) to such points as have been less notoriously and fully discussed.

To shew that the Alien act *is an exercise of power not delegated to the Federal Government,* the report makes some preliminary observations, and answers arguments urged in justification of this power.

The first observation is, "that the powers not delegated to the United States, by the constitution, nor prohibited by it to the states, being reserved to the states respectively or to the people,"* *it is incumbent to prove, that the constitution grants every power exercised by the Federal Government.*

[20] It is sufficiently understood, that their amendment of the constitution here relied on, like other amendments, made little, if any, alteration of the constitution. Borrowed from the confederation, it proceeded from a false jealousy, rising from a false principle, and applying to a compact made by the people, of power to be exercised by representatives of the people, restrictions in a compact made by the governments, of power exercised by representatives of governments.

* Constitution, Amendment 10.

However this may be, it will not be pretended, that this amendment deprives the government of the United States of any power given it by the constitution; nor that Congress, under the constitution, has less power than Congress had before; nor that any nation would be so absurd, as to form a government without power to manage its general interests, and provide for its common defense and general welfare. Nor will it be denied, that the government of the United States has power to carry on intercourse with foreign nations, make war or peace, or form treaties of alliance and commerce; and that no individual state has any authority to interfere in any foreign affairs; nor that the government of the United States is intrusted with the management of its general interests, with providing for the common defense and general welfare, with the protection of each state against invasion, and domestic violence, with the preservation of the peace and safety of the United States, and with power to make all laws necessary and proper for executing its powers and duties. Nor will it be denied, that aliens may be dangerous to the peace and safety of the United States; nor that the government of every other nation has power to remove aliens, when and how it chooses, on all reasonable occasions, in any reasonable manner, without any respect to the rules by which it is governed in the punishment or restraint of its own subjects. The declaration of Independence, which raised the United States to the rank of a nation, gave to any government, which the people of the United States should establish with the charge of common defence and foreign intercourse, all the rights which the law of nations gives to every sovereign government. The people have established the government of the United States with this sovereign charge, and the law [21] of nations gives it all sovereign rights with respect to other nations. The restrictions of the constitution are not restrictions of external and national right, but of internal and municipal right. And power over aliens is to be measured, not by internal and municipal law, but by external and national law. It affects not the people of the United States, parties and subjects to the constitution; but foreign governments, whose subjects the aliens are. Foreign governments, parties to the code of [inter]national law, may call the government of the United States to account for the abuse of its right under this law; but the constitution of the United States restrains it not. The government of the United States being exclusively vested with the power of peace and war and foreign intercourse, must be exclusively vested with the means (and the admission or expulsion of aliens may be one of the means) of producing or affecting either. And being charged with the common defence and protection against invasion and domestic violence, the government of the United States, with a discretion to judge of the proper means, must be vested with all means conducive to these ends, and confident, according to their respective objects, with the municipal law, and the law of nations. The constitution could never intend to make the government of the United States, as the report would make it, a government of duties without powers: for it was framed expressly to add powers to duties. The constitution was established by the people of the United States, "to form a more perfect union, insure domestic tranquility, provide for the common defence, and promote the general welfare." Any construction of this constitution, not unavoidable, which would deprive the government of any proper means to promote those ends will be rejected. Whatever is fairly involved in any power granted by the constitution, is a power granted by the constitution, and cannot be restrained by the provision that the powers not delegated are reserved. And all powers of peace and war, and foreign intercourse, and therefore the means of producing or affecting either, are delegated to the United States by the constitution, and prohibited by it to the individual states.

[22] The next observation is, *that there is a distinction, by the law of nations, between alien enemies, and alien friends.* To be sure there is: Alien friends have by the law of nations certain hospitable rights subject to the reasonable discretion of the government under which they live; and alien enemies have no rights. But the question is, whether every government may not, when it judges it proper for its own safety, order and compell "aliens, members of a friendly nation," to depart out of its territory. Every government has, by the law of nations, authority to do this. The right of a nation to the exclusive enjoyment of its own territory is, like the right of an individual to the exclusive enjoyment of his own house, a perfect right, subject only to the right of hospitality, an imperfect right, at the discretion of the owner. This is a doctrine too well established by the law of nations, to need any authorities to support it: a very slight inspection of any book of this law will justify it. And, on this principle, it was thought necessary, to stipulate in the confederation,* that "the people of each

* Article 4.

state shall have free ingress and regress to and from any other state, and enjoy therein all the privileges of trade and commerce."

A third observation is, that "admitting the object of the alien act to be preventive, not penal justice, and within the power of the Federal Legislature; *this power has not been exercised in a constitutional manner.*"

I hope, it has already appeared, that this power is given to the government of the United States: and, as its object is not municipal justice, either penal or preventive, but public national defence, and as it affects no party to the constitution, but a party to the law of nations; its exercise is to be regulated, not by the constitution or municipal law, but by the general law of nations. Has the constitution prescribed, that aliens, like "the citizens of each states, shall be entitled to all privileges and immunities of citizens in every state?" Was the denial or retraction of an imperfect right, a favour or indulgence, ever called a *punishment?* Or has the law of [23] nations ever called the removal of aliens a banishment: It were well if the Virginia Assembly would allow to Congress as much preventive vigilance, with respect to dangerous aliens, as they have themselves exercised in their assumed authority on the design to expound general phrases; and would as readily suppose that aliens may be dangerous, as that the government of the United States may be corrupt.

Having made these observations, the report proceeds to answer the arguments by which the alien act has been justified.

The first answer suggests a doubt, *whether the discretionary power of admitting aliens be vested in the Federal Government, or in the state governments;* that is, whether, though Congress has power to establish an uniform rule of naturalization, every state has not a power to naturalize, without any regard to the uniform rule of Congress. Can the Virginia committee discover in the Federal Government a design so grossly to pervert the constitution, as is manifested in this doubt? This committee, and the Secretary of the commonwealth of Pennsylvania, in a note to one of the laws of that state, are the only patrons of this doubt that I know.

"But it cannot be a true inference, that, because the admission of an alien is a favour, the favour may be revoked. A grant of land or a pardon may be a favour, but irrevocable. Admission of an alien to naturalization is as much a favour, as admission to residence."

If the favour be complete in one act, as a grant of land, or a pardon, to be sure, it cannot be revoked. But if the enjoyment of the benefit depend on the continuance of the benevolence, the favor may be revoked. If I convey my house gratuitously, and thereby part with all my right in it; I cannot devest the right I have conveyed. But if I give a stranger a lodging in it for a night, I may turn him out the next day. Admission of an alien to residence is not admission to naturalization: the first is revocable, like a permission; the other absolute, like a grant. The author of the report, who had ingenuity to devise the illustration, did not want judgment to discern the [24] fallacy of the reasoning. Admission of aliens to residence is not a grant of naturalization: this, until the grant be absolutely made, must depend on the continuance of the benevolence of the government towards them.

I pass by the four following answers to justifications of this act, either because the justifications have been sufficiently and publickly established before, or because I think them not necessary.

The next is an answer to the justification, "that the means of preventing invasions are included in the power of protecting against them."

One would have thought it would not be denied, for it is evident, that a power to protect against invasion did include a power to use all proper means to prevent it, or defeat its success; and what means more proper to protect against invasion can there be, than the means given by the alien act: a power to remove "aliens dangerous to the peace and safety of the United States, or concerned in any treasonable or secret machinations against the government thereof." As aliens are not entitled to the privileges of citizens, any farther than the constitution and laws direct, and as the constitution says nothing of them, the legislature has a right to prescribe in what manner they shall be dealt with. As the legislature has referred to the discretion of the President, to determine who of them shall be deemed dangerous, or concerned in any treasonable or secret machinations against the government, and as such removed; and as their removal is consistent with the law of nations, by which only it can be judged, and is a proper means of preventing or defeating an invasion, which is clearly the same as protecting against an invasion; their removal in this manner seems clearly within the power and duty of Congress to protect against invasions by a just and natural construction of the constitution. To adopt an illustration used by the report, a municipal power to *punish* involves a municipal power to *prevent*: for the judge who can try a breach of the peace, can bind over to keep the peace. What a municipal judge can do in the manner prescribed by the municipal law, the legislature can do or direct to be done, [25] with respect to an alien, in any manner consistent with the law of nations. Will the report deny that a power to protect against an evil includes a power over the means proper to prevent it? What would the committee think of a physician engaged for a yearly sum, who should tell his employer, when seized with a fever, *I saw this fever coming on you, and could have prevented it; but I am engaged only to cure, and not to prevent diseases?*

The committee seem aware of such absurd reasoning, and only refuse to grant, "that a power to act on a case when it occurs, includes a power over *all* the means that *may tend* to prevent its occurrence." Is not this confounding power with discretion, a reasonable with a wanton discretion, and inferring a want of power from a possibility of its abuse? On such reasoning what power might not be denied?

To lessen the force of the clause in the constitution enjoining the government of the United States to protect against invasion, the report considers it as *"either a specification of the power of war in general, before granted, or as a duty superadded to a power;"* and reasons thus, *"Invasion is an operation of war. To protect against invasion is an exercise of the power of war. A power, therefore, not incident to war, cannot be incident to a particular modification of war. And as the removal of alien friends has appeared to be no incident to a general state of war, it cannot be incident to a particular modification of war."* If this reasoning means any thing it must be this: a power not incident to war is not incident to war; or a power not incident to all war, is incident to no war, or is not incident to invasion. The first proves nothing: for the proof and the position are the same. The second proves too much, and is therefore false: for there may be powers incident to some wars, or to invasion, which are not incident to all war. One of the steps of the syllogism is false, and therefore the conclusion cannot be considered as true. For it is not true, according to the law of nations, that the removal of alien members of a friendly nation, if they are supposed dangerous, is not incident to a state of war, or to every state of reasonably apprehended danger. The report says, [26] that, *"without this clause of the constitution, the power to protect against invasion is included in the power to declare war."* This on the principle so much relied on by the report, *that general phrases are limited by the particular specifications and every power not specified is refused,* is saying, that to declare war is to protect against invasion. Presumptions it would seem are admissable to lessen, but not to enlarge, the powers of Congress.

Without assenting to the reasoning by which the next answer is supported (for I think it exceptionable) I shall not discuss it; because it seems not material to the main point. Can it be supposed that the constitution meant to deny the government of the United States the important right of using, towards other nations, all means, consistent with the law of nations, for the common defence of the states, and their protection against invasion. Nothing appears from the constitution, that can shew, that the people of the United States meant to deny their own government any right, which, by the law of nations, any other sovereignty enjoys with respect to foreign nations: and the alien law affects only foreign nations. The limits of power of any government, towards its own subjects, were never meant to be applied as limits of power of that government towards the subjects of other governments. And the question, whether a government conducts itself well towards a subject of another government, is not a question of municipal, but of national law: it cannot arise between the subject of another government and the government of which he complains, but between this and his own government. How then can the constitution of any one government be made a rule to decide this question?

If the candor and "respect," which the report professes, has been justly "felt," the captious censure on an expression in the report of a committee of Congress would have found no place in it. The constitution is the act of the people of the United States, and is the supreme law of the land; and no individual state ever had power of the common defence, or of foreign intercourse, war, or peace.

[27] Not having access, at present, to the alien law of Virginia, from which a justification of the alien law of the United States has been drawn, I cannot satisfactorily discuss the answer to this justification. From the misapplication of the pronoun *who,* in the statement of that law in the report, it is difficult to say, whether it be the alien or his government, that is the object of suspicion of *hostile designs.* If it be the alien, the Virginia law is the same as the law of Congress. If it be the state, an apprehension of hostility is not hostility; there is no war, and the alien is an alien friend, who, from the reasoning in the report, ought to be treated as a citizen, and not punished, but for an offence actually committed. And the cruelty so much deplored

in the report, would be the same under both acts, if a harmless alien were removed, whether his government were hostile or friendly.

What remains of the report respecting the alien act, as to its union of legislative and judicial with executive powers, and the influence of this union, having been sufficiently and publicly discussed elsewhere; I shall content myself with observing, that this union can only be dangerous, when it is constitutionally and permanently established; not when it is only occasionally permitted by the legislature, for a convenient and practicable execution of legislative power, and always under the control of the legislature, which is under the control of the people.

On this resolution, as it respects the Sedition act, the report states, "that it affirms; *1st. that this act exercises a power not delegated by the constitution: 2nd. that this power is expressly prohibited by one of the amendments to the constitution; and 3rd. that this power ought, more than any other, to produce universal alarm; because levelled against that right of free examination of public characters and measures, and free communication thereon, which has ever been justly deemed the only effectual guardian of every other right.*"

I think, I am disposed to treat all public authority, not perverted to improper purposes, with respect, and to examine the report with candour. But so extravagant seem the positions, and so dangerous their consequences, [28] in many parts of this report, that I cannot reconcile them with the ingenuity shewn in it, and, at the same time with sincerity.

First, On the first point, the report begins with observing, "that the Federal Government being composed of powers specifically granted, with a reservation of all others to the states; *the positive authority, under which the Sedition act could be passed, must be produced.*" I have already mentioned, that this principle was introduced into the constitution, which is a government made by the people, from a false imitation of the confederation, a government made by the legislatures of the states. From this it seems to be contended, that the Federal Government has no power, but such as the constitution *expressly* gives. There is nothing in the constitution to justify this; and the report afterward admits, "that particular parts of the common law may have a sanction from the constitution, so far as they are necesssarily comprehended in the technical phrases, which express the powers delegated to the government; so far as such other parts may be adopted as necessary and proper for carrying into execution the powers expressly delegated."

In justifying the Sedition law, it has been urged, that it created no new offence; for every thing punishable under it was punishable at common law. Referring to this argument, the report censures, as *"novel and extravagant, the doctrine lately advanced, that the common or unwritten law makes a part of the law of these states in their united and national capacity."* And, to justify this, it reviews the colonial state of this country, and the effects of the declaration of independence, the confederation, and the constitution of the United States.

The report admits, "that, prior to the revolution, the common law was the separate law of each colony, but not operating through the whole as one society; because there was no common legislature or judiciary for the colonies." This confounds the term *common* with the term *general,* and argues, from the circumstance of the *unwritten law* being called the *common law,* that there could be no common law, because there was no general legislature [29] or judiciary over all the colonies. This is an abuse of words. It also confounds principles: for it might as well be contended, that there can be no religion where there is no revelation; and no obligation, where there is no power to enforce it.

What are now the United States were separate colonies, settled under the authority of England, and, as part of its territory, subject to its laws: for it is of the nature of colonies, to take with them the laws, rights, and duties of the mother country. The mother country may give its colonies power, more or less, to make laws for their separate internal government, or may combine two or more of them in a confederacy, with power to make laws for the confederacy. But the government of the mother country remains the controlling head, and sovereign power, in a legislative and judicial capacity; unless it devest itself of this authority; or until the colony, as in our case, grow to such strength, as to be able to support itself, and deny the right and oppose the force of the mother country. As a colony of England, therefore, each state was subject to the law of England, the general and controlling law of all; except so far as each had authority from England to alter this general law, according as their several circumstances required.

The law of England is of two kinds written and unwritten. The written is called the *statute law,* because composed of statutes or acts of parliament. The unwritten is called the *common law*, because founded on an implied common consent, from long acquiescence in its authority and use. The authority of both is thus equally the will of the community. The *common law* is founded on the law of nature and the revelation of God, to which all men are subject; on the law of nations, to which every nation is, as a nation, and the individuals composing it, subject towards every other; and on certain maxims or usages, which have long prevailed, and been sanctioned by judicial authority, as naturally rising out of the circumstances by which the subjects of that government were connected with each other, and therefore imposing duties on the individuals of that nation towards each [30] other. Of these maxims or usages some are general, and prevail in every part of England; and some, from the separate authorities formerly existing there, or from other circumstances, are particular, and prevail only in certain parts. Parliament may adopt some part of this *common law*, and, by putting it in an act of Parliament, make it *statute law;* or may alter or annul it by act of parliament. Any part of the common law may also cease, or become obsolete, by the circumstances ceasing to exist, which manifestly were the reasons of its establishment: and this will be considered as a repeal by the same authority which enacted. The colonies, therefore, severally carried with them all the common law of England, which was applicable to their circumstances, with power, so far as given by the mother country to alter this law, by the acts of their several legislatures. Thus, the circumstances of each colony more or less differing, and each having a distinct legislature; the common law throughout the colonies would be, in part, general maxims or usages prevailing in all the colonies; and, in part, maxims or usages prevailing only in one or several of the colonies. The government of the mother country was the general superintending government.

The declaration of Independance, though it annulled the power of Britain over the colonies, established no superintending government in its room; and each colony became a free and independant state. But this could not alter any of the law of the several states, except what necessarily resulted from the change of situation. There was a common law in each state before the declaration of Independence, and it remained after this declaration.

From every organisation of individuals, of domestic or commercial connections, of societies, and of governments, certain powers and duties arise; a sort of common law for the good of all concerned in the organisation. Men can neither live without law, nor put every law in express words. Incidental powers, without being expressed, result from every civil organisation: for it is the will of those concerned that it should be effectual for its [31] purposes. Thus, before the confederation, which gave the power, Congress formed treaties; by a sort of common law, which gave to Congress, as the only general organ, the authority usually annexed to such a government. The same idea seems to be expressed in the reports "In the interval between the commencement of the revolution, and the final ratification of the articles of confederation, the nature and extent of the union was determined by the circumstances of the crisis." It would not indeed be "alledged, that the common law could have *birth* during that state of things." It was *born* long before; "in a time whereof the memory of man runneth not to the contrary." The colonists brought it with them from their native land, with their other possessions, for their common protection against murderers, against thieves, and against *libellers;* for the recovery of their debts, the execution of their contracts, and the redress of their wrongs. The people of every state modify it according to their several circumstances; and, so modified, it has been constantly preserved, and will be forever preserved as a rule of right, and standard of action. There never was a time in any society or government, in which a common law did not exist: it is incidental to the constitution of every regular state, and inseparable from its existence. However the condition of men, societies, or governments may be modified; whatever shape or station they assume, certain rights, powers, and duties, forming a common law, is attached to each.

The confederation was not intended to give any legislative or judicial authority to the Federal government, except in a very few instances. But proving that there existed no one general authority over the whole, does not prove, "that the common or unwritten law makes *not* a part of the law of these states in their united and national capacity." The confederation altered not the rules or nature of offences, trespasses, or duties: the common law remained as it was, except such alteration as resulted from the change in the government.

The last question made by the report in this review of our state is, *"whether the common law, be introduced as a* [32] *national law by the present constitution of the United States."* Its introduction is admitted, so far as necessarily comprehended in technical phrases, or necessary and proper for the execution of given powers; but beyond this its admission is denied by the report.

It states, that from the provision of the constitution, "that the judicial power shall extend to all cases *in law and equity,* arising under this constitution, the laws of the United States, and treaties made under their authority;"* it has been inferred, that, besides cases arising under the laws and treaties of the United States, other cases are presumed to arise, by a common law, thus established by the constitution. This inference appears just, and little, if at all, different from the admission made by the report. Every organisation of authority must have the means of protection and execution of the powers vested in it. This is a *common law* in all countries, and in all cases; and no supposition of other possible or probable constructions can lessen the force of this reasoning.

From the expression "cases in law *and equity*," and a subsequent expression "that the appellate jurisdiction of the Supreme Court is of law and *fact,*" the report would exclude criminal cases from federal jurisdiction; for criminal cases *in equity* would be a language unknown to the law; and the *fact* in criminal cases is not a subject of appeal.

There is something in a guilty mind and a bad cause, which will now and then betray itself. In the manner of Samson with the Philistines, we might ask the reporter how he came by the exposition of this riddle. *"Criminal cases in equity is a language unknown to the law."* To what law? To the common law surely. *The fact in criminal cases is not a subject of appeal.* On what authority is this asserted? Not on the authority of the constitution; for it gives appellate jurisdiction in *all* cases, with exceptions which the report says "do not mean criminal cases." It is asserted on the authority of the *common law* only; and yet the report says *"the common law has no authority under the constitution of the United States."*

[33] The report having thus palpably admitted the common law as part of the law under the constitution, and having admitted, that particular parts of the common law comprehended under technical phrases are sanctioned by the constitution; the phrase, *all cases in law and equity* being a common law technical phrase, and adopted in the constitution; we may fairly conclude that under this phrase the common law jurisdiction of the Federal courts is sanctioned.

---

* Article III, Section 2.

But on the authority of the common law, which directs that, in criminal cases there is no appeal from the finding of *fact* by a jury, to conclude, because the appelative jurisdiction of the Supreme Court is both as to law and fact, that criminal cases are not within the jurisdiction of the Federal Courts, is not fair: for it amounts to this, that no words in a description shall extend beyond the meaning of one word. This appellate jurisdiction may be as to fact in civil cases, and as to law in criminal cases: for it will not be denied, that on a judgment on a conviction in a criminal case in an inferior court, a writ to Error will lie in the Supreme Court. And, though, in case of an acquittal in a criminal case, by the *common law,* a new trial cannot be granted; yet, in case of a conviction, a new trial may be granted by the *common law;* and if the inferior court refuse a new trial, the Supreme Court may have appellate jurisdiction as to *fact* to grant it, where the conviction is contradicted or not supported by evidence.

The constitution provides that "all civil officers of the United States shall be removed from office on impeachment for, and conviction of treason, bribery, or other high crimes and misdemeanors."* But the party convicted shall nevertheless be liable to indictment, trial, judgment, and punishment according to law.† And the trial of *all* crimes, except in cases of impeachment, shall be by jury, and in the state were the crimes shall have been committed; or when not committed within any state, at such place as the Congress may by law have directed."‡ Can it be supposed, that the general expressions [34] here used are to be limited to the particular offences enumerated in the constitution; treason, piracy and felony at sea, counterfeiting and bribery: Is not the phrase *high crimes and misdemeanors* a technical phrase at common law? Is not a libel a misdemeanor at common law? And may we not, from the expressions used in the clauses of the constitution just cited, fairly conclude, that all offences, which are subjects of impeachment, or, when committed at sea, of indictment in the Admiralty courts, are when committed at land, and against the authority of the United States, subjects of indictment in the common law courts of the United States? This opinion is fortified by the amendments to the constitution proposed by the conventions of some of the states, which speak in such general terms of the trial of crimes,

* Art. II. Sect. 4
† Art. I, Sect. 3.
‡ Art. III. Sect. 2.

of offences, of all suits at common law, of criminal proceedings by states; and of making laws touching religion, as seem to suppose general legislative authority in Congress, and general common law jurisdiction in the courts of the United States.

Whenever a government was established for the United States, with judicial organisation for the trial of offences, there resulted a common law jurisdiction in the Federal Courts, over all offences against the authority of this government. Government, the sovereignty, is as it were the *person* of civil society. And, like individuals in a state of nature, governments in the civil state will not submit their wrongs to the determination of any other, but to themselves alone. Every offence is an offence against the sovereign. The sovereign alone examines, tries, judges, punishes, or pardons it, according to its own organisation. The state courts cannot try an offence against the Federal government only: there is no law empowering them. Prosecutions there are in the name of the respective states, and punished or pardoned by them. The courts of the United States cannot try an offence only against any of the individual states. Thus the rights and honour of the several governments are respectively reserved to themselves, and full judicial authority vested in each for their several protection.

[35] It is not necessary for me to controvert the position, "that section a of article III. of the constitution is a compleat enumeration of the powers of the Federal courts": for it is fairly proved from the report itself, that this enumeration includes the *common law*. But the report is evidently wrong in saying that the second paragraph of the 6th. article is an enumeration of those powers.

If the common law be *not a law of the United States, and a guide to the Judges of the United States,* and if the description of the law of the United States in the constitution be a *precise and compleat enumeration,* excluding the rules of the common law, helpless indeed would be the suitors in the Federal courts, outlawed, as it were, from the protection of natural rights, the rules of common justice, of debts, contracts, and property, and of the redress of wrongs. Are not the Federal courts, in trying claims or injuries arising in any state, bound to apply to them the law of the state where they originate, and is not the common law part of the law of each state? May not an action for a libel be brought in a Federal court, by a citizen of one state, against a citizen of another state? Is it not an action at common law, to be decided by the rules of the common law? If this libel be for describing the plaintiff as an impious atheist, a blasphemer of God, will the common law, the principles of religion, be no guide to the Federal judges? Have "the rights of man" no authority in the federal courts, because they are not enumerated in the Federal constitution? Or had they no authority, by a *common law*, till they were recorded in some constitution? By what law is a promise, contract, or grant valid? What law defines impeachable misdemeanors? By what law do legislative and judicial bodies punish contempts? Is it not by the common law? Have the legislative and judicial organs of the government of the United States no such power? Are they destitute of all such means of protecting their own dignity and authority? And if they have such means, from what law are they derived? From the common law surely.

[36] Confusion has been introduced into the reasoning of the report by an ambiguous application of the phrase common law, using it sometimes as a limit of jurisdiction, and sometimes as a rule of judgment.

Considering the common law as a limit of jurisdiction, the Legislature of the United States, as of every nation, has authority to make all laws necessary or proper for the defence of its own authority, but no other common law jurisdiction; and the courts of the United States have authority to determine all cases arising under any law of the United States, and all cases of misdemeanor, or offence against the authority of the United States. This plainly results from the nature of government, and is fairly deducible from the constitution. But the constitution expressly gives to the courts of the United States a further jurisdiction, either, on the principles of common law, for the protection of the peace, dignity and authority of the government, as in cases of certain crimes, and in the case of foreign ministers, and in cases of maritime law; or for impartiality, as in disputes between citizens of different states, or for titles derived from different states.

As a rule of judgment, the *common law,* in all cases where it is applicable, is an universal guide to the Judges of the Federal courts. It is no objection to the application of this rule, *that it may differ in different states.* The common law of England, so far as it rests on general and local customs, differs in different portions of that territory. The Judges apply it, as it exists, as a rule to the case before them. The statute law of each state may differ; the Federal Judges will apply it, as the courts of the state having jurisdiction over the case would apply it. So the common law of each state will be applied by the

Judges of the Federal court, as the judges of the state, having jurisdiction over the case would apply it.

It is no objection to the common law being considered by the constitution as a guide to the Federal courts, that *this would give it a constitutional establishment, make it part of the constitution, irrevocable by the legislature.* The constitution considers the law of each state, both common and [37] statute law, a guide to Federal courts; but leaves all law to be modified by legislative authority, saving always the paramount authority of the United States. The Federal courts, like the state courts, must take the statute law of each state, as it stands in the existing statutes; and the common law of each state, as it stands in established usages and decisions. Whatever parts of the common law are altered by the change of circumstances of the United States, by the constitution or laws of the United States within their constitutional limits, will no longer remain law over cases affected by the alteration.

The picture drawn of the common law, and the difficulties and consequences stated in the report, from the introduction of this law into the Federal code, seem so merely the work of a busy imagination, that any farther discussion of them would be useless.

Its preamble declares, that the people of the United States ordained their constitution, "in order to form a more perfect union, establish justice, ensure domestic tranquility, provide for the common defence, promote the general welfare, and secure the blessings of liberty;" and from this, an argument was drawn for the power of Congress to pass the Sedition-act. The report says, *"a preamble usually contains the general motives for the particular measures, and is always understood to be explained and limited by them."* I will say, that, wherever the body of an instrument admits of two constructions, one of which will better than the other promote the intentions expressed in the preamble, that construction which will best promote the intentions is the just construction of the instrument. And it is a less evil, that the restrictions be not adhered to, in the most rigid sense, than that the only government established by the people with general powers should, where a reasonable construction will prevent this, be deprived of a power necessary or proper to promote the general welfare.

[38] The constitution enables Congress "to make all laws, which shall be necessary and proper for carrying into execution all powers vested by it in the government of the United States, or in any

department or office thereof:" and requires that the President of the United States "shall take care that the laws be faithfully executed," and that "the United States, shall protect each state against invasion and domestic violence." Hence it has been inferred, that, to enable the President to take care that the laws are duly executed, and to suppress insurrections, Congress has power to make laws to suppress the means, by which insurrections and obstructions to the execution of laws are usually excited; and, as seditious libels are the most usual and efficacious means, that Congress may make laws to suppress them. All this seems natural and logical enough. But the report says, *that a power for faithful execution does not imply a power to provide that no opposition be promoted; and that a power to protect against insurrection, does not imply a power to prevent it. There is no doubt that libels on the government will excite insurrections; but government shall not suppress libels; for it may suppress the insurrections. Let the libels go on till they have excited an insurrection, and then the government can take all necessary and proper measures for its suppression. If then the combination be such that the government has not force to suppress it, the government is not to blame; it has used constitutional means, and the constitution is overturned in due form.*

The report, admitting that the grant of a power involves the means of rendering it effectual, *limits those means to such as are strictly necessary for its execution.* It, therefore admits that the grant of the crop growing in a field includes a power to cut down, carry off, and secure the grain; *but not to repair the fences, nor keep off the cattle from destroying it before it is ripe.*

Though Congress has power to make all laws necessary and proper for carrying into execution the powers vested in the Federal Government, yet the report will not admit that this implies a power to make all laws which *may have a tendency, whether proper or not,* for the execution of such powers. I shall not dispute this point.

[39] Though Congress has power to make all laws necessary and *proper* for carrying their powers into execution; yet the report contends, that Congress shall make no laws but such as are *necessary* for this purpose. And, if the law which they make or means which they prescribe be not necessary, but only proper; they have no authority for the law or the means, and they are invalid; *for the judiciary alone can determine the propriety of the law or the means!*

The report has admitted, that a power to punish implies a power to prevent the mischief. The judiciary will execute their preventive authority, by all the means prescribed by law, whether common or statute law. The legislature will execute their preventive power by statutes. The discretion of the choice of means, necessary or proper, for executing their powers lies with the legislature. If the legislature choose means palpably unnecessary and improper, the judiciary can then only exercise their judgment, by the authority of construction of all laws vested in this branch of government. But the legislature of Virginia ought not, in the exercise of usurped power of judging of the means used by the Congress, or courts of the United States, for the execution of their powers, presume themselves wiser than the constituted authorities. A power over the end implies a power over the means; and a power to make laws, for carrying any power into execution, implies a power to make laws for preventing or removing obstructions to the execution: and it is indifferent, whether those obstructions be acts of violence or acts naturally leading to violence. The experience of other goverments, and of our own, has shewn us, that libels on the powers of government are obstructions to the execution of those powers, and naturally lead to insurrections. Denying the Federal government the power of supressing libels is, therefore, denying it *proper* means, and may be denying it *all* means, of executing its powers. For, if the libels proceed, the obstruction of the powers of government may be too strong for removal. This is vesting in the people "the holy right of insurrection," while the government is vested with the right of suppressing it; and leaving with the [40] people the best means of exercising their right, while the government is stript of the best means of exercising the right vested in it. With such a disposition of powers, we should soon see a very unequal contest, with very fatal effects; and the most summary exercise of the people's sovereign power over their servants, that the most modern professor of liberty could desire. It would indeed bind the government, *hand and foot,* from all resistance, till, in this condition, the knife was at its throat. This is the end to which the clamours against the Sedition act and a standing army naturally tend. If the people would preserve their government free they have their choice of the alternative; indictments to suppress sedition, or a standing army to suppress insurrection. A government, possessing force, independent of public opinion, may more safely suffer public opinion to be tampered with. Samson, while he retained his strength, might slumber in the lap of Delilah, amidst the ambush of the Philistines, or be incircled with the walls of Gaza. Let every government watch where its strength lies, and guard it from corruption. If the strength of a government, as of ours, lies in the opinion of the people, the corruption of public opinion will ruin the government. No injury to public opinion is too slight to be overlooked; for every injury to it is a wound in a mortal part. "Lilliputian ties" intwined in Gulliver's hair made him surrender at discretion, though spears and arrows did him no material hurt.

Second, On the resolution, as it respects the Sedition act the report next states, that *the power exercised by this act is expressly prohibited by one of the amendments of the constitution.*

The amendment or additional article of the constitution here referred to is the third, which provides, "that Congress shall make no law respecting an establishment of religion, or prohibiting the free exercise thereof; *or abridging the freedom of speech or of the press.*"

The report observes, that, "to vindicate the Sedition act it has been contended; 1st. That the *freedom of the press* is to be determined by the meaning of this expression [41] in the common law; and 2d. that the article supposes the power over the press to be in Congress, and prohibits them only from *abridging* the freedom allowed to it by the common law."

In answer to the first of these, the report says, *"It is deemed to be a sound opinion, that the sedition act, in its definition of some of the crimes created, is an abridgment of the freedom of publication recognized by principles of the common law in England."* The meaning of this is, that there are offences declared by this act, for which an indictment would not lie at common law. The report prudently declines supporting this opinion; and I may safely assert, that it is not a sound opinion, and that this act does not create any new offence, and that every offence declared by it would have been an offence indictable at common law in the Federal Courts, if this act had never been made, and would be indictable if this act were repealed.

The people of England, and the common law writers there, say, the press is free there; the report says, it is as free there as here; here and there, it is subject to no previous restraint; here and there, the abuse of it is, by the common law subject to penalties. Yet the report will not admit, that the common law idea of the freedom of the press is the American idea! The circumstances being compleatly the same, it will surely be incumbent on the author of the report to point out the difference in the *ideas*; and to shew why punishment of the abuse would not as effectually check the freedom of the press *there* as *here*.

The sagacious contrast *between the principles of the American government and the principles of the British government* can give no force to the reasoning in the report, unless it be meant to establish, that, because the sovereign American people can change their government when they please; every individual is at liberty, *by lies and without any just reason*, to incite the people to change their government whenever *he* pleases. Or unless it be meant to establish, that the American people ought to have less confidence in a President chosen for four years, than in an hereditary King, or in Senators chosen for six years, than in a hereditary House of Lords; or in Representatives [42] chosen for two years, than in members of the House of Commons chosen for seven years; or, in a word, that it is more an offence to abuse the government there, than to mislead the people by abusing their government here. In any shape in which it is possible to put his report, its author will be obliged to maintain, that among the rights of the American people, one is, that every individual has a liberty to use the press to produce mischief, by publishing falsehood or indecency. For it is well known, that, as by the common law of England, so by the common law of America, and by the Sedition act, every individual is at liberty to expose, in the strongest terms, consistent with decency and truth all the errors of any department of the government.

To contend, *that where the government is elective, there ought to be a liberty of the press beyond the bounds of decency and truth;* is to contend, that, where the people have a right to choose their magistrates, every individual has a right to misrepresent the character and conduct of the magistrates, to pervert the judgment of the people, and render it impossible for them to make a right choice. The degree of the restraint ought to be in proportion to the danger of the offence. To mislead the judgment of the people, where they have *all* power, must produce the greatest possible mischief.

The *"practice, here and in England,"* will not change the law, any more than trespasses will give a right to the soil. It is possible, that, both here and there, too much indulgence has been given to libels: but, in either country, when a libel has been tried and found, has the practice prevented a judgment? Not only libels, but thefts, robberies, and murders have been common in both countries; and the trials and punishments have not been so numerous as the offences. It is not from a corrupt practice, but from a settled practice allowed by judicial decisions, that the common law is to be taken.

That the liberty of the press is an excellent engine to destroy a *bad* government, and the licentiousness of the [43] press to destroy *any* government, all experience will confirm. But where the government is, like ours, founded on the people, I venture to assert, that a degree of liberty beyond that given to the press by the common law and the Sedition act, will tend only to make the people miserable, to corrupt and destroy the government, and to introduce anarchy, and, in the end, despotism. Some means of destroying a bad may not be the means of preserving a good government. To preserve a good government the confidence of the people is necessary; but falsehood, if it may be propagated with impunity, may be as fatal to a good, as truth to a bad government. To preserve our best blessings in an useful state, we must restrain unlimited indulgence. The care and industry of man must be constantly exerted for a proper enjoyment of the gifts of Providence. To make the fruit of the tree good and abundant, we must prune its natural luxuriance. And to preserve the liberty, we must restrain the licentiousness of the press.

When it is known, that our Sedition act, like the common law, forbids the publication of only "false, scandalous and malicious writings against the government," and permits the publisher, if he can, "to give in evidence the truth of the matter;" every candid mind will regret the misrepresentation in the following sentence. *"Had Sedition acts* forbidding *every* publication been uniformly inforced against the press, *might not the United States have been languishing at this day under the infirmities of a sickly confederation; or, possibly, miserable colonies groaning under a foreign yoak?"* By this the author must mean, either that our Sedition act forbids *every* publication against the government; or that there is as much ground of censure of the government now as before the constitution and revolution; or that there would have been no constitution or revolution, if *lies* had not been published of the confederation and the British government; or that American juries are not to be trusted with the examination of truth.

The last argument in the report on this point is founded on a fallacy. "The freedom of conscience and of religion are the same by the common law of England, and of America. The difference between the actual freedom [44] there and here is made, not by the common law, but by statutes there; and our constitution restrains Congress from making *"any"* such statute here, "respecting an establishment of religion, or prohibiting the free exercise thereof." The right of conscience is a natural right of a superior order for the exercise of which we are answerable to God. The right of publication is more within the control of civil authority, and was thought a more proper subject of general law.

There is nothing therefore in the reasoning of the report that can shew, that the meaning of the words *"freedom of the press"* is not to be ascertained by the common law. It is a common law phrase. The common law of England is the foundation of our law. Their language is ours. We use the terms of the English law in the English sense of those terms. And where we mean to restrain, enlarge, or alter this sense, we do so in express terms. Where this is not done, a law phrase is nearly as well understood to mean the same thing here as in England, as a mathematical phrase is so understood. The freedom of the press is plain language, to be understood in the common acceptance of this term here and in England. There and here absolute freedom of the press did not exist. In every state, Libels were punishable at common law. With this state of freedom of the press, the people were content, and only restrain Congress from *abridging* this freedom. Forbidding power to abridge, implies a previous general power over the subject, and leaves a power to punish an abuse of this freedom without abridging it. If this were not so why is there so sudden a change in the manner of expression in this amendment? Why as respecting religion, was it not declared that *Congress shall make no law respecting the freedom of the press?*

This however is denied by the resolution; and, on arguments drawn from discussions of the constitution previous to its adoption, from propositions of amendment made by some of the state conventions at the time of its adoption, and from the proposition of amendment made by Congress after its adoption; the reports asserts *"that this amendment is a positive denial to Congress of any power whatever on the subject."*

[45] It is very clear, that the power exercised by Congress is not included by this amendment; and I think it has been shewn, that it is fairly involved in powers actually given, and necessarily results from the organization of the government; and that it gives no new jurisdiction to the Federal courts; for by the common law, the principles of right and wrong, morality, the rules of religion; the criminal courts of every

government must have jurisdiction over this offence. A libel is an offence against all those laws, a violation of the rights of man, one of which is reputation, and is punished under every government in the courts of the government offended by it. No evil can arise from the exercise of this power by Congress as a general authority: it depends on local information; the honor and safety of the general government is involved in it; it is proper, that there should be a general law uniformly affecting this case, and that the courts of the general government injured by the offence, should be the organs of its correction. Under all these circumstances, the construction will be favorable to the power, and an useful power will not be taken away but by strong and express words, and such do not exist, in the amendment.

In the discussion of the constitution, some of its opponents may have charged it with powers which it had not, and some of its advocates may have denied or dissembled powers really in it. Each, with perhaps honest views, may have laboured to carry his point, and if he succeeded knew that false arguments would not affect the determination, and might be forgotten. On similar ground, many in the state conventions acceded to the propositions of amendment. Those propositions gave some justification, to their arguments; with, or without them, the ratification was equally valid, and they made it more palatable; they were supposed harmless, or, if mischievous, they had no force then, and could be opposed again after the constitution was established. At any rate a proposition that a thing should be done, will not control the construction of the act as done, any more than a preamble will control an act. A contract is to be taken not [46] from the previous conversations of the parties, but from the words in which it is expressed in the writing. Virginia was but one of the parties, and, admitting that there *might have been,* in the convention of that state, a desire to give the Federal government *no power respecting the press;* this might have been contradicted by the other states. Exclusive of Rhode Island, six states ratified the constitution absolutely. Three annexed propositions of amendment, but not including this respecting the press, though one of them, New Hampshire proposed, that "Congress shall make no laws touching religion, or to infringe the rights of conscience." And only three states proposed the amendment respecting the press. So that the constitution was compleatly ratified without any view to this amendment, and must be understood to give all the powers which this amendment was intended to restrain; and the amendment restrains only the power to abridge. It is not necessary, therefore to shew, as might be done, that the declaration by the Virginia Convention, admitting it sincere, is founded on a principle, which, though true, will not support it. And were it every way supportable, it is susceptible of a construction, which would defeat that contended for by the report. It combines two powers with certain attributes, which, *reddendo singula singulis* may be taken thus; the liberty of conscience cannot be modified, and the liberty of the press cannot be abridged, by authority of the United States. But in any construction, how can a law, which only abridges the unlimited degree of punishment for abuse of the press, be said to modify the liberty of the press?

The author of the report must have known that the Virginia Convention in endeavouring to establish the liberty of the press, understood this liberty as every one else does to be a liberty from previous restraint and not from subsequent penalties for its abuse; and did not understand it in the sense contended for by him in the report, *a freedom from all restraint previous and subsequent* and by him said to be the sense of the Virginia Convention. "A law inflicting penalties on printed publications would," says the report, "have a similar effect with a law authorising a previous restraint." Now this Virginia Convention, [47] together with the amendment on the freedom of the press, proposes an amendment, "That every freeman ought to find a certain remedy by recourse to the laws for all injuries and wrongs he may receive in his person, property, *or character.*" If for all injuries to his character, he ought especially to find a remedy for the worst of all a libel. A verdict in an action for damages may be (and we have a late remarkable instance of it) a severer penalty than any that would probably be inflicted by a sentence on an indictment; it may be a severer penalty than can be inflicted by the Sedition Act. Yet this Virginia Convention, which, the report says meant to make the press free from all restraint previous and subsequent, subjects it to this subsequent penalty at common law without limitation. If the opinion of the Virginia Convention were material on this point, it appears, that it meant to leave the press free from all restraints for abuse. And (since the report will argue from the opinion of Conventions) it appears from this and other amendments proposed, that a general legislative authority was supposed to exist in Congress, and a general common law jurisdiction in the courts of the United States. And it appears that the Virginia Convention believed, that without the proposed amendment which I have cited, Congress might make a law, denying the right of action for a libel, and therefore might make a law respecting the freedom of the press; and that the Federal Courts might deny that an action lies for a libel, and, therefore, that they had common law jurisdiction, by which alone such action could be brought before them.

The preamble to the proposition of amendment by Congress is no evidence that the amendment declared the press to be wholly exempt from the power of Congress. There are other amendments proposed, *which might correspond with the desire of the states, and might extend the ground of public confidence.* This amendment was desired only by three states. If it was the intention of Congress to satisfy the desire of those states, by proposing this amendment, it must be presumed that they proposed it in terms corresponding with the desire. None of these states ever desired [48] that the licentiousness or abuse of the press should not be restrained or punished; and Virginia expressly desired the contrary. They desired that the freedom of the press should not be violated or restrained. By the freedom of the press, they must be understood to mean the freedom of the press as it then existed at common law in all the states. The amendment corresponds with this desire, and the Sedition law with this amendment, for it neither violates nor abridges the freedom of the press in the known and established sense of that expression. The intention of those who made the amendment must be collected from the plain meaning of the words used in it. Some may have intended greater restraint, and others less: the question is what is done. *Congress must leave the freedom of the press as it was. There shall be no previous restraints on this freedom; but there may be subsequent penalties on the abuse of it.*

Third, The last point discussed in this resolution is, *"that the power exercised by Congress, in this act, ought, more than any other, to produce universal alarm, because levelled against that right of free examination of public characters and measures, and free communication thereon, which has ever been justly deemed the only effectual guardian of every other right.*

On this point, the report, having stated part of the act, makes various observations on it.

"The constitution supposes that the President, the Congress, and each of its Houses may not discharge their trusts. Hence they are made responsible to their constituents, at the returning periods of election. Should it happen, that

either of these branches has not discharged its trust, it is proper, that according to the degree of their faults, they should be brought into contempt and hatred of the people. Whether this has happened, can only be determined by a free examination and communication among the people. And whenever it has happened, it is the right and duty of intelligent and faithful citizens, to discuss and promulge it freely, as well, for control, as for remedy; and those who are to apply the remedy must feel a contempt or hatred against the transgressing party. During the continuance of this act, two elections of the entire House of Representatives, an election of two-thirds of the Senate, and an election of a President were [49] *to take place: and, during all these elections, the remedial rights of the people were to be exercised, and the responsibility of their public agents to be skreened under the penalties of their act."*

Who, reading these observations, would not suppose, that the people of the United States were by this *alarming sedition-act,* restrained from a free and fair discussion of the public conduct of their public agents, with an honest intent of bringing them into disrepute when they deserved it? But does this act forbid this? No: it forbids, as the report itself shews, "a knowingly and willingly publishing a false, scandalous, and malicious writing, with intent to defame the government," &c. Do the people of the United States wish to retain a right, wilfully, maliciously, and falsely, to publish scandal against their officers? Is this one of the rights of man under a free government? Does the restraint of this right alarm them? Or have they made a constitution to protect it?

It is evident, that the freedom contended for in these observations and the report generally, is a freedom from all restraint; subsequent, as well as previous; from the state governments, as well as from the Federal government: from action, as well as from indictment. For "it is equally a restraint" (says the report) "whether it precede or follow the publication; and so is it equally a penalty, whether assessed by a jury* or by a court, by a state court or by a Federal court." This freedom is a contradiction to all experience, to common understanding, to natural justice, to the rules of religion, and to the judicial decisions of every state. It is a violation of the rights of man, one of the dearest of which is reputation.

The Sedition act enables the person persecuted for a libel, "to

---

* In Virginia Juries assess fines.

give in evidence the *truth* of the matter contained in it," and enables the jury "to determine the law and the fact, under the direction of the court, as in other cases." But the report says, *"its baneful tendency is little diminished by this privilege."* And why is its baneful tendency not diminished? Why is it not entirely removed? Because a restraint from publishing truth would [50] have a baneful tendency; is there any baneful tendency to restrain the publication of falsehood? Because the press ought to be permitted to publish every truth interesting to the public; ought it to be permitted to publish every lie? Because "an intelligent and faithful citizen" has a right, honestly, decently, and freely, to examine the public conduct of every officer, and, by exposing the truth, expose the officer to contempt and hatred; has every impudent or malicious man a right, wilfully, falsely, and scandalously to defame every officer. It is not a free, but a false publication that is prohibited by this act.

But is is objected by the report, that *"where simple and naked fact alone are in question, there is sufficient difficulty of meeting a prosecution from government with the proof necessary in a court of law."* This will infer, that in order to save offenders from the trouble of producing the necessary proof in their defence, there should be no prosecutions, but a general impunity for crimes, for murders, rapes, robberies, thefts, misdemeanors in office, &c. Libels of public officers, where the people have a right of election, are offences of great magnitude and dangerous tendency. And it is as safe for a person accused of a libel to have the accusation tried by a jury, as for a person accused of any other offence.

As to *"opinions, inferences, and conjectural observations,"* they must be drawn from facts. If a man wilfully, maliciously, and with intent to defame, publish an opinion not supported by fact, it is an offence. If there be fact to justify it, he may give it in evidence. If there be none, why should not a wilful, false, and malicious inference be a libel, as well as a wilful, false and malicious assertion. The inference implies the assertion.

As to the intent to defame, the report reasons absurdly, *"that in proportion to the guilt of the officer will be the certainty and criminality of the intent to defame him."* Nothing like this can be drawn from the act. The intent to defame is never criminal, where the matter of the accusation is true. All depends on the truth or falsehood of the matter of the publication. If the publication of the [51] officer's official conduct be true, the intent to defame, however malicious will not make the publication a libel. So that the intent to defame is not criminal unless the publication be false, and is criminal in proportion to the innocence or merit of the officer. There is good reason why the authors of publications against officers should be responsible, that they publish nothing but truth. For if falsehood might be published of officers, and the publishers were liable to no restraint, the whole of an officer's time might be taken up in examining or refuting slander; or the people concerned in the officer's character might be misled by false information.

No less absurd, and more pernicious in its application, is the reasoning of the report, from *"the right of electing the members of the government."* It proceeds on a confusion of freedom with falsehood; as if a discussion could not be free, without being false, or the restraint of a false were restraint of a free discussion. If *"the value and efficacy of the right of election depends on the knowledge of the comparative merits and demerits of the candidate,"* the greater ought to be the restraint on falsehood in examining their character. A free discussion will not be pretended to include a false one: it means a full and fair discussion. A full and fair discussion is not forbidden by the Sedition act. It forbids only a false discussion with a malicious intent. It forbids not diffusing information, but diffusing corruption, among the people, misleading their judgment, and seducing them from their duty. It puts not the officer in a state of greater protection than the citizen. Any truth may be published of the officer, which may be published of the citizen; and every truth may be published of the official character of the officer. Would the committee desire more? Because a man is an officer, shall every slander of him be published with impunity? Because Mr. Adams is President of the United States, shall leave be given to mislead the people, by publishing falsehood or slander of him; in order that another candidate, not in such responsible station, may be on equal terms for a chance of election to that office?

[52] A free means not a false discussion, any more than the liberty, means the abuse, of the press. The greatest injury *"to the right of election,"* and the greatest danger to *"the blessings of a government founded on this right,"* is slander; which perverts the opinions and choice of the people, and leads them to prefer bad to good men. In proportion to the freedom of the government ought to be restraint on libels. And the sedition-act no farther abridges the liberty of the press, than by declaring that false publications are subject to penalties.

To whom then is the sedition-act *alarming?* To slanderers, to libellers, to robbers of reputation, to disturbers of the peace, to violators of the rights of man. It is, as law ought to be, *"a terror only to evil doers."*

The three following resolutions and the report on them contain only matter less important or already considered. Perhaps Pennsylvania deserves the rebuke which may be implied in the declaration of the patriotism of Virginia, in *"maintaining the authority and laws of the Union, without a single exception of internal resistence of commotion."* And while I cheerfully give all due praise to the people of Virginia for this uniform submission, I cannot allow any share of this merit to the authors or promoters of the resolutions or the report. And of the people, for this respect for public authority, we shall find room to praise not only the patriotism but the prudence. There is among them a force, which, if the bands of public authority were relaxed might be fatal indeed.

The resolutions conclude as they commenced, with a profession of affection for the states, and anxiety for the Union. I will not say (for they profess otherwise) that the object of the resolutions is to dissolve the Union; but I may with little hazard of contradiction, say, that they are (especially accompanied with the report) well calculated for this purpose. On the ground that *"a wilful and material breach of a part is a breach of the whole compact; having deliberately determined that palpable and alarming infractions of the constitution have been made;"* they lay a sufficient foundation for the dissolution of the Union. [53] And I will say also, that, in making this deliberate and solemn determination, the legislature of Virginia is mistaken, and has usurped a power not given to it by the people; but given to the judiciary, or reserved to the people themselves, as parties to the compact, in their highest sovereign capacity. This is a deliberate, palpable, dangerous, and alarming exercise of powers not granted by the constitution: for the powers of the legislature of Virginia are no farther valid, than they are authorized by the constitutions of that state and of the Union. And the people are in duty bound to "interpose, for arresting the progress of the evil, and maintaining within their respective limits the authorities, rights, and liberties appertaining to them."

[54]   *POSTSCRIPT*

When I wrote what is said in page 12 of the opinion of General Washington, on the power of Congress to provide for the general welfare, I alluded to this opinion as officially delivered to Congress. I had not then seen his will giving a donation to A NATIONAL UNIVERSITY, in the hope that Congress would establish such an institution. This is a deliberate declaration of a WISE and VIRTUOUS man, in whom LOVE of COUNTRY was the ruling passion; made in the full strength of this passion, in a solemn moment when he was preparing to part with all earthly things, and to meet his GOD.

[68]

JOEL BARLOW 1754–1812

To His Fellow Citizens of the United States.
Letter II: On Certain Political Measures
Proposed to Their Consideration

PHILADELPHIA, 1801

In 1788 a business venture took Barlow to Europe, and there, mainly in France, he remained for nearly twenty years, entranced by the French Revolution and its parallels with American experience in launching a new political system. These observations stirred him to a series of shrewd analyses of the French effort to build a new order. Several of them took the form of letters, one of which is reproduced here. While not as famous as his *Advice to the Privileged Orders* (1792), which warned against ruling for class interest, or his epic poem *The Columbiad,* or his *Letters to the National Convention of France on the Defects in the Constitution of 1791* (for which he was awarded an honorary French citizenship), the "letter" reproduced here is a discussion of Federalism in a general, international context that justifies a federal structure for all nations of a considerable population and does so with a sophistication equal to his other more well known writings.

Fellow Citizens,

In my first letter to you I signified an intention of addressing you a second time on political subjects; and of suggesting certain measures which appear to me to be within your power, for securing your own liberty both civil and commercial, and for laying the foundation of a pacific intercourse among all maritime nations, on a plan which may perpetuate itself and become universal. Some of my observations may appear superfluous, as being already familiar to the minds of thinking men; and some of my theories may be thought impracticable because they are not familiar. Could I know beforehand what would really prove superfluous, and what impracticable, I would certainly retrench all that should come under both these descriptions; though it might go to the whole contents of my work; for my object is to aid the exertions of those who wish to do good; and not to embarrass them in the choice of means.

The art of governing a nation is the art of substituting a moral to a physical force. It is only in [2] their rudest state, antecedent to government and previous to any experience, that men can be supposed to be impelled or restrained altogether by the action of other men, applied as bodily strength. *The right of the strongest* among individuals, or in sections of the same society, supposes the absence of that controling power which is held over them by the society at large; and which, being confided to the hands of the magistrate, constitutes the moral force with which the government usually acts.

As the absolute independence of one man upon another is incompatible with a state of society, personal strength becomes no longer necessary to personal protection; but, on the contrary, it is a general maxim, that individual safety is best secured where individual exertion is least resorted to. Our submitting to any force whatever, whether physical or moral, is the choice of self-interest; resulting in the first case from real defect, and in the last, either from calculation or from habit. The consciousness of public power gives rise to public opinion; and while experience teaches us to calculate their energy, it brings on the habit of respecting their authority. We thus refrain from mutual injury by an habitual sense of convenience, which resembles the instinct of self-preservation, and is almost as strong in us, as that sensitive horror which prevents our stepping off a precipice. Hence great societies may be moved, millions of persons protected, industry and virtue universally encouraged, idleness and violence completely restrained, without lifting the hand of one man upon another.

These reflections open to our view an immense career of improvement, and explain the theory of the whole progress of society, past, present and to come. Great strides have been taken in this [3] wonderful career; and a considerable elevation in the ascending scale of improvement is already attained. Whoever will compare the present state of the species with what it was when every thing was decided by bodily strength; when man, after having forced a bit of food from the elements, or robbed it from the savage beast, was still obliged to dispute its possession with his fellow man: whoever looks back to that state of painful privation, precarious toil, and perpetual danger, which saddened the existence of unassociated men, and will then turn to himself, and contemplate what he now enjoys in his protected industry, in the comforts of life assured to himself and family, in the love and good will of his neighbors, and even of distant nations, where virtue and talents are respected, must be convinced of a progress in human affairs, and of a tendency towards perfection. And he will not deny the truth of this general theory, though the period of a few years, taken in any one section of the great circle, may not present to his discernment any perceivable amelioration.

The perfectibility of human society is not a subject of idle speculation, fit only to adorn the pages of a book. It is a truth of the utmost importance in its practical tendency. No maxim is more essential to the legislator of a nation or to the negotiator of treaties; and it ought especially to be present in the minds of all men who are called to administer a representative government. If such men have talents and information worthy of their place, and a proper zeal for performing its duties, they will not content themselves with the thoughtless routine of official functions, just necessary to escape impeachment; they will not think it enough to avoid crimes themselves, or to punish them in others; but they will call forth the energies of their own genius, and that of their fellow citizens, [4] to interrogate the native resources of their country, the elements of national happiness; they will second the designs of nature, by accelerating the progress of improvement, by exploring the objects of industry, multiplying the means of subsistence, creating new inducements for peace and harmony with neighbouring states, and removing every occasion for jealousy and war.

An enlightened magistrate will not be satisfied with himself; as having done his duty, unless he can say on quitting the administration, that he leaves the nation better than he found it. Neither can he be said to have served his own country well, unless he has communicated benefits to other countries to which her relations extend. There is no absolute independence of nations any more than of individuals. Men are every where surrounded with wants, and every where incumbered with superfluities; the necessity of asking aid, and the ability of granting it, are mutual, perpetual, and universal; they keep up a constant exchange of commodities, a circulation of the vital fluid of society. Our mutual wants and aids are the elements of our civilization; they have already civilized individuals to a great degree, convinced them of their relative dependence, and taught them the art as well as the convenience of living together in peace. They have made some progress too in civilizing states; and their energy must be infallible in carrying on the work of harmony and happiness, till nations shall stand in the same relation to each other as families do at present in the best regulated community.

The *civilization of States* is the great object to be aimed at in the present age of the progress of human affairs. It is that part of general improvement which has been the least understood, and the least investigated, both as to the means of [5] bringing it forward, and the consequences that would result from its success. So little has it been studied, so ill have the principles of society been applied to it, even in theoretical discussion, that its possibility is still regarded as a problem. Many persons imagine that states or nations never can be civilized more than they are at present; that among them the savage principle, or *the right of the strongest,* will always be resorted to. And as it is evident that individual improvement being constantly interrupted by the quarrels of nations, cannot be carried much farther, unless those nations will agree to live in peace, they say there is no reason to hope that human society will ever attain a greater degree of perfection than what we see at present. This would evidently be the case, if nations were never to civilize, that is, if a sense of mutual dependence were not to produce the same effects in the great sections of society, called states, as it does in the small sections called families. But why should we despair of these effects? The mutual dependence of men is universal, and it is perpetual: it is not only sure to serve as a permanent source of reciprocal confidence, but as an increasing source; it increases with our factitious wants; it becomes more sensible in proportion to our knowledge of distant countries and of their productions, in proportion to the acquisitions we make in science, to the accumulation of superfluities, and the infinite researches of industry.

A particular *people,* whatever extension we give to the meaning of the word, whether it means a parish or an empire, is every where a physical and moral agent, whose interests are analogous and reciprocal with those of another people of a like description, who inhabit a neighbouring territory. Each of them has a real interest in the prosperity of the other; because prosperity creates [6] certain relative superfluities, which, being exchanged between the parties, supply their relative wants. This interchange of commodities creates an interchange of affections; it begins among individuals, and extends in regular progression with their knowledge, to every country and every portion of mankind.

Nature has certainly placed no barrier in this long course of improvement. Whatever barriers are perceived in it are unnatural and accidental: they will therefore be removed by the development of the human faculties, though by slow degrees. There is no reason why civilization, after having softened the temper of individuals, and harmonized the component parts of a state as acting among themselves, should forever stop short at that point, and leave the state savage without, while it is social and peaceful within. For in this case it acts by its physical force abroad, and by its moral force at home; which supposes on the one side a want of experience, which borders on the rudest condition of savage man; and on the other it indicates a sense of convenience and the habits of social life.

To make this matter a little plainer, and show that our hopes of progressive civilization are well founded, let us recur to first principles, and explain the causes which seem to impede its progress in certain stages of its career. What do we mean by the word *nation?* and what is that precise portion of mankind which necessarily forms a body politic, independent and unsocial, beneficent within and ferocious without? It is certain that the necessary limits of a nation are not geographical; neither are they numerical. In both these respects they are perpetually changing, and are already exceedingly various. One of them, the Chinese, is supposed to contain three hundred millions [7] of inhabitants; another, the Dutch, which does not exceed three millions, is established in the four quarters of the world; its different branches being separated by the widest oceans, and yet united in interest, friendly and social, like a family. The territory now covered by one Federal Republic, the United States, was lately inhabited by at least two hundred different nations at a time, all independent, sovereign, and savage towards each other, as the nations of Europe are this day. France itself, a few centuries ago, was composed of a great number of independent states; which have been united one after another, under the name of provinces, for the purposes of exterior defence and the splendor of the crown: but never till the present revolution, were they completely incorporated in one national body, for the objects of interior commerce, or attached to each other by a similarity of political rights and pecuniary burthens.

It seems then that the tendency of civilization is to diminish the number of nations, and to increase their size and prosperity. But this kind of progression, as applied to independent nations, is limited by the nature of things. The few men to whom the government of a state must be confided, cannot extend their knowledge nor multiply their attentions to such a degree as the affairs of a great people would require. France, in her present limits, presents a mass of population and territory sufficient for at least twenty integral and well constituted states. Her legislative body is representative; it is twice as numerous as any legislative body ought to be; and yet, it is not the fifth part so numerous as a proper representation of the people would require. It is incumbered with much more business than it can treat with that attention which the business deserves; and yet not half the affairs which are necessary to the people are ever [8] brought up for its deliberation. This republic, for the purposes of interior or local legislation and police, should be organised into about twenty subordinate republics; while, for the purposes of general legislation, exterior relations, defence, commerce, canals, roads, and every common concern, they should remain concentrated in one great union, or community, with a national legislative and executive, restricted in their powers to the simple objects of great national interest; which objects should be defined with the utmost precision in their general constitution.[1]

[1] The terms *federal, confederacy,* and others from the same original, have been proscribed in France during the organization of the republic, because their *ordinary* meaning refers to a different state of things from what the condition of France admits; and different from what would be their *appropriate* meaning in this country, were the system adopted which I should recommend; and which appears to me the only one capable of preserving liberty here, and of civilizing Europe. To *federalize,* applied to states, usually signifies to bring towards a union, but not into unity, those that were before distinct and independent. But as France was already one integral state, to *federalize* France would seem to be to divide and dismember that which was before united, which, in the vocabulary of the revolution, was another word for anarchy and intestine war. The federality which I would propose for France and for Europe would not carry with it any such idea. The integrity of the republic, for every purpose of safety, and harmony of parts, would not be altered by it.

JOEL BARLOW 1754–1812

In pursuance of such a system there would be no danger that France would become too extensive or too populous for her internal convenience. And the several nations that are now forming republics in her neighbourhood ought to constitute them on the same plan as those of France, and make part of the general confederation. This system should be adopted, and this confederation joined by every European people, as fast as they become free; though it should extend through this [9] quarter of the world. It would present a great union of Republics, which might assume the name of the United States of Europe and guarantee a perpetual harmony among its members.

This beneficent system of federalizing appears to be the only resource that nature has offered us at least in the present state of political science for avoiding at once the two dangerous extremes of having the republic too great for any equitable administration within, or too small for security without. On this principle, if wisely pursued, no confederated republic will be too great, and no member of it too small, as all subjects of jealousy will be done away by the nature of the association. The new republics of Europe must resort to this principle if they mean to hold the ground they have gained, in changing their feudal for their representative constitutions. Could we flatter ourselves that they would resort to it at the end of the present war, then we might hope to see [10] the moral force of nations take place of their physical force, the civilization of states keep pace with that of individuals, and their commercial relations established on the principles of peace.

There has been a great deal of false reasoning on this subject. It is now believed by most of the philosophers in Europe to be a great misfortune to our United States, that they were in several states, and not in one state. This would truly be a misfortune, had we not adopted the federal principle, but now it is one of our greatest advantages.

I am sorry to see that M. Liancourt, in his Late Travels in America, has given countenance to this European sentiment, which I consider a very unfortunate one for the progress of society. His book which contains a vast quantity of facts and information, will have a tendency to accredit this doctrine in the minds of many persons who had not before adopted it. If that able and labourous inquirer after truth will reflect on the calamities which I shall notice in this letter, as what would be the consequence of a dissolution of our federal system, and will contemplate the principle of that system in its vast extent, as a new means of civilizing states and preventing wars. I hope he will find occasion for changing his opinions.

See vol. 7, page 221 of his Travels. Paris edition.

Infinite credit is due to the conductors of our American Revolution for the wisdom and energy with which they seized the occasion of establishing our interior and federal governments in the forms which they now possess. The two most consoling principles that political experience has yet brought to light, are those on which we have founded our constitutions—I mean *representative democracy,* and the *federalizing of States.* It is true that neither of these principles was wholly of our own discovery. But what little experience had been made of either of them by other nations was extremely imperfect, was attended with little success, and had by no means united the opinions even of the most sanguine in their favor. In no one instance had the two principles been brought together and wrought into one system, nor had they ever been attempted both by the same people.

Democracy had been disgraced by the pretended experience of some of the states of Greece, though in reality no such things as democracy ever did exist in Greece or Rome. It has been concluded, and very justly, that *pure democracy,* or the immediate autocracy of the people, is unfit for a great state; it might be added, that it is unfit for the smallest state imaginable, even a little town. But *representative democracy* is applicable to a state of any size, and under any circumstances where men have the use of their reason; though neither this nor any other principle hitherto discovered is sufficient *of itself* to regulate the concerns of a great people; as no one integral government is capable of bestowing equal and adequate benefits on every part of an extensive and populous country. But [11] happily for mankind, the representative principle is a fit companion and a sure guide of the other previous experiment which our country has adopted with such singular propriety, the principle of *confederation.* The union of these two theories, as organised in America, is a vast improvement on the wisdom of former ages; and I cannot but hope that they will be so far cherished by us, and imitated by others, as to change, very greatly the face of human society.

It is essential to the interests of America, and would be a compliment to her wisdon, to see her political system, in both its parts, adopted by other countries. It would be the surest pledge of peace from abroad, and the strongest guarantee against a relapse of principle at home. But, for ourselves, there is one maxim which ought not to be forgotten, that these two pillars of the edifice, the representative principle and the federal principle, should never be separated. Though one of them alone may promise liberty and the other of them alone may promise peace, yet we cannot be confident that either liberty or peace will become extensive or permanent, unless these well assorted principles are united in one system, and kept inseparable in their practice.

Let us convince ourselves of this truth by examining the effect of each principle apart, as operating without the aid of the other. First, the federalizing of states, whose governments were monarchical, or aristocratical, has not obtained any brilliant success, either in ancient or modern times. The Amphictyonic Council of the Greeks was a body of so little consequence in a political view, that it would not be worth noticing in this place were it not for a certain practice among writers on governments, of seeking models for every thing in the annals of that pompous people. The [12] Amphictyons had no regular constituted authority, except in matters of religion. They never prevented a foreign war offensive or defensive. It would be difficult indeed to say they never prevented a domestic war among the states, because such a thing might be done with so little rumour as to escape the notice of history, but it is certain that they excited several domestic wars, and those of the most cruel and exterminating kind, being wars of religion. On the whole, it appears that this congressional institution, notwithstanding its solemn pretensions of confederating the States of Greece, was more detrimental than beneficial to the people. Whenever their common country was invaded, whether by Persians, Macedonians or Romans, about half the states in every instance, joined the invading enemy. The power of the Amphictyons was effectual only in directing, on certain occasions, the united avengeance of several powerful states against the weaker one, for having slighted the authority of the priests, for having put into cultivation certain lands which religion had devoted to sterility, or neglected some frivolous or barbarous duty enjoined by an insidious oracle.

As to the Corinthian, the Peloponesian and the Arcananian leagues, they were only allies or coalitions against an enemy, temporary in their nature, and not extensive in their effects. The other examples from Greece which are sometimes cited as confederations, such as the Arcadian, the Beotian, the Eolian and the primitive Achaian, present something more regular and permanent in their constitutions. But they were each of them too diminutive to merit the name of an association of states. The primitive Achaian, for instance, was the union of twelve small boroughs into one small republic. It may be considered rather as a model of representative democracy in a single state, [13] than as a federal system, and in this view perhaps it approaches nearer to modern republican representation than any other example left us by the ancients.

The subsequent, or great Achaian league, was indeed an association of states, whose object was laudable and well defined. It suffered less from a defect in its federal principle than from the corruption of its members. It retrieved in a partial degree the liberties of Greece from the rapacity of Alexander's successors, preserved them with considerable energy for no more than a hundred years, and finally yielded them with some appearance of dignity to the irresistable fortunes of Rome.

The Lycian league was not unlike the latter Achaian, either in its object or its destiny. It caused itself to be respected by the Romans as long as the Romans retained any respect for themselves; but no institutions could stand before the corruptions of their monstrous and debilitated empire.

The Etruscans and some other early tribes in Italy, had likewise their several confederations. But their constitutions are so little known, and they refer to a state of society so different from ours that for every purpose, except for displaying an empty erudition, their investigation would be as useless to us as that of some of the native tribes of North America, the Six Nations or the Tascallans. Examples of these imperfect associations are not rare. It is probable that the history of the human race would present them in every corner of the earth, if its affecting and monotonous page could be completely laid open before us. They shew the feeble efforts of inexperienced societies to defend themselves against the effects of each other's inexperience.

The German Empire, the Swiss Canton, and the United Netherlands present us three great examples [14] of the confederation of states in modern Europe; the former still subsisting, the two latter but lately overturned. It requires but little observation to discern the constitutional defects in the Germanic body: it is a confederation of princes, and not of nations. With this radical vice in its organization, it is impossible that its object should be peace, or its policy justice; and without pursuing these, no society of men can be tolerably happy, no union of states can be sincere, no portion of the earth can greatly increase its population, or present that progressive augmentation of benefits which nature has placed within our reach, and science is teaching us how to realise. National happiness is never the object of a state where the interest of those who govern is in any measure different from that of the people. The pursuits, therefore, of the Germanic Princes are mutual encroachment instead of mutual assistance; the object of their union is war, and not peace; their constitution is military, and not commercial. Hence all the compulsory provisions that are made in it have reference to warlike preparations, contingencies of men and money, for recruiting armies and discouraging industry. There is no public provision made for the encouragement of useful arts and manufactures, no power lodged in the federal Diet for establishing a general system of canal or river navigation, for equalizing the duties on the objects of commerce, allowing a free exchange of the produce of labor, even in the most necessary articles of life.

There is no inhibition which prevents any prince or state from beginning a war without the consent of the Diet, from building forts and raising armies with the manifest intention to invade each other's territory, from entering into foreign alliances and other treaties, for involving the empire in destructive [15] wars. But, on the contrary, every facility and every temptation are held out for intestine wars among the states, as if no federal tie subsisted between them, while their interior commerce from state to state is shackled with all those restrictions which hostile jealousy has invented among the most independent and ferocious monarchies of Europe.

Many other defects might be easily pointed out in the Germanic constitution. We may find some of them in the books that treat on this subject; but where is the advantage of searching them? The fundamental defect, which is the source of all the rest, is not noticed in any book, but stares us in the face on the first reflection: a confederation of Princes stands no chance of being beneficial to the people. You might as well expect to render service to the sheep by confederating the wolves that should be set to watch them.

The Swiss Cantons and the United Netherlands have been more fortunate in their federal systems. Considering the feebleness of that means with which they began the quantity of force against which they rose; and the weight of effort that has been frequently made to destroy them, they exhibit wonderful monuments of the efficacy of organized liberty in political bodies. Though the Swiss Cantons had scarcely the appearance of a federal constitution, the acts of union being little more than treaties of alliance, which external danger generally kept them from violating; and though that of the United Netherlands was very imperfect, yet these were not the radical defects which brought on the decline and overthrow of either of their celebrated systems. The original defect, in each case, lay in the constitutions of the particular states of which the union was composed. The representative principle was originally [16] unknown, and never understood in either country. Without this principle, the people can not exercise their rights, unless it be in the form of mobs: the necessary consequence of which is to throw the active power into the hands of a few, where it soon becomes habitual and hereditary, no longer the property of the nation, and no longer exercised for her benefit. It would be as impracticable to establish a rational system of federal government among aristocratical states as among principalities of monarchies. For the principle is the same in each; the supposed interest of the people.

The plan for a perpetual peace, projected two centuries ago by Henry IV, new modeled and proposed with great zeal in the early part of the present century by the abbe de St. Pierre, and afterwards embellished with the nervous eloquence of J. J. Rousseau, must have been a fruitless experiment, if attempted on the model of either of its illustrious patrons. The project was to league all the Christian Powers of Europe in one confederation, guaranteeing to each its own form of government, and its limits as then existing, to establish a permanent Diet, composed of delegates from every state, with power to settle all disputes that might arise between the several states, to prevent any of them from raising armies on their own account, building forts or fleets to act against each other, or forming any foreign alliances, but all exterior relations and all measures of defence should be directed and managed by the general Diet, in the name of the Confederacy.

It is possible that by the means which Henry had in his power, this sublime conception might have been realised so far as to organize the constitution and begin the operation, had not an untimely death prevented the experiment by depriving the [17] world of its author. Rousseau has detailed the reasons why this project could not be carried into effect at any period since the days of Henry, nor by any influence short of that which he possessed among the powers of Europe. But the same writer supposes that were it once adopted, its benefits would be so conspicuous and universal as to secure its continuance. I question the probability of this supposition. What could secure the members of this Diet from corruption? There is but one effectual mode of securing them; and that is to make it the interest of none of the parties to corrupt them; no other principle can be relied upon with safety. In an association of this magnitude, it is not enough that it should be the interest of each of the associated states to preserve the constitution; but it should be the interest of those who govern the associated states. Now as long as these were governed by hereditary princes, who had an interest in extending their private dominions to the detriment of each other, it must be expected that they would seek to encroach as much as possible and violate the constitution by every means in their power. And, as the federal government, if well administered, would prevent their doing it by force, the more effectual way would be to corrupt the members of the Diet, so as to palsy the operation of the constitution, suspend its protection of the weaker associates, and re-establish the right of the strongest, as in the present state of Europe. This is a favorite state of society for princes, a state of hazard, inviting them to plunder, and so far exposing them to be plundered in their turn, as to afford a constant pretext for armies and navies. It is what they call independence; and notwithstanding it leads them every day to commit crimes for which they would hang a hundred [18] subjects, they will not agree to be restrained by law; though the same law would restrain their neighbors who prey upon themselves; though it would greatly increase their revenues, by increasing the population and the quantity of productive labour within their dominions; and though it would greatly lessen their expenses, by reducing to almost nothing their constant preparations for defences.

But if the powers of government in every associated state were in the hands of the people, in whom the right resides, and if these powers were exercised in all cases by an equal representation, freely chosen and frequently renewed, then would there be no person interested in extending the limits of any one state to the detriment of another; then would no person attempt to corrupt the Diet to violate the compact; and throw Europe back into a state of national animosity and princely plunder; then the farmer would be on his own farm, and the artisan in his own shop; and whether his habitation were included in the limits of Prussia or of Austria, whether it were called protestant or catholic, would not be to him a matter of interest; he would find equal protection in each district, by laws made and obeyed by his own delegates.

A Confederation of States whose interior governments should be founded on these principles might indeed extend through Europe with the project of Henry IV, and be as lasting as was imagined by the fervid benevolence of St. Pierre; but it would not be a confederation of hereditary proprietors of nations.

Hence we may conclude, so far as the experience of mankind will enable us to judge from practice, and so far as the nature of the case will strengthen our conclusions from theory, that no [19] considerable advantage ought to be expected from the federal principle among states unless the states themselves are constituted on the representative principle; so as that the system in both its branches may be the work of the people, carried on for their benefit, by persons of their own choice and under their own control.

Second, in the other branch of the present examination, to discover the effect of the representative principle, without the aid of federalizing, we shall receive but little light from the experience of any nation. There is no example, within my knowledge, of a complete representative government of an elder date than those of our own country; and those were effectually federalized as soon as they were formed, and before. It is true that the government of Connecticut and Rhode Island were as perfectly representative before the American revolution as they are now; and some other of their sister colonies had been at some periods nearly so. But their commonality with the monarchy of Great Britain answered some of the purposes of a federal union. They were not independent, and no state on earth, in my opinion, ought to be called independent. For no state can really be so in fact, it is only a source of false ideas and of endless calamities to have them so in form.

France and the other new republics in Europe cannot be said as yet to have had much experience of the representative principle. Their practical governments are hitherto revolutionary, and must of necessity continue so till the end of the revolutionary war which has been excited to destroy them.

There being therefore no example of real representative government, except in the American States, and those being united by strong federal [20] ones; we are driven to theoretical inquiry alone for the opinion we ought to form of the operation of the republican principle among individual and unconfederated states.

We should begin by observing that such states must necessarily be small, for the reasons already noticed, otherwise the representative energy cannot be well preserved, nor the benefits of equal government be experienced by every portion of the people. If the states are small, their territories contiguous, and their governments independent, they will necessarily be rivals; there will probably be mutual restrictions on their trade for the sake of revenue; there will be forts and armies and generals; it will not be long before some citizens in each state will conceive themselves to have a private property in their respective governments, and an interest in extending the dominion of their own state, to the detriment of the others; they will have sycophants to flatter this fatal ambition, places and patronage at their disposal, and a number of new departments and their appendages to be granted at the moment of a rupture with their neighbours.

The first cannon fired between two rival states in this situation may be taken as the signal of the departure of liberty from them both. The power in each state becomes military; military power is necessarily concentrated in a few hands where it soon becomes hereditary. The rest of the history of such states might as well be written before they exist, as after they are extinguished. But it would not be worth writing at all; it would be but the repetition of some indifferent chapter in the great history of despotism and war.

Since then, my fellow citizens, it is to you that we must turn for the best practical lessons on the subject of government; in both the principles [21] on which your system is founded, you will at least acknowledge the importance of maintaining those principles. And I hope at the same time that you will not be averse to making such improvements in your situation as the nature of your system will admit, without changing its theory. Your objects are: 1, to secure the continuance of interior liberty, in the United States; and 2, to take such an attitude in vindicating your commercial liberty, has to gain the confidence of other Powers, and lay the foundation of perpetual peace, at least between you and them, possibly between all commercial nations. These two objects are so essential to your own prosperity, and at the same time so accordant with that desire which is natural to uncorrupted minds, of extending benefits to other sections of the human race, that you will indulge me in a few observations upon each.

The means of securing interior liberty in the United States

I will not go into an examination of the state Constitutions, nor propose to your consideration those amendments of which some of them appear susceptible, because it is at all times a delicate subject; and to give it a candid discussion requires a moment of less fermentation than the present. It is not a work of immediate necessity; though some parts of it should not be neglected till your population is very greatly increased; and till certain habits founded on constitutional defects become too inveterate to be easily removed. But there are other objects of a more general concern [22] which may be noticed with less danger of giving offence; and which doubtless demand an early attention.

The face of things in North America is changing so exceedingly fast that every political step you take ought to have a special reference to the time to come, as well as to the time present. No government should have so little to do with temporizing, and so much to do with system, as that of the United States. The science of political perspective ought to be rendered familiar to those who aspire to be your guides; so that the great events which are sure to happen, may be classed and measured, and their places assigned them, before they come into being. Without this precaution, it would be impossible to go right with it, the task of governing would be so easy that honest men would scarcely go along. The approaching changes in our situation should be distinctly noticed, and their consequences profoundly meditated. 1. Our nation is young in respect to the date of its independence, the habits of thinking incident to this condition, and the trial we have had of our political institutions. 2. One half of the territory within our limits remains unoccupied, on the other half the population is small, compared with what it is capable of becoming; and the increase must be rapid. 3. Extensive and flourishing colonies are springing up beyond our frontiers in every direction. These are of various extraction, principally Spanish, French and English; all of them from the impulse given them by their mother countries, are doubtless unfriendly to us, but all of them, from real interest, similarity of circumstances, and future inevitable events, are capable of becoming our natural and best friends, and, with proper management, our fellow citizens. Not many years can pass before [23] these colonies will shake off their foreign dependence, and burst the ties which now bind them to European governments.

These are some of the principal circumstances to be consulted in supporting the interior of our system. The events are easy to foresee: they must be provided for; and it depends on you from this moment to say whether they shall redound to our advantage, and to the extensive benefit of ages and nations; or whether they shall bring destruction to our hopes, and overturn the fairest fabric of human policy that the world has hitherto seen.

I will waste no arguments in proving that it is essential to the interest of the United States, to continue their federal union, whatever may be the increase of population and the addition of new states within our present limits. Taking this to be a position which will not be denied by those for whom I write, I will content myself with noticing the means by which alone the union can be preserved.

First: The United States, to maintain their federal system entire, through all their limits, and, under approaching circumstances, *must be out of debt,* or nearly so. The annual call for money, for federal purposes, must be moderate. Otherwise the people in different districts, who see with what simplicity and economy their own state governments are carried on, and who know that much the greater part of their real interests are regulated, they will begin to calculate, and enquire whether their part of the expences of the confederation, does not exceed its benefits. Such enquiries indeed would be of a nature not to be pursued with the utmost fairness, nor could we expect calculations of this sort to be conducted with all that foresight which the subject would require. There is no doubt but prudence would [24] dictate to any district of the Union to submit to very great expences, rather than withdraw from it, and become a rival nation. But experience teaches us that in political resentments we are not to expect much prudence or true policy.

To keep the frontier districts attached to the Union, we must rely more on their passions and their sense of present convenience, than on their prudence and their calculation of future convenience. We should not forget that the United States are to be held together by interest, not by force. And the federal government should conduct its operations in such a manner as that this interest shall always be felt by every state and act upon the inhabitants, as a steady principle of union; since there is no other on which we can depend.

In the old governments of Europe the people of different districts are held together under one head by the co-operation of several causes which do not exist with us. A military force, or a standing army, acts as a constant pressure on them, both by the terror it excites, and the great number of places it offers to the nobility and the ambitious of every class. To this is added a superstitious veneration for a reigning family, who never fail to be painted to their subjects as the centre of every virtue and the particular favorites of heaven; so that withdrawing from their government is considered as rebellion against God. Then comes the machinery of a state religion, which is kept in continual play by a host of artful men, who teach that every thing beyond their own dominion is heretical and reprobate. And farther to discourage every wish for a change, the people are so hemmed in by nations as miserable as themselves, that they perceive that great taxes and other vexations are not to be avoided by shifting their allegiance, and looking to the [25] right, instead of the left, for the centre of their government.

We shall deceive ourselves exceedingly if we suppose that any of these causes are to operate in the western and southern districts of the United States. Our system of policy does not admit of standing armies, and if it did, we could not support one sufficiently strong to restrain a whole people who have arms in their hands, who should think themselves oppressed, and determine to be free. No superstition, that is likely to be lasting or extensive, is yet established among us, in favor of any one man or family; for not withstanding the pains that are taken to deify some of our citizens, and to propagate an opinion that they can do no wrong, these efforts are ridiculed by the mass of people whom they were intended to deceive. As to religion, the sects are so numerous in America, and the people are so convinced, that whatever concern they may have in it must be personal and not political, that the general government cannot hope to establish a uniformity of worship, and therefore can never make it a powerful engine of state. And with regard to the last article above mentioned, that of being surrounded by nations habituated to oppression, this is totally wanting in our country. If therefore the federal government becomes oppressive to the people of the frontier states, or only appears to be so, there is no other example of oppression in their neighbourhood with which to compare it; their reasoning in this case will be very short. Nothing binds us to this boasted Union; it is at least an inconvenience to us; let us shake it off and be our own Union; or, if we are not strong enough for that, let us form another with the Spanish or English colony in our neighbourhood, where every encouragement is held out [26] to us; where, having no national debt, we shall have no taxes, but for the current expences of a government, which, being of our own formation, shall be kept within the bounds of economy.

JOEL BARLOW 1754–1812

These good people will not perhaps reflect on the immense inconveniencies which would afterwards arise both to them and us from our new condition of two or more rival nations, bordering on each other, having each an extensive line of forts and garrisons, standing armies and frequent wars to maintain; which would inevitably plunge us all into the gulf of monarchy, nobility and priesthood, from which we never could arise, or regain the ground we should have lost.

Should this letter reach the inhabitants of the frontier states and districts of our common country, I beg, on the one hand, that they will not be offended at the apprehension that I express, that a disposition may one day arise in them to dissolve their union with their sister states, and they will pardon my fears if no such event is likely to occur. But, on the other hand, if these apprehensions are well founded, I entreat them to listen for a moment to the voice of the most disinterested friend that will probably ever discuss the subject.

Let them look at the condition of Europe, and contemplate its history through the bloody series of modern ages. It is divided into rival states, that call themselves *independent;* which is another word for the ferocity of savage life, and a licence for organized violence. These states are separated from each other by triple or quadruple ranges of fortified towns, whose inhabitants, from age to age subjected to military law, are shut up at night like cattle, and pursue their labours by day under the shade of the bayonet, within the view of an insolent soldiery, whose ranks are supplied by draining the country of its best young men, and whose [27] pay and provisions are drawn from the hard industry of those who remain behind.

The commerce of these independent nations is so harrassed with duties and imposts, in passing through different dominions, that very little of it can be carried on. A barrel of sugar, brought into the middle of Germany, must have paid at least six or eight different taxes. And when the consumer has any produce of his own labor to send abroad, it is loaded with as many more burthens, before it can arrive at market.

Such is their condition in their best times, the times of peace; but in the years of war, which are about half the years of every generation of these unhappy men, immense armies are set in motion; whole countries are overspread and exhausted by the marches of successive hordes of friends and enemies, confederates and allies; whose undistinguished voracity excites equal terror among the inhabitants.

Sieges, battles, hospitals, prisons, pestilence and famine sweep off half the population of each country and force their princes at last to a temporary cessation of butchery, which they call peace. Perhaps the halves of some provinces are severed from one dominion and annexed to another; and this they call conquest. This occasions a new line of frontier, and new ranges of fortifications to be run through an interior country, cutting up the cultivated fields and forcing the owners (who cannot fly from the devastation) to work at the new trenches and ramparts, to prepare this transfiguration of nature, and be ready for another war.

This picture is not overcharged; and if it should be thought inapplicable to the present subject, because modern Europe is governed by hereditary princes, and the projected independent governments of America expect to be republics, let us look back [28] for another example to the states of ancient Greece. Those states were most of them called republics, and were independent of each other; and among the five or six hundred years of their political existence, from the commencement of history 'till they became a Roman province, I believe there was not a single year when they can be said to have been completely at peace among themselves. No, the evil is not altogether in the nature of the inferior government, though this in itself, when bad, is a great source of calamities; a still greater source, if possible, is in the independence and rivalship of neighbouring governments. What a long and uninterrupted series of wars between England and Scotland was arrested by the union of the two crowns, and afterwards of the two kingdoms! And how much more extensive and more lamentable would have been the scenes of slaughter among the American States had we left them independent of each other, after effecting their independence from Great Britain.

Since then we have found the means of avoiding these disasters—since we have established a union of interest and of states which may bid defiance to every possible enemy but ourselves, shall we not have the wisdom to preserve this union? Shall we, on the one side, indulge in the prodigality of increasing our debt and in a proud indifference to the opinions of an irritable and powerful portion of the nation, and on the other side, will that portion run wild with an untimely resentment and not consent to a small and temporary sacrifice, rather than plunge themselves and their brethren with all their intermingled posterity, into calamities which are inseparable from a disjunction of the states, and the frightful experiment of independent and rival governments, whose tempers will have been already imbittered by the act of separation?

[29] It is doubtless to be lamented that the debt of the United States has risen to such a formidable size, and that there still seems to be a disposition to increase it, from pretences so frivolous as to be clearly seen through by those whom they were intended to blind and mislead. It is impossible that the smallest portion of the American people has been made to believe that there was any conceivable danger of an invasion from France; and the resentment occasioned by the creation of that part of the debt which has been raised on this pretence must therefore be sharpened by the impudent attempt to impose on their understanding.

That great and wanton augmentation of the federal debt in the year 1790, which arose from the assumption of those of the individual states, was founded on a very singular argument; it was said that this measure would have a tendency to cement the federal union. Why was it not foreseen that precisely the contrary must be the effect. While the state remained the debtor and its own citizens the creditor for neither of them could find relief by withdrawing from the union; the citizens in fact were all debtors, and as many of them as chose to be were creditors. But now they would both find relief by withdrawing, for by that act all the citizens of such a state would cease to be debtors, while the creditors would remain the same. These would have only to sell their stock and receive payment; and then that state would have nothing more to do with the burthens of the late war, nor with the subsequent accumulation of the national debt. If there can be an argument proper to engage a state or district to withdraw from the union, this is certainly one.

Perhaps I mistake the present temper of the American people, but it appears to me that the greatest risk we run of a dismemberment of the empire [30] arises from the magnitude of the debt. There are many other reasons why its progress ought to be arrested where it is, and the capital diminished as fast as possible; but the greatest of all reasons is the preservation of the federal system, on which our liberty and happiness most essentially depend. This argument, I apprehend, has not been sufficiently attended to [in] America.

Besides the magnitude of our debt, the manner of funding it has had a pernicious influence on the policy of our government with foreign powers. The payment of the interest was made to depend in a great measure on the duties to be levied on imported merchandise, which were by law appropriated for fifteen years to this object. This made every stock holder a partizan of our commercial connections with that country whose commerce with us was supposed principally to secure this revenue; however injurious those connections might become to the general interest of the United States. It is greatly owing to this unfortunate measure that our commerce has suffered so much during the present war from English and French depredations. For no one will deny that the latter were occasioned by our tame submission to the former.

Second: As the government belongs to the people, and not the people to the government, it is proper that the latter should be as accommodating as possible with regard to the place of its residence. The existing law by which the Congress has pledged itself to remove to the Federal City at a certain time, ought to suffer no delay in its execution, after that time arrives. If that law had carried the Federal City eighty or a hundred miles farther up the Potowmac, it would have been still more central, and doubtless would have had a greater effect in preserving the union entire.

[31] The article is trifling in itself; but every thing in this world goes by appearance. It would have been a mark of attention, a complaisance, an accommodation to our western brethren, that would have been worth millions in fixing their affections. It is doubtless too late to think of changing the resolution already taken by the legislature; but it would doubtless be impolitic to admit of a new delay, as many persons apprehend, in carrying it into effect.

Third: The opening of roads, and the improvement of water communication between the central and the frontier states should be objects of constant solicitude, not only to the state legislatures and to Congress, as far as may be in their power, but to patriotic individuals and companies, wherever they can reconcile private interest with so great a public benefit.

A facility of intercourse for the objects of commerce, travelling and the transportation of letters would have a powerful effect in assimilating our manner, and inspiring that confidence and friendship so necessary to the political union of men who feel themselves able at all times to change their connexions at pleasure.

A system of small canals, as projected by one of our most estimable citizens, on a plan so extensive as to take the place generally of public roads in the most frequented routes, may one day be presented to the consideration of the federal government. This is not the moment to enter into a development of the project, either in its political or fiscal operation. I will only observe that in both these views it would greatly serve to harmonise the interests of the states, and to strengthen their present union.

Fourth: A universal attention to the education of youth, and a republican direction given to the elementary articles of public instruction, are among [32] the most essential means of preserving liberty in any country where it is once enjoyed; especially in the United States. The representative system must necessarily degenerate, and become an instrument of tyranny, rather than of liberty, where there is an extraordinary disparity of information between the generality of the citizens and those who aspire to be their chiefs. And as to the federal ties between the different states, how shall they be maintained, but by extending the views and enlightening the minds of those whose votes are frequently to be consulted, and whose actions are always irresistible by their numbers, and the direction which they take.

Ignorance is every where such an infallible instrument of despotism, that there can be no hope of continuing even our present *forms* of government, either federal or state, much less that spirit of equal liberty and justice on which they were founded, but by diffusing universally among the people that portion of instruction which is sufficient to teach them their duties and their rights.

We must not content ourselves with saying, that education is an individual interest and a family concern; and that every parent, from a desire to promote the welfare of his children, will procure them the necessary instruction, as far as may be in his power, which will be enough for their station. These assertions are not true; parents are sometimes too ignorant, and often too inattentive or avaricious, to be trusted with the sole direction of their children; unless stimulated by some other motive than a natural sense of duty to them. Neither is it merely a family concern; it is a civil and even a political concern. The legislator and the magistrate neglect an essential part of their duty, if they do not provide the means and carry them into effect, for giving instruction to every member of the state.

[33] This may be done with very little expence, and with much less trouble than is generally imagined. The subject appears to me to

be too much neglected in the United States in general, considering that the preservation of liberty depends in a great measure upon it.

Fifth: What shall we say of those gigantic colonies that are forming on our frontiers, to the westward of the Mississipi, and to the northward of the lakes? These are germs of empire, which offer an immense field of meditation to the American politician. How soon, and by what combination of events, are they to become independent states.—When that day arrives, are they to be our rivals, and consequently our enemies, after the example of the states of Europe. Or can the way be prepared and they be persuaded to adopt our principles, to form with us a great union of political interests, and make of the whole but one confederated empire? These questions hurry the mind into an awful train of thought, which is difficult to methodize and delicate to communicate. Yet no branch of the enquiry is useless; since it contemplates an event the most important that can probably affect our Constitution; and one which a prudent conduct on our part may modify in a very considerable degree. I do not mean that it will be our duty to interfere in their present concerns, or to take any part in any dispute that may happen between them and their present governments, with a view to hasten or retard the moment of their separation. But it is essential, that we should so conduct our own affairs as to set such an example of rational liberty and public happiness, as they cannot fail to admire, and must therefore wish to partake.

Our frontier states, which border on theirs, must necessarily entertain an intimate and extensive intercourse [34] with them. Reciprocal migrations and intermarriages will be numerous between them; their commerce will be active; their manners, language and modes of education will be the same on both sides. The probability is, that if we do not induce them to join themselves to us, they will induce some of our extensive districts to quit us, and join with them.

But if at that day, the United States should be clear of debt, and should exhibit the singular phenomenon of a wise, impartial, and energetic government, reserving so much power to individual states as shall enable the people to regulate the great mass of their most interesting concerns at home, where they are best understood, and yet continuing a sufficient force in the federal head to insure at all times the means of giving protection and obtaining respect,—there can be no insuperable objection, and there may be a powerful inducement, for those new nations, to form their state governments after the model of ours, and to join our confederation.

I am aware of the inconvenience that might arise from the magnitude of this projected empire; as the colonies in question are spreading over a surface at least equal to that of the present United States. The objection is weighty, but my answer is at hand; by encountering this inconvenience, which is new, and therefore formidable in appearance, we avoid those that are infinitely more serious; though from being familiar and thought unavoidable they are less attended to. There is no political inconvenience so great as the neighbourhood of independent and rival nations. Their commercial restrictions, their military preparations, their fortified frontiers, their interfering jurisdictions, their whimsical and undefinable points of honor, give so many occasions of dispute in the minds of passionate or ambitious men, that such nations, if not always at [35] war, must be always in such a warlike postures as to present a perpetual image of the savage state, degrade the morals and devour the substance of the people.

Besides, I apprehend, that if we well consider the nature of a federal government, we shall have less reason to dread the extension of its limits. The objects of its legislation are few, according to our present system; and I have no doubt but this might still be simplified, without risk of lessening its energy. If its simplification should be found practicable, this circumstance may add to the inducements that our neighbours may one day have to join us in confederation, and may diminish on our side the inconvenience which many will apprehend from the first view of the case.

Though the Achaian and the Lycian confederacies were the most perfect that history has transmitted to us, we ought to recollect, that the former was overturned by refusing to admit the state of Sparta as a member; and the destruction of the latter was brought on by its excluding sixty cities which desired to join it.

The interest we shall have in inducing new nations to join our union, instead of being our rivals, is a strong argument, in addition to many others, for preserving at least as much power to our individual states as they now possess, and for not suffering any encroachment from the federal government. It is convenient, as well as inviting, for every section of a free people to regulate as many of their own affairs at home as is consistent with the interest of the whole. And when their federalizing with us depends on their own choice, they will be more likely to do it if the requisite sacrifice of power should be small, than if it should be great.

I hope none will infer from the observations in this article, that I am an advocate of *conquest,* in [36] any case whatever; and still less that I would extend the limits of a dominion by colonies and foreign possessions. Nothing is more destructive to liberty, both at home and abroad, than this sort of policy. There is no doubt (all other circumstances being equal) but small dominions are preferable to large ones. It is only to avoid the greater evils of the independence and rivalship of states, that I would consent to an extension of limits. And this would be scarcely tolerable, but on the federal plan; which I regard as one of the most useful and most consoling experiments to be found in the history of government. There is no knowing yet to what extent it may be carried.

Sixth: The more I reflect on the nature of political liberty, the more I am convinced that a military establishment of any magnitude is extremely incompatible with it. The most effectual way of preventing this, as well the surest mode of providing for the defence of the country, is by a universal attention to arming and disciplining the militia. When every citizen is a soldier, and every soldier will be a citizen, military exercise, to a certain degree, should be considered as a part of education; and though a subordinate part, it should not be neglected.

But it is happy for us that military life, as an exclusive object, is not yet become a profession in the United States. There are very few evils of a political kind that would be more subversive of their liberty. Ambition, which has been so destructive to national happiness, could scarcely be taken in a bad sense, but for its usual association with military fame. And if excellence in warlike achievements, in themselves considered, without regard to the cause, should once become an object of pursuit with the young men of America, it would soon be found impossible to keep us out of unnecessary [37] wars, and all the miseries and degradations of character that they entrain. The epidemy would seize, as usual, the richest and most influential families; the rage would become fashionable; it would be made an object of real profit, as well as of supposed honor. And how many votes, in the freest governments in Europe, have been given for war, from no other motive than that of providing places for sons, brothers, cousins, or the voters themselves?

War has hitherto been considered in America, I believe by every class of people, as a calamity to be avoided, in all possible cases by all rational means. It probably may be avoided, as long as we are out of the neighbourhood of independent nations; and as long as the ambition of our leading men shall be directed to the true interests of society.

[69]

AN IMPARTIAL CITIZEN

A Dissertation Upon the Constitutional
Freedom of the Press

BOSTON, 1801

T he first years of the nineteenth century witnessed a vituperative
dispute between the supporters of Jefferson and the recently ousted
Federalists. In certain respects it was a broader continuation of the
bitter debate over the Alien and Sedition Acts. Jefferson's opponents
attacked him mercilessly in the press as the agent of "leveling" in the
society, an agent for the excesses of the French Revolution, and far
worse. The viciousness of the charges hurled by both sides in the press
reached unprecedented levels, and the subject of what was acceptable
free speech and what constituted abuse of such in writing became
a major topic of discussion. This anonymous pamphlet is unusual
in its comprehensiveness, thoroughness, and level of analysis as well
as for its temperateness in an era, and on a
topic, not noted for it.

ADVERTISEMENT BY THE AUTHOR.

The freedom of the press is of vast importance to the United States; it depends,
for its constitutional definition, upon natural, simple principles; there is no
abstruse learning on the subject. It ought to be settled, and understood by the
body of freemen, whose votes in elections, and whose verdicts as jurymen, are
to maintain it, according to its constitutional principles.

This essay is the first attempt of the kind in America. Whoever reads the
production, will find, that it is not written under the influence of any party.
Some of each party will be displeased with it. But as it is composed with a

sincere desire to enlighten, and inform the whole body of the people, in a matter of great consequence to their liberty and safety, the author is by no means anxious in regard to the opinions of men, who have forsaken principle, and devoted themselves to party. He will, indeed, consider himself as unfortunate in this production, unless it shall be abused, mutilated, misunderstood, and misapplied, as is usual in such cases. Should he be charged with being ambitious to be President, Governor, Judge, Senator, or any thing else, he allows the charge;—only read the book, and attend to the truths it contains, and his wishes are accomplished.

[3]   A PREFACE BY THE AUTHOR.

Where shall the true art of exercising power without tyranny, or authority without pusillanimity be found? The idea of power is noble, and sublime; we tremble at it, when we conceive it to be uncontrollable and irresistible. We stand in awful diffidence before it; because our first conceptions of its form admit of no modifications or restraint. But the moment it has become familiar to our senses, and we have conceived the idea of rendering it subservient to our will, the apprehension of terror vanishes, and we soon treat it with indifference and contempt. Strength is the first indication of power, but when the horse is broken to the bit, or the ox subdued to the yoke, the sublime and terrible, which had before associated themselves with the dread of strength, are done away. The tyger and the wolf excite emotions of terror, but the mastiff and the spaniel recline on our bosoms.

The ancient nations were well acquainted with all the feelings of the human heart. Homer carried his hero, under the contested protection of a multitude of gods, through dangers and distresses, through voyages and shipwrecks, through victories and defeats, to lay the foundation of the Grecian empire. The Greeks brought their civil institutions from Egypt, where, as it was then believed, the gods had promulgated laws for mankind. This was done, that the laws [4] should be respected by the people. The Romans founded an empire, by the man who had been nursed by a wolf; and their poet, in imitation of Homer, to render their origin respectable, and their religious and civil institutions sacred, detailed the perils, and wars, and the interposition of the gods, which carried the first of their race to the spot, which was admired by earth, and protected by heaven.

Before the christian religion was respected in Europe, fabulous deities were called in, to take a part in the inauguration of kings; and the laws were framed by the Druids, who lived sequestered from the world, and were considered as having an intercourse with heaven. As soon as christianity was established, the divine right of kings was proclaimed, as from heaven; and miraculous signs, and terrible wonders, were observed at the birth of princes, and the coronation of monarchs.

The English nation have had so many changes in the dynasty of their throne, that they were compelled, by a sense of decency, to abandon the divine right of earthly sovereigns, and the peculiar efficacy of the royal blood. A sacred regard to a constitution, much talked of, no where on paper, and highly respected, because it has never been seen, forms the main bond of that vigorous and efficient government.

But where shall we, placed in the going down of the sun; we, who have been familiar with our own origin, and have created ourselves; we, who are but of yesterday, find a substitute equal to the exigency of our situation? Composed of millions, who widely differ in their educations, habits, manners, pursuits and [5] designs, what shall hold us together as a nation? Our constitution of national government is in our own hands, like the school books; we know the men who formed it. They have not, like Solon, banished themselves from the country, nor like the Druids, sequestered themselves from the world. They remain among us, as men of like passions, subjected to the same errors, follies and weakness, as other men. So far are they from boasting of an inspiration in this work, that neither two of them can agree to understand the instrument in the same sense.

We not only have this thing in our own hands, familiar to our senses, but it informs us, that it is in our own power, subject to any alterations we may choose to make in it. How then shall we dress it in the sublime and noble? How shall we decorate it in the venerable habiliments of a mysterious and supernatural origin? How shall we raise and maintain a permanent awe and reverence for it? Shall we change it for a more incontestible power, by adopting an hereditary executive, in the room of an elective chief magistrate? Behold the divine right of kings is done away! their persons are no longer sacred! but the throne is the rallying point of faction, and the supporter of the standard of civil war. Round this the partizans collect their forces, under various pretexts, but to gain the same object, the prostration of power, and the plunder of the people.

Shall we restore the days of ignorance, and fanaticism, and return to the dark ages, when rulers shall be considered as gods, though we see them die as men? Alas! the days of religious enthusiasm, founded [6] in the ignorance of mankind, are the days of tyranny and calamity.

Shall we rely on our boasted dissemination of knowledge and learning, and fly to our churches, colleges, academies and schools, as the ancients did, in their distress, to the temples of their gods? Here we find that learning is but the spy of sorrow, and that a great part of it is expended in describing troubles which can never happen, or in attempts to overturn the civil state, that contending parties may gain a lucrative and powerful standing.

Since then the real happiness of our country has no kind of connexion with those boisterous struggles; since every violent contention serves to distract the people, and weaken the social compact, since the destruction of our constitution will annihilate our existence as a nation, and render us wretched as citizens, and miserable as men, we will attach ourselves to that glorious system; we will hold in contempt the few, who fill the atmosphere with seditious libels, base calumnies, and false reasonings, and, rallying round the constitution, we will, in the character of brethren, live and die like freemen, honorably associated for civil happiness, and the promotion of our country's honour and interest.

[7]   DISSERTATION

When the constitution of the United States was formed, there was no provision in regard to the freedom of the press; the general convention left it to the common understanding, and established opinion of the people. But the conventions, which were called in the several states, to ratify the instrument, exhibited proposals for an explicit recognition of the privilege, as it had been used and approved in the country. Upon this, the first Congress, by way of amendment to the Constitution, resolved, that "Congress shall make no law respecting an establishment of religion, or prohibiting the free exercise thereof, or abridging the freedom of speech, *or of the press,* or of the right of the people, peaceably to assemble, and to petition the government for a redress of grievances."

Previously to this, there had been express provision made, in several of the states, to prevent an abridgment of the liberty of the press. In New Hampshire, it was declared, that "the liberty of the press is essential to the security of the freedom of a state: it ought therefore to be inviolably preserved."

In Massachusetts it is thus expressed in the declaration of rights prefixed to the constitution; "The liberty of the press is essential to the security of freedom in a state: it ought not, therefore, to be restrained in this commonwealth."

As new constitutions were not formed in the states of Rhode Island, and Connecticut, there was not, in either of those states, any declaration upon the subject. The freedom of the press was well understood in those states; [8] and the common, public opinion of the citizens in them, was established in unison with the declarations made by the others.

The convention which formed the constitution of the state of New York, and the people whose authority ratified it, contented themselves with declaring, ordaining, and determining, "that such parts of the common law of England, with the statutes adopted, and the acts of their own legislature, as together did form the law of the colony in the year 1775 shall continue, subject to the alterations of the legislature." They then considered the freedom of the press as established by the common law; and were under no apprehensions, that a legislature, frequently elected by the people, would ever be induced to lay an undue restraint upon a privilege so important, as that of a free communication of sentiment on public measures.

The state of Pennsylvania, is more explicit in its constitution on this subject. The provision there is, "that the printing presses shall be free to every one who undertakes to examine the proceedings of the legislature, or any branch of government; and no law shall ever be made to restrain the right thereof. The free communication of thoughts and opinions, is one of the invaluable rights of man; and every citizen may freely write and print, on any subject, being responsible for the abuse of that liberty. In the prosecutions for publications of papers, investigating the official conduct of officers, or men of public capacity, or where the matter published is proper for public information, the truth thereof may be given in evidence. And, in all indictments for libels, the jury shall have a right to determine the law and the facts, under the direction of the court, as in other cases."

The state of Maryland said no more than "that the liberty of the press ought to be inviolably preserved."

An Impartial Citizen

The state of Virginia seems to rest the guardianship of this important privilege on the common understanding, and the enlightened prudence of the people.

In North Carolina it was declared, "that the freedom [9] of the press, is one of the great bulwarks of liberty, and therefore ought never to be restrained."

South Carolina committed the privilege to the keeping of the common law, as understood by the people.

In Georgia it was declared, that "freedom of the press, and trial by jury, should remain inviolate."

In Vermont it was declared, "that the people have a right of freedom of speech, and of writing and publishing their sentiments, concerning the transactions of government; and therefore the freedom of the press ought not to be restrained."

In the States of Tennessee and Kentucky, the declarations on the freedom of the press are the same. "That the printing presses shall be free to every person who undertakes to examine the proceedings of the legislature, or any branch or officer of government: and no law shall ever be made to restrain the right thereof. The free communication of thoughts and opinions, is one of the invaluable rights of man; and every citizen may freely speak, write, and print on any subject, being responsible for the abuse of that liberty. But in prosecutions for the publication of papers investigating the official conduct of officers, or men in public capacity, the truth thereof may be given in evidence; and in all indictments for libels, the jury shall have a right to determine the law, and the facts, under the direction of the court, as in other cases."

This subject is treated as a matter of great importance by the Congress of the general government, as well as by the conventions of the greater part, and by all the people of the United States. Their wishes seem to be concentrated in a principle, which they conceive to be highly interesting to the whole nation, and of great account in the establishment, and preservation of free governments. The systems they were forming, were to be rested, for support, on the opinions of the people at large; and it would therefore have been a great degree of remissness in their procedure, to have left any thing in the [10] way of a free, open, and universal communication of sentiments upon public men, and public measures, where the same should be necessary to maintain the principles of the constitutions they were forming.

The conventions of the states; and the Congress of the United States, use the word *press* as descriptive of the free communication of ideas and sentiments, by the art of printing. This kind of figure, in speech, where the continent is used for the contents; the appellation of the cause as a description of the effect; or the power which produces, for the product obtained, is very common in all languages. By the freedom of the press they undoubtedly intended *an unrestrained use, and free improvement of the privilege of writing, and printing, in the communication of sentiments and opinions, on matters of public concernment, governmental measures, and political procedure.* Not a licentious and destructive abuse of the privilege, in such a manner, as that wicked and malicious men should gratify their resentment, malevolence, and revenge, to the overthrow of family reputation, and the ruin of their neighbor's character.

In order to define the meaning of the liberty of the press, as established in the country, I shall,

First, Endeavor to shew how far it may be considered as free, in regard to the rights of individual members of the community, in their private capacities.

Secondly, How far it may be restrained, consistently with the principles of the constitutions of our governments, in regard to men, in their public official character and conduct.

Thirdly, How far it may be restrained in regard to the measures of government, and in questions of elections.

Fourthly, Shall make some observations, on a late act of Congress, which has furnished so much fuel for the fire of party zeal.

It seems to be an agreed principle, that government is instituted for the public good; and to preserve, in safety, the lives, the happiness, the interests, the characters, and the estates of all those, who are combined to [11] maintain it; and who have consented to become the subjects of it. In the social compacts, which we denominate constitutions, no more is surrendered or given up, than what is supposed to be necessary to the safety, and well being of the whole. So much is consequently retained, as cannot, in the nature of the government, be defended and protected by the powers of the association. The right of conscience, as to the forms and principles of devotion, cannot be ceded, and given up, because this is a matter between a man and God, the high and holy creator and preserver of all things, and man can have no control over it. Reputation, and character, are of great consequence to the happiness and enjoyment of human life, and therefore, these are never sacrificed to government, but are jewels of inestimable value, deposited carefully, to the safe keeping of the constitution, and the protection of the laws. The whole society has an interest in the reputation of each individual member, as in a part of the wealth and happiness of the community.

There is an invaluable right, which the society has in the good character of each individual of which it is composed. In order to demonstrate this, nothing more is necessary, than to conceive of the distress and misery of a community, composed of men, who have no moral principle, and who are totally regardless of character, integrity, and truth. It has been said, and perhaps was never disputed, that the founders of Rome were a banditti, a collection of robbers; but this cannot be understood, as meaning any thing more, than that they were regardless of the natural rights of other tribes, and did not attend to the law of nations, which in later times has governed, in some measure, the conduct of independent nations towards each other. The hordes, clans, or tribes of all that part of the world were then hostile to each other; and the Romans, no doubt, made an accession of strength by receiving fugitives from justice into their society; there must have been, nevertheless, a great degree of public and private virtue, to lay the foundation, and to raise so powerful an association, as that of the Roman empire. The Romans not only began [12] very early, to inculcate the principles of morality and virtue, but they made a good character the qualification to office, and the preliminary condition of public confidence.

The laws of all civilized nations provide for the protection of character, by the punishment of slander, as a crime against the public, and by giving a remedy in damages at the suit of the party injured. In our laws, the words which are considered as slander, are very well defined, and are classed, as those which have a tendency to expose the person of whom they are uttered to a prosecution for an offence against the public, and those which injure him, or have a tendency to injure him in his prospects, business, or profession. A distinction is also made between those words above described, and words which proceed from sudden heat and passion; such as calling one a rascal, liar, villain, &c. These are lightly provoking, and frequently produce very fatal consequences between the parties, and which might, perhaps, be avoided by the provision of a legal remedy.

The distinction between words proceeding from malice, and those which are only from sudden heat and passion, is lost, when they are committed to paper; because that every act of writing is deliberate, and the party has time to reflect, and is therefore deprived of the excuse of a sudden gust of passion or resentment. This distinction is founded in the nature of man, and is therefore a constituent part of the laws of every society.

But there is yet something more in the nature of this distinction. Words vanish in air, unless the injury really done by speaking them has, from peculiar circumstances, an abiding effect on the character against whom they are spoken; but words written, or signs made to impress the senses, may do a lasting injury. Hence it has been always holden, that erecting a gallows at a man's door, is punishable, and so is the making of any other sign, or picture, as expressive of his deserving an infamous punishment, or the drawing signs, or pictures, expressive of his having committed crimes, or of his being a scandalous, abandoned, or wicked man. These have not [13] only a tendency to injure him personally, but they have also a strong tendency to injure his family, and connexions, who may have good characters, even if his is not good.

This kind of abuse has no tendency to correct the morals of the man against whom it is uttered, but may stimulate him to revenge; and thereby endanger the peace of the society. If the man is proveably guilty of crimes, let him be exposed to punishment, according to the laws; if there is no proof, he ought not to have a slanderous accusation exhibited without proof, in a manner which will not admit of a defence; and which might, by creating a prejudice against him, deprive him of a defence on a future trial. If the charge by way of libel is only for foibles, or weakness of character, it is a crime against the community to publish it; because no one is without his failings, and if you have a right to expose those of one man, you have a right to expose those of all, and that respect yielded from one member of the community to the character of another, and which forms a strong band in social life, would be subverted; the bands of society essentially weakened, examples to virtue and goodness, would appear to be generally beclouded by the infirmities naturally incident to human kind, so as to form excuses for licentiousness, and apologies for voluntary errors. It is therefore prudent, on principles of social economy, to let those instances, which mark the imperfection of human nature, remain without comment, or public exposure. This is not a new idea, either in theory or practice. We all know the force of example, and the overbearing power of fashion. We all know the restraint resulting from the disapprobation of men whom we consider, as having attained to a high degree of perfection in morals and propriety of conduct. We all venerate the eye of prudence, and stand reproved by the countenance of matured discretion. Why then should an unprofitable and malignant licentiousness be allowed to subvert a most urgent stimulus to virtue, and to weaken, or destroy, one of the most powerful restraints upon vice?

[14] All men will say, that this ought not to be, in a free and equal government; and that every government will, for its own sake, and for the sake of justice, defend the characters of all its members and subjects, from that kind of slander, which, from mere circumstances of human weakness, will expose a man, and his posterity, to contempt and ridicule; and much more, from that slander, which, when rendered permanent by ink and paper, or by signs and pictures, will wrap a character in infamy, spread it abroad in disgrace, and hand it down to posterity in the habiliments of guilt. Yet it may be, that some honest advocate for the freedom of the press will say, that though slander committed to paper with the pen, ought to be punished, yet there is a sacred respect due to the press, and that the slander which issues from the type is a different thing.

If that slander, which comes from the press, is less injurious than that which comes immediately from the quill, it must be, because that which is printed is not so worthy of credit, as that is, which is seen in manuscript only. This idea is not only opposed to the freedom, but to the usefulness of the press; for if it is agreed, that what issues from the press does not deserve credit, merely because it is produced under that form, then there is a want of confidence in this manner of communication, and consequently the press has lost all its valuable usefulness. But a production from the type, if the press has equal credit with a manuscript communication, as the circle of communication is, in that way, increased in its diameter, so the injury is increased in its magnitude; and therefore the slander from the press is the most injurious, and most to be dreaded.

But still there may be a question, whether a restraint can be laid on the press, so as to protect the individuals of society, in their private capacity, from libels and slander, and yet preserve the freedom of printing, so as fully to answer the intentions of the people, in their attempts to preserve the freedom of the press, as essential to the support of a free government.

The affirmative of this argument would rest on the [15] advocate for an unrestrained liberty of the press. He would have to prove, that such a restraint, as would protect individual characters from printed slanders, is incompatible with that freedom of printing, which is necessary to the maintenance of a free form of government. All I can say, is, that I do not discover the least degree of incompatibility in the question. How can the privilege of slandering our neighbours with impunity, be of necessity to the maintenance of a free government? To the support of a tyranny, it may be necessary, because, that every thing which derogates from the respectability of the people, increases the power of the despot, and serves to evince the necessity of a despotism.

Even though the libel is true, yet being unjustifiably published, because it is not done in support of a claim of right, or in a legal prosecution, the truth of it cannot be given in evidence, as a justification; because there is no necessity for the publication of it. This has always been the principle in the European governments, from the time of the Romans* to the present day. In England we find the principle sacredly maintained, from the earliest times. In the 5th of Coke's Reports it was decided, that a libel is a malicious defamation, expressed either in printing or writing, page 121; the same Report also determines that to be a libel, which is in signs, or pictures, if it is defamatory. Skinner's Reports, 123, maintain the same principle. Hobart, 253, has the same doctrine; and Hawkins, 93, and all the later writers and decisions, give us the same as law.

The first settlers in this country, considered themselves as subjects of the English government, and declared, "that they came here as free born subjects of the kingdom of Great Britain; endowed with all the privileges belonging to such."† And further declared, "that no person should suffer in his life, limb, or liberty, [16] *good, name* or estate,

---

* "Vel si quis ad infamiam alicujus libellum aut carmen, aut historiam scripserit, composuerit," &c.

"By the Roman law, the author or publisher of an infamous libel might be punished with death if it brought another man's life into danger; but if it did not he was deprived of capacity of giving testimony."

† Old Colony Laws.

under color of law, but by some express law of the general court of this colony, *or the good and equitable laws of our nation,* suitable for us, in matters which are of a civil nature, as by the court here hath been accustomed, wherein we have had no particular law of our own."

This declaration proves, that the first settlers of the country, claimed the principles of the English common law, so far as these were suitable to the situation of the country, as their privilege; and they trusted in the wisdom and prudence of their courts of justice, to determine what part of those principles was suited to their circumstances. No law was ever made before the revolution, to give an action for slander, whether the same was uttered in words, in writing, in print, or otherwise; yet such actions have been maintained on the principles of common law, ever since the first settlement of the country. This must have been done on the idea of the efficiency of the common law, which had been adopted and practised upon here. The common law, is a system of commonly received opinions, established by the common consent of the people, without acts of the legislature, and defined by practice in the courts of law. The idea of having a government, which does not give a remedy in such cases, must be the result of an opinion, either, that character is of no value, or that each subject is left as in a state of nature, by the force of his own arm, to protect that which is most dear to him, to his family, and to his posterity. Where this is the state of society, there ought to be no law against *duels,* or *assassination;* for those who have strength and kill to do it, ought to be allowed to defend their reputation by open combat; while those of less courage, or weaker bodies, ought to be indulged in private assassination, by way of revenge, on the principle of the *lex talionis.*

It is a fact, that among the advocates for an unrestrained license of the press, we find some of the most resentful persons, when they are themselves, attacked in that mode of slander. It would, indeed, be a strange, unreasonable conclusion, that though a man was to have a [17] remedy, in all cases, against *written* slander, yet that the *type* should render the evil so sacred, that when the same libel shall be issued from the press, the virtue of that form shall render the publication of it a justifiable act.

It may be well to examine, whether any of the declarations, made by the people on this subject, can have a construction tending to maintain so unreasonable and dangerous a hypothesis.

The constitution of the United States provides, that Congress shall "make no law abridging the freedom of speech or of the press." It would be as reasonable to conclude, that, as Congress can make no law to abridge the freedom of speech, every one is at liberty to utter, in words spoken, what slander he pleases, with impunity, as to conclude, that because Congress can make no law to abridge the freedom of the press; every one may be allowed to print and publish, of his neighbor, what slanders he pleases to publish. But take this, declaration upon the same principles of construction, as other declarations, acts and productions are taken; that is according to the subject matter of it, and it can have no other meaning than this, that the measures of the government of the United States shall, at all times, and on all occasions, be open to a public examination in the press. How such an examination is to be conducted, according to the provisions of the constitution, is to be the subject of another section.

The constitution of Massachusetts, declares, that "the liberty of the press is essential to the security of freedom in a state." But this can never have a construction, to render printed slander against those whom the constitution has agreed to defend, as justifiable; when the same constitution declares, "that the end of government is to furnish the individuals who compose it, with the power of enjoying, in safety, and tranquillity their natural rights, and the blessings of life." To believe, that men, under the pressure of calumny, and overborne with slander, can enjoy the blessings of life in tranquillity, is to suppose, that they have lost all sense of [18] honor and reputation, and are no more than savage barbarians.

The same declaration in New Hampshire, will have the same construction. The state of Pennsylvania, provides for the freedom of writing and printing, but, also provides, that he who prints, or writes, shall be responsible for the abuse of the liberty he has exercised.

The other states make the same declaration, that the liberty of the press is essential to a free government, and that it ought therefore to be inviolably preserved. But none of them intimate an idea, that such a due, and proper restraint, as shall be adequate to the preservation of the characters of individuals from slander, would be an undue restraint, or by any means amount to such a restraint, as would endanger the freedom of the government, or be subversive of the principles of civil liberty.

Since the history of the human race exhibits full evidence, that in every age of the world, a good name has been esteemed as precious ointment, and as of the highest value, it would be a very strange, and unfortunate circumstance, if in this enlightened day, and in this free and highly civilized country, we could not maintain our governments, without a constitutional license to calumny and detraction.

The freedom of the press, in regard to men in public stations, is of, at least, as much consequence, as it is in regard to private individuals. The idea, that a man's being in office, renders him a fit mark for the malignant arrows of slander, is no less injurious to the rights of individual citizens, than it is to the government at large. It cannot be considered as of no importance to a man, whether he shall have, an opportunity to improve his talents in his country's service; whether he shall share in the honors of his government, or enjoy the confidence of his nation. Every one has a right, by fair and honest means, to possess himself of a place in the administration of government, and to obtain an office, which, while it renders him useful to the public, will promote the honor and happiness of his family. But if, as soon as he is in office his enemies, and others, have a right [19] to defame his character, and to charge him with corruption and wickedness in his public conduct, or even to represent him, through the press, as a weak, unsuitable person for the office, the best part of the community, the men, who hold a good character, as of high value, will not run the hazard of holding an office or place; and of course, the worst and most unsuitable men will be called forward to take the care of the government: and thus by the power of their own slanders, gain an opportunity to plunder the people.

There can be no man of any consideration, who will sacrifice his own reputation, by advancing it as a principle, that the press shall be free to abuse and slander a man, merely because he holds a public office; but there are some who believe, that a libel against a magistrate, or public officer, may be justified, by proving the charge in the libel to be true. There are declarations in the constitutions of Pennsylvania, and the Tennessee states, which maintain the idea, that, "in prosecutions for publications of papers, investigating the official conduct of officers, and men of public capacity, or where the matter published is proper for public information, the truth thereof may be given in evidence."

These states having made this provision, there can be no doubt but that men may publish what they shall please within them, on the official conduct of men in office, provided they have their proof ready at hand to maintain the charge. But even this is a restraint upon the press; for if any thing is published which cannot be proved, the author and publisher, are liable to prosecutions and severe punishment. I do not know what the law, in this respect, had before been in Pennsylvania; the other state did not exist previously to its present constitution which formed it; but in the other states, such a provision if taken in a literal sense, unconnected with the subject matter, would have been an express alteration of the common law, as before used and practiced in them.

In the other states, there may be question, whether the liberty of the press, guarded in their constitutions, [20] as an important privilege, has or has not the same meaning as is expressed in the constitution of Pennsylvania. New Hampshire says the liberty of the press ought to be inviolably *preserved*. Massachusetts says it ought not to be *restrained*. Maryland says the liberty of the press ought to be inviolably *preserved*. North Carolina and Georgia say the press ought not to be *restrained*. The states not mentioned, leave it to the public opinion, according to the principles of the common law, as used and practiced upon in them.

As by the common law of England, adopted and practiced upon in the several states before the revolution, the truth of a libel, or written or printed slander, could not be given in evidence to justify the publication, the question is, whether such an alteration is made, by the declarations recited, or by the nature of the governments in the nation, and in the several states, as shall place this principle of a footing similar to what it is, in the states of Pennsylvania, Kentucky and Tennessee. The restraint guarded against, is not defined in any of those states, and it is said, that the liberty of the press shall be inviolably preserved, there is do definition of what that liberty of the press is. But the main object is apparent; that there shall be no such restraint upon the printing, and publishing sentiments, and opinions upon public men and measures, as shall prevent a free and necessary communication of ideas, for the preservation of liberty and the support of the principles of the constitution. I therefore conclude, that these constitutions have not changed the common law principle adopted and uniformly acknowledged in the country; nor do they differ essentially from those of the other states.

When we come to consider the evils, and injuries, which would result from a justification of a written or printed libel, or defamation against a public officer, and see that no public advantage can possibly arise from it, every reasonable man will be contented with the old settled form of principle.

I here mean to make a distinction between a charge made in a publication against an officer, for his having [21] corruptly taken bribes, or having acted wrong and unjustly from corrupt motives, and the act which may have proceeded either from such motives or from others indiscriminately. In the next section, under the liberty of the press, in regard to the measures of government, I mean to maintain, that it cannot be criminal to publish what the government in fact does, and that therefore the truth of the publication may be given in evidence, as a justification under the prosecution. But I am now speaking of a charge of corruption, for which a magistrate, or public officer, may be removed from his office, or punished *criminaliter,* for the fraud or corruption; or be displaced for weakness, incapacity, or impropriety of conduct in his official capacity.

There may be a question, what good a publication, charging a public officer with corruption, can do? If he feels himself guilty, he will never procure a prosecution for the libel. If the publisher of the charge has the evidence to maintain it, he may lay it before a legal and proper tribunal, with much less trouble than he can go to the press. Unless the charge is altogether groundless, and he knows it to be so, he runs no hazard by a prosecution before a grand jury and a competent court. Even though he shall fail, unless his attempt is groundless and malicious, he is not liable to damages. What advantage, can then result from printing a charge, which, if true, can be inquired into by a court of justice, where the man charged will have a fair chance to defend himself, if he is innocent, and the public the advantage of punishing him, if he is guilty?

If a citizen has a privilege of consequence enough to contend for, it is that of a fair, impartial, and candid trial when he becomes the subject of a criminal prosecution. But if he can be, before, charged in a gazette, with the same crime, the public opinion will be forestalled, and there can be no certainty of obtaining a fair trial by a jury. The *publication* of the corruption, or weakness of an officer's conduct, can be no foundation for his removal; for the gazette is no evidence in itself, nor can any court take cognizance of a charge made in that manner. It [22] may be said, that an unrestrained license to publish on the conduct of public men, would operate as a restraint upon them, and thus promote the public good; but this is not true; an unrestrained license to publish slander against public officers, would very soon be improved, by men who wish their removal, and by others who resent the uprightness of their conduct, or who have private quarrels with them on other occasions, in such a manner that the slanders uttered from the press, though rendered of less consequence, and received as matters of course, would, while they wound the feelings of him to whom they shall be pointed, pass unnoticed as to public prosecutions, and answer no possible valuable purpose to the community.

If the officers of government are guilty of corruption or fraud, there are tribunals to punish them; the grand jury may indict, and the house of representatives, on the supported complaint of an individual, may impeach before the senate; and, in nearly all the states, there may be a removal from office for weakness and incapacity; but, where there is no power of removal, the publication of the officer's incapacity can do no good; and, where there is such power, the publication can furnish no grounds for a removal.

Yet it may be asked, why the truth, in regard to the officer's corruption and fraud, shall not be published? The answer is, that if it could be rendered certain, that nothing but the truth would, under such license, be published, there might be less objection to it. For then the mere publication would amount to proof of his guilt, and he might be removed, or otherwise punished without a trial. But this idea is against the tenor of all our constitutions. No man is to be condemned until his crime has been fully and plainly described to him, nor until he has had an opportunity to be heard in his own defence. Should a charge be made in the gazette against a public officer, he would be, if he was innocent, under some necessity to commence, or to procure to be commenced, a prosecution against the printer or author, or against both, more especially if they could give the [23] truth of the charge in evidence to defend themselves; otherwise he might be supposed to be afraid to bring his conduct into legal disquisition. This would give a first, or principal, magistrate business enough to do, without attending to matters of state. Every transaction must be opened and explained before a jury, and the secrets of the state, in many instances at least, be exposed, in order to maintain prosecutions against men of no consequence, but who would hope to rise, even from a conviction and punishment.

There is therefore, no doubt, but that the declaration, on this subject, in Pennsylvania, has a restrained meaning, and is not intended to be taken altogether in its literal sense. Whatever a government, or officer of state does in his civil capacity, must be open, and public acts. The president's appointments, his embassies and treaties, the laws, resolves, and orders of the legislature, the judgments and decisions of the judges and magistrates, are all public acts; they not only may be, but they ought to be made public through the press. If they are wrong, the people ought to know it, if they are right, they ought to be given to the public. But these ought to be accurately and truly published; and there ought not to be a publication, or assertion of public acts or proceedings, which had never been made or done. When a publication of this kind is made, it is fit and reasonable that the truth should be a justification. If the acts done or passed are wrong, yet as errors may happen without corruption, the existence of the act can be no justification of a charge of bribery or corruption, or of an intent, or combination to overthrow the government, or to subvert the liberties of the people; and therefore the proof of the act can be no justification of a charge of treason or corruption in them, or him who effected it. There can therefore be no reason to believe that Pennsylvania ever intended any thing more, than a mere license to publish what had been in fact done by the government, or by its officers, in an official capacity, independent of any charge for gross immoralities, corruptions or frauds, by them personally committed.

[24] To explain this idea more fully, it may be observed, that a league or combination in a president, governor, or other magistrate, to subvert or change the form or nature of the government by force, and without the consent of the people, given in the form which is provided by the constitution, is treason of itself, treason, even though there should never, in fact, be an open attempt, or an overt act in pursuance of it. There could be no necessity for gazette publications on this point, because a public prosecution for a crime of the first magnitude ought to be immediately commenced. But should there be such publication made, on full proof, the nature of the case, and public jeopardy, would justify it. The league, or combination being fairly stated, the public would be left to determine, how far the danger had been extended, and the tribunals of justice, how far it amounted to treason, and whether the nature of the combination *truly given* through the press is not a justifiable act.

When a judge, magistrate, or any officer, civil or executive, shall take a bribe in his office, to induce him to do wrong, or shall, by extortion, take that, which he has no right to take, in order to induce him to do that, which it was his duty to do without, whether any thing is done in consequence of it, or not, it is a crime in itself, and is not the subject of a gazette essay, but a matter for an indictment, or impeachment, and ought to be taken up in that way. The act done in consequence of such bribe, or the corrupt refusal, when it is the officer's duty to act, are distinct facts from the crimes of bribery or extortion. They may be criminal, or they may be only an error of judgment; and as they may, or may not proceed from corruption, so they are, or are not punishable as crimes, as they are, or are not connected with corrupt motives. But bribery and extortion, are crimes in themselves, simply considered, without a connexion with any consequent act or denial. Whatever an officer, therefore, does, or whatever he denies to do, may be published, without the danger of being charged with a libel, unless the fact published is false. But publishing, that he had received a bribe, is charging [25] him with a crime in an open and public manner, where no proof can be offered against him, where he can by no means make a defence, and where there is no existing tribunal to render judgment.

Should it be said, that the person who is made the subject of the libel, may have his action, or prosecution against the printer, and that the truth of the libel may, on that be investigated, the answer is, that this would be unreasonable and unjust, because it would involve all public servants of the people in litigatious suits to discharge themselves from accusation, which would never be produced against them by a grand jury, or by a judicial inquest. Besides this, if there could be one libel, there could be a hundred for the same thing; and if these publications, had any weight in the public opinion, they would create a prejudice, which would deprive the party injured of a fair and impartial trial. This is in its nature, an opposition to the principle expressed in the constitution of Massachusetts, and maintained by the tenor of all the others, that no man shall be held to answer to a charge for a crime, until the same shall be fairly and fully described to him.

The simple fact of an officer's having done, or refused to have done, any thing in his office, is not a charge of criminality against him, yet if it is false and malicious, and he shall be injured, or receive any special damage by such publication, he may have his remedy by an action for the libel, and be recompensed in such sum of money as a jury shall adjudge to be adequate.

The transactions of government, may, in some instances be wrong, and even unconstitutional, and yet the authors, and agents have no corrupt intentions. These may all be published, and their consequences be detailed, and dilated upon, without charging the men who effect the measure with crimes. When the earl of Chatham in his nervous language said, that the earl of Bute had brought the king and kingdom of Great Britain to the brink of ruin, he did not charge him with a crime, because, as the earl of Bute had been prime minister, this might all have been done by him, from error and weakness; [26] and without any corrupt intention. But had Chatham charged Bute with having done this, *with a traitorous intention* to overthrow the government, or dethrone the king, he would have charged him with a crime: or had he charged him with a *conspiracy* against his sovereign, or of having *corruptly received a stipend from another sovereign,* there must have been an inquiry into the fact. Should it so happen, that when the measures of any department of the government, shall be published, the people shall be alarmed, and dark jealousies shall arise; should there be false consequences drawn, and erroneous reasonings be exhibited on the tendency and consequences of those measures, there can be no possible way to cure such an evil, but by giving to patience, and experience their perfect work.

There are other cases, where the exercise of the liberty of the press may injure individual citizens, and yet the truth of what is published, or the causes and circumstances of the publication, must excuse the author and printer from punishment. A man allows his friends to propose him to an office under the suffrages of the people; and others undertake to examine his character, and to shew that he is unfit for the office. In this case, there are no decisions, or legally established opinions, to guide our inquiries, and we can therefore only reason on the question, according to what is conceived to be the principles of reason and justice; and we may gain understanding from the practice of nations on the subject. On the one hand, it will not do to say, that when a man is proposed as a suitable character to fill an office to be given by the suffrages of the people, that his incapacity, incompetency, or inability to sustain it, shall not be asserted with as much publicity as the proposal of his election is. This would be, to allow any one, however unsuitable he may be, to palm himself upon the people, to the great injury of the nation. We therefore, have a right, through the medium of the press, to communicate our opinions, in regard to the character of every candidate, and to assign our reasons for those opinions. The press is as free for him and his friends, to combat our [27] opinions, and to shew that our reasons are not supported on good foundations, or to vindicate his character from false aspersions, tending to shew him to be no proper candidate, as it is for us to call his eligibility or competency into question. On the other hand, it will not do, to allow men, merely because one is nominated to office, to charge him falsely, and maliciously, with crimes, and scandalous conduct, for which he ought by law to be punished, or which would, if he is guilty, amount to a disqualification to office. Yet if he is thus guilty, he who proclaims this to the public, and thus prevents a villain from obtaining the public confidence, to which he has no just pretensions, does his country an essential service.

In this case the party who may be charged with a libel against another, is taken out of the reach of the principle, that he who publishes a libel against another, cannot be allowed to justify the publication by the truth of the facts. This question would be decided on the same principles, as that where a suit or prosecution is brought before a proper tribunal authorised to discuss, and decide on the question. The candidate opens his claim to the public, every member of the community has an interest in the event, the whole people are to decide on the question, he constitutes them his judges, and there is no other way to bring the question before the public, than by the press; and therefore every one in the community, has a right, in the same way, to lay his objections before the people, in order to prevent the election.

In all cases of criminal prosecutions, each citizen has a right to exhibit his complaint against another, and no action or prosecution lies against him for it, unless it is done maliciously, and groundlessly. Whether it was done maliciously, or not, will appear, generally, from those circumstances which shew, whether it were groundless or not. So in the case of an election, the publisher of any thing against the candidate, which in itself, is defamatory and scandalous, ought to be responsible; and heavy and aggravated damages ought to be given, unless [28] he can justify himself on the truth of the publication. But if he publishes the truth only, he ought to be allowed to justify his conduct upon the proof of the facts; and in such case the plaintiff by

An Impartial Citizen

his action, will only expose his own folly and weakness, in attempting to gain an office, to which his misconduct and vices have rendered him incompetent.

In these observations, two lessons are contained. One is, that he, who allows himself to be proposed as a candidate on an election, ought to consider whether his character can bear the test of public scrutiny. The other is, that when an election is in question, every one who writes, or publishes, against the candidate, ought to have his proof ready at hand to meet him before a tribunal of civil justice, if he charges him with a crime, or with scandalous, or infamous conduct; or even, if he charges him with weakness, incapacity, or a want of integrity, and thereby defeats his election, it would be reasonable to suppose, if this was proved to have been done maliciously, falsely, without any foundation, that an action would be maintained, and proper damages be given by a jury.

The liberty of the press, as it respects the government and measures of administration in a state, is not so easy to be adjusted; yet, perhaps, a little careful attention will place it on reasonable grounds, and exhibit it on constitutional principles.

The United States in all their constitutions clearly intended to preserve a free communication of sentiments, and opinions, in every state, as to matters of governmental concernment. The public opinion, in the most arbitrary government, has its irresistible influence and acknowledged effect. The great art of government, in a despotism, is to gain the public opinion in favour of tyranny. This is done by promotions, by bribery, by corruption, and by terror. We have many examples in ancient, and modern history, where the change of public opinion has effected a revolution, has totally altered the dynasty of nations, dethroned one family and set up another; taken away the father and enthroned the son, [29] and even changed and rechanged the form of the government. The princes and despots of the world are afraid to acknowledge the force of public opinion, and yet all their movements are predicated upon a conviction of its force. In America, we have made the public opinion the guide and safety of our systems of civil government; but to avoid the errors, and wildness, with which the public opinion has been generally conducted in other countries, we have marked the place of its current in our civil constitutions; that so it may move on, in the form of frequent elections, curing, by silent votes, the mischiefs, which in Europe demand the remedy of a civil commotion. There can be, then, no danger in appealing to the public, on the transactions of a government, where the manner and measure of the public will are thus regulated. The idea that the body of the people are incapable of judging in the public concerns of state, is in itself an opposition to the principles of the governments in America; because they are all founded in the sentiment, that the people at large, will maintain them on the considerations of interest. It cannot therefore be wrong to spread the concerns of the state before the people, that their opinions may be formed on the measures of the administration. And I should conceive it to be very clear, and a well established truth, that this was all that was intended by the state of Pennsylvania, when that state provided for a justification, in prosecutions for libels, from the truth of the fact, as to public men, and public measures. It is hard to be believed, that it is intended there, that a tale of bribery and corruption of a public officer, may be made the subject of a gazette publication, and then be justified, upon proof of the facts charged, when there should be a prosecution. This would be, to compel every man in public office, to engage in a lawsuit with every evil minded printer, or malicious writer, on the peril of losing his reputation, and compel him to try those facts, on an action for slander, which ought to be tried only on impeachment.

The press ought, by the tenor of all the constitutions, to be free in the publication of all the measures of the [30] government. The restraints laid upon the press in all the governments on the continent of Europe, was the stimulus which produced an express declaration in so many of the governments in North America. If the measures exhibited are right, the people will ultimately support them, if the measures are wrong, they will have their influence in the then next election.

To explain this principle more fully, we begin with the lowest magistrate. Whatever, he in fact does, or whatever decision he may make, he does it as a servant of the public, and the people at large ought to be possessed of it. To publish what he has officially done, is one thing, and to charge him with having received a bribe to do either right or wrong, is another. The former may be from error or mistake, but the latter is in itself a crime in him, in his private capacity, because it is received by him as a man, to corrupt him as an officer, and thereby to contaminate the stream of public jurisprudence. If the opinion of a judge is published, and a prosecution commenced for the publication as a libel, the truth may be given in evidence, because we are all interested in the opinion and judgment of the judges, and though the opinion or judgment may be wrong and erroneous, yet it is an opinion in which the public have a concern, and therefore there is no impropriety in the publication of it.

Whatever shall be done by the legislature, is a proper subject for public communication through the medium of the press. The legislature ought to pass no act, which will not bear the public scrutiny. If their acts are wrong, they ought to be repealed; if they are unconstitutional, the judges ought to declare them to be so, and refuse to carry them into execution. Therefore, as the measures of government are proper for communications through the medium of the press, and the publication of them, if truly and impartially made, is for the use, advantage, and safety of the state, the truth of them ought to be a justification to the author and printer.

The publication of what is done by the judiciary, or legislative power, must in itself be a justifiable and proper [31] thing. But should the printer, at the same time suggest or publish, that what was done, was done from corrupt motives, or from a traitorous design to overthrow the constitution, he ought to be punished, unless he can prove the fact of corruption, or the conspiracy or combination to destroy the government. If the writer or printer asserts, that the measure is unconstitutional and wrong, even though he is mistaken, or wilfully errs, he cannot be punished; because he has a right to have and give an opinion, and he submits it to the public, who are a proper tribunal to decide upon it; and the act done may be wrong and unconstitutional, and yet not be the effect of corruption or treason.

It does not follow that all publications on the measures of government, which are not true, are liable to prosecution and punishment. The indictment must set forth that the publication was *false,* and that it was *falsely and maliciously made* by the party charged. The malice or evil intention of him, who made the publication is a material part of the charge; for if it was done by involuntary error or mistake, there is no criminality in it; and of this the jury are to judge, as they do of the charge of fraud in other cases, or the charge of malice on a suit for defamation, or a malicious prosecution, or the charge of malice aforethought, as a constituent part of the crime of murder. But if the false publication proceed from *malice* to the government, or its officers, or from a seditious temper against the powers of the state, and the fact published be in itself false, there can be no reason why the author and publisher should not receive adequate and condign punishment.

The late act of Congress was intended to have been passed on proper principles, and the Congress had an undoubted right to pass an act against seditious libels; but it will not follow from thence, that the act was drawn on the rules of prudence, or executed with that discretion which might procure the confidence, and merit the support of the people.

Some of the men who contended against it, rested their opposition too much on principles quite incompatible [32] with every species of a free government; and though the act was finally suffered to expire, yet this circumstance can furnish no argument against a constitutional restraint on the press.

The act of Congress was made in June 1798. It was to continue in force until the third of March, 1801. The second section enacted, "That if any person shall write, print, utter or publish, or shall cause or procure to be written, printed, uttered or published, or shall knowingly and willingly assist or aid in writing, printing, uttering or publishing any false, scandalous and malicious writing or writings against the government of the United States, or either house of Congress of the United States, or the president of the United States, with intent to defame the said government, or either house of the said Congress, or the said president, or to bring either of them into contempt or disrepute; or to excite against them or either or any of them, the hatred of the good people of the United States, &c. such person being thereof convicted, shall be punished by fine, not exceeding two thousand dollars, or by imprisonment, not exceeding two years."

There is a section providing that it shall be lawful for a defendant, when under prosecution for writing or publishing any libel, to give in evidence in his defence the truth of the matter contained in the publication charged as a libel.

By this act, the crime is publishing any *false, scandalous and malicious writing*. This clause, taken in its literal sense, excludes the necessity of a provision for giving the truth in evidence in the defence, because the writing must be in itself *false,* in order to make the publication a crime; and therefore it would be natural to justify the fact by the truth. But though the facts asserted might be true, yet the conclusions drawn from them might not be so, of this the jury were made the judges, under the direction of the court. The crime did not seem to be completed, unless the publication was made to defame the Congress, or one branch of it, or to defame the president, or to bring him or the senate or house into contempt [33] or disrepute, or to excite against him, or them, the hatred of the people. Thus the act provided for the president and Congress, leaving all the other officers, and departments of government, without protection from slanders and libels, unless they could have found protection in the common law. The common law would have afforded equal protection to the president and Congress, as it did to the others.

This act seemed to have its origin in an apprehension, that the president and Congress, or a majority of the latter, were in danger from their fellow-citizens, or some of them, and was received, however it might have been intended, as a measure adopted to maintain a party influence long enough to gain some point, contemplated as of great political importance.

The writing and publishing falsely, and maliciously, against any one officer in the national government, a libel, with an intent to subvert the government of the United States, to bring it into hatred or contempt, or in that way, wilfully, and wickedly, uttering, and publishing any falsehood, in fact, with an intent to alarm the people, or to cause them to withdraw their love and support from the government, must in itself be a crime against the government, and ought to be punished. But the libel against a president or Congress, or officer of the government, must be in regard to something said to have been done by him, or them, officially, or otherwise, the government cannot be injured by it, and it remains as an offence against him, or them in their private capacities, and they are, as to a remedy, on the same foot of privilege, and point of protection, as other citizens. Where the private reputation of an officer of the general government is injured, or his property trespassed upon, he has his remedy as a private citizen. But where his official conduct is libelled, maliciously and falsely, *with a view to injure the general government,* or where he is opposed in the exercise of legal, official authority, derived from that government, there the injury is to the government itself, and it ought to be considered as possessing powers for its own defence and support.

[34] Nothing could have been [more] necessary, nor is there any thing more necessary at this time, than to pass an act, that if any

person shall, by writing, printing, or in any other manner, utter and publish, any false, malicious, and scandalous libel of and concerning the legislature of the United States, or of and concerning the conduct of any member of the same in his legislative business, or of and concerning the president, vice president, or any officer or servant of the government, in regard to his official conduct, *with an intent to subvert, or weaken the government* he shall be punished by fine or imprisonment, not exceeding, &c.

There is yet one point attended with more difficulty. The truth may be published in regard to the measures of the administration of states, and yet such false constructions may be given to them in the publication, as will alarm the people, raise a jealousy against the state, breed sedition, and tend to bring on an insurrection. The question is, as this is an evil, how it can be prevented by the government.

Every man has a privilege to reason on the measures of government. Some reason in one way, and some in another; one part may be right and the other may be wrong; but if he who happened to be wrong in his reasoning, could be punished for his error, there would be an end of all free inquiry on the measures of administration. Some men may form wrong conclusions with very honest hearts, while others form the same from wrong heads and seditious minds; but there can be no way, in which a just, and exact scrutiny can be made, and therefore, there can be no punishment in such cases, without a dangerous infringement on the right of private judgment, in public concerns.

The evils attending these errors, whether involuntary or corrupt, are not so dangerous as they may be at first conceived to be. The writer, or the publisher lays the fact of the measure, fairly and fully before the public, and then offers his opinion, as to its effects and consequences. If he believes the act, decision or measure, to be unconstitutional, he says so, and exhibits his reasons: [35] the body of the people have the constitution in their hands, they hear the reasons of others on the subject; and they can ultimately form an opinion for themselves, and they generally decide with ability and propriety; because they have no corrupt motive, no sinister end in view, nor any wrong bias from interest on their minds. If he says that the measure, though constitutional, has a tendency to injure the public weal, yet if he assigns no reasons for his opinion, the public will not regard him; and if he does, others will canvass his reasons, and the people will finally be able to form a correct and proper judgment on the case.

It will sometimes happen, that inflammatory pieces, with little or no foundation, will have a warm effect on the public mind. Elections are sometimes procured and sometimes prevented in this way; and good men are frequently grieved at the effects of a misunderstanding in the public opinion; but such is our state of imperfection here, that we can have no good, which is not tinctured with evil. This is necessarily incidental to the freedom of the press, as established and contemplated by all the constitutions in our nation; and being an evil in itself of less magnitude, than what would result from a restraint on the freedom of the press in such cases, it must be endured.

There can be no standard, besides that of the public opinion, established to decide on the reasonings and conclusions, which men and parties will draw, in adverse or diverging lines from the same premises. Therefore to punish a man for reasoning wrong, would be to deny him the privilege of reasoning at all: and to deprive him of this privilege, in a matter, wherein he has an interest in common with the rest of his fellow citizens, would be to deprive him of one of the most valuable rights secured by the form of all our governments. It would be like the claim of that authority which burned one philosopher for suggesting principles, the belief of which ultimately crowned another with laurels: or that which effected the execution of another philosopher, for suggesting, that the earth was not a *plane* but a *globe*.

[36] Wherever one man, or one body of men can erect and maintain a coercive tribunal in favor of their own opinions, and in opposition to that of those who differ from them, there is an end of all free inquiry: and the right of private judgment no longer exists. The world has seen, does now see, and will forever see, melancholy instances of this truth. The wise man says, that which hath been will be again; and there is nothing new under the sun. A survey of the whole Mussulman empire rises up in testimony of this fact. Wherever the Roman catholic religion has had a full perception of its consequences, the effect has been the same as that of Mahomet in Turkey. Thus we see Italy, the garden of Europe, has become the imbecile sport of neighboring powers, from a want of mental energy; and by reason of that torpid weakness of nerves, which never fails to be the consequence of indolence of mind. We behold in Spain, the ass

crouching between two burdens; the church and the throne. The former has a servile dependence upon the latter; and in due form of law, lays the people, bound hand and foot, on the altar of superstition, that the sacrifice may be divided between the church and the state. This same kind of tyranny was maintained, in a great degree, under the late French monarchy; but as it inculcated a superstitious regard to the monarch, as to the Lord's anointed, it was necessary to overthrow the church, in order to overturn the throne.

The holy religion, which was by these powers vilely corrupted, and profanely debased, contains no authority for such tyranny. The whole tenor and spirit, as well as all the precepts and examples of it, are in favor of the rights of conscience. We are there taught, to call no man master in matters of conscience, for one is our master even our Father who is in heaven. The whole host of martyrs, are now bearing testimony in favor of this right. The states of America have done themselves infinite honor in recognizing this sacred principle, given to the human race on their creation, and more fully explained in that divine system which hath brought life and immortality to light.

[37] There never has been an instance, of the freedom of enquiry in matters of religion, being restrained, where the civil liberty of the people survived it. Nor has there ever been an instance, of the people being denied the right of enquiry on the principles, and, administration, of civil government, where the rights of conscience have been preserved. Neither of these can subsist without the other. I do not mean, that, because a man has a right to think for himself, he has a right to vex and disturb others in the exercise of the same privilege. The whole of my argument tends to prove the reverse. The idea of each man's having a right to think for himself, suggests in the strongest manner, that in this respect, all are equal, and that it will be unjust in one, to subvert the right of another.

The laws made against blasphemy, and profanity, when fully understood, and properly, and cautiously executed, are quite compatible with these ideas. The laws against blasphemy, at least any one which I have seen, allow every one to have his own opinion in regard to the incomprehensible author and creator of the universe. If any one has a belief that there is a Being, who has created all things, and on whom he himself is dependant for his existence, he cannot think of him but with awe and reverence. If all the community are in this belief, they can have no right to grieve and vex each other, by contumelious reproaches of him. If the greater part of the community have this belief, and the reproach and ridicule of it, are not essential to the happiness and comfort of the minority, they ought to be restrained from the exercise of such contumely and reproach, as will afflict, or disturb the majority. This can be no injury to them, because they are left to have, and enjoy their own opinions in peace and in quietness; they are left to the exercise of the right of defending them in argument, by necessary means, only avoiding that mode of conversation, which is unnecessary to them, injurious to others, and vexatious to men of decency and good manners, who are not careful about any religion.

The laws which are made to prevent blasphemy, against [38] what christians denominate revealed religion, are on the same principles. The *contumeliously* reproaching of God, Jesus Christ, or the Trinity, or the books of the old or new testament, is a crime. But the opinion which any one may have, on these subjects, or any arguments he may offer in support of his opinion can be no crime against the laws. Yet there can be no reason, why one man shall be allowed to treat the opinion of a majority of a community, on those original ideas of religion, with contempt and ridicule. It can by no means be proof of the truth of his own opinion, of the gravity of his own mind, or the seriousness of his own inquiries to treat the religious opinions of his neighbors with contumely and reproach.

A society of men may believe with well grounded reason, that the apprehension of punishment in another state of existence after this is terminated, will lay a powerful restraint upon the actions of men here, that it will have a tendency to prevent secret crimes, or the crimes openly done, under the hope of protection from secrecy, and that it may have a tendency to establish truth, by the prevention of falsehood and perjury. This idea is as old as the world itself, and all nations have adopted it. The United States have universally adopted the same opinion, and it has been by the people here, counted upon as a main pillar of their several governments. There may be philosophers in the present day, who ridicule the idea, and assert that death is an eternal sleep. It is well for the world, in my opinion, that there are such men; for when the levity of their characters, and the atrocity of their actions are seen, we are convinced that the world would be a most miserable place of existence, if all men were to adopt their sentiments. Though these men, like other evils, may be useful in attaching mankind more sacredly to what is right and good in itself, yet like other evils their opinion may, and ought to be restrained within such bounds as may not injure, or overthrow the social compact. If they please themselves with the idea of a termination of their existence in the article of death, yet if they commit no crime against the laws of civil society, [39] no body can punish them. If their mode of belief takes off their restraint on their actions, so far as to involve them in guilt, they must suffer like other men. The promulgation of their opinion can be of no consequence to them, because if the end of this life is the end of our existence, there can be no necessity for our urging each other to receive opinions in which we can have no possible concern, and consequently, in which, as men, on their own hypothesis we, or they, can have no interest. The conclusion is therefore reasonable, that when the majority shall conceive a restraint upon contumelious treatment of a generally received religion to be necessary, which restraint can do no injury to one individual, but may advance the interest and security, and promote the happiness of the whole, his own included, they have a right to lay it.

The conclusion by me made from these arguments, is simply this, that in all matters of religion, and civil authority we have the freedom of the press sacredly assured to us by the constitutions of governments which we have formed; or, in other words, that while we have yielded to the community, the power of restraining us, so far, as is for the promotion of our own security and happiness, with that of all enrolled in the same social compact, we have reserved the privilege of exercising such rights, as will have a tendency to preserve from corruption, that system, by which that power is ceded, and by which these rights are secured.

Productions addressed to the understanding of mankind, on the subject of civil government have never been deemed to be seditious; but essays made on false facts to influence the minds of the people, to create unnecessary jealousies, and to disaffect the people to the government, always have been, and no doubt always will be, held as highly criminal.

Reasoning with decency on the being and attributes of God, on the divinity of Jesus Christ, or the efficacy of the Holy Ghost, or the evidence of the bible, have never been considered as criminal, but contumeliously reproaching the Deity, reviling the scriptures, &c. have [40] been, and no doubt will always be considered as criminal in these governments; because such conduct tends to dissolve the bands of civil society, and of course, to subvert that security to the people, which their governments were formed to establish.

It may, nevertheless happen, under the best form of government, that the means provided in the constitution for its own support, may be prostituted, either in acts of legislation, or in judicial procedures, to base and unworthy purposes. There can be no necessity for a civil government, when the imperfection of human nature is done away; and while men govern men, there will of course, be imperfections and errors in the administration of government. When parties run high, the ruling majority, ever right in their own opinion, can never conceive that the rod in their hand is too heavy for the shoulders of those who oppose them. They will not reflect, that their severity has a direct tendency to change the public opinion, on which they stand; and that those, whom they now scourge, may have an opportunity to lay the lash on their shoulders in turn.

The late act of Congress against sedition was the offspring of a warm party spirit. The execution of it seemed to be tinctured with the same baneful drug. While some were punished for abusing the president, there was no provision against abusing the vice president; but this was done in the most licentious manner. The way to make interest, and to gain an influence with some of the men who promoted the sedition law, was to violate its principles, by abusing some of the principal officers of the government. While some were punished for abusing the senate, as a body, others were attempting to make their way into office, by villifying, ridiculing, and libelling the members of that body, who were in the minority.

The act, was in itself, pointed, and particular, which no doubt produced those effects in its execution, that put an end to its existence. No act was necessary for any other purpose than that of providing the mode and [41] quantum of punishment. One of the judges observed, in one of the trials for a libel, that there was no criminal common law in the United States. He could not mean by this, that a nation had formed a government, without the powers of protecting itself. If he intended, that the government had powers to protect itself, but that these powers must be first defined by the legislature, before the judiciary authority could concern themselves with them, he involves himself in this difficulty, that there is no where, in the catalogue of powers given to Congress, any one in regard to sedition. If he says, that the restraint of sedition is necessary to the preservation of the government, and that therefore the power is given by implication, the answer is, that whatever has a tendency to overthrow the constitution and civil authority, is a crime against the government, and may be punished by a reasonable restraint; and that fines, imprisonment, and sureties for good behavior are reasonable restraints, and may be administered without any act of Congress for the purpose. If these are not adequate, the legislature of the nation may increase the punishment.

There never was a necessity for Congress to do any thing more than to provide for the punishment of sedition, without an attempt to define it by statute. This crime, in this respect, is like treason, murder and other offences, which are defined by precedents, and by the nature of things, and can never submit to a legislative description. Congress ought therefore to have simply provided a punishment for sedition, and seditious libels, without saying more on the subject. If they had thought it necessary to make provision, as was done in that act, that in all cases for a libel against the government, or any officer of it, for misconduct in his official capacity, with an intent to injure or to oppose the government, the party charged should be allowed to produce evidence of the facts contained in the libel, in his justification, they might have done it. But this ought to be restrained to such facts only, as the officers of government should commit in their public capacity, and not to such matters as would be disgraceful, and immoral in them, as private men. [42] To allow everyone to produce evidence that a judge or magistrate had given a wrong judgment, and to use that, as proof that he had received a bribe, would be inadmissible. To prove that a president had made a wrong appointment, or that a member of the legislature had given a wrong vote, and to offer this as evidence of corruption, would be unreasonable and unjust.

The conduct and tenor of executive and judicial appointments, ought to be the subject of scrutiny. Where the appointments are bestowed upon persons of a particular way of thinking, or on the leaders of a party, we have a just right to discover from this, the drift of the administration, and as clear a privilege openly to promulge the truth, as to the facts of appointments, and to give out our opinion of the tendency of the measures. Where there is a division of federalists and democrats, as the parties are now called, and the president, or the governor will make an attachment to the one party or the other a qualification to office, and a condition for a place, we have a right to charge him with being of that party. Nay, further, we have a right to condemn the practice as being a species of corruption, destructive to the rights of private judgment on public concerns; and as a mode, which cannot fail to create factions, and to maintain dangerous and bitter parties, as long as the government shall exist.

The patronage of the president, as has been asserted by some politicians, must be maintained by some means or other, and there are no other than those of filling offices and places with men who are devoted to his opinions.

When this idea is properly examined, it will appear to be quite unnatural to our systems of civil government, and derogatory to all the principles, which have been advanced, in order to maintain our late glorious revolution. It will appear to be a legitimate offspring of that tyranny which has so often deluged the world in blood. It is introduced at no other door, than that, which opens to receive the dangerous charge against the people of America, that they are incapable of preserving and enjoying a free government.

[43] The president can have no interest separate from that of the people. The idea of bribing, by appointments, a part of the people, to defend the interests of the whole, is absurd and unnatural. An honest man and a patriot, will promote and defend the interest of his country, whether he is in office or not; while a man of no principle, he who acts or engages for the sake of an office, will betray his country, and subvert the liberties of, the people, where it shall be for his sinister emolument to do it. The constitution is to be maintained, not because it is the source of honor and emolument, but because it is established by the nation for the public happiness and security.

There can be no incompatibility in the interests of the state governments, and that of the United States. The latter, as now established, sinks of course when the state governments shall cease to exist. They will become the destroying angel of each other, for as soon as that is overturned, the preserving balance will be done away and they must sink to ruin by their wars and depredations on each other.

How far the idea of creating an interest, and maintaining an influence by a presidential patronage, in the late administration, was adopted, I do not undertake to determine. There are charges openly made on this score by men in the interest of the present administration, and the same is as warmly reciprocated. How far either charge is true, the public must judge for themselves.

BOSTON, 1801

It has been said that the president cannot administer the government on his own principles and plans, unless his agents and servants shall coincide with him in opinions upon civil and political subjects. This assertion, in the latitude it is intended, cannot be true, or be consistent with political propriety. Could this assertion be maintained, every president ought to exhibit his political creed, not that the people might know his sentiments, and correct them, as by the standard of public opinion, but that they should implicitly conform themselves to it, as to the fixed, unerring and unalterable standard of political [44] truth. We should all be released from the labor of forming opinions for ourselves, and have only to embrace the creed of the chief magistrate. Those who expect to live by the president's patronage, finding the offices all full, will begin to intrigue for a new president; whose political principles are in direct opposition to the one in office. The men who view themselves as candidates, will of course open a controversy with him, and either explicitly, or implicitly, form contracts to promote the leaders of their party. Thus the constitution will be forsaken, and the plans and machinations of parties form the plan of administration.

Mr. Adams in his book, intitled A Defence of the Constitutions of Government of the United States of America, observes very truly, that a *majority may be a faction*. Whatever number of men shall associate together, for any other purpose than that of maintaining the government on the principles, and by the forms of the constitution, is a faction. What necessity can there be for associations, either by express compact, or by implicit intrigue? We are all united in a form of government, which interests all alike, and which must be supported by the will of the whole. Does any one say, that parties, intrigues, armies and a separate order of men, are necessary, because the people have not virtue enough to govern themselves, in an elective republic? *He who says this, is an antifederalist, and commits treason against the constitution.*

The agents and servants of the government, and the secretaries of the departments, foreign ministers and consuls, the executive and judicial officers, and the men employed in the business of legislation; the secretary of state, the secretaries of war and of the navy, are properly confidential friends of the president; and will of course, be men whose opinions are coincident whith those of him who appoints them. The foreign ministers and consuls are men who are under the president's confidential orders, and ought to be with him in political sentiments. The legislators are so far from being in the rank of agents of the chief magistrate, that he is by the form of the constitution considered as their agent, to carry in [45] to effect the acts they pass. The judges and judicial officers, the executive officers, including in this description the officers of the revenue, are not his agents and servants, but are the agents and servants of the nation according to the established form of the government and the laws of the land. This distinction is of great importance under the form of a free government; because the immediate, confidential friends of the president are to be guided by his pleasure, as dictated by him alone, while the judicial and executive officers are under the direction of the laws. These are personally amenable for their own conduct, and responsible for every deviation from the legal path of their duty: nay, further, the express orders of the president himself, is no justification for their neglect of duty, or error in proceeding.

Since the laws alone are to govern the conduct of those officers, of what moment can it be to the people whether their opinions coincide with the president, either in religion or politics? To the president it may be of consequence in an ensuing election, because their being in office may give them an influence in his support. It is of consequence to the people that the officers of their government should be well informed, and upright men. If they are so, and the president is a good man, and a suitable person for his elevated station, they and he cannot differ in sentiment; but if he thinks, and reasons erroneously, it is of consequence that they should not unite with him. It is therefore, a salutary, and just conclusion, that no man ought to be denied an office in the judicial, or executive line, or be removed from such office, because his opinions and sentiments, are not assimilated to that of the chief magistrate.

Men who are opposed in opinion to the government, as it is established, cannot be safely trusted with its administration. Those who have no confidence in an elective republic, but believe an hereditary monarchy, and a line of descending nobility as necessary, can never administer an elective republic with firmness and patience. Those men who are opposed to all settled rules, and averse [46] to all the maxims, which experience and wisdom have established, can never administer any government well. Yet this is a case very wide from those opinions, which divide the body of the people in our country; the extremes on each side ought to be rejected, but whether a man is in favor of

Adams, Jefferson, Burr or Pinckney, ought by no means to be considered as a qualification, or as a disqualification to office.

Should the idea obtain, that men are to be appointed to, or secluded from office, on account of political opinions upon the administration of the government, there would be an eternal warfare between the *outs* and *ins*. Contentions would be sharpened, and the hopes and fears of men in office, or those who want offices, would have the full effect of bribery and corruption. The number who are in office, will always be a minority, and those who are out, and under disappointment, must ultimately prevail: these will have their day of triumph and an opportunity to share in the coveted emoluments of the treasury.

It may be suggested here, that in a struggle of this kind, the respectable and honest part of the community, will take no part. The men who are partizans, have a claim to the offices, as they may have gained a victory, and the only men who could be safely trusted with the government, are placed at a distance, while these champions, for their own emolument, assume the gown of the patriot, and urge the people to civil discord; and perhaps to bloody dissensions: the men who dare to condemn, in a Washington, that which they would not justify in an Adams; who will condemn in a Jefferson's administration, the measures which they censured in that of his predecessor, and applaud in the one, what they approved in the other. These men are the true federalists, independent of all parties; and though neither are friendly to them, yet they will have a tribute of respect, from the community, of more value, than the eulogies of designing partizans; and will enjoy more substantial satisfaction, than can be derived from offices and stipends.

[47] It is asserted with confidence, that there are men in the United States, who have no faith or confidence in the present federal constitution; and from a variety of publications in several parts of the union, there is some reason to believe the fact. There seems in some productions to be a design to disaffect the southern with the northern states. Others seem to be endeavoring to divide the New England states from the others. Whatever pretensions such men may make, they are by no means *federalists*. The general constitution is a league, or covenant, between all the states, and he, whoever he is, that shall attempt in any manner to dissolve it, is an *antifederalist*.

The people of the United States are secure in their persons and property. And therefore these men who delight in theoretic, speculative politics, ought to have modesty enough to be quiet, until those, who have a confidence in our present government, shall have given it a fair trial.

By the constitution of the United States, Congress have a right to exercise, over a territory ten miles square, where the seat of government is, exclusive legislative jurisdiction. What may be done under this clause for the punishing of libels, made or published within that territory, cannot now be satisfactorily ascertained: but we must take up the subject as the law now is in the general government, and in the state governments.

The remedies for libels are on a civil process, or on indictment. The former is by an action upon the case for damages. In this action, the plaintiff sues in his private capacity, as a private citizen, and can make no use of any public official character he may sustain, excepting merely in aggravation of damages. The court, where such actions are to be litigated are the same as those where any action for breach of contract, or other civil injury may be maintained.

The remedy, or redress on an indictment is on a different footing. There, unless the national constitution has changed it, the prosecution is to be, not only in the state, but in the county where the offence is committed.

[48] The indictment cannot be for a libel, simply, against a public officer. The description of the offence may be aggravated by a malicious intention in the party charged, to deprive the party libelled of offices, or honors: but still it is no more an offence against the government in kind, than it would be if the person libelled had never possessed an office; or if the indictment was for an assault and battery on the same person. These injuries can never be considered as offences against the general government, even though the libels are against the officers of the same; but must remain within the jurisdiction of the state governments, because the party injured, although he is an officer of the federal government, yet remains a subject of, and under the protection of the state where he resides. This will appear to be conclusive, on a review of the powers given to the Congress of the United States.

"The Congress shall have power, 1st, to lay and collect taxes, duties, imposts and excises, to pay debts, and provide for the common defence and general welfare of the United States: but all duties, imposts and excises shall be uniform throughout the United States."

2. "To borrow money on the credit of the United States."

3. "To regulate commerce with foreign nations, and among the several states."

4. "To establish an uniform rule of naturalization, and uniform laws on the subject of bankruptcies, throughout the United States."

5. "To coin money: regulate the value thereof; and of foreign coin; and for the standards of weights and measures."

6. "To provide for the punishment of counterfeiting the securities, and current coin of the United States."

7. "To establish post offices, and post roads."

8. "To promote the progress of science and the useful arts, by securing, for a limited time, to authors and inventors, the exclusive right of their respective writings and discoveries."

[49] 9. "To constitute tribunals inferior to the supreme court."

10. "To define and punish piracies and felonies on the high seas, and offences against the law of nations."

11. "To declare war; grant letters of marque and reprisal; and make rules concerning captures on the land and water."

12. "To raise and support armies. But no appropriation of money for that use shall be for a longer term than two years."

13. "To provide and maintain a navy."

14. "To make rules for the government, and regulations for the land and naval forces."

15. "To provide for calling forth the militia, to execute the laws of the union, suppress insurrections, and repel invasions."

16. "To provide for organizing, arming and disciplining the militia, and for governing such part of them as may be employed in the service of the United States: reserving to the states respectively, the appointment of officers, and the authority of training the militia according to the discipline prescribed by Congress."

17. "To exercise exclusive legislation in all cases whatsoever over such district (not exceeding ten miles square) as may, by cession of particular states, and the acceptance of Congress, become the seat of the government of the United States; and to exercise like authority over all places purchased by the consent of the legislature of the state in which the same shall be, for the erection of forts, magazines, arsenals, dock yards, and other needful buildings."

18. "To make laws which shall be necessary and proper for carrying into execution the aforegoing powers, and all other powers vested by this constitution in the government of the United States, or in any department or office thereof."

None of these powers seem to include the authority to punish libels; and therefore, some very good men, [50] have their doubts whether the general government can make laws on this subject.

It is very clear, that considering a libel as a private injury, the congress can have no authority to enact a law for its definition, or punishment. But yet it does by no means follow, that a libel may not be so conceived, and published, as to be a crime against the government itself, independent of the personal injury done to the particular subject of it; and when that is the case, the government ought to possess the powers of punishing it on principles of preserving the constitution.

Any laws which may be necessary to the carrying into effect the powers vested in the national government, may be made by the Congress; but if there is no government, or no Congress, there can be no laws made. It is therefore necessarily implied, that all things which ought to be done to preserve, and maintain that government, which is vested with those authorities, and which may make laws for their execution, may make laws to preserve its own existence. Should it be said, that the state governments will preserve and defend the existence of the federal government, this would by no means be accepted as an answer; because a government, depending on another government for its existence, is merely a corporation—it can have no sovereignty— and can be no band of union for a nation.

The late act of Congress was deficient in its principles on these essential points. It went beyond what the constitution would warrant. Some of the libels pointed out by the act, were such, as were written and published against the president, to bring him personally into disrepute, or contempt: or to excite against him personally, the hatred of the people.

The constitution of the United States has expressly provided, that crimes shall be tried in the state where they shall be committed. And that in civil actions for damages, where one of the parties is a citizen of a state, of which the other is not a citizen, the action may be commenced and prosecuted in a court of the United States at the election of the parties. There is, [51] in this provision, no distinction in persons or officers. When the general government was formed, the people might, if they had thought it proper, have made provision for a president, vice president, and all the officers of the general government, to bring their suits and prosecutions in the federal courts; but no such provision was made. Perhaps the reason was, that the general government is as much the government of the people, as the others; and must derive its support from the same source.

The character of the first magistrate of the nation is highly to be respected; and though it may not be safe in any keeping, but that of the federal government, yet as the constitution has not placed it there, a question, on a legal principle, does not arise on the subject. Those who are advocates for the late act of Congress against libels, may feel themselves hurt at these observations; and may endeavor to support their measure by arguments, supposed to result from powers, necessarily implied in the constitution. Their arguments will be before the public, and I am without anxiety at the event, be it what it may; for I am ready to receive and abide the public judgment. It has been said, that the power of self preservation is an incidental, constituent part of the government; because a national government must be a sovereign government of course, and a sovereignty, relying on another sovereignty, for civil support, is an inadmissible idea in politics: but it will by no means follow, that the right to vindicate the president's personal character against libels, is necessarily incident to the constitution. The want of personal character in a chief magistrate, would be an unfortunate circumstance; but governments have existed very frequently and very well, under this difficulty. Should the president bring a civil action for a libel, or other slander, he would stand on the same level with other actions, and have his trial by the same rules and in the same courts where they have their's. Should there be a criminal prosecution for a libel, published against him personally, it could not be prosecuted any where but in the state courts, and in the county where the offence happens. But if the libel is pointed at him personally, and yet written, [52] printed, or published, *with an intent to injure, oppose or subvert the government of the United States* it takes a new denomination of criminality, and becomes punishable of necessity in the judiciary of that government against which the crime is committed.

The argument, that the Congress have a right to protect the character of the president, would with the same propriety be extended to every officer and servant of the general government. There can be no government without officers, and there can be no government without subjects and property. The case with us is, whether right or wrong, must remain under the process of experiment; that we have, from a number of separate sovereign states, carved out a national general sovereignty, limited, as to its authority, over the same persons and the same property, as the state governments have in protection, and what power is not expressly, or by a necessary implication given to that, is retained to the several states. Had the Congress enacted, that if any person should print, write, or publish, any libel against the president, or either house of Congress, *with an intent to obstruct, injure, oppose, or subvert, the government of the United States, or to raise sedition against the same,* he should be punished, &c. it would have described a new offence, which ought to be punished by that government. But when they enact, that, when any person shall publish a libel, *with an intent to defame the said president, or to excite against him the hatred of the good people of these states,* without connecting it with an intent to injure the government, it will be very difficult to maintain the measure by the constitution.

It may be said, that the injury done to the president may be an injury done to the United States. That may or may not be true: and it may be said that libels against the judges and other servants of the public, are injuries to the government. Nay, every immoral and vicious thing is an injury to the nation: but the creators of the federal government, are the creators and the supporters of the others, and are equally interested in all, and did not choose to invest the general government with all the authority [53] claimed in the late sedition law, passed by the late Congress.

This observation will, no doubt, be made and be echoed and reechoed from one champion to another, *that if the federal government cannot protect their president from libels, but must send him to the state courts for defence, we had better give up the national system at once.* This observation, when made, will be the result of the want of consideration. A moment's reflection will evince, that the general government is supported by the same people, who support the others. That these will have their influence; and whenever the general government shall be guided by men, who shall attempt a separate interest, the public opinion will gradually remove them, until the connecting balance shall be restored to its constitutional perfection.

The sum of the argument, on the whole, is this, that the

constitutional freedom of the press does not open the flood gates of slander on the members of the civil society, and allow each man to calumniate his neighbor with impunity.

That a man's reputation ought to be guarded, as of the next consequence to his life.

That whatever is in fact done by a government, or by any officer of it, in his official capacity, or under a pretence of official authority, may be published to the world, without the writer or printer's being chargeable for a libel.

That the reputation of men in office, is as dear to them, as that of other citizens are to them, and as much under the protection of the laws, as the reputation of men in private life is; and that, therefore, a charge against them of bribery or corruption, ought not to be published, otherwise than in a judicial prosecution against them, before a proper tribunal, where they may be removed from office, or otherwise punished according to the demerit of their crime.

That where a man appears as a candidate for an elective office, he exhibits his character for a public scrutiny, and every one has a right to publish any thing against his [54] election, which is not false in fact; but must be answerable for all falsehoods and groundless slanders, as well in civil, as in a criminal prosecution.

That though every one has a right to publish the proceedings of the government, in all its departments, yet if the publications are made of measures, which have never happened, the writers and printers are amenable, provided that any injury is done, or may be done, to the government by it. The fact of writing or publishing being proved, the burden of proof rests on the defendant, to prove the truth of the facts published, which if he cannot do, he must submit to punishment; unless he can show, that it was innocently done from mere error and mistake.

That though no one can justify the false publication of facts, in regard to the measures of the government, yet if facts are truly published, no one can be punished for reasoning erroneously upon them, or for publishing his reasons, however wrong he may be in his conclusions.

That the general government's having the power of punishing libels against the government itself, by a necessary inference from the constitution, does by no means give it the power of punishing those which are published against its president or other officers, who are also the subjects of the state governments; unless the libel is made and published, with an intent to injure the government itself. Which intent, must be averred in the indictment, and be found by the traverse jury, or jury of trials, otherwise he cannot be convicted. As this distinction most plainly results from the constitution, there can be no doubt but that every candid, sober man will be ready to give it a full force in his mind; because, were whatever he may wish the constitution, he must be content to take it as it is.

And finally, that a reasonable, constitutional restraint, judiciously exercised, is the only way, in which the freedom of the press can be preserved, as an invaluable privilege to the nation.

FINIS.

[70]

JEREMIAH ATWATER 1773–1835

A Sermon

MIDDLEBURY, VERMONT, 1801

Born in New Haven, Jeremiah Atwater graduated from Yale and for five years remained there as a tutor. During that time he was ordained as a minister, but preaching ran second to education for the succeeding twenty years. At the age of twenty-seven he was selected as first president of Middlebury College, well up on the northern frontier of Vermont, where his success was such that within a decade he was enticed to leave Middlebury to put new life into Dickinson College, in Carlisle, Pennsylvania. This sermon before the governor and legislature of Vermont was delivered two years before Atwater took over the presidency of Middlebury. The title page bears a quote from Montesquieu: "The natural place of Virtue is near to Liberty; but it is not nearer to extreme liberty than to servitude." The quote nicely summarizes Atwater's moderate tone and careful balancing of principles.

1st PETER—II Chap. 16th Verse.

As free, and not using your liberty for a cloak of maliciousness.

Called to speak before this respectable Assembly, I have need of much of the candor, and must beg the patient indulgence of my audience, on the present occasion.

The time has been, when the feelings of all have been powerfully interested in the events, which have happened on the theatre of Europe. But the European world is now at peace, and our sympathy with foreign governments, it is to be hoped, is lessened. The affairs which now occupy our minds, are the concerns of our own country, and its government. What happens in all free countries, has happened here, that differences of opinion have arisen. What lies at the bottom of these differences, is, I apprehend, difference of views, relative to the nature and end of government itself. To entertain right [6] ideas on this point will, by all, be judged of the highest importance. Errors here, cannot fail to produce those evils which ever attend error. It is desirable, not only that we should know the true end of government; but that we should understand the foundation of our own free, republican system, that we may unite in our endeavours, to give to it permanency, and guard against the evils, which threaten its overthrow. Whether in treating on a subject of this sort, in times like these, I may flatter myself with the idea of escaping censure, or not, still, this may, with truth, be said, that to attempt to irritate and add fuel to the flame of party, would be improper, and incompatible with the friendly feelings, with which we ought to assemble on this anniversary.

In the chapter containing the text, the apostle directed those to whom he wrote, how to conduct in the civil relation. He supposes that there may be such a thing, as an abuse of liberty, and warns them to guard against it. What I now propose, is, to consider the restraint which the idea of government always supposes, and the nature of this restraint in a republican government; the connexion of such a system in our own country, with the peculiar state of society, and the moral principles and habits of the people; and the necessity and the means of preserving [7] them. The apostle, in the context, informs us, that rulers are appointed for the punishment of evil doers, and for the praise of those who do well. Government may then, I conceive, be considered, as having its origin, primarily, in the vices of man. If all men were virtuous, there would be little need of it. But such is man's nature, so prone is he to invade the rights of others, that he needs restraint: The selfish passions need curbing and regulating. The necessity of government arises from the necessity of such restraint. This is a very obvious truth: But at the same time, apt to be overlooked in an age, when multitudes, feeling that restraints have, in many instances, been unnecessarily imposed, in the paroxysm of passion seem disposed to throw off all restraint. To exclaim against restraint, and to extol unbounded liberty, has ever been a popular theme. The man who can flatter restlessness with change; poverty with an equalization of station and property; vice with the indulgence of passion; and discontent with the removal of restraints which are displeasing, has ever found friends among those, who are dissatisfied with the existing order of things.

Liberty is a sound dear to us all: But what do we understand by it? One, perhaps, denotes by it, a license to do what he pleases, and considers [8] every kind and degree of restraint, as tyranny, whether that restraint originates with the individual himself, or is imposed by civil rulers. Self-government, as commanded by christianity, is viewed as a counteraction of natural freedom, and civil government as an intrusion on natural rights, equally odious. It is the perfection of Rousseau's celebrated system, entitled the Social Contract, that "every person while united with all, shall obey only himself, and remain as free, as before the union." Such a liberty as this must be pronounced, in the highest degree, detrimental to the interests of mankind. It reduces man back to the very state of barbarism, from which government is supposed to have redeemed him. Liberty, if considered as a blessing, must be taken in a qualified sense. The freedom which it implies, must be a limited, not absolute freedom; unless we will pronounce government itself a curse; for the very idea of government always supposes some restraint. But to this restraint the perversity of man's nature has ever been opposed, and vicious men have ever been most loud in exclaiming in favor of unbounded liberty; because such a liberty is no other than the liberty of sinning, the liberty of indulging lawless passion, and of invading a neighbor's rights. It would arm the idle and profligate against the virtuous and industrious, [9] and instead of a rational liberty, would be seen and felt to be, the worst of tyrannies; no better than a state of nature, and destitute of the least security for life or property. Let any one point out, if he can, an instance in the history of the world, where the human race have arrived to any tolerable degree of perfection or happiness, in a state of this kind. It cannot be done. Let speculative men then cease to extol the state of nature, and to be in love with the life of savages. To restrain such an absurd liberty, government was instituted. Restraint, in some degree or other, is its very object: And to exclaim in favor of liberty as wholly opposite to restraint, is to oppose the very end for which government itself is instituted. Restraint then must be allowed to be necessary. The only question is, of what sort it shall be? Now, altho' there are various forms of government; they may all be resolved into two kinds. One kind is supported by force; The other is dependant on opinion. The first is adapted to the worst view of human nature. It considers man, as corrupt, and is prepared to encounter his vices. Fear is the great principle which it addresses. Partaking, generally, of the monarchical form, it is simple in its structure, and easily organized. The greater part of the governments of the world have been [10] of this sort. Originating immediately from the vices of men, it too often operates to continue those vices. The evils of it are, an opposition of interests between rulers and ruled, and the tyrannical oppression and extortion which always follow. Various circumstances modify this kind of government. The government of Turkey is different from that of China, and that of Prussia different from either. The essential principles of each, however, are the same. The evils of this system have made the friends of mankind wish for a better system, in which the happiness of society should be primarily consulted, and not the aggrandizement of rulers; in which rulers should impose no restraints, but such as are necessary, and the ruled should willingly submit to them. If no burdens were imposed, but necessary ones, they could not, with any propriety, be deemed oppressive. Mankind, being unwilling to make themselves unhappy, might, it has been thought, be freely entrusted with the power of governing themselves. Though, in this case, no absolute security could be afforded for wisdom in the people; still, a degree of it would be expected, in their judgment concerning their own interests. In a pure democracy, the people, as a body, act. But this must ever be impossible, but in a very small State. To extend a free government [11] farther, the representative system has, in modern ages, been adopted. But whatever be the form, the people are supposed the source of power, and to have a constant check, or control over rulers. The essential principle of such a government is, that the people are willing to be controlled by reason, and to submit to all necessary restraints and burdens, without the compulsion of force. Such a system is dependant altogether on opinion; and as soon as there is not such a willingness, as soon as it becomes necessary to depend on force, as in despotic countries, the system is overthrown.

Can such a government exist for any length of time? Some have thought not. It has been pronounced utopian; and it is said, that in few countries, has this sort of government flourished. It is said, that no such government will stand; because it is calculated on a wrong view of human nature: That it supposes a degree of knowledge, a moral character and moral habits which, ordinarily, are not found: That to understand the business of government thoroughly, requires a degree of skill, of which, the people, generally are not possessed: That, as a body, they know not enough to be able to judge of public measures: That even tho' they did, still, a disposition to acquiesce always in what is reasonable [12] would be wanting. Knowledge alone, it is said, is not sufficient: That the people must be not only enlightened, but disposed to obey: That as long as the nature of man continues as it is, there will be no security for the general prevalence of such a disposition: That in all countries, such a system must be alike impracticable for any length of time: That the essential qualities of human nature being the same, the same obstacles will be every where presented. The great enemies of such a system, it is said, are the vices of men: That as long as human passions exist, they will have their operation, and be the fruitful sources of contention, turbulence, and discontent: That demagogues will arise, who will deceive the people for the sake of exalting their own consequence: That ambition in aspiring individuals, and the love of power, which is inherent in man, tend to engender faction: That rival towns or states, actuated by jealousy, will set themselves in opposition to each other, as they find their interests to disagree: That there is no absolute security for wisdom in the people: That they can never, for any considerable time, be brought, willingly, to submit even to wholesome restraints: That, thirsting for novelty, they will ever be given to change, and consider the laws which they themselves have made, as easily unmade: That notwithstanding what is [13] said about the diffusion of information, still, the people will easily suffer themselves to be duped and blinded by the crafty and designing: That truth will be perverted, and the channels of information obstructed: That heat, passion, and prejudice, will drown the still voice of reason, and public offices be the purchase of venality, or the sport of faction.

Some have had a totally different view of human nature. If men, as they suppose, are naturally inclined to do what is right, without being compelled to it; if they are inclined, on all occasions, to respect the rights of others, to do justice, and yield all due submission and obedience to proper restraints and wholesome laws, what should prevent the republican system from being carried into effect? Information, according to their opinion, is the only thing wanted among the people. Let it only be known what is right and necessary, and it will, at once, be acquiesced in: Whatever is for the public interest will be favoured, and all the evils, under which mankind have laboured, will, with justice, be ascribed to corrupt governments as their cause.

But I must acknowledge, that to me, human nature appears different from what is here represented; whether we obtain our knowledge of it from scripture, civil history, or observation.—[14] Selfishness has ever been a prominent trait in the character of mankind; which will make men consult their own private good at the expense of others. Man is always prone to what will center in himself only; hating restraint of any sort, and considering it, of itself, as an evil; aspiring at domination over others; fond of possessing power, and prone to abuse it. Human nature appears in its true colours, without artificial disguise, in children. It is, in general, very hard to make children submit to what is proper. They are self-willed and extremely apt to rebel. What children are, in a family, mankind are, as subject to the restraints of law and order.

But must we then despair of the human race, and sit down with the melancholy conclusion, that no improvements can ever take place in the political state of the world? The most remarkable instance of popular governments, which have secured freedom to the people, while they have been allowed a control over it, is to be found in our own country. Mankind have been astonished at beholding free systems of government prevailing here, while they have flourished so badly in all former ages, and in all other parts of the world. If the before-mentioned objections to the practicability of the republican system do not apply here, this must be owing to some peculiar circumstances.

[15] It has been observed, that government always supposes restraint on the passions of individuals. If mankind can be placed in such a situation, that this restraint shall be imposed from any other cause, there will be little need of much severity on the part of government: There will be little need of force, or fear, to awe men to submission. Human nature, though radically the same in different countries, may still be variously modified; and the character which man has sustained, may be greatly altered, by placing him in a new and different situation, and allowing free scope to all the means necessary for effecting a change.—Whatever of this kind has been peculiar here; whatever there is, which has fitted us for a free government, must be sought for in the genius and habits of the

people, and in the circumstances attending the first settlement of the country.

The state of society in Europe, and the governments established there, originated from the feudal system, and the genius of European institutions cannot be understood, without a recurrence to that system. The circumstances attending the settlement of this country, were, in like manner, altogether peculiar, and gave rise to a peculiar state of society. The object of our ancestors was different from what usually influences men, in settling a new country: It was, to [16] worship God, agreeably to the dictates of their own consciences. Though they fled from unrighteous oppression, they did not bring with them an abhorrence of those salutary restraints, which are necessary in all countries. They acquiesced in civil government, as ordained of God, and were firm supporters of law and order. They reverenced the Deity, and framed their lives on Christian principles. They made mistakes, it is true, on the subject of religious toleration; but their errors were those of the age in which they lived. The Bible they revered, and endeavored to enact their laws in accordance with it. Patriotism warmed their hearts and stimulated them to aim at the public good.— Where will you find legislators, laying a better foundation for the greatness and happiness of a nation? Where will you find men, actuated by a more sincere regard to posterity, and possessed of a more ardent desire to transmit to them, undiminished, the blessings they enjoyed? They possessed sober, industrious habits, and were strangers to the temptations of luxury. In their manners, they were distinguished for simplicity, and in speaking their sentiments, they had no artificial disguise. They revered truth and detested hypocrisy. Averse to ceremony in public worship, they had, while in England, been reproachfully styled Puritans by their adversaries. [17] But this name of reproach they accounted their highest honor. The friends of freedom in the country from which they emigrated, the historian* has not failed to do them and their ancestors merited honor, in ascribing to them the freedom which is to be found in the British constitution. Their manners, their habits, and their employments fitted them for the republican system of government.

It cannot be denied, that the institutions which they established, have had great influence, in producing that moral restraint of reason

* Hume.

and opinion, which is grounded on religion and knowledge. The influence of the first was secured by the erection of houses for public worship, and the prevalence of the last, by the early establishment of schools and colleges. By these and other means, a state of society has been produced altogether peculiar, different from what has been known in Europe, and superior to what is often known in any part of the world.

Our present enjoyment of civil and religious liberty results from the wise institutions established by our ancestors. Even when colonies, our governments were free, and our present systems are but a continuation of them. The kind of government has grown out of our circumstances, and its success and permanency show how well it [18] is fitted for our peculiar situation. The state of society naturally admitted a free government: No other would have been consonant with the manners, sentiments, and character of the people.

Now, it is evident that the more virtuous a people are, the less need is there of the restraints of civil government, to promote order. Our country, we have seen, admits of our enjoying a mild and free government. The important enquiry is, to what this is owing? Is it owing to this, which some have contended, that man needs no restraint; but will, unless made vicious by government, always act as a reasonable being, and be obedient and virtuous, because it is his highest interest to be so? This is a theoretical idea, which has no foundation in fact. It proceeds from a totally wrong view of human nature, and is fraught with mischief to society. If man is here formed a good citizen, it is not because he needs no restraint; but because, from his youth, he has been taught to restrain those passions, which it is the principal business of law and government to restrain. This restraint is begun in the family. Children are early inured to family government, and are taught habits of subordination and respect. In the school, the same system is continued, while the seeds of knowledge and virtue are sown in the youthful mind. Higher seminaries of learning also, accord [19] with the same system, as do the instructions of the bible and the desk. Man, from the cradle to the grave, is constantly learning new lessons of moral instruction, and is trained to virtue and order by perpetual and salutary restraints. To all which may be added the restraint of public opinion, which, in a country where christianity is believed, compels even profligates to be outwardly virtuous. Habits and institutions, like these, tho' by many deemed unworthy of notice, and underrated, as subordinate means of securing virtue and order, are here found to possess distinguished efficacy. Influencing reason and opinion, they operate more silently, but far more powerfully than force, or fear. Like the great law of gravity, in the natural world, they tend to the preservation of universal harmony and order in society. They govern man far more effectually, than the most cruel codes of penal laws. When they have produced their effect, and taught man the course of conduct which he ought to pursue, little is left for the magistrate: The business of government is already anticipated.

From the moral culture of the heart, is derived the chief force of moral obligation, and of course, the chief support of human laws. Thence proceed all the endearing ties of gratitude and love, which unite man to man, in the discharge [20] of reciprocal duties, and which unite man to his Maker, in the discharge of the more solemn duties of piety. To be satisfied of the importance of these truths, we feel under no necessity of going abroad for light and information; for few can be found, who will not blush to deny them, in a country like this, where a constant experience of their benefits has produced a general conviction of their truth.

Property, in this country, is pretty equally divided among the people, and the principles of a just and equal distribution are recognized and established by the laws, which regulate the descent of estates. An ocean of three thousand miles has separated us from the vices of an old and corrupt world. With a soil, not so spontaneously productive as to encourage idleness, but sufficiently fertile to repay the annual loan of industry, the innocent employments of an agricultural life have blessed us with health and happiness.

The feudal distinctions of tenant and lord are here unknown. In most European countries, the dependance of the peasants on the rich, produces, on the one side, idleness and pride, and on the other, depression and humiliating debasement. The dependance of our citizens is only on each other, for the supply of mutual wants; which produces mutual confidence and good-will in the interchange of kind offices. Men, respectable [21] for knowledge and worth, without the pride generally attached to their character in other countries, can here freely associate with their less informed fellow-citizens, for diffusing among them useful information. It is the false pride of ignorance, which always elates empty minds; but, in them, good sense carries with itself the antidote to arrogance and vanity. The traveller, reposing confidence in the moral habits of the people, feels himself safe from lawless assaults, and in every village that he enters, meets with the marks of civility and cordial welcome, from the cheerful sons of toil.

Facts of this kind are open to the observation of all, and cannot but be peculiarly interesting to Americans. The astonishing effects of our institutions strike foreigners with surprise, while we, who experience their benefits, are apt to be insensible of their importance.

At no period, was it ever more necessary, that this importance should be understood and felt, than at present. A general attention to the subject of politics, both at home and abroad, has led to the discovery of moral theories, concerning the means of producing national and individual happiness, which, while they come to us, not recommended by the sanction of experience, do, at the same time, strike at the root of our own systems. Principles in their nature visionary, have been [22] held out by speculative men, as improvements upon our own systems, and are already fast gaining ground in popular estimation. A wild way of thinking has arisen, in connexion with events which have recently happened in the world: New ideas on political subjects have been adopted by men of speculative minds, tending to annihilate all that is practical in virtue, and to substitute, in the room, the boldness of unauthorised conjecture. It must be allowed by all, that it is of importance, that we should understand the true genius and spirit of our institutions, and their effects on the state of society, lest, in an age of innovation, we make shipwreck of our political happiness, by venturing on the uncertainty of untried hypothesis. This is the more necessary at a period, when, by an application of our principles of civil liberty to European nations, in a different state of society, mistakes concerning their nature have unavoidably happened. Those who have become converts to liberty, after having recently smarted under the lash of tyranny, like the first converts to christianity, who passed as suddenly from the superstitious darkness of heathenism, could not fail, influenced by feeling rather than reason, to mistake the nature and application of principles, adopted with precipitancy and passion, before opportunity was afforded to study them, with coolness and care, or to trace their extensive and important effects on society. [23] It has been the wish of benevolent minds, that the principles of our liberty might be universally adopted: And as mankind easily believe what they wish to be true, without waiting to enquire, whether liberty can be any blessing to those who have not habituated themselves to that moral restraint which is a necessary substitute for force, the conclusion has been rested in, as certain, that other nations in a totally different situation, could, as easily as ourselves, enjoy what we enjoy, without that previous discipline in the school of virtue, which has laid the foundation of our peculiar state of society. Benevolent men, pleased at beholding this country enjoying rational freedom, but failing to notice that peculiar state of society on which it is grounded, with a well-intentioned but ill-timed zeal, have hastened to make the experiment of giving liberty, like ours, to nations unprepared to receive it: And they have fallen victims to their precipitancy. Ambitious men, treading in their steps, taking advantage of popular passion and revolutionary phrenzy, anxious to acquire, by disorganizing, a distinction which they never would acquire by merit, and to attain a promotion to which they never could have aspired by keeping to the line of duty and honor, and madly estimating their importance by the confusion which they spread, proceeded on to level, with blind violence, the distinctions of virtue, to overthrow the wisdom [24] of ages, and to fill the world with wretchedness and ruin.

These scenes are now past, and Americans, it is to be hoped, will learn from them, a profitable lesson. It is plain that our political happiness is valuable, only, in proportion to the security of its continuance. If this security depends on the preservation of our civil and religious institutions, it follows that the means, by which this can be effected, highly merit our attention. Manly and vigorous resolution duly exerted, in enquiries concerning their nature and influence, will lead to such a knowledge of their importance, as will make it impossible to overlook, or neglect them: While ignorance and sloth, joined with knavery and cunning, by blinding us to their real value, cannot fail to induce us to withhold the attention, necessary for their preservation, and thus precipitate our national ruin. In a situation like ours, no endeavours of false and designing men will be wanting, to warp and seduce us from our principles. What they cannot effect, by the force of ridicule, or the blandishments of persuasion and flattery, they will endeavor to accomplish by sophistry and intrigue.

That we may be guarded against the dangers of innovation, let us be cautious, in what manner we apply ourselves to the study of politics. On [25] this, as on other subjects, common sense will ever be our best guide. This most useful faculty always proceeds, by slow steps and clear deductions from known principles. Carefully consulting facts, it admits no conclusions, as certain, which are not warranted by them. Safe from the fascination of sound, it looks only at things. Experience is its only guide, in examining or adopting.

In private life, it often requires much skill and experience, to hit upon the proper means of accomplishing any good. These qualities are still more necessary, in searching for the means of national happiness. Practical rules, in all situations, are safe; because tried. Theory is novel, and therefore, dangerous. Whenever it is resorted to, it is the source of innumerable errors.

In common life, the projector, who idly wastes his time and estate, by venturing on theoretical plans, which promise no certainty, is, by all, laughed at and pitied. In political matters, where the lives and happiness of millions are at stake, such trifling ought to excite other feelings than those of pity. The speculatist in his closet, may not feel the evils, which flow from the ill success of his plans; but to the great body of mankind, on whom the suffering devolves, they are too serious, not to turn to sadness the wantonness [26] of sport, and touch with remorse even the heart of [the] adamant.

It is only by proceeding in the course of experiment, that advances have ever been made in real knowledge. It was by discarding theory, and by philosophising upon the principles of common sense, that Bacon and Newton were led to the vast improvements which they made in natural philosophy: And it has been by adhering to common sense, that, in a few years, we have been able to know more of the true nature of government, than we could have learned by studying for ages, all the absurd declamations of all the theoretical politicians that ever existed.

It shuns with equal care, the errors of prejudice and the flights of enthusiasm. Are we required to divest ourselves of all prejudice and passion, when about to investigate truth in other sciences, and shall we wrap ourselves up completely in them, when about to apply to the study of politics? The science is interesting to the happiness of our species, and ought therefore to be studied with a candor, proportionate to its importance. Prejudice is a sandy foundation, on which no system can be stable or lasting.—Warmth of passion is apt to warp the mind from truth, and lead it astray into the bewildering [27] paths of error. The republicanism of our countrymen, if it have no other foundation than this, is mere sound. It may animate the soldier in battle; but can do little towards informing his mind, or guiding his conduct, as a citizen.

Prejudice and enthusiasm have ever proved wretched guides, which lead, only to bewilder, and govern, only to destroy: They are equally useless in their influence, and transient in their being. When the events which called them forth, have ceased to impress the mind with their novelty, they die; and with them, the opinions which they created, and the spirit which they inspired. But it is far otherwise with the evils, which they occasion. They inflict wounds, not in the power of time itself to heal, and embitter the cup of life to millions of the human race.

The preservation of our institutions, and the influence which they shall have, depend much on the character of those, who are to direct our national affairs. Human nature is so constituted, that the sentiments and conduct of one part of society are always, in some degree, under the influence of the other. This ever must be the case, while the endowments of the mind and the advantages for improving them continue, as at present, infinitely various. If good men only, could be influential, virtue and order might, in [28] them, uniformly meet with powerful support. But while the world is sufficiently vicious, to allow influence to men of gross immorality, such men will ever be directing their endeavors to increase the stock of vice, by assimilating others to themselves.

Political promotion, in this country, depends on the suffrages of the people. It is for them to determine, on the one hand, the rewards which shall crown the virtuous; and on the other, the success which shall attend the vicious. These rewards, we trust, will be rightly bestowed, if the people properly feel respect for the man, who unites goodness with greatness, and at the same time, detest the villain, the evils of whose villainy are increased by the very abilities which he possesses: If they properly feel, how much permanent good will accrue to our country from the patriotic labors of the one, and how much misery cannot fail to be entailed on it, by the plots and vices of the other.

With these views, let us for a moment, contrast some of the prominent features of their respective characters.

The love of his country is, in the good man, the ruling principle, and the public good is the pole-star, which guides his conduct, in the turbulent [29] ocean of political life. His firmness in support of a cause, which he deems a right one, fear cannot weaken: His resolution danger cannot shake. Aiming steadily at the public welfare, he is discouraged by no difficulty and retarded by no obstacle. Opposition only stimulates his powers and invigorates his exertions. As the fabled Phoenix rises from its own ashes, the fire of his soul is kindled, by attempts to extinguish it. With wisdom to contrive, with strength of arm to execute, difficulties serve but to encourage his zeal and add new energy to his determinations. Always consistent in his political conduct, and steadily pursuing an uniform course, he commands the tribute of respect even from his enemies. Moral principle and inherent worth give him a commanding dignity, which overawes the licentious. His character reflects honor on himself and his country. To society he is an ornament and a benefactor, and from his labors results more permanent benefit, than would accrue from the splendor of conquest, or the accumulation of national wealth.

But what shall we say of characters, in every thing, the reverse! men distinguished for nothing, but baseness, sophistry, corruption, temporising and fickleness; apparently influenced by no higher motives, than pride, selfishness, and [30] ambition. When the seductions of error and folly have led men to sacrifice the principles of integrity to personal interest, and thro' motives of avarice or ambition, to counteract the honest convictions of their own minds; when temptation has led to deviate from the plain road of uprightness, the transition is easy and rapid into the by-paths of intrigue and baseness. A crouching and fawning disposition takes the place of manliness of manners and personal independence. Whatever charms a course of fair and open conduct may have before possessed, they have now lost their influence. Too careless faithfully to examine, too uncandid impartially to judge, the mind becomes wholly divested of any relish for truth. Confounding those obvious distinctions, which common sense has ever been sufficient to discover, and common honesty to observe, it no longer discriminates real worth from meanness, and the true honor of pursuing noble ends, by means equally noble, from the baseness of meanly flattering and temporising, to accomplish dishonorable ends, by means no less dishonorable.

If to such men our country is to look, for upholding its most essential interests, it were madness to flatter ourselves, that we can long continue to enjoy them. Not only the happiness, but [31] the dignity of our nation, which, with our own citizens, is to be the ground of attachment to their country and its government, and which is to claim from foreign nations the tribute of respect, must depend on the character of those, who are to fill our offices of trust and importance. But if on such men we depend, we lean upon the staff of a broken reed, which will surely pierce the hand which it supports.

It was not by such men, that our present happy institutions were planned and established. It was not by such men, the glorious revolution was accomplished, which gave us independence as a nation. Bad men, as they are unwilling to lend their aid to accomplish things so noble, are equally unable to comprehend the greatness of soul and sublimity of virtue, which inspired the breasts of those, to whom, under Providence, we are indebted for their existence. Under the influence of principles, which they contributed to establish, we have erected a new empire, unknown to former times. The spirit of enterprise has given a highly elastic spring to the exertions of our citizens: Our commerce has been greatly extended and our wealth proportionably augmented.

Prosperity so unparalleled, has not failed to excite the envy and the jealousy of other nations, [32] who found, that while they were exhausting their resources in unprofitable wars, we were reaping the fruits of peace. The mind dwells with pleasure, on the picture of our prosperity, and with pain do we reflect, that any circumstances of an unpropitious kind darken the prospect of our glory. With pain are we forced to acknowledge, that it is the natural tendency of prosperity to corrupt the human heart.* But prosperity must be considered as a

---

* "Often, while employed in writing these papers, have I wished for a warning voice of more power. The present moment, however auspicious to the United States, is critical: and, though apparently the end of all their dangers, may prove the time of their greatest danger. I have, indeed, since finishing this address, been mortified more than I can express by accounts which have led me to fear that I have carried my ideas of them too high, and deceived myself with visionary expectations. And should this be true—should the return of peace, and the pride of independence lead them to security and dissipation—should they lose those virtuous and simple manners by which alone republics can long subsist—should false refinement, luxury and impiety, spread among them; excessive jealousy distract their governments; and clashing interests, subject to no strong control, break the federal union: The consequence will be, that the fairest experiment, ever tried in human affairs, will miscarry; and that a revolution that had revived the hopes of good men, and promised an opening to better times, will become a discouragement to all future efforts in favor of liberty, and prove only an opening to a new scene of human degeneracy and misery."

Dr. Price's address to the inhabitants of the United States.

curse rather than a blessing, when it proves the means of corrupting the purity of our national morals and of leading us to reject those wise institutions, established [33] by our ancestors. I have no hesitation in declaring, that whenever, from this or any other cause, there shall exist in the community, a relaxation of every religious and moral principle, together with a general licentiousness of manners and christianity shall here cease to influence the minds of men, there will be an end to the republican system of government. It is an all-important truth and cannot be too forcibly impressed on our minds, that christianity is necessary to fit a nation for enjoying freedom. A government, like ours, cannot flourish, unless there exist among the citizens, a love of justice, benevolence, obedience and contentment. Suppose an individual destitute of these, and what does he become? Without justice, he is prompted to invade his neighbor's rights, to injure his good name, to disturb his domestic peace and defraud him of his property. Without benevolence, he has no concern for others, no solicitude for his country's welfare. But wrapped up in indolent self-enjoyment, and making himself the centre of all, he is fitted to be the slave of venality, or sensual appetite. Without obedience and contentment, he becomes turbulent, proud, and assuming. He has no disposition to remain in that subordinate state, which the good of society requires; but rushing forward into the foremost station, he proudly arrogates to himself the honors, belonging [34] to others, and disturbs the peace and harmony of society. We have now only to extend the idea farther and to imagine a nation composed of individuals universally of this character, and we are presented with the picture of a people altogether unqualified for freedom. The Romans, when they became corrupt, notwithstanding their boasted love of liberty, tamely acquiesced in the government of Julius Caesar, and in a more recent instance, a nation, not behind the Romans in pretensions to freedom, have as quietly submitted to an authority no less despotic. Let Americans open their eyes to the evidence which is before them, and derive wisdom from the instructive lesson which the example of other nations affords them. A corrupt people are fitted to be political slaves, and if we become vicious, to attempt to preserve our liberties will be an absurd and a fruitless task.

When we reflect on these things, and look on our own situation, we cannot but be deeply impressed with a sense of our danger. It cannot be denied, that immorality has, of late, very greatly increased, and that the principles and habits of our ancestors are, by many, ridiculed and despised. Is there not a visible contempt of christianity? Has it not become fashionable to reject the whole system of revealed truth as a [35] cunningly devised fable? Has not infidelity, instead of being confined to the higher circles, of late, pervaded the lowest class? These things are written as with a sun-beam, and they must be worse than blind who do not perceive them.

Ingratitude to God for the great things which he has done for us, is likewise too apparent to need any proof; as also, a spirit of discontent and wanton abuse of the blessings conferred on us. The example of the Jewish nation is useful for our contemplation. Our land, like theirs, was originally settled for the purposes of religion, and the events in their history, are written for our instruction. The uneasiness and discontent which they manifested, God severely punished. Murmuring that they should be under the divine government, and desiring a king, that they might be like the nations around them, God gave them a king in his displeasure. A people, ungrateful for a good government and virtuous rulers, deserve to have the blessing taken away from them. Groundless murmurings have ever been the certain means of bringing down upon a people divine judgments, to punish them for their unthankfulness, and all their unworthy returns for divine goodness. Some may be disposed to look no higher than to mere political causes, for the evils with which a nation may, [36] at any time, be visited. But christians will remember, that there is a governing Providence of God over nations, and whatever instruments are used, still the divine hand is to be ultimately regarded.

It cannot be denied, that in our own country, there are some things which bear very evident marks of the displeasure of the Almighty. I do not exaggerate. Every one's observation must have taught him, that our country, once peaceful and happy, is now rent with divisions. The little cloud that arose, at first, like a man's hand, is spread over the horizon and portends evil.—What shall we say? "Shall a trumpet be blown in the city and the people not be afraid? Shall there be evil in the city and the Lord hath not done it? All power is of God. He putteth down one and setteth up another: He raiseth up, as well as removeth, the mighty man, the judge, the prudent, and the counsellor." It is the same Being, that "turneth wise men backward, and sendeth civil discord into kingdoms."

The anxious mind will be solicitous to know what is to be the issue of these things. We cannot look into futurity. Should we be a virtuous people, we may still hope for the kind protection of that Almighty arm which has often been made bare in our defence. Good men have [37] with pleasure, indulged the idea of our arriving to great national happiness and glory, and that this new and rising empire would be built up and made to flourish, so long as the sun and moon should endure. But from present appearances, have we not reason to apprehend, that the solemn denunciation of the Most High comes addressed to us? "At what instant I shall speak concerning a nation and concerning a kingdom, to build and to plant it; if it do evil in my sight, that it obey not my voice, then I will repent of the good wherewith I said I would benefit them." It is righteousness alone that exalteth a nation, and it is only by returning to that piety, righteousness and sobriety which adorned and blessed the ancestors of our nation, that we can hope to escape divine judgments and prevent the ruin, threatened to a sinful people. If we truly reform, and put away those evil doings which provoke the Lord to jealousy, then may we expect that he will return to us in mercy, and rejoice over us, to bless us and to do us good. To encourage us in so doing, the Almighty has further given us these words of promise: "At what instant I shall speak concerning a kingdom, to pluck up and to pull down and to destroy, if that nation, against which I have pronounced, turn from their evil ways, I also will repent of the evil, that I thought to do unto them." Let us [38] then, as a nation, accept the punishment of our iniquity, and return to the God of our fathers, from whom we have revolted. In this way only, can we expect that divisions will cease, and party spirit subside. In this way only, can we hope that he, who hath the hearts of all men in his hands, will give judgment to them who sit in judgment; and make us to be perfectly joined together, in the same mind and in the same judgment; causing our eyes to see our Jerusalem a quiet habitation, a tabernacle that shall not be taken down, none of whose cords shall be broken, neither any of the stakes thereof removed.

May we all repent, and do our first works, remembering that mercy, when despised, will be followed with judgment. Inattention to God and a continued abuse of his goodness will provoke him to empty us from vessel to vessel, and for the iniquities of our land, many will be the rulers thereof: Unstable as water, we shall not excel. But if we notice the Divine hand which has been lifted up against us, and turn unto God by repentance and works of righteousness; if we speak the truth one to another, and love as brethren, we may still hope, that God will be in the midst of us, and sit in the assembly of our rulers, that he will prosper the work of their hands, and make their administration productive [39] of the public good. God shall fill Zion with judgment and righteousness, and wisdom and knowledge shall be the stability of our times and strength of salvation: And the fear of the Lord shall be our treasure; and he shall lift us high among the nations.

[71]

JOHN LELAND 1754–1841

The Connecticut Dissenters' Strong Box: No. 1

NEW LONDON, 1802

J ohn Leland was identified in connection with Pamphlet No. 62
earlier in this collection. He was preaching from Baptist pulpits in
Massachusetts when he wrote this commentary and petition relating
to freedom of religion in Connecticut. Having long advocated the
separation of Church and State, he was here agitating for the removal
of provisions on religious belief from the Connecticut Constitution.
The pamphlet entitled "The Connecticut Dissenters' Strong Box:
No. 1" contained what follows and a short sample petition to be used
by anyone else wishing to dissent, a reproduction of the Connecticut
ecclesiastical laws, extracts from nineteen other state constitutions
concerning the rights of conscience, and a few random remarks at the
end. Only the essay at the beginning of the pamphlet is
reproduced here.

---

*The Rights of Conscience inalienable; and therefore Religious
Opinions not cognizable by Law: Or, The high-flying Churchman,
stript of his legal Robe, appears a Yaho.*

There are *four* principles contended for, as the foundation of civil
government, viz. birth, property, grace, and compact. The *first* of these
is practised upon in all hereditary monarchies, where it is believed
that the son of a monarch is entitled to dominion upon the decease of
his father, whether he be a wise man or a fool. The *second* principle is
built upon in all aristocratical governments, where the rich landholders
have the sole rule of all their tenants, and make laws at pleasure which

are binding upon all. The *third* principle is adopted by those kingdoms and states that require a religious test to qualify an officer of state, proscribing all non-conformists from civil and religious liberty. This was the error of Constantine's government, who first established the christian religion by law, and then proscribed the pagans and banished the Arian heretics. This error also filled the heads of the anabaptists in Germany (who were re-sprinklers): they supposed that none had a right to rule but gracious men. The same error prevails in the see of Rome, where his holiness exalts himself above all who are called gods, (i.e. kings and rulers) and where no protestant heretic is allowed the liberty of a citizen. This principle is also plead[ed] for in the Ottoman empire, where it is death to call in question the divinity of Mahomet or the authenticity of the Alcoran.

The same evil has twisted itself into the British form of government; where, in the state-establishment of the church of England, no man is eligible to any office, civil or military, without he subscribes to the 39 articles and book of common prayer; and even then, upon receiving [4] a commission for the army the law obliges him to receive the sacrament of the Lord's supper; and no non-conformist is allowed the liberty of his conscience without he subscribes to all the 39 articles but about 4. And when that is done his purse-strings are drawn by others to pay preachers in whom he has no confidence and whom he never hears.

This was the case with several of the southern states (until the revolution) in which the church of England was established.

The *fourth* principle (compact) is adopted in the American states as the basis of civil government. This foundation appears to be a just one by the following investigation:

Suppose a man to remove to a desolate island and take a peaceable possession of it without injuring any, so that he should be the honest inheritor of the isle. So long as he is alone he is the absolute monarch of the place, and his own will is his law, which law is as often altered or repealed as his will changes. In process of time from this man's loins ten sons are grown to manhood and possess property. So long as they are all good men each one can be as absolute, free, and sovereign as his father; but one of the ten turns vagrant, by robbing the rest; this villain is equal to if not an overmatch for any one of the nine— not one of them durst engage him in single combat: reason and safety both dictate to the nine the necessity of a confederation to unite their strength together to repel or destroy the plundering knave. Upon entering into confederation some *compact* or agreement would be stipulated by which each would be bound to do his equal part in fatigue and expense; it would be necessary for these nine to meet at stated times to consult means of safety and happiness; a shady tree or small cabin would answer their purpose; and in case of disagreement four must give up to five.

In this state of things their government would be perfectly democratical, every citizen being a legislator.

[5] In a course of years, from these nine there arises nine thousand; their government can be no longer democratical, prudence would forbid it. Each tribe or district must chuse their representative, who (for the term that he is chosen) has the whole political power of his constituents. These representatives, meeting in assembly, would have power to make laws binding on their constituents; and while their time was spent in making laws for the community each one of the community must advance a little of his money as a compensation therefor. Should these representatives differ in judgment the minor must submit to the major, as in the case above.

From this simple parable the following things are demonstrated:

1. That the law was not made for a righteous man, but for the disobedient. 2. That righteous men have to part with a little of their liberty and property to preserve the rest. 3. That all power is vested in and consequently derived from the people. 4. That the law should rule over rulers, and not rulers over the law. 5. That government is founded on *compact*. 6. That every law made by the legislators inconsistent with the *compact*, modernly called a *constitution*, is usurpive in the legislators and not binding on the people. 7. That whenever government is found inadequate to preserve the liberty and property of the people they have an indubitable right to alter it so as to answer those purposes. 8. That legislators in their legislative capacity cannot alter the constitution, for they are hired servants of the people to act within the limits of the constitution.

From these general observations I shall pass on to examine a question, which has been the strife and contention of ages. The question is, *"Are the Rights of Conscience alienable, or inalienable?"*

The word *conscience* signifies *common science*, a court of judicature which the Almighty has erected in every human breast; a *censor morum* over all his actions. Conscience will ever judge right when it is rightly informed, and speak [6] the truth when it understands it. But to advert to the question—"Does a man upon entering into social compact surrender his conscience to that society to be controlled by the laws thereof, or can he in justice assist in mak[ing] laws to bind his children's consciences before they are born?" I judge not, for the following reasons:

1. Every man must give an account of himself to God, and therefore every man ought to be at liberty to serve God in that way that he can best reconcile it to his conscience. If government can answer for individuals at the day of judgment, let men be controlled by it in religious matters; otherwise let men be free.

2. It would be sinful for a man to surrender that to man which is to be kept sacred for God. A man's mind should be always open to conviction, and an honest man will receive that doctrine which appears the best demonstrated; and what is more common than for the best of men to change their minds? Such are the prejudices of the mind, and such the force of tradition, that a man who never alters his mind is either very weak or very stubborn. How painful then must it be to an honest heart to be bound to observe the principles of his former belief after he is convinced of their imbecility? and this ever has and ever will be the case while the rights of conscience are considered alienable.

3. But supposing it was right for a man to bind his own conscience, yet surely it is very iniquitous to bind the consciences of his children; to make fetters for them before they are born is very cruel. And yet such has been the conduct of men in almost all ages that their children have been bound to believe and worship as their fathers did, or suffer shame, loss, and sometimes life; and at best to be called dissenters, because they dissent from that which they never joined voluntarily, Such conduct in parents is worse than that of the father of Hannibal, who imposed an oath upon his son while a child never to be at peace with the Romans.

4. Finally, religion is a matter between God and individuals, [7] religious opinions of men not being the objects of civil government nor any ways under its control.

It has often been observed by the friends of religious establishment by human laws, that no state can long continue without it; that religion will perish, and nothing but infidelity and atheism prevail.

Are these things facts? Did not the christian religion prevail during the three first centuries, in a more glorious manner than ever it has since, not only without the aid of law, but in opposition to all the laws of haughty monarchs? And did not religion receive a deadly wound by being fostered in the arms of civil power and regulated by law? These things are so.

From that day to this we have but a few instances of religious liberty to judge by; for in almost all states civil rulers (by the instigation of covetous priests) have undertaken to steady the ark of religion by human laws; but yet we have a few of them without leaving our own land.

The state of Rhode-Island has stood above 160 years without any religious establishment. The state of New-York never had any. New-Jersey claims the same. Pennsylvania has also stood from its first settlement until now upon a liberal foundation; and if agriculture, the mechanical arts and commerce, have not flourished in these states equal to any of the states I judge wrong.

It may further be observed, that all the states now in union, saving two or three in New-England, have no legal force used about religion, in directing its course or supporting its preachers. And moreover the federal government is forbidden by the constitution to make any laws establishing any kind of religion. If religion cannot stand, therefore, without the aid of law, it is likely to fall soon in our nation, except in Connecticut and Massachusetts.

To say that "religion cannot stand without a state establishment" is not only contrary to fact (as has been proved already) but is a contradiction in phrase. Religion must have stood a time before any law could have been made about it; and if it did stand almost three [8] hundred years without law it can still stand without it.

The evils of such an establishment are many.

1. Uninspired fallible men make their own opinions tests of orthodoxy, and use their own systems, as Procrustes used his iron bedstead, to stretch and measure the consciences of all others by. Where no toleration is granted to non-conformists either ignorance and superstition prevail or persecution rages; and if toleration is granted to restricted non-conformists the minds of men are biassed to embrace that religion which is favored and pampered by law (and thereby hypocrisy is nourished) while those who cannot stretch their consciences to believe any thing and every thing in the established creed are treated with contempt and opprobrious names; and by such means some are pampered to death by largesses and others confined from doing what good they otherwise could by penury. The first lie under a temptation

to flatter the ruling party, to continue that form of government which brings the sure bread of idleness; the last to despise that government and those rulers that oppress them. The first have their eyes shut to all further light that would alter the religious machine; the last are always seeking new light, and often fall into enthusiasm. Such are the natural evils of establishment in religion by human laws.

2. Such establishments not only wean and alienate the affections of one from another on account of the different usages they receive in their religious sentiments, but are also very impolitic, especially in new countries; for what encouragement can strangers have to migrate with their arts and wealth into a state where they cannot enjoy their religious sentiments without exposing themselves to the law? when at the same time their religious opinions do not lead them to be mutinous. And further, how often have kingdoms and states been greatly weakened by religious tests! In the time of the persecution in France not less than twenty thousand people fled for the enjoyment of religious liberty.

[9] 3. These establishments metamorphose the church into a creature, and religion into a principle of state; which has a natural tendency to make men conclude that *bible religion* is nothing but a *trick of state*. Hence it is that the greatest part of the well informed in literature are overrun with deism and infidelity: nor is it likely it will ever be any better while preaching is made a trade of emolument. And if there is no difference between *bible religion* and *state religion* I shall soon fall into infidelity.

4. There are no two kingdoms or states that establish the same creed or formularies of faith (which alone proves their debility). In one kingdom a man is condemned for not believing a doctrine that he would be condemned for believing in another kingdom. Both of these establishments cannot be right—but both of them can be, and surely are, wrong.

5. The nature of such establishments, further, is to keep from civil office the best of men. Good men cannot believe what they cannot believe; and they will not subscribe to what they disbelieve, and take an oath to maintain what they conclude is error: and as the best of men differ in judgment there may be some of them in any state: their talents and virtue entitle them to fill the most important posts, yet because they differ from the established creed of the state they cannot—will not fill those posts. Whereas villains make no scruple to take any oath.

If these and many more evils attend such establishments—What were and still are the causes that ever there should be a state establishment of religion?

The causes are many—some of them follow.

1. The love of importance is a general evil. It is natural to men to dictate for others; they choose to command the bushel and use the whip-row, to have the halter around the necks of others to hand them at pleasure.

2. An over-fondness for a particular system or sect. This gave rise to the first human establishment of religion, by Constantine the Great. Being converted to the christian [10] system, he established it in the Roman empire, compelled the pagans to submit, and banished the christian heretics, built fine chapels at public expence, and forced large stipends for the preachers. All this was done out of love to the christian religion: but his love operated inadvertently; for he did the christian church more harm than all the persecuting emperors did. It is said that in his day a voice was heard from heaven, saying, "Now is the poison spued into the churches." If this voice was not heard, it nevertheless was a truth; for from that day to this the christian religion has been made a stirrup to mount the steed of popularity, wealth and ambition.

3. To produce uniformity in religion. Rulers often fear that if they leave every man to think, speak and worship as he pleases, that the whole cause will be wrecked in diversity; to prevent which they establish some standard of orthodoxy to effect uniformity. But is uniformity attainable? Millions of men, women and children, have been tortured to death to produce uniformity, and yet the world has not advanced one inch towards it. And as long as men live in different parts of the world, have different habits, education and interests, they will be different in judgment, humanly speaking.

Is conformity of sentiments in matters of religion essential to the happiness of civil government? Not at all. Government has no more to do with the religious opinions of men than it has with the principles of the mathematics. Let every man speak freely without fear—maintain the principles that he believes—worship according to his own faith, either one God, three Gods, no God, or twenty Gods; and let government protect him in so doing, i.e. see that he meets with no personal abuse or loss of property for his religious opinions. Instead of discouraging of him with proscriptions, fines, confiscation or death;

let him be encouraged, as a free man, to bring forth his arguments and maintain his points with all boldness; then if his doctrine is false it will be confuted, and if it is true (though ever so novel) let others credit it. When every [11] man has this liberty what can he wish for more? A liberal man asks for nothing more of government.

The duty of magistrates is not to judge of the divinity or tendency of doctrines, but when those principles break out into overt acts of violence then to use the civil sword and punish the vagrant for what he has done and not for the religious phrenzy that he acted from.

It is not supposable that any established creed contains the whole truth and nothing but truth; but supposing it did, which established church has got it? All bigots contend for it—each society cries out "The temple of the Lord are we." Let one society be supposed to be in possession of the whole—let that society be established by law—the creed of faith that they adopt be so consecrated by government that the man that disbelieves it must die—let this creed finally prevail over the whole world. I ask what honor *truth* gets by all this? None at all. It is famed of a Prussian, called John the Cicero, that by one oration he reconciled two contending princes actually in war; but, says the historian, "it was his six thousand horse of battle that had the most persuasive oratory." So when one creed or church prevails over another, being armed with (a coat of mail) law and sword, truth gets no honor by the victory. Whereas if all stand upon one footing, being equally protected by law as citizens (not as saints) and one prevails over another by cool investigation and fair argument, then truth gains honor, and men more firmly believe it than if it was made an essential article of salvation by law.

Truth disdains the aid of law for its defence—it will stand upon its own merits. The heathens worshipped a goddess called truth, stark naked; and all human decorations of truth serve only to destroy her virgin beauty. It is error, and error alone, that needs human support; and whenever men fly to the law or sword to protect their system of religion and force it upon others, it is evident that they have something in their system that will not bear the light and stand upon the basis of truth.

[12] 4. The common objection "that the ignorant part of the community are not capacitated to judge for themselves" supports the popish hierarchy, and all protestant as well as Turkish and pagan establishments, in idea.

But is this idea just? Has God chosen many of the wise and learned? Has he not hidden the mystery of gospel truth from them and revealed it unto babes? Does the world by wisdom know God? Did many of the rulers believe in Christ when he was upon earth? Were not the learned clergy (the scribes) his most inveterate enemies? Do not great men differ as much as little men in judgment? Have not almost all lawless errors crept into the world through the means of wise men (so called)? Is not a simple man, who makes nature and reason his study, a competent judge of things? Is the bible written (like Caligula's laws) so intricate and high that none but the letter-learned (according to common phrase) can read it? Is not the vision written so plain that he that runs may read it? Do not those who understand the original languages which the bible was written in differ as much in judgment as others? Are the identical copies of Mathew, Mark, Luke and John, together with the epistles, in every university, and in the hands of every master of arts? If not, have not the learned to trust to a human transcription, as much as the unlearned have to a translation? If these questions and others of a like nature can be confuted, then I will confess that it is wisdom for a conclave of bishops or a convocation of clergy to frame a system out of the bible and persuade the legislature to legalise it. No. It would be attended with so much expence, pride, domination, cruelty and bloodshed, that let me rather fall into infidelity; for no religion at all is better than that which is worse than none.

5. The ground work of these establishments of religion is *clerical influence*. Rulers, being persuaded by the clergy that an establishment of religion by human laws would promote the knowledge of the gospel, quell religious disputes, prevent heresy, produce uniformity, and [13] finally be advantageous to the state, establish such creeds as are framed by the clergy; and this they often do the more readily when they are flattered by the clergy that if they thus defend the truth they will become *nursing fathers* to the church and merit something considerable for themselves.

What stimulates the clergy to recommend this mode of reasoning is,

1. Ignorance—not being able to confute error by fair argument.

2. Indolence—not being willing to spend any time to confute the heretical.

3. But chiefly covetousness, to get money—for it may be observed

that in all these establishments settled salaries for the clergy recoverable by law are sure to be interwoven; and was not this the case, I am well convinced that there would not be many if any religious establishments in the christian world.

Having made the foregoing remarks, I shall next make some observations on the religion of *Connecticut*.

If the citizens of this state have any thing in existence that looks like a religious establishment, they ought to be very cautious; for being but a small part of the world they can never expect to extend their religion over the whole of it, without it is so well founded that it cannot be confuted.

If one third part of the face of the globe is allowed to be seas, the earthy parts would compose 4550 such states as Connecticut. The American empire would afford above 200 of them. And as there is no religion in this empire of the same stamp of the Connecticut *standing order*, upon the Saybrook platform, they may expect 199 against 1 at home, and 4549 against 1 abroad.

Connecticut and New-Haven were separate governments till the reign of Charles II. when they were incorporated together by a charter, which charter is still considered by some as the basis of government.

At present [1791] there are in the state about 168 [14] presbyterial, congregational and consociated preachers, 35 baptists, 20 episcopalians, 10 separate congregationals, and a few of other denominations. The first are the *standing order* of Connecticut, to whom all others have to pay obeisance. Societies of the *standing order* are established by law; none have right to vote therein but men of age who possess property to the amount of 40£. or are in full communion in the church. Their choice of ministers is by major vote; and what the society agree to give him annually is levied upon all within the limits of the society-bounds, except they bring a certificate to the clerk of the society that they attend worship elsewhere and contribute to the satisfaction of the society where they attend. The money being levied on the people is distrainable by law, and perpetually binding on the society till the minister is dismissed by a council or by death from his charge.

It is not my intention to give a detail of all the tumults, oppression, fines and imprisonments, that have heretofore been occasioned by this *law-religion*. These things are partly dead and buried, and if they do not rise of themselves let them sleep peaceably in the dust forever. Let it suffice on this head to say, that it is not possible in the nature of things to establish religion by human laws without perverting the design of civil law and oppressing the people.

The certificate that a dissenter produces to the society clerk [1784] must be signed by some officer of the dissenting church, and such church must be protestant-christian, for heathens, deists, Jews and papists, are not indulged in the certificate law; all of them, as well as Turks, must therefore be taxed to the standing order, although they never go among them or know where the meeting-house is.

This certificate law is founded on this principle, "that it is the duty of all persons to support the gospel and the worship of God." Is this principle founded in justice? Is it the duty of a deist to support that which he believes to be a cheat and imposition? Is it the duty of a Jew to [15] support the religion of Jesus Christ, when he really believes that he was an impostor? Must the papists be forced to pay men for preaching down the supremacy of the pope, whom they are sure is the head of the church? Must a Turk maintain a religion opposed to the *alcoran,* which he holds as the sacred oracles of Heaven? These things want better confirmation. If we suppose that it is the duty of all these to support the protestant christian religion, as being the best religion in the world—yet how comes it to pass that human legislatures have right to force them so to do? I now call for an instance where Jesus Christ, the author of his religion, or the apostles, who were divinely inspired, ever gave orders to or intimated that the civil powers on earth ought to force people to observe the rules and doctrine of the gospel.

Mahomet called in the use of law and sword to convert people to this religion; but Jesus did not, does not.

It is the duty of men to love God with all their hearts, and their neighbors as themselves; but have legislatures authority to punish men if they do not? So there are many things that Jesus and the apostles taught that men ought to obey which yet the civil law has no concerns in.

That it is the duty of men who are taught in the word to communicate to the teacher is beyond controversy, but that it is the province of the civil law to force men to do so is denied.

The charter of Charles II. is supposed to be the basis of government in Connecticut; and I request any gentleman to point out a single clause in that charter which authorises the legislature to make any religious laws, establish any religion, or force people to build meeting-houses or pay preachers. If there is no constitutional clause, it follows that the laws are usurpasive in the legislators and not binding on the people. I shall here add, that if the legislature of Connecticut have authority to establish the religion which they prefer to all religions, and force men to support it, then every legislature or legislator has the same authority; and if this be true, the separation of the christians [16] from the pagans, the departure of the protestants from the papists, and the dissention of the presbyterians from the church of England, were all schisms of a criminal nature; and all the persecution that they have met with is the just effect of their stubbornness.

The certificate law supposes, 1. That the legislature have power to establish a religion: This is false. 2. That they have authority to grant indulgence to non-conformists: this is also false, for religious liberty is a *right* and not a *favor*. 3. That the legitimate power of government extends to force people to part with their money for religious purposes. This cannot be proved from the new testament.

The certificate law has lately passed a new modification. Justices of the peace must now examine them; this gives ministers of state a power over religious concerns that the new testament does not. To examine the law part by part would be needless, for the whole of it is wrong.

From what is said this question arises, "Are not contracts with ministers, i.e. between ministers and people, as obligatory as any contracts whatever?" The simple answer is, Yes. Ministers should share the same protection of the law that other men do, and no more. To proscribe them from seats of legislation, &c. is cruel. To indulge them with an exemption from taxes and bearing arms is a tempting emolument. The law should be silent about them; protect them as citizens (not as sacred officers) for the civil law knows no sacred religious officers.

In Rhode-Island, if a congregation of people agree to give a preacher a certain sum of money for preaching the bond is not recoverable by law.*

---

* Some men, who are best informed in the laws of Rhode Island, say, that if ever there was such an act in that state there is nothing like it in existence at this day; and perhaps it is only cast upon them as a stigma because they have ever been friends to religious liberty. However, as the principle is supposable I have treated it as a real fact; and this I have done the more willingly because nine tenths of the people believe it is a fact.

JOHN LELAND 1754–1841

This law was formed upon a good principle, but, [17] unhappy for the makers of that law, they were incoherent in the superstructure.

The principle of that law is, that the gospel is not to be supported by law; that civil rulers have nothing to do with religion in their civil capacities. What business had they then to make that law? The evil seemed to arise from a blending religious *right* and religious *opinions* together. Religious *right* should be protected to *all* men, religious *opinion* to none; i.e. government should confirm the first unto all— the last unto none; each individual having a *right* to differ from all others in *opinion* if he is so persuaded. If a number of people in Rhode-Island or elsewhere are of opinion that ministers of the gospel ought to be supported by law, and chuse to be bound by a bond to pay him, government has no just authority to declare that bond illegal; for in so doing they interfere with private contracts, and deny the people the liberty of conscience. If these people bind nobody but themselves, who is injured by their religious opinions? But if they bind an individual besides themselves, the bond is fraudulent, and ought to be declared illegal. And here lies the mischief of Connecticut religion. My lord, major vote, binds all the minor part, unless they submit to idolatry, i.e. pay an acknowledgment to a power that Jesus Christ never ordained in his church; I mean produce a certificate. Yea, further, Jews, Turks, Heathens, Papists and Deists, if such there are in Connecticut, are bound, and have no redress: and further, this bond is not annually given, but for life, except the minister is dismissed by a number of others, who are in the same predicament with himself.

Although it is no abridgment of religious liberty for congregations to pay their preachers by legal force, in the manner prescribed above, yet it is antichristian; such a church cannot be a church of Christ, because they are not governed by Christ's laws, but by the laws of state; and such ministers do not appear like ambassadors of Christ, but like ministers of state.

[18] The next question is this: "Suppose a congregation of people have agreed to give a minister a certain sum of money annually for life, or during good behaviour, and in a course of time some or all of them change their opinions and verily believe that the preacher is in a capital error, and really from conscience dissent from him—are they still bound to comply with their engagements to the preacher?" This question is supposable, and I believe there have been a few instances of the kind.

If men have bound themselves, honor and honesty call upon

them to comply, but God and conscience call upon them to come out from among them and let such blind guides† alone. Honor and honesty are amiable virtues; but God and conscience call to perfidiousness. This shows the impropriety of such contracts, which always may, and sometimes do lead into such labyrinths. It is time enough to pay a man after his labour is over. People are not required to communicate to the *teacher* before they are *taught*. A man called of God to preach, feels a necessity to preach, and a woe if he does not. And if he is sent by Christ, he looks to him and his laws for support; and if men comply with their duty, he finds relief; if not, he must go to his field, as the priests of old did. A man cannot give a more glaring proof of his covetousness and irreligion, than to say, "If you will give me so much, then I will preach, but if not be assured I will not preach to you."

So that in answering the question, instead of determining which of the evils to chuse, either to disobey God and conscience, or break honor and honesty, I would recommend an escape of both evils, by entering into no such contracts: for the natural evils of imprudence, that men are fallen into, neither God nor man can prevent.

A minister must have a hard heart to wish men to be [19] forced to pay him when (through conscience, enthusiasm, or a private pique) they dissent from his ministry. The spirit of the gospel disdains such measures.

The question before us is not applicable to many cases in Connecticut: the dissenting churches make no contracts for a longer term than a year, and most of them make none at all. Societies of the *standing order* rarely bind themselves in contract with preachers, without binding others beside themselves; and when that is the case the bond is fraudulent: and if those who are bound involuntarily can get clear, it is no breach of honor or honesty.

A few additional remarks shall close my piece.

I. The church of Rome was at first constituted according to the gospel, and at that time her faith was spoken of through the whole world. Being espoused to Christ, as a chaste virgin, she kept her bed pure for her husband, almost three hundred years; but afterwards she played the whore with the kings and princes of this world, who with

† The phrase of *blind guides*, is not intended to cast contempt upon any order of religious preachers; for, let a preacher be orthodox or heterodox, virtuous or vicious, he is always a *blind guide* to those who differ from him in opinion.

their gold and wealth came in unto her, and she became a strumpet: and as she was the first christian church that ever forsook the laws of Christ for her conduct and received the laws of his rivals, i.e. was established by human law, and governed by the legalised edicts of councils, and received large sums of money to support her preachers and her worship by the force of civil power—she is called the MOTHER OF HARLOTS: and all protestant churches, who are regulated by law, and force people to support their preachers, build meeting-houses and otherwise maintain their worship, are DAUGHTERS of this HOLY MOTHER.

II. I am not a citizen of Connecticut—the religious laws of the state do not oppress me, and I expect never will personally; but a love to religious liberty in general induces me thus to speak. Was I a resident in the state, I could not give or receive a certificate to be exempted from ministerial taxes; for in so doing I should confess that the legislature had authority to pamper one religious order in the state, and make all others pay obeisance to [20] that *sheef*. It is high time to know whether all are to be free alike, and whether ministers of state are to be lords over God's heritage.

And there I shall ask the citizens of Connecticut, whether, in the months of April and September, when they chuse their deputies for the assembly, they mean to surrender to them the rights of conscience, and authorise them to make laws binding on their consciences. If not, then all such acts are contrary to the intention of constituent power, as well as unconstitutional and antichristian.

III. It is likely that one part of the people in Connecticut believe in conscience that gospel preachers should be supported by the force of law; and the other part believe that it is not in the province of civil law to interfere or any ways meddle with religious matters. How are both parties to be protected by law in their conscientious belief?

Very easily. Let all those whose consciences dictate that they ought to be taxed by law to maintain their preachers bring in their names to the society clerk by a certain day, and then assess them all, according to their estates, to raise the sum stipulated in the contract; and all others go free. Both parties by this method would enjoy the full liberty of conscience without oppressing one another, the law use no force in matters of conscience, the evil of Rhode-Island law be escaped, and no persons could find fault with it (in a political point of view) but those who fear the conscience of too many would lie dormant, and therefore wish to force them to pay. Here let it be noted, that there are many in the world who believe in conscience that a minister is not entitled to any acknowledgment for his services without he is so poor that he cannot live without it (and thereby convert a gospel debt to alms). Though this opinion is not founded either on reason or scripture, yet it is a better opinion than that which would force them to pay a preacher by human law.

IV. How mortifying must it be to foreigners, and how far from conciliatory is it to citizens of the American [21] states, who, when they come into Connecticut to reside must either conform to the religion of Connecticut or produce a certificate? Does this look like religious liberty or human friendship? Suppose that man (whose name need not be mentioned) that fills every American heart with pleasure and awe, should remove to Connecticut for his health, or any other cause—what a scandal would it be to the state to tax him to a presbyterian minister unless he produced a certificate informing them that he was an episcopalian?

V. The federal constitution certainly had the advantage, of any of the state constitutions, in being made by the wisest men in the whole nation, and after an experiment of a number of years trial, upon republican principles; and that constitution forbids Congress ever to establish any kind of religion, or require any religious test to qualify any officer in any department of the federal government. Let a man be Pagan, Turk, Jew or Christian, he is eligible to any post in that government. So that if the principles of religious liberty, contended for in the foregoing pages, are supposed to be fraught with deism, fourteen states in the Union are now fraught with the same. But the separate states have not surrendered that (supposed) right of establishing religion to Congress. Each state retains all its power, saving what is given to the general government by the federal constitution. The assembly of Connecticut, therefore, still undertake to guide the helm of religion: and if Congress were disposed yet they could not prevent it by any power vested in them by the states. Therefore, if any of the people of Connecticut feel oppressed by the certificate law, or any other of the like nature, their proper mode of procedure will be to remonstrate against the oppression and petition the assembly for a redress of grievance.

VI. Divines generally inform us that there is such a time to come (called the *Latter-Day Glory*) when the knowledge of the Lord shall cover the earth as the waters do the sea, and that this day will appear upon the destruction [22] of the antichrist. If so, I am well convinced that Jesus will first remove all the hindrances of religious establishments, and cause all men to be free in matters of religion. When this is effected, he will say to the kings and great men of the earth, "Now see what I can do; ye have been afraid to leave the church and gospel in my hands alone, without steadying the ark by human law; but now I have taken the power and kingdom to myself, and will work for my own glory." Here let me add, that in the southern states, where there has been the greatest freedom from religious oppression, where liberty of conscience is entirely enjoyed, there has been the greatest revival of religion; which is another proof that true religion can and will prevail best where it is left entirely to Christ.

[72]

ZEPHANIAH SWIFT MOORE
1770–1820

An Oration on the Anniversary of the
Independence of the United States of America

WORCESTER, 1802

Born into a family with Massachusetts residence for a hundred years, Moore was moved at the age of eight to a farm in Vermont. Recognized as precocious, he was sent for a brief period to preparatory school and then to Dartmouth College, where he graduated with distinction. Four years later he held a pastorate in the Congregational Church, which he surrendered after fourteen years to become professor of ancient and modern languages at Dartmouth, then president of Williams College, and, finally, founder and first president of Amherst College. This address, delivered when Moore was thirty-two years old, is notable for its discussion of public opinion and illumination of the theoretical connections between virtue, education, and successful popular government. References to "foreign influence," the undermining of religion and morals, and leaders of the French Revolution establish Moore as a Federalist opposed to Jefferson's policies. While partisan, the essay rises above mere factional name-calling to stake out a theoretical position.

AN ORATION

Among the most interesting events, recorded in the history of the world, is that, which gave rise to this day's festival. The Declaration of the Independence of the United States of America, on the FOURTH OF JULY, 1776, involved in its consequences the happiness of millions, will extend its influence to the latest ages, and ought to be had in everlasting remembrance. We then emerged from our colonial and dependent existence, and took a rank among the Independent nations of the world. To maintain the rank, we had taken, was deemed impossible by the nations of Europe; and they with confidence asserted, we were preparing for an exemplary punishment. That they should not realize what they so confidently expected, wisdom, fortitude, and union were necessary, and the protection of Him, who is the GOD of armies.

[4] Compared with our enemies, we were few in number. We possessed little property, except the soil and its appendages, and were thinly scattered over an extensive country. We were destitute of an army, and a navy; were without any bond of general union; and without any coercive method to raise money, or levy troops.

The nation, with whom we had to contend, was opulent, numerous, powerful, and warlike. They were furnished with all the apparatus of war, both by sea and land; and, if they found it necessary, could add to their strength by forming alliances. The disparity was, indeed, great. It was seen, it was known, it was felt by all.—We look back, feel a kind of astonishment, and are almost ready to say, that the courage and intrepidity of the United States were rashness and frenzy.

But the cause was important. It was the cause of justice and rational liberty against the unjust encroachments of arbitrary power. A consciousness of this animated every heart. We were encouraged by able patriots; we raised armies without compulsion, and supported them almost without means. From various sources we procured arms and all the furniture of war, and were soon able to meet the veteran troops of Greatbritain on equal ground. In many instances we were successful; in disastrous seasons we retained our courage; and, putting ourselves under the protection of Him, who made the stripling David victorious over the brazen shielded [5] Goliath, we captured whole armies of invaders, reduced our enemies to the necessity of withdrawing their forces and acknowledging our Independence, and negotiated and established a peace on terms equal to our wishes, and superior to our hopes.

The most critical period of our national existence had now arrived. Without law and without government, every man did that, which was right in his own eyes. Our firmest patriots trembled for our safety.

But anarchy, that many headed monster, under whose ravages we must soon have been wasted and destroyed, for a moment, slept without his chains.

Public opinion was not contaminated by the poisonous draughts of foreign influence. Modern sentiments of liberty and equality, which are designed to inflame the corrupt and dissocial passions of the human heart, to exhibit the restraints of social order, law, and religion, as unjust and tyrannical, and to render men hostile to every thing which opposes their inclinations, were then unknown.

The revolutionary war had not its origin in the blinding influence of corrupt, insidious, and designing men. It was not excited by the lawless and ambitious desire of rendering America mistress of the world. It does not name for its leaders a DANTON, a MARAT, or a ROBERSPIERE;—but a WASHINGTON, an ADAMS, and other worthies, whose patriotism was pure, and whose only object was their country's good. "The American revolution owed its rise and progress to a just sense [6] in the Americans of their civil rights, of what was due to themselves and posterity, and to a virtuous and patriotic determination to resist the first encroachments of lawless power."

So soon, therefore, as the war was closed, and an honorable peace obtained, the great object of the states, individually and collectively, was to form and adopt constitutions of government, which should preserve to the citizens the free enjoyment of their natural rights, under the protection of equal laws, and impartial justice. Simplicity of manners, habits of industry and economy, together with increasing means of information and moral instruction, afforded a flattering prospect, that government and the blessings of rational liberty would be permanent.

When the government of the United States was organized, and commenced its operation, force and elasticity were given to all its motions by the great and dignified characters, who presided, and to whom its administration was entrusted. We saw with pleasing astonishment the revival of confidence, credit and commerce. The merchant, farmer and mechanic rejoiced under an impressive sense of the vivifying effects of the wise arrangements, which were made.

Under the Presidency of WASHINGTON and ADAMS, our rulers, without the useful aid and instruction of precedent and experience, exploring a new and untried path, in which it would require more wisdom and foresight, than fall to the lot of man, to commit no errors, established peace, and [7] formed advantageous treaties with the nations of Europe, and with the tribes, who inhabit the western wilderness. They preserved our neutrality in midst of the conflicts of the European powers, and their artful, and even violent attempts to involve us in their contentions. They reduced our deranged finances to a regular system, and raised a revenue, which, though little felt by the people, has been sufficient for the support of government, has answered many unforeseen demands, and effected a considerable reduction of the public debt. To the same wise and judicious system may we attribute the existence of our navy, which has repelled many wanton encroachments upon our neutral rights, and been the principal means of our present commercial prosperity.

With great propriety did President JEFFERSON observe, in his Inaugural Speech, that our national Government, at the close of the late administration, was "in the full tide of successful experiment."

Since that period, it is acknowledged by all, a new order of things has been introduced, and many deviations from the prosperous path of the former administration. To determine with accuracy the ultimate effect of these upon our national happiness, time and experience are necessary. While we wait the decision of these, we ought not to forget, that confidence is one of the principal nerves of republicanism, and that circumspection ought never to be changed into jealousy.

[8] Our progress, since the revolution, in population, in wealth, and in the useful arts, has never been equalled by any nation, of which we have an account in the records of time. In tracing this progress, and the causes, which have had influence in raising us to a high state of prosperity, and a dignified rank among the nations of the earth, there is a kind of pleasure, which is more easily felt than described. We cannot but devoutly wish the progress may continue, and that future generations may not point back to us, as another example of those, who have in vain attempted to perpetuate a popular government.

In tracing the rise, progress, and consequences of the American revolution, we cannot but admit, that our freedom from political corruption and the purity of public opinion, have had commanding influence. In the revolutions in Europe and in the rise and decline of empires, the invariable influence of public opinion is clearly seen, and its intimate connexion with rational happiness, or misery, is strikingly exhibited.

For a nation to secure and perpetuate their prosperity and

happiness, they must be in favor of those means, which are connected with prosperity; and in order for this, the public mind must be uncontaminated.—For a moment, therefore, let us turn our attention to the influence of public opinion, and the importance of its being rightly formed.

In the formation of laws and constitutions of [9] civil government, public opinion is the capital director. To conform these to the humors, habits, and opinions of a people, is deemed an important part of legislative wisdom. Legislators ever have been and ever will be influenced by the public mind. For a legislative body to act in opposition to that, is an Herculean task, which has seldom been attempted, and, when attempted in elective governments, has never been followed with success. Men in their legislative capacity will strongly incline to omit those virtues, which are disagreeable, and to spare those vices, which are agreeable to those for whom they legislate. In proportion, therefore, as laws and systems of government affect the happiness of a people, so does public opinion. From this they receive their complexion.

So powerful is the influence of public opinion, that it will direct the conduct of a community against its own laws. Hence, in almost every country, we find statutes which are obsolete, and the breach of which cannot be punished. Hence, also it is, that statutes, which operate against public opinion, have very little effect. We may instance in the statute against duelling, which has no effect in places, where the public voice is against its execution upon offenders. As the administration, therefore, of the government of a people, has influence upon their prosperity, in the same proportion is their prosperity affected by public opinion.

The opinions of a community must be revolutionized, [10] before a revolution can take place in the form or administration of their government. The ancient monarchy of France could not be overthrown, till public opinion was in favor of its destruction. The Swiss Cantons must be revolutionized in opinion, before a change could take place in their government, and political state. The same is true of Geneva. The Declaration of our Independence was an expression of the public will. Without that, it could not have been asserted, nor supported.

In the various stages of the Roman Republic, not only the form and administration of government, but those to whom the management of the Republic was entrusted, were varied and changed, according to

the variations and changes in public opinion. The same is true of all
the popular governments, which have ever existed. In such governments, where the people are the source of honor and authority, and
the election of rulers frequent, a change of the officers of government
is effected by a change of the public mind. From a corruption of that,
the virtuous, patriotic, and faithful may be neglected, and the affairs
of state entrusted to the corrupt, the selfish, and the unfaithful. The
noisy demagogue may triumph over the man of eminent talents and
unsullied patriotism. The wickedly ambitious may be raised to the
chair of state, while those who have devoted their time and talents to
the service of their country, are rejected and loaded with calumny.
Hence, as the [11] public mind is pure or corrupt, so will be the
character of those, who are chosen to places of honor and authority.
Do the character and conduct of rulers hold an intimate relation to
the welfare of a community? Public opinion must, then, be important.

The actions of nations, as well as of individuals, are more
frequently determined by their character, than by their interest. Their
conduct takes its complexion more from their acquired habits,
principles, and opinions, than from a deliberate regard for the public
good. It is with the great body of a people in a community, as with
individuals. On great and important occasions only, do they take an
extended survey of the whole course of their conduct, and admit the
dictates of reason to impress a new bias upon their movements. As
the prevailing habits and opinions of a people are, so will their conduct
be directed, either for, or against their interest and prosperity.

These observations are verified by the known principles of human
nature, and the general history of the world. Opinions have directed
the conduct of communities. Under their influence they have pursued
those means, which have raised them to dignity and happiness; or
those, which have sunk them in misery and ruin.

Public opinion being thus powerful, and its influence so great
upon the condition and happiness of a people, whatever has influence
in its formation, must be considered as highly important. To guard
[12] against its corruption, and to use every effort for its purity, is
the part of a faithful citizen.

To be free from political impurity, and friendly to the means of
perpetuating our prosperity, it is necessary that we be virtuous. Virtue
is the life and support of a free government; for none, but a virtuous
people, can long be governed by persuasion.

If we look back to the ancient republics, we find that their years of prosperity continued no longer, than they retained their virtues. While they retained these, they were free from political feuds, and public opinion was properly formed and directed. With their vices they began their decline, and hastened to their exit.

There was a period, when the Athenians were active, brave, and polished in their manners; when their increase in numbers and wealth was rapid; when they were without a rival in their knowledge and improvements in the arts and sciences; free from broils and contentions, and in a state flourishing and highly prosperous. This period was while they were virtuous. Their customs, manners, and opinions became corrupt. They ceased to be in favor of the means, connected with their prosperity. They were disturbed and broken by factions. They were enfeebled and enslaved, reduced to the lowest stage of savage stupidity and ignorance, and became an easy prey to their enemies. The Romans, after they had subdued the Greeks, and all other nations within the reach of [13] their arms, subdued and enslaved themselves by their vices and political corruptions. These subverted the foundation of their civil liberties and freedom, prepared them for the rod of arbitrary power, and involved them in ruin.

Vice is to the body politic, what a gangrene is to the natural body. This destroys the cords and ligatures, which unite the parts, and strengthen the members to perform their office; and brings on an extinction of life and motion. That destroys the numerous moral ties and connexions, which, like veins and nerves, give strength and freedom to the body politic, and, by disolving these, brings on great and fatal convulsions, and hastens to dissolution.

Virtue, then, is necessary to the existence and preservation of a republican government, and the perpetuity of public happiness. The real importance of virtue to the welfare of society consists in this, that it is an uniform direction of the public will to that which is good. When a people are virtuous, their disposition and opinions, the source of their conduct, being steadily directed to that which is good and right, their conduct must, of course, be right and good. Virtue of necessity aims at the public good; invariably seeks the common welfare; and gives no pain, where it is not necessary for the promotion of that welfare. Wherever, and how long soever it exists, the happiness, of which it is the parent, will also exist. Under its salutary influence public opinion will be uncontaminated, [14] and the body politic retain a state of health and vigor. The public mind was never corrupted on the soil of virtue. On that soil grows nothing, which is impure.

How, then, is the public mind to be formed to virtue? How is the public voice to be influenced to speak in its favor? Is it to be done by disseminating the principles, and pursuing the practices of philosophical illumination? Is it to be done by teaching, "that death is an eternal sleep? that reason dethrones both the kings of earth, and the kings of heaven? that man, when free, wants no other divinity than himself? that every republic, but a republic of atheists, is a chimera? that the end sanctifies the means? that moral obligation is a dream? religion a farce? and the founder of christianity the spurious offspring of pollution? Is it to be done by sending abroad the fairer part of creation in the attire of a female Greek? by making marriage the mockery of a register's office? and by enrolling your sons as conscripts for plunder and butchery?" Are a people to be made virtuous, by teaching them to contemn every thing that is virtuous, and to abhor every thing that can make them virtuous?—No, fellow citizens, virtue never was promoted by these means. It never was the offspring of these principles. They engender corruption. They enkindle a flame, not to be extinguished. Their spread is devastation and ruin. Their influence is death to every republican virtue.

As if designing to warn us against these principles,[15] and to persuade us to be friendly to the means of virtue, that great and excellent man, President WASHINGTON, in the language and character of a father, observed, "of all the dispositions and habits, which lead to political prosperity, religion and morality are indispensable supports. In vain would that man claim the tribute of patriotism, who should labor to subvert these great pillars of human happiness, these firmest props of the duties of men and citizens. The mere politician, equally with the pious man, ought to respect, and to cherish them. A volume could not trace all their connexions with public and private felicity. Let it be simply asked, Where is the security for property, for reputation, for life, if a sense of religious obligation desert the oaths, which are the instruments of investigation in courts of justice? And let us with caution indulge the supposition, that morality can be maintained without religion. Whatever may be conceded to the influence of refined education, on minds of peculiar structure, reason and experience both forbid us to expect, that national morality can prevail, in exclusion of religious principle."

"It is substantially true, that virtue, or morality, is a necessary spring of popular government. The rule, indeed, extends, with more or less force, to every species of free government. Who, that is a sincere friend to it, can look with indifference upon attempts to shake the foundation of the fabric?"

In opposition to these sentiments of our political [16] father, much is said by utopian projectors in favor of knowledge, as what, if universally disseminated, will promote the purity of public opinion, and ensure national prosperity. Great expectations have been raised, that an end will be put to wars, and universal good will pervade the earth, in consequence of philosophical illumination, and certain systems of education, and modes of government. But these speculations proceed upon false data. They suppose, that the cause of political corruption, and of the evils that exist in society, is the ignorance, and not the depravity of man.

But we ask, Was ignorance the cause of the decline and downfal of the ancient republics? Was it ignorance, that rendered the Romans an easy prey to the Goths and Vandals? Was ignorance the cause of the cruelties of Nero, or the barbarities of Roberspiere? Is that the cause of contentions in common life? The source of discord in families, neighborhoods, and societies? Have the bloody scenes, acted in France, been the production of ignorance? If not, let us treat with merited contempt the visionary theories of the GODWINS of the present day, and cherish a respect for the religion of heaven.

In the formation of the public mind, much is done by education. Impressions, made in early life, are not easily erased; and habits of thinking and acting, formed in youth, are seldom laid aside. By education the tender youth may be fitted for treason, stratagem, and death; or they may be trained up [17] for order, peace, and happiness. Much depends on the systems of education, which are adopted, and carried into practice. If these be right, they will be directed not only to the improvement of the intellectual, but of the moral powers, and to the formation of a virtuous character. Virtue will be exhibited in all its charms; vice in all its deformity. The social affections will be strengthened, and that tenderness, humanity, and benevolence taught and enforced, which cement mankind together, and without which the whole fabric of social institutions would be dissolved.

Aware of the influence of education in forming the public mind, the disorganizers of the present day, and such there are, and ever will be in every popular government, whose love of licentiousness and hatred of law and justice are perpetual, in their endeavors to corrupt the minds of the young, have manifested a zeal, which would highly become a better cause. Instead of imbuing the mind with right tastes, affections, and habits, which is the great effort of practical wisdom, they have used every exertion to infuse an everlasting hatred to the laws of social order and virtue. Fatal, indeed, must be the effect of such exertions, if they be not counteracted. A more direct method to destroy the sacred and civil institutions of our country, cannot be named, than that of infusing into the minds of the young the principles of disorder, and training them up for anarchists.

In Egypt, Persia, and Rome, when they were most [18] famous and prosperous, the education of youth occupied a large portion of the time and attention of their legislators and magistrates, as well as of parents and teachers. Their efforts were diligent and successful, and worthy of imitation. "The children of the Persians, during the period of their national glory, were taught virtue, as those of other nations were taught letters."

So great is the influence of education, that it demands the attention of every citizen, of every friend to our national prosperity. It may be made a source of our corruption and final dissolution, or a means of the purity and perpetuation of our republic.

Another cause, which operates with great force in forming the public mind, is the information communicated from the press, through the medium of newspapers and pamphlets.—In this country, almost every man considers himself a politician, and a judge of the affairs of state; and the political sentiments of a large proportion of the community, are derived from the information and essays in the weekly papers. Hence, these papers are of the utmost consequence to the public, and ought ever to be vehicles of truth. The public good ought ever to be their object; and that never can, for a moment, be promoted by falsehood, calumny, or deceit.

The editors of papers must view themselves in a high sense accountable to their country, as the formation of public opinion, in no small degree, depends upon them. In their power it is, to do much [19] in corrupting, and much in promoting the purity of the public mind. They cannot answer it to their own consciences, nor at the bar of their country, if they become the dupes of a party, the tools of the wickedly ambitious, the contemners of virtue, or the calumniators of the wise and patriotic.

A *free* press is one of the greatest blessings of our independence, and one, which we ought highly to prize. But a *licentious* press is a sink of iniquity, a poisonous fountain, whose streams are more to be dreaded, than the ravages of war, or the destruction of the pestilence. It is to be regretted, that any of the presses in this country, should ever be prostituted to the vile purposes of strengthening foreign influence, of corrupting public opinion by weakening the ties of religion and morality, and of calumniating those, who have devoted their lives to the service of their country, and to whose wise and faithful exertions we are, in a very high degree, indebted for our present state of prosperity. While the encouragement given to the publications of such presses, argues that the opinions of many are already corrupted, it tends to increase the corruption with great rapidity. If the streams of truth and patriotism flow from the press, they will have a most salutary effect, in cleansing from political impurity, and promoting the health of the body politic.

So great is the influence of the information communicated from the press, in the formation of public opinion, that it ought not, it cannot be viewed [20] with indifference by any, who are friendly to public happiness.—It is ardently to be wished, that undisguised truth might ever shine in the columns of the weekly gazettes; and that candor, honesty, and patriotism might be the steady guide of those pens, which are employed in political discussion.

Another source of the corruption of public opinion is to be looked for in the exertions of those, who are under the influence of restless, unworthy, aspiring ambition.—In every country there are those, who wish to rise to places of honor and authority, to which, from their merit, they can have no claim. Under a popular government, like ours, the number of such is likely to be great. While steady virtue reigns, and the public mind is pure, they have no prospect of obtaining their object. Hence, they do not hesitate to use their influence, and all the arts of which they are capable, to contaminate the public mind, that they may rise on the tide of corruption to places of honor and power. Men of this class are apt to proclaim their own patriotism, and to say with a rebellious son of old, "O that I were made judge in the land, that every man, which hath any suit or cause, might come unto me, and I would do him justice."

ZEPHANIAH SWIFT MOORE 1770–1820

The arts and intrigues of such men, were among the principal causes of political corruption in the ancient popular governments; and the principal means of hastening their decline and final ruin. They were the deceivers of the people; the leaders of faction; the destroyers of their country.

[21] So long as the laws, by which the moral world is governed, remain as they now are, the character and example of rulers will have influence in forming the public mind. The opinions and conduct of rulers extend their influence through intermediate steps to the lowest class of citizens. The licentious conduct of Charles II, of England, in a very few years, corrupted almost every class of people. It gave a fatal blow to their morals, enfeebled their minds, checked their spirit of enterprise, and made their progress in corruption exceeding rapid. To his we might add the example of many others.

On the other hand, we adduce the character and example of an ALFRED and a WASHINGTON, as having had a most salutary influence upon the opinions and morals of their respective nations. The example of such rulers checks the progress of political impurity, and tends to form the public mind to that which is right. Before such characters licentiousness retires, and vice dares not rear her brazen front.

Such being the influence of the character and example of those, who are in places of honor and authority, it must be highly important, that they be such, as tend to the purity, and not to the corruption of public opinion.

As those, therefore, who justly appreciate National Independence, and who wish to transmit to future generations civil and sacred institutions, the most valuable, let us be vigilant against every source of impurity, and every thing, that tends to vitiate. The [22] necessity of this does, and will increase with our numbers and wealth. Let us trace, and retrace the means of perpetuating our national prosperity; and pursue them with the order of freemen, and with that zeal, which true patriotism never fails to inspire. Let us use every effort to promote the purity of public opinion. The motives to this are infinite. On this depend the preservation of our freedom, and those constitutions of government, of which we boast. Upon this depend the condition of unborn millions, and the future of our country.

In looking over the historical map of the world, we see empire, for many centuries, has been travelling from the east toward the west. Nations have successively risen to their height of grandeur and prosperity; and in succession have they hastened to their dissolution. In their turns they have boasted of their indissolubility, and fondly dreamed that they lived on the confines of a golden age. Arms and wealth, national pride, a high sense of honor, and deep policy, have been pursued by the magistrate and politician, and esteemed the sure means of perpetuating national existence and happiness. The history of the world evidences, that none of these have been sufficient to give the public mind its proper direction, and to obtain the end in view.

The fathers of America chose a different path, in which to seek the desired object. The cultivation of science, the dissemination of religious knowledge, and the practice of virtue, were by them pursued, [23] as the only sure means of rightly forming the public mind, and perpetuating national freedom and happiness. They well knew, that civil liberty could not be preserved without these means; and that good citizens must be made, by making good men. To tread in their path, it is necessary that we be friendly to institutions for the promotion of science, religion, and virtue; that we encourage a *free,* but frown upon a *licentious* press; and that we be faithful in the choice of rulers.

From the dangerous tendency of party spirit and animosity to corrupt and oppress, and to deprive us of every thing we hold dear as men and citizens, let us feel that our laws, constitutions, and interests are one. As we dread the horrors of war, the domination of tyrants, and final ruin, with firmness let us reject the sentiment, that a separation between the sister States must ever take place. As a means of cementing and perpetuating their union, let us cherish a profound respect for the Federal Constitution, and view "the preservation of the general government in its whole constitutional vigor, as the sheet anchor of our peace at home, and safety abroad." A government without a constitution is a government of men, and not of law; and whether in the hands of one, or many, is a despotism. The constitution of the United States is the bond of our union, and the palladium of our public liberties. Every attempt to weaken, or destroy that, is the attempt of an enemy, and ought to be resisted with unshaken firmness.

[24] Having ourselves experienced the evils of war, and enjoyed the unnumbered blessings of peace, we, this day, "sincerely participate in the repose granted our European brethren from the alarms and calamities of a war," which has been, indeed, bloody, expensive, and ruinous.—Long may their peace continue. May their condition be

ameliorated by a reform in their habits and opinions, and by their being fitted for governments, which combine freedom with energy.

Citizens of a country, the freest and happiest the world has hitherto seen, a country which has been the peculiar favorite of Heaven, and in whose history are recorded many signal interpositions of Divine Providence, we have motives innumerable to gratitude and obedience to the Supreme Ruler. Let us maintain a deep and habitual reverence for his government, in which it is a fixed maxim, "That righteousness exalteth a nation; but sin is a reproach to any people." Let us revere the Christian Religion, as being above every thing else adapted to the preservation of our freedom and systems of policy; as affording the only ground, on which to hope for an amelioration of the condition of man; and as enabling us to look forward with consolation and transport, to rising periods of order, peace, and safety, in which truth shall triumph, justice preside over the concerns of men, and benevolence reign in every heart.

FINIS.

[73]

NOAH WEBSTER 1758–1843

An Oration on the Anniversary of the
Declaration of Independence

NEW HAVEN, 1802

Noah Webster, distant kin of the God-like Daniel, was no match
for the younger (by twenty-three years) Webster in eloquence or
in public acclaim. At the same time, the case can be made that Noah
Webster contributed more to the original conceptions of republican
government than did the more famous Daniel Webster. Not only did
Noah have a twenty-three-year head start, but his use of the printed
word allowed him to reach an audience larger than that of the orator
Daniel Webster and to produce a more long-lasting effect. The current
selection is a good case in point. Noah Webster wrote on almost every
topic relevant to history, politics, education, and morals, and always
he combined a fierce patriotism with an iconoclastic eye. Much as
David Hume turned a clear-sighted eye on the standard ideas of his
own time in England, Webster here reconsiders the popular assumptions
then current among Americans concerning their political system, and
departs rather markedly in his conclusions. That Webster's conclusions
are not far from those which many political scientists today would
reach indicates that intellectual realism was one of the strains
present in the writing of the founding era.

AN ORATION

The history of the first English settlements in America, and of the
measures which prepared the way for a revolution in the colonies, is
too interesting not to be well understood by men of common curiosity

and reading in this State. That history unfolds a series of great events, evidently suited to accomplish important purposes in the economy of Divine Providence . . . . events which every American of expanded views must contemplate with admiration; and every Christian, with delight. To recapitulate even the most remarkable of those events, however amusing and instructive the recital, would require more time than the appropriate business of this anniversary would afford. The day we are assembled to commemorate, summons the attention of American citizens to the history and the real objects of the revolution; to the national rights vindicated; to the dignity of character attached to the new sovereignty; to the duties imposed on the citizens, by their new rank and station among nations; to the errors which have been committed in framing the constitutions of the States and the federal compact; and especially to the means of preserving and perpetuating the benefits of Independence.

[6] In the lapse of twenty six years, since the date of our sovereignty, a large proportion of the inhabitants of the United States have been changed. Most of the civil and military characters, conspicuous in the revolution, are now in their graves; and a new generation has arisen to guide the public councils, and to guard the blessings which their fathers have purchased. The experience of the same period of time, has drawn in question some opinions respecting the superior excellence of a republican government; and clouded the brilliant prospect which animated the hopes of the revolutionary patriots. Numerous unexpected difficulties in the management of this species of government, and multifarious disappointments, under the best administrations have arisen in thick succession, to confound the wisdom, and blast the hopes, of the most discerning friends of their country. To trace the causes of these disappointments, is to prevent a repetition of them, or prepare ourselves to meet them with advantage.

It is worthy of observation, that nations sometimes begin their political existence, as young men begin the world, with more courage than foresight, and more enthusiasm than correct judgment. Unacquainted with the perils that await their progress, or disdaining the maxims of experience, and confident of their own powers, they expect to attain to supereminent greatness and prosperity, by means which other nations have found ineffectual, and bid defiance to calamities by which others have been overwhelmed . . . . . Nations, like individuals, may be misled by an ardent enthusiasm, which allures them from the standard of practical wisdom, and commits them to the guidance of visionary projectors. By fondly cherishing the opinion that they enjoy some superior advantages of knowledge, or local situation, the rulers of a state may lose the benefit of history and observation, the surest guides in political affairs; and delude themselves with the belief, that they have wisdom to elude [7] or power to surmount the obstacles which have baffled the exertions of their predecessors.

Such are the mistakes of reformers; and such have been the illusions of the enthusiastic friends of the revolution. Their imagination has been warmed with the belief, that the sequestered position of America, would exempt her citizens from the troubles which harrass Europe; that a general diffusion of knowledge, and superior attainments in policy, would enable them to form constitutions of government, less defective than any which have preceded them; and that their public virtue would secure a faithful, uncorrupt, and impartial administration. Whenever a doubt has been suggested, respecting the duration of a free republic, it has been repelled by one general answer, that the system of representation, supposed to be a modern improvement in free constitutions, is calculated effectually to obviate the evils which other states have experienced, from legislatures consisting of popular assemblies.

But does the wide ocean that rolls between the two continents, detach our citizens from a deep interest in the affairs of Europe? Will our commerce, a productive source of our wealth, permit a separation of interests? And will not our prejudices and our wants, in spite of reason and patriotism, continue, for a long period, to link us to the policy, the opinions, and the interest of European nations?

But if we had the power to insulate our country, our interest, and our hearts, can we assure ourselves that our citizens possess supereminent wisdom, to frame systems of government, which shall be proof against the insidious advances of corruption, and the bold assaults of faction? What has prevented the enlightened sages of antiquity, from viewing man in all his attitudes; and learning all the possible modes, by which the human passions operate on [8] society and government? After the experience of four or five thousand years, and numberless forms of government, how should it happen to be reserved for the Americans to discover the great secret, which has eluded all former inquiry, of infusing into a political constitution, the quality of imperishable durability? Is not the pretension to such superior light and wisdom in our citizens, rather an evidence of pride, self-sufficiency, and *want of wisdom?* If Moses, with an uncommon portion of talents, seconded by divine aid, could not secure his institutions from neglect and corruption, what right have we to expect, that the labors of our lawgivers will be more successful?

But great expectations are formed from *representation* in government, which is supposed to be a modern discovery, destined to give permanency to republics. If representation were a modern invention, every good citizen would wait impatiently for the result of a fair experiment; solicitous that the inventors might not be ultimately numbered among a multitude of dreaming projectors, who commence their schemes, "acribus initiis, incurioso fine,"* with ardent zeal and splendid promises, which end in nothing. But representation is not a modern discovery. It was for ages practiced, not only in France, Spain, Denmark, and Sweden, as it has been in Switzerland and Great-Britain, but in many of the small states of antiquity; not, perhaps, in the same form prescribed by our constitutions, but in a variety of modes, in which the principles of it were fully and fairly tested.

Representation, by enabling a state to govern, without assembling all its citizens, lessens the chance of sudden and violent convulsions; but it neither humbles pride, subdues ambition, nor controls revenge and rivalry. It still [9] leaves a state subject to the operation of all the turbulent, restless passions of man; changing only their direction. It is a popular opinion, but probably a great mistake, that corruption in a state is introduced by men in power; whereas, in fact, it usually originates with the candidates for preferment. Men in office, if respected and rewarded, have few temptations to abuse their trust; but strong and irresistible motives for fidelity and diligence. Their subsistence and their reputation are the most ample guaranty for a faithful discharge of their duties. Men, therefore, who *seek,* not those who *possess,* the honors and emoluments of government, are the first to introduce corruption. It is extremely important that this truth should be duly weighed; for popular jealousy is usually directed exclusively against the officers of government, when in fact, it ought to be employed to guard against the arts and address of *office-seekers.*†

* TACITUS. An. lib. 6. 18.
† By corruption is here intended, not only the influence of money or favors, but an undue bias given to the minds of the electors, from violent passions and strong prejudices, which impel them to abandon *principle* to follow *men.* No man will

NEW HAVEN, 1802

This truth being admitted, for it is authorized by history and observation, we have a clear rule by which to estimate [10] the hazard to which a state is exposed, by a corruption of its true principles. The passions of men being every where the same, and nearly the same proportion of men in every society, directing their views to preferment, we observe that, in all governments, the object and efforts are the same, but the direction of those efforts is varied, according to the form of government, and *always applied to those who have the disposal of honors and offices.* In a monarchy, office-seekers are courtiers, fawning about the ministers or heads of departments . . . . in a pure democracy, they are orators, who mount the rostrum, and harangue the populace, flattering their pride, and inflaming their passions . . . . in a representative republic, they are the *friends of the people,* who address themselves to the electors, with great pretensions to patriotism, with falsehoods, fair promises, and insidious arts. In a monarchy, the minister may be corrupted, and the nation not be materially affected. In a democratic state, the populace may be corrupted by the arts or seduced by the eloquence of a popular orator. In a single hour, an Athenian assembly might be converted from the adorers, into the persecutors of their best magistrates and ablest generals . . . . In the

---

deny that men in power sometimes abuse their trust; nor is it the intention of the writer to discountenance a proper watchfulness over public officers. This vigilance, however, is much better exercised by the legislature, than by candidates for office, printers, clerks and spies. The latter are incessantly exciting groundless alarms and popular suspicions, about officers whose conduct, on a regular inquiry, is found to be unimpeachable. Fraud and delinquency in public officers occasionally occur, and when detected, are universally reprobated and the guilty persons punished. About *real* crimes, there is rarely any difference of opinion . . . . parties and factions arise on doubtful questions and imaginary evils. But the natural growth of corruption in a state, from the mismanagement of men in power, is extremely slow, compared with the vast increase under the impulse of the violent passions [10] raised among electors by the candidates for office. When the electors inlist under *men,* they desert the true principles of elective governments . . . . they follow *their leaders* and *their party,* without examining *measures* or *principles.* This has been the ruin of many states. It is an evil that seems to be *innate* in a republican government, that the electors never remain *free* and *unbiased.* This is a *perversion* of the true principles of an elective government, which is here called *corruption.* and it arises from factions originating mostly with office-seekers. For this evil, no remedy has ever been devised. One general effort of a party to change the administration in a government like ours, does more to introduce and confirm this species of corruption, than all that can be done by men in power, for half a century.

morning, a Themistocles and a Phocion might be idolized by the people; and at evening, sentenced to exile, or condemned to swallow poison. [11] But does a representative government effectually guard the magistrates from similar abuses of popular power? If the electors cannot assemble, to listen to the seductions of an artful orator, has modern invention supplied no means, by which their minds may be perverted, and their passions inflamed? What are gazettes, handbills and pamphlets, but substitutes for orators? A species of silent messengers, walking by night and by day, stealing into farm houses and taverns, whispering tales of fraud about public officers, exciting suspicion, spreading discontent, weakening confidence in government! What is the difference between the misguided zeal of an Athenian assembly, and of the citizens of America, except in the means and the time employed to effect the object? The one resembles a tornado, suddenly collecting and exhausting its force in undistinguishing, but momentary ravages; the other is like the slowly gathering tempest, whose lingering approach is announced by chilling blasts, and a lowering sky.

Whatever may be the form of government, therefore, corruption and misrepresentation find access to those who have the disposal of offices; by various means and different channels indeed, but proceeding primarily from demagogues and office-seekers, of bold designs and profligate principles.

It is said, however, that we have constitutions of government, or fundamental compacts, which proscribe abuses of power, by defining the exact limits of right and duty, and controlling both rulers and people. But how long will a constitutional barrier resist the assaults of faction? From the nature of things, the words of a fundamental code must be general, to comprehend cases which cannot possibly be specified; and of course, liable to be extended, or frittered away by construction. The danger from this quarter is imminent, and hardly admitting of a remedy, when popular jealousy is excited against the constitution, and the rights or the prejudices of the people are to be favored, by enlarging [12] or abridging its powers. When a magistrate becomes more popular than the constitution, he may "draw sin as it were with a cart-rope"* in the work of extending his power over the instrument which was intended to restrain usurpation. Whatever vanity

* Isaiah v. 18.

and self-confidence may suggest, in favor of the restraints of a paper compact, all history and uniform experience evince, that against men who command the current of popular confidence, the best constitution has not the strength of a cobweb. The undisguised encroachments of power give the alarm and excite resistance . . . . but the approaches of despotism, under cover of popular favor, are insidious and often deceive the most discerning friends of a free government.

"Virtue," says the learned, but visionary Montesquieu, "is the foundation of a republic." . . . . "Virtue will maintain a free government," is echoed and reechoed by the political enthusiast . . . . Where is this virtue, and what is it? Among the ancient Greeks and Romans, it was personal bravery, and enthusiastic love of military glory, and a heroic contempt of death, in the service of their country. This species of virtue, so often displayed by the citizens of ancient democracies, is not exclusively the property of republicans. It was found as vigorous and pure under the old monarchy of France, as in Athens or Sparta; and is still as energetic a principle in Denmark, Sweden, or Great-Britain. It proceeds from early habits, and a strong attachment to the place where men are born, and to the customs, manners, and government, in which they are educated. It is the growth of every soil, and the production of every age. Yet this species of virtue, never yet preserved a republic from decay.

If by virtue, writers mean *pure morals,* we shall all agree that such virtue is the true, safe, and permanent foundation of a republic; and so it is, of every other species of [13] government. But when have pure morals adorned the character of a whole nation? A free government founded on exact and universal morality might be durable, if such morality could be enforced, and guarded from declension: . . . . but this presupposes what history and observation, do not authorize us to expect.

Some enthusiasts preach to us the *self denial* of the Spartans, their frugal meals, their rigid discipline, and contempt of riches. Others urge the example of the Chinese, who restrain commerce to preserve their manners from corruption, and their religion and government from innovation. But such examples are inapplicable; for they suppose a condition of society, which would admit of such restraints; or a rigor of despotism which no free nation would now bear. An attempt to restrain commerce, in a state where commercial habits prevail, would occasion a revolution. Even an attempt to introduce the iron money of Sparta into modern Turkey or Russia, would probably shake the throne, and convulse the empire, of the prince who should hazard the experiment.

If there is a possibility of founding a perfectly free government, and giving it permanent duration, it must be raised upon the pure maxims, and supported by the undecaying practice, of that religion, which breathes "peace on earth, and good will to men." That religion is perfectly republican . . . . it is calculated to humble the pride and allay the discontents of men . . . . it restrains the magistrate from oppression, and the subject from revolt . . . . it secures a perfect equality of rights, by enjoining a discharge of all social duties, and a strict subordination to law. The universal prevalence of that religion, in its true spirit, would banish tyranny from the earth. Yet this religion has been perverted, and in many countries, made the basis of a system of ecclesiastical domination, which has enslaved the minds of men, as political power had before enslaved their bodies. To correct [14] these evils, a set of fanatical reformers, called philosophers, charging that oppression to the religion itself, which sprung only from its abuses, have boldly denied the sacred origin of Christianity, and attempted to extirpate its doctrines and institutions. Strange, indeed, that the zealous advocates of a republican government, should wage an inveterate war against the only system of religious principles, compatible with rational freedom, and calculated to maintain a republican constitution! . . . .

But vain are the speculations of closet-philosophy! Baseless and fleeting are the illusions of theory! All forms of government have been tried, from the theocracy of the Israelites, to the splendid paper constitutions of the French reformers. And where are they? What have been their duration and success? Like the vast cities of antiquity, the most of them are known only in story, or their moss-grown ruins alone are left, as proofs that they once existed. Some of them, like the massy pillars of Palmyra, broken and defaced, still exhibit evidence of their ancient splendor, and appear magnificent even in ruins. Others, like the stupendous walls of Babylon, have been so totally swept away by the ravages of time, that not a stone or a moldering column remains to tell where they stood.

If such has been the fate of all former systems of government, must we indulge the melancholy thought, that such is to be the fate of ours? Let us examine the foundations of our systems . . . . to determine, if possible, whether they will sustain the magnificent edifice of freedom and happiness, which their projectors have contemplated.

The eminent characters who have conducted the revolutions in England and America, have laid it down as a fundamental principle in government, that by nature all men are *free, independent,* and *equal;* and this principle, [15] without definition or limitation, forms a main pillar of our constitutions.

If there were but a single man on earth, he certainly could have no masters, but the elements and the inflexible laws of nature. But political axioms, if not mere empty sounds, must have reference to a social state. How then, can men, exposed to each others power, and wanting each others aid, be *free* and *independent?* If one member of a society is free and independent, all the members must be equally so. In such a community, no restraint could exist, for this would destroy freedom and independence. But in such a state of things, the will of each individual would be his only rule of action, and his *will* would be supported by his *strength.* Force then would be the ultimate arbiter of right and wrong, and the wills of the weaker must bend to the power of the stronger. A society, therefore, existing in a state of nature, if such a state can be supposed in which there should be no law but individual wills, must necessarily be in perpetual anarchy or despotism. But no such state of society can exist. The very act of associating destroys the natural freedom and independence of each member of the society, anterior to any compact limiting their respective powers and rights; for it is a principle, resulting from the very nature of society, independent of any mutual agreement for the purpose, that one individual shall not exercise his own power to another's prejudice. Of course, by the very constitution of society, the will of each member is restrained by the laws of general utility, or common good, the details of which are to be regulated by the supreme power. Whatever may be the abstract reasoning of men on this subject, the practice has been, and by the nature of man, must continue to be, that the members of a state or body politic, hold their rights subject to the direction and control of the sovereignty of the state. It is needless to discuss questions of natural right as distinct from a social state, for all rights are social, and subordinate to [16] the supreme will of the whole society. Nor, without such a supreme controlling power over all the members of a state, can an individual possess and enjoy liberty.

In the supposed state of nature, every man being free from the restraint of *law,* every man would be subject to the restraint of *force,* and of course would be a slave. Civil liberty, therefore, instead of being derived from *natural freedom* and *independence,* is the creature of society and government. Man is too feeble to protect himself, and unless he can protect himself, he is not free. But to secure protection, man must submit to the restraints of a sovereign power; subordination, therefore, is the very essence of civil liberty. Yet how often has the abstract, undefined proposition, that "all men are by nature free and independent," furnished the motive or the apology, for insurrection!

Equally fallacious is the doctrine of *equality,* of which much is said, and little understood. That one man in a state, has as good a right as another to his life, limbs, reputation and property, is a proposition that no man will dispute. Nor will it be denied that each member of a society, who has not forfeited his claims by misconduct, has an equal right to protection. But if by *equality,* writers understand an equal right to distinction, and influence; or if they understand an equal share of talents and bodily powers; in these senses, all men are *not* equal. Such an equality would be inconsistent with the whole economy of nature. In the animal and vegetable world, however strong the general resemblance in the individuals of a species, each is marked with a distinct character; and this diversity is one of the principal beauties of creation, and probably an important feature in the system. There are, and there must be, distinctions among men . . . . they are established by nature, as well as by social relations. Age, talents, virtue, public services, the possession of office and certain natural relations, carry with them just claims to distinction, to influence [17] and authority. Miserable, indeed, would be the condition of men, if the son could disengage himself from the authority of his father; the apprentice from the command of his master; and the citizen from the dominion of the law and the magistrate.*

* No doctrine has been less understood or more abused, than that of political *equality.* It is admitted that all men have an equal right to the enjoyment of their life, property and personal security; and it is the duty as it is the object, of government to protect every man in this enjoyment. The man who owns a single horse or cow, has as strong a claim to have that property protected, as the man who owns a ship or a thousand acres of land. So far the doctrine of *equal rights,* is vindicable. But that all men have an equal claim to distinction and authority, is contradicted by the opinions and practice of people in every country. Whatever

Again . . . . It is asserted as an axiom in politics, that the sovereign power resides in the *people*. Unfortunately our language does not, like the Roman, distinguish the *populus* from the *plebs;* the free citizens from those who have not the privilege of suffrage. But if we restrict the word *people* to the free citizens or electors, what act of sovereign power do they or can they exercise? They cannot assemble for debate; but sovereignty consists in the single will of a body acting together, deliberating, deciding, and capable of carrying its decrees into effect. Do the people possess this power?

[18] To avoid this absurdity, some writers allege that the sovereign power is *derived from* the people. This proposition is more correct. The people possess the right of electing agents or substitutes to meet and constitute the supreme power . . . . and farther than this right of electing, which is exercised by a private act of each individual, the people cannot possibly have a share in the sovereign power. This right

---

absurdities men may write, publish and repeat, respecting natural and political equality; in practice, they are usually correct, and would always be so, if they could be left to act from their unbiassed sentiments. All men naturally respect age, experience, superior wisdom, virtue and talents . . . . and when they are to make appointments, they pursue this natural sentiment, and select men who are best qualified for the places. If most men should be asked, are you qualified for the office of chief magistrate . . . . of judge . . . . of ambassador . . . . of president of a college . . . of commander of a ship of war? They will acknowledge their unfitness . . . . they abandon all claims to these distinctions. But the same men will maintain that they have all an *equal right* to suffrage; that is, to an *equal* influence [18] in government. But all men are not equally competent to judge of proper characters to fill offices. This is however not the main objection to the principle. Government is chiefly concerned with the *rights of person* and *rights of property*. Personal rights are few, and are not subject to much difficulty or jealousy. All men are agreed in the *principle* of protecting *persons,* and differ very little in the *mode*. But the *rights of property,* which are numerous, and form nineteen twentieths of all the objects of government, are beyond measure intricate, and difficult to be regulated with justice. Now if all men have an equal right of suffrage, those who have *little* and those who have *no* property, have the power of making regulations respecting the property of others . . . . that is, an equal right to control the property with those who own it. Thus, as property is *unequally* and suffrages *equally* divided, the principle of equal suffrage becomes the basis of *inequality of power*. And this principle, in some of our larger cities, actually gives a *majority of suffrages* to the men who possess not a *twentieth of the property*. Such is the fallacy of abstract propositions in political science! In truth, this principle of *equal suffrage* operates to produce extreme *inequality of rights;* a monstrous inversion of the natural order of society . . . . a species of oppression that will ultimately produce a revolution.

of election is certainly a precious right, and one which, if used with discretion, is the safety and glory of a free state; but the exercise of it cannot, with propriety, be denominated, an act of sovereignty.

Closely connected with this axiom, are the principles recognized by some of the State Constitutions, that "the people have a right to meet together to consult upon the common good, give instructions to their representatives, and request of the legislature a redress of wrongs." But [19] are the rights here described compatible with each other? Are they consistent with the nature of a representative republic? The electors appoint deputies or substitutes, and by that act, delegate away their own power; how then can they meet and exercise the same power? And it is to be observed in this species of delegation, that the agent is appointed, for this very reason, that the electors in person cannot deliberate and act upon public affairs, in their several towns or districts; for if they could, no substitution would be necessary. The right in the electors to meet and deliberate on the common good, is directly incompatible with the act of delegation, which they have before exercised. And it ought not to be forgotten, that the insurgents in Massachusetts, in 1786, cited the clause in the declaration of rights, prefixed to the Constitution of that State, recognizing this right of meeting and consulting for the common good, in justification of their opposition to the law.

It should be remarked farther, that the same clauses in the constitutions, which authorize the people to *instruct* their representatives, permit them only to *request* of the legislature a redress of grievances. But a right to *instruct,* is a right to *direct* and *control*. *Instruction* implies *superior power;* whereas, *request* implies a *want of such power,* or *subordination*. Such are the contradictions which disfigure our constitutions!

In the same spirit of exalting the *people* over the legislature and the magistrate, it is asserted that the officers of government are the *servants of the people,* and *accountable to them*. Is not the direct tendency of such language to degrade all authority, to bring the laws and the officers of government into contempt, and to encourage discontent, faction and insurrection? Such language is not correct . . . . the proposition is not true either in theory or fact. The legislative officers are declared, by the constitution, not to be liable to be called in question for their opinions or [20] votes . . . . their inviolability is guaranteed in the most express manner. How then can they be accountable to the people? The two propositions are a contradiction in terms. The power of the people to omit chusing a representative at a subsequent election, is, by no means, a power to call him to account for his conduct. Nor are executive and judicial officers responsible to the people . . . . if guilty of crimes and misdemeanors, they are answerable to the laws in courts of justice, and to no other tribunal.

It is not unfrequent, that the citizens of our country express their surprize at the popular tumults which have disturbed our tranquility. They are astonished that in this free country, the people should be so lost to a sense of their duty, as to resist the laws. But their surprize must cease, when, upon examination, they find that the people have a *constitutional* right to direct and control the legislature. The transition from the right of *instruction* to the right of *resistance,* is extremely easy; and if all officers of government are the *servants* of the *people,* how can it be expected that the *masters* should not, at times, take the government out of the hands of the *servants!*

Equally absurd is the doctrine that the universal enjoyment of the right of suffrage, is the best security for free elections and a pure administration. The reverse is proved by all experience, to be the fact; that a liberal extension of the right of suffrage accelerates the growth of corruption, by multiplying the number of corruptible electors, and reducing the price of venal suffrages.

It has also been a received maxim, that a frequent rotation of officers, is among the means of guarding a state from the malpractices of the public agents. But this principle has been extended too far, and experience has compelled some of the states to recede from it in their revised constitutions. It has been found that a short and precarious tenure [21] of offices, is the direct means of degrading them, and making them an object of desire only to worthless and incompetent men.

Such are the brilliant theories which have dazzled the founders of our states! Such the illusions by which the admirers of a republican government have been fascinated and misled! But it is the fate of man to be confounded by his own wisdom, and to see the elegant structures raised by his fancy, demolished by the rough hand of experiment. Nor is mortification the only evil to be expected from the fallacy of political doctrines. Errors, wrought into constitutions, have a sanction that gives them high authority, which it requires a long period of time, and perhaps the experience of several public calamities, to destroy.

There is another evil, connected with the very nature of elective governments, which is little suspected by the mass of people, but which of itself balances half the good that is secured by elections; this is, the dependence which the representatives feel upon their immediate constituents. This evil is augmented in proportion to the frequency of the elections and the smallness of the districts in which the candidates are chosen. The fear of losing a future election, subdues the firmness of mind which is a primary quality in a public officer . . . . it even lays snares for his integrity. It contracts his views to the spot in which his electors reside, and often deters him from acting for the interest of the whole community . . . . it makes him the humble instrument of party politics, and local intrigue . . . . it converts him from the rank of a dignified legislator of a state or nation, into a servile, political pettifogger. And to complete the evil, the opinions of each representative must be made known to his constituents, by placing the yeas and nays on the journals of the house of which he is a member. With such a system of elections and legislation, the weakness of man forbids us [22] to expect, that representatives will not often forsake the public interest, to secure a temporary popularity.

But the occasional sacrifices of conscience and the public good to popular fame, are not the darkest shades in the picture. The man who only flatters and cringes to gain applause, is a saint, compared with the man who tramples on law and constitution to secure the popularity his arts have obtained, and to retain the confidence of a party. There is something extremely contemptible in the factitious character of a popularity-seeker, or mere man of the people.

> "All tongues speak of him, and the bleared sights,
> Are spectacled to see him. Your prattling nurse
> Into a rapture lets her baby cry,
> While she chats him. The kitchen malkin pins
> Her richest lockram 'bout her reechy neck,
> Clambering the walls to see him; stalls, bulks, windows,
> Are smothered up, leads filled, and ridges horsed,
> With variable complexions . . . all agreeing,
> In earnestness to see him . . . . such a pother,
> As if that whatsoever god, who leads him,
> Were slily crept into his human powers,
> And gave him graceful posture,"

SHAKESPEAR, CORIOLANUS.

NEW HAVEN, 1802

The natural consequence of too much popularity is, that it enables the possessor to violate the laws and constitution of his country, and sacrifice its interests with impunity . . . . During the war in Europe, in the beginning of the last century, the Duke of Marlborough, by an unusual tide of victory, was borne so high in popularity, that he had influence enough to prolong that war, for the purpose of enriching himself; and a commission was actually prepared, which would have made him general for life, but it was [23] rendered ineffectual by a single member of the ministry, who had firmness enough to refuse his seal.*

To be a tyrant with any tolerable degree of safety, a man must be fully possessed of the confidence of the *people*. Charles the first of England extended the royal prerogative to an unwarrantable length, and lost his head . . . . but that prince could not have sent a detachment of three hundred men to drive the commons of England from their hall, and have effected his purpose. That act of despotism was reserved for the republican Cromwell, the *friend of the people*. James the second was an arbitrary man, a catholic, and odious to the English nation . . . . he was, therefore, compelled to abdicate his throne. But his successor, William, a friend of the whigs, ascended the throne upon a tide of popularity; and *he* could deliberately sign an illegal and barbarous warrant for the murder of the whole village of Glencoe, in Scotland, and never be called in question for the murderous deed!†
"Oh, 'tis excellent," says the poet,

> "To have a giant's strength; but it is tyrannous
> To use it like a giant."
>> MEASURE FOR MEASURE.

The open advocate of a strong government is subject to popular odium, his encroachments are eyed with jealousy, or resisted by force. But the hypocritical pretender to patriotism acquires, in the confidence of the people, a giant's force, and he may use it like a giant. The people, like artless females, are liable to be seduced, not by the men they hate or suspect, but by those they love.

> . . . . "Our natures do pursue,

> Like rats that raven down their proper bane
> A thirsty evil, and when we drink, we die."
>> MEASURE FOR MEASURE.

* Johnson's Life of Swift.
† Smollet. continuation of Hume. Anno. 1691.

[24] Nor is it among the least evils proceeding from the ambition of popular favor, that the *friends of the people* are willing to secure it, by relaxing the energy of the laws. They know that legal restraints are odious, and will hazard the public peace, rather than not gratify the licentious propensities of their partizans. But,

> "Mercy is not itself that oft looks so;
> Pardon is still the nurse of second woe."

> "We have strict statutes and most biting laws,
> (The needful bits and curbs for headstrong steeds:)
> Which for these fourteen years we have let sleep;
> Even like an overgrown lion in a cave,
> That goes not out to prey: now, as fond fathers
> Having bound up the threat'ning twigs of birch,
> Only to stick it in their children's sight
> For terror, not for use; in time the rod
> Becomes more mocked than feared; so our decrees,
> Dead to infliction, to themselves are dead;
> And liberty plucks justice by the nose;
> The baby beats the nurse, and quite athwart
> Goes all decorum." . . . .
>
> MEASURE FOR MEASURE.

But why this gloomy picture of errors committed, and evils felt or expected? Ought we to renounce our predilection for a republican government, and abandon, in despair, the experiment which our fathers have begun? By no means. Not only our duty enjoins, but necessity impels us to prosecute plans of national grandeur and happiness, which were contemplated by the revolution. To advance, indeed, requires courage and firmness; but to retreat is impossible, and would be infamy.

To ourselves, however, and to posterity, it will be useful to inquire, with candor and impartiality, into the causes of our disappointments. The real truth is, our revolutionary [25] schemes were too visionary . . . . and our hopes too sanguine. A republican government, in which the supreme power is created by choice, is unquestionably the most excellent form of government in theory; and with all its imperfections, is, in fact, the most eligible form, for nations in the early stages of society. In old, corrupt, and very populous nations, it is probable that the state of society must always prevent the mass of citizens, from acquiring that portion of property, knowledge and independence of mind, which are absolutely essential to render an elective government a public blessing. Government takes its form very much from the character of the people to be governed; and a republican or free government, necessarily springs from the state of society, manners and property in the United States. No other form is proper for the country . . . . no other will suit the present state of society . . . . no other can be imposed upon our citizens. It would be as difficult to establish a monarchy in the United States, as to found a durable republic in France; and the difficulty would, in both, proceed from a common cause, the unfitness of each species of government for the people of the respective countries. The French project, of *conquering all nations into liberty,* or of giving them all a republican government, has had its admirers. . . . We have seen the tragedy and its catastrophe. As well might the reformers of government attempt to fit all nations with one kind of garment . . . . compelling a Laplander to wear, in winter, the muslins of India, or the tribes that pant beneath a sultry sun on the banks of the Senegal, to wrap themselves in the furs of Siberia.

But although a republican government is admitted to be the best, and most congenial to our state of society, its innate perfections and unavoidable abuses, render it far less durable, than its enthusiastic admirers have supposed. This conclusion, drawn from experience, should silence the [26] complaints of men, who look for more perfection in government than it is susceptible of receiving; it should allay the animosities and temper the discussions of our citizens; . . . . it should produce a more indulgent spirit towards the faults of men in power, and the errors of private individuals.

The consideration, also, that the intended effects of a free government, are mostly defeated by an abuse of its privileges, should make us more solicitous to acquire a deep and correct knowledge of its true principles, and more vigilant in guarding against the impositions of designing men . . . . men who seek offices by fair promises, and flatter only to deceive. Most men are more willing to command than to obey . . . . and more men are desirous to obtain public favor, than are willing to deserve it, by severe study and laborious services. One truth, also, ought to be deeply impressed on the minds of freemen, that men of real worth are always the last to seek offices for themselves . . . . and the last to clamor against men of worth who possess them.

But while considerations like these should abate the expectations of the enthusiast, we should carefully avoid despondence, and faithfully exert our talents to realize the blessings of freedom, under our present form of government. The real object of the revolution was, to secure to the United States, the privilege of governing themselves . . . . not to dissolve all government and resign our country to be the sport of licentious passions and wild misrule. The real object of Independence ought not to be abandoned . . . . it must be steadily and perseveringly pursued. Weak or wicked men may occasionally rise to distinction in the public councils; but whoever may be the men in power, let the government be obeyed. As the poet enjoins:

"Respect to your great place; and let the devil
Be sometimes honored for his burning throne."
MEASURE FOR MEASURE.

[27] To know the real worth of men, their talents and views must be put to the test. The weak and the corrupt, exalted to high and responsible stations, are tried and exposed . . . . and from their elevations, they fall like Lucifer, never again to rise. Nor are combinations of profligate men very formidable in society; as their influence can never be of long duration. Were the power of such combinations equal to the turpitude of the members, they would, in every age, overwhelm the earth. But it is the decree of heaven that the league of iniquity should dissolve, like a rope of sand; for the same perfidious principles which impel men to betray their country and its religion, will make them treacherous to each other.

While we thus attend to the objects of the revolution, with the errors and dangers to which our government is exposed, let us employ a moment in calling to mind the gloomy scenes, and vicissitudes of the war, the wants, the feebleness and the distractions of the Colonies; the distresses of the army, and the solicitude of our citizens. This solemn anniversary has demands upon the sensibilities of the heart, no less than upon the faculties of the mind; and by mingling the recollections of manly sorrow, with the joys of the day, we unite the purposes of virtue with convivial pleasure, and give dignity to the festival. . . Let this anniversary renew the deep, but tranquil grief of the aged sire, who bore the bleeding carcase of a brave son, from the field of victory to a grave.* . . . Let it revive the keen anguish of the mother, whose heart was wrung by the loss of a favorite son, and of the widow, bereaved of an affectionate husband. . . . Let it soften the heart of the orphan, whose hopes of protection and support were blasted by the [28] premature fate of a kind father! Yet while we yield, for the moment, to the sensibilities of our nature, let the proud recollection of the glory won, and the blessings acquired, in the field of battle, arrest the sympathies of the soul, and check the rising flood of sorrow, While our hearts melt with the recollection of the severe sufferings, and glorious fate, of our departed friends, let us be animated with new zeal to imitate their virtues, and with fresh desires to cherish the honor and interest of the country, which they shed their blood to defend.

Let the youth of our country, who were not spectators of the distresses of the war; but who have entered upon the stage of life in time to see the silver locks of the revolutionary patriots, and to witness the scars and the poverty of the war-worn soldier . . . . let these ponder the history and listen to the tale of their fathers' sufferings, and their country's danger. Let them read the animated and energetic addresses of the first American Congress, whose firmness and eloquence would have honored a Roman Senate. . . Let them early imbibe the manly and dignified sentiments of that illustrious council which pointed out the road to independence. . . . Let them catch a portion of the patriotic flame . . . . and by learning to revere the sentiments, may they be led to follow the example, of those venerable sages. . . . Let them review, in imagination, the heroic achievements of the American troops. . . . Let them see, at Bunker's hill, a few hardy farmers, twice repulsing the numerous, well-marshalled columns of the foe, and holding the issue of the contest in suspense. . . . Let them transport their imaginations to the hills of Bennington, the fields of Saratoga, the almost inaccessible cliffs of Stony Point, and the plains of Yorktown where the armies of America closed their triumphs; there let them admire the heroism of the citizen soldier, and catch the spirit of victory. Then let them cast their eyes [29]

---

* Alluding to a fact which took place at Bennington.

upon a shattered army, retreating before a triumphant foe. . . . See the magnanimous WASHINGTON, almost deserted and driven to despair, rallying a small band of half-clothed, dispirited troops, whose naked feet, lacerated with the frost bound clods, stained the road with blood, as they marched to the victories of Trenton and Princeton! Let scenes like these lead them to compassionate the distresses of a half-famished soldiery, who suffered and bled to defend the blessings which we now enjoy, and whose services are yet unrewarded. And when our youth see a needy soldier, grown old in poverty, or the widows and orphans of soldiers, doomed to want by the loss of their protectors, and the depreciation of government paper, let them open the liberal hand of bounty, and by relieving their wants, still divide with them the burthens and the distresses of the revolution. Let them consider that upon them has devolved the task of defending and improving the rich inheritance, purchased by their fathers. Nor let them view this inheritance of National Freedom and Independence, as a fortune that is to be squandered away, in ease and riot, but as an estate to be preserved only by industry, toil and vigilance. Let them cast their eyes around upon the aged fathers of the land, whose declining strength calls for their support, and whose venerable years and wisdom demand their deference and respect. Let them view the fair daughters of America, whose blushing cheeks and modest deportment invite their friendship and protection; whose virtues they are to cherish and reward by their love and fidelity; and whose honor and happiness it is their duty to maintain inviolable. Let them learn to merit the esteem and affections of females of worth, whose rank in life depends much on the reputation of their husbands, and who therefore never fail to respect men of character, as much as they despise those who waste their lives in idleness, gaming and frivolous pursuits.

[30] And let us pay the tribute of respect to the memory of the illustrious hero who led our armies in the field of victory, and the statesman who first presided over our national councils. Let us review the history of his life, to know his worth and learn to value his example and his services. Let us, with a solemn pleasure, visit his tomb; there to drop a tear of affection, and heave a fervent sigh, over departed greatness. . . . There let us pluck a sprig of the willow and the laurel that shade the ashes of a WASHINGTON, and bear it on our bosoms,

to remind us of his amiable virtues, his distinguished achievements, and our irreparable loss! . . . . Then let us resume our stations in life, and animated by his illustrious example, cheerfully attend to the duties assigned us, of improving the advantages, secured to us by the toils of the revolution, and the acquisition of independence.

FINIS.

[74]

SAMUEL KENDAL 1753–1814

Religion the Only Sure Basis of
Free Government

BOSTON, 1804

Throughout the founding era clergymen played an important role in American politics, instructing their congregations on the organization of government, indoctrinating them in moral principles and the conditions of justice, and generating a common holding of political theory in the minds of political leaders and passive citizens. Death before the age of fifty cut short what promised to be a remarkably productive career, considering the unusually large number of Samuel Kendal's sermons that were put into print immediately before and after his death. Kendal was pastor of a Congregational church in Weston, Massachusetts, but his counterpart was to be found in every colony and state and in every denomination that appealed to a sophisticated congregration—Presbyterian, Congregationalist, Baptist, Methodist, Unitarian, or what have you; and whether responding to the Stamp Act as loyal yet unhappy Englishmen, rousing the populace for the war, upholding patriotic fervor during the struggle, helping to bring order and consistency to the chaotic 1780s, engaging in the debate around the Constitution, adapting to new nationhood, or fighting against the anti-clericism that arose during the late 1790s and early 1800s, the clergy helped produce and hold together the core of American political theory. While ministers were prominent in adapting that theory to new problems and events, they also injected, although thoughtfully and with sophistication, the basic commitments from an earlier era into the evolving present. Comparing this sermon with earlier ones will be illustrative.

BOSTON, 1804

AN ELECTION SERMON

DEUTERONOMY, XXXII. 46, 47.

SET YOUR HEARTS UNTO ALL THE WORDS WHICH I TESTIFY AMONG
YOU THIS DAY; WHICH YE SHALL COMMAND YOUR CHILDREN TO
OBSERVE AND DO, ALL THE WORDS OF THIS LAW.
FOR IT IS NOT A VAIN THING FOR YOU; BECAUSE IT IS YOUR LIFE;
AND THROUGH THIS THING YE SHALL PROLONG YOUR DAYS IN
THE LAND WHITHER YE GO OVER JORDAN TO POSSESS IT.

This important advice was given by the Jewish Legislator, just before his death, to the whole congregation of Israel. Moses had exhibited to his nation unequivocal proof of his attachment to their interest, freedom and happiness. Although acknowledged as the son of Pharaoh's daughter, educated at Egypt's court, and assured of the honors and offices which commonly gratify the ambition of men, he disclaimed kindred and alliance with the oppressors of his people, and boldly demanded their release from servitude. By a series of wonders, wrought in the name of Jehovah, he effected their emancipation, and conducted them to the land promised to their fathers.

To form and carry into operation a system of government, and habituate a newly emancipated people to rule and order were important objects to be accomplished. In these, as in the deliverance of the Hebrews, Moses was under the immediate supernatural direction of Heaven. The government was a theocracy; religion the basis on which the [6] whole structure rested. Their institutions, civil and religious, happily combined to improve the nation, and to guard it against being corrupted by admitting strangers to an equal participation of all its privileges. In its advancement from bondage to an independent rank among the nations of the earth, the people were led by the hand of Moses and Aaron; by the civil magistrate and the minister of religion. Each was a chosen instrument to carry on the merciful designs of Providence in respect to ancient Israel; and each the world hath ever found necessary to promote the peace, order and improvement of society.

Arrived at the borders of the promised land, and apprized that he should not be permitted to pass Jordan, Moses gave the people a new edition of the law in the book before us; and, to aid their memory,

rehearsed the mercies and judgments of God, and the duties and
dangers of Israel, in a divine song; in which, with an eloquence worthy
of his subject, he celebrated the praises of Jehovah, and warned the
nation against departing from the statutes he had appointed unto
them.

Having concluded his song, the prophet said to the congregation,
assembled to hear his last instruction, "Set your hearts unto all the
words which I testify among you this day; which ye shall command
your children to observe and do, all the words of this law."

The two great commandments in this law, on which all the rest
depend, according to our Savior, are to love the Lord our God with
all the heart, and our neighbor as ourselves. It therefore related to
religious, moral and social duty. In this view of it the people were
directed by their great deliverer, whose character and achievements,
situation and prospects, gave weight to his counsel, sincerely to regard
its rules and precepts, and to teach and command their children to
observe them. [7] The reason assigned for the injunction we have in
these words: "For it is not a vain thing for you; because it is your life;
and through this thing ye shall prolong your days in the land whither
ye go over Jordan to possess it."

By the life of a community we understand its political existence,
independence, freedom and happiness. In the preservation, or loss, of
these, whatever may be ascribed to natural causes, we often observe
the powerful effect of moral causes. To show the influence of these
upon national freedom and prosperity is more particularly the duty of
the ministers of religion. To this the subject directs our attention.
The importance of the injunction in the text will appear from the
truth and weight of the reason by which it is enforced. Our main
object, therefore, will be to illustrate this general truth, viz.

That religion, and the moral and social virtues, of which *that* is
the great spring, are, under God, the life and security of a free people.

In attempting this, the speaker must rely on the candor of our
civil fathers, and of this numerous and respectable assembly. What
he proposes is, briefly to hint at the necessity and end of civil
government; then show that religion is the only sure basis of good
government; that its influence upon communities is salutary; that it
is the only rational ground of mutual confidence; and that the Christian
system is most favorable to liberty and social order.

The necessity, or at least the expediency, of civil government might be inferred from the universal adoption of it among all nations whose history is known. But we perceive for ourselves that it is impossible for society to exist without it; and conclude, as man is a social being, the Creator designed he should be a subject of law and government.

[8] The end of government is the protection, improvement and happiness of the community. To accomplish this end, as in the natural, so in the political body, there must be a head, or governing power, which shall direct the operations of the members, combine their strength for the common defence, and unite their exertions for the public good.

That is the best government which most effectually restrains the dissocial passions, prevents crimes, and, with the least restriction of natural liberty, preserves order, dispenses justice, and procures to the whole the greatest happiness. To these ends the fundamental principles of every government, and all the laws of the state, should be adapted. The government, whose object or tendency is any other than the public good, or whose administration is guided by other motives than the general interest, neither comports with the design of Heaven, nor merits the esteem and confidence of men.

But such is the imperfection of man, that nothing depending on human authority only is adequate to the proposed end of civil government. The language of experience is, that to control the passions, and habituate men to the love of order, and to act for the public good, some higher authority than that which is merely human must influence their minds. Their views are often too limited to comprehend the reasonableness of yielding private interest and inclination to public utility, or the connexion between surrendering a portion of their natural liberty, and enjoying civil liberty, under the protection of law. The institution of government many seem to imagine designed, not for their own, but the benefit of a chosen few; and though they may dread the sanctions of the law, and the power of the magistrate; yet, feeling no moral obligation to obey, and hoping to evade legal justice, they have but slender motives to obedience while [9] unrestrained passion, or personal interest, impels them to counteract the established system of rule and order; or, if they have correct notions of the general design and tendency of good government, yet viewing it merely as an ordinance of man, and reflecting on the imperfection of legislators, they have but a feeble sense of obligation to observe laws, which oppose their immediate advantage. Fond of self government, they reluctantly delegate the necessary power to others; and when they have consented to it, a jealousy of their rulers often renders them hostile to their administration. Some higher and better established principle of action, than a view to public interest and convenience, must operate on the minds of most men, to render them good members of a civil community.

But what must this higher principle be? The ideas of some seem to have been that there must be a system of political morality established, whose object shall be to fix certain rules of social duty, to the observance of which all shall be obliged by the authority of the state. But if such system is to rest solely on the authority of human laws, and to be the result of human wisdom only, its fitness will be always liable to doubts, and a violation of its principles and rules thought no great crime. It being, as I think it must be, conceded that morality is essential to the support and due administration of government, let it be considered whether the laws of morality must not have some higher origin than the consent of political bodies, and be enforced by other authority than that to whose aid they are deemed necessary. Nothing is gained if they are not supposed to proceed from some superior power, to which human beings are amenable. This can be no other than God. Religious faith, or sentiment, must then be called in to the support of that morality, which is essential to the order and well-being [10] of society; and is, therefore, the basis on which good government ultimately rests.

Belief in the being and providence of God, and that he hath given to men a perfect law, the transgression of which is an offence against him, will furnish motives to virtue suggested by no other consideration. Exclude the thought of a God, of a providence, and of future retribution, and we sap the foundation of morality and social order, and brutalize the human character.

All nations, however ignorant of the true God, and of the worship most acceptable to him, have practically acknowledged the importance of religious sentiment. Sensible that it was the support of virtue, the sages of antiquity inculcated reverence for the imaginary deities of their country; and deemed it hazardous to weaken the influence of religious opinions; though many could not but perceive that the objects of adoration were really no gods.

As every thing in the natural world evinces the existence of a supreme intelligent Agent, so every faculty of the human soul indicates that man was formed for the exercises of religion. If not sufficiently enlightened for that which is pure and rational, he adopts that which is wild and extravagant. Perceiving this universal propensity to some religion, and despairing, probably, of leading the world, by the bare light of philosophy, to a discovery of the divine perfections, the wisest and best men were careful to improve the general sentiment as a motive to every moral and social virtue. Among the Romans, before they had learned to contemn the gods, an oath was a greater security for the faithful performance of a trust, than any bond that could be entered into by the more corrupted and atheistic Greeks. Their idea was, that men will not be induced to perform the duties which result from their social relations, unless they [11] suppose themselves under the inspection of some invisible powerful agent, to whom they are responsible.

Absurd opinions in religion, it is true, were embraced, and gods of different characters adored; and each walked in the name of his god; but in all nations some things have been deemed virtuous, and others vicious; and their religion has a tendency to encourage the one, and to repress the other. Their morals received support, and their government aid, when they were most free, from their religious opinions; and it is more than probable that notwithstanding all their darkness and pagan superstition, tradition had scattered some rays of the true light, which were the principal cause of their brightest virtues.

Some moderns, contrary to the sentiments of the best men in all ages, have impiously asserted, that the idea of a God is subversive of free governments, and tends to support tyrannic rule; and more than intimated that it hath degraded human beings, kept most nations enslaved, and concealed from them the true liberty, dignity and perfectability of man. But judging from the visible disastrous effects of these principles, the conclusion is, that so far as their advocates, according to their ideas, have disincumbered the public mind of religious sentiments, and freed the passions from their restraining influence, they have prepared the way for cruelty and crimes of every description. The experiment has been made in Europe. Heaven forbid that it should be repeated in America!

As the body politic, like the natural body, consists of many members, it is certain all cannot hold the same place, and perform the same functions; but will have parts assigned according to their relative situations and connexion with the body; and the grand *desideratum* is, to infuse into the whole some general principle of action, which, preserving [12] the unity of the body, shall induce each to perform the duties of his station. What beside religious sentiment will uniformly have this effect? Will a principle of honor, or regard to public opinion, supposing it to be enlightened and correct? However these might prevail with a few of a refined taste, enlarged understanding, and superior education, early habituated to respect the precepts of virtue, they have been always found insufficient to regulate the generality of mankind. The idea of a God, and the hopes and fears connected with it, are indispensably necessary to secure the practice of that virtue, which is requisite to the preservation, order and happiness of society. Impress on the public mind a full belief in an all-seeing God, whose law and government are perfect, whose honor is concerned in the obedience of his creatures, and who will render a just recompense to all; and it will be a steady motive to those virtues which are the ornament and life of society, and the glory of man. Add to this general sentiment a persuasion that we have a clear expression of the divine will in the sacred Scriptures, and it must have a happy influence upon public manners, and be a source of individual consolation and hope. The great, rich and honorable, it will teach moderation, humility and condescension; the poor and lowly, it will elevate to dignity of thought, design and action; and present to each a prospect of that state of equality in which they shall appear before their righteous Judge.

In the present world there is neither a real nor apparent equality in the conditions of men. Different abilities, success, power, station and influence, are visible in every community. This arrangement is not an human invention; it is the work of Providence; and an attempt to change the present order of things and reduce all to perfect equality, would be to wage war with Heaven, and exalt the [13] wisdom of man above that of the Creator. The natural rights of men are equal; but their actual advantages and improvement are unequal, and lead to different stations; in which religion teaches them to be content, and faithfully perform their part, as members of the same body, having like care one for another.

Rulers are the constituted head. Their elevation is honorable, their office important, and their characters dignified with the title of gods, and ministers of God. But being men of like passions with other men, in proportion to the importance of their trust, and to their burdens and temptations, they need the influence, support and direction of religious principle. This is equally necessary to secure their fidelity, and to enable them to bear the trials incident to their stations. Realizing that they are subjects of the divine government, elevated to rule over their brethren, as God's vicegerents, and entrusted with authority, for the exercise of which they are responsible to that Being, who "standeth in the congregation of the mighty, and judgeth among the gods," they will make the divine character, law and government, as far as possible, the model of their own. The same principle that induces the ruler to be faithful will incline the people to honor and obey him, as one who exercises "The powers that are ordained of God," and under his wise administration to "lead quiet and peaceable lives in all godliness and honesty."

Let it be added; religion is the only rational ground of mutual confidence. Every person has some governing principle of action; either a supreme regard to the Deity, or to himself. If the former, as God is immutable and his law perfect, *he* will be just whose conduct is regulated by such a standard. His sense of accountability at a tribunal where no artifice can disguise the truth, no subtilty evade a righteous decision, preserves his integrity. [14] But, destitute of this, the predominant passion, or private interest, will determine the conduct of a man; and as it is impossible to foresee what these will be at a given period, because liable to vary with situations and circumstances, there can be no reasonable confidence that he will observe any fixed rule of duty. Public opinion may have considerable influence upon him; and were this never affected by the same passions and prejudices, or by the same want of information, that occasion the errors of individuals, it would merit all the respect it ever received. But it is variable; and sometimes takes its complexion from designing men, who allege its authority in support of measures justifiable on no other ground. It cannot, then, be a fixed standard of right conduct in all cases; because, according to its own concession, it is sometimes misguided; in which case, he who is governed by it may act in opposition to what he perceives the laws of justice and the public good require. But a religious or moral principle leads to the discharge of duty, without considering how the performance of it may affect a man's popularity; and is the only security that men will, at all times, be faithful in their stations.

The dependence of government upon religious sentiment is recognized in the legal administration of an oath, the solemnity and obligation of which will be diminished as the influence of that sentiment shall be destroyed. Impress it more deeply, and its effect will be more evident and salutary. If the great principles of religion were to actuate the whole political body, we should soon see society advancing to its highest perfection.

Christianity is designed to give these principles their full effect. It presents a clear view of the divine character, and of the duty and destiny of man; and furnishes the strongest motives to virtue by inspiring new and more sublime hopes than [15] the light of nature ever imparted. Not in the least diminishing the grandeur of the thought which surrounding phenomena suggest of a God, it introduces to the mind the idea of goodness, or grace, as the connecting link between men and their Creator; by which they may rise to a resemblance of the great standard of moral excellence; to the dignity and privileges of sons of God. It represents our liberty and happiness to be objects of the divine care, exhibits astonishing examples of benevolence, and requires in us the same heavenly temper. It offers a remedy for our moral disorders, and support under natural evils. It enforces every precept of virtue by the consideration that present behaviour will affect our future condition; that God is the witness, and will be the judge of our conduct; that no distinctions, however honorable here, will avail us in the day of final audit; that truth and faithfulness lead to glory, vice and folly to shame and confusion. It forbids the indulgence of the selfish passions, and encourages a generous philanthropy. In its great Founder we behold a perfect pattern of all righteousness; its doctrines enlighten the mind and improve the heart; and its whole spirit is that of harmony and love, which has a benign aspect upon the state of civil society.

It is objected that Christianity hath been the occasion of cruel wars and bloodshed. But until it can be shown that these are the natural effects of Christian principles, or agreeable to the spirit and precepts of the gospel, the objection proves no more than that the best gift of Heaven is capable of being perverted by ignorant or designing men. With equal truth and justice might it be affirmed that patriotism is not a virtue, because under its name scenes of disorder have been introduced, and states enslaved; or that liberty has nothing in it lovely, because the excess of it leads to anarchy and despotism, as that Christianity is unfriendly to the [16] peace and improvement of society, because some have assumed it as a mask for their enormities. The most ingenuous among its enemies have conceded that such objections cannot be fairly urged against the system.

The maxims, as well as the general spirit of this religion, are equally favorable to rational liberty, and to good government. Christianity, indeed, authorizes no particular form of civil government in preference to another; but it speaks of government in general as an ordinance of God, points out its design, and enjoins submission to it, "not only for wrath, but also for conscience' sake." It teaches us to consider rulers as the "ministers of God, sent for the punishment of evil doers, and for the praise of them that do well." It forbids us, though "free, to use our liberty for a cloak of maliciousness;" and commands us to "render to Caesar the things which are Caesar's, and to God the things that are God's;" and not, like the Pharisees, under pretence of religion, to stir up sedition, or, like the Herodians, make a compliment of our religion to Caesar, that we may be in favor with him. By placing all the moral and social virtues on their proper basis, urging them by the highest motives, and introducing charity as the great bond of perfectness, it provides against the evils which result from defect in all human institutions. Under its governing influence, the magistrate will ever keep in view the design of his appointment; the people, the reasons for their submission; and both a nobler motive to their respective duties than ever actuated an unbeliever.

True piety and pure morals, it is maintained by many, would preserve the freedom and happiness of a nation to the latest period of time. Not to say any thing of the divine promises, facts seem to justify the supposition. Corruption of morals and manners has always preceded the fall of states, [17] kingdoms and empires; and with its usual attendants, lust of power, party spirit, intrigue and faction, sanctified by the specious name of patriotism, or disguised under the flattering pretence of liberty, has been the visible cause of their loss of freedom and independence, or of their entire ruin. But should it be admitted that the political body, like the natural, has its infancy, youth and manhood, and must at length sink under the inevitable infirmities of age; that like all earthly things it is subject to decay; still it may be true that religion and virtue, as a suitable regimen and sober habits preserve natural life, will prolong the term of its health, prosperity and glory. But, as certain vices destroy the human constitution, and bring men to an early grave; so impiety and general corruption of manners hurry on the decline of political bodies, especially of free republics, or, by inducing some violent disorder, cut them off in the meridian of their splendor.

These truths admitted, the following inferences will be natural.

The *first* is, that genuine patriotism, as well as personal considerations of infinite moment, requires a strict adherence to the advice given to Israel. Indifference to religion, or to the means of extending and perpetuating the knowledge and influence of its principles and duties, is totally incompatible with enlightened zeal for the freedom and best interest of our country. General information, reverence for the worship of God, and its necessary institutions, and virtuous habits, in a political view, are of the highest importance. Without these it will be impossible long to maintain our free constitutions. Ignorance, or corruption of morals, will have an immediate effect upon the government whose powers emanate from the people, and whose administration is guided by the public will. [18] Through want of information a virtuous people may be induced, under the idea of amendments, to co-operate in schemes subversive of the principles of their government; but when freed from the salutary restraints of religion and virtue, they are in danger of being hurried through the turbid sea of licentious liberty to the rugged and inhospitable shores of despotism. Deceived and demoralized, they will be prepared to second the views of ambition, and to aid any aspiring genius that may grasp at unlimited power. To remain free, a people must be enlightened and virtuous; and in order to this, they must cherish institutions calculated to promote knowledge and virtue. These, in free states, are the sources of political life, and claim our high consideration and respect.

It is worthy of observation, that one part of the law to which our text refers was designed to secure the nation from the corrupting influence of "aliens from the commonwealth of Israel," who, though permitted to enjoy certain privileges, were not allowed to exercise all the rights of citizens; and that Israel seldom failed to suffer by departing from the law in this respect. This provision the wisdom of God ordained for the safety of his chosen people; and it merits consideration in every age and nation.

Natural as well as moral causes operate the destruction of republics. The Roman commonwealth, fallen indeed from her republican virtues, was at length crushed by her own weight. Extending her territorial possessions, she lost her freedom. This might have been expected; for the central force in all cases must be proportionate to the extent of its intended operation, and to the repelling power to be overcome. In free republics it is limited, that liberty may be more secure; but extending the space over which it must operate induces the necessity of increasing the momentum; which may effect [19] a radical change in the government, more or less injurious to liberty, introduce monarchy, a more to be dreaded aristocracy, or, which is commonly a disastrous event, lead to the division of a large into a number of small rival states.

But it belongs rather to the politician than to the minister of religion to contemplate and guard against such dangers. They are increased by neglect to improve the public mind in knowledge, virtue and religion, and to strengthen the general attachment to the principles of the government, and aversion to frequent innovations. As ours is a vastly extended republic, composed in some measure of jarring materials, of the bond and of the free, the feelings of every true patriot and friend of republican government, must be deeply interested in preserving pure the sources and vehicles of information, and in extending, among the bond as well as the free, the means of religious and moral instruction.

The example of our venerable ancestors is recommended by the success of their exertions. In their view every thing possible was to be attempted to disseminate knowledge, and fix in the public mind the principles of religion and virtue. As soon as the desert became so far a fruitful field, as to afford sustenance to a few families, they formed into little societies, whose most prominent feature was reverence for the institutions of religion, and care of the education of the youth. Heaven smiled upon their laudable efforts; and we feel an honest pride in paying a tribute of respect to their memory, and in acknowledging the advantages we have derived from their attention to these things; the effect of which upon the present state of society in New-England, compared with what it is in those sections of our country where the same views did not actuate the first settlers, is as happy as it is visible. Our fathers have transmitted to us a fair inheritance; and [20] through the efficacy of the same means, if as generally adopted, we may hope to hand it down to posterity.

We next infer, *secondly,* that lessening the influence of religious sentiment, to which neglect, or contempt of sacred institutions tends, is extremely hazardous to the public weal. Persuade men that they are under no law to God, that his existence and providence are doubtful, their accountability and a future state uncertain, and they will be prepared, if passion or interest urge, to trample on the authority of all law and government. To secure order and justice, the arm of the magistrate must be strengthened, and liberty abridged, in proportion as the influence of religion is diminished.

To effect designs, the execution of which required the unrestrained indulgence of the worst passions of the heart, their authors have used means to pervert or destroy this influence. If atheism do not best comport with their purpose, they will, if possible, pervert the sentiment, and make religion consist, not in rational piety and humble obedience, but in passion and blind devotion; and render it subservient to their views by infusing into the mind the unhallowed fire of enthusiasm, or the gloomy severity of bigoted superstition; either of which detracts from the credit of religion in general; though less disastrous in its effects than the total annihilation of religious principle.

To prevent a return of the revolted tribes to the house of Judah, Jeroboam "set up golden calves, and made priests of the lowest of the people;" thus corrupting religion to secure his reign over Israel; the melancholy consequences of which are seen in almost every page of their history. For a purpose not very dissimilar, in later times, a still bolder step hath been taken, and an attempt made to establish absolute atheism; the success of which, though [21] partial, hath blackened the character and multiplied the miseries of man.

Eradicate all sense of accountability to the moral Governor of the world, and what security could there be that iniquity will not be framed and established by law? Oaths of office, or of evidence, will not bind men to be faithful, or true. The streams of justice will be polluted, or turned from their course, and passion, interest, or prejudice, decide the fate of innocence. The judge, it is true, who neither fears God, nor regards man, who has no sense of religious or moral obligation, to avoid the inconvenience of importunity, may avenge a poor widow; but will never do justice from a higher motive. As it may best accord with his convenience, he will neglect the oppressed, or aid the oppressor. There is nothing in his conscience to ensure the faithful administration of justice. Life, every thing dear in life, or valuable in society, depending on him, is at hazard. Place in the several departments like characters, and what confidence can there be in government? Would not civil commotions and scenes of violence soon commence, and continue till some one, more artful, ambitious and successful than the rest, elevate himself upon the ruins of liberty and republican virtue?

Convinced of the salutary influence of Christianity upon the state of civil society, and of its tendency to preserve a free government, suspicion justly attaches to the political principles and views of its avowed enemies and revilers. Enlightened friends of the people, and of equal laws, can never wish to bring into discredit and contempt, the benign religion of the gospel. By doing this among a people educated in the belief of it, they destroy the influence of religious sentiment in general; because the mind has been in the habit of associating the doctrines of revelation with the first principles of religion, and of supposing the existence and providence [22] of God no more certain than the divine mission and authority of Jesus Christ. Though some are able to distinguish between natural and revealed religion, and, rejecting the latter, profess to embrace the former; yet it will be found, with many at least, that speculative deism and practical atheism are nearly allied. The prevalence of either will excite concern in the virtuous patriot, not for the ark of God only; but for the honor, freedom and safety of his country. Under this impression, the injunction of the Jewish lawgiver will command his attention, religion and its institutions his reverence and support, as the best means of improving society, giving stability to a free government, and permanency to every social enjoyment.

Religion and virtue, we infer, *thirdly,* will be a prominent feature in the character of wise and good rulers. These are important qualifications for their stations. To concede the general utility of such a principle of action, and yet suppose it unnecessary that rulers should be under its influence, is too great an inconsistency to be seriously maintained. The piety and virtue requisite for the preservation of the body politic ought to be visible in the head. If this be sick, the whole heart will be faint. Void of religious principle, or sense of moral obligation, can we believe that civil rulers will be the ministers of God for good? May we not rather apprehend that they will be an encouragement to evil doers, and a terror to these who do well? But a steady eye to a presiding Deity, with humble reliance on the wisdom of his providence, will direct, animate and support them in all the duties of their office, make them faithful, and render them superior to the trials that may await them.

Moses provided able men, such as feared God, men of truth, hating covetousness, to be rulers of thousands, of hundreds, of fifties, and of tens; a clear indication that in every department men [23] should be placed, who will act in the fear of God. Destitute of this, their influence and example will tend to subvert the foundations of social order, to weaken the springs of political life, and to corrupt the whole system.

But must our civil rulers be Christians? It certainly cannot be less important to the general interest that they should be, than that other members of the community should be under the influence of this religion; and the constitution of this commonwealth requires of them, previous to their entering on the duties of their office, a declaration of their belief in the Christian religion, and full persuasion of its truth. As that does not contemplate evasion, an unbeliever, whatever he might be tempted to affirm, would not possess the qualification which the constitution makes requisite. As an expression of the public sentiment this provision has merit; but religious tests are feeble barriers against unprincipled men. They take no hold on the conscience of one who mentally consigns himself to an everlasting sleep, and never acts with reference to a judgment to come. It ought, however, to be presumed, unless there should be decisive proof to the contrary, that no man will ever hazard his reputation for veracity, and the confidence of his fellow-men, so much, as to make the declaration in opposition to his inward conviction, and common profession. We may feel assured, at least, that he would not, after such a declaration, place himself in the ranks of the avowed enemies of Christianity. Should this happen, what ground of confidence would be left? The speaker feels almost constrained to apologize for a suggestion so dishonorable to human nature. A possible case only is supposed. Should it ever exist, no apology would be due.

If Christianity tend to enrich the heart with every amiable and beneficial virtue, and highly to improve the present condition of man, it is of vast importance [24] that rulers should feel its influence, and reflect the light of it on every beholder.

We infer, *fourthly,* that wise and good rulers will guard and promote the interest of religion and literature. One is the parent, the other the handmaid of virtue. To extend the knowledge and influence of those truths, on the observance of which the freedom and happiness of the state depend, merits and will command their attention. Like Moses, they will endeavor to make the people know the statutes of God, and his law. Tending to the public good, this is one end of their appointment. They will regard the immutable laws of justice in the structure of all the laws of the State, which must result from the divine law, applied to the circumstances of the people. When made, the wise and virtuous ruler, by a punctual observance of them, will add to their dignity and authority in the view of the community.

To prevent is more noble than to punish crimes. The means, therefore, to improve the understanding, mend the heart, restrain the dissocial passions, and call into exercise the benevolent affections, will receive countenance and support from the faithful ruler. On the side of religion and virtue he will give the whole weight of his example and influence. As these have a powerful effect in forming the public sentiment and manners, he will respect the law of God, honor the Savior, reverence the institutions of religion, encourage attendance upon them, and discountenance every practice that would defeat their design.

The opinion of some, that government ought to take no notice of religion, that it is the exclusive concern of the Deity to preserve the worship of himself in the world, and that it would be presumption in legislators to enact any laws relating to it, is not correct, nor consistent with the practice under the freest governments. Improper it would be, and what it is to be hoped we shall never see in [25] our country, to enact "laws to dictate what articles of faith men shall believe, what mode of worship they shall adopt, or to raise and establish one mode or worship, or denomination of Christians above, or in preference to another." In these respects let the mind be perfectly free, and all denominations equally under the protection and countenance of the law. But the support of institutions calculated to promote religious knowledge in general, give efficacy to the precepts of the gospel, instil the principles of morality, and improve the social affections, may be a proper subject of legislation. Blasphemy is punished by law, not because God is unable to vindicate the honor of his name; but because it is a crime which weakens the bands of society by lessening the solemnity and obligation of an oath; and legal aid may be given to religious institutions which strengthen those bands of society by extending the knowledge and influence of the sentiments,

SAMUEL KENDAL 1753–1814

which give to an oath its whole force upon the conscience. Moral instruction is not less important than instruction in the arts and sciences; and the means of it demand as much the care of the guardians of the public weal. Motives of sound policy, as well as the best feelings of his heart, will therefore induce every good ruler to give them all necessary encouragement.

Religion and virtue being the life of a free people, and deriving countenance, or discouragement, from the example, influence and authority of rulers, we observe, *lastly,* that it is of the highest importance carefully to exercise the right of election. Incalculable mischief may result from the neglect, or abuse of this privilege. Through the one, weak or wicked men may be exalted to bear rule by a minor part of the community; through the other, our happy constitutions may be destroyed, and our liberty sacrificed to passion and party zeal. From either great evil is to be apprehended. The elections [26] indicate what information and virtue a people possess, and how far they are influenced by a regard to the public good. Difference in political opinions is no certain proof that either side does not aim at the general welfare; but when base means are employed by either, the purity of their motives is liable to suspicion.

If the enlightened and virtuous part of the community will not improve their right, and give their suffrages to the able and faithful only; or if the majority suffer themselves to be governed by other considerations than those of public benefit, the ill consequences may be soon felt, but not easily remedied. The passions and prejudices of men may be quickly excited, and their confidence withdrawn from their best friends, by trifling circumstances, which, if they actually exist, imply no delinquency. Against these we should be guarded as much as possible. No avoidable circumstance should be permitted to exist, which might operate against the choice of the best men. The freedom of elections should be preserved with the utmost vigilance. In exercising this important right, the object should be to bring into the government the greatest wisdom, virtue and experience to be found; that the people may behold in their rulers a constant example of those things, which are the main pillars of their freedom. Attention should fix on able men; but such, at the same time, as fear God. Great abilities and popular talents, without a moral principle to direct their application, should be trusted, if trusted at all, with great caution. Men of integrity, of steady habits and strict virtue, are the only men that have a title to public confidence. In a Christian country, the general sentiment and suffrage, it may be expected, will create a more effectual bar against men of antichristian principles and policy than any constitutional test. These principles, and this policy, in whatever light they may appear, undermine [27] civil liberty and social order; and, if they prevail, will inevitably effect a change for worse in the state of society.

A free people have the means of their preservation in their own hands; and if they fall it will be through their own indiscretion. Bad men cannot rise and continue in office without their consent, or a faulty neglect of their privileges. If they voluntarily choose such to rule over them, they manifest a criminal indifference to their own, and the happiness of posterity. To honor such is to dishonor God. It would indicate a corruption of morals, and be an abuse of the right of suffrage; and this tends still further to pervert the public taste and sentiment. In elective governments the people and the constituted organs of their will, have a reciprocal influence in forming the general character; the one in elevating to office, the other in exercising the powers of their elevation; and it should be employed by both to prevent a corruption of manners. In nothing can a nation honor themselves more, or secure their liberty better, than in committing the administration of their government to able and faithful men, as eminent for their moral virtues as for their political wisdom. Should a people, merely because of a coincidence in political opinions, give their suffrages to men with whom they could not confide their individual concerns, they might well be jealous of their rulers; but would deserve all they could apprehend. For a Christian, under the influence of such a motive, to favor the choice of a known enemy to his Lord, and to the religion on which he builds his hope of happiness, is something worse than inconsistency. Constitutionally in office, to such an one the Christian will be *subject for conscience' sake;* but will never willingly aid in his advancement.

In scanning men and their measures, let justice and candor preside. This we owe to them, and [28] to our own reputation. The office of the magistrate, the station of the legislator, their private rights and the public good, forbid all calumny, misrepresentation and abuse. But a fair and candid investigation of the characters and qualifications of candidates for office, of rulers and their administration, is a duty imposed by a proper regard to our own, and to the happiness of posterity; of which we are the present guardians. That character is unworthy, which will not bear the light of truth; that suspicious, which seeks defense in a suppression of the truth; but that entitled to protection, which is assailed by the base art of falsehood, and groundless insinuation.

On the due observance of these things the freedom and glory of our country are suspended. If we depart from the principles of our ancestors, neglect religion and its institutions, are not attentive to the instruction of our youth in religious and moral duty, as well as in human literature, indulge a spirit of innovation, are indifferent to the moral character of rulers, and yield to the temptations to luxury and dissoluteness of manners, which increasing wealth presents, we shall soon find ourselves unable to support the constitutions which have been the pride of our nation, and the admiration of the world. But if we diligently attend to all these things, set our own hearts unto all the words of the divine law, and command our children to observe and do them, it will be our life, and we shall prolong our days in this good land. The mouth of the Lord hath spoken it.

Our fathers passed through the sea, were under the cloud, and in the wilderness. God was their shield, and he hath been our helper. A retrospect of the past, a just estimation of the present, and a rational prospect of the future, impose on us a sacred obligation to guard the inestimable treasure committed to our trust. Our own and the happiness of [29] generations yet unborn is concerned in the choice we make, and the course we pursue. The friends of liberty and good government view passing events here with anxious expectation. Heaven hath distinguished America from every other quarter of the globe, by bestowing upon it, in richer abundance, the bounties of providence, and the blessings of civil and religious liberty. All that we could reasonably desire, and more than we had a right to expect, hath been put into our possession. While other countries have groaned under oppression, witnessed war and desolation, seen their governments and their altars prostrated, or felt the scourge of usurped dominion, ours hath been rising, beyond a parallel, in wealth, importance and honorable fame. Delivered from foreign control, and possessing free constitutions of government, the work of our own hands, administered for a series of years with equal ability and integrity, we have presented to admiring nations the fairest hopes, that here, in her last, safest retreat, liberty had erected her standard, and would long display her banners. To realize our own, and justify their expectations, we must continue, what we have been esteemed, an enlightened, sober, virtuous and united people.

But are there no clouds that darken the once fair prospect? No appearances of danger that we, with a motion accelerated in proportion to the height of our elevation, shall follow the path all other republics have trodden, and hasten to a similar catastrophe? Have we not fallen already, in a considerable degree, from the religion, virtue, and simplicity of manners, which were the characteristics of the New-England states, and will ever be essential to lasting freedom and prosperity? Have we not become divided, and in the zeal, or triumph of parties, lost sight of the public good, and overlooked the best means and instruments of its promotion? Is there nothing to be apprehended from [30] a too hasty admission of foreigners, little acquainted with the nature, and less with the enjoyment of civil liberty, to all the rights of citizens? Nothing from the influence of *people of a strange language* upon our government? Is there no reason to fear the relative weight and importance of the small states will be diminished by a change in the principles of the general government! Or that the whole constellation will be attracted to a common centre, or revolve in prescribed orbits within the sphere of its influence? Are there no symptoms, on the one hand, of a design to possess a disproportionate influence in the general scale; and, on the other, of alarm and discontent, which may lead to a disunion, attended with serious if not ruinous consequences? Many whom we all once esteemed wise, discerning and patriotic, are persuaded of the affirmative; and we may say, without implicating the motives, or criminating the measures of any, that some respect is due to their opinions. If men of ability, who have given illustrious proof of their patriotism, are apprehensive, it at least merits consideration, whether there be not some just ground of apprehension. Whatever it may be, whether discovered by all or not, the surest way to escape evil, and enjoy safety under the divine protection, is, to imbibe the genuine spirit of religion, reverence its institutions, extend its light and influence, promote general knowledge, cherish the social affections, banish party prejudices, cultivate harmony, and, realizing our dependence on the Supreme Ruler, gratefully improve the blessing we continue to possess.

In the divine goodness we have at this time abundant reason to rejoice. The heads of our tribes, after the laudable example of our fathers, have met in this city of our anniversary solemnities; and now present themselves before the Lord, to seek his direction and blessing on the important concerns of civil government. As aforetime, our [31] nobles are yet of ourselves, and our Governor hath proceeded from the midst of us.

Re-elected to the first magistracy, HIS EXCELLENCY hath received renewed assurance of the public approbation of confidence. He is still the man whom the people delight to honor. But whether they have honored most his talents and virtues, or their own discernment and moral taste, is a question too delicate for solution. May his integrity continue to guide and preserve him; and that God, who beholdeth with favor him that is upright in heart, crown his administration with success, his days on earth with peace, and his future existence with ineffable glory.

HIS HONOR will accept our cordial congratulations, on his re-election to the second office in the government. Next to the approbation of his own mind, that of the multitude of his brethren must afford the highest satisfaction. Their acknowledgment of his past fidelity, and continued reliance on his abilities and zeal to promote the general welfare, will be esteemed the best reward in their power to give, and a motive to such further exertions, as shall fully answer all their reasonable expectations. Faithful and approved of God, may he at last receive a crown of righteousness.

The HONORABLE COUNCIL, from the dignity of their station and characters, and in consideration of their past important and acceptable services, merit our respectful attention. In conscious rectitude, and in the approbation of God, may they ever have a source of the highest human happiness; and when released from the labors of this, receive in a better world the full reward of faithful servants.

May this branch of the government be always composed of men of candor, clear understanding, sound judgment, and uncorruptible integrity.

[32] To the Hon. SENATE, and HOUSE of REPRESENTATIVES, we now tender our high respects. Called by the voice of the people to be legislators, and guardians of their rights and liberties, may they realize the importance of the trust, and fulfil their duty with all good fidelity. In the true spirit of ministers of God for good, may they enter on the interesting transactions of this day, and pursue the public business of the year. Attached to the original principles of the state

and general government, may they adopt measures that will have the best tendency to render both permanent blessings. In all elections, whether under the federal or state constitution, may they fix their choice, so far as constitutional limitations will permit, on men most capable and best disposed to promote the public good. In all their deliberations, discussions and decisions, may they manifest a spirit of candor and dignified moderation; and, however they may differ in opinion, give to each other, and to the public, proof of their strict probity and genuine patriotism. In all things may they be under the guidance and blessing of the great Fountain of wisdom, and receive his final approbation.

VENERABLE FATHERS in each department, to your care the people of this respectable commonwealth have committed their dearest civil interests. By calling you to your respective stations they have expressed a confidence that you will be watchful and faithful. You have every rational motive to be so; but the highest must be a sense of accountability to that God, by whom actions are witnessed and weighed, and from whom all will receive a just reward. Though ye are called gods on earth, you must all die like men, and, with those over whom you now bear rule, appear in judgment, to receive according to your works.

In contemplating the happy influence of religion upon the state and government of society, it is not [33] intended to diminish its importance in a personal view, and in respect to the solemn period when all civil societies shall be disbanded, secular honors and distinctions known no more, and the whole world arraigned at Jehovah's awful tribunal. In this august event we have the highest personal concern; and from the individual anticipation of it, society derives peculiar advantage. What the public good requires, your own particular happiness more strongly demands. In your honorable stations, and in the private walks of life, may you ever be actuated by the great principles of our holy religion, enjoy its consolations, exemplify its duties, and extend its benign influence; that you may at last share its richest rewards.

FELLOW-CITIZENS of this numerous assembly, you doubtless feel a lively interest in the freedom, prosperity and glory of our common country; and in guarding and transmitting to posterity the fair inheritance we have received from our fathers. Like them, then, fear God, and keep his commandments. We have risen up, and call them blessed. But if we abandon their principles, despise their attention to religion and its institutions, and refuse to follow their virtuous examples, our posterity, denied what we inherit, will have reason to execrate our folly.

Personal salvation, public safety, and the happiness of generations to come, impose on us a sacred obligation to set our hearts unto all the words of the divine law, and to command our children to observe them. The man of religion and virtue is a public benefactor. By teaching his children to follow the example, he increases the benefit; and by exciting others to imitation enhances the obligation. In proportion to the sphere of your influence, you all possess means of your own security, and of promoting our national prosperity and glory. [34] Let this consideration, as well as the still more animating one, that by it you may prepare yourselves and others for a state of endless felicity, be a motive to employ all your influence in the cause of religion and virtue. To these God hath promised his protection and blessing. They will be our life, and the lengthening out of our tranquillity. "The work of righteousness shall be peace, and the effect of righteousness, quietness and assurance forever."

[75]

JAMES WILSON 1742–1798

On Municipal Law

PHILADELPHIA, 1804

Born in Scotland in 1742, James Wilson came to America in 1766; was a member of the Pennsylvania convention in 1775, as well as the Continental Congress; one of the most influential members of the Constitutional Convention in 1787; and an associate justice of the United States Supreme Court when he died, in 1798. For a man of such brilliance (he was the first professor of law at the College of Philadelphia—later the University of Pennsylvania), and such importance to our founding, Wilson is little known by the general public and little read by academics. One of the most ardent advocates of popular sovereignty throughout his life, although generally known as a conservative, Wilson here argues a strong case for the doctrine of government based upon consent. This doctrine was implicit in American political theory for over a century and a half by the time he wrote, but few attempted to proceed analytically on the subject as Wilson does here. In 1804 Bird Wilson directed the publication of *The Works of James Wilson* by Lorenzo Press. Its contents were a comprehensive and detailed discussion of politics. Only Chapter V of the more-than-850-page volume is reproduced here, as it is the most representative of his life's work and the best discussion of consent by an American during the era. This particular piece was originally published some ten years before being published in the volume of collected works. The 1804 version is used here.

OF MUNICIPAL LAW

I now proceed to the consideration of municipal law—that rule, by which a state or nation is governed. It is thus defined by the learned

JAMES WILSON 1742–1798

Author of the Commentaries on the Laws of England. "A rule of civil conduct, prescribed by the *supreme power* of the state, commanding what is right and prohibiting what is wrong."[a] In my observations upon Sir William Blackstone's definition of law in general, I did him the justice to mention, that he was not the first, and that he has not been the last, who has defined law upon the same principles, or upon principles similar, and equally dangerous. Here it is my duty to mention, and, in one respect, I am happy in mentioning, that he was the first, though, I must add, he has not been the last, who has defined municipal law, as applied to the law of England, upon principles, to which I must beg leave to assign the epithets, dangerous and unsound. It is of high import to the liberties of the United States, that the seeds of despotism be not permitted to lurk at the roots of our municipal law. If they shall be suffered to remain there, they will, at some period or another, spring up and produce abundance of pestiferous fruit. Let us, therefore, examine, fully and minutely, the extent, the grounds, the derivation, and the consequences of the abovementioned definition.

"Legislature," we are told, "is the greatest act of superiority, that can be exercised by one being over another. Wherefore it is requisite to the very essence of a law, that it be made by the supreme power. Sovereignty and legislature are, indeed, convertible terms; one cannot subsist without the other."[b] "There must be in every government, however it began, or by whatsover right it subsists, a supreme, irresistible, absolute, uncontrolled authority, in which the *jura summi imperii,* or the rights of sovereignty reside." "By sovereign power is meant the making of laws; for wherever that power resides, all others must conform to and be directed by it, whatever appearance the outward form and administration of the government may put on. For it is at any time in the option of the legislature to alter that form and administration, by a new edict or rule, and to put the execution of the laws into whatever hands it pleases: and all the [169] other powers of the state must obey the legislative power in the execution of their several functions, or else the constitution is at an end."[c] "In the British parliament, is lodged the sovereignty of the British constitution."[d]

[a] 1. Bl. Com. 44.
[b] 1. Bl. Com. 46.
[c] Id. 48. 49.
[d] Id. 51.

"The power of making laws constitutes the supreme authority."[e] "In the British parliament," therefore, which is the legislative power, "the supreme and absolute authority of the state is vested."[f] "This is the place, where that absolute despotick power, which must, in all governments, reside somewhere, is intrusted by the constitution of these kingdoms." "Its power and jurisdiction is so transcendent and absolute, that it cannot be confined, either for causes or persons, within any bounds."[g] "It can change and create afresh even the constitution of the kingdom and of parliaments themselves. It can, in short, do every thing that is not naturally impossible." "What the parliament doth, no authority upon earth can undo."[h] "So long as the English constitution lasts, we may venture to affirm, that the power of parliament is absolute and without control."[i] "Hence the known apothegm of the great Lord Treasurer Burleigh, that England could never be ruined but by a parliament."[j]

It is obvious, that though this definition of municipal law, and this account of legislative authority be applied particularly to the law of England and the legislature of Great Britain; yet they are, in their terms and in their meaning, extended to every other state or nation whatever—"to every government, however it began, or by whatever right it subsists." Indeed, the opinion of Mr. Locke and other writers, "that there remains still inherent in the people a supreme power to remove and alter the legislature," is considered to be so merely theoretical, that "we cannot adopt it nor argue from it, under any dispensation of government at present actually existing."[k]

The doctrines contained in the foregiong quotations from the Commentaries on the laws of England, may be comprised under the two general propositions, which follow. 1. That in every state, there is and must be a supreme, irresistible, absolute, uncontrolled authority, in which the rights of sovereignty reside. 2. That this authority, and these rights of sovereignty must reside in the legislature; because "sovereignty and legislature are convertible terms," and because "it is

[e] Id. 52.
[f] 1. Bl. Com. 147.
[g] Id. 160.
[h] Id. 161.
[i] Id. 162.
[j] Id. 161.
[k] Id. 161.

requisite to the very essence of a law, that it be made by the supreme power." In the first general proposition, I have the pleasure of agreeing entirely with Sir William Blackstone. Its truth rests on this broad and fundamental principle—that, by the constitutions of nature, men and nations are equal and free. In the second general proposition, I am under the necessity of differing altogether from the learned Author of the Commentaries. I differ from him, not only in the opinion, that the foregoing chain of reasoning must be [170] applicable to every government and to every system of municipal law; I differ from him likewise in the opinion, that the foregoing chain of reasoning can be justly applied even to the government of Great Britain and to the municipal law of England. I think I can safely pledge myself to show, that, in both, I differ from him on the most solid and satisfactory ground.

It deserves to be remarked, that, for his definition of municipal law, he cites the authority of no English court, nor of any English preceding writer, lawyer, or judge. Indeed, so far as I know, he could cite no such authority. So far as I have examined the English law books and authorities, upon this important subject—and I have examined them, as it has been my duty to do, with no small degree of attention—this definition stands entirely unsupported in point of authority. I may, however, be mistaken—I pretend not to have read, far less to remember, every thing in the law. If I am mistaken, I will thank the friendly monitor, that will advise me of the mistake. As at present advised, I can say, that, so far as I know, this definition is unsupported by authority in the English law. I shall hereafter have occasion to show that, concerning acts of parliament, to which the definition is particularly applied, our law authorities hold, and even parliament itself holds, a very different language.

The introduction of the principle of superiority into the definition of law in general, we traced, when we examined that subject, from Sir William Blackstone to Baron Puffendorff. The introduction of the same principle into the definition of municipal law, can be traced to the same source. "Human laws," says he, "are nothing else, but the decrees of the supreme power, concerning matters to be observed by the subjects."[1] The celebrated Heineccius, in his system of Universal Law, gives a definition much to the same purpose—"Civil laws," says

---

[1] Puff. 688. b. 7. c. 6. s. 3.

he, "are the commands of the supreme power in a state."[m] Why was this principle transplanted into the law of England?

It deserves to be further remarked, that, for all the strong sentiments and expressions concerning the necessary connexion, and indeed the convertibility of the sovereign and the legislative powers, no authority is produced from the English law; and—I speak under the guard as before—so far as I know, none could be produced, except in one instance, of which I shall soon take notice. The observation, which I have already made with regard to the definition of municipal law, may, therefore, be applied, with equal propriety, to the necessary connexion between the sovereign and the legislative powers. This connexion is not attempted to be supported by authority in the English law. I excepted one instance. It is this—"The power and jurisdiction of parliament is so transcendent [171] and absolute, that it cannot be confined, either for causes or persons, within any bounds."[n] For this, the authority of my Lord Coke in his fourth Institute is quoted. I have examined the passage. It stands thus. "Of the power and jurisdiction of the parliament, *for making of laws in proceeding by bill,* it is so transcendent and absolute, as it cannot be confined, either for causes or persons, within any bounds."[o] From this authority, I think it may be fairly and justly inferred—that, by the British constitution, the legislative authority of that nation is, without any exception of causes or persons, vested in the British parliament. In the same manner, by the constitution of Pennsylvania, the legislative power of this commonwealth is vested in a general assembly. But can it be inferred from this authority, that the sovereign power of Great Britain is vested in her parliament? Can it be inferred from the constitution of Pennsylvania, that her sovereign power is vested in her general assembly? I think, therefore, I may now venture to say, that both in his definition of municipal law, and in his opinion concerning the convertibility of the legislative and the sovereign authority, Sir William Blackstone stands unsupported by authority. Is he supported by reason and by principle? By neither, in my humble opinion.

The discussion of this question necessarily leads me to consider the establishment of government, and the division of its powers. That this subject may be fully understood,—for, in the United States, it

[m] 2. Hein. s. 150. p. 152.
[n] 1. Bl. Com. 160.
[o] 4. Ins. 36.

ought to be understood fully—I shall examine the sentiments, which have been generally entertained and received concerning it, and then compare those sentiments with what I consider as the true state of things. No sooner is government mentioned, than the fine flattering images of power, dominion, and sovereignty dance in the fancy, and the beautiful and magnificent effects of its establishment. But the truth is, that sovereignty, dominion, and power are the parents, not the offspring of government. Let us, however, see what has been thought, and what ought to be thought, concerning those splendid objects.

The theory of the establishment of government has been generally such as I am about to explain.

It has been supposed, that, if a multitude of people, who had formerly lived independent of each other, wished to unite in a political society, and to establish a government, they would find it necessary to take the following steps. 1. Each individual would engage with all the others to join in one body, and to manage, with their joint powers and wills, whatever should regard their common preservation, security, and happiness. In consideration of this engagement, made by each individual with all the others, all those others would engage with each individual to protect and [172] defend him from injury, and to secure him in the prosecution of every just and laudable pursuit. These reciprocal engagements from each individual to all the others, and from all the others to each individual form the political association. Those who do not enter into them are not considered as a part of the society.

The society being formed, some measures must be taken in order to regulate its operations; otherwise it could never adopt or pursue a system of measures for promoting, jointly and effectually, the publick security and happiness. These measures involve the formation of government.

A third step, we are told, must also be taken, before government can be completed. In addition to the engagement of political association, another engagement must be made: to that engagement, there must be a new party. What he is—whence he comes—from what source his equal and independent powers of contracting originate, have never, to this moment, been explained. Such an account of him as I have received, I will give: if it is not satisfactory, you must not blame me. "This party is one or more persons, on whom the supreme authority is conferred," says one.[p] By another, we are told, that this party is one or more persons, on whom "the sovereignty is conferred."[q] The sovereignty of supreme authority! How has it started up all of a sudden? Why does it make its first appearance in a derivative state? Where do we find it originally?—for it must exist originally before it can be conferred. To these questions we receive no explicit answer. We are told at one time, that "there are, in each individual, the seeds, as it were, of the supreme power."[r] We are told, more cautiously, at another time, that the voluntary consent and subjection of the respective members of the society, is the "nearest and immediate cause, from which sovereign authority, as a moral quality, results."[s] But, to make the most of these different pieces of information, let us suppose that this cause will produce its proper effects; that these seeds will yield, in due time, their natural fruits; and that this conferred sovereignty existed originally in those who conferred it. What is this sovereignty? Is it divisible or indivisible? Was the whole or only a part of it conferred? Was it conferred unconditionally, or upon certain conditions? Was it conferred gratuitously, or for a valuable consideration? Why hear we nothing concerning these important steps, which, upon the opinion generally received, must have been taken previously to the complete formation of a government? This, I confess, is far from being satisfactory: let us, however, take it as it is; and proceed to the remaining step, which, we are told, is taken for the complete establishment of government. This is an engagement by those, who are to be the future governours, that they will consult most carefully and act most honestly for [173] the common security and happiness; and a reciprocal engagement by those, who are, in future, to be governed, that they will observe fidelity and allegiance to those invested with the sovereign authority.

It is admitted not to be probable, that, in the formation of the several governments, these three steps have been actually and regularly taken; yet, we are told, in every just institution of power, there must have been such transactions as implicitly contain the full force and import of all of them.[t]

[p] 2. Burl. 28.
[q] Puff. 640. b. 7. c. 2. s. 8.
[r] 2. Burl. 42.
[s] Puff. 654. b. 7. c. 3. s. 1.
[t] 2. Hutch. 227.

That the two first steps have been sometimes taken, and must be always supposed, in the regular structure of a government, I readily agree; because it is not easy to discover how a government could be formed without them. But with regard to the third, I see no necessity for it: I see no propriety in it: it is derogatory, in my humble judgment, from the genuine principles of legitimate sovereignty, and inconsistent with the best theory, and the best exercise too, of supreme power. But the full illustration of these dignified subjects is reserved for another place.

With regard, however, to the British constitution, we must allow the supposition, that a contract took place at its establishment. For this we have high political authority. A full assembly of the lords and commons, met in convention in the year 1688, declared that James the second had broke the original contract between the king and people.[u] What the terms of that contract were, at what time it was made, and what duties it enjoined, have been subjects of dark and doubtful disputation. For this reason, as we are told by Sir William Blackstone, it was, after the revolution, judged proper to declare these duties expressly, and to reduce that contract to a plain certainty. So that, whatever doubts might be formerly raised, by weak and scrupulous minds, about the existence of such an original contract, they must now entirely cease; especially with regard to every prince, who has reigned since that revolution.[v]

But, after all, what will this prove with regard to the supreme power of parliament? Do we hear, in the British constitution, of any contract between *them* and the people? How came *they* to be invested with such immense authority? The usual theories of government support no hypothesis of this kind, even in favour of the British legislature; far less, in favour of the legislature of every other government, "however formed, or by whatever right subsisting."

Let us trace this matter a little farther: let us endeavour to form some just conceptions concerning this supreme and sovereign power, concerning which so much has been said, and concerning which so little has been said justly. Let us turn our eyes, for a while, from books and systems: let us fix them upon men and things. While those, who were about to form a society, continued separate and independent

[u] 1. Bl. Com. 211, 212.
[v] Id. 233.

men, they possessed [174] separate and independent powers and rights. When the society was formed, it possessed jointly all the previously separate and independent powers and rights of the individuals who formed it, and all the other powers and rights, which result from the social union. The aggregate of these powers and these rights composes the sovereignty of the society or nation. In the society or nation this sovereignty originally exists. For whose benefit does it exist? For the benefit of the society or nation. Is it necessary for the benefit of the society or nation, that, the moment it exists, it should be transferred?— This question ought, undoubtedly, to be seriously considered, and, on the most solid grounds, to be resolved in the affirmative, before the transfer is made. Has this ever been done? Has it ever been evinced, by unanswerable arguments, that it is necessary to the benefit of a society to transfer all those rights and powers, and the results of all those rights and powers, which the members once possessed separately, but which the society now possess jointly? I think such a position has never been evinced to be true. Those powers and rights were, I think, collected to be exercised and enjoyed, not to be alienated and lost. All these powers and rights, indeed, cannot, in a numerous and extended society, be exercised personally; but they may be exercised by representation. One of those powers and rights is to make laws for the government of the nation. This power and right may be delegated for a certain period, on certain conditions, under certain limitations, and to a certain number of persons. I ask—Is it necessary that, along with this power and this right, all the other powers and rights of the nation should be delegated to the same persons? I ask farther—is it necessary, that all those other powers and rights should be delegated without any right of resumption?—Another of those powers and rights is that of carrying the laws into execution. May not the society delegate this right for another period, on other conditions, with other limitations, and to other persons? A third right and power of the society is that of administering justice under the laws. May not this right be delegated for still another period, on still other conditions, under still other limitations, and to still other persons? Or may not this power and right be partly delegated and partly retained in personal exercise? For, in the most extended communities, an important part of the administration of justice may be discharged by the people themselves. All this certainly may be done. All this certainly has been done, as I shall have the pleasure of showing, when I come to examine the

JAMES WILSON 1742–1798

American governments, and to point out, by an enumeration and comparison of particulars, how beautifully, how regularly, and how usefully we have established, by our practice in this country, principles concerning the reservation, the distribution, the arrangement, the direction, and the uses of publick authority, of which even the just theory is still unknown in other nations.

[175] Let us now pause and reflect. After what we see can be done, after what we see has been done, in the delegation and distribution of the rights and powers of society; can we subscribe to the doctrine of the Commentaries—that the authority, which is legislative must be *supreme?* Can we consent, that this doctrine should form a first principle in our system of municipal law? Certainly not. This definition is not calculated for the meridian of the United States.

I go farther—It is not calculated for the meridian of Great Britain. In order to show this, as it ought to be shown, it will be necessary to enter into a disquisition concerning the component parts and powers of the British parliament, and the origin, kinds, and properties of the English municipal law; the greatest and best proportion of which was never made by a parliament at all.

The British parliament consists of three distinct branches; the king, the house of lords, and the house of commons. To that species of English law, which is called a statute, the assent of all the three branches is necessary. When it has received the assent of all the three, it becomes a law and is obligatory upon the nation; but it is obligatory upon different parts of it for different reasons. "An act of parliament," says my Lord Hale, "is made, as it were, a tripartite indenture, between the king, the lords, and commons; for without the concurrent consent of all those three parts of the legislature, no such law is or can be made."[w] What is an indenture? The Commentaries will tell us, that it is a species of deed, to which there are more parties than one.[x] What is the first requisite of a deed? The Commentaries will also tell us, "that there be persons able to contract, and be contracted with."[y] If a deed is a contract or agreement; if an indenture is a species of deed, to which there are more parties than one; if an act of parliament may be called an indenture tripartite, because there are three parties to it—the king, the lords, and the commons; we find,

[w] Hale's Hist. 2.
[x] 2. Bl. Com. 295.
[y] Id. 296.

that an act, which, considered indistinctly and dignified by the name
of law, requires the whole supreme power of the nation to give it
birth, is, when viewed more closely and analyzed into the component
parts of its authority, properly arranged under the class of contracts.
It is a contract to which there are three parties; those, who constitute
one of the three parties, not acting even in publick characters. A peer
represents no one; he votes for himself; and when he is absent, he may
transfer his right of voting to another. This may be thought a very
free way of treating what is represented as necessarily an emanation of
sovereign authority; but it is treating it truly; and give me leave to
add, it is treating it accurately. Besides; I shall not be ashamed of
treading in a path, though even a foot path, to which I am directed
by the finger of the enlightened Lord Hale. That path, to which he
points, will lead to instruction. Let us pursue it— [176] To this
indenture there are three parties: to an indenture the power of
contracting in each of the parties is necessary. What is the power of
contracting in the different parts? The king contracts for himself, and
as representing the executive authority of the nation. The peers engage
in their private and personal rights. The members of the house of
commons bind themselves and those whom they represent. They
represent, or are supposed—how justly is immaterial to our present
argument—to represent "all the commons of the whole realm."[z] We
all know, that one may execute an instrument, either in person, or
by an attorney: we all know that an instrument may be executed by
a person in his own right and as attorney also. Perhaps it would not
be improper if, on some occasions at least, the forms, as well as the
principles, of private, were copied into publick, transactions. Permit
me to mention an instance, in which this was lately done. In the
ratification of the constitution of the United States by the convention
of Pennsylvania, the distinct characters, in which the members of that
convention acted, are distinctly marked. "We the delegates of the
people of the commonwealth of Pennsylvania, in general convention
assembled, do, in the name and by the authority of the same people,
and for ourselves, assent to and ratify the foregoing constitution for
the United States of America."

The foregoing, though a very familiar, must, I think, be admitted
to be a very intelligible and satisfactory illustration and analysis of the

[z] 4. Ins. 1.

manner, in which acts of parliament are made and become obligatory. For my own part, I cannot conceive how the truth, or the real dignity of a subject, can suffer by being closely inspected. When the exclamation—procul este—is made, I am led to suspect, that a secret conscious want of dignity or integrity is the cause. The plain and simple analysis, which I have given, of the nature and obligation of acts of parliament is evidently countenanced by the expressive legal language of my Lord Hale—It is supported and confirmed by the very respectable authority of my Lord Hardwicke. "The binding force—" I use his very words, as they are reported—"the binding force of these acts of parliament arises from that prerogative, which is in the king, as our sovereign liege lord; from that personal right, which is inherent in the peers and lords of parliament to bind themselves and their heirs and successours in their honours and dignities; and from the delegated power vested in the commons, as the representatives of the people; and, therefore, Lord Coke says, 4. Inst. 1. these represent the whole commons of the realm, and are trusted for them. By reason of this representation, every man is said to be a party to, and the consent of every subject is involved in, an act of parliament."[a] "Every man in England," says the Author of the Commentaries himself, [177] "is, in judgment of law, party to the making of an act of parliament, being present thereat by his representatives."[b] What is there in all this, that necessarily implies the irresistible energy of power, which is sovereign and supreme, without limits and without control?

We have already seen all the parties to an act of parliament. Let us, again, take a deliberate and distinct view of them: where shall we find the sovereign and supreme power? In the king? It is true, that he is called by my Lord Hardwicke "sovereign liege lord," and that his prerogative, as such, is assigned, and with much propriety, as one of the sources, from which "the binding force of acts of parliament arises." The legal and constitutional import of the expressions, sovereign liege lord, is well known. They present the king to his subjects as the object of their allegiance: they present him to foreigners as exercising the whole authority of the nation in foreign transactions. To foreign transactions, the British parliament is no party: to foreign nations, the British parliament is totally unknown. Alliances, treaties

[a] 2. Atk. 654.
[b] 1. Bl. Com. 185.

of peace, even declarations of war, are made in the name, and by the constitutional authority, of the king alone. But, it has never been pretended, that the prerogative of the king, as sovereign liege lord, extended so far as to bind his subjects by his laws. Even Henry the eighth, tyrant as he was, knew that an act of parliament was necessary, if even that could be sufficient, to endow his proclamations with legal obligatory force. But the king, by assenting to an act of parliament, can bind himself; and he can bind all that portion of the sovereign power of the nation, which is intrusted to his management and care. And it is certainly proper, that, as he represents the executive and the foreign powers of the nation, he should be consulted in the making of the national laws. From this short and clear deduction, we evidently see, that the absolute, uncontrolled power, mentioned by Sir William Blackstone as inseparable from legislative authority, is not to be found in the king. Is it to be found in the house of lords? That will not be pretended. Their votes bind not a single person in the nation, except themselves and the heirs and successours of their honours and dignities. Let us go to the house of commons: is this supreme power, which elsewhere we have searched for in vain, to be found among the members of this house? In what character? In their own right? This will not be alleged. As representatives? As representatives, they act, not by their own power, but by the power of those whom they represent. This power, therefore, whatever it is, cannot be found among the members of the house of commons, it must be looked for among their constituents. There, indeed, we shall find it: and the moment we find it, we shall discover its nature and extent. The king and the commons assembled in parliament are invested by the whole nation, [178] except the house of lords, who act in their own right, not with "transcendent and absolute power and jurisdiction" *generally,* as one would naturally conclude from the unqualified expressions of Sir William Blackstone; but with this "transcendent and absolute power and jurisdiction for the *making of laws,*" as we find in the determinate language of my Lord Coke. To the making of laws, this power and jurisdiction of the British parliament is strictly and rigidly confined. A single law the British parliament cannot execute: in a single cause, the British parliament cannot administer justice. Why then should "absolute depotick power," to use the language of the Commentaries, be ascribed to the British parliament? Has this doctrine a solid foundation? I presume it has not. But though it has not a solid foundation, it has produced, as I shall hereafter show, the most pernicious effects. I will acknowledge freely, that the bounds, which circumscribe the authority of the British parliament, are not sufficiently accurate: I will acknowledge farther, that they are not sufficiently strong. But can this suggest a reason or a motive for denying their existence? It strongly suggests, indeed, reasons and motives of a very different kind. It suggests the strongest reasons and motives for circumscribing the authority of the British parliament by limits more accurate, for fortifying those limits with an additional degree of strength, and for rendering the practice more conformable than it now is, to the theory of its institution—for rendering the house of commons in fact, what it is presumed to be in law, "a representation of all the commons of the whole realm." If any thing coming from this chair could be supposed, by possibility, to produce the smallest effect in that nation, I would warmly recommend to it the accomplishment of those great objects, as consummations most devoutly to be wished. The maxim of the great Lord Burleigh has prevailed long enough: let it make way for a better. Instead of saying, that "England can never be ruined but by a parliament;" let it be said, and truly said, that "England can never be ruined but by herself."

The learned Author of the Commentaries distinguishes between a law and a counsel; and also between a law and an agreement. I will examine the principle of these distinctions, in order that its strength or weakness may appear. It will be necessary to mention what is said in the Commentaries upon this subject. "Municipal law is called a *rule,* to distinguish it from *advice* or *counsel,* which we are at liberty to follow or not, as we see proper, and to judge of the reasonableness or unreasonableness of the thing advised: whereas our obedience to the law depends not upon our approbation, but upon the maker's will. Counsel is only matter of persuasion; law is matter of injunction: counsel acts only upon the willing; law upon the unwilling also.

"It is also called a *rule,* to distinguish it from a *compact* or *agreement:* for a compact is a promise proceeding *from* us; law is a command directed [179] *to* us. The language of a compact is, 'I will, or will not, do this;' that of a law is, 'thou shalt, or shalt not, do this.' It is true, that there is an obligation, which a compact carries with it, equal, in point of conscience, to that of a law; but then the original of the obligation is different. In compacts, we ourselves determine and promise what shall be done, before we are obliged to do it; in laws, we are obliged to act, without ourselves determining or promising any thing at all."[c]

The examination of the principle, which lies at the root of these distinctions, is an interesting subject indeed. If these distinctions can be supported, we may bid a last adieu to the maxim which I have always deemed of prime importance in the science of government and human laws—a free people are governed by laws, of which they approve. Before we part from this darling position, let us, at least, cast behind us, a "longing, lingering look."

Upon these passages in the Commentaries, I make remarks similar to those, which I made upon the passages examined some time ago. No authority in the English law is adduced—none, so far as I know, could be adduced to support them. These sentiments concerning law, as well as the definitions of municipal law, and law in general, may be traced to the performance of Baron Puffendorff. Let us see what this performance says. *"Law* differs from *counsel* in this, that by the latter a man"—"has no proper power, so as to lay any direct obligation on another; but must leave it to his pleasure and choice whether he will follow the counsel or not." "But law, though it ought not to want its reasons, yet these reasons are not the cause why obedience is paid to it, but the power of the exacter, who, when he has signified his pleasure, lays an obligation on the subject to act in conformity to his decree." "We obey laws, not principally on account of the matter of them, but upon account of the legislator's will. And thus law is the injunction of him, who has a power over those, to whom he prescribes; but counsel comes from him, who has no such power." "Counsel is only given to those, who are willing to have it; but law reaches the unwilling."[d]

"Neither are those ancients accurate enough in their expressions, who frequently apply to laws the name of *common agreements.*" "The points of distinction between a compact or covenant and a law, are obvious. For a *compact* is a *promise,* but a *law* is a *command.* In *compacts,* the form of speaking is, I will do so and so; but in *laws,* the form runs, do thou so, after an imperative manner. In *compacts,* since they depend, as to their original, on our will, we first determine what is to be done, before we are obliged to do it; but in *laws,* which suppose

[c] I. Bl. Com. 44. 45.
[d] Puff. 58. 59. b. I. c. 6. s. I.

the power of others over us, we are, in the first place, obliged to act, and afterwards the manner of acting is determined. And, therefore, he is not bound by a *compact* [180] who did not freely tie himself by giving his consent: but we are, for this reason, obliged by a *law;* because we owed an antecedent obedience to its author."[e]

You now see, that these distinctions between a law and an agreement, a law and a compact are adopted from Baron Puffendorff: whence he derived them, it is immaterial to inquire. But it is material to show, as I think I can do unanswerably, that these distinctions, if they could be supported, would overturn the beautiful temple of liberty from its very foundations. It is material also to show, as I think I can do unanswerably, that the fair temple of liberty stands unshaken and undefaced; and that the sole legitimate principle of obedience to human laws is human consent. This consent may be authenticated in different ways: in its different stages of existence, it may assume different names—approbation—ratification—experience: but in all its different shapes—under all its different appellations, it may easily be resolved into this proposition, simple, natural, and just—All human laws should be founded on the consent of those, who obey them. This great principle I shall, in the course of these lectures, have occasion to follow in a thousand agreeable directions. My present business, while I examine the principles of municipal law as delivered in the Commentaries, is to apply them and the examination of them to the law of England. In that law, we shall find the stream of authority running, from the most early periods, uniform and strong in the direction of the principle of consent—consent, given originally—consent, given in the form of ratification—and, what is most satisfactory of all, consent given after long, approved, and uninterrupted experience. This last, I think, is the principle of the common law. It is the most salutary principle of obedience to human laws, that ever was diffused among men. With such a Byzantium before him, is it not astonishing, indeed, that the attention—must I say the attachment?—of Sir William Blackstone should have been attracted towards a Chalcedon?[f]

The ancient coronation oath of the kings of England obliged them, to the utmost of their power, to cause those laws to be observed, "which the men of the people have made and chosen."[g]

---

[e] Puff. 59. b. 1. c. 6. s. 2.

[f] 3. Gibbon. 6. 7. Tac. Ann. XII. 62.

[g] 1. Bl. Com. 236, note. "que lez gentez du people avont faitez et esliez."

Let us next pay the respect, which is due to the celebrated sentiment of the English Justinian, Edward the first. "Lex justissima, ut quod omnes tangit, ab omnibus approbetur." It is a most just law, that what affects all should be approved by all. This golden rule is, with great propriety, inserted in his summons to his parliament. The Lord Chancellor Fortescue, in his most excellent tractate concerning the English laws, informs his royal pupil, that the statutes of England are framed, not by the will of the prince, but by that and by the assent of the whole kingdom. "Angliæ, statuta, [181] nedum principis voluntate, sed et totius regni assensu, ipsa conduntur." And if a statute, though passed with the greatest caution and solemnity, should be found, on experience, not to reach those purposes, which were intended by its framers, it can soon be reformed; but not without the same assent of the peers and commonalty of the kingdom, from which it originally flowed. "Et si statuta hæc, tanta solennitate et prudentia edita, efficaciæ tantæ, quantæ conditorum cupiebat intentio, non esse contingant, correcto reformari ipsa possunt; et non sine communitatis et procerum regni illius assensu, quali ipsa primitus emanarunt."[h] "To an act of law, statute or common, every man," says Lord Chief Justice Vaughan, "is as much consenting, and more solemnly, than he is to his own private deed."[i] Authorities to the same purpose might, without end, be heaped upon authorities from the law books. I forbear to trouble you with any more of them. Let us have recourse to what I may properly call a perpetually standing authority upon this very important subject—the writ for choosing members of parliament. It commands the sheriff of each county to cause two knights, the most fit and discreet of the county, and two citizens from every city, and two burgesses from every borough within the county, to be chosen according to law—"So that the said knights have full and sufficient power for themselves,[j] and the commonalty of the said county, and

[h] Fortes. c. 18.
[i] Vaugh. 392.
[j] It is the wisdom of the English law, that acts of parliament are equally binding to the makers of them as to the rest of the people. The makers are empowered for themselves, as well as for their constituents; and themselves, as well as their constituents must taste the sweet or bitter fruits of their own works. This suggests a powerful motive for caution and justice in their determinations (2. Whitlocke 87.) But this doctrine ill agrees with the new and foreign theory, introduced into the Commentaries—"A law always supposes some superiour, who is to make it." 1. Bl. Com. 43.

the said citizens and burgesses for themselves and the commonalty[k] of the said cities and boroughs, severally from them, to do and consent to those things, which, by the favour of God, shall happen to be ordained by the common council of the kingdom: so that for default of such power, or through improvident election of the said knights, citizens, or burgesses, the said affairs remain not undone."[l] Can language be more explicit to show the principle, upon which acts of parliament must be made, and consequently the principle, upon which alone they ought to be obeyed? It is directed, that the members have full and sufficient powers *for themselves,* and for their constituents *from their constituents.* This is precisely according to the analysis, which we have already given of the power of parliament. Why are those powers [182] necessary? To do and *consent* to those things, which shall be ordained by parliament. Those powers are absolutely necessary; for, without them, the business of the nation would remain undone. Is it possible, that any one, who has ever seen this venerable and authentick legal instrument, could suppose, that the sovereign power of the nation was vested in the parliament of Great Britain? Is it possible, that one who has seen this writ could forget the rock, from which the members were hewn, and the hole of the pit from which they were dug? The humble servants, who must come furnished with "full and sufficient power from" their masters "the commonalty of the county, and the burgesses and the citizens separately—" *"Divisim,"* one by one—have those humble servants, when assembled together, the uncontrolled powers of the nation in their hands? When they are intrusted with the legislative, may they, therefore, assume also the executive and the judicial powers of their country?

We now see, in a very striking point of view, the strong and expressive import of the language of my Lord Hale, when he says, that an act of parliament is, as it were, a tripartite indenture, between the king, the lords, and the commons. They form three parties: each party has power to contract. The king contracts in his own right— for the king is also a man—and in consequence of the powers devolved on him by that original contract, long supposed, but, at the revolution

---

[k] It is a great trust reposed in members of parliament, to have the power of the whole commonalty of a county, or city, or borough conferred on them. The acts of the members are the acts of the commonalty, from whom they have their power, and who are bound by them. 2. Whitlocke 89.
[l] 1. Whitlocke 2. 3.

of 1688, expressly recognized to have been made between him and the people. The lords of parliament contract solely in their own right. The members of the house of commons contract in their own right, for themselves, and in right of their constituents, for the commonalty of the whole realm. Thus we find every party and every power to form a contract, a compact, or an agreement—for these terms are synonimous—in the strictest and most proper sense of the words. The vital principle of every contract is the consent of the mind. My Lord Hale did not draw the obligatory principle of an act of parliament from a foreign fountain: he drew it, pure and clear, from its native springs.

Sir William Blackstone tells us, that the original of the obligation, which a compact carries with it, is different from that of a law. The original of the obligation of a compact we know to be consent: the original of the obligation of an act of parliament we have traced minutely to the very same source.

But acts of parliament are not the only—let us add, they are not the principal—species of law, known and obligatory in England. That kingdom boasts in the common law. In the countenance of that law, every lovely feature beams consent. This law is of vast importance. By it, the proceedings and decisions of courts of justice are regulated and directed. It guides the course of descents and successions to real estates, and limits their extent and qualifications: it appoints the forms and solemnities of [183] acquiring, of securing, and of transferring property: it prescribes the manner and the obligation of contracts: it establishes the rules, by which contracts, wills, deeds, and even acts of parliament are interpreted.[m] This law is founded on long and general custom. A custom, that has been long and generally observed, necessarily carries with it intrinsick evidence of consent. Caution and prudence are universally recommended in the introduction of new laws: can caution and prudence be so strongly exemplified—can their fruits be so certainly reaped in any other laws, as in those that are established by custom? The prospect of convenience invites to the first experiment: a first experiment, successful, encourages to make a second. The successful experiments of one man or one body of men induce another man or another body of men to venture upon similar trials. The instances are multiplied and extended, till, at length, the custom becomes universal and established. Can a law be made in a

---

[m] Hale's Hist. 24.

manner more eligible? Experience, the faithful guide of life and business, attends it in its every step. Other laws demand to be taken upon trust: a good countenance is their only recommendation. Those, who introduce them, can only say, in their favour, that they look well. A customary law, with a modesty appropriate to conscious merit, asks for admittance only upon trial, and claims not to be considered as a part of the political family, till she can establish a character, founded on a long and intimate acquaintance. The same means, by which the character of one law is known and approved, are employed to try and discriminate the character of every other. In favour of every one that is recommended, it can be said, not only, that it has lived unexceptionably by itself, but also that it has lived in peace and harmony with all the others. In this manner, a system of approved and concording laws is gradually, though slowly, collected and formed. By a process of this kind, the immortal Newton collected, arranged, and formed his just and beautiful system of experimental philosophy. By the same kind of process, our predecessors and ancestors have collected, arranged, and formed a system of experimental law, equally just, equally beautiful, and, important as Newton's system is, far more important still. This system has stood the test of numerous ages: to every age it has disclosed new beauties and new truths. In improvement, it is yet progressive; and what has been said poetically on another occasion, may be said in the strictest form of asseveration on this,—it acquires strength in its progress. From this system, we derive our dearest birthright and richest inheritance. The rise, the progress, the history, and the component parts of this invaluable system; its extension to America, and the principles of its establishment in the several states and in the national government, it will be my duty and my pleasure to trace and to exhibit in the course of these lectures. My present business is, to ascertain the origin [184] of its obligatory force. Surely, this may be done with ease. The common law is founded on long and general custom. On what can long and general custom be founded? Unquestionably, on nothing else, but free and voluntary *consent*. The regions of custom afford a most secure asylum from the operations of absolute, despotick power. To the cautious, circumspect, gradual, and tedious probation, which a law, originating from custom, must undergo, a law darted from compulsion will never submit.

"Sic volo, sic jubeo, stet pro ratione voluntas,"* is the motto of edicts, proclaimed, in thunder, by the voice of a human superiour. Far dissimilar are the sentiments expressed in calm and placid accents by a customary law. I never intruded upon you: I was invited upon trial: this trial has been had: you have long known me: you have long approved me: shall I now obtain an establishment in your family? A customary law carries with it the most unquestionable proofs of freedom in the country, which is happy enough to be the place of its abode.

Some truths are too plain to be proved. That a law, which has been established by long and general custom, must have received its origin and introduction from free and voluntary consent, is a position that must be evident to every one, who understands the force and meaning of the terms, in which it is expressed. My object is to imprint, as well as to prove, this great political doctrine. Perhaps this cannot be done better, than by laying before you the sentiments, which an English parliament held upon this subject, above two hundred years ago. You will see how strongly they support the principle—that the obligation of human laws arises from consent. The sentiments were expressed on an occasion similar to one, which will still suggest matter of very interesting recollection to many minds— They were expressed when an attempt was made to establish, in England, a foreign jurisdiction. With becoming indignation against it, the parliament declare—"This realm is free from subjection to any man's laws, but only to such as have been devised, made, and obtained within this realm, for the wealth of the same, or to such as, by sufferance of your grace and your progenitors, the people of this your realm have taken at their free liberty, with their *own consent* to be used amongst them, and have *bound themselves* by *long use and custom* to the observance of the same, not as to the observance of laws of any foreign prince, potentate, or prelate, but as to the customed and ancient laws of this realm, originally established as laws of the same, by the said sufferance, consents, and customs, and none otherwise."[n]

Some writers, when they describe that usage, which is the foundation of common law, characterize it by the epithet *immemorial*. The parliamentary [185] description is not so strong. "Long use and custom" is assigned as the criterion of law, "taken by the people at

* [Thus I will, thus I command, let my will stand as the reason.]
[n] St. 25. H. 8. c. 21. s. 1.

their free liberty, and by their own consent." And this criterion is surely sufficient to satisfy the principle: for consent is certainly proved by long, though it be not immemorial usage.

That consent is the probable principle of the common law, is admitted by the Author of the Commentaries himself. "It is one of the characteristick marks of English liberty," says he,[o] "that our common law depends upon custom, which carries this internal evidence of freedom along with it, that it probably was introduced by the voluntary consent of the people." I search not for contradictions: I wish to reconcile what is seemingly contradictory. But, if the common law could be introduced, as it is admitted it probably was, by the voluntary consent of the people; I confess I can not reconcile with this—certainly a solid—principle, the principle that "A law always supposes some superiour, who is to make it," nor another principle, that "sovereignty and legislature are indeed convertible terms."

A power, far beneath the sovereign power, may be invested with legislative authority; and its laws may be as obligatory as any other human laws. Of this, instances occur even in the government of Great-Britain.

It is necessarily and inseparably incident to all corporations, to make by-laws, or private statutes, for their government. These laws are binding upon themselves, unless contrary to the laws of the land, and then they are void.[p] From these positions, we clearly infer, that laws, obligatory upon those for whom they are made, may be enacted by a power, so far from being absolute and supreme, that its laws are void, when contrary to those enacted by a superiour power: so far do sovereignty and legislature, in this instance at least, appear to be from convertible terms: so far is it from being requisite to the very essence of a law, that it be made by the supreme power. Sir William Blackstone tells us, that in the provincial establishments in America, the assemblies had the power of making local ordinances; that subordinate powers of legislation subsisted in the proprietary governments; and that, in the charter governments, the assemblies made laws, suited to their own emergencies:[q] and yet, in these instances, he certainly did not admit, that "by sovereign power is meant the making of laws."

I hope I have now shown, that the definition of municipal law

[o] 1. Bl. Com. 74.
[p] 1. Bl. Com. 475.
[q] 1. Bl. Com. 108.

in the Commentaries is not calculated even for the meridian of Great-Britain: it is still less calculated for that of many other governments: for, in many other governments, the distinction is still more strongly marked between the sovereign and legislative powers.

[186] In the original constitution of Rome, the sovereign power, the *dominium eminens,* as it is called by the civilians, always resided in the collective body of the people. But the laws of Rome were not always made by that collective body. To the senate was indulged a privilege of legislation; partial and subordinate, it is true; but still a privilege of legislation. An act of the senate was not considered as a permanent law; but it was allowed to continue in force for one year; not longer, unless it was ratified by the people. To the plebeians, exclusive of the senators and patricians, a privilege of legislation was also indulged; but their laws bound only themselves. While we are taking notice of the different bodies, that possessed the power of legislation in Rome, it is proper to mention one very great defect, which existed in the constitution of that celebrated republick. A power, inferiour to that which made a law, could dispense with it. The senate, by its own decree, could dispense with a law, made by the whole collective body of the people. This power, dangerous in every free government, was often exercised, in Rome, to accomplish the most pernicious purposes.[r]

In the United States, and in each of the commonwealths, of which the union is composed, the legislative is very different from the supreme power. Instead of being uncontrollable, the legislative authority is placed, as it ought to be, under just and strict control. The effects of its extravagancies may be prevented, sometimes by the executive, sometimes by the judicial authority of the governments; sometimes even by a private citizen, and, at all times, by the superintending power of the people at large. These different points will afterwards receive a particular explication. At present, perhaps, this general position may be hazarded—That whoever would be obliged to obey a constitutional law, is justified in refusing to obey an unconstitutional act of the legislature—and that, when a question, even of this delicate nature, occurs, every one who is called to act,

---

[r] In the government of Media, an opposite extreme prevailed. When an edict was once published, it was not in the power of the legislator to alter or repeal it. The same power, which is sufficient to make, should be sufficient to abrogate a law. 3. Gog. Or. Laws. 11.

has a right to judge: he must, it is true, abide by the consequences of a wrong judgment.

Puffendorff, from whom the idea of a superiour, as forming a necessary ingredient in the idea of law, seems to have been transplanted into the Commentaries, insists much upon what he calls a maxim— *that a person cannot oblige himself;* "and this maxim," he tells us, "is not confined to single men, but extends to whole bodies and societies:"[s] "for a person to oblige himself under the notion of a lawgiver, or of a superiour, is an impossibility."[t] Hence the inference seems to be drawn, that "obligations are laid on human minds by a superiour." To different [187] minds, the same things, sometimes, appear in a very different manner. If I was to make a maxim upon this subject, it would be precisely the reverse of the maxim of Baron Puffendorff. Instead of saying, that a man cannot oblige himself; I would say, that no other person upon earth can oblige him, but that he certainly can oblige himself. Consent is the sole principle, on which any claim, in consequence of human authority, can be made upon one man by another. I say, in consequence of human authority; for, in consequence of the divine authority, numerous are the claims that we are reciprocally entitled to make, numerous are the duties, that we are reciprocally obliged to perform. But none of these can enter into the present question. We speak of authority merely human. Exclusively of the duties required by the law of nature, I can conceive of no claim, that one man can make upon another, but in consequence of his own consent. Let us, upon this occasion, as we have done upon some others, simplify the object by a plain and distinct analysis. Let us take for the subject of our analysis the very question we are upon—Whether a man can be bound by any human authority, except his own consent? Let us suppose, that one demands obedience from me to a certain injunction, which he calls a law, by performing some service pointed out to me: I ask him, why am I obliged to obey it? He says it is just I should do it. Justice, I tell him, is a part of the law of nature; give me a reason drawn from human authority. He tells me, he had promised it. Very well, perform your promise. Suppose he rises in his tone, and tells me, he orders it. Equal and free, I see no reason for obeying the order of one, who is only equal and free. Repelled from

[s] Puff. 63. b. 1. c. 6. s. 7.
[t] Id. 688. b. 7. c. 6. s. 2.

this attack upon my independence, he assails me on a very different quarter; and, softening his accents, represents how generous, nay how humane, it would be, to do as he desires. Humanity is a duty; generosity is a virtue; but neither is to be referred to human authority. Let invention be put upon the rack, and the severest torture will not draw from it a discovery of any external human authority, by which I am obliged to obey the supposed law, or to perform the supposed service. He tells me, next, that I promised to do it. Now, indeed, I discover a human source of obligation. If I promised to do it, I am bound to do it; unless the promise is either unlawful, or discharged; dissolved by an equal, or prohibited by a superiour authority. But this promise originated from consent; for if it was the abortion of compulsion—the effect sometimes of exterior and superiour human *power,* but never of human *authority*—I am not bound to consider it as my act and deed.

Let us now vary the supposition a little. Suppose this demand to be made upon me by one, of whose superiour judgment and unimpeached veracity I had the strongest and best founded belief: suppose me at that period of life—for there is such a period of life—when I should [188] believe implicitly whatever was taught me by one, whom I knew I could so well trust: suppose this person, respected for his knowledge and integrity, should tell me, that he really thought it my duty to comply with the demand. I think I should probably feel a sense of obligation arise within me. But why? because this respectable person says it? No. But for a reason, which may be easily mistaken for this: because I believe, that what this respected person says must be true. Here, indeed, is a species of external human authority, exerted and obeyed for the wisest purposes: But this is very different from that external human authority, which is assigned by some as the source of obligation in human laws. This species of authority is said to have been carried to a very great height by Pythagoras, the celebrated philosopher. He delivered it as a maxim, and it was received as such in his school, that whatever he said must be true. *Ipse dixit* was an undisputed authority. But if folly and falsehood had been as inseparably associated with the character of Pythagoras, as veracity and wisdom were, in the minds of his followers, I ask—would his *ipse dixit* have been received as an undisputed authority? I presume not. To recur, then, to the supposition, which I last made; I should feel the sense of obligation arise in me, not because I should think it his will, that I should comply with the demand; but because I should believe in his opinion, that it was my duty to do so. This refers to a very different source. For let me suppose a little farther, that, after feeling this sense of obligation arise within me, I should come to learn, either from my own observation, or from authority still superiour to that of the person in whom I placed confidence, that this confidence was misplaced; that what he told me proceeded either from mistake, or from something worse than mistake; his will might continue the same, and my opinion concerning it might continue the same, but my sense of obligation would be greatly altered. These remarks, I hope, will be sufficient to show, that no exterior human authority can bind a free and independent man.

The next question is—can a man bind himself? Baron Puffendorff lays it down as a maxim, that he cannot: and on this maxim, applied to publick bodies as well as private individuals, he builds a very interesting series of argumentation—just, indeed, and unanswerable, if the basis, on which it rests, be solid and sound.

We have, at last, reached the bottom of the business. We are now come to the important question, the resolution of which must, in my opinion, decide the fate of all human laws. I say, in my opinion; for I have already given my reasons for thinking, that if a man cannot bind himself, no human authority can bind him. For one man, equal and free, cannot be bound by another, who is no more. The consequence necessarily is, that if a man can be bound by any human authority, it must be [189] by himself. A farther consequence necessarily is, that if he cannot bind himself, there is an end of all human authority, and of all human laws. How differently, sometimes, things turn out, from what was expected from them! The idea of superiority, it was probably thought, would strengthen the obligation of human laws. When traced minutely and accurately, we find, that it would destroy their very existence. If no human law can be made without a superiour; no human law can ever be made.

First principles ought to be admitted with caution indeed. When you first read, in the Commentaries, this principle—"a law always supposes some superiour, who is to make it;" you did not suspect, I presume, that this principle is subversive of all human laws. You now perceive, that, if a man can be bound by human authority, it must be by his own. But is he his own superiour? The creative imagination of a Theobald himself could not suggest the fancy. He could only go so far as to say

None but himself can be his *parallel*.

Even the master of a show, who boasted, that his elephant was "the greatest elephant in the world," thought it necessary, for preventing mistakes, to add—except himself.

But to resume seriously the important question—can a man bind himself? Simple facts have sometimes led to the greatest discoveries. The sublime theory of gravitation was first suggested to Newton by an apple falling from a tree.

At the end of the second volume of the Commentaries are precedents of some useful instruments, known to the law of England. Among others, there is a precedent of a common bond. In that bond, there are these words written—*I bind myself*. This form of a bond has been known and used and approved in England from time immemorial. If a man cannot bind himself, then all the bonds, which have been executed in England, have been mere nullities. The substantial parts of that bond are parts of the common law of England. The part, which I have mentioned, is certainly a most substantial one. All parts of the precedent are not substantial: many of them may be omitted or altered without vitiating the force of the bond. The law does not require any particular form of words: but one thing it strictly requires—such words as declare the intention of the party, and denote his being bound: such words will be sufficient: such words will be carried into effect by the judgment of the law.

Let us examine the obligatory principle of a bond by legal tests, by triers at the common law. Suppose one applies to a court of justice to enforce the obligation of a bond, and proposes it as the foundation of his demand. In what manner is he directed by the law to express the legal import of the instrument? He is directed to declare, that, by this instrument, [190] the party who executed it, "acknowledged himself to be bound,"[u] or "bound himself."[v] The precedents are in both forms. When the action is properly instituted, the party, against whom it is instituted, is next called upon, with all legal solemnity, to make his defence—for against no man ought a decision to be

[u] Boh. Ins. Leg. 102.
[v] 2. Mod. Ent. 178.

JAMES WILSON 1742–1798

pronounced till he has an opportunity of being heard. He appears: the instrument is produced. What can he say, why a decision should not be pronounced against him? The common law furnishes him with forms to suit almost every case, certainly every case that has been brought before a court of justice. If the case of the present defendant is so very peculiar, that nothing similar to it ever happened before; the common law will protect him in forming a defence, suited to his very peculiar case. Among all the different kinds of pleas, fitted for every case that has happened, for almost every case that can happen, are there any furnished, which bear towards this principle—that the defendant could not oblige himself? There are. But they are furnished only for those, who, by reason of their infancy, or any other cause, appear to want a common degree of understanding. For without understanding it, no obligation can be legitimately formed. There are others too, that respect another situation, which it will be proper to examine particularly; because it is probable, that it will throw much light upon the principle of obligation to human laws. The understanding, though necessary, is not, of itself, sufficient to form a legitimate obligation: in a legitimate obligation, the *will* must concur; compulsion will not be received as a substitute for consent. The common law is a law of liberty. The defendant may plead, that he was compelled to execute the instrument. He cannot, indeed, deny the execution of it; but he can state, in his plea, the circumstances of compulsion attending its execution;[w] and these circumstances, if sufficient in law, and established in fact, will procure a decision in his favour, that, in such circumstances, he did not bind himself. If he never executed the instrument at all; he can state the fact; and unless the execution of it be proved against him, he will, upon this plea likewise, obtain a decision, that he did not bind himself. But if he can do none of these things—if he executed the instrument; if he executed it voluntarily; if he executed it knowingly; the law will pronounce, that he bound himself. This has been the regular course of the law during time immemorial—a course, uninterrupted and unrepealed. In the municipal law of England, therefore, the doctrine is established—that a man can bind himself. This doctrine is established by strict legal inference from the principles and the practice of the common law. The consequence is, that, on the principles of the municipal law of England, a superiour

[w] 5. Rep. 119.

is not necessary to the existence of obligation. A man can [191] bind himself. But is his bond a law? Yes, it is a law binding upon himself. Farther it ought not to bind. But shall a private contract be viewed in the venerable light of a law? Why not, if it has all its essential properties? Suppose this contract to have been made by millions, contracting on each side: it would have been dignified by the name of a treaty: as such, had the United States been the contractors on one side, it would have become a law of the land: as such, it would have become an important part of the law of nations. Is the act of millions more binding upon those millions, than the act of one is binding upon that one? Light will break in upon us by degrees.

By the law of England, a man can bind himself. The law of England speaks not a language contrary to that of the law of nature. By this law also, a man can bind himself. "If among men," says Barbeyrac,[x] "the immediate reason why one ought to be subject to the command of another is ordinarily this, that he has voluntarily consented to it"—and we have shown, that this is not only *ordinarily*, but *always* the reason—"then," continues he, "this consent, and all other engagements whatever are only obligatory through that maxim of natural law, which tells us, that every one ought to observe what he has engaged himself to." This maxim is, indeed, a part of the law of a superiour; but this maxim is founded upon the previous truth—that a man can engage himself: I need not surely prove, that an engagement must be made before it can be observed. "That we should be faithful to our engagements," says the very learned President Goguet,[y] "is one of those maxims, which derive their origin from those sentiments of equity and justice, which God has engraven on the hearts of all men: they are taught us by that internal light, which enables us to distinguish between right and wrong." The same important lesson is delivered to nations, as well as to men.[z]

We see now, that, both by the law of England, and by the superiour law of nature, men and nations can bind themselves. Can they be bound without their consent? Is it necessary to dig for another foundation, on which the obligatory force of human laws can be laid? Can any other solid foundation be found?

[x] Puff. 67. n. 2. to b, 1. c. 6. s. 12.
[y] 1. Gog. Or. Laws. 7. 8.
[z] Vat. Pref. 12.

That this foundation is sufficient to support the whole beautiful structure of human law, will abundantly appear.

"The union of families," says the same respectable author, whom I quoted just now, "could not have taken place but by an agreement of wills. When we view society as the effect of unanimous concord, it necessarily supposes certain covenants. These covenants imply conditions. These conditions are to be considered as the first laws."[a] We have already [192] seen the sentiments of the excellent Hooker— that "human edicts, derived from any other human source, than the consent of those, upon whom they are imposed, are nothing better than mere tyranny. Laws they are not, because they have not the publick approbation."[b] "The mother of civil law," says Grotius,[c] "is that very obligation, which arises from consent." "So that the civil law," says his commentator, Barbeyrac,[d] "is, at the bottom, no more than a consequence of that inviolable law of nature—every man is obliged to a religious observance of his promise." "The legislative power of a civil society," says Dr. Rutherford, in his Institutes of Natural Law,[e] "is acquired by the immediate and direct consent of the several individuals, who make themselves members of such society. And the legislative body acquires it, as by the immediate and direct consent of the collective body of the society, so by the remote and indirect consent of the several members."

I hope I have now performed my engagement: I hope I have evinced, from authority and from reason, from precedent and from principle, that *consent* is the sole obligatory principle of human government and human laws. To trace the varying but powerful energy of this animating principle through the formation and administration of every part of our beautiful system of government and law, will be a pleasing task in the course of these lectures. Can any task be more delightful than to pursue the circulation of liberty through every limb and member of the political body? This kind of anatomy has a peculiar advantage—it traces, without destroying, the principle of life.

Before I conclude, it will be proper to take a concise view of the consequences, necessarily resulting from the doctrine, that the legis-

[a] 1. Gog. Or. Laws. 7.
[b] Hooker. b. 1. s. 10. p. 19. 20.
[c] Pref. 20. s. 16.
[d] Id. note to s. 16.
[e] Vol. 2. 222.

lative power must be "absolute, uncontrolled, irresistible, and supreme." 1. the power, which makes the laws, cannot be accountable for its conduct; it cannot be submitted either to human judgment, or to human punishment. For both these, says Puffendorff,[f] suppose a superiour; but a superiour to the supreme, in the same order of men, and the same notion of government, is a contradiction. 2. If to every human law, a superiour is necessary: and if the power, which makes a human law, must be supreme; the consequence unquestionably is, that that power cannot be bound by the laws, which it makes: for where shall we find a superiour to what is supreme? "When a civil power," says Puffendorff,[g] "is constituted supreme, it must, on this very score, be supposed exempt from human laws; or, to speak more properly, above them. Human laws are nothing else but the decrees of the supreme power, concerning matters to be observed, by the subjects, for the publick good of the state. That no such edicts can directly oblige the sovereign is manifest; because his very [193] name and title supposeth, that no bond or engagement can be laid on him by any other mortal hand: and for a person to oblige himself, under the notion of a lawgiver, or of a superiour, is an impossibility." 3. If the legislative power be absolute, uncontrolled, and supreme; all opposition to its acts must be unlawful. this, indeed, is not so much a consequence, as a part of the doctrine. In the language of the Commentaries, this power is "irresistible,"[h] Many recollect the numerous and the extravagant inferences, which, at a former period, were drawn from the supposed absolute, irresistible, uncontrolled, and supreme power of the British parliament. They will fall under our notice, when we come to examine the principles, the rise, and the progress of the American constitutions and governments.

I have already mentioned, that though Sir William Blackstone was the first, he has not been the last, who defined municipal law, as applied to the law of England, upon unsound and dangerous principles. This doctrine has been adopted by his successour in the Vinerian chair, though with some degree of apparent hesitation. "Every state,' says he, "must, like individuals, be subject to certain rules." The necessity of rules infers the necessity of political superiours."[i] "The giving of

[f] B. 7. c. 6. s. 2. p. 687.
[g] B. 7. c. 6. 5. 3. p. 688.
[h] 1. Bl. Com. 49.
[i] El. Jur. (4to) 26. 27.

laws to a people, forms the most exalted degree of human sovereignty; and is, perhaps, in effect, or in strict propriety of speech, the only truly supreme power of the state."[j] The sensible and decided Mr. Paley, in his principles of moral and political philosophy, has propagated the same doctrine without limitation and without reserve. "As a series of appeals," says he, "must be finite, there necessarily exists, in every government, a power, from which the constitution has provided no appeal; and which power, for that reason, may be termed absolute, omnipotent, uncontrollable, arbitrary, despotick; and is alike so, in all countries. The person, or assembly, in whom this power resides, is called the sovereign or the supreme power of the state. Since to the same power universally appertains the office of establishing publick laws, it is also called the legislature of the state."[k] It is not improbable, that the doctrine is disseminated wherever the Commentaries are generally received as authority.

I have already intimated, that there is a period in our lives, when we receive implicitly whatever we are taught, especially by those, in whom, we think, we can confide. "It is the intention of nature," says the ingenious Dr. Reid,[l] "that we should be carried in arms before we are able to walk upon our legs; and it is likewise the intention of nature, that our belief should be guided by the authority and reason of others, before it can be guided by our own reason." At this very period of life, the Commentaries, as a book of authority, are put into the hands of young gentlemen, [194] to form the basis of their law education. Is it surprising, that the reception of its doctrines should be indiscriminate, as well as implicit? Indeed the former is the unavoidable consequence of the latter. But doctrines received implicitly, at this period of life, are not so easily dismissed in its subsequent stages. "For," says the same experienced judge of human nature,[m] "the novelty of an opinion, to those who are too fond of novelties; the gravity and solemnity, with which it is introduced; the opinion we have entertained of the author; and, above all, its being fixed in our minds at that time of life, when we received implicitly what we are taught; may cover its absurdity, and fascinate the understanding for a time"—I will add—for a long time. These observations explain,

[j] El. Jur. (4to) 43.
[k] 2. Paley 185.
[l] Inq. 433.
[m] Reid. Ess. In. 568.

and, while they explain, they justify my conduct in examining, so fully and so minutely, the definitions of law in general and of municipal law given in the Commentaries on the laws of England. This full and minute examination has, at the same time, given me a fit opportunity of discovering, of illustrating, and, I, hope, of establishing very different principles, as the foundation of the science of law. In this, as in every other science, it is all important, that the foundation be properly and surely laid.

Permit me to close this subject with sentiments, which a very learned and ingenious judge expressed, on an occasion somewhat similar to this, and in a situation somewhat similar to mine. The principles of the revolution in England have been dear to whigs: they have been opposed inveterately and pertinaciously by tories. Some passages in the law performances of the great and good Lord Chief Justice Hale were conceived, on both sides, and justly, to militate against the principles of that revolution. These passages were cited with uncommon exultation, and were, no doubt, disseminated by the votaries of the abdicated family with extraordinary zeal. Seventy years after the revolution, and sixteen years after the last rebellion, which was raised in order to overturn its happy establishment, Mr. Justice Foster thought it his duty to publish some observations on those passages, with a view to detect and expose their mistakes, which were great, and to defend the principles, on which the revolution and the subsequent establishment were founded. Concerning these observations, and their publication, he thus speaks, "The cause of the Pretender seems now to be absolutely given up. I hope in God it is so. But whether the root of bitterness, the principles which gave birth, and growth, and strength to it, and have been, twice within our memory, made a pretence for rebellion, at seasons very critical, whether those principles be totally eradicated, I know not. These I encounter, by showing that certain historical facts, which the learned Judge hath appealed to in support of them, either have no foundation in truth, or, were they true, do not warrant the conclusions drawn from them.

[195] "The passages I animadvert upon have been cited with an uncommon degree of triumph by those, who, to say no worse of them, from the dictates of a misguided conscience, have treated the revolution and present establishment as founded in usurpation and rebellion; and they are in every student's hand. Why, therefore, may not a good

subject, be it in season or out of season, caution the younger part of the profession against the prejudices, which the name of Lord Chief Justice Hale, a name ever honoured and esteemed, may otherwise beget in them? I, for my part, make no apology for the freedom I have taken with the sentiments of an author whose memory I can love and honour, without adopting any of his mistakes on the subject of government.

"It cannot be denied, and I see no reason for making a secret of it, that the learned Judge hath, in his writings, paid no regard to the principles, upon which the revolution and present happy establishment are founded. The prevailing opinion of the times, in which he received his first impressions, might mislead him. And it is not to be wondered at, if the detestable use the parliamentary army made of its success in the civil war did contribute to fix him in the prejudices of his early days. For, in the competition of parties, extremes, on one side, almost universally produce their contraries on the other. And even honest minds are not always secured against the contagion of party prejudice.

"But, it matters not with us, whether his opinion was the effect of prejudices early entertained, or the result of cool reflection; since the opinion of no man, how great or good soever, is or ought to be the sole standard of truth."[n]

The next great title in my course of lectures is MAN, the subject of all, and the author, as well as the subject of part of those kinds of law, of which I have now given a general and summary view. Man I shall consider as an individual, as a member of society, as a member of a confederation, and as a part of the great commonwealth of nations.

On a slight glance of this subject, it may seem, perhaps, not to be very intimately connected with a system of lectures on law. And, indeed, it must be owned, that as law, or what is called law, is sometimes taught, and sometimes practised, there is but a slender and very remote alliance between law and man. But, in the real nature of things, the case is very different.

You have not, I am sure, forgotten, that, in an early address, which I made to you, I recommended, most earnestly, to the utmost degree of your attention, an outline of study, supported with all the countenance and authority of three distinguished and experienced characters—Bacon, Bolingbroke, Kaims: it will not, I am sure, be

[n] Fost. Pref. 6. 7.

forgotten, that metaphysical knowledge, or the philosophy of the human mind, formed a very conspicuous [196] part of that outline; one of those "vantage grounds," which everyone must climb, who aims to be really a master in the science of law.

"Natura juris a natura hominis repetenda est,"* is the judgment of Cicero. It is a judgment, not more respectable on account of the high authority, which pronounces it, than on account of its intrinsick solidity and importance.

You have heard me mention, that a proper system of evidence is the greatest *desideratum* in the law. From a distinct and accurate knowledge of the human mind, and of its powers and operations, the principles and materials of such a system must be drawn and collected.

Whatever produces belief may be comprehended under the name of evidence. Belief is a simple and undefinable operation of the mind; but, by the constitution of our nature, it is intimately and inseparably associated with many other powers and operations. This association should be minutely traced: all its properties and consequences should be distinctly marked. Belief attends on the perceptions of our external senses, on the operations of our internal consciousness, on those of memory, on those of intuition, on those of reason: it is attendant, likewise, on the veracity, the fidelity, and the judgment of others. Hence the evidence of sense, the evidence of recollection, the evidence of consciousness, the evidence of intuition, the evidence of demonstration, probable evidence, the evidence of testimony, the evidence of engagements, the evidence of opinion, and many other kinds of evidence; for this is, by no means, a complete enumeration of them.

It is difficult, perhaps it is impossible, to discover any common principle, to which all these different kinds of evidence can be reduced. They seem to agree only in this, that, by the constitution of our nature, they are fitted to produce belief.

It is superfluous to add, that the social operations of the mind should be well known and studied by him, who wishes to reach the genuine principles of legal knowledge.

* [The nature of the law is to be sought from the nature of man himself.]

[76]

FISHER AMES 1758–1808

The Dangers of American Liberty

BOSTON, 1805

Graduate of Harvard University and a lawyer by training and occupation, Ames was elected to represent a district bordering on Boston in the first Congress chosen under the United States Constitution. After serving four terms in the House of Representatives he terminated his legislative service because of ill health. He was noted as a lucid writer and a speaker of unusual persuasive power. A bitter opponent of Thomas Jefferson and his supporters, Ames wrote this essay a decade after retirement from public life but despite urging by friends refused to publish it, thinking it not sober and moderate enough to represent his approach to politics and life. Superficially the essay can be read as a jeremiad against the leveling ideas emanating from France and supposedly supported by the Jeffersonians, but a careful reading shows Ames to be a Federalist with their standard concern for faction, instability, and majority tyranny, who at the same time has a theoretical stance interpenetrated with the traditional values of many Anti-Federalists (Whigs) whom he opposed. It seems appropriate to end this book with an essay by a man who could address himself to problems uppermost in the minds of Americans at any time during the half-century we have identified as the founding era and who unobtrusively synthesizes much of American political theory into a continuing critique of bigness, impersonality, corruption, venality, and the loss of community and public virtue. The stance is reasoned, the rhetoric impassioned, and the result peculiarly American.

BOSTON, 1805

THE DANGERS OF AMERICAN LIBERTY

Sic tibi persuade, me dies et noctes nihil aliud agere, nihil curare, nisi ut mei cives salvi liberique sint. *Ep. Famil.* 1. 24.

Be assured, therefore, that neither day nor night have I any cares, any labors, but for the safety and freedom of my fellow citizens.

I am not positive that it is of any immediate use to our country that its true friends should better understand one [345] another; nor am I apprehensive that the crudities which my ever hasty pen confides to my friends will essentially mislead their opinion in respect either to myself or to public affairs. At a time when men eminently wise cherish almost any hopes, however vain, because they choose to be blind to their fears, it would be neither extraordinary nor disreputable for me to mistake the degree of maturity to which our political vices have arrived, nor to err in computing how near or how far off we stand from the term of their fatal consummation.

I fear that the future fortunes of our country no longer depend on counsel. We have persevered in our errors too long to change our propensities by now enlightening our convictions. The political sphere, like the globe we tread upon, never stands still, but with a silent swiftness accomplishes the revolutions which, we are too ready to believe, are effected by our wisdom, or might have been controlled by our efforts. There is a kind of fatality in the affairs of republics, that eludes the foresight of the wise as much as it frustrates the toils and sacrifices of the patriot and the hero. Events proceed, not as they were expected or intended, but as they are impelled by the irresistible laws of our political existence. Things inevitable happen, and we are astonished, as if they were miracles, and the course of nature had been overpowered or suspended to produce them. Hence it is, that, till lately, more than half our countrymen believed our public tranquillity was firmly established, and that our liberty did not merely rest upon dry land, but was wedged, or rather rooted high above the flood in the rocks of granite, as immovably as the pillars that prop the universe. They, or at least the discerning of them, are at length no less disappointed than terrified to perceive that we have all the time floated, [346] with a fearless and unregarded course, down the stream of events, till we are now visibly drawn within the revolutionary suction of Niagara, and every thing that is liberty will be dashed to pieces in the descent.

We have been accustomed to consider the pretension of Englishmen to be free as a proof how completely they were broken to subjection, or hardened in imposture. We have insisted, that they had no constitution, because they never made one; and that their boasted government, which is just what time and accident have made it, was palsied with age, and blue with the plague-sores of corruption. We have believed that it derived its stability, not from reason, but from prejudice; that it is supported, not because it is favorable to liberty, but as it is dear to national pride; that it is reverenced, not for its excellence, but because ignorance is naturally the idolater of antiquity; that it is not sound and healthful, but derives a morbid energy from disease, and an unaccountable aliment from the canker that corrodes its vitals.

But we maintained that the federal Constitution, with all the bloom of youth and splendor of innocence, was gifted with immortality. For if time should impair its force, or faction tarnish its charms, the people, ever vigilant to discern its wants, ever powerful to provide for them, would miraculously restore it to the field, like some wounded hero of the epic, to take a signal vengeance on its enemies, or like Antaeus, invigorated by touching his mother earth, to rise the stronger for a fall.

There is of course a large portion of our citizens who will not believe, even on the evidence of facts, that any public evils exist, or are impending. They deride the apprehensions of those who foresee that licentiousness will prove, as it ever has proved, fatal to liberty. They consider her as a nymph, who need not be coy to keep herself pure, but that on the contrary, her chastity will grow robust by frequent scuffles with her seducers. They say, while a faction is a minority it will remain harmless by being outvoted; and if it should become a majority, all its acts, however profligate or violent, are then legitimate. For with the democrats the people is a sovereign who can do [no] wrong, even when he respects [347] and spares no existing right, and whose voice, however obtained or however counterfeited, bears all the sanctity and all the force of a living divinity.

Where, then, it will be asked, in a tone both of menace and of triumph, can the people's dangers lie, unless it be with the persecuted federalists. They are the partisans of monarchy, who propagate their principles in order, as soon as they have increased their sect, to introduce a king; for by this only avenue they foretell his approach. Is it possible the people should ever be their own enemies? If all government were dissolved to-day, would they not reëstablish it to-morrow, with no other prejudice to the public liberty than some superfluous fears of its friends, some abortive projects of its enemies? Nay, would not liberty rise resplendent with the light of fresh experience, and coated in the sevenfold mail of constitutional amendments?

These opinions are fiercely maintained, not only as if there were evidence to prove them, but as if it were a merit to believe them, by men who tell you that in the most desperate extremity of faction or usurpation we have an unfailing resource in the good sense of the nation. They assure us there is at least as much wisdom in the people as in these ingenious tenets of their creed.

For any purpose, therefore, of popular use or general impression, it seems almost fruitless to discuss the question, whether our public liberty can subsist, and what is to be the condition of that awful futurity to which we are hastening. The clamors of party are so loud, and the resistance of national vanity is so stubborn, it will be impossible to convince any but the very wise, (and in every state they are the very few,) that our democratic liberty is utterly untenable; that we are devoted to the successive struggles of factions, who will rule by turns, the worst of whom will rule last, and triumph by the sword: But for the wise this unwelcome task is, perhaps, superfluous: they, possibly, are already convinced.

All such men are, or ought to be, agreed that simple governments are despotisms; and of all despotisms a democracy, though the least durable, is the most violent. It is also true, that all the existing governments we are acquainted [348] with are more or less mixed, or balanced and checked, however imperfectly, by the ingredients and principles that belong to the other simple sorts. It is nevertheless a fact, that there is scarcely any civil constitution in the world, that, according to American ideas, is so mixed and combined as to be favorable to the liberty of the subject—none, absolutely none, that an American patriot would be willing to adopt for, much less to impose on, his country. Without pretending to define that liberty, which writers at length agree is incapable of any precise and comprehensive definition, all the European governments, except the British, admit a most formidable portion of arbitrary power; whereas in America no plan of government, without a large and preponderating commixture of democracy, can for a moment possess our confidence and attachment.

It is unquestionable that the concern of the people in the affairs of such a government tends to elevate the character, and enlarge the comprehension, as well as the enjoyments of the citizens; and supposing the government wisely constituted, and the laws steadily and firmly carried into execution, these effects, in which every lover of mankind must exult, will not be attended with a corresponding depravation of the public manners and morals. I have never yet met with an American of any party who seemed willing to exclude the people from their temperate and well-regulated share of concern in the government. Indeed it is notorious, that there was scarcely an advocate for the federal Constitution who was not anxious, from the first, to hazard the experiment of an unprecedented, and almost unqualified proportion of democracy, both in constructing and administering the government, and who did not rely with confidence, if not blind presumption, on its success. This is certain, the body of the federalists were always, and yet are, essentially democratic in their political notions. The truth is, the American nation, with ideas and prejudices wholly democratic, undertook to frame, and expected tranquilly and with energy and success to administer, a republican government.

It is and ever has been my belief, that the federal Constitution was as good, or very nearly as good, as our country could bear; that the attempt to introduce a mixed monarchy [349] was never thought of, and would have failed if it had been made; and could have proved only an inveterate curse to the nation if it had been adopted cheerfully, and even unanimously, by the people. Our materials for a government were all democratic, and whatever the hazard of their combination may be, our Solons and Lycurguses in the convention had no alternative, nothing to consider, but how to combine them, so as to insure the longest duration to the Constitution, and the most favorable chance for the public liberty in the event of those changes, which the frailty of the structure of our government, the operation of time and accident, and the maturity and development of the national character were well understood to portend. We should have succeeded worse if we had trusted to our metaphysics more. Experience must be our physician, though his medicines may kill.

The danger obviously was, that a species of government in which the people choose all the rulers, and then, by themselves or ambitious demagogues pretending to be the people, claim and exercise an effective control over what is called the government, would be found on trial no better than a turbulent, licentious democracy. The danger was that their best interests would be neglected, their dearest rights violated, their sober reason silenced, and the worst passions of the worst men not only freed from legal restraint, but invested with public power. The known propensity of a democracy is to licentiousness, which the ambitious call, and the ignorant believe to be, liberty.

The great object, then, of political wisdom in framing our Constitution, was to guard against licentiousness, that inbred malady of democracies, that deforms their infancy with gray hairs and decrepitude.

The federalists relied much on the efficiency of an independent judiciary, as a check on the hasty turbulence of the popular passions. They supposed the senate, proceeding from the states, and chosen for six years, would form a sort of balance to the democracy, and realize the hope that a federal republic of states might subsist. They counted much on the information of the citizens; that they would give their unremitted attention to public affairs; that either dissensions [350] would not arise in our happy country, or if they should, that the citizens would remain calm, and would walk, like the three Jews in Nebuchadnezzar's furnace, unharmed amidst the fires of party.

It is needless to ask how rational such hopes were, or how far experience has verified them.

The progress of party has given to Virginia a preponderance that perhaps was not foreseen. Certainly, since the late amendment in the article for the choice of president and vice-president, there is no existing provision of any efficacy to counteract it.

The project of arranging states in a federal union has long been deemed, by able writers and statesmen, more promising than the scheme of a single republic. The experiment, it has been supposed, has not yet been fairly tried; and much has been expected from the example of America.

If states were neither able nor inclined to obstruct the federal union, much indeed might be hoped from such a confederation. But Virginia, Pennsylvania, and New York are of an extent sufficient to form potent monarchies, and of course are too powerful, as well as too proud, to be subjects of the federal laws. Accordingly, one of the first schemes of amendment, and the most early executed, was to exempt them in form from the obligations of justice. States are not liable to be sued. Either the federal head or the powerful members must govern. Now, as it is a thing ascertained by experience that the great states are not willing, and cannot be compelled to obey the union, it is manifest that their ambition is most singularly invited to aspire to the usurpation or control of the powers of the confederacy. A confederacy of many states, all of them small in extent and population, not only might not obstruct, but happily facilitate the federal authority. But the late presidential amendment demonstrates the overwhelming preponderance of several great states, combining together to engross the control of federal affairs.

There never has existed a federal union in which the leading states were not ambitious to rule, and did not endeavour to rule by fomenting factions in the small states, and thus engross the management of the federal concerns. Hence it was, that Sparta, at the head of the Peloponnesus, filled all [351] Greece with terror and dissension. In every city she had an aristocratical party to kill or to banish the popular faction that was devoted to her rival, Athens; so that each city was inhabited by two hostile nations, whom no laws of war could control, no leagues or treaties bind. Sometimes Athens, sometimes Sparta took the ascendant, and influenced the decrees of the famous Amphyctionic council, the boasted federal head of the Grecian republics. But at all times that head was wholly destitute of authority, except when violent and sanguinary measures were dictated to it by some preponderant member. The small states were immediately reduced to an absolute nullity, and were subject to the most odious of all oppressions, the domination of one state over another state.

The Grecian states, forming the Amphyctionic league, composed the most illustrious federal republic that ever existed. Its dissolution and ruin were brought about by the operation of the principles and passions that are inherent in all such associations. The Thebans, one of the leading states, uniting with the Thessalians, both animated by jealousy and resentment against the Phocians, procured a decree of the council of the Amphyctions, where their joint influence predominated, as that of Virginia now does in congress, condemning the Phocians to a heavy fine for some pretended sacrilege they had committed on the lands consecrated to the temple of Delphi. Finding the Phocians, as they expected and wished, not inclined to submit, by a second decree they devoted their lands to the god of that temple, and called upon all Greece to arm in their sacred cause, for so they affected to call it. A contest thus began which was doubly sanguinary, because it combined the characters of a religious and civil war, and raged for more than ten years. In the progress of it, the famous Philip of Macedon found means to introduce himself as a party; and the nature of his measures, as well as their final success, is an everlasting warning to all federal republics. He appears, from the first moment of his reign, to have planned the subjugation of Greece; and in two-and-twenty years he accomplished his purpose.

After having made his escape from the city of Thebes, [352] where he had been a hostage, he had to recover his hereditary kingdom, weakened by successive defeats, and distracted with factions from foreign invaders, and from two dangerous competitors of his throne. As soon as he became powerful, his restless ambition sought every opportunity to intermeddle in the affairs of Greece, in respect to which Macedonia was considered an alien, and the sacred war soon furnished it. Invited by the Thessalians to assist them against the Phocians, he pretended an extraordinary zeal for religion, as well as respect for the decree of the Amphyctions. Like more modern demagogues, he made use of his popularity first to prepare the way for his arms. He had no great difficulty in subduing them; and obtained for his reward another Amphyctionic decree, by which the vote of Phocis was forever transferred to Philip and his descendants. Philip soon after took possession of the pass of Thermopylae, and within eight years turned his arms against those very Thebans whom he had before assisted. They had no refuge in the federal union which they had helped to enfeeble. They were utterly defeated; Thebes, the pride of Greece, was razed to the ground; the citizens were sold into slavery; and the national liberties were extinguished forever.

Here let Americans read their own history. Here let even Virginia learn how perilous and how frail will be the consummation of her schemes. Powerful states, that combine to domineer over the weak, will be inevitably divided by their success and ravaged with civil war, often baffled, always agitated by intrigue, shaken with alarms, and finally involved in one common slavery and ruin, of which they are no less conspicuously the artificers than the victims.

If, in the nature of things, there could be any experience which would be extensively instructive, but our own, all history lies open for our warning,—open like a churchyard, all whose lessons are solemn, and chiselled for eternity in the hard stone,—lessons that whisper, O! that they could thunder to republics, "Your passions and vices forbid you to be free."

But experience, though she teaches wisdom, teaches it too late. The most signal events pass away unprofitably for the [353] generation in which they occur, till at length, a people, deaf to the things that belong to its peace, is destroyed or enslaved, because it will not be instructed.

From these reflections, the political observer will infer that the American republic is impelled by the force of state ambition and of democratic licentiousness; and he will inquire, which of the two is our strongest propensity. Is the sovereign power to be contracted to a state centre? Is Virginia to be our Rome? And are we to be her Latin or Italian allies, like them to be emulous of the honor of our chains on the terms of imposing them on Louisiana, Mexico, or Santa Fe? Or are we to run the giddy circle of popular licentiousness, beginning in delusion, quickened by vice, and ending in wretchedness?

But though these two seem to be contrary impulses, it will appear, nevertheless, on examination, that they really lead to but one result.

The great state of Virginia has fomented a licentious spirit among all her neighbors. Her citizens imagine that they are democrats, and their abstract theories are in fact democratic; but their state policy is that of a genuine aristocracy or oligarchy. Whatever their notions or their state practice may be, their policy, as it respects the other states, is to throw all power into the hands of democratic zealots or jacobin knaves; for some of these may be deluded and others bought to promote her designs. And, even independently of a direct Virginia influence, every state faction will find its account in courting the alliance and promoting the views of this great leader. Those who labor to gain a factious power in a state, and those who aspire to get a paramount jurisdiction over it, will not be slow to discern that they have a common cause to pursue.

In the intermediate progress of our affairs, the ambition of Virginia may be gratified. So long as popular licentiousness is operating with no lingering industry to effect our yet unfinished ruin, she may flourish the whip of dominion in her hands; but as soon as it is accomplished she will be the associate of our shame, and bleed under its lashes. For democratic license leads not to a monarchy regulated by laws, but to the ferocious despotism of a chieftain, who owes [354] his elevation to arms and violence, and leans on his sword as the only prop of his dominion. Such a conqueror, jealous and fond of nothing but his power, will care no more for Virginia, though he may rise by Virginia, than Bonaparte does for Corsica. Virginia will then find, that, like ancient Thebes, she has worked for Philip, and forged her own fetters.

There are few, even among the democrats, who will doubt, though to a man they will deny, that the ambition of that state is inordinate, and unless seasonably counteracted, will be fatal; yet they will persevere in striving for power in their states, before they think it necessary, or can find it convenient to attend to her encroachments.

But there are not many, perhaps not five hundred, even among the federalists, who yet allow themselves to view the progress of licentiousness as so speedy, so sure, and so fatal, as the deplorable experience of our country shows that it is, and the evidence of history and the constitution of human nature demonstrate that it must be.

The truth is, such an opinion, admitted with all the terrible light of its proof, no less shocks our fears than our vanity, no less disturbs our quiet than our prejudices. We are summoned by the tocsin to every perilous and painful duty. Our days are made heavy with the pressure of anxiety, and our nights restless with visions of horror. We listen to the clank of chains, and overhear the whispers of assassins. We mark the barbarous dissonance of mingled rage and triumph in the yell of an infatuated mob; we see the dismal glare of their burning and scent the loathsome steam of human victims offered in sacrifice.

These reflections may account for the often lamented blindness, as well as apathy of our well-disposed citizens. Who would choose to study the tremendous records of the fates, or to remain long in the dungeon of the furies? Who that is penetrating enough to foresee our scarcely hidden destiny, is hardy enough to endure its anxious contemplation?

It may not long be more safe to disturb than it is easy to enlighten the democratic faith in regard to our political propensities, since it will neither regard what is obvious, nor yield to the impression of events, even after they have happened. [355] The thoughtless and ignorant care for nothing but the name of liberty, which is as much the end as the instrument of party, and equally fills up the measure of their comprehension and desires. According to the conception of such men, the public liberty can never perish; it will enjoy immortality, like the dead in the memory of the living. We have heard the French prattle about its rights, and seen them swagger in the fancied possession of its distinctions long after they were crushed by the weight of their chains. The Romans were not only amused, but really made vain by the boast of their liberty, while they sweated and trembled under the despotism of the emperors, the most odious monsters that ever infested the earth. It is remarkable that Cicero, with all his dignity and good sense, found it a popular seasoning of his harangue, six years after Julius Caesar had established a monarchy, and only six months before Octavius totally subverted the commonwealth, to say, "It is not possible for the people of Rome to be slaves, whom the gods have destined to the command of all nations. Other nations may endure slavery, but the proper end and business of the Roman people is liberty."

This very opinion in regard to the destinies of our country is neither less extensively diffused, nor less solidly established. Such men will persist in thinking our liberty cannot be in danger till it is irretrievably lost. It is even the boast of multitudes that our system of government is a pure democracy.

What is there left that can check its excesses or retard the velocity of its fall? Not the control of the several states, for they already whirl in the vortex of faction; and of consequence, not the senate, which is appointed by the states. Surely not the judiciary, for we cannot expect the office of the priesthood from the victim at the altar. Are we to be sheltered by the force of ancient manners? Will this be sufficient to control the two evil spirits of license and innovation? Where is any vestige of those manners left, but in New England? And even in New England their authority is contested and their purity debased. Are our civil and religious institutions to stand so firmly as to sustain themselves and so much of the fabric of the public order as is [356] propped by their support? On the contrary, do we not find the ruling faction in avowed hostility to our religious institutions? In effect, though not in form, their protection is abandoned by our laws and confided to the steadiness of sentiment and fashion; and if they are still powerful auxiliaries of lawful authority, it is owing to the tenaciousness with which even a degenerate people maintain their habits, and to a yet remaining, though impaired veneration for the maxims of our ancestors. We are changing, and if democracy triumphs in New England, it is to be apprehended that in a few years we shall be as prone to disclaim our great progenitors, as they, if they should return again to the earth, with grief and shame to disown their degenerate descendants.

Is the turbulence of our democracy to be restrained by preferring to the magistracy only the grave and upright, the men who profess the best moral and religious principles, and whose lives bear testimony in favor of their profession, whose virtues inspire confidence, whose services, gratitude, and whose talents command admiration? Such magistrates would add dignity to the best government, and disarm the malignity of the worst. But the bare moving of this question will be understood as a sarcasm by men of both parties. The powers of impudence itself are scarcely adequate to say that our magistrates are such men. The atrocities of a distinguished tyrant might provoke satire to string his bow, and with the arrow of Philoctetes to inflict the immedicable wound. We have no Juvenal; and if we had, he would scorn to dissect the vice that wants firmness for the knife, to elevate that he might hit his object, and to dignify low profligacy to be the vehicle of a loathsome immortality.

It never has happened in the world, and it never will, that a democracy has been kept out of the control of the fiercest and most turbulent spirits in the society; they will breathe into it all their own fury, and make it subservient to the worst designs of the worst men.

Although it does not appear that the science of good government has made any advances since the invention of printing, it is nevertheless the opinion of many that this art has risen, like another sun in the sky, to shed new light and joy on the political world. The press, however, has left the [357] understanding of the mass of men just where it found it; but by supplying an endless stimulus to their imagination and passions, it has rendered their temper and habits infinitely worse. It has inspired ignorance with presumption, so that those who cannot be governed by reason are no longer to be awed by authority. The many, who before the art of printing never mistook in a case of oppression, because they complained from their actual sense of it, have become susceptible of every transient enthusiasm, and of more than womanish fickleness of caprice. Public affairs are transacted now on a stage where all the interest and passions grow out of fiction, or are inspired by the art, and often controlled at the pleasure of the actors. The press is a new, and certainly a powerful, agent in human affairs. It will change, but it is difficult to conceive how, by rendering men indocile and presumptuous, it *can* change societies for the better. They are pervaded by its heat, and kept forever restless by its activity. While it has impaired the force that every just government can employ in self-defence, it has imparted to its enemies the secret of that wildfire that blazes with the most consuming fierceness on attempting to quench it.

Shall we then be told that the press will constitute an adequate check to the progress of every species of tyranny? Is it to be denied that the press has been the base and venal instrument of the very men whom it ought to gibbet to universal abhorrence? While they were climbing to power it aided their ascent; and now they have reached it, does it not conceal or justify their abominations? Or, while it is confessed that the majority of citizens form their ideas of men and measures almost solely from the light that reaches them through the magic-lantern of the press, do our comforters still depend on the all-restoring, all-preserving power of general information? And are they not destitute of all this, or rather of any better information themselves, if they can urge this vapid nonsense in the midst of a yet spreading political delusion, in the midst of the "palpable obscure" that settles on the land, from believing what is false, and misconstruing what is true? Can they believe all this, when they consider how much truth is impeded by party on its way to the public understanding, and even after having [358] reached it, how much it still falls short of its proper mark, while it leaves the envious, jealous, vindictive will unconquered?

Our mistake, and in which we choose to persevere because our vanity shrinks from the detection, is, that in political affairs, by only determining what men ought to think, we are sure how they will act; and when we know the facts, and are assiduous to collect and present the evidence, we dupe ourselves with the expectation that, as there is but one result which wise men can believe, there is but one course of conduct deduced from it, which honest men can approve or pursue. We forget that in framing the judgment every passion is both an advocate and a witness. We lay out of our account, how much essential information there is that never reaches the multitude, and of the mutilated portion that does, how much is unwelcome to party prejudice; and therefore, that they may still maintain their opinions, they withhold their attention. We seem to suppose, while millions raise so loud a cry about their sovereign power, and really concentre both their faith and their affections in party, that the bulk of mankind will regard no counsels but such as are suggested by their conscience. Let us dare to speak out; is there any single despot who avowedly holds himself so superior to its dictates?

But our manners are too mild, they tell us, for a democracy—then democracy will change those manners. Our morals are too pure—then it will corrupt them.

What, then is the necessary conclusion, from the view we have taken of the insufficiency or extinction of all conceivable checks? It is such as ought to strike terror, but will scarcely raise public curiosity.

Is it not possible, then, it will be asked, to write and argue down opinions that are so mischievous and only plausible, and men who are even more profligate than exalted? Can we not persuade our citizens to be republican again, so as to rebuild the splendid ruins of the state on the Washington foundation? Thus it is, that we resolve to perpetuate our own delusions, and to cherish our still frustrated and confuted hopes. Let only ink enough be shed, and let democracy rage, there will be no blood. Though the evil is fixed [359] in our nature, all we think will be safe, because we fancy we can see a remedy floating in our opinions.

It is undoubtedly a salutary labor to diffuse among the citizens of a free state, as far as the thing is possible, a just knowledge of their public affairs. But the difficulty of this task is augmented exactly in proportion to the freedom of the state; for the more free the citizens, the bolder and more profligate will be their demagogues, the more numerous and eccentric the popular errors, and the more vehement and pertinacious the passions that defend them.

Yet, as if there were neither vice nor passion in the world, one of the loudest of our boasts, one of the dearest of all the tenets of our creed is, that we are a sovereign people, self-governed—it would be nearer truth to say, self-conceited. For in what sense is it true that any people, however free, are self-governed? If they have in fact no government but such as comports with their ever-varying and often inordinate desires, then it is anarchy; if it counteracts those desires it is compulsory. The individual who is left to act according to his own humor is not governed at all; and if any considerable number, and especially any combination of individuals, find or can place themselves in this situation, then the society is no longer free. For liberty obviously consists in the salutary restraint, and not in the uncontrolled indulgence of such humors. Now of all desires, none will so much need restraint, or so impatiently endure it, as those of the ambitious, who will form factions, first to elude, then to rival, and finally to usurp the powers of the state; and of the sons of vice, who are the enemies of law, because no just law can be their friend. The first want to govern the state; and the others, that the state should not govern them. A sense of common interest will soon incline these two original factions of every free state to coalesce into one.

So far as men are swayed by authority, or impelled or excited by their fears and affections, they naturally search for some persons as the sources and objects of these effects and emotions. It is pretty enough to say, the republic commands, and the love of the republic dictates obedience to the heart of every citizen. This is system, but is it nature? The republic is a creature of fiction; it is everybody in the [360] fancy, but nobody in the heart. Love, to be any thing, must be select and exclusive. We may as well talk of loving geometry as the commonwealth. Accordingly, there are many who seldom try to reason, and are the most misled when they do. Such men are, of necessity, governed by their prejudices. They neither comprehend nor like any thing of a republic but their party and their leaders. These last are persons capable of meriting, at least of knowing and rewarding their zeal and exertions. Hence it is, that the republicanism of a great mass of people is often nothing more than a blind trust in certain favorites, and a no less blind and still more furious hatred of their enemies. Thus, a free society, by the very nature of liberty, is often ranged into rival factions, who mutually practise and suffer delusion by the abuse of the best names, but who really contend for nothing but the preeminence of their leaders.

In a democracy, the elevation of an equal convinces many, if not all, that the height to which he is raised is not inaccessible. Ambition wakes from its long sleep in every soul, and wakes, like one of Milton's fallen angels, to turn its tortures into weapons against the public order. The multitude behold their favorite with eyes of love and wonder; and with the more of both, as he is a new favorite, and owes his greatness wholly to their favor. Who among the little does not swell into greatness, when he thus reflects that he has assisted to make great men? And who of the popular favorites loses a minute to flatter this vanity in every brain, till it turns it?

The late equals of the new-made chief behold his rise with very different emotions. They view him near, and have long been accustomed to look behind the disguises of his hypocrisy. They know his vices and his foibles, and that the foundations of his fame are as false and hollow as his professions. Nevertheless, it may be their interest or their necessity to serve him for a time. But the instant they can supplant him, they will spare neither intrigues nor violence to effect it. Thus, a democratic system in its very nature teems with faction and revolution. Yet, though it continually tends to shift its head, its character is immutable. Its constancy is in change.

[361] The theory of a democracy supposes that the will of the people ought to prevail, and that, as the majority possess not only the better right, but the superior force, of course it will prevail. A greater force, they argue, will inevitably overcome a less. When a constitution provides, with an imposing solemnity of detail, for the collection of the opinions of a majority of the citizens, every sanguine reader not only becomes assured that the will of the people must prevail, but he goes further, and refuses to examine the reasons, and to excuse the incivism and presumption of those who can doubt of this inevitable result. Yet common sense and our own recent experience have shown, that a combination of a very small minority can effectually defeat the authority of the national will. The votes of a majority may sometimes, though not invariably, show what ought to be done; but to awe or subdue the force of a thousand men, the government must call out the superior force of two thousand men. It is therefore established the very instant it is brought to the test, that the mere will of a majority is inefficient and without authority. And as to employing a superior force to procure obedience, which a democratic government has an undoubted right to do, and so indeed has every other, it is obvious that the admitted necessity of this resort completely overthrows all the boasted advantages of the democratic system. For if obedience cannot be procured by reason, it must be obtained by compulsion; and this is exactly what every other government will do in a like case.

Still, however, the friends of the democratic theory will maintain that this dire resort to force will be exceedingly rare, because the public reason will be more clearly expressed and more respectfully understood than under any other form of government. The citizens will be, of course, self-governed, as it will be their choice as well as duty to obey the laws.

It has been already remarked, that the refusal of a very small minority to obey will render force necessary. It has been also noted, that as every mass of people will inevitably desire a favorite, and fix their trust and affections upon one, it clearly follows that there will be of course a faction opposed to the public will as expressed in the laws. Now, if [362] a faction is once admitted to exist in a state, the disposition and the means to obstruct the laws, or, in other words, the will of the majority, must be perceived to exist also. If then it be true, that a democratic government is of all the most liable to faction, which no man of sense will deny, it is manifest that it is, from its very nature, obliged more than any other government to resort to force to overcome or awe the power of faction. This latter will continually employ its own power, that acts always against the physical force of the nation, which can be brought to act only in extreme cases, and then, like every extreme remedy, aggravates the evil. For, let it be noted, a regular government, by overcoming an unsuccessful insurrection, becomes stronger; but elective rulers can scarcely ever employ the physical force of a democracy without turning the moral force, or the power of opinion, against the government. So that faction is not unfrequently made to triumph from its own defeats, and to avenge, in the disgrace and blood of magistrates, the crime of their fidelity to the laws.

As the boastful pretensions of the democratic system cannot be too minutely exposed, another consideration must be given to the subject.

That government certainly deserves no honest man's love or support, which, from the very laws of its being, carries terror and danger to the virtuous, and arms the vicious with authority and power. The essence, and in the opinion of many thousands not yet cured of their delusions, the excellence of democracy is, that it invests every citizen with an equal proportion of power. A state consisting of a million of citizens has a million sovereigns, each of whom detests all other sovereignty but his own. This very boast implies as much of the spirit of turbulence and insubordination as the utmost energy of any known regular government, even the most rigid, could keep in restraint. It also implies a state of agitation that is justly terrible to all who love their ease, and of instability that quenches the last hope of those who would transmit their liberty to posterity. Waiving any further pursuit of these reflections, let it be resumed, that if every man of the million has his ratable share of power in the community, then, instead of restraining the vicious, [363] they also are armed with power, for they take their part; as they are citizens, this cannot be refused them. Now, as they have an interest in preventing the execution of the laws, which, in fact, is the apparent common interest of their whole class, their union will happen of course. The very first moment that they do unite, which it is ten thousand to one will happen before the form of the democracy is agreed upon, and while its plausible constitution is framing, that moment they form a faction, and the pretended efficacy of the democratic system, which is to operate by the power of opinion and persuasion, comes to an end. For an *imperium in imperio* exists; there is a state within the state, a combination interested and active in hindering the will of the majority from being obeyed.

But the vicious, we shall be told, are very few in such an honest nation as the American. How many of our states did, in fact, pass laws to obstruct the lawful operation of the treaty of peace in 1783? and were the virtuous men of those states the framers and advocates of those laws? What shall we denominate the oligarchy that sways the authority of Virginia? Who is ignorant that the ruling power have an interest to oppose justice to creditors? Surely, after these facts are remembered, no man will say, the faction of the vicious is a chimera of the writer's brain; nor, admitting it to be real, will he deny that it has proved itself potent.

It is not however the faction of debtors only that is to be expected to arise under a democracy. Every bad passion that dreads restraint from the laws will seek impunity and indulgence in faction. The associates will not come together in cold blood. They will not, like their federal adversaries, yawn over the contemplation of their cause, and shrink from the claim of its necessary perils and sacrifices. They will do all that can possibly be done, and they will attempt more. They will begin early, persevere long, ask no respite for themselves, and are sure to triumph if their enemies take any. Suppose at first their numbers to be exceedingly few, their efforts will for that reason be so much the greater. They will call themselves the people; they will in their name arraign every act of government as wicked and weak; [364] they will oblige the rulers to stand forever on the defensive, as culprits at the bar of an offended public. With a venal press at command, concealing their number and their infamy, is it to be doubted that the ignorant will soon or late unite with the vicious? Their union is inevitable; and, when united, those allies are powerful enough to strike terror into the hearts of the firmest rulers. It is in vain, it is indeed childish to say, that an enlightened people will understand their own affairs, and thus the acts of a faction will be baffled. No people on earth are or can be so enlightened as to the details of political affairs. To study politics, so as to know correctly the force of the reasons for a large part of the public measures, would stop the labor of the plough and the hammer; and how are these million of students to have access to the means of information?

When it is thus apparent that the vicious will have as many opportunities as inducements to inflame and deceive, it results, from the nature of democracy, that the ignorant will join, and the ambitious will lead their combination. Who, then, will deny that the vicious are armed with power, and the virtuous exposed to persecution and peril?

If a sense of their danger compel these latter, at length, to unite also in self-defence, it will be late, probably too late, without means to animate and cement their union, and with no hope beyond that of protracting, for a short time, the certain catastrophe of their destruction, which in fact no democracy has ever yet failed to accomplish.

If then all this is to happen, not from accident, not as the shallow or base demagogues pretend, from the management of monarchists or aristocrats, but from the principles of democracy itself, as we have attempted to demonstrate, ought we not to consider democracy as the worst of all governments, or if there be a worse, as the certain forerunner of that? What other form of civil rule among men so irresistibly tends to free vice from restraint, and to subject virtue to persecution?

The common supposition is, and it is ever assumed as the basis of argument, that in a democracy the laws have only to command individuals, who yield a willing and conscientious obedience; and who would be destitute of the force to [365] resist, if they should lack the disposition to submit. But this supposition, which so constantly triumphs in the newspapers, utterly fails in the trial in our republic, which we do not denominate a democracy. To collect the tax on Virginia coaches we have had to exert all the judicial power of the nation; and after that had prevailed, popularity was found a greater treasure than money, and the carriage tax was repealed. The tax on whiskey was enforced by an army, and no sooner had its receipts begun to reimburse the charges of government, and in some measure to equalize the northern and southern burdens, but the law is annulled.

With the example of two rebellions against our revenue laws, it cannot be denied that our republic claims the submission, not merely of weak individuals, but of powerful combinations, of those whom distance, numbers, and enthusiasm embolden to deride its authority and defy its arms. A faction is a sort of empire within the empire, which acts by its own magistrates and laws, and prosecutes interests not only unlike, but destructive to those of the nation. The federalists are accused of attempting to impart too much energy to the administration, and of stripping, with too much severity, all such combinations of their assumed importance. Hence it is ridiculously absurd to denominate the federalists, the admirers and disciples of Washington, a faction.

But we shall be told, in defiance both of fact and good sense, that factions will not exist, or will be impotent if they do; for the majority have a right to govern, and certainly will govern by their representatives. Let their right be admitted, but they certainly will not govern in either of two cases, both fairly supposable, and likely, nay sure, to happen in succession: that a section of country, a combination, party, or faction, call it what you will, shall prove daring and potent enough to obstruct the laws and to exempt itself from their operation; or, growing bolder with impunity and success, finally by art, deceit, and perseverance, to force its chiefs into power, and thus, instead of submitting to the government, to bring the government into submission to a faction. Then the forms and the names of a republic will be used, and used more ostentatiously than ever; but its [366] principles will be abused, and its ramparts and defences laid flat to the ground.

There are many, who, believing that a penful of ink can impart a deathless energy to a constitution, and having seen with pride and joy two or three skins of parchment added, like new walls about a fortress, to our own, will be filled with astonishment, and say, is not our legislature divided? our executive single? our judiciary independent? Have we not amendments and bills of rights, excelling all compositions in prose? Where then can our danger lie? Our government, so we read, is constructed in such a manner as to defend itself and the people. We have the greatest political security, for we have adopted the soundest principles.

To most grown children, therefore, the existence of faction will seem chimerical. Yet did any free state ever exist without the most painful and protracted conflicts with this foe? or expire any otherwise than by his triumph? The spring is not more genial to the grain and fruits, than to insects and vermin. The same sun that decks the fields with flowers, thaws out the serpent in the fen, and concocts his poison. Surely we are not the people to contest this position. Our present liberty was born into the world under the knife of this assassin, and now limps a cripple from his violence.

As soon as such a faction is known to subsist in force, we shall be told, the people may, and because they may they surely will, rally to discomfit and punish the conspirators. If the whole people in a body are to do this as often as it may be necessary, then it seems our political plan is to carry on our government by successive, or rather incessant revolutions. When the people deliberate and act in person, laying aside the plain truth, that it is impossible they should, all delegated authority is at an end; the representatives would be nothing in the presence of their assembled constituents. Thus falls or stops the machine of a regular government. Thus a faction, hostile to the government, would ensure their success by the very remedy that is supposed effectual to disappoint their designs.

Men of a just way of thinking will be ready to renounce the opinions we have been considering, and to admit that [367] liberty is lost where faction domineers; that some security must be provided against its attacks; and that no elective government can be secure or orderly, unless it be invested by the Constitution itself with the means of self-defence. It is enough for the people to approve the lawful use of them. And this, for a free government, must be the easiest thing in the world.

Now the contrary of this last opinion is the truth. By a free government this difficulty is nearly or quite insuperable; for the audaciousness and profligacy of faction is ever in proportion to the liberty of the political constitution. In a tyranny individuals are nothing. Conscious of their nothingness, the spirit of liberty is torpid or extinct. But in a free state there is, necessarily, a great mass of power left in the hands of the citizens, with the spirit to use and the desire to augment it. Hence will proceed an infinity of clubs and associations, for purposes often laudable or harmless, but not unfrequently factious. It is obvious, that the combination of some hundreds or thousands for political ends will produce a great aggregate stock or mass of power. As by combining they greatly augment their power, for that very reason they will combine; and as magistrates would seldom like to devolve their authority upon volunteers who might offer to play the magistrate in their stead, there is almost nothing left for a band of combined citizens to do, but to discredit and obstruct the government and laws. The possession of power by the magistrate is not so sure to produce respect as to kindle envy; and to the envious it is a gratification to humble those who are exalted. But the ambitious find the public discontent a passport to office—then they must breed or inflame discontent. We have the example before our eyes.

Is it not evident, then, that a free government must exert a great deal more power to obtain obedience from an extensive combination or faction than would be necessary to extort it from a much larger number of uncombined individuals? If the regular government has that degree of power which, let it be noted, the jealousy of a free people often inclines them to withhold; and if it should exercise its power with promptness and spirit, a supposition not [368] a little improbable, for such governments frequently have more strength than firmness, then the faction may be, for that time, repressed and kept from doing mischief. It will, however, instantly change its pretexts and its means, and renew the contest with more art and caution, and with the advantage of all the discontents which every considerable popular agitation is sure to multiply and to embitter. This immortal enemy, whom it is possible to bind, though only for a time, and in flaxen chains, but not to kill; who may be baffled, but cannot be disarmed; who is never weakened by defeat, nor discouraged by disappointment, again tries and wears out the strength of the government and the temper of the people. It is a game which the factious will never be weary of playing, because they play for an empire, yet on their own part hazard nothing. If they fail, they lose only their ticket, and say, draw your lottery again; if they win, as in the end they must and will, if the Constitution has not provided within, or unless the people will bring, which they will not long, from without, some energy to hinder their success, it will be complete; for conquering parties never content themselves with half the fruits of victory. Their power once obtained can be and will be confirmed by nothing but the terror or weakness of the real people. Justice will shrink from the bench, and tremble at her own bar.

As property is the object of the great mass of every faction, the rules that keep it sacred will be annulled, or so far shaken, as to bring enough of it within the grasp of the dominant party to reward their partisans with booty. But the chieftains, thirsting only for dominion, will search for the means of extending or establishing it. They will, of course, innovate, till the vestiges of private right, and of restraints on public authority, are effaced; until the real people are stripped of all privilege and influence, and become even more abject and spiritless than weak. The many may be deluded, but the success of a faction is ever the victory of a few; and the power of the few can be supported by nothing but force. This catastrophe is fatal.

The people, it will be thought, will see their error and return. But there is no return to liberty. What the fire [369] of faction does not destroy, it will debase. Those who have once tasted of the cup of sovereignty will be unfitted to be subjects; and those who have not, will scarcely form a wish, beyond the unmolested ignominy of slaves.

But will those who scorn to live at all unless they can live free, will these noble spirits abandon the public cause? Will they not break their chains on the heads of their oppressors? Suppose they attempt it, then we have a civil war; and when political diseases require the sword, the remedy will kill. Tyrants may be dethroned, and usurpers expelled and punished; but the sword, once drawn, cannot be sheathed. Whoever holds it, must rule by it; and that rule, though victory should give it to the best men and the honestest cause, cannot be liberty. Though painted as a goddess, she is mortal, and her spirit, once severed by the sword, can be evoked no more from the shades.

Is this catastrophe too distant to be viewed, or too improbable to be dreaded? I should not think it so formidably near as I do, if in the short interval of impending fate, in which alone it can be of any use to be active, the heart of every honest man in the nation, or even in New England, was penetrated with the anxiety that oppresses my own. Then the subversion of the public liberty would at least be delayed, if it could not be prevented. Her maladies might be palliated, if not cured. She might long drag on the life of an invalid, instead of soon suffering the death of a martyr.

The soft, timid sons of luxury, love liberty as well as it is possible they should, to love pleasure better. They desire to sleep in security, and to enjoy protection, without being molested to give it. While all, who are not devoted to pleasure, are eager in the pursuit of wealth, how will it be possible to rouse such a spirit of liberty as can alone secure, or prolong its possession? For if, in the extraordinary perils of the republic, the citizens will not kindle with a more than ordinary, with a heroic flame, its cause will be [370] abandoned without effort, and lost beyond redemption. But if the faithful votaries of liberty, uncertain what counsels to follow, should, for the present, withhold their exertions, will they not at least bestow their attention? Will they not fix it, with an unusual intensity of thought, upon the scene; and will they not fortify their nerves to contemplate a prospect that is shaded with horror, and already flashes with tempest?

If the positions laid down as theory could be denied, the brief history of the federal administration would establish them. It was first confided to the truest and purest patriot that ever lived. It succeeded a period, dismal and dark, and like the morning sun, lighted up a sudden splendor that was gratuitous, for it consumed nothing, but its genial rays cherished the powers of vegetation, while they displayed its exuberance. There was no example, scarcely a pretence of oppression; yet faction, basking in those rays, and sucking venom from the ground, even then cried out, "O sun, I tell thee, how I hate thy beams." Faction was organized sooner than the government.

If the most urgent public reasons could ever silence or satisfy the spirit of faction, the adoption of the new Constitution would have been prompt and unanimous. The government of a great nation had barely revenue enough to buy stationery for its clerks, or to pay the salary of the door-keeper. Public faith and public force were equally out of the question, for as it respected either authority or resources, the corporation of a college, or the missionary society were greater potentates than congress. Our federal government had not merely fallen into imbecility, and of course into contempt, but the oligarchical factions in the large states had actually made great advances in the usurpation of its powers. The king of New York levied imposts on Jersey and Connecticut; and the nobles of Virginia bore with impatience their tributary dependence on Baltimore and Philadelphia. Our discontents were fermenting into civil war; and that would have multiplied and exasperated our discontents.

Impending public evils, so obvious and so near, happily roused all the patriotism of the country; but they roused [371] its ambition too. The great state chieftains found the sovereign power unoccupied, and like the lieutenants of Alexander, each employed intrigue, and would soon have employed force, to erect his province into a separate monarchy or aristocracy. Popular republican names would indeed have been used, but in the struggles of ambition they would have been used only to cloak usurpation and tyranny. How late, and with what sourness and reluctance, did New York and Virginia renounce the hopes of aggrandizement which their antifederal leaders had so passionately cherished! The opposition to the adoption of the federal Constitution was not a controversy about principles; it was a struggle for power. In the great states, the ruling party, with that sagacity which too often accompanies inordinate ambition, instantly discerned, that if the new government should go into operation with all the energy that its letter and spirit would authorize, they must cease to rule—still worse, they must submit to be ruled, nay, worst of all, they must be ruled by their equals, a condition of real wretchedness and supposed disgrace, which our impatient tyrants anticipated with instinctive and unspeakable horror.

To prevent this dreaded result of the new Constitution, which, by securing a real legal equality to all the citizens, would bring them down to an equality, their earliest care was to bind the ties of their factious union more closely together; and by combining their influence and exerting the utmost malignity of their art, to render the new government odious and suspected by the people. Thus, conceived in jealousy and born in weakness and dissension, they hoped to see it sink, like its predecessor, the confederation, into contempt. Hence it was, that in every great state a faction arose with the fiercest hostility to the federal Constitution, and active in devising and pursuing every scheme, however unwarrantable or audacious, that would obstruct the establishment of any power in the state superior to its own.

It is undeniably true, therefore, that faction was organized sooner than the new government. We are not to charge this event to the accidental rivalships or disgusts of leading men, but to the operation of the invariable principles [372] that preside over human actions and political affairs. Power had slipped out of the feeble hands of the old congress; and the world's power, like its wealth, can never lie one moment without a possessor. The states had instantly succeeded to the vacant sovereignty; and the leading men in the great states, for the small ones were inactive from a sense of their insignificance, engrossed their authority. Where the executive authority was single, the governor, as for instance in New York, felt his brow encircled with a diadem; but in those states where the governor is a mere cipher, the men who influenced the assembly governed the state, and there an oligarchy established itself. When has it been seen in the world, that the possession of sovereign power was regarded with indifference, or resigned without effort? If all that is ambition in the heart of man had slept in America, till the era of the new Constitution, the events of that period would not merely have awakened it into life, but have quickened it into all the agitations of frenzy.

Then commenced an active struggle for power. Faction resolved that the new government should not exist at all, or if that could not be prevented, that it should exist without energy. Accordingly, the presses of that time teemed with calumny and invective. Before the new government had done any thing, there was nothing oppressive or tyrannical which it was not accused of meditating; and when it began its operations, there was nothing wise or fit that it was not charged with neglecting; nothing right or beneficial that it did, but from an insidious design to delude and betray the people. The cry of usurpation and oppression was louder then, when all was prosperous and beneficent, than it has been since, when the judiciary is violently abolished, the judges dragged to the culprit's bar, the Constitution changed to prevent a change of rulers, and the path plainly marked out and already half travelled over, for the ambition of those rulers to reign in contempt of the people's votes, and on the ruins of their liberty.

He is certainly a political novice or a hypocrite, who will pretend that the antifederal opposition to the government is to be ascribed to the concern of the people for their liberties, [373] rather than to the profligate ambition of their demagogues, eager for power, and suddenly alarmed by the imminent danger of losing it; demagogues, who leading lives like Clodius, and with the maxims of Cato in their mouths, cherishing principles like Catiline, have acted steadily on a plan of usurpation like Cæsar. Their labor for twelve years was to inflame and deceive; and their recompense, for the last four, has been to degrade and betray.

Any person who considers the instability of all authority, that is not only derived from the multitude, but wanes or increases with the ever changing phases of their levity and caprice, will pronounce that the federal government was from the first, and from its very nature and organization, fated to sink under the rivalship of its state competitors for dominion. Virginia has never been more federal than it was, when, from considerations of policy, and perhaps in the hope of future success from its intrigues, it adopted the new Constitution; for it has never desisted from obstructing its measures, and urging every scheme that would reduce it back again to the imbecility of the old confederation. To the dismay of every true patriot, these arts have at length fatally succeeded; and our system of government now differs very little from what it would have been, if the impost proposed by the old congress had been granted, and the new federal Constitution had never been adopted by the States. In that case, the states being left to their natural inequality, the small states would have been, as they now are, nothing; and Virginia, potent in herself, more potent by her influence and intrigues, and uncontrolled by a superior federal head, would of course have been every thing. Baltimore, like Antium, and Philadelphia, like Capua, would have bowed their proud necks to a new Roman yoke. If any of her more powerful neighbors had resisted her dominion, she would have spread her factions into their bosoms, and like the Marsi and the Samnites, they would at last, though perhaps somewhat the later for their valor, have graced the pomp of her triumphs, and afterwards assisted to maintain the terror of her arms.

[374] So far as state opposition was concerned, it does not appear that is has been overcome in any of the great states, by the mild and successful operation of the federal government. But if states had not been its rivals, yet the matchless industry and close combination of the factious individuals who guided the antifederal presses would, in the end, though perhaps not so soon as it has been accomplished by the help of Virginia, have disarmed and prostrated the federal government. We have the experience of France before our eyes to prove that, with such a city as Paris, it is utterly impossible to support a free republican system. A profligate press has more authority than morals; and a faction will possess more energy than magistrates or laws.

On evidence thus lamentably clear, I found my opinion, that the federalists can never again become the dominant party; in other words, the public reason and virtue cannot be again, as in our first twelve years, and never will be again the governing power, till our government has passed through its revolutionary changes. Every faction that may happen to rule will pursue but two objects, its vengeance on the fallen party, and the security of its own power against any new one that may rise to contest it. As to the glory that wise rulers partake, when they obtain it for their nation, no person of understanding will suppose that the gaudy, ephemeral insects, that bask and flutter no longer than while the sun of popularity shines without a cloud, will either possess the means or feel the passion for it. What have the Condorcets and Rolands of to-day to hope or to enjoy from the personal reputation or public happiness of to-morrow? Their objects are all selfish, all temporary. Mr. Jefferson's letters to Mazzei or Paine, his connection with Callender, or his mean condescensions to France and Spain, will add nothing to the weight of his disgrace with the party that shall supplant him. To be their enemy will be disgrace enough, and so far a refuge for his fame, as it will stop all curiosity and inquiry into particulars. Every party that has fallen in France has been overwhelmed with infamy, but without proofs or discrimination. If time and truth have furnished any materials for the vindication of the ex-rulers, there has nevertheless been no instance of the return of the [375] public to pity, or of the injured to power. The revolution has no retrograde steps. Its course is onward from the patriots and statesmen to the hypocrites and cowards, and onward still through successive committees of ruffians, till some one ruffian happens to be a hero. Then chance no longer has a power over events, for this last inevitably becomes an emperor.

The restoration of the federalists to their merited influence in the government supposes two things, the slumber or extinction of faction, and the efficacy of public morals. It supposes an interval of calm, when reason will dare to speak, and prejudice itself will incline to hear. Then, it is still hoped by many, *Nova progenies cœlo demittitur alto,* the genuine public voice would call wisdom into power; and the love of country, which is the morality of politics, would guard and maintain its authority.

Are not these the visions that delight a poet's fancy, but will never revisit the statesman's eyes? When will faction sleep? Not till its labors of vengeance and ambition are over. Faction, we know, is the twin brother of our liberty, and born first; and as we are told in the fable of Castor and Pollux, the only one of the two that is immortal. As long as there is a faction in full force, and possessed of the government, too, the public will and the public reason must have power to compel, as well as to convince, or they will convince without reforming. Bad men, who rise by intrigue, may be dispossessed by worse men, who rise over their heads by deeper intrigue; but what has the public reason to do but to deplore its silence or to polish its chains? This last we find is now the case in France. All the talent of that country is employed to illustrate the virtues and exploits of that chief who has made a nation happy by putting an end to the agitations of what they called their liberty, and who naturally enough insist that they enjoy more glory than any other people, because they are more terrible to all.

The public reason, therefore, is so little in a condition to reëstablish the federal cause, that it will not long maintain its own. Do we not see our giddy multitude celebrate with joy the triumphs of a party over some essential articles of our Constitution, and recently over one integral and independent [376] branch of our government? When our Roland falls, our Danton will be greeted with as loud a peal and as splendid a triumph. If federalism could by a miracle resume the reins of power, unless political virtue and pure morals should return also, those reins would soon drop or be snatched from its hands.

By political virtue is meant that love of country diffused through the society, and ardent in each individual, that would dispose, or rather impel every one to do or suffer much for his country, and permit no one to do any thing against it. The Romans sustained the hardships and dangers of military service, which fell not, as amongst modern nations, on the dregs of society, but, till the time of Marius, exclusively on the flower of the middle and noble classes. They sustained them, nevertheless, both with constancy and alacrity, because the excellence of life, every Roman thought, was glory, and the excellence of each man's glory lay in its redounding to the splendor and extent of the empire of Rome.

Is there any resemblance in all this to the habits and passions that predominate in America? Are not our people wholly engrossed by the pursuit of wealth and pleasure? Though grouped together into a society, the propensities of the individual still prevail; and if the nation discovers the rudiments of any character, they are yet to be developed. In forming it, have we not ground to fear that the sour, dissocial, malignant spirit of our politics will continue to find more to dread and hate in party, than to love and reverence in our country?

What foundation can there be for that political virtue to rest upon, while the virtue of the society is proscribed, and its vice lays an exclusive claim to emolument and honor? And as long as faction governs, it must look to all that is vice in the state for its force, and to all that is virtue for its plunder. It is not merely the choice of faction, though no doubt base agents are to be preferred for base purposes, but it is its necessity also to keep men of true worth depressed by keeping the turbulent and worthless contented.

How then can love of country take root and grow in a soil, from which every valuable plant has thus been plucked up and thrown away as a weed? How can we forbear to [377] identify the government with the country? and how is it possible that we should at the same time lavish all the ardor of our affection, and yet withhold every emotion either of confidence or esteem? It is said, that in republics majorities invariably oppress minorities. Can there be any real patriotism in a state which is thus filled with those who exercise and those who suffer tyranny? But how much less reason has any man to love that country, in which the voice of the majority is counterfeited, or the vicious, ignorant, and needy, are the instruments, and the wise and worthy are the victims of oppression?

When we talk of patriotism as the theme of declamation, it is not very material that we should know with any precision what we mean. It is a subject on which hypocrisy will seem to ignorance to be eloquent, because all of it will be received and well received as flattery. If, however, we search for a principle or sentiment general and powerful enough to produce national effects, capable of making a people act with constancy, or suffer with fortitude, is there any thing in our situation that could have produced, or that can cherish it? The straggling settlements of the southern part of the union, which now is the governing part, have been formed by emigrants from almost every nation of Europe. Safe in their solitudes, alike from the annoyance of enemies and of government, it is infinitely more probable that they will sink into barbarism than rise to the dignity of national sentiment and character. Patriotism, to be a powerful or steady principle of action, must be deeply imbued by education, and strongly impressed both by the policy of the government and the course of events. To love our country with ardor, we must often have some fears for its safety; our affection will be exalted in its distress; and our self-esteem will glow on the contemplation of its glory. It is only by such diversified and incessant exercise that the sentiment can become strong in the individual, or be diffused over the nation.

But how can that nation have any such affinities, any sense of patriotism, whose capacious wilderness receives and separates from each other the successive troops of emigrants from all other nations, men who remain ignorant, or learn [378] only from the newspapers that they are countrymen, who think it their right to be exempted from all tax, restraint, or control, and of course that they have nothing to do with or for their country, but to make rulers for it, who, after they are made, are to have nothing to do with their makers; a country, too, which they are sure will not be invaded, and cannot be enslaved? Are not the wandering Tartars or Indian hunters at least as susceptible of patriotism as these stragglers in our western forests, and infinitely fonder of glory? It is difficult to conceive of a country, which, from the manner of its settlement, or the manifest tendencies of its politics, is more destitute or more incapable of being inspired with political virtue.

What foundation remains, then, for the hopes of those who expect to see the federalists again invested with power?

Shall we be told, that if the nation is not animated with public spirit, the individuals are at least fitted to be good citizens by the purity of their morals? But what are morals without restraints? and how will merely voluntary restraints be maintained? How long will sovereigns, as the people are made to fancy they are, insist more upon checks than prerogatives? Ask Mr. . . . and Judge Chase.

Besides, in political reasoning it is generally overlooked, that if the existence of morals should encourage a people to prefer a democratic system, the operation of that system is sure to destroy their morals. Power in such a society cannot long have any regular control; and, without control, it is itself a vice. Is there in human affairs an occasion of profligacy more shameless or more contagious than a general election? Every spring gives birth and gives wings to this epidemic mischief. Then begins a sort of tillage, that turns up to the sun and air the most noxious weeds in the kindliest soil; or, to speak still more seriously, it is a mortal pestilence, that begins with rottenness in the marrow. A democratic society will soon find its morals the encumbrance of its race, the surly companion of its licentious joys. It will encourage its demagogues to impeach and persecute the magistracy, till it is no longer disquieted. In a word, there will not be morals without justice; and though justice might possibly support a democracy, yet a democracy cannot possibly support justice.

[379] Rome was never weary of making laws for that end, and failed. France has had nearly as many laws as soldiers, yet never had justice or liberty for one day. Nevertheless, there can be no doubt that the ruling faction has often desired to perpetuate its authority by establishing justice. The difficulties however lie in the nature of the thing; for in democratic states there are ever more volunteers to destroy than to build; and nothing that is restraint can be erected without being odious, nor maintained if it is. Justice herself must be built on a loose foundation, and every villain's hand is of course busy to pluck out the underpinning. Instead of being the awful power that is to control the popular passions, she descends from the height of her temple, and becomes the cruel and vindictive instrument of them.

Federalism was therefore manifestly founded on a mistake, on the supposed existence of sufficient political virtue, and on the permanency and authority of the public morals.

The party now in power committed no such mistake. They acted on the knowledge of what men actually are, not what they ought to be. Instead of enlightening the popular understanding, their business was to bewilder it. They knew that the vicious, on whom society makes war, would join them in their attack upon government. They inflamed the ignorant; they flattered the vain; they offered novelty to the restless; and promised plunder to the base. The envious were assured that the great should fall; and the ambitious that *they* should become great. The federal power, propped by nothing but opinion, fell, not because it deserved its fall, but because its principles of action were more exalted and pure than the people could support.

It is now undeniable that the federal administration was blameless. It has stood the scrutiny of time, and passed unharmed through the ordeal of its enemies. With all the evidence of its conduct in their possession, and with servile majorities at their command, it has not been in their power, much as they desired it, to fix any reproach on their predecessors.

It is the opinion of a few, but a very groundless opinion, that the cause of order will be reëstablished by the splitting of the reigning jacobins; or, if that should not take place [380] soon, the union will be divided, and the northern confederacy compelled to provide for its own liberty. Why, it is said, should we expect that the union of the bad will be perfect, when that of the Washington party, though liberty and property were at stake, has been broken? And why should it be supposed that the Northern States, who possess so prodigious a preponderance of white population, of industry, commerce, and civilization over the Southern, will remain subject to Virginia? Popular delusion cannot last, and as soon as the opposition of the federalists ceases to be feared, the conquerors will divide into new factions, and either the federalists will be called again into power, or the union will be severed into two empires.

By some attention to the nature of a democracy, both these conjectures, at least so far as they support any hopes of the public liberty, will be discredited.

There is no society without jacobins; no free society without a formidable host of them; and no democracy whose powers they will not usurp, nor whose liberties, if it be not absurd to suppose a democracy can have any, they will not destroy. A nation must be exceedingly well educated, in which the ignorant and the credulous are few. Athens, with all its wonderful taste and literature, poured them into her popular assemblies by thousands. It is by no means certain that a nation, composed wholly of scholars and philosophers, would contain less presumption, political ignorance, levity, and extravagance than another state, peopled by tradesmen, farmers, and men of business, without a metaphysician or speculatist among them. The opulent in Holland were the friends of those French who subdued their country, and enslaved them. It was the well dressed, the learned, or at least the conceited mob of France that did infinitely more than the mere rabble of Paris to overturn the throne of the Bourbons. The multitude were made giddy with projects of innovation, before they were armed with pikes to enforce them.

As there is nothing really excellent in our governments, that is not novel in point of institution, and which faction has not represented as old in abuse, the natural vanity, presumption, and restlessness of the human heart have, from the [381] first, afforded the strength of a host to the jacobins of our country. The ambitious desperadoes are the natural leaders of this host.

Now, though such leaders may have many occasions of jealousy and discord with one another, especially in the division of power and booty, is it not absurd to suppose, that any set of them will endeavor to restore both to the right owners? Do we expect a self-denying ordinance from the sons of violence and rapine? Are not those remarkably inconsistent with themselves, who say, our republican system is a government of justice and order, that was freely adopted in peace, subsists by morals, and whose office it is to ask counsel of the wise and to give protection to the good, yet who console themselves in the storms of the state with the fond hope that order will spring out of confusion, because innovators will grow weary of change, and the ambitious will contend about their spoil. Then we are to have a new system exactly like the old one, from the fortuitous concourse of atoms, from the crash and jumble of all that is precious or sacred in the state. It is said, the popular hopes and fears are the gales that impel the political vessel. Can any disappointment of such hopes be greater than their folly?

It is true, the men now in power may not be united together by patriotism, or by any principle of faith or integrity. It is also true, that they have not, and cannot easily have, a military force to awe the people into submission. But on the other hand, they have no need of an army; there is no army to oppose them. They are held together by the ties, and made irresistible by the influence of party. With the advantage of acting as the government, who can oppose them? Not the federalists, who neither have any force, nor any object to employ it for, if they had. Not any subdivision of their own faction, because the opposers, if they prevail, will become the government, so much the less liable to be opposed for their recent victory; and if the new sect should fail, they will be nothing. The conquerors will take care that an unsuccessful resistance shall strengthen their domination.

Thus it seems, in every event of the division of the ruling party, the friends of true liberty have nothing to hope. Tyrants may thus be often changed, but the tyranny will remain.

[382] A democracy cannot last. Its nature ordains, that its next change shall be into a military despotism, of all known governments, perhaps, the most prone to shift its head, and the slowest to mend its vices. The reason is, that the tyranny of what is called the people, and that by the sword, both operate alike to debase and corrupt, till there are neither men left with the spirit to desire liberty, nor morals with the power to sustain justice. Like the burning pestilence that destroys the human body, nothing can subsist by its dissolution but vermin.

A military government may make a nation great, but it cannot make them free. There will be frequent and bloody struggles to decide who shall hold the sword; but the conqueror will destroy his competitors and prevent any permanent division of the empire. Experience proves, that in all such governments there is a continual tendency to unity.

Some kind of balance between the two branches of the Roman government had been maintained for several ages, till at length every popular demagogue, from the two Gracchi to Caesar, tried to gain favor, and by favor to gain power by flattering the multitude with new pretensions to power in the state. The assemblies of the people disposed of every thing; and intrigue and corruption, and often force disposed of the votes of those assemblies. It appears, that Catulus, Cato, Cicero, and the wisest of the Roman patriots, and perhaps wiser never lived, kept on like the infatuated federalists, hoping to the last, that the people would see their error and return to the safe old path. They labored incessantly to reestablish the commonwealth; but the deep corruption of those times, not more corrupt than our own, rendered that impossible. Many of the friends of liberty were slain in the civil wars; some, like Lucullus, had retired to their farms; and most of the others, if not banished by the people, were without commands in the army, and of course without power in the state. Catiline came near being chosen consul, and Piso and Gabinius, scarcely less corrupt, were chosen. A people so degenerate could not maintain liberty; and do we find bad morals or dangerous designs any obstruction to the election of any favorite of the reigning party? It is remarkable, that when by a most singular concurrence of circumstances, [383] after the death of Caesar, an opportunity was given to the Romans to reëstablish the republic, there was no effective disposition among the people to concur in that design. It seemed as if the republican party, consisting of the same class of men as the Washington federalists, had expired with the dictator. The truth is, when parties rise and resort to violence, the moment of calm, if one should happen to succeed, leaves little to wisdom and nothing to choice. The orations of Cicero proved feeble against the arms of Mark Antony. Is not all this apparent in the United States? Are not the federalists as destitute of hopes as of power? What is there left for them to do? When a faction has seized the republic, and established itself in power, can the true federal republicans any longer subsist? After having seen the republic expire, will it be asked, why they are not immortal?

But the reason why such governments are not severed by the ambition of contending chiefs, deserves further consideration.

As soon as the Romans had subdued the kingdoms of Perseus, Antiochus, and Mithridates, it was necessary to keep on foot great armies. As the command of these was bestowed by the people, the arts of popularity were studied by all those who pretended to be the friends of the people, and who really aspired to be their masters. The greatest favorites became the most powerful generals; and as at first there was nothing which the Roman assemblies were unwilling to give, it appeared very soon that they had nothing left to withhold. The armies disposed of all power in the state, and of the state itself; and the generals of course assumed the control of the armies.

It is a very natural subject of surprise, that when the Roman empire was rent by civil war, as it was perhaps twenty times from the age of Marius and Sylla to that of Constantine, some competitor for the imperial purple did not maintain himself with his veteran troops in his province; and found a new dynasty on the banks of the Euphrates or the Danube, the Ebro or the Rhine. This surprise is augmented by considering the distractions and weakness of an elective government, as the Roman was; the wealth, extent, and power of the rebellious provinces, equal to several modern [384] first rate kingdoms; their distance from Italy; and the resource that the despair, and shame, and rage of so many conquered nations would supply on an inviting occasion to throw off their chains and rise once more to independence; yet the Roman power constantly prevailed, and the empire remained one and indivisible. Sertorius was as good a general as Pompey; and it seems strange that he did not become Emperor of Spain. Why were not new empires founded in Armenia, Syria, Asia Minor, in Gaul or Britain? Why, we ask, unless because the very nature of a military democracy, such as the Roman was, did not permit it? Every civil war terminated in the reunion of the provinces, that a rebellion had for a time severed from the empire. Britain, Spain, and Gaul, now so potent, patiently continued to wear their chains, till they dropped off by the total decay of the Western empire.

The first conquests of the Romans were made by the superiority of their discipline. The provinces were permitted to enjoy their municipal laws, but all political and military power was exercised by persons sent from Rome. So that the spirit of the subject nations was broken or rendered impotent, and every contest in the provinces was conducted, not by the provincials, but by Roman generals and veteran troops. These were all animated with the feelings of the Roman democracy. Now a democracy, a party, and an army bear a close resemblance to each other; they are all creatures of emotion and impulse. However discordant all the parts of a democracy may be, they all seek a centre, and that centre is the single arbitrary power of a chief. In this we see how exactly a democracy is like an army: they are equally governments by downright force.

A multitude can be moved only by their passions; and these, when their gratification is obstructed, instantly impel them to arms. *Furor arma ministrat.* The club is first used, and then, as more effectual, the sword. The disciplined is found by the leaders to be more manageable than the mobbish force. The rabble at Paris that conquered the Bastile were soon formed into national guards. But from the first to the last, the nature, and character, and instruments of power remain the same. A ripe democracy will not long [385] want sharp tools and able leaders; in fact, though not in name, it is an army. It is true, an army is not constituted as a deliberative body, and very seldom pretends to deliberate; but whenever it does, it is a democracy in regiments and brigades, somewhat the more orderly as well as more merciful for its discipline. It always will deliberate when it is suffered to feel its own power, and is indiscreetly provoked to exert it. At those times, is there much reason to believe it will act with less good sense, or with a more determined contempt for the national interest and opinion, than a giddy multitude managed by worthless leaders? Now though an army is not indulged with a vote, it cannot be stripped of its feelings, feelings that may be managed, but cannot be resisted. When the legions of Syria or Gaul pretended to make an emperor, it was as little in the power as it was in the disposition of Severus to content himself with Italy, and to leave those fine provinces to Niger and Albinus. The military town-meeting must be satisfied; and nothing could satisfy it but the overthrow of a rival army. If Pompey, before the battle of Pharsalia, had joined his lieutenants in Spain, with the design of abandoning Italy, and erecting Spain into a separate republic or monarchy, every Roman citizen would have despised, and every Roman soldier would have abandoned him. After that fatal battle, Cato and Scipio never once thought of keeping Africa as an independent government; nor did Brutus and Cassius suppose that Greece and Macedonia, which they held with an army, afforded them more than the means of contesting with Octavius and Antony the dominion of Rome. No hatred is fiercer than such as springs up among those who are closely allied and nearly resemble each other. Every common soldier would be easily made to feel the personal insult and the intolerable wrong of another army's rejecting his emperor and setting up one of their own—not only so, but he knew it was both a threat and a defiance. The shock of the two armies was therefore inevitable. It was a sort of duel, and could no more stop short of destruction than the combat of Hector and Achilles. We greatly mistake the workings of human nature when we suppose the soldiers in such civil wars were mere machines. Hope and fear, love and hatred, [386] on the contrary, exalt their feelings to enthusiasm. When Ortho's troops had received a check from those of Vitellius, he resolved to kill himself. His soldiers, with tears, besought him to live, and swore they would perish, if necessary, in his cause. But he persisted in his purpose, and killed himself; and many of his soldiers, overpowered by their grief, followed his example. Those whom false philosophy makes blind will suppose that national wars will justify, and therefore will excite, all a soldier's ardor; but that the strife between two ambitious generals will be regarded by all men with proper indifference. National disputes are not understood, and their consequences not foreseen, by the multitude; but a quarrel that concerns the life, and fame, and authority of a military favorite takes hold of the heart, and stirs up all the passions.

A democracy is so like an army that no one will be at a loss in applying these observations. The great spring of action with the people in a democracy is their fondness for one set of men, the men who flatter and deceive, and their outrageous aversion to another, most probably those who prefer their true interest to their favor.

A mob is no sooner gathered together than it instinctively feels the want of a leader, a want that is soon supplied. They may not obey him as long, but they obey him as implicitly, and will as readily fight and burn, or rob and murder, in his cause, as the soldiers will for their general.

As the Roman provinces were held in subjection by Roman troops, so every American State is watched with jealousy, and ruled with despotic rigor by the partisans of the faction that may happen to be in power. The successive struggles to which our licentiousness may devote the country, will never be of state against state, but of rival factions diffused over our whole territory. Of course, the strongest army, or that which is best commanded, will prevail, and we shall remain subject to one indivisible bad government.

This conclusion may seem surprising to many; but the event of the Roman republic will vindicate it on the evidence of history. After faction, in the time of Marius, utterly obliterated every republican principle that was worth any thing, Rome remained a military despotism for almost six [387] hundred years; and, as the reëstablishment of republican liberty in our country after it is once lost is a thing not to be expected, what can succeed its loss but a government by the sword? It would be certainly easier to prevent than to retrieve its fall.

The jacobins are indeed ignorant or wicked enough to say, a mixed monarchy, on the model of the British, will succeed the failure of our republican system. Mr. Jefferson in his famous letter to Mazzei has shown the strange condition both of his head and heart, by charging this design upon Washington and his adherents. It is but candid to admit, that there are many weak-minded democrats who really think a mixed monarchy the next stage of our politics. As well might they promise, that when their factious fire has burned the plain dwelling-house of our liberty, her temple will rise in royal magnificence, and with all the proportions of Grecian architecture, from the ashes. It is impossible sufficiently to elucidate, yet one could never be tired of elucidating the matchless absurdity of this opinion. An unmixed monarchy, indeed there is almost no doubt, awaits us; but it will not be called a monarchy. Caesar lost his life by attempting to take the name of *king*. A president, whose election cannot be hindered, may be well content to wear that title, which inspires no jealousy, yet disclaims no prerogative that party can usurp to confer. Old forms may be continued till some inconvenience is felt from them; and then the same faction that has made them forms can make them less, and substitute some new organic decree in their stead.

But a mixed monarchy would not only offend fixed opinions and habits, but provoke a most desperate resistance. The people, long after losing the substance of republican liberty, maintain a reverence for the name; and would fight with enthusiasm for the tyrant who has left them the name, and taken from them every thing else. Who, then, are to set it up? and how are they to do it? Is it by an army? Where are their soldiers? Where are their resources and means to arm and maintain them? Can it be established by free popular consent? Absurd. A people once trained to republican principles will feel the degradation of submitting to a king. It is far from certain that their opposition [388] would be soothed, by restricting the powers of such a king to the one half of what are enjoyed by Mr. Jefferson. That would make a difference, but the many would not discern it. The aversion of a republican nation to kingship is sincere and warm, even to fanaticism; yet it has never been found to exact of a favorite demagogue, who aspired to reign, any other condescension than an ostentatious scrupulousness of regard to names, to appearances, and forms. Augustus, whose despotism was not greater than his cunning, professed to be the obsequious minister of his slaves in the senate; and Roman pride not only exacted, but enjoyed to the last, the pompous hypocrisy of the phrase, the majesty of the Roman *commonwealth*.

To suppose, therefore, a monarchy established by vote of the people, by the free consent of a majority, is contrary to the nature of man and the uniform testimony of his experience. To suppose it introduced by the disciples of Washington, who are with real or affected scorn described by their adversaries as a fallen party, a despicable handful of malecontents, is no less absurd than inconsistent. The federalists cannot command the consent of a majority, and they have no consular or imperial army to extort it. Every thing of that sort is on the side of their foes, and of course an unsurmountable obstacle to their pretended enterprise.

It will weigh nothing in the argument with some persons, but with men of sense it will be conclusive, that the mass of the federalists are the owners of the commercial and moneyed wealth of the nation. Is it conceivable that such men will plot a revolution in favor of monarchy, a revolution that would make them beggars as well as traitors if it should miscarry; and if it should succeed ever so well, would require a century to take root and acquire stability enough to ensure justice and protect property? In these convulsions of the state, property is shaken, and in almost every radical change of government actually shifts hands. Such a project would seem audacious to the conception of needy adventurers who risk nothing but their lives; but to reproach the federalists of New England, the most independent farmers, opulent merchants, and thriving mechanics, as well as pious clergy, with such a conspiracy, requires a degree of impudence [389] that nothing can transcend. As well might they suspect the merchants of a plot to choke up the entrance of our harbors by sinking hulks, or that the directors of the several banks had confederated to blow up the money vaults with gunpowder. The Catos and the Ciceros are accused of conspiring to subvert the commonwealth—and who are the accusers? The Cloddii, the Antonies, and the Catilines.

Let us imagine, however, that by some miracle a mixed monarchy is established, or rather put into operation; and surely no man will suppose an unmixed monarchy can possibly be desired or contemplated by the federalists. The charge against them is, that they like the British monarchy too well. For the sake of argument, then, be it the British monarchy. To-morrow's sun shall rise and gild it with hope and joy, and the dew of to-morrow's evening shall moisten its ashes. Like the golden calf it would be ground to powder before noon. Certainly, the men who prate about an American monarchy copied from the British, are destitute of all sincerity or judgment. What could make such a monarchy? Not parchment. We are beginning to be cured of the insane belief that an engrossing clerk can make a constitution. Mere words, though on parchment, though sworn to, are wind, and worse than wind, because they are perjury. What could give effect to such a monarchy? It might have a right to command, but what could give it power? Not an army, for that would make it a military tyranny, of all governments the most odious, because the most durable. The British monarchy does not govern by an army, nor would their army suffer itself to be employed to destroy the national liberties. It is officered by the younger sons of noble and wealthy parents, and by many distinguished commanders who are in avowed opposition to the ministry. In fact, democratic opinions take root and flourish scarcely less in armies than in great cities, and infinitely more than they are found to do, or than it is possible they should, in the cabals of any ruling party in the world.

Great Britain, by being an island, is secured from foreign conquest; and by having a powerful enemy within sight of her shore is kept in sufficient dread of it to be inspired with patriotism. That virtue, with all the fervor and elevation [390] that a society which mixes so much of the commercial with the martial spirit can display, has other kindred virtues in its train; and these have had an influence informing the habits and principles of action, not only of the English military and nobles, but of the mass of the nation. There is much, therefore, there is every thing in that island to blend self-love with love of country.

It is impossible that an Englishman should have fears for the government, without trembling for his own safety. How different are these sentiments from the immovable apathy of those citizens, who think a constitution no better than any other piece of paper, nor so good as a blank on which a more perfect one could be written!

Is our monarchy to be supported by the national habits of subordination and implicit obedience? Surely when they hold out this expectation, the jacobins do not mean to answer for themselves. Or do we really think it would still be a monarchy, though we should set up, and put down at pleasure, a town-meeting king?

By removing or changing the relation of any one of the pillars that support the British government, its identity and excellence would be lost, a revolution would ensue. When the house of commons voted the house of peers useless, a tyranny of the committees of that body sprang up. The English nation have had the good sense, or more correctly, the good fortune, to alter nothing, till time and circumstances enforced the alteration, and then to abstain from speculative innovations. The evil spirit of metaphysics has not been conjured up to demolish, in order to lay out a new foundation by the line, and to build upon plan. The present happiness of that nation rests upon old foundations, so much the more solid, because the meddlesome ignorance of professed builders has not been allowed to new lay them. We may be permitted to call it a *matter of fact* government. No correct politician will presume to engage, that the same form of government would succeed equally well, or even succeed at all, anywhere else, or even in England under any other circumstances. Who will dare to say that their monarchy would stand, if this generation had raised it? Who indeed will believe, if it did stand, that the weakness produced by [391] the novelty of its institution would not justify, and even from a regard to self-preservation, compel, an almost total departure from its essential principles?

Now is there one of those essential principles, that it is even possible for the American people to adopt for their monarchy? Are old habits to be changed by a vote, and new ones to be established without experience? Can we have a monarchy without a peerage? or shall our governors supply that defect by giving commissions to a sufficient number of nobles of the quorum? Where is the American hierarchy? Where, above all, is the system of English law and justice, which would support liberty in Turkey, if Turkey could achieve the impossibility of supporting such justice?

It is not recollected that any monarchy in the world was ever introduced by consent; nor will anyone believe, on reflection, that it could be maintained by any nation, if nothing but consent upheld it. It is a rare thing for a people to choose their government; it is beyond all credibility, that they will enjoy the still rarer opportunity of changing it by choice.

The notion, therefore, of an American mixed monarchy is supremely ridiculous. It is highly probable our country will be eventually subject to a monarchy, but it is demonstrable that it cannot be such as the British; and whatever it may be, that the votes of the citizens will not be taken to introduce it.

It cannot be expected that the tendency towards a change of government, however obvious, will be discerned by the multitude of our citizens. While demagogues enjoy their favor, their passions will have no rest, and their judgment and understanding no exercise. Otherwise it might be of use to remind them, that more essential breaches have been made in our constitution within four years than in the British in the last hundred and forty. In that enslaved country every executive attempt at usurpation has been spiritedly and perseveringly resisted, and substantial improvements have been made in the constitutional provisions for liberty. Witness the habeas corpus, the independence of the judges, and the perfection, if any thing human is perfect, of their administration of justice, the result of the famous Middlesex election, [392] and that on the right of issuing general search warrants. Let every citizen who is able to think, and who can bear the pain of thinking, make the contrast at his leisure.

They are certainly blind who do not see that we are descending from a supposed orderly and stable republican government into a licentious democracy, with a progress that baffles all means to resist, and scarcely leaves leisure to deplore its celerity. The institutions and the hopes that Washington raised are nearly prostrate; and his name and memory would perish, if the rage of his enemies had any power over history. But they have not—history will give scope to her vengeance, and posterity will not be defrauded.

But if our experience had not clearly given warning of our approaching catastrophe, the very nature of democracy would inevitably produce it.

A government by the passions of the multitude, or, no less correctly, according to the vices and ambition of their leaders, is a democracy. We have heard so long of the indefeasible sovereignty of the people, and have admitted so many specious theories of the rights of man, which are contradicted by his nature and experience, that few will dread at all, and fewer still will dread as they ought, the evils of an American democracy. They will not believe them near, or they will think them tolerable or temporary. Fatal delusion!

When it is said, there may be a tyranny of the *many* as well as of the *few,* every democrat will yield at least a cold and speculative assent; but he will at all times act, as if it were a thing incomprehensible, that there should be any evil to be apprehended in the uncontrolled power of the people. He will say arbitrary power may make a tyrant, but how can it make its possessor a slave?

In the first place, let it be remarked, the power of individuals is a very different thing from their liberty. When I vote for the man I prefer, he may happen not to be chosen; or he may disappoint my expectations if he is; or he may be outvoted by others in the public body to which he is elected. I may then hold and exercise all the power that a citizen can have or enjoy, and yet such laws may be made and such abuses allowed as shall deprive me of all liberty. I may be tried by a jury, and that jury may be culled and picked out [393] from my political enemies by a federal marshal. Of course, my life and liberty may depend on the good pleasure of the man who appoints that marshal. I may be assessed arbitrarily for my faculty, or upon conjectural estimation of my property, so that all I have shall be at the control of the government, whenever its displeasure shall exact the sacrifice. I may be told that I am a federalist, and as such bound to submit, in all cases whatsoever, to the will of the majority, as the ruling faction ever pretend to be. My submission may be tested by my resisting or obeying commands that will involve me in disgrace, or drive me to despair. I may become a fugitive, because the ruling party have made me afraid to stay at home; or, perhaps, while I remain at home, they may, nevertheless, think fit to inscribe my name on the list of emigrants and proscribed persons.

All this was done in France, and many of the admirers of French examples are impatient to imitate them. All this time the people may be told, they are the freest in the world; but what ought my opinion to be? What would the threatened clergy, the aristocracy of wealthy merchants, as they have been called already, and thirty thousand more in Massachusetts, who vote for Governor Strong, and whose case might be no better than mine, what would they think of their condition? Would they call it liberty? Surely, here is oppression sufficient in extent and degree to make the government that inflicts it both odious and terrible; yet this and a thousand times more than this was practised in France, and will be repeated as often as it shall please God in his wrath to deliver a people to the dominion of their licentious passions.

The people, as a body, cannot deliberate. Nevertheless, they will feel an irresistible impulse to act, and their resolutions will be dictated to them by their demagogues. The consciousness, or the opinion, that they possess the supreme power, will inspire inordinate passions; and the violent men, who are the most forward to gratify those passions, will be their favorites. What is called the government of the people is in fact too often the arbitrary power of such men. Here, then, we have the faithful portrait of democracy. What avails the boasted power of individual citizens? or of what [394] value is the will of the majority, if that will is dictated by a committee of demagogues, and law and right are in fact at the mercy of a victorious faction? To make a nation free, the crafty must be kept in awe, and the violent in restraint. The weak and the simple find their liberty arise not from their own individual sovereignty, but from the power of law and justice over all. It is only by the due restraint of others, that I am free.

Popular sovereignty is scarcely less beneficent than awful, when it resides in their courts of justice; there its office, like a sort of human providence, is to warn, enlighten, and protect; when the people are inflamed to seize and exercise it in their assemblies, it is competent only to kill and destroy. Temperate liberty is like the dew, as it falls unseen from its own heaven; constant without excess, it finds vegetation thirsting for its refreshment, and imparts to it the vigor to take more. All nature, moistened with blessings, sparkles in the morning ray. But democracy is a water-spout that bursts from the clouds, and lays the ravaged earth bare to its rocky foundations. The labors of man lie whelmed with his hopes beneath masses of ruin, that bury not only the dead but their monuments.

It is the almost universal mistake of our countrymen, that democracy would be mild and safe in America. They charge the horrid excesses of France not so much to human nature, which will never act better, when the restraints of government, morals, and religion are thrown off, but to the characteristic cruelty and wickedness of Frenchmen.

The truth is, and let it humble our pride, the most ferocious of all animals, when his passions are roused to fury and are uncontrolled, is man; and of all governments, the worst is that which never fails to excite, but was never found to restrain those passions, that is, democracy. It is an illuminated hell, that in the midst of remorse, horror, and torture, rings with festivity; for experience shows, that one joy remains to this most malignant description of the damned, the power to make others wretched. When a man looks round and sees his neighbors mild and merciful, he cannot feel afraid of the abuse of their power over him; and surely if they oppress me, he will say, they will spare their own [395] liberty, for that is dear to all mankind. It is so. The human heart is so constituted, that a man loves liberty as naturally as himself. Yet liberty is a rare thing in the world, though the love of it is so universal.

Before the French Revolution, it was the prevailing opinion of our countrymen, that other nations were not free, because their despotic governments were too strong for the people. Of course, we were admonished to detest all existing governments, as so many lions in liberty's path; and to expect by their downfall the happy opportunity, that every emancipated people would embrace, to secure their own equal rights for ever. France is supposed to have had this opportunity, and to have lost it. Ought we not then to be convinced, that something more is necessary to preserve liberty than to love it? Ought we not to see that when the people have destroyed all power but their own, they are the nearest possible to a despotism, the more uncontrolled for being new, and tenfold the more cruel for its hypocrisy?

The steps by which a people must proceed to change a government, are not those to enlighten their judgment or to soothe their passions. They cannot stir without following the men before them, who breathe fury into their hearts and banish nature from them. On whatever grounds and under whatever leaders the contest may be commenced, the revolutionary work is the same, and the characters of the agents will be assimilated to it. A revolution is a mine that must explode with destructive violence. The men who were once peaceable like to carry firebrands and daggers too long. Thus armed, will they submit to salutary restraint? How will you bring them to it? Will you undertake to reason down fury? Will you satisfy revenge without blood? Will you preach banditti into habits of self-denial? If you can, and in times of violence and anarchy, why do you ask any other guard than sober reason for your life and property in times of peace and order, when men are most disposed to listen to it? Yet even at such times, you impose restraints; you call out for your defence the whole array of law, with its instruments of punishment and terror; you maintain ministers to strengthen force with opinion, and to make religion the auxiliary of morals. With all this, however, crimes [396] are still perpetrated; society is not any too safe or quiet. Break down all these fences; make what is called law an assassin; take what it ought to protect, and divide it; extinguish, by acts of rapine and vengeance, the spark of mercy in the heart; or, if it should be found to glow there, quench it in that heart's blood; make your people scoff at their morals, and unlearn an education to virtue; displace the Christian sabbath by a profane one, for a respite once in ten days from the toils of murder, because men, who first shed blood for revenge, and proceed to spill it for plunder, and in the progress of their ferocity, for sport, want a festival—what sort of society would you have? Would not rage grow with its indulgence? The coward fury of a mob rises in proportion as there is less resistance; and their inextinguishable thirst for slaughter grows more ardent as more blood is shed to slake it. In such a state is liberty to be gained or guarded from violation? It could not be kept an hour from the daggers of those who, having seized despotic power, would claim it as their lawful prize. I have written the history of France. Can we look back upon it without terror, or forward without despair?

The nature of arbitrary power is always odious; but it cannot be long the arbitrary power of the multitude. There is, probably, no form of rule among mankind, in which the progress of the government depends so little on the particular character of those who administer it. Democracy is the creature of impulse and violence; and the intermediate stages towards the tyranny of one are so quickly passed, that the vileness and cruelty of men are displayed with surprising uniformity. There is not time for great talents to act. There is no sufficient reason to believe, that we should conduct a revolution with much more mildness than the French. If a revolution find the citizens lambs, it will soon make them carnivorous, if not cannibals. We have many thousands of the Paris and St. Domingo assassins in the United

States, not as fugitives, but as patriots, who merit reward, and disdain to take any but power. In the progress of our confusion, these men will effectually assert their claims and display their skill. There is no governing power in the state but party. The moderate and thinking part of the [397] citizens are without power or influence; and it must be so, because all power and influence are engrossed by a factious combination of men, who can overwhelm uncombined individuals with numbers, and the wise and virtuous with clamor and fury.

It is indeed a law of politics, as well as of physics, that a body in action must overcome an equal body at rest. The attacks that have been made on the constitutional barriers proclaim, in a tone that would not be louder from a trumpet, that party will not tolerate any resistance to its will. All the supposed independent orders of the commonwealth must be its servile instruments, or its victims. We should experience the same despotism in Massachusetts, New Hampshire, and Connecticut, but the battle is not yet won. It will be won; and they who already display the temper of their Southern and French allies, will not linger or reluct in imitating the worst extremes of their example.

What, then, is to be our condition?

Faction will inevitably triumph. Where the government is both stable and free, there may be parties. There will be differences of opinion, and the pride of opinion will be sufficient to generate contests, and to inflame them with bitterness and rancor. There will be rivalships among those whom genius, fame, or station have made great, and these will deeply agitate the state without often hazarding its safety. Such parties will excite alarm, but they may be safely left, like the elements, to exhaust their fury upon each other.

The object of their strife is to get power *under* the government; for, where that is constituted as it should be, the power *over* the government will not seem attainable, and, of course, will not be attempted.

But in democratic states there will be factions. The sovereign power being nominally in the hands of all, will be effectively within the grasp of a few; and therefore, by the very laws of our nature, a few will combine, intrigue, lie, and fight to engross it to themselves. All history bears testimony, that this attempt has never yet been disappointed.

Who will be the associates? Certainly not the virtuous, who do not wish to control the society, but quietly to enjoy its protection. The enterprising merchant, the thriving [398] tradesman, the careful farmer, will be engrossed by the toils of their business, and will have little time or inclination for the unprofitable and disquieting pursuits of politics. It is not the industrious, sober husbandman, who will plough that barren field; it is the lazy and dissolute bankrupt, who has no other to plough. The idle, the ambitious, and the needy will band together to break the hold that law has upon them, and then to get hold of law. Faction is a Hercules, whose first labor is to strangle this lion, and then to make armor of his skin. In every democratic state, the ruling faction will have law to keep down its enemies; but it will arrogate to itself an undisputed power over law. If our ruling faction has found any impediments, we ask, which of them is now remaining? And is it not absurd to suppose, that the conquerors will be contented with half the fruits of victory?

We are to be subject, then, to a despotic faction, irritated by the resistance that has delayed, and the scorn that pursues their triumph, elate with the insolence of an arbitrary and uncontrollable domination, and who will exercise their sway, not according to the rules of integrity or national policy, but in conformity with their own exclusive interests and passions.

This is a state of things which admits of progress, but not of reformation; it is the beginning of a revolution, which must advance. Our affairs, as first observed, no longer depend on counsel. The opinion of a majority is no longer invited or permitted to control our destinies, or even to retard their consummation. The men in power may, and no doubt will give place to some other faction, who will succeed, because they are abler men, or possibly, in candor we say it, because they are worse. Intrigue will for some time answer instead of force, or the mob will supply it. But by degrees force only will be relied on by those who are *in,* and employed by those who are *out.* The vis major will prevail, and some bold chieftain will conquer liberty, and triumph and reign in her name.

Yet it is confessed, we have hopes that this event is not very near. We have no cities as large as London or Paris; and of course the ambitious demagogues may find the ranks of their standing army too thin to rule by them alone. It [399] is also worth remark, that our mobs are not, like those of Europe, excitable by the cry of no bread. The dread of famine is everywhere else a power of political electricity, that glides through all the haunts of filth, and vice, and want in a city, with incredible speed, and in times of insurrection rives and scorches with a sudden force, like heaven's own thunder. Accordingly, we find the sober men of Europe more afraid of the despotism of the rabble than of the government.

But as in the United States we see less of this description of low vulgar, and as in the essential circumstance alluded to, they are so much less manageable by their demagogues, we are to expect that our affairs will be long guided by courting the mob, before they are violently changed by employing them. While the passions of the multitude can be conciliated to confer power and to overcome all impediments to its action, our rulers have a plain and easy task to perform. It costs them nothing but hypocrisy. As soon, however, as rival favorites of the people may happen to contend by the practice of the same arts, we are to look for the sanguinary strife of ambition. Brissot will fall by the hand of Danton, and he will be supplanted by Robespierre. The revolution will proceed in exactly the same way, but not with so rapid a pace, as that of France.

A SELECTED LIST OF POLITICAL WRITINGS BY AMERICANS BETWEEN 1760 AND 1805

THE FOLLOWING BIBLIOGRAPHY is based upon a comprehensive reading of the political literature of the founding era and is designed to assist those interested in the study of American political theory by identifying items worthy of attention. If the topic of the piece is not apparent from its title, the editors have, in most instances, provided annotation. If an item lacks annotation, as is the case with many sermons, this is because the content is either so broad as to defy easy categorization, or the content is so typical for such a piece that there is no point in repetitiously noting that fact. The information is sufficient for an investigator to be able to identify those pieces dealing with a specific topic he or she might wish to study. We enter no comment on the pieces printed in this collection.

The editors have roughly divided the items in the bibliography into three categories. If there is no asterisk, the piece is deemed of interest to someone studying American political theory, but the level of analysis is low. One asterisk identifies pieces with substantial theoretical content, and two asterisks indicate pieces that these editors feel are candidates for inclusion among the best theoretical writing by Americans during the founding era. Major bibliographies compiled by historians on some part of what is here defined as the founding era usually will be found to have a 20 to 30 percent overlap with the following bibliography. The items cited by such historians but not included below are not lacking in historical interest or importance, but simply do not have sufficient *theoretical* content or interest for inclusion here. A dagger at the end of a citation indicates a piece that is reproduced in these volumes.

A SELECTED LIST OF POLITICAL WRITINGS

A. ITEMS WHERE THE AUTHOR IS KNOWN

1   Adams, John. *A Defence of the Constitutions of Government of the United States.* 1787. In Charles Francis Adams, ed., *Works of John Adams,* (Boston, 1851), IV.**

2   Adams, John [Novanglus]. (Untitled Essays). *Boston Gazette,* January 23, 30, February 20–April 17, 1775.*
Written in response to essays by Massachusettensis [Daniel Leonard]. Reproduced in Merrill Jensen, ed., *Tracts of the American Revolution, 1763–1776* (Indianapolis: Bobbs-Merrill, 1978).

3   Adams, John. *Thoughts on Government.* 1776. From Charles Francis Adams, ed., *Works of John Adams* (Boston, 1851), IV: 189–202.**†

4   Adams, Samuel. *The Rights of the Colonists.* Boston, 1772. 11 pp. Reproduced in *The Annals of America,* I: 217–220.

5   Adams, Zabdiel. *An Election Sermon.* Boston, 1782. 59 pp.**†

6   Addison, Alexander. *Analysis of the Report of the Committee of the Virginia Assembly.* Philadelphia, 1800. 52 pp.**†

7   Addison, Alexander. *A Charge to the Grand Juries of the County Courts in Pennsylvania.* Philadelphia, 1798. 24 pp.
Alien and Sedition Acts, free speech, and free press.

8   Addison, Alexander. *Liberty of Speech and of the Press: Charges to a Grand Jury.* Albany, 1790. 16 pp.

9   Alden, Timothy. *The Glory of America.* Portsmouth, N.H., 1802. 47 pp.

10 Allen, Ira. *Some Miscellaneous Remarks and Short Arguments on a Small Pamphlet . . . and Some Reasons Given Why the District of the New Hampshire Grants Had Best Be a State.* Hartford, 1777. 26 pp.

11 Allen, Ira. *A Vindication of the Conduct of the General Assembly of the State of Vermont.* Dresden. N.H., 1779. 48 pp.

12 Allison, Patrick. *Candid Animadversions on a Petition. . . .* Baltimore, 1793. 47 pp.

13 Ames, Fisher. *The Dangers of American Liberty.* Boston, 1805. 55 pp.**†

14 Ames, Fisher. *Laocoon No. 1.* 1799. From Seth Ames, ed., *Works of Fisher Ames* (Boston, 1854), II: 109–115.
Defends Federalists against charges by Jeffersonians.

15 Atwater, Jeremiah. *A Sermon.* Middlebury, Vt., 1801. 39 pp.**†

16 Austin, Benjamin [Honestus]. *Observations on the Pernicious Practice of the Law.* Boston, 1786, 52 pp.

A SELECTED LIST OF POLITICAL WRITINGS

Lawyers are not needed for good government, but they have insinuated themselves into it with pernicious consequences.

17 Austin, Benjamin Jr. To the Printers. *Massachusetts Centinel*, January 9, 1788.
Supports proposed United States Constitution.

18 Avery, David. *Two Sermons on the Nature and Evil of Professors of Religion Not Bridling the Tongue*. Boston, 1791. 66 pp.
The tongue as the principal medium for displaying corruption, and the effect it has on people and society.

19 Backus, Charles. *A Sermon*. Hartford, 1793. 38 pp.

20 Backus, Isaac. *Government and Liberty Described*. Boston, 1778. 20 pp.

21 Backus, Isaac. *A Letter . . . Concerning Taxes to Support Religious Worship*. Boston, 1771. 22 pp.
Opposes such taxation.

22 Backus, Isaac. *Truth is Great and Will Prevail*. Boston, 1781. 44 pp.

23 Backus, Simon. *A Dissertation on the Right and Obligation of the Civil Magistrate*. Middletown, Conn., 1804. 38 pp.**
Importance of religion to make oaths and compacts operative, preserve public virtue, and support self-government.

24 Baldwin, Ebenezer. *The Duty of Rejoicing Under Calamities and Afflictions*. New York, 1776. 42 pp.
A "God is an American" morale-booster during the War.

25 Baldwin, Henry. *A General View of the Origin and Nature of the Constitution and Government of New York*. New York, 1780. 197 pp.

26 Baldwin, Thomas. *A Sermon* (Election Day). Boston, 1802. 36 pp.

27 Ball, Heman. *Vermont Election Day Sermon*. Bennington, 1804. 31 pp.
A standard rehearsal of Whig political principles.

28 Bancroft, Aaron. *Massachusetts Election Day Sermon*. Boston, 1801. 29 pp.
Prosperity and political success of American colonies laid to the moral virtues of the people. Continued success depends upon preserving these virtues.

29 Barlow, Joel. *Advice to the Privileged Orders. . . .* New York, 1794. 31 pp.**
Principles that ought to govern the collection of public revenue.

30   Barlow, Joel. *A Letter to the National Convention of France on the Defects in the Constitution of 1791.* New York, 1792. 31 pp.**†

31   Barlow, Joel. *To His Fellow Citizens of the United States. Letter II: On Certain Political Measures Proposed to Their Consideration.* Philadelphia, 1801. 37 pp.**†

32   Barnes, David. *A Discourse on Education.* Boston, 1803. 27 pp.**
Comprehensive discussion of education—school, home, etc.

33   *The Barrington-Bernard Correspondence, 1760–1770.* Selections from 1765–1768. From Edward Channing and Archibald Cary Coolidge, eds., *The Barrington-Bernard Correspondence, 1760–1770,* Harvard Historical Studies, vol. XVII (Cambridge, Mass,: Harvard University, 1912), pp. 92–103, 244–293.

34   Barton, William. *The Constitutionalist: Addressed to Men of All Parties.* Philadelphia, 1804. 49 pp.**
Judiciary has a special responsibility to enforce Constitution.

35   Baxter, Joseph. *The Duty of a People to Pray to and Bless God for Their Rulers. . . .* Boston, 1772. 36 pp.
The duties of rulers.

36   Bean, Joseph. *Massachusetts Election Day Sermon.* Boston, 1774. 36 pp.

37   Beers, William P. *An Address to the Legislature and People of the State of Connecticut.* New Haven, 1791.*
Cosmopolitan, contrasted with localist, spirit in political factions. Size of electorate and of the legislature important.

38   Belknap, Jeremy. *The History of New England,* 3 vols.; vol. I, pp. 60–99; vol. III, pp. 252–287. Boston, 1791–1792.
Equality and public virtue as the basis for true republicanism.

39   Belsham, William. *An Essay on the African Slave Trade.* Philadelphia, 1790. 15 pp.
Opposed to it.

40   [Benezet, Anthony.] *Brief Considerations on Slavery.* Burlington, Vt., 1773. 16 pp.*

41   Benezet, Anthony. *A Caution and Warning to Great Britain . . . the Calamitous State of the Enslaved Negroes in the British Dominion.* Philadelphia, 1767. 52 pp.

42   Benezet, Anthony. *A Mite Cast into the Treasury: Or, Observations on Slave-Keeping.* Philadelphia, 1772. 14 pp.**
Major spokesman for the Quaker position.

43   Benezet, Anthony. *Serious Considerations on Several Important Subjects.* Philadelphia, 1778. 48 pp.
Compendium of Quaker political principles.

A Selected List of Political Writings

44 Benezet, Anthony. *Some Observations on . . . Indian Natives of the Continent.* Philadelphia, 1784. 59 pp.

45 Benezet, Anthony. *Thoughts on the Nature of War. . . .* Philadelphia, 1766. 14 pp.*
    Statement of the Quaker position.

46 Bernard, Francis. *Select Letters on the Trade and Government of America.* London, 1774. 130 pp.
    Prominent American explains how colonists see their government and place within the Empire.

47 Binney, Barnabas. *An Oration* [re] *. . . the Liberty of Choosing Our Own Religion.* Boston, 1774. 44 pp.

48 Bishop, Abraham. *Oration . . . . Before the Republicans of Connecticut.* New Haven, 1801. 47 pp.*
    Characteristics of Federalists as seen by a partisan Republican.

49 Bishop, Abraham. *Proofs of a Conspiracy Against Christianity and the Government of the United States.* Hartford, 1802. 135 pp.**
    A tirade against the Federalists, professionals, well-to-do, and those who attack Jefferson. Good on equality, Federalist rhetoric, elitism, and corruption.

50 Bland, Richard [Common Sense]. *The Colonel Dismounted: Or the Rector Vindicated. . . .* Williamsburg, Va., 1764. 53 pp.**
    Discusses constitution of the colony. Reproduced in Bernard Bailyn, ed., *Pamphlets of the American Revolution* (Cambridge, Mass., Belknap Press, 1965).

51 Bland, Richard, *An Inquiry into the Rights of the British Colonies.* Williamsburg, Va., 1766. 31 pp.**†

52 Bollan, William. *The Freedom of Speech and Writing Upon Public Affairs, Considered, With an Historical View.* London, 1766.

53 Bowdoin, James. *A Philosophical Discourse, Addressed to the American Academy of Arts and Sciences. . . .* Boston, 1780. 16 pp.
    On the encouragement of knowledge.

54 Bowen, Nathaniel. *An Oration . . . in Commemoration of American Independence.* 1802.
    A rehearsal of the reasons for separating from England.

55 Boucher, Jonathan. *On the Necessity of Popular Support of Government.* 1763. From *A View of the Causes and Consequences of the American Revolution* (London, 1797), pp. 308–321.

56 Bradbury, Thomas. *The Ass: or, the Serpent, A Comparison Between the Tribes of Issachar and Dan, in Their Regard for Civil Liberty.* First

printed in London, 1712; reprinted in Newburyport, Mass., 1774. 22 pp.**†

57 Braxton, Carter [A Native of This Colony]. *An Address to the Convention of the Colony and Ancient Dominion of Virginia on the Subject of Government in General, and Recommending a Particular Form to Their Attention. Virginia Gazette,* June 8 and 15, 1776.**†

58 Brown, Charles Brockden. *Alcuin, A Dialogue.* New Haven, 1798. 38 pp.

On the essential equality of the sexes. Reprinted in *The Annals of America,* vol. IV. 40 pp.

59 Brown, William L. *An Essay on the Natural Equality of Men.* Philadelphia, 1793. 191 pp.

60 Burk, John. *The History of Virginia from its First Settlement to the Present Day.* Williamsburg, Va. 1805.

61 Burke, Aedanus. *An Address to the Freemen of . . . South Carolina.* Charleston, 1783.

Proper treatment of colonials who maintained friendly relations with the British within territory held by British forces.

62 Burke, Aedanus. *Considerations on the Society or Order of Cincinnati.* Charleston, 1783. 33 pp.

63 Burnet, Matthias. *Connecticut Election Day Sermon.* Hartford, 1803. 29 pp.*

Five conditions needed for order, peace, and security.

64 Callender, John. *An Historical Discourse on the Civil and Religious Affairs . . . of Rhode Island.* 1739. Republished in 1783.

On liberty of conscience.

65 Carmichael, John. *A Self-Defensive War Lawful, Proved in a Sermon.* Lancaster, Penn., 1775. 25 pp.

66 Case, Stephen [A Moderate Whig]. *Defensive Arms Vindicated and the Lawfulness of the American War Made Manifest.* 1783. 53 pp.*

67 Chalmers, James [Candidus]. *Plain Truth: Addressed to the Inhabitants of America, Containing, Remarks on a Late Pamphlet Entitled Common Sense.* Philadelphia, March 13, 1776. 40 pp.

In response to Thomas Paine's pamphlet, Chalmers defends the British monarchical constitution and attacks the idea of republicanism.

68 Champion, Judah. *Christian and Civil Liberty.* Hartford, 1776.

The basis for civil liberty lies in Christian thought.

69 [Chandler, Thomas B.] *An Address from the Clergy of New York and New Jersey to the Episcopalians in Virginia.* New York, 1771. 58 pp.

70 Chandler, Thomas B. *The Appeal Farther Defended.* New York, 1771. 240 pp.

71 Chandler, Thomas B. *A Friendly Address . . .* [re] *Our Political Confusions.* New York, 1774. 55 pp.

72 [Chandler, Thomas B.] *What Think Ye of the Congress Now?* New York, 1775. 48 pp.

73 Chase, Samuel [Publicola]. To the Voters of Anne-Arundel County. *Maryland Journal,* February 13, 1787. See also May 18, July 13, July 18, and August 31, the last few being entitled "To Aristides."*
A running battle with Aristides [Alexander Hanson] in which Publicola defends the right of the people to instruct their representatives.

74 Chauncy, Charles. *The Appeal of the Public Answered in Behalf of the Non-Episcopal Churches of America.* Boston, 1768. 205 pp.

75 Chipman, Nathaniel. *Sketches of the Principles of Government.* Rutland, Vt. 1793.*
An analysis of the United States Constitution, and the principles that give it strength, by a Federalist.

76 Clarendon, Earl of, to William Pym. *Boston Gazette,* January 27, 1766.*
An English Whig lays out the basic Whig principles.

77 Clark, Jonas. *Massachusetts Election Day Sermon.* Boston, 1781. 42 pp.*
Uses an extended biological metaphor to stress the communitarian underpinnings to a just relationship between governors and the governed.

78 Clinton, George, [Cato]. No. IV: To the Citizens of the State of New York. *New York Journal,* November 8, 1787.*
Critical analysis of the proposed Constitution.

79 Clinton, George [Cato]. No. VI: To the People of the State of New York. *New York Journal,* December 13, 1787.**
Problems of taxation, dangers of aristocracy. Cato's pamphlets are reproduced in Cecelia Kenyon, ed., *The Antifederalists* (Indianapolis: Bobbs-Merrill, 1966).

80 Cobbett, William. *The Democratic Judge: or the Equal Liberty of the Press.* Philadelphia, 1798. 102 pp.

81 Cooper, David. *An Inquiry into Public Abuses, Arising for Want of a Due Execution of Laws.* Philadelphia, 1784.

82 [Cooper, David.] *Serious Address to the Rulers of America.* Trenton, 1783. 22 pp.

83 Cooper, Thomas. *An Account of the Trial of Thomas Cooper.* Philadelphia, 1800. 64 pp.

Cooper edits the proceedings of the trial against him under the Alien and Sedition Acts.

84 Coram, Robert. *Political Inquiries, to which is Added a Plan for the Establishment of Schools Throughout the United States.* Wilmington, 1791. 107 pp.**†

85 Coxe, Tench [An American Citizen]. *An Examination of the Constitution of the United States of America.* . . . Philadelphia, 1788. 33 pp.*

Theoretical support for the proposed Constitution.

86 Coxe, Tench [An American Citizen]. On the Federal Government, No. 1 and No. 3. *New York Packet,* October 5 and 16, 1787, respectively.*

Reproduced in Paul Leicester Ford, ed., *Pamphlets on the Constitution of the United States* (New York: Da Capo Press, 1968). Summarizes American political history showing how it leads naturally to the Constitution.

87 Cumings, Henry. *A Sermon* (Election Day). Boston, 1783. 55 pp.

88 Daggett, David. *Sun-Beams May be Extracted from Cucumbers, But the Process Is Tedious: An Oration.* New Haven, 1799. 28 pp.*

A witty, sarcastic response by a Federalist to what he perceived to be the utopianism on the part of the opposition.

89 Dana, James. *Connecticut Election Day Sermon.* Hartford, 1779. 46 pp.*

Foundations of good government are rooted in the word of God. Good on virtue, oaths, and basic principles of government.

90 Dana, Samuel W. *Essay on Political Society.* Philadelphia, 1800. 234 pp.

On the supremacy of the Constitution and how it is to be enforced. Pages after 193 contain discussion of judicial review.

91 Dickinson, John. *Essay on the Constitutional Power of Great Britain.* Philadelphia, 1774. 127 pp.*

Relationship of colonies to Britain.

92 Dickinson, John. *The Late Regulations Respecting the British Colonies on the Continent of America.* . . . Philadelphia, 1765. 38 pp.

A response to the Stamp Act. Reproduced in Bernard Bailyn, ed., *Pamphlets of the American Revolution.*

93 Dickinson, John. Letters of a Farmer [On British Policy Affecting the American Colonies]. 1767. In *The Political Writings of John Dickinson,* I:167–276.*

Letter XII especially good on basic principles. Letters I, II, IV, VI, IX, and X are reproduced in Jensen, ed., *Tracts of the American Revolution.*

94 Dickinson, John [Fabius]. Letters to the Editor. *Delaware Gazette,* 1788.*

These nine letters in support of the Constitution are reproduced in Ford. ed., *Pamphlets on the Constitution of the United States.*

95 Dickinson, Samuel F. *An Oration in Celebration of American Independence.* Northampton, Mass., 1798. 23 pp

How political institutions and conduct of government respond to manners and taste.

96 Doggett, Simeon. *A Discourse on Education.* New Bedford, 1796.

Reproduced in Frederick Rudolph, ed., *Essays on Education in the Early Republic* (Cambridge, Mass.: Belknap Press, 1965), pp. 147–166.*

97 Dorr, Edward. *The Duty of Civil Rulers: A Connecticut Election Sermon.* Hartford, 1765. 34 pp.**

Favors support of Church by State, and protection of Church and religion from injurious behavior.

98 Downer, Silas [A Son of Liberty]. A Discourse at the Dedication of the Tree of Liberty. Providence, 1768. 16 pp.**†

99 Drayton, William Henry. The Charge to the Grand Jury. *South Carolina and American General Gazette,* May 8, 1776.

Precursor to the Declaration of Independence in laying out grounds for breaking with England.*

100 Dulaney, Daniel. *Considerations on the Propriety of Imposing Taxes in the British Colonies . . . By Parliament.* Annapolis, 1765. 55 pp.*

Against virtual representation and the right of Parliament to tax colonists. Reproduced in Bailyn, ed., *Pamphlets of the American Revolution.*

101 Dwight, Theodore. *An Oration on the Anniversary of American Independence.* Hartford, 1801. 31 pp.*

A Federalist opposed to "levelling" by Jeffersonians. Opposes separating State and religion—discusses public schools, moral and religious instruction, literacy, religion, etc.

102 Dwight, Theodore. *An Oration, Spoken Before the Connecticut Society, for the Promotion of Freedom and the Relief of Persons Unlawfully Holden in Bondage.* Hartford, 1794. 24 pp.**†

103 Dwight, Timothy. *A Discourse on Some Events of the Last Century.* New Haven, 1801. 55 pp.*

Summation of the state of American people, especially in morals and religion. A diatribe against the Enlightenment, self-interest, commercialism—all put at the door of freemasonry.

104 Dwight, Timothy. *The Nature and Danger of Infidel Philosophy.* . . . New Haven, 1798. 95 pp.*

An earlier and inferior version of the previous piece.

105 Dwight, Timothy. *Sermon Before the Connecticut Society of Cincinnati.* New Haven, 1795. 40 pp.*

Excellent discussion of virtue and politics.

106 Dwight, Timothy. *The True Means of Establishing Public Happiness.* New Haven, 1795. 40 pp.

The importance of religion and virtue.

107 Dwight, Timothy. *Virtuous Rulers A National Blessing.* New Haven, 1791. 42 pp.

108 Eliot, Andrew. *Massachusetts Election Day Sermon.* Boston, 1765. 49 pp.**

On qualities of good public officials and their relations with the citizenry. Subtle and practical.

109 Ellsworth, Oliver. The Landholder, VII. *Connecticut Courant,* December 17, 1787,

On religious tests.

110 Emerson, William. *An Oration . . . In Commemoration of the Anniversary of American Independence.* Boston, 1802. 25 pp.**

Discusses prevailing attitudes about equality, liberty, rights; and how manners and way of life support these commitments.

111 Emmons, Nathanael. *A Discourse. Delivered on the National Fast,* Wrentham, Mass., 1799. 31 pp.**†

112 Emmons, Nathanael. *A Discourse . . . in Commemoration of American Independence.* Wrentham, Mass., 1802. 24 pp.*

Character of American political system—mixed regime; similarity of American independence to Jewish independence.

113 Evans, Israel. *New Hampshire Election Day Sermon.* Concord, N.H., 1791. 35 pp.*

Interrelationships of religion, liberty, and just government.

114 Farmer, A. W. *A View of the Controversy Between Great Britain and Her Colonies.* . . . New York, 1774. 37 pp.*

A reply to Alexander Hamilton's *Full Vindication,* which, in turn, had been a reply to an earlier pamphlet by Farmer—*Free Thoughts on the Proceedings.* . . . Very much a Tory.

A SELECTED LIST OF POLITICAL WRITINGS

115 Findley, William. *History of the Insurrection in the Four Western Counties of Pennsylvania.* . . . Philadelphia, 1796. 328 pp.

116 Fish, Elisha. *A Discourse.* Worcester, 1775. 28 pp.

117 [Fitch, Thomas.] *Reasons Why the British Colonies in America, Should Not Be Charged With Internal Taxes, by Authority of Parliament.* New Haven, 1764. 39 pp.*
Reproduced in Bailyn, ed., *Pamphlets of the American Revolution.*

118 Fobes, Peres [Perez]. *An Election Sermon.* Boston, 1795. 42 pp.**†

119 Ford, Timothy [Americanus]. *The Constitutionalist: Or, An Inquiry How Far It Is Expedient and Proper to Alter the Constitution of South Carolina. City Gazette and Daily Advertiser,* Charleston, 1794. 55 pp.**†

120 Ford, Timothy. *An Enquiry into the Constitutional Authority of the Supreme Federal Court Over the Several States.* Charleston, 1792. 40 pp.

121 Foster, Dan. *A Short Essay on Civil Government.* Hartford, 1775. 73 pp.
Origin and nature of government.

122 Franklin, Benjamin. An Account of the Supremest Court of Judicature in Pennsylvania, viz., The Court of the Press. *Philadelphia Federal Gazette,* February 12, 1789.**†

123 Franklin, Benjamin. Advice to a Young Tradesman from an Old One. *Worcester Magazine,* Third Week in August, 1786, pp. 247–248.*
The capitalist ethic and behavior appropriate to it.

124 French, Jonathan. *A Sermon.* Boston, 1796. 23 pp.

125 [Gale, Benjamin.] *Brief, Decent, but Free Remarks on Several Laws.* Hartford, 1782. 55 pp.

126 Galloway, Joseph. *A Candid Examination of the Mutual Claims of Great Britain and the Colonies.* . . . New York, 1775, 62 pp.**
Galloway's rebuttal of the case for separation. Reproduced in Jensen, ed., *Tracts of the American Revolution.*

127 Galloway, Joseph. *A Letter to the People of Pennsylvania.* . . . Philadelphia, 1760. 17 pp.
Justifies an independent judiciary.

128 Galloway, Joseph. *A Reply to an Address.* . . . New York, 1775. 42 pp.
Galloway answers someone who severely attacked his *Candid Examination.* . . . Says colonies integral part of Great Britain.

129 Gerry, Elbridge [A Columbian Patriot]. *Observations on the New Constitution, and on the Federal and State Conventions*. Boston, 1788.*
Reproduced in Ford, ed., *Pamphlets on the Constitution of the United States*.

130 Gordon, William. *The History of the Rise, Progress, and Establishment of the Independence of the United States of America*. 3 vols. New York, 1794.

131 Gray, Robert. *New Hampshire Election Day Sermon*. Dover, N.H., 1798. 29 pp.
The requisites for a great nation.

132 [Grey, Isaac.] *A Serious Address to Quakers*. Philadelphia, 1778. 44 pp.

133 Griffith, David. *Passive Obedience Considered: A Sermon*. Williamsburg, Va., 1776. 26 pp.
The right of resistance—drawn from biblical passages.

134 Hamilton, Alexander, James Madison, and John Jay [Publius]. *The Federalist Papers*. Published between October 27, 1787 and May 28, 1788 with individual essays appearing primarily, but not exclusively, in four New York papers: the *Independent Journal*, the *New York Packet*, the *New York Daily Advertiser*, and the *New-York Journal and Daily Patriotic Register*. The eighty-five essays have been published together in book form a number of times, with the best available being Jacob E. Cooke, ed., *The Federalist* (Cleveland: Meridian Books, 1961).**

135 Hammon, Jupiter. *Address to the Negroes of New York*. New York, 1787. 20 pp.

136 Hanson, Alexander. To the People of Maryland. *Maryland Journal*, April 13, June 22, and August 14, 1787, (last one titled "To Publicola").
Formerly writing under "J.B.F." Hanson continues debate with Publicola [Samuel Chase] and argues against the people giving binding instructions to their representatives.

137 Hanson, Alexander [Aristides]. *Remarks on the Proposed Plan of a Federal Government*. Annapolis, 1788. 42 pp.*
Reproduced in Ford, ed., *Pamphlets on the Constitution of the United States*.

138 Hart, Levi. *Liberty Described and Recommended: in a Sermon Preached to the Corporation of Freemen in Farmington*. Hartford, 1775. 23 pp.**†

139 Haven, Jason. *Massachusetts Election Day Sermon*. Boston, 1769. 54 pp.

Civil order and disobedience.

140   Hawkins, Benjamin, et. al. *Articles of a Treaty . . .* [with] *the Head Men and Warriors of the Cherokees.* April, 1786.*

141   Hay, George [Hortensius]. *An Essay on the Liberty of the Press.* Philadelphia, 1799.
Legalistic discussion of requiring security of good behavior for publishers under indictment for libel.

142   Hay, James. [A Virginian Born and Bred]. *Remarks on the Bill of Rights and Constitution . . . of the State of Virginia.* 1796. 35 pp.
Arguments for writing a new state constitution to remedy the defects of the 1776 document.

143   Hemmenway, Moses. *Massachusetts Election Day Sermon.* Boston, 1784. 52 pp.**
Liberty in (1) state of nature, (2) civil society, and (3) the Church; limits on rulers in each of these; rights and duties of individuals; sources of authority.

144   Hicks, William [A Citizen]. The Nature and Extent of Parliamentary Power Considered. *Pennsylvania Journal,* January 21–February 25, 1786.
American colonists equal to British people.

145   Hillhouse, William. *A Dissertation, In Answer to a Late Lecture on the Political State of America.* New Haven, 1789. 23 pp.
A Federalist defends proposed Constitution.

146   Hilliard, Timothy. *An Oration* (July 4). Portland, Maine, 1803. 20 pp.

147   Hilliard, Isaac. *The Rights of Suffrage.* Danbury, 1804. 64 pp.

148   Hitchcock, Gad. *An Election Sermon.* Boston, 1774. 56 pp.**†

149   Hitchcock, Gad. *A Sermon* [Thanksgiving]. Boston, 1775. 44 pp.**
On liberty—natural, civil, and religious.

150   [Hoar, David] *Natural Principles of Liberty, Virtue, etc.,* Boston, 1782. 12 pp.

151   Holdfast, Simon. *Facts Are Stubborn Things, Or Nine Plain Questions.* Hartford, 1803. 23 pp.
A Federalist defends Connecticut's long-standing commitment to restricted suffrage, and to state support for education.

152   Hopkins, Samuel. *A Dialogue Concerning the Slavery of the Africans.* New York, 1776. 71 pp.*
Rebuttal of all arguments for continued slavery.

A SELECTED LIST OF POLITICAL WRITINGS

153 Hopkins, Stephen. The Rights of Colonies Examined. *Providence Gazette,* December 22, 1764.**†

154 Hotchkiss, Frederick W. *On National Greatness.* New Haven, 1793. 23 pp.

155 Howard, Martin Jr. *A Letter from a Gentleman at Halifax, To His Friend in Rhode Island, Containing Remarks Upon a Pamphlet Entitled "The Rights of Colonies Examined".* Newport, R.I. 1765.
Attacks the pamphlet by Stephen Hopkins.

156 Howard, Simeon. *Massachusetts Election Day Sermon.* Boston, 1780. 48 pp.*
Characteristics of good rulers: need for educated population; emphasis upon virtue. Government should encourage piety.

157 Howard, Simeon. *A Sermon Preached to the Ancient and Honorable Artillery Company in Boston.* Boston, 1773. 43 pp.**†

158 Humphreys, Daniel. *The Inquirer: Being an Examination of the Question Whether the Legitimate Powers of Government Extend to the Care of Religion.* Boston, 1801. 47 pp.*

159 Huntington, Enoch. *Political Wisdom, Or Honesty the Best Policy.* Middletown, Conn., 1786. 20 pp.
The qualities desirable in public officials.

160 Huntington, Joseph. *God Ruling the Nations for the Most Glorious Ends.* Hartford, 1784. 34 pp.*
Efforts by elected officials to rule justly are being thwarted by public distrust.

161 Hurt, John. *The Love of Our Country, A Sermon Preached Before the Virginia Troops.* Philadelphia, 1777. 23 pp.

162 Inglis, Charles. *The Letters of Papinian: in which the Conduct, Present State and Prospects, of the American Congress, Are Examined.* New York, 1779. 150 pp.

163 Inglis, Charles. *The True Interest of America Impartially Stated, In Certain Strictures on a Pamphlet Intitled "Common Sense".* Philadelphia, 1776. 71 pp.
A Tory attacking Paine's pamphlet rehearses all the costs likely to be incurred with independence.

164 Iredell, James [Marcus] *Answer to Mr. [George] Mason's Objections to the New Constitution. . . .* 1788.*
Reproduced in Ford, ed., *Pamphlets on the Constitution of the United States.*

165   Jackson, Jonathan [A Native of Boston]. *Thoughts Upon the Political Situation of the United States of America. . . .* Worcester, 1788. 209 pp.**
A Whiggish analysis of the Massachusetts Constitution in comparison with the proposed United States Constitution.

166   Jay, John [A Citizen of New York]. *An Address to the People of the State of New York on the Subject of the Constitution Agreed Upon at Philadelphia, the 17th of September, 1787. 1788.**
Reproduced in Ford, ed., *Pamphlets on the Constitution of the United States.*

167   Jefferson, Thomas. *Notes on the State of Virginia,* edited by William Peden. Chapel Hill, 1955.**

168   Jefferson, Thomas. *A Summary View of the Rights of British America.* Williamsburg, Va., 1774. 23 pp.*
Reproduced in Jensen, ed., *Tracts of the American Revolution.*

169   Johnson, John Barent. *An Oration on Union.* New York, 1794. 24 pp.

170   Johnson, Stephen. *A Connecticut Election Sermon.* New London, 1770. 39 pp.**
Good on general Whig principles.

171   Johnson, Stephen. *Integrity and Piety the Best Principles of a Good Administration of Government.* New London, 1770. 39 pp.

172   Jones, David. *Defensive War in a Just Cause* [is] *Sinless.* Philadelphia, 1775. 27 pp.

173   Keith, Isaac S. *The Friendly Influence of Religion and Virtue.* Charleston, 1789. 24 pp.

174   Kendal, Samuel. *Religion the Only Sure Basis of Free Government.* Boston, 1804. 34 pp.**†

175   Kendal, Samuel. *A Sermon.* Boston, 1794. 35 pp.*
Liberty dependent upon a regime of order.

176   Kent, James. *Dissertations . . . Preliminary Part of a Course of Law Lectures.* New York, 1795. 87 pp.**
Main forms of government and their respective merits; development of self-government in America; principles of law governing nations.

177   Kent, James. *An Introductory Lecture to a Course of Law Lectures.* New York, 1794. 23 pp.**†

178   Keteltas, Abraham. *God Arising and Pleading His People's Cause.* Boston, 1777. 32 pp.

179   Kirkland, John T. *A Sermon*. . . . Boston, 1795. 35 pp.
      Wars are evil, but some good effects arise from them.

180   Knox, Samuel. *An Essay on the Best System of Liberal Education,
      Adapted to the Genius of the Government of the United States*. . . .
      1799.*
      Reproduced in Rudolph, ed., *Essays on Education in the Early Republic*,
      pp. 271–372.

181   Knox, William. *Massachusetts Election Day Sermon*. Boston, 1769.
      100 pp.

182   De Lafitte Du Courteil, Amable-Louis-Rose. *Proposal to Demonstrate
      the Necessity of a National Institution in the United States of America,
      for the Education of Children of Both Sexes*. . . . Philadelphia, 1797.*
      Reproduced in Rudolph, ed., *Essays on Education in the Early Republic*.

183   Lathrop, John. *Innocent Blood Crying to God: Boston Massacre Sermon*.
      Boston, 1771. 21 pp.

184   Lathrop, John. *A Sermon Preached to the Artillery Company in Boston*.
      Boston, 1774. 39 pp.*
      Circumstances under which Christians are justified in going to war.

185   Lathrop, Joseph. *The Happiness of a Free Government*. Springfield,
      Mass., 1794. 22 pp.

186   Lathrop, Joseph. *A Miscellaneous Collection of Original Pieces*. Spring-
      field, Mass., 1786. 168 pp.**†

187   Lathrop, Joseph. *A Sermon*. Springfield, Mass., 1787. 24 pp.

188   Lee, Arthur. *An Appeal to the Justice and Interests of the People of Great
      Britain*. New York, 1775. 32 pp.

189   Lee, Charles. *Defense of the Alien and Sedition Laws*. Philadelphia,
      1798. 47 pp.

190   Lee, Richard Henry. *Letters from the Federal Farmer to the Republican*.
      Letters II and III out of 18 published in 1787.**
      Reproduced in Ford, ed., *Pamphlets on the Constitution of the United
      States*.

191   Leib, Michael. *Patriotic Speech*. New London, 1796. 24 pp.

192   Leland, John. *A Blow at the Root*. 1801. In L. F. Greene, ed.,
      The Writings of John Leland (New York: Arno Press, 1969),
      pp. 235–55.*

193   Leland, John. *The Connecticut Dissenters' Strong Box: No. 1*. New
      London, 1802. 40 pp.**†

194   Leland, John. *An Elective Judiciary*. . . . 1805. In L. F. Greene,
      ed., *The Writings of John Leland*, pp. 285–300.

A SELECTED LIST OF POLITICAL WRITINGS

195 Leland, John. *The Rights of Conscience Inalienable.* . . . 1791. In L. F. Greene, ed., *The Writings of John Leland,* pp. 179–192.

196 Leland, John [Jack Nips] *The Yankee Spy.* Boston, 1794. 20 pp.**†

197 Leonard, Daniel [Massachusettensis] *The Origin of the Contest With Great Britain.* New York, 1775. 86 pp.**
Balanced, detailed analysis urging caution and accommodation.

198 Leonard, Daniel [Massachusettensis]. To All Nations of Men. *Massachusetts Spy,* November 18, 1773.*†

199 Lewis, Isaac. *A Sermon Preached Before* . . . *the Governor* . . . *and Legislature.* Hartford, 1797. 31 pp.*
Basic principles, religion, virtue, and godliness.

200 Linn, William. *A Discourse on National Sins.* New York, 1798. 37 pp.
Religion, government, prosperity, and how all can be undercut by sin.

201 Livingston, Philip. *The Other Side of the Question* . . . *A Defence of the Liberties of North America.* Boston, 1774. 29 pp.

202 Livingston, Robert. *The Address of Mr. Justice Livingston to the House of Assembly in Support of His Right to a Seat.* New York, 1769.
New York Assembly cannot, according to Livingston, deny a seat in that body to justices of the colony's supreme court.

203 Livingston, Robert R. *An Oration.* New York, 1787. 22 pp.

204 Livingston, William. *Observations on Government, Including Some Animadversions on Mr. Adams's "Defence of the Constitutions. . . . "* New York, 1787. 56 pp.**

205 Livingston, William. *On the Use, Abuse, and Liberty of the Press.* 1753.
Reproduced in Leonard W. Levy, ed., *Freedom of the Press from Zenger to Jefferson: Early American Libertarian Theories* (Indianapolis: Bobbs-Merrill, 1966).

206 Logan, George. *Five Letters Addressed to the Yeomanry.* Philadelphia, 1792. 28 pp.
Presses for social and economic equality.

207 Lyman, Joseph. *A Sermon,* (Election Day). Boston, 1787. 61 pp.

208 MacClintock, Samuel. *A Sermon Preached Before the Honorable the Council.* Portsmouth, N.H., 1784. 47 pp.*
Comprehensive on Whig principles from religious point of view.

209 McKeen, Joseph. *Massachusetts Election Day Sermon.* Boston, 1800. 30 pp.**

Qualities and conduct of good rulers and relation of religion to same. Wisdom and virtue preferred to brilliance.

210 Madison, James. *An Extensive Republic Meliorates.* 1787. In Gaillard Hunt, ed., *The Writings of James Madison* (New York: G. P. Putnam's Sons, 1901), 2:365–369.**

211 Madison, James. Letter to T. Jefferson, Oct. 24, 1787. In Gaillard Hunt, ed., *The Writings of James Madison* (New York: G. P. Putnam's Sons, 1901), 2:18–35.**

Incisive summary of much debate at constitutional convention.

212 Madison, James. *Vices of the Political System of the United States.* 1787. In Gaillard Hunt, ed., *The Writings of James Madison,* 2:36–69.**

213 Madison, James, et. al. *Memorial and Remonstrance Against Religious Assessments* [in Virginia]. 1785. In Gaillard Hunt, ed., *The Writings of James Madison* (New York: G. P. Putnam's Sons, 1901), 2:183–191.**†

214 Mason, John Mitchell. *The Voice of Warning to Christians.* 1800.

Jefferson cannot fulfill obligations of office because he is an atheist.

215 Mason, Jonathan. *An Oration.* New York, 1780. 40 pp.

The necessity of patriotism for maintaining freedom, justice, etc.

216 Maxcy, Jonathan. *An Oration.* Providence, 1799. 16 pp.**†

217 Mayhew, Jonathan. *On the Limits of Obligation to Obey Government.* 1750.**

No state of nature or compact—good of the people. Reproduced in Bailyn, ed., *Pamphlets of the American Revolution.*

218 Mellen, John. A Great and Happy Doctrine. Boston, 1795. 34 pp.

219 Mellen, John. *Massachusetts Election Day Sermon.* Boston, 1797. 36 pp.**

Origin of government, basis for political obligation, basis for resistance, guide for good rulers and for deposing them.

220 Messer, Asa. *An Oration . . . in the Baptist Meeting House on the 4th of July. . . .* Providence, 1803. 14 pp.*

On the relation of knowledge, virtue, and religion to popular government.

221 Miller, Samuel. *A Discourse* [to] *the Society for Manumission of Slaves.* New York, 1797. 36 pp.

222 Minot, George Richard. *The History of the Insurrections in Massachusetts, in the year 1776 and the Rebellion Consequent Thereon.* Worcester, 1788. 192 pp.

A SELECTED LIST OF POLITICAL WRITINGS

223 Moore, Zephaniah Swift. *An Oration on the Anniversary of the Independence of the United States of America.* Worcester, 1802. 24 pp.**†

224 Morse, Jedidiah. *A Sermon Exhibiting the Present Dangers and Consequent Duties of the Citizens of the United States.* Charlestown, Mass., 1799. 59 pp.
Defense of the right and duty of ministers to preach on political subjects; posits a French plot to undermine United States government, and silencing ministry part of this.

225 Moultrie, William. *Memoirs of the American Revolution so far as it Related . . . North and South Carolina, and Georgia,* vols. I and II. 1802.

226 Nicholas, George. *A Letter . . . Justifying the Conduct of the Citizens of Kentucky* [re: Kentucky Resolutions of 1798]. Lexington, Ky., 1798. 42 pp.

227 Niles, Nathaniel. *Two Discourses on Liberty.* Newburyport, Mass., 1774. 38 pp.**†

228 Osgood, David. *A Discourse.* Boston, 1795. 40 pp.*

229 Osgood, David. *A Sermon.* Boston, 1788. 20 pp.

230 Osgood, David. *A Thanksgiving Sermon.* Boston, 1794. 20 pp.

231 Otis, James. *The Rights of the British Colonies Asserted and Proved. Boston Gazette,* July 23, 1764.**
Reproduced in Bailyn, ed., *Pamphlets of the American Revolution.*

232 Otis, James. *A Vindication of the British Colonies Against the Aspersions of the Halifax Gentleman, in His Letter to a Rhode Island Friend.* Boston, 1765.*
Response to pamphlet by Martin Howard. Reproduced in Bailyn, ed., *Pamphlets of the American Revolution.*

233 Page, John. *An Address to the Citizens of the District of York, in Virginia.* Richmond, 1794.

234 Paine, Thomas. *Common Sense Addressed to the Inhabitants of America.* Philadelphia, January 9, 1776. 45 pp.**
Reproduced in Jensen, ed., *Tracts of the American Revolution.*

235 Parker, Samuel. *A Sermon.* Boston, 1793. 42 pp.

236 Parsons, Jonathon. *A Consideration of Some Unconstitutional Measures Adopted and Practiced in This State.* Newburyport, Mass., 1784. 24 pp.

237 Parsons, Theodore. *A Forensic Dispute on the Legality of Enslaving the Africans.* Boston, 1773. 48 pp.

A SELECTED LIST OF POLITICAL WRITINGS

238 Parsons, Theophilus. *The Essex Result*. Newburyport, Mass., 1778. 68 pp.**†

239 Payson, Phillips. *A Sermon*. Boston, 1778. 30 pp.**†

240 Payson, Seth. *A Sermon*. Portsmouth, N.H., 1799. 23 pp.

241 Peck, Jedidiah. *The Political Wars of Otsego: Downfall of Jacobinism and Despotism*. . . . Cooperstown, N.Y., 1796. 123 pp.
Dangers of levelling spirit.

242 Perkins, John. [A Well-Wisher to Mankind]. *Theory of Agency: Or, An Essay on the Nature, Source and Extent of Moral Freedom*. Boston, 1771. 43 pp.**†

243 Pinkney, William. *Speech in the House of Delegates of Maryland*. Philadelphia, 1790. 22 pp.
Supports legislation (a) prohibiting shipment of slaves to the West Indies, (b) removing restrictions on manumission of slaves.

244 Pope, Nathaniel. *A Speech*. Richmond, 1800. 37 pp.
Concerning the Sedition Act.

245 Porter, Nathaniel. *A Discourse* (Election Day Sermon). Concord, N.H., 1804. 34 pp.*
On the qualities and conduct of good rulers.

246 Prescott, Benjamin. *A Free and Calm Consideration of the Unhappy Misunderstanding. . . Between the Parliament of Great Britain and These American Colonies*. Salem, Mass., 1774. 52 pp.*

247 Price, Richard. Observations on the Nature of Civil Liberty. *New York Gazette and Weekly Mercury*, July 22, 1776.*

248 Quincy, Josiah. *Observations on the . . . Boston Port Bill With Thoughts on Civil Society and Standing Armies*. Boston, 1774. 82 pp.*

249 Quincy, Josiah. *An Oration*. Boston, 1798. 31 pp.

250 Ramsay, David. *An Address to the Freemen of South Carolina, On the Subject of the Federal Constitution*. . . . Charleston, 1788, 12 pp.
Reproduced in Ford, ed., *Pamphlets on the Constitution of the United States*, (Brooklyn, 1888), pp. 373–380.

251 Ramsay, David. *The History of the American Revolution*. Philadelphia, 1789. 390 pp.**†

252 Ramsay, David. *The History of the Revolution of South Carolina*. 2 vols. Trenton, 1785.*

253 Ramsay, David. An Oration on the Advantages of American Independence. *Pennsylvania Gazette*, January 20, 1779.
The arts and sciences in a new republic.

A Selected List of Political Writings

254 Randolph, Edmund. *Letter on the Federal Constitution.* October 16, 1787.*

Found in Ford, ed., *Pamphlets on the Constitution of the United States* (Brooklyn, 1888), pp. 261–276.

255 Reese, Thomas. *An Essay on the Influence of Religion, in Civil Society.* Charleston, 1788. 87 pp.

256 Rice, David. *Slavery Inconsistent With Justice and Good Policy.* Augusta, Ky., 1792. 23 pp.**†

257 Ross, Robert. *A Sermon* [on] *the Union of the Colonies.* New York, 1776. 28 pp*.

The reasons for separating from Britain.

258 Rush, Benjamin. [A Pennsylvanian]. *An Address to the Inhabitants of the British Settlements in America Upon Slave-Keeping.* Philadelphia, 1773. 28 pp.**†

259 Rush, Benjamin. *Considerations on the Injustice and Impolicy of Punishing Murder by Death.* Philadelphia, 1792. 19 pp.

260 Rush, Benjamin. *Considerations Upon the Present Test-Law of Pennsylvania.* Philadelphia, 1784. 23 pp.

In opposition to oaths. Rush was a prominent Quaker.

261 Rush, Benjamin. *Essays Litarary, Moral and Philosophical.* Philadelphia, 1798.

262 Rush, Benjamin. *On the Superiority of a Bicameral to a Unicameral Legislature.* Philadelphia, 1777. 24 pp.*

263 Rush, Benjamin. *A Plan for the Establishment of Public Schools and the Diffusion of Knowledge in Pennsylvania; To Which Are Added, Thoughts upon the Mode of Education, Proper in a Republic.* Philadelphia, 1786. 23 pp.*†

264 Rush, Benjamin. *Thoughts Upon Female Education, Accommodated to the Present State of Society, Manners, and Government in the United States of America.* Philadelphia, 1787. 17 pp.*

265 Rush, Benjamin. *A Vindication of the Address. . . .* Philadelphia, 1773, 54 pp.

Response to a critique of the piece preceeding this one.

266 Rush, Justice [Jacob]. The Nature and Importance of an Oath— the Charge to a Jury. In *The Rural Magazine or Vermont Repository, Rutland, Vt.,* vol. II, pp. 469–475. 1796.**†

267 Sanders, Daniel Clarke. *A Sermon.* Vergennes, Vt., 1798. 26 pp.*

On virtue and patriotism.

A Selected List of Political Writings

268   De Saussure, Henry. [Phocion]. *Letters on the Question of the Justice and Expediency of . . . Alterations of the Representation in the Legislature of South Carolina. . . .* Charleston, 1795. 33 pp.*
      Property should be represented as well as people.

269   De Saussure, Henry W. *Address to the Citizens of South Carolina.* Charleston, 1800. 34 pp.
      On the obligation of high officials to support the policies of the administration in which they serve.

270   Scott, John. *War Inconsistent with the Doctrine and Example of Jesus Christ.* Philadelphia, 1799. 26 pp.

271   Seabury, Samuel. *An Alarm to the Legislature.* New York, 1775. 13 pp.
      A Tory attacks the extralegal government being developed by colonists.

272   Sherman, Roger. *Remarks on a Pamphlet Entitled "A Dissertation on the Political Union."* New Haven, 1784. 43 pp.

273   Sherwood, Samuel, *A Sermon Containing Scriptural Instructions to Civil Rulers.* New Haven, 1774. 42 pp.

274   Shute, Daniel. *An Election Sermon.* Boston, 1768. 55 pp.**†

275.   Smalley, John. *On the Evils of a Weak Government: A Sermon.* Hartford, 1800. 51 pp.**
      Especially good on the advantages of republican government.

276   Smith, Elihu H. *A Discourse to the Society for Promoting the Manumission of Slaves.* New York, 1798. 30 pp.

277   Smith, John. *An Oration. . . In Commemoration of the Anniversary of American Independence.* Suffield, Mass., 1799. 15 pp.

278   Smith, Melancthon [A Plebian]. *An Address to the People. . . of New York Showing the Necessity of Making Amendments to the Proposed U.S. Constitution.* New York, 1788. 22 pp.*
      Reproduced in Ford, ed., *Pamphlets on the Constitution of the United States.*

279   Smith, Samuel Harrison. *Remarks on Education: Illustrating the Close Connection Between Virtue and Wisdom.* Philadelphia, 1798. 92 pp.**
      Reproduced in Rudolph, ed., *Essays on Education in the Early Republic.*

280   Smith, William. *A Sermon on the Present Situation in American Affairs.* Philadelphia, 1775. 32 pp.

281   Smith, William Loughton. *A Comparative View of the Constitutions of the Several States.* Charleston, 1796. 34 pp.

282   Stearns, Josiah. *Two Sermons.* Newburyport, Mass., 1777. 19 pp. (First sermon only.)

A Selected List of Political Writings

The right of oppressed people to resist their rulers, and the duty of Americans to do so.

283 Stearns, William. *A View of the Controversy Subsisting Between Great Britain and the American Colonies.* Watertown, Mass., 1775. 33 pp.

284 Stearns, William and Daniel Bigelow, eds. Editorial. *Massachusetts Spy,* June 21, 1776.
On freedom of the press.

285 Stevens, John. *Observations on Government, Including Some Animadversions on Mr. Adams' Defence of the Constitutions of Government of the United States of America.* New York, 1787. 56 pp.**

286 Stillman, Samuel. *Massachusetts Election Day Sermon.* Boston, 1779. 38 pp.**
Good on general Whig principles.

287 Stoddard, Amos. *An Oration.* Portland, Mass., 1799. 30 pp.
Justifies Alien and Sedition Acts by reference to plot against American religion and morals.

288 Stone, Timothy. *Election Sermon.* Hartford, 1792. 35 pp.**†

289 Story, Isaac. *The Love of Our Country Recommended and Enforced.* Boston, 1775. 23 pp.

290 Strong, Cyprian. *Connecticut Election Day Sermon.* Hartford, 1799. 46 pp.
Ultimate purpose of a civil government is to advance the progress of a spiritual kingdom.

291 Strong, Nathan. *The Reasons and Design of Public Punishment. A Sermon* (at the execution of Moses Dunbar). Hartford, 1777. 18 pp.

292 Sullivan, James. *Observations Upon the Government of the United States of America.* Boston, 1791. 55 pp.

293 Sullivan, James [Cassius].Ten essays in the *Massachusetts Gazette,* September 18–December 25, 1787.
Reproduced in Ford, ed., *Pamphlets on the Constitution of the United States.*

294 Swanwick, John. *Considerations on an Act of the Legislature of Virginia . . . For the Establishment of Religious Freedom.* Philadelphia, 1786, 26 pp.
Defends a State-established church.

295 Swift, Dean. Causes of a Country's Growing Rich and Flourishing. *Worcester Magazine,* June, 1786.*†

296 Taggart, Samuel. *An Oration on the . . . Anniversary of Independence.* Northampton, Mass., 1804. 30 pp.*

297 Tennent, William. *Mr. Tennent's Speech on the Dissenting Petition.* . . . Charleston, 1777. 28 pp.

298 Thacher, Oxenbridge. *Considerations on Election of Counsellors.* . . . Boston, 1761. 8 pp.

299 Thacher, Oxenbridge. *The Sentiments of a British American.* Boston, 1764. 16 pp.*
Against the Stamp Act tax. Reproduced in Bailyn, ed., *Pamphlets of the American Revolution.*

300 Thatcher, Peter. *An Address to . . . The Massachusetts Charitable Fire Society.* Boston, 1805. 24 pp.

301 Thatcher, Peter. *A Sermon.* Boston, 1793. 27 pp.
Prepare for defense regardless of likelihood of being attacked.

302 Thayer, Nathaniel. *A Discourse.* Boston, 1798. 30 pp.

303 Thomas, Barnard. *A Sermon.* Boston, 1789. 27 pp.
War is not all bad; some good comes of it.

304 Thomson, John. *An Enquiry Concerning the Liberty and Licentiousness of the Press, and the Uncontroulable Nature of the Human Mind.* New York, 1801. 79 pp.**
One of the best on freedom of expression. Partially reproduced in Levy, ed., *Freedom of the Press from Zenger to Jefferson,* pp. 284–316.

305 Trumbull, Benjamin. *A Discourse Delivered* [to] *the Freemen of the Town of New Haven.* New Haven, 1773. 38 pp.**
Rulers, magistrates, public officials—all should come from among, enjoy the confidence of, and be dependent on the people they govern.

306 Tucker, John. *An Election Sermon.* Boston, 1771. 54 pp.**†

307 Tucker, Josiah. *The True Interest of Britain Set Forth in Regard to the Colonies.* Philadelphia, 1776. 66 pp.

308 Tucker, St. George. *A Dissertation on Slavery With a Proposal for the Gradual Abolition of it in the State of Virginia.* Philadelphia, 1796. 106 pp.**

309 Tucker, St. George. *A Letter to a Member of Congress Respecting the Alien and Sedition Laws.* Philadelphia, 1799. 48 pp.*
Response to a perception of French attempts to undermine the United States. Sees America as "the chosen land."

310 Tucker, Thomas Tudor [Philodemus]. *Conciliatory Hints, Attempting, by a Fair State of Matters, to Remove Party Prejudice.* Charleston, 1784. 34 pp.**†

311 Turner, Charles. *Massachusetts Election Day Sermon.* Boston, 1773. 45 pp.*

Public officials, including kings, should be servants of the people.

312   Wales, Samuel. *The Dangers of Our National Prosperity.* Hartford, 1785. 39 pp.*

Virtue more important than prosperity to a people.

313   Warren, Mercy. [A Columbian Patriot]. *Observations on the New Constitution and on the Federal and State Conventions.* Boston, 1788. 22 pp.*

314   Wattes, Thomas. Charge Delivered to the Grand Juries of Beaufort. . . . *City Gazette and Daily Advertiser,* Charleston, June 5, 1789.

A standard statement of general political principles of the time.

315   Webster, Noah. *Attention! or, New Thoughts on a Serious Subject; Being an Inquiry into the Excise Laws of Connecticut.* Hartford, 1789. 18 pp.*

316   Webster, Noah. *Effects of Slavery on Morals and Industry.* Hartford, 1793. 49 pp.**

United States will benefit economically from gradual elevation of slaves to free tenantry.

317   Webster, Noah. *An Examination into the Leading Principles of the Federal Constitution. . . With Answers to the Principle Objections. . . .* Philadelphia, 1787. 55 pp.**

Reproduced in Ford, ed., *Pamphlets on the Constitution of the United States.*

318   Webster, Noah. *On the Education of Youth in America.* Boston, 1790. 37 pp.*

Reproduced in Rudolph, ed., *Essays on Education in the Early Republic.*

319   Webster, Noah. *An Oration on the Anniversary of the Declaration of Independence.* New Haven, 1802. 30 pp.**†

320   Webster, Noah. *Sketches of American Policy.* Hartford, 1787. 45 pp.*

Advocates strong central government.

321   Webster, Peletiah. *A Dissertation on the Political Union and Constitution of the Thirteen United States.* Philadelphia, 1783. 47 pp.

322   Webster, Peletiah. *Political Essays,* Philadelphia, 1791. 504 pp.

323   Webster, Peletiah. *Remarks on the Address of Sixteen Members of the Assembly of Pennsylvania . . . with some Strictures on their Objections to the Constitution Recommended by the late Federal Convention.* Philadelphia, 1787. 28 pp.

324   Webster, Peletiah. [A Citizen of Philadelphia]. *The Weakness of Brutus Exposed: or, Some Remarks in Vindication of the Constitution*

Proposed by the Late Federal Convention, Against the Objections and Gloomy Fears of that Writer Humbly Offered to the Public. Philadelphia, 1787. 22 pp.*

Reproduced in Ford, ed., *Pamphlets on the Constitution of the United States.*

325 Webster, Samuel. *Massachusetts Election Day Sermon.* Boston, 1777. 44 pp.**

Obligations of both citizens and rulers, and what accounts for tyranny and the right to resist.

326 Weems, M.L. *The True Patriot: or an Oration on the Beauties and Beatitudes of a Republic. . . .* Philadelphia, 1802. 56 pp.

327 Wells, Richard. *A Few Political Reflections Submitted to the Consideration of the British Colonies.* Philadelphia, 1774. 77 pp.

A moderate assessment of what America should do.

328 Wells, Richard. *The Middle Line, or . . . Hints for Ending the Differences Between Great Britain and the Colonies.* Philadelphia, 1775. 48 pp.**

Clever, practical, moderate, but still sees the Americans as equal to the British.

329 West, Samuel. *On the Right to Rebel Against Governors.* Boston, 1776. 63 pp.**†

330 Wheaton, Levi. *An Oration Delivered to the Society of Blackfriars.* Boston, 1797. 22 pp.

A plea for reason, patience, and charity on the parts of citizenry and public officials.

331 Whitaker, Nathaniel. *The Reward of Toryism.* Newburyport, Mass., 1783. 32 pp.

332 White, William. *A Sermon on the Duty of Civil Disobedience.* Philadelphia, 1799. 26 pp.

333 Whiting, William [Impartial Reason]. *Address to the Inhabitants of Berkshire County.* Boston, 1778. 11 pp.**†

334 Whitman, Benjamin. *An Oration . . . On the Anniversary of American Independence.* Boston, 1803. 24 pp.*

Supports an elitist theory of democracy.

335 Williams, Abraham. *An Election Sermon.* Boston, 1762. 28 pp.**†

336 Williams, Samuel. *A Discourse on the Love of Our Country.* Salem, Mass., 1775. 29 pp.**

A good summary of basic political principles.

337 Williams, Samuel. *The Influence of Christianity on Civil Society.* Boston, 1780. 32 pp.**

Christian beliefs and commitments are essential to the maintenance of free government.

338 Williams, Samuel. *The Natural and Civil History of Vermont*. Walpole, N.H., 1794. 400 pp.**†

339 Wilson, Alexander. *Oration on the Power and Value of Natural Liberty*. Philadelphia, 1801. 23 pp.*

A bit "preachy," but good on the nature of liberty. Presents the attachment to equality as incompatible with liberty.

340 Wilson, James. *On Municipal Law*, Part V of *The Works of James Wilson*, edited by Bird Wilson. Originally published in Philadelphia, 1804. 30 pp.**†

341 Witherspoon, John. *The Dominion of Providence Over the Passions of Men*. Philadelphia, 1776. 78 pp.

The duties of patriots in the struggle for independence.

342 Witherspoon, John. *On Training Children and Their Parents*. Philadelphia, 1775. 37 pp.*

Reproduced in Wilson Smith, ed., *Theories of Education in Early America* (Indianapolis: Bobbs-Merrill, 1973), pp. 184–220.

343 Witter, Ezra. *Two Sermons on the Party Spirit and Divided State of the Country, Civil and Religious*. Springfield, Mass., 1801. 28 pp.*

Divisions in nation traced to the split in the 1780s over a stronger central government, furthered by false doctrines bred in Europe.

344 Woodward, Israel B. *American Liberty and Independence. A Discourse*. Litchfield, Conn., 1798. 26 pp.*

On the consequences and rewards of being independent of other peoples. Compares American with French views on freedom.

345 Woolman, John. *Considerations on Keeping Negroes . . . Part Second*. Philadelphia, 1762. 52 pp.*

Part I published in 1754. The two published together as *Some Considerations on the Keeping of Negroes* (New York: Grossman, 1976).

346 Woolman, John. *A Plea for the Poor*. Philadelphia, 1763. 24 pp.*

347 Wortman, Tunis. *An Oration on the Influence of Social Institutions Upon Human Morals and Happiness*. New York, 1796. 31 pp.*

Democratic philosophy of social reform.

348 Wortman, Tunis. *A Solemn Address to Christians and Patriots . . . In Answer to a Pamphlet "Serious Considerations."* New York, 1800. 20 pp.*

Preachers dabbling in politics and civil rulers interposing in church affairs result in both becoming corrupted.

349 Wortman, Tunis. *A Treatise Concerning Political Inquiry, and the Liberty of the Press.* New York, 1800. 296 pp.*

350 Yates Robert [Sydney]. To the Citizens of the State of New York. *Daily Patriotic Register,* New York, June 13 and 14, 1788.

351 Zubly, John Joachim. *An Humble Enquiry into the Nature of the Dependency of the American Colonies. . . .* Charleston, 1769. 28 pp.

352 Zubly, John Joachim. *The Law of Liberty. . . .* Philadelphia, 1775. 41 pp.

353 Zubly, John Joachim, [A Freeman]. *Calm and Respectful Thoughts on the Negative of the Crown on a Speaker Chosen and Presented by the Representatives of the People.* Savannah, 1772. 24 pp.

B. ITEMS WHERE THE AUTHOR IS DISPUTED OR UNKNOWN

354 *The Address and Petition of a Number of the Clergy of Various Denominations . . . Relative to the Passing of a Law Against Vice and Immorality.* Philadelphia, 1793. 13 pp.
Proposes outlawing theatrical exhibitions, among other things.

355 *An Address of the Convention for Framing a New Constitution of Government of the State of New Hampshire.* Portsmouth, N.H., 1781. 64 pp.
Why the old constitution is deficient.

356 Aequus. From the Craftsman [London]. *Massachusetts Gazette and Boston Newsletter,* March 6, 1766.**†

357 Agricola. [untitled essay]. *Massachusetts Spy,* October 22, 1772.**
Very Lockian statement of basic principles on government.

358 Agrippa [James Winthrop?] *Massachusetts Gazette,* November 23– February 5, 1788.
Reproduced in Ford, ed., *Pamphlets on the Constitution of the United States.*

359 Amendments Proposed to the Federal Constitution Proposed by the New York State Convention. *Boston Gazette,* August 18, 1788.*

360 Amicus. To the Printer. *Columbian Herald,* Columbia, S.C., August 28, 1788.
Anti-Federalist statement on the right of recall.

361 Amicus Republicae. *Address to the Public, Containing Some Remarks on the Present Political State of the American Republicks, etc.* Exeter, 1786. 36 pp.**†

A Selected List of Political Writings

362   [anon.] *Address of a Convention of Delegates from the Abolition Society, to the Citizens of the United States.* Philadelphia, 1794. 7 pp.

363   [anon.] *An Address . . . Respecting the Alien and Sedition Laws.* Richmond, 1798. 63 pp.

364   [anon.] *An Address to the Inhabitants of the County of Berkshire Respecting Their Present Opposition to Civil Government.* Hartford, 1778. 28 pp.*

365   [anon.] *The Alarm: or, an Address to the People of Pennsylvania, on the Late Resolve of Congress, for Totally Suppressing All Power and Authority Derived from the Crown of Great Britain.* Philadelphia, 1776. 4 pp.**†

366   [anon.] Ambition. *City Gazette and Daily Advertiser,* Charleston, June 6, 1789.*†

367   [anon.] *Boston Gazette,* September 17, 1764**†

368   [anon.] *A Candid Examination of the Address of the Minority of the Council of Censors.* Philadelphia, 1784. 40 pp.

369   [anon.] *Declaration and Address of His Majesty's Loyal Associated Refugees, Assembled at Rhode Island.* New York, 1779. 36 pp.

370   [anon.] *A Declaration of Independence Published by the Congress at Philadelphia in 1776 With a Counter-Declaration Published at New York in 1781.* New York, 1781. 24 pp.
The Tories declare their independence from revolutionary America.

371   [anon.] Discussion of Revision of South Carolina's Code of Law. *City Gazette and Daily Advertiser,* Charleston, February 3, 1789.

372   [anon.] *Dissertation Upon the Constitutional Freedom of the Press.* Boston, 1801. 54 pp.

373   [anon.] An English Patriot's Creed, Anno Domini, 1775. *Massachusetts Spy,* January 19, 1776.*†

374   [anon.] *An Essay of a Frame of Government for Pennsylvania.* Philadelphia, 1776. 16 pp.*
Summary of Whig ideas, with specific proposals for a state constitution.

375   [anon.] *An Essay Upon Government.* Philadelphia, 1775. 125 pp.**
Origin of government; society, government, and property defined; authority and obligations of rulers; and the rights and obligations of citizens.

376   [anon.] *A Few Salutary Hints Pointing out the Policy and Consequences of Permitting British Subjects to Engross Our Trade and Become Our Citizens.* Charleston, 1786. 16 pp.

377   [anon.] *Four Letters on Interesting Subjects.* Philadelphia, 1776. 24 pp.**†

A SELECTED LIST OF POLITICAL WRITINGS

378   [anon.] *A Friend to the Judiciary.* New York, 1801. 60 pp.
Concerning the independence of the judiciary.

379   [anon.] *An Impartial Review of the Rise and Progress of the Controversy Between . . . Federalists and Republicans.* Philadelphia, 1800. 50 pp.

380   [anon.] *A Letter from a Virginian to the Members of the Continental Congress.* Boston, 1774. 31 pp.*
A restrained, even-tempered plea for Congress to be patient and to seek accommodation with Britain.

381   [anon.] *Letter to a Member of the General Assembly of Virginia on the Subject of a Conspiracy of the Slaves.* Richmond, 1801. 21 pp.

382   [anon.] Letter to the Editor. *Boston Gazette,* July 22, 1765.*
"No taxation without representation" applied to western Massachusetts towns vis-a-vis Massachusetts legislature.

383   [anon.] Letter to the Editor. *Massachusetts Spy,* April 4, 1771.*
The nature of government.

384   [anon.] Letter to the Editor. *Massachusetts Spy,* August 22, 1771.
The nature of government.

385   [anon.] Letter to the Editor. *Boston Gazette,* December 31, 1787.*
Short, pithy summary of views on education.

386   [anon.] *A Letter to the People of Pennsylvania, Occasioned by the Assembly's Passing that Important Act, for Constituting the Judges of the Supreme Courts and Common-Pleas, During Good Behavior.* Philadelphia. 1760. 39 pp.*
Reproduced in Bailyn, ed., *Pamphlets of the American Revolution.*

387   [anon.] *A Memorial and Remonstrance Presented to the General Assembly of the State of Virginia . . . in Consequence of a Bill . . . for the Establishment of Religion by Law.* Worcester, 1786. 16 pp.*

388   [anon.] *Northampton* [Mass.] *Returns to the Convention on the Constitution.* 1780. In Oscar Handlin and Mary Handlin, eds. *The Popular Sources of Political Authority* (Cambridge, Mass.: Harvard University Press, 1966), pp. 572–587.*
Comprehensive critique of the Massachusetts Constitution of 1780, especially interesting on property requirement in voting for lower house.

389   [anon.] *No Standing Army in the British Colonies.* New York, 1775. 18 pp.

390   [anon.] Number I and Number II. *City Gazette and Daily Advertiser,* Charleston, March 16, 17, and 18, 1789.
Parliamentary privilege and freedom of the press.

A Selected List of Political Writings

391 [anon.] On the Management of Children in Infancy. *South Carolina Gazette,* November 1, 1773.*
Brief statement on child-rearing up to literacy at age seven.

392 [anon.] *The People the Best Governors: Or a Plan of Government Founded on the Just Principles of Natural Freedom.* New Hampshire, 1776. 11 pp.**†

393 [anon.] *The Political Establishment of the United States of America.* Philadelphia, 1784. 25 pp.*
Inadequacy of the Articles of Confederation—a new constitution is required.

394 [anon.] *The Power and Grandeur of Great Britain Founded on the Liberty of the Colonies. . . .* New York, 1768. 24 pp.**
The British government does not impose taxes; the people make voluntary contributions for revenue.

395 [anon.] *Proposals to Amend and Perfect the Policy of the Government of the United States of America.* Baltimore, 1782. 36 pp.*

396 [anon.] Review [in two parts] of John Adams's "Defence of the Constitutions . . . of America," taken from the *Monthly Review* (in London) and reprinted in the *New York Packet,* September 25 and 28, 1787.

397 [anon.] *Rudiments of Law and Government Deduced from the Law of Nature.* Charleston, 1783. 56 pp.**†

398 [anon.] *Serious Considerations on Several Important Subjects, viz. On War . . . Observations on Slavery . . . Spiritous Liquors.* Philadelphia, 1778. 48 pp.

399 [anon.] To the Printers. *Boston Gazette,* July 15, 1765.
Americans are equal to the British at home.

400 [anon.] To the Printer. *Boston Gazette,* December 2, 1765.*
Succinct statement of general principles in response to the Stamp Act.

401 [anon.] [two untitled essays]. *The United States Magazine,* January, Providence, 1779 vol. I, pp. 5–41, 155–159.*
The first summarizes traditional attitudes toward government. The second outlines reasons for distaste for established religion.

402 A. Z. Virtuous Pennsylvanians. *South Carolina Gazette,* November 29, 1773.

403 Benevolus. Poverty. *City Gazette and Daily Advertiser,* Charleston, December 8, 1789.*†

404 Berkshire's Grievances. *Statement of Berkshire County Representatives,* and *Address to the Inhabitants of Berkshire.* Pittsfield, Mass., 1778.**†

405 *Bills of Rights and Amendments Proposed by Massachusetts and Virginia* [to the Proposed United States Constitution]. 1788.*

Reproduced in Kenyon, ed. *The Antifederalists,* pp. 421–39.

406 Bostonians. Serious Questions Proposed to All Friends to The Rights of Mankind, With Suitable Answers. *Boston Gazette,* November 19, 1787.*†

407 Britannus Americanus. *Boston Gazette,* March 17, 1766.**†

408 Brutus [Thomas Treadwell? Robert Yates?] Against the New Federal Constitution. *Worcester Magazine,* December, 1787.

List of objections to the proposed constitution.

409 Brutus [Thomas Treadwell? Robert Yates?] No. I: To the Citizens of the State of New York. *New York Journal and Weekly Register,* October 18, 1787.*

Not reproduced in the volume edited by Kenyon (as are several of the other essays by Brutus), this one expresses the fears that under the new Constitution the government will be too far from the people, and the country too heterogeneous.

410 Brutus [Thomas Treadwell? Robert Yates?] No. II. *New York Journal and Weekly Register,* November 1, 1787.*

411 Brutus [Thomas Treadwell? Robert Yates?] No. IV: To the People of the State of New York. *New York Journal and Weekly Register,* November 29, 1787.*

Not reproduced in Kenyon, this essay explores the relationship between the people and their representatives.

412 Brutus [Thomas Treadwell? Robert Yates?] No. V: To the People of the State of New York, *New York Journal and Weekly Register,* December 13, 1787.*

Not reproduced in Kenyon, it proposes that the Constitution is an original compact among the people dissolving other compacts, rather than an agreement among the states.

413 Brutus [Thomas Treadwell? Robert Yates?] No. VI: To the People of the State of New York, *New York Journal and Weekly Register,* December 27, 1787.*

Reproduced in Kenyon, ed., *The Antifederalists.* Will the states be absorbed?

414 Brutus Junior. Letter to the Editor. *New York Journal,* November 8, 1787.

415 By a Gentleman Born and Bred. *Remarks on the Bill of Rights, Constitution and Some Acts of the General Assembly of the State of Virginia.* Richmond, 1801. 35 pp.

A SELECTED LIST OF POLITICAL WRITINGS

416   Cato. Discourse Upon Libel. *Massachusetts Spy,* April 19, 1771.

417   Centinel [Samuel Bryan?] No. I & No. II: To the People of Pennsylvania. *Maryland Journal,* October 30, and November 2, respectively, 1787.

     A widely-read Anti-federalist. Reproduced in Kenyon, ed., *The Antifederalists.*

418   Cincinnatus. Number I, Number II, Number V, and Number VI: To James Wilson, esq. *New York Journal,* November 1, 8, 29, and December 6, respectively, 1787.

     An Anti-Federalist response to James Wilson's defense of the proposed Constitution. Number II especially notable on freedom of the press and trial by jury. Number VI speaks to taxation and public finance.

419   A Citizen. To the Citizens of Richmond, Not Freeholders. *Virginia Argus,* Richmond, July 31, 1801.

     In favor of broad suffrage.

420   A Citizen of Connecticut. *An Address to the Legislature and People of Connecticut on the Subject of Dividing the State into Districts for the Election of Representatives in Congress.* New Haven, 1791. 37 pp.

421   Columbus. *A Letter to a Member of Congress, Respecting the Alien and Sedition Laws.* Boston, 1799.

422   Common Sense. [untitled essay]. *Massachusetts Gazette,* January, 1788.

     Arguments in support of the proposed Constitution.

423   A Constant Customer. Extract of a Letter from a Gentleman in the Country to His Friend. *Massachusetts Spy,* February 18, 1773.*†

424   *The Constitution of the Pennsylvania Society for Promoting the Abolition of Slavery . . . to Which are Added the Acts . . . of Pennsylvania for the Gradual Abolition of Slavery.* Philadelphia, 1788. 29 pp.

425   Continental Congress. Appeal to the Inhabitants of Quebec, October 26, 1774, *Journals of the Continental Congress,* vol. I, pp. 105–113.**†

426   Council of Censors of Pennsylvania. Minority Report. *To the Freemen of Pennsylvania.* Philadelphia, 1784, 12 pp.

     Anti-constitutionalists in Pennsylvania list the failures of the 1776 Pennsylvania Constitution.

427   A Countryman. Letter to the Editor. *New York Journal,* Dec. 6, 1787.*

     The social disruptions caused by the war.

428   A Countryman. Letter II. *New York Journal,* Dec. 13, 1787.

Discusses section in the Constitution on the importation of slaves. Confused by the terms *Federalist* and *anti-Federalist.*

429   D.D. Extract from a Thanksgiving Sermon, Delivered in the County of Middlesex. *Worcester Magazine,* January, 1787.*

Defense of the Massachusetts government against the charges by Daniel Shays.

430   Deliberator. To the Printers. *Freeman's Journal,* Philadelphia, February 20, 1788.

In opposition to the proposed Constitution.

431   Demophilus [George Bryan?] *The Genuine Principles of the Ancient Saxon, or English*[,] Constitution, Philadelphia, 1776. 46 pp.**†

432   De Witte, John [pseud.] To the Editor. *American Herald,* Worcester, December 3, 1787.

An Anti-Federalist essay.

433   An Elector. To the Free Electors of This Town. *Boston Gazette,* April 28, 1788.**†

434   F.A. A Letter to a Right Noble Lord. *Boston Gazette,* July 22, 29, August 5, 12, 26, and September 2, 1765.

Six-part essay in response to a member of Parliament who defended the Stamp Act.

435   A Farmer. To the Editor. *Maryland Gazette and Baltimore Advertiser,* March 7, 1788.

The new Constitution will not abate war or prevent despotism.

436   Farmer. To the Printer. *Pennsylvania Packet,* Philadelphia, November 5, 1776.*

Exposition of Whig ideology in relatively concise form.

437   A Federalist. Letter to the Editor. *Boston Gazette,* December 3, 1787.

A general defense of the proposed Constitution.

438   A Federalist. To the People of Pennsylvania. *Maryland Journal,* November 6, 1787.

In response to Centinel.

439   Form of Ratification of the Federal Constitution by the State of New York. *Boston Gazette,* August 11, 1788.*

440   Freeborn American. To the Printers. *Boston Gazette and Country Journal,* March 9, 1767.

The duties of a free press.

A Selected List of Political Writings

441 Freeholders of Boston. Instructions to Their Representatives. *Boston Gazette,* May 28, 1764.*
Summary of Whig ideas and values.

442 Freeholders of Newbury-Port. Instructions to Their Representatives. *Boston Gazette,* November 4, 1765.
Summary of basic values.

443 Freeholders of Plymouth. Instructions to Their Representatives. *Boston Gazette,* November 4, 1765.

444 Freeman, [Untitled essay reproduced from the June 6 issue of the *New York Gazette*]. *Georgia Gazette,* September 19, 26, and October 3, 1765.**
Virtual representation, the nature of representation, and the relationship of the American people to the British people.

445 Freeman. Another Letter from Freeman. *Georgia Gazette,* October 26, 1769.*
In response to Libertas, supports the position that the people are sovereign and can withdraw support from a legislature that breaks the contract.

446 Hamden. On Patriotism. *South Carolina Gazette,* November 29, 1773.
Brief discussion of private interest versus public good.

447 Hermes. *The Oracle of Liberty, and Mood of Establishing a Government.* Philadelphia, 1791, 39 pp.

448 Historicus. *Royal South Carolina Gazette,* Charleston, March 28, 1782.
An untitled essay laying out the Tory view of republican government.

449 Homespun. A Countryman. *South Carolina Gazette,* October 31, 1774.*
Brief discussion of how deliberation on public affairs should proceed, who should be allowed to deliberate, etc.

450 Hortensius. *An Essay on the Liberty of the Press,* Richmond, 1799. 30 pp.*

451 An Impartial Citizen. *A Dissertation Upon the Constitutional Freedom of the Press.* Boston, 1801. 54 pp.**†

452 Instructions of the Town of New-Braintree to its Representative. *Worcester Magazine,* June, 1786

453 J. Letter to the Printer. *The Boston Evening Post,* May 23, 1763, Supplement.

A Selected List of Political Writings

454 J.B.F. To the Electors of Anne-Arundel County. *Maryland Journal and Baltimore Advertiser,* February 23, 1787.

In response to Samuel Chase's piece in the same paper, J.B.F. attacks the practice of instructing representatives.

455 The Journeyman Carpenters. An Address. *American Daily Advertiser,* Philadelphia, May 11, 1791.

Justifies their strike and striking in general.

456 Junius, Camillus. [untitled]. *The Argus, or Greenleaf's New Daily Advertiser,* New York, March 15 and April 6, 1796.*

Freedom of speech—the legislature has no "privilege" against criticism.

457 A Landholder. For the New Federal Constitution. *Worcester Magazine,* December, 1787.

458 Leonidas. *A Reply to Lucius Junius Brutus' Examination of the President's Answer to the New Haven Remonstrance.* New York, 1801. 62. pp.*

Leonidas is attacking Brutus, a Federalist: topics range from the limits to majority rule to presidential power of appointment and removal.

459 L.Q. To the Printers. *Boston Gazette,* May 16, 1763.

A reply to T.Q., whose discussion on the separation of powers (prohibition on multiple office holding) appeared in the April 18 edition of the same paper.

460 Majority and minority reports on the repeal of the Sedition Act. February 25, 1799. *Annals of Congress,* 5th Cong., 3rd Session, pp. 2987–2990, 3033–3014.*

461 Medium. On the Proposed Federal Constitution. *Worcester Magazine,* December, 1787.

462 A Member of the General Committee. To Freeman. *South Carolina Gazette,* October 18, 1769.

Counters a critic of the Stamp Act.

463 *A Memorial and Remonstrance Presented to the General Assembly of the State of Virginia . . . In Consequence of a Bill . . . for the Establishment of Religion by Law.* Worcester, 1786. 16 pp.*

464 *Memorial Presented to Congress . . . by Different Societies Promoting Abolition of Slavery.* 1792. 31 pp.

465 Monitor. No. VI, *Massachusetts Spy,* January 9, 1772.**

A community has the right to reward every virtue and punish every vice. A list of virtues is included.

466 Monitor. To the New Appointed Councellors of the Province of Massachusetts-Bay. *Massachusetts Spy,* August 18, 1774.**†

A Selected List of Political Writings

467 Monitor. [untitled]. *Massachusetts Gazette,* October 30, 1787.
Supports the proposed Constitution.

468 M.Y. A Letter from a Son of Liberty in Boston to a Son of Liberty
in Bristol County. *Boston Evening Post,* May 12, 1766.
Defends lawyers as members of the legislature against those who would
exclude lawyers from political office.

469 A Native of this Colony. An Address to the Convention of the
Colony . . . of Virginia, on the Subject of Government in General
and Recommending a Particular Form to Their Attention. *Virginia
Gazette,* June 8, 1776.**
The basic principle underlying each form of government, with a good
discussion of virtue (public versus private).

470 Nestor. To the Publick. *Worcester Magazine,* December, 1786.**
The blessings of civil society and the need for seeking the common
good to remain a civil society (of the five essays, the first is best).

471 Nov Anglicanus. To the Inhabitants of the Province. *Boston Gazette,*
May 14, 1764.
A response to the Stamp Act.

472 An Observer. To the Editor. *American Herald,* Worcester, December
3, 1787.
A rejoinder to Federalist paper number five.

473 An Officer of the Late Continental Army. Against the Federal
Constitution. *Worcester Magazine,* December, 1787.

474 An Old Whig. To the Printer. *Massachusetts Gazette,* November
27, 1787.

475 An Old Whig. To the Printer. *Freeman's Journal,* Philadelphia,
November 28, 1787.
On constitutional conventions.

476 An Old Whig. To the Printer. *Maryland Gazette and Baltimore
Advertiser,* November 2, 1788.
An opponent of the proposed Constitution predicts that the "necessary
and proper" clause will be used to expand the powers granted Congress
in Article I.

477 One of the Subscribers. Letter to the Editor. *New York Packet,*
September 21, 1789.*
Propositions for reforming the system of public education in Boston,
for both sexes.

478 An Other Citizen. On Conventions. *Worcester Magazine,* September,
1786.*

Opposed to the county conventions called by those opposed to the operation of Massachusetts courts. These conventions eventually led to Shays's Rebellion.

479   P. . . . To the Printers. *New York Mercury,* January 28, 1765.
A typical response to the Stamp Act.

480   Penn, William [pseud.] To the Printer. *Independent Gazetteer,* Philadelphia, January 3, 1788.
An Anti-Federalist keying on the topic of presidential veto.

481   *Personal Slavery Established by the Suffrages of Custom and Right Reason.* Philadelphia, 1773. 26 pp
A reply to a piece by Anthony Benezet, this essay outlines the standard arguments used in favor of slavery.

482   Philadelphiensis [Benjamin Workman?] To the Printer. *Freeman's Journal,* Philadelphia, February 6, 20, and April 9, 1788.
An Anti-Federalist focusing on the executive branch.

483   Philanthropos. [untitled]. *Pennsylvania Gazette,* Philadelphia., January 16, 1788.
In support of the proposed Constitution.

484   Philodemos. [untitled]. *Boston American Herald,* May 12, 1788.
In support of the proposed Constitution.

485   Philo Patriae [William Goddard?] *The Constitutional Courant: Continuing Matters Interesting to Liberty, and No Wise Repugnant to Loyalty.* Burlington, N.J. [?], 1765.

486   Philo Publicus. *Boston Gazette,* October 1, 1764.*†

487   Philo Publius [untitled]. *New York Daily Advertiser,* December 1, 1787.
In support of the proposed Constitution.

488   The Preceptor. Vol. II Social Duties of the Political Kind. *Massachusetts Spy,* May 21, 1772.**†

489   *Proposed Amendments* [to the Federal Constitution] *Made by the Maryland Convention.* Annapolis, 1788.

490   A Republican. To the Printer. *New Hampshire Gazette,* Exeter, February 8 to March 22, 1783.*
Summary of the Whig perspective.

491   Republicus. To the Printer. *The Kentucky Gazette,* March 1, 1788.
Against the proposed Constitution, especially the electoral college.

492   Resolves of the Lower House of the South Carolina Legislature. *South Carolina Gazette and Country Journal,* December 17, 1765.*

A SELECTED LIST OF POLITICAL WRITINGS

Resolutions in opposition to the Stamp Act; wording and logic very similar to that found in proposals by northern colonies.

493 Resolves of the Massachusetts House of Representatives. *Boston Gazette*, November 4, 1765.

In opposition to the Stamp Act. Good summary of basic American political principles. See previous item.

494 Rusticus. Letter to the Editor. *New York Journal*, September 13, 1787.

In opposition to the proposed Constitution.

495 Salus Populi. To the Freemen of the Province of Pennsylvania. *South Carolina and American General Gazette*, Charleston, April 3, 1776.

Justifies breaking with England.

496 [Several Quakers]. *An Address to the Inhabitants of Pennsylvania by the Freemen of Philadelphia Who Are Now Confirmed.* Philadelphia, 1777. 52 pp.

497 Sidney. Letter to the Editor. *New York Journal*, September 13, 1787.

In opposition to the proposed Constitution.

498 Spartanus. *Freemans Journal or New Hampshire Gazette*, Portsmouth, June 15 and 29, 1776.*

A strongly democratic statement.

499 Theophrastus. A Short History of the Trial by Jury. *Worcester Magazine*, October, 1787.**†

500 *To the Supporters and Defenders of American Freedom and Independence in the State of New York.* New York, 1778.

Urges no traffic with or toleration of Tories, loyalists, or collaborators with Britain.

501 T.Q. On Separation of Powers: How Much Separation is Enough? *Boston Gazette and Country Journal*, April 4, 18, and June 6, 1763.*†

See the piece by L.Q.

502 The Tribune. No. xvii. *South Carolina Gazette*, October 6, 1766.**†

503 Tribunus. Letters from Tribunus to Republicanus. *Worcester Magazine*, May, 1787.

Two articles discussing public credit.

504 Tullius. *Three Letters on the Nature of the Federal Union,* etc., Philadelphia, 1783. 28 pp.

505 U. *Boston Gazette*, August 1, 1763.*†

506 U. To the Printers. *Boston Gazette,* August 29, 1763.
Diatribe against "private revenge."

507 Velerius. *Massachusetts Centinel,* Boston, November 28, 1787.
Supports the proposed Constitution.

508 *The Virginia Report of 1799–1800, Touching the Alien and Sedition Laws,* Richmond, 1850.

509 Virginiensis [Charles Lee?] *Defense of the Alien and Sedition Laws.* Philadelphia, 1798. 47 pp.

510 *The Votes and Proceedings of the Freeholders and Other Inhabitants of the Town of Boston, In Town Meeting Assembled, According to Law. November 20, 1772,* [Samuel Adams?].*
Reproduced in Jensen, ed., *Tracts of the American Revolution.*

511 Vox Populi. To the Printer. *Massachusetts Gazette,* Boston, October 30, 1787.
Against the proposed Constitution, with a special concern for the dangers in congressional control of elections.

512 The Worcester Speculator. No. VI. *Worcester Magazine,* October, 1787.**†

513 Worcestriensis. To the Honorable . . . (No. II). *Massachusetts Spy,* August 14, 1776.*
The importance of education to a republic.

514 Worcestriensis. Number III. *Massachusetts Spy,* August 21, 1776.*
The importance of religion.

515 Worcestriensis. Number IV. *Massachusetts Spy,* September 4, 1776.**†

A LIST OF NEWSPAPERS EXAMINED

Anyone attempting to read comprehensively the newspapers published in America between 1760 and 1805 runs into several problems. First of all, a significant percentage of issues did not survive, and those that do are often available only on microfilm of poor quality and in various libraries. The Library of Congress has the most complete collection, but even there the problem is that few papers were published for as long as half the period under study. The strategy forced upon the researcher is to select judiciously from those papers available, with the aim of constructing a continuous set of newspapers over the period from each of the major cities and towns that generated the most

A Selected List of Political Writings

activity. The problem is eased somewhat by the significant number of newspapers that did not usually publish political essays and letters, or if they did, tended to reprint essays from newspapers elsewhere. Most of the newspapers that were not read comprehensively, and are so indicated below, were in fact examined and determined to fall into this last category. An estimated four thousand political essays and letters were examined in the newspapers from the era. Because it was the practice in even the most sophisticated publications to reprint pieces from papers in other colonies, in some instances a political essay was encountered four or five times in various newspapers, from South Carolina to New Hampshire. In the list below, those newspapers that were consulted comprehensively for the period 1760–1805 are marked with an asterisk. The rest are listed to show which major papers were not so examined, and to help provide a reasonably complete list of newspapers for the period.

CONNECTICUT

American Mercury (Hartford)*
Connecticut Courant (Hartford)*
Connecticut Gazette (New London)*
Connecticut Journal (New Haven)
Middlesex Gazette (Middletown)
New Haven Chronicle
New Haven Gazette*
Norwich Packet
Spectator*
Weekly Monitor (Litchfield)

DELAWARE

Wilmington Courant
Wilmington Gazette

GEORGIA

Augusta Chronicle
Georgia Gazette (Savannah)*
State Gazette of Georgia (Savannah)*

MARYLAND

Maryland Chronicle (Frederick)
Maryland Gazette (Annapolis)*
Maryland Gazette and Baltimore Advertiser*
Maryland Journal (Baltimore)*
Weekly Museum (Baltimore)*

A SELECTED LIST OF POLITICAL WRITINGS

MASSACHUSETTS

American Herald (Worcester)*
Berkshire Chronicle
Boston Censor*
Boston Chronicle*
Boston Evening Post*
Boston Gazette*
Boston Gazette and Weekly Republican Journal*
Cumberland Gazette (Portland, Maine)
Essex Journal (Salem)
Hampshire Chronicle (Springfield)
Hampshire Gazette (Northhampton)
Hampshire Herald (Springfield)
Independent Chronicle (Boston)
Massachusetts Centinel (Boston)*
Massachusetts Gazette (Boston)*
Massachusetts Spy (Worcester)*
Post Boy and Advertiser (Boston)*
Salem Mercury
Western Star (Stockbridge)
Worcester Magazine*

NEW HAMPSHIRE

Freemans Oracle and New Hampshire Advertiser (Exeter)*
New Hampshire Gazette and General Advertiser (Exeter)
New Hampshire Mercury (Portsmouth)
New Hampshire Recorder and Weekly Advertiser (Keene)*
New Hampshire Spy (Portsmouth)

NEW JERSEY

Brunswick Gazette (New Brunswick)
New Jersey Gazette (Trenton)
New Jersey Journal (Elizabethtown)
Plain Dealer (Bridgetown)*

NEW YORK

Albany Gazette*
Albany Register
American Magazine (New York)
Goshen Repository
Hudson Gazette
Independent Journal (New York)
New York Daily Advertiser (New York)*
New York Gazette (New York)*

A SELECTED LIST OF POLITICAL WRITINGS

New York Gazette and Weekly Mercury (New York)*
New York Journal (New York)*
New York Mercury (New York)*
New York Museum (New York)
New York Packet (New York)*
Northern Centinel or Lansingburg Advertiser
Poughkeepsie Journal*

NORTH CAROLINA
North Carolina Chronicle (Fayetteville)
North Carolina Gazette*
State Gazette of North Carolina (Newberne and Edentown)*

PENNSYLVANIA
American Museum (Philadelphia)
Freeman's Journal (Philadelphia)*
Independent Gazetteer (Philadelphia)*
Lancaster Journal*
Pennsylvania Evening Post and Daily Advertiser (Philadelphia)*
Pennsylvania Gazette (Philadelphia)*
Pennsylvania Herald (Philadelphia)
Pennsylvania Journal (Philadelphia)*
Pennsylvania Ledger (Philadelphia)*
Pennsylvania Mercury (Philadelphia)
Pennsylvania Packet (Philadelphia)*
Pittsburg Gazette

RHODE ISLAND
Newport Herald
Newport Mercury*
Providence Gazette*
United States Chronicle (Providence)

SOUTH CAROLINA
City Gazette, or Daily Advertiser (Charleston)*
The Columbian Herald or the Independent Courier (Charleston)
Royal South Carolina Gazette (Charleston)*
South Carolina and American General Gazette (Charleston)*
South Carolina Gazette (Charleston)*
South Carolina Gazette and Country Journal (Charleston)*
South Carolina State Gazette and Timothy's Daily Advertiser (Charleston)*
South Carolina Weekly Chronicle
State Gazette of South Carolina (Charleston)*

VIRGINIA

The Norfolk and Portsmouth Chronicle
Virginia Gazette (Winchester)*
Virginia Gazette and Petersburg Advertiser
The Virginia Gazette and Weekly Advertiser (Richmond)
The Virginia Herald and Independent Advertiser
Virginia Independent Chronicle (Richmond)*
The Virginia Journal and Alexandria Advertiser*

COLLECTIONS OF WRITING FROM THE FOUNDING ERA

There are a number of good, more-specialized collections that have proved to be very useful, and any student of American political theory would want to be at least familiar with their respective contents. In some instances we have drawn upon them for pieces found in this collection.

Almon, John, ed. *A Collection of Papers Relative to the Dispute Between Great Britain and America, 1764–1775.* New York: Da Capo Press, 1971.

Bailyn, Bernard, ed. *Pamphlets of the American Revolution.* Cambridge, Mass.: Belknap Press, 1965.

Borden, Morton, ed. *The Antifederalist Papers.* East Lansing, Mich.: Michigan State University Press, 1965.

Cooke, J. E., ed. *The Federalist.* Cleveland: Meridian Books, 1961.

Elliott, Jonathan, ed. *The Debates in the Several State Conventions on the Adoption of the Federal Constitution.* Philadelphia: J. B. Lippincott, 1901.

Farrand, Max, ed. *The Records of the Federal Convention of 1787.* New Haven: Yale University Press, 1937.

Ford, Paul Leicester, ed. *Pamphlets on the Constitution of the United States.* Brooklyn: 1888.

Handlin, Oscar, and Mary Handlin, eds. *The Popular Sources of Political Authority.* Cambridge, Mass.: Harvard University Press, 1966.

Hyneman, Charles S. and George W. Carey, eds. *A Second Federalist.* New York: Appleton-Century-Crofts, 1967.

Jensen, Merrill, ed. *Tracts of the American Revolution, 1763–1776.* Indianapolis: Bobbs-Merrill, 1978.

A SELECTED LIST OF POLITICAL WRITINGS

Kenyon, Cecilia, ed. *The Antifederalists*. Indianapolis: Bobbs-Merrill, 1966.

Levy, Leonard W., ed. *Freedom of the Press from Zenger to Jefferson: Early American Libertarian Theories*. Indianapolis: Bobbs-Merrill, 1966.

Lewis, John D., ed. *Anti-Federalists Versus Federalists: Selected Documents*. San Francisco: Chandler, 1967.

Mark, Irving and Eugene L. Schwaab, eds. *The Faith of Our Fathers: An Anthology Expressing the Aspirations of the American Common Man, 1790–1860*. New York: Octagon Books, 1976.

Padover, Saul K., ed. *The World of the Founding Fathers*. New York: A. S. Barnes and Company, 1977.

Pole, J. R., ed. *The Revolution in America, 1754–1788: Documents and Commentaries*. Stanford, Calif.: Stanford University Press, 1970.

Rudolph, Frederick, ed. *Essays on Education in the Early Republic*. Cambridge, Mass.: The Belknap Press, 1965.

Smith, Wilson, ed. *Theories of Education in Early America, 1655–1819*. Indianapolis: Bobbs-Merrill, 1973.

Storing, Herbert, ed. *The Complete Antifederalist*. 7 vols. Chicago: University of Chicago Press, 1981.

Thornton, John Wingate, ed. *The Pulpit of the American Revolution*. Boston: Gould and Lincoln, 1860.

INDEX

INDEX

INDEX

INDEX

INDEX

INDEX

INDEX

INDEX

INDEX

This book was set in Garamond Number 3, a typeface indirectly derived from the designs of Claude Garamont, a French punch-cutter who died in the mid-sixteenth century. Garamont worked for many printers in Paris, and in his lifetime his types were widely used. Because of their legibility and beauty, these types have been used as models by many contemporary designers.

———————

This book is printed on paper that is acid-free and meets the requirements of the American National Standard for Permanence of Paper for Printed Library Materials, Z39.84, 1984 ∞

Book design by Betty Binns Graphics, New York, New York
Editorial service by Harkavy Publishing Service, New York, New York
Typography by Monotype Composition Co., Inc., Baltimore, Maryland
Printed and bound by R. R. Donnelley and Sons, Crawfordsville, Indiana